The Photographic History of The Civil War

TWO VOLUMES IN ONE.
Soldier Life and Secret Service

JOHN C. BABCOCK

A SECRET SERVICE MAN FROM '61 TO '65

PHOTOGRAPHED IN 1862 WITH HIS FLEET HORSE "GIMLET"

"Avoid the camera" is the rule of the twentieth century secret-service man. But on that sunny day of October, 1862, the dashing young scout was guilty of no impropriety in standing for his portrait: direct "half-tone" reproductions were yet unknown, photography itself under the limits of its first pioneer years, and the photographer was Alexander Gardner, himself a trusted secret-service employee. It was correspondence about this very photograph which, forty-eight years later, brought the editors of the PHOTOGRAPHIC HISTORY into touch with Babcock himself. He had enlisted in the Sturges Rifle Corps, of Chicago, but was soon detailed to McClellan's secret service with Pinkerton. He remained after the latter left, did most of the scouting and news gathering under Burnside, and continued in the bureau, as reorganized by Colonel Sharpe, until the end of the war. No small part of his success was due to "my horse 'Gimlet,' that I rode in the Secret Service from 1861 to 1865." "Gimlet" looks an ideal mount for the man who had to be "the eyes of the army"—alert, nervous, eager to be off, bearing the news that would influence the fortunes and lives of thousands.

[4]

The Photographic History of The Civil War

Complete and Unabridged

Two Volumes in One.

Volume 4
*Soldier Life and Secret Service
Prisons and Hospitals

Contributors

CHARLES KING
Brigadier-General, U. S. V.

RANDOLPH H. McKIM
Army of Northern Virginia, C. S. A.

ALLEN C. REDWOOD
Army of Northern Virginia, C. S. A.

JOHN W. HEADLEY
Captain, C. S. A.

WILLIAM B. SHAW

A. W. GREELY
Major-General, U. S. A.

T. S. C. LOWE
Balloon Corps, Army of the Potomac

FENWICK Y. HEDLEY
Brevet-Captain, U. S. V.

L. R. STEGMAN
Late Colonel 102d New York, U. S. V.

GEORGE H. CASAMAJOR

ROY MASON

THE BLUE & GREY PRESS

PHOTOGRAPHIC HISTORY OF THE CIVIL WAR

Vol. 4
Soldier Life and Secret Service
Prisons and Hospitals

Two Volumes in One.

Printed in the United States of America.

ISBN: 1-55521-201-8

CONTENTS

Introduction

Contents

PHOTOGRAPHIC DESCRIPTIONS THROUGHOUT THE VOLUME
    Roy Mason
    Louis R. Stegman

PREFACE

IN General King's "Introduction," the reader steps behind the scenes of warfare, where the machinery is found to be very different from the popular notion. It is soon plain that the most brilliant and profound calculations of strategy will amount to little unless there are leaders in the field with the faculty for gathering news and other military information against obstacles which might dumfound the ablest newspaper editor—coupled with the ability to distribute supplies and transport men on a scale more immense than the grandest engineering construction operations of the twentieth century. These two practical functions of the general are properly treated in one volume under the heads of "Secret Service" and "Soldier Life."

The obtaining of military information through scouts and spies is of little use unless there are available the clothing, food, and transportation whereby soldiers are made "fit." An understanding of these problems uncovers the human realities behind military phrases otherwise burdensome. How the grandest moves on the campaign chess-board can be thwarted by the blunder of a credulous scout, or the mud from a few days' rain, is made clear in General King's preface and the pages that follow.

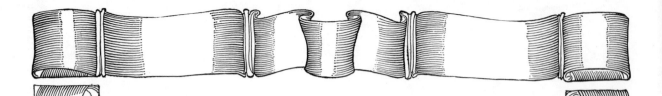

THE STATES AND THEIR QUOTAS

As Illustrated and Described in This Volume

The index below refers the reader to pages of this volume upon which appear photographs showing representatives of every State engaged on either side in the Civil War, with some account of the volunteers in '61:

The matter above referred to appears in this volume merely as illustrating the respective chapters. It is entirely independent of the extensive charts, tables, and statistics covering State activities, as well as those of the armies, corps, famous brigades and regiments, which will be found in the volume devoted to biography.

[12]

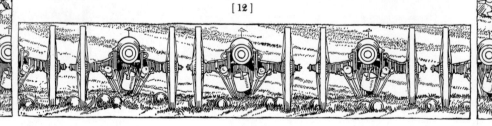

INTRODUCTION

THE TWO PRACTICAL PROBLEMS
OF THE GENERAL

READING THE DISTANT MESSAGE

AN OFFICER OF THE FEDERAL SIGNAL CORPS

HOW

THE SECRET SERVICE

GAVE RISE TO THE COMPLETE

PHOTOGRAPHIC RECORD OF "SOLDIER LIFE"

It is quite astonishing to discover that the immense collection of photographs reflecting the "soldier life" of 1861–65 so intimately and vividly had its rise in secret-service work. It is literally true, however, that Alexander Gardner's privileges of photographing at headquarters and within the Federal lines, at a thousand historic spots and moments, resulted entirely from the desire of the authorities to insure the strictest secrecy for their movements. Obviously, any commander was pretty much at the mercy of the individual who copied the maps, charts, and the like for his secret service. Through an untrustworthy or careless employee the most zealously guarded secrets of contemplated destinations or routes might reach the adversary. The work of preparing these maps, therefore, was confided to Alexander Gardner, the brilliant Scotchman

[14]

PHOTOGRAPHER
AND SOLDIER, 1862,
AS THE ARMIES PAUSED
AFTER McCLELLAN'S ATTEMPT ON RICHMOND

brought to America and instructed in the photographic art by Brady himself. He proved so trustworthy that he was permitted in his spare time to indulge his hobby of photographing the soldiers themselves— a useless hobby it seemed then, since there was no way of reproducing the pictures direct on the printed page. But Gardner, first and last an artist, worked so patiently and indefatigably that, before the campaign was over, he had secured thousands of outdoor views which, with the many that Brady took in '61 and part of '62, and later in the path of Grant's final campaign from the Wilderness to Richmond, form the nucleus of the collection presented herewith. Needless to say, Gardner did not break faith with his employers or pass any of these photographs to Southern sympathizers, or through the Confederate lines.

MATTHEW B. BRADY UNDER FIRE IN THE WORKS BEFORE PETERSBURG

Shells were flying above the entrenchments before Petersburg at the time the photograph above was taken —June 21, 1864—but so inured to this war-music have the veterans become that only one or two of them to the right are squatting or lying down. The calmness is shared even by Brady, the indomitable little photographer. He stands (at the left of the right-hand section above) quietly gazing from beneath the brim of his straw hat—conspicuous among the dark forage caps and felts of the soldiers—in the same direction in which the officer is peering so eagerly through his field-glass. Brady appears twice again in the

[Brady]

THREE OF THE "BRADY" PHOTOGRAPHS TAKEN IN GRANT'S LAST CAMPAIGN

two lower photographs of the same locality and time. "I knew Mr. Brady during that time," writes William A. Pinkerton, the son of Allan Pinkerton, who was in charge of the secret-service department throughout the war, "but had no intimate acquaintanceship with him, he being a man and I being a boy, but I recollect his face and build as vividly to-day as I did then: a slim build, a man, I should judge, about five feet seven inches tall, dark complexion, dark moustache, and dark hair inclined to curl; wore glasses, was quick and nervous. You can verify by me that I saw a number of these negatives made myself."

[Brady]

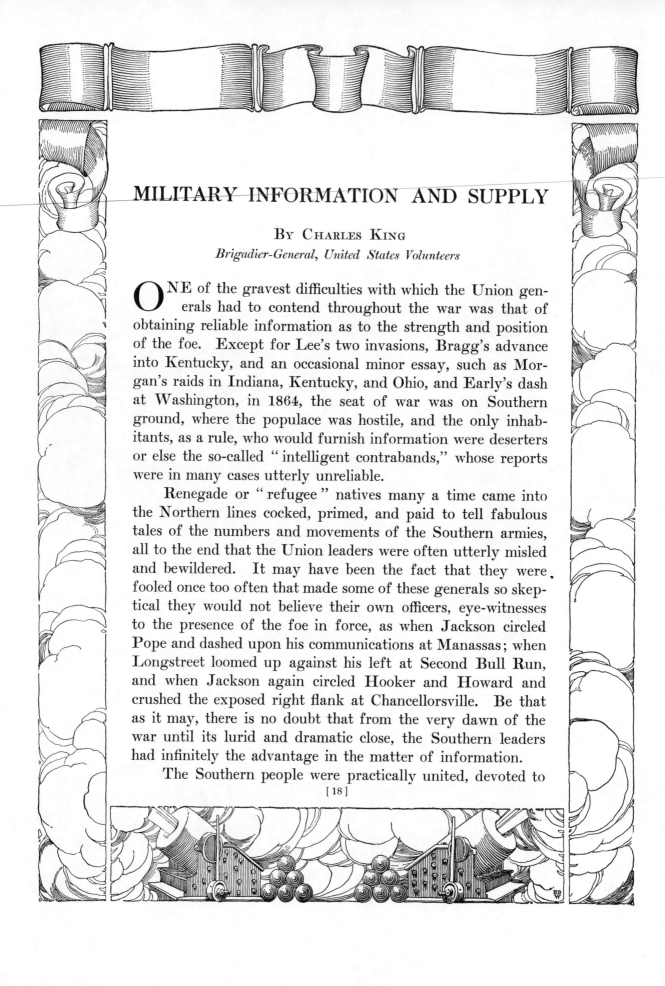

MILITARY INFORMATION AND SUPPLY

By Charles King
Brigadier-General, United States Volunteers

ONE of the gravest difficulties with which the Union generals had to contend throughout the war was that of obtaining reliable information as to the strength and position of the foe. Except for Lee's two invasions, Bragg's advance into Kentucky, and an occasional minor essay, such as Morgan's raids in Indiana, Kentucky, and Ohio, and Early's dash at Washington, in 1864, the seat of war was on Southern ground, where the populace was hostile, and the only inhabitants, as a rule, who would furnish information were deserters or else the so-called "intelligent contrabands," whose reports were in many cases utterly unreliable.

Renegade or "refugee" natives many a time came into the Northern lines cocked, primed, and paid to tell fabulous tales of the numbers and movements of the Southern armies, all to the end that the Union leaders were often utterly misled and bewildered. It may have been the fact that they were fooled once too often that made some of these generals so skeptical they would not believe their own officers, eye-witnesses to the presence of the foe in force, as when Jackson circled Pope and dashed upon his communications at Manassas; when Longstreet loomed up against his left at Second Bull Run, and when Jackson again circled Hooker and Howard and crushed the exposed right flank at Chancellorsville. Be that as it may, there is no doubt that from the very dawn of the war until its lurid and dramatic close, the Southern leaders had infinitely the advantage in the matter of information.

The Southern people were practically united, devoted to

SCOUTS AND GUIDES OF THE ARMY OF THE POTOMAC, 1862

The scouts and guides of the Army of the Potomac were attached to the secret-service department conducted by Major A. Pinkerton. It was more than difficult for the Union generals to obtain reliable information as to the strength and position of the enemy. The Southern people were practically united, devoted to their cause and all that it comprised. The only inhabitants, as a rule, who would furnish information were deserters or else the so-called "intelligent contrabands," whose reports were in many cases utterly untrust-worthy. Therefore it became necessary for these men of indomitable courage to brave the halter in order to obtain information. During the campaign of the army in front of Fredericksburg, they proved of incalculable value. Each man was provided with a pass from the commanding general, written with a chemical preparation that became visible only when exposed to solar rays. On the back was penciled some unimportant memoranda, to deceive the adversaries, should the scout fall into their hands. If captured, he could drop this paper, apparently by accident, without exciting suspicion; and if successful in his expedition, the pass, after a moment's exposure to the heat, enabled the bearer to re-enter his own lines and proceed without delay to headquarters. The scouts generally passed as foragers within their own lines, always coming in with vegetables, poultry, and the like, to preserve their *incognito*,

their cause and all that it comprised. The North was filled with spies, special correspondents, paid agents, Southern sympathizers by the score, "copperheads" innumerable, and among the border States and in Louisiana and Mississippi, whither Union armies had penetrated in force, the blue lines enclosed hundreds of homesteads of Southern families whose men were with their regiments in Virginia or Tennessee, leaving the women and the faithful blacks, the household servants, to look after what was left of their once fertile and productive fields and the hospitable old mansions of their forefathers.

It followed that the South often knew pretty much everything worth knowing of the disposition and preparations of the Union forces—often, indeed, of their carefully guarded plans. It followed that, on the other hand, the Northern generals had as often to guess at the opposing conditions, since so very much of the information paid for proved utterly worthless.

With an overwhelming force at his back, well organized and equipped, better disciplined than were the Southern troops late in 1861, and their equal at least in experience, McClellan's splendid divisions, fully one hundred and forty thousand strong, were held up in front of Washington by not more than forty-seven thousand Confederates, all because agents induced the overcautious commander to believe he was confronted by fully two hundred thousand men. Again, on the Peninsula, when McClellan could have smashed through to Richmond by simple weight of numbers—such had been the casualties of battle in the Southern lines—the specter of Southern superiority in numbers unnerved the young leader, and the story of thousands of Southern reenforcements drove him to the change of base and the shelter of the gunboats on the James. A few weeks later and the same tactics told on Pope and his subordinates. "Old Jack" was at their heels or on their flanks, with sixty thousand men—"the flower of the Southern infantry," said prisoners who had ridden, apparently accidentally, into the Federal lines.

GUARDING
FEDERAL
ARMY SUPPLIES

AT
FORT FISHER
NORTH CAROLINA

AT   AT
NASHVILLE CITY POINT

European history abounds in illustrations of all that is scientific and systematic as clockwork in the logistics of warfare—all made possible because of their military roads.   But in the Civil War it was almost impossible to calculate with any great degree of certainty the movement of a single regiment for more than a few miles, much less the movement of a cumbrous wagon-train.   The way of the armies lay through seas of mud, through swamp, morass, and tangled wildwood, and over roads that would seem impossible to a European army.   From the mountains to the sea, the quartermaster's easiest route lay along the great open waterways.   The upper photograph shows a quartermaster's sentry at Fort Fisher, N. C., on the Atlantic seaboard.   In the lower one to the left stands a sentry guarding the quartermaster's stores at Nashville, Tenn., on the Cumberland, while the sentry on the right is at City Point, Va., on the James.

Again, after Antietam, what tremendous tales of Southern strength must have held McClellan an entire month along the north bank of the Potomac, while Stuart, with less than two thousand troopers, rode jauntily round about him unscathed. It was not until well along in 1863, when the Federals began to wake up to the use of cavalry, that fairy tales gave way to facts, and Hooker and Meade could estimate the actual force to be encountered, so that by the time Grant came to the Army of the Potomac in 1864, he well knew that whatsoever advantage Lee might have in fighting on his own ground, and along interior lines, and with the most devoted and brilliantly led army at his back, the Union legions far outnumbered him. Then, with Grant's grim, invincible determination, there were no more footsteps backward.

Yet even Grant had very much to contend with in this very matter. Southern families abounded in Washington; Southern messengers of both sexes rode the Maryland lanes to Port Tobacco; Southern skiffs ferried Southern missives in the black hours of midnight under the very muzzles of the anchored guns in the broad reaches of the Potomac; Virginia farm boys, or girls—born riders all—bore all manner of messages from river to river and so to the Southern lines southeast of Fredericksburg, and thus around to Gordonsville and the Confederate army.

The Northern newspapers, under the inspiration of professional rivalry, kept the Southern cabinet remarkably well informed of everything going on within the Union lines, and not infrequently prepared the Confederate generals for the next move of the Union army. It was this that finally led the vehement Sherman to seek to eliminate the newspaper men from his military bailiwick, about as hopeless a task as the very worst assigned to Hercules. Grant, with his accustomed stoicism, accepted their presence in his army as something inseparable from American methods of warfare, adding to the problems and perplexities of the generals commanding,

MAP
PHOTO-
GRAPHING
FOR THE ARMY
IN THE FIELD

THE
PROCESS
THAT TOOK
GARDNER INTO
THE SECRET SERVICE

Alexander Gardner's usefulness to the secret service lay in the copying of maps by the methods shown above—and keeping quiet about it. A great admirer of Gardner's was young William A. Pinkerton, son of Allan Pinkerton, then head of the secret service. Forty-seven years later Mr. Pinkerton furnished for the PHOTOGRAPHIC HISTORY some reminiscences of Gardner's work: "It was during the winter of '61–'62 that Gardner became attached to the Secret Service Corps, then under my father. I was then a boy, ranging from seventeen to twenty-one years of age, during all of which time I was in intimate contact with Gardner, as he was at our headquarters and was utilized by the Government for photographing maps and other articles of that kind which were prepared by the secret service. I have quite a number of his views which were made at that time." These negatives, more than a thousand in number, are among the collection so long buried in obscurity before becoming represented in these volumes. Mr. Pinkerton adds: "I used to travel around with Gardner a good deal while he was taking these views and saw many of them made."

heralding their movements, as did the Virginia maids and matrons, and impeding them, as did the Virginia mud.

Other writers have described the "Intelligence Bureau" of the rank and file, by means of which the troops seemed well supplied with tidings of every Union move of consequence— tidings only too quickly carried by daring and devoted sons of the South, who courted instant death by accepting duty in the secret service, and lived the lonely life, and in many an instance died the lonely, unhallowed death of the spy. Men who sought that calling must have had illimitable love for and faith in the cause for which they accepted the ignominy that, justly or unjustly, attaches to the name. Men like Major André and Nathan Hale had succeeded in throwing about their hapless fate the glamour of romance and martyrdom, but such halos seem to have hovered over the head of few, if any, who, in either army during the bitter four years' war, were condemned to die, by the felon's rope, the death of the spy.

The Old Capitol Prison in Washington was long the abiding place of men and women confined by order of our "Iron Secretary" on well-founded suspicion of being connected with the Southern system, and in the camp of the Army of the Cumberland, two sons of the Confederacy, men with gentle blood in their veins and reckless daring in their hearts, were stripped of the uniforms of officers of the Union cavalry, in which they had been masquerading for who can say what purpose, tried by court martial, and summarily executed.

Secret service at best was a perilous and ill-requited duty. In spite of high pay it was held in low estimation, first on general principles, and later because it was soon suspected, and presently known, that many men most useful as purveyors of information had been shrewd enough to gain the confidence, accept the pay, and become the informants of both sides. Even Secretary Stanton was sometimes hoodwinked, as in the case of the "confidential adviser" he recommended to Sheridan in the fall of 1864.

THE PHOTOGRAPHERS WHO FOLLOWED THE ARMY

In the early years of the war the soldiers were so mystified by the peculiar-looking wagon in which Brady kept his traveling dark-room that they nicknamed it the "What-is-it?" wagon, a name which clung to the photographer's outfit all through the war. The upper photograph, with the two bashful-looking horses huddling together before the camera, shows Brady's outfit going to the front, in 1861. The lowest photograph demonstrates that even the busy photographer occasionally slept in his camp with the army. The left-

hand of the three center pictures shows the "What-is-it?" again, on the Bull Run battlefield; in the next appears the developing tent of Barnard, Colonel O. M. Poe's engineer-corps photographer, before one of the captured Atlanta forts, in September, 1864; and in the last stands Cooley, photographer to the Army of the Tennessee, with his camera, on the battered parapet of Sumter in 1865. In spite of these elaborate preparations of the enterprising photographers, among the million men in the field few knew that any photographs were being taken. These volumes will be the first introduction of many a veteran to the photography of fifty years before.

Sheridan had the born soldier's contempt for such characters, and though setting the man to work, as suggested, he had him watched by soldier scouts who had been organized under Colonel Young of Rhode Island, and when later there was brought to him at midnight, in complete disguise, a young Southerner, dark, slender, handsome, soft-voiced, and fascinating in manner—a man who " had had a tiff with Mosby," they said, and now wished to be of service to the Union and act in concert with Stanton's earlier emissary, " Mr. Lomas of Maryland," Sheridan's suspicions were redoubled. The newcomer gave the name of Renfrew—that under which the Prince of Wales (Baron Renfrew) had visited the States in the summer of 1860—and was an artist in the matter of make-up and disguise. Sheridan kept his own counsel, had the pair "shadowed," and speedily found they were sending far more information to the foe than they were bringing to him. They were arrested and ordered to Fort Warren, but in most mysterious fashion they escaped at Baltimore. A few weeks later and Stanton found reason to believe that his friend Lomas was closely allied with the conspirators later hanged for the assassination of Abraham Lincoln, and then it dawned upon Sheridan that Renfrew was probably none other than John Wilkes Booth.

At best, therefore, the information derived from such sources could never be relied upon, at least by Union generals, and Sheridan's scout system was probably the most successful of all those essayed during the war. It was also most daring and hazardous, for the men took their lives in their hands, and the chance of immediate and ignominious death when they donned, as they had to, the Confederate uniform and penetrated the Confederate lines. There, if suspected and arrested, their fate was sealed. Yet it was one of these who successfully bore to General Grant, Sheridan's urgent " I wish you were here," when, on the 5th of April, 1865, the latter saw slipping away the chance of penning Lee's harassed and panting army

THE ARMY PHOTOGRAPHER AHEAD OF THE WRECKING–TRAIN

When the Confederate cavalry made life a burden for the United States Military Railroad Construction Corps in the vicinity of Washington, the enterprising photographers on their part were not idle. This photograph shows the engine "Commodore" derailed and lying on its side. Even before the wrecking crew could be rushed to the scene, the photographer had arrived, as is attested by the bottle of chemicals, the developing tray, and the negative rack in the right foreground, as well as the photograph itself. Every negative had to be developed within five minutes after the exposure, a fact which makes all the more marvellous the brilliant work that was accomplished. In the buggy and wagon shown in the lower picture, Brady safely transported glass plates wherever an army could march.

THE BÊTE NOIR OF THE SECRET SERVICE

At the headquarters of the New York *Herald* in the field, August, 1863, sit some of the men who had just conveyed to the breathless nation the tidings of the great battle as it surged to and fro for three days on the field of Gettysburg. No Union general could object to dissemination of such news as this; but wide protest was made against the correspondents' activity at other times, their shrewd guesses at the armies' future movements, that kept the Southern Cabinet so remarkably well-informed of everything going on within the Union lines, and not infrequently prepared the Confederate generals for the next move. "Of course," wrote General Sherman to his wife, in a letter from camp in front of Vicksburg, dated April 10, 1863, "the newspaper correspondents, encouraged by the political generals, and even President Lincoln, having full swing in this and all camps, report all news, secret and otherwise . . . All persons who don't have to fight must be kept out of camp, else secrecy, a great element of military success, is an impossibility . . . Can you feel astonished that I should grow angry at the toleration of such suicidal weakness, that we strong, intelligent men must bend to a silly proclivity for early news that should advise our enemy days in advance?" The newspaper correspondents pitched their tents in the wake of the army, but they themselves were more than likely to be found with the advance-guard. Not a few of the plucky newspaper men fell on the field of battle, while others, like Richardson of the *Tribune*, endured imprisonment.

at Amelia Court House. The courier had to ride southward across a dozen miles of dubious country. It was nip and tuck whether "Yank" or "Reb" first laid hands on him, and when he finally reached the wearied leader, and, rousing to the occasion, Grant decided to ride at once through the darkness to Sheridan's side, and set forth with only a little escort and the scout as guide, two staff-officers, thoroughly suspicious, strapped the latter to his saddle, linked his horse with theirs, and cocked their revolvers at his back. That scout rode those long miles back to Jetersville with these words occasionally murmured into his ears, "At the first sight or sound of treachery, you die." Not until they reached Sheridan at midnight were they sure it was not a device of the desperate foe. Volumes could be written of the secret service of the Union armies—what it cost and what it was really worth—but the South, it is believed, could more than match every exploit.

Serious as was this problem, there were others beyond that of the strategy of a campaign of even greater moment—problems the Union generals, especially in the West, were compelled to study and consider with the utmost care. Napoleon said, "An army crawls upon its belly." Soldiers to march and fight their best must be well fed. Given sound food and shoe leather, and the average army can outdo one far above the average, unfed and unshod. East and West, the armies of the Union suffered at the start at the hands of the contractors, because of "shoddy" coats and blankets and "pasteboard" shoes, but in the matter of supplies the Army of the Potomac had generally the advantage of the armies of the West—it was never far removed from its base.

From the farms, granaries, mills, and manufactories of the Eastern and Middle States, in vast quantities, bacon, flour, coffee, sugar, and hardtack for the inner man; blankets, caps, coats, shirts, socks, shoes, and trousers for his outer self were shipped by canal and river to the sea and then floated up the Potomac to the great depots of Aquia and Washington, and

[30]

THE HARPER'S WEEKLY ARTIST SKETCHING THE GETTYSBURG BATTLEFIELD, 1863

Photo-engraving was unknown in the days of 1861 to 1865, and it remained for the next generation to make possible the reproduction in book form of the many valuable photographs taken by Matthew B. Brady and Alexander Gardner in the North, and George S. Cook, J. D. Edwards, A. D. Lytle, and others in the South. The public had to be content with wood-cuts, after sketches and drawings made by the correspondents in the field. On this page appears A. R. Waud, an active staff artist, in war and peace, for *Harper's Weekly*.

WAUD AT HEADQUARTERS, 1864,

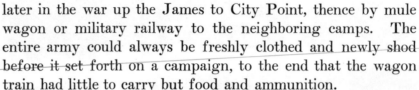

later in the war up the James to City Point, thence by mule wagon or military railway to the neighboring camps. The entire army could always be freshly clothed and newly shod before it set forth on a campaign, to the end that the wagon train had little to carry but food and ammunition.

The seasoned soldier bore with him none of the white tentage that looked so picturesque among the green hills around Washington. The little *tente d'abri* of the French service, speedily dubbed the "pup tent" by our soldier humorists, was all he needed in the field, and generally all he had. So, too, with his kitchen and its appliances. The huge pots, pans, kettles, and coffee-boilers seen about the winter cantonments were left behind when the army took the field, and "every man his own cook" became the rule. Each man had speedily learned how to prepare his own coffee in his own battered tin mug, season it with brown sugar, and swallow it hot. Each man knew the practical use of a bayonet or ramrod as bread or bacon toaster. It was only in the matter of beans that community of cooking became necessary, and the old plains-bred regulars could teach the volunteers—ready pupils that they were—famous devices for reducing these stubborn but most sustaining pellets to digestible form. There never was a time when the Eastern army, after the first few months, was not well fed and warmly, if clumsily, clothed.

But in the West it was far different, far more difficult. Almost from the start the armies of the Ohio, the Cumberland, the Tennessee, and the forces beyond the Mississippi, setting forth from such bases as Louisville, Cairo, and St. Louis, pushed far southward through hostile territory, spinning behind them, spiderlike, a thin thread of steel, along which, box by box, car by car, were to roll to them the vast quantities of supplies without which no army can exist. The men of Grant and Buell, trudging on to Shiloh, had the Tennessee for a barge and steamboat route, and so fared well upon their hostile mission; but the men who later marched with "Old

MAIL AND NEWSPAPERS AT "A. OF P." HEADQUARTERS

It was important for the people at home to receive news of the armies that their enthusiasm might be kept high and their purses wide open; but it was also desirable that the soldier boys should receive their news. Whether in swamp, morass, or on a mountain-top, the men in camp rushed to read their newspapers, and yearned to know what was going on at home. They wanted to know what the people thought of them, how they were describing the situation of the armies, what they told of their battles, and were voracious readers of all and every class of publications, magazines as well as newspapers. In 1864, the post-office at the headquarters of the Army of the Potomac was

a leading institution. Thousands of letters passed through it every week, and so systematically was this department conducted under the supervision of Army Postmaster William B. Haslett, with a mail-pouch for every corps and detached command, that their distribution was seldom delayed when the army was not on the march. Shrewd merchants, men who were willing to take chances to earn an honest dollar, followed the army with wagons or little trucks, selling to the men every sort of publication, but especially the journals of the day. In the lower photograph is shown quite an elaborate outfit then for the sale of Philadelphia, New York, and Baltimore newspapers.

Rosey" to Tullahoma and then beyond the Tennessee, well-nigh starved to death in their Bragg-beleaguered camps about Chattanooga, until Hooker came to their relief and established the famous "cracker line" beyond reach of shot and shell.

Then came long weeks in which, day by day, the freight trains, squirming slowly down that long, sinuous, single-track road from the Ohio River, reached the wide supply camps at Chattanooga, dumped their huge crates of bacon and hard-tack, or the big boxes of clothing, accouterments, and ammunition, and went rumbling and whistling back, laden with sick or wounded soldiery, creeping to the sidings every thirty miles or so to give the troop and "cracker" trains right of way. Nearly four long months it took Sherman, newly commanding in the West, to accumulate the vast supplies he would need for his big army of one hundred thousand men, ere again he started forth another two hundred miles into the bowels of the land, and every mile he marched took his men further from the bakeries, the butcher-shops, the commissary and quartermaster's stores from which the "boys" had received their daily bread or monthly socks, shoes, and tobacco. Another long, sinuous, slender thread of railway, guarded at every bridge, siding, and trestle, was reeled off as fast as Sherman fought on southward, until at last he reached the prize and paused again to draw breath, rations, and clothing at Atlanta before determining the next move.

And then, as in the Eastern armies, there loomed up still another factor in the problems of the campaign—a factor that European writers and critics seem rarely to take into account. From the days of the Roman Empire, Italy, France, Switzerland, and even England were seamed with admirable highways. The campaigns of Turenne, of Frederick the Great, of Napoleon were planned and marched over the best of roads, firm and hard, high and dry. The campaigns of Grant, Lee, Sherman, Johnston, Sheridan, Stuart, Thomas, Hood, Hooker, Burnside, and Jackson were ploughed at times

"LETTERS FROM HOME"—THE ARMY MAIL WAGON

HOW THE SOLDIERS GOT THEIR LETTERS FROM HOME

Letters from home were a great factor in keeping up the *morale* of the army. Wheresoever the armies might be located, however far removed from railroads or from the ordinary means of communication, the soldier boy always expected to receive his mails. The carrying of letters from his tent to his beloved ones was also a vital necessity. Each regiment in the field had a special postmaster, generally appointed by the colonel, who received all mail and saw to its proper distribution among the men, also receiving all mail forwarded to the home address. He sold stamps to the men, received their letters, and at stated periods made trips to what would be established as a sort of main post-office. The

man designated as the postmaster of the regiment was generally relieved from all other duties. Each regiment in the Army of the Potomac had a post-boy, who carried the letters of his command to the brigade headquarters. There the mails of the different regiments were placed in one pouch and went up to division headquarters, and thence to corps headquarters, where mail-agents received them and delivered them at the principal depot of the army to the agent from general headquarters. At times it was an arduous task for the mail wagons to transport the accumulated mail over bad roads, and several trips might have to be made for the purpose of securing all that was lying at some distant depot.

through seas of mud, through swamp, morass, and tangled wildwood. Southern country roads, except perhaps the limestone pikes of Kentucky and northern Tennessee, were roads only in name, and being soft, undrained, and unpaved, were forever washed out by rains or cut into deep ruts by gun and wagon wheels. Then there were quicksands in which the mule teams stalled and floundered; there were flimsy bridges forever being fired or flooded; scrap-iron railways that could be wrecked in an hour and rebuilt only with infinite pains and labor and vast expenditure of time and money.

Just what Frederick, or Napoleon, or Turenne would have done with the best of armies, but on the worst of roads, with American woods and weather to deal with, is a military problem that would baffle the critics of all Christendom. It is something for the American people to remember that when Grant and Sheridan cut loose from their base for the last week's grapple with the exhausted but indomitable remnant of Lee's gallant gray army, it rained torrents for nearly three entire days, the country was knee-deep in mud and water, the roads were utterly out of sight.

It was the marvelous concentration march of Meade's scattered army corps, however, that made possible the victory of Gettysburg. It was when they struck the hard, white roads of Pennsylvania that the men of the Army of the Potomac trudged unflinchingly their thirty miles or more a day, and matched the records of Napoleon's best. It was " Stonewall " Jackson's unequaled " foot cavalry " that could tramp their twenty-four hours through Virginia mountain trails, cover their forty miles from sun to sun, and be off again for another flank attack while yet their adversary slept. Moltke said the armies of the great Civil War were " two armed mobs," but Moltke failed to realize that in the matters of information and logistics, the Union generals had, from first to last, to deal with problems and conditions the best of his or Frederick's field-marshals never had met nor dreamed of.

[36]

THE BUSINESS SIDE
OF THE
WAR DEPARTMENTS

EMBARKING TROOPS
NINTH ARMY CORPS
LEAVING ACQUIA CREEK
IN FEBRUARY, 1863

GOVERNMENT BAKERIES AT ALEXANDRIA

COMMISSARY BUILDINGS AT ALEXANDRIA

ONE OF THE GOVERNMENT MESS–HOUSES AT WASHINGTON

GROUPS AT THE QUARTERMASTER-GENERAL'S OFFICE IN WASHINGTON

EMPLOYEES, TRANSPORTATION OFFICE, ASSISTANT QUARTERMASTER'S OFFICE, AND WAREHOUSE NO. 1—WASHINGTON

SUPPLIES ON THE TENNESSEE

BRANDY STATION, VA.

NEW YORK FERRY ON THE POTOMAC

STORES AT STONEMAN'S STATION

COL. J. B. HOWARD, Q. M.

SIBLEY, WALL, AND "A" TENTS

SUPPLIES AT WHITE HOUSE

"ARMY BREAD"

SUPPLIES AT CITY POINT

By water, rail, and horse the busy quartermasters traveled during the war. All kinds of river and sea-going craft were employed as transports for army supplies. In the left-hand corner appears a Tennessee River side-wheel steamer of the type that was said to be able to "run in a heavy dew," so light was its draught! And in the upper right-hand corner of this page a New York ferry-

GRAND REVIEW AT WASHINGTON

boat is seen at the City Point dock, on the James River, in Virginia. Both boats were engaged in bringing food and other supplies to the Federal armies in the field. Sitting on the box above is Captain T. W. Forsythe, provost-marshal. It was fitting that the army wagons, which had played so important a part in all the aggressive movements of the troops, should have a place in the Grand Review.

OFFICE OF U. S. REPAIR SHOPS

GOVERNMENT TRIMMING SHOP

GOVERNMENT PAINT SHOP

OUTSIDE THE REPAIR SHOPS

BLACKSMITH EMPLOYEES

WHEELWRIGHT SHOP

GOVERNMENT WHEELWRIGHT SHOP

During the progress of the war, repair shops were established by the Federal Government at various points inside its lines, including Washington, Cincinnati, St. Louis, Louisville, Kentucky, and Nashville, Tennessee. The Washington shops above pictured were among the largest of their kind. The huge buildings were used for the purpose of repairing army wagons, artillery wagons, ambulances, caissons, and every kind of vehicle used by the Government for transportation. The materials for prompt repair were always on hand in these immense establishments. The mechanics and artisans were selected from the best the country afforded. All of these repair depots were maintained by the Government at great expense.

HORSES AND WAGONS OF FIELD REPAIR-TRAIN IN SEPTEMBER, 1863

FIELD FORGE, PETERSBURG

BUILDING WINTER-QUARTERS

FIELD WHEELWRIGHTS

GOVERNMENT WORKSHOPS, CORRALS, AND RESERVOIR AT CAMP NELSON, KENTUCKY

"Wagon busted, axle broken and wheel gone to smash!" was a frequent exclamation that met the repair gangs accompanying the armies. Miry or rocky roads were usually accountable for the disasters to the wheeled vehicles. Even the best of wagons were liable to break under the heavy strain of the poor roads. Hence the above cry, with the usual accompanying direction: "About a mile down the road—have shoved her over into a field." The repair wagons would make for the scene of trouble, and if possible the break would be temporarily patched up. If not, the wagon would be abandoned. The repair department had many other activities at headquarters, and kept excellent workmen of many trades working constantly at fever-heat, especially when the army was engaged in a hard campaign.

MULE-CHUTE AT CAMP NELSON

UNITED STATES "FRANKLIN SHOP S" AT NASHVILLE, TENNESSEE

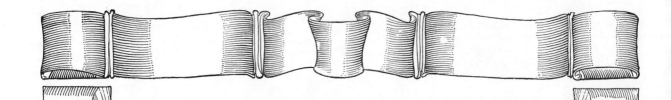

THE BUSINESS SIDE OF WAR–MAKING

By William B. Shaw

IT is one of the purposes of this " Photographic History " to show more clearly than has been shown before what the Civil War meant to the common man, on either side of Mason and Dixon's Line, whether volunteer or non-combatant. It must be remembered that thousands of men and women, North and South, rendered loyal service to their respective Governments throughout the four years of strife, without so much as lifting a musket. This series of photographs shows not only how battles were fought, but how the armies were made fit to fight them, how campaigns were conducted, how soldiers were made out of raw recruits, how railroads and bridges were destroyed and rebuilt, how rivers were dammed and their channels deflected, how blockades were maintained and eluded—in short, how the *business* of war went on in America for four full years of three hundred and sixty-five days each, practically without interruption.

Clearly, there would have been no wisdom in recruiting and organizing great armies without making provision for feeding and clothing them. Even more futile would have been an attempt to use such armies in aggressive movements without suitable equipment. The essential requisite to every army's success on the march or on the field of battle is good nourishment; yet so lacking in the picturesque was the machinery for feeding the armies in the Civil War, that historians have given it but slight attention. To equip, clothe, shelter, and transport a million men in arms at once was the task that confronted the Washington Government in the second year of the war. The country's long period of peace had not prepared it

"HOME ON FURLOUGH"—ABOARD THE ARMY TRANSPORT

After McClellan's Peninsula campaign in 1862, thousands of Northern soldiers were debilitated by swamp miasma. It was necessary that all the men who had been attacked by typhoid and various forms of intermittent fever should be taken from the environment of the Virginia camps to their homes in the North for recuperation. The photograph is that of a transport on the River James carrying a number of these furloughed men, most of whom had become convalescent in the hospitals and so were able to make the homeward journey. The lower photograph shows a transport steamer crowded with troops for Grant's concentration of the army at City Point.

for such an undertaking. A wholly new military establishment had to be created. The supply departments of the old army organization were fitted for the work of provisioning and equipping a dozen regiments; they were suddenly called upon to provide for a thousand. The fact that department and bureau chiefs rose to the situation and responded to these new and unprecedented demands is usually regarded quite as a matter of course.

Every American schoolboy knows the names of the men who led the armies, whether to victory or to defeat, but who saw that the soldiers were clothed and fed? Hundreds of faithful officers were engaged in that duty throughout the four weary years of war; without their services the battles that brought enduring fame to victorious generals could never have been fought, much less won. The feats that these men performed were largely unknown to the public and even to the armies themselves. Frequently in the face of appalling difficulties, we are told, a whole army corps was saved from starvation and defeat by the ready resourcefulness of a commissary. More than once the intelligent cooperation of the Quartermaster's Department made possible a rapid movement of troops, crowning with success the brilliant plans of a commander to whom history has awarded all the credit for skilful execution.

At the outbreak of the war the army's two great supply departments were directed by the quartermaster-general and the commissary-general of subsistence, respectively. The Quartermaster's Department was charged with the duty of providing means of transportation, by land and water, for all the troops and all materials of war; it furnished the horses for artillery and cavalry, and for the supply trains; supplied tents, camp and garrison equipage, forage, lumber, and all materials for camps; it built barracks, hospitals, wagons, and ambulances; provided harness, except for artillery and cavalry horses; built or chartered ships and steamships, docks and

[44]

TRANSPORT ON THE TENNESSEE

AN OCEAN–LINER TRANSPORT

OCEAN TRANSPORT AT CHARLESTON

THE DECK OF THE "ARAGO"

Army transports represented all types of river craft and sea-going vessels. Steamboats, propellers, tugs, barges, and canal boats were all utilized for this important service. The vessels shown upon this page were used for moving regiments, brigades, divisions, and even entire corps from point to point along the rivers and up and down the Atlantic coast-line. The

TRANSPORT ON THE APPOMATTOX

Arago had been one of the great side-wheel ocean-liners plying between New York and Liverpool in the days preceding the war. She was especially desirable for the transportation of large bodies of troops along the Southern coast. The *Washington Irving* in the lower picture was a North River passenger-boat loaned or leased to the Federal Government.

wharves; constructed and repaired roads, bridges, and even railroads; clothed the soldiers, and supervised the payment of all expenses attending military operations which were not regularly assigned by law or regulation to some other department.

Upon the Subsistence Department fell the duty of securing food for the army. During a great part of the war, the Washington Government was expending approximately one million dollars a day upon the maintenance and equipment of troops, and the prosecution of campaigns. The greater part of this expenditure was made through these two departments, the Quartermaster's and the Subsistence.

The matter of railroad transportation concerned both of these intimately. The total railroad mileage of the United States at the outbreak of the war was 30,635—about one-eighth of what it was in 1910. The railroads of 1861 connected the Mississippi valley with the seaboard, it is true, but they had not yet been welded into systems, and as a means of transportation for either men or materials they were sadly inadequate when judged by twentieth-century standards. Deficient as they were, however, they had reached the Mississippi River some years in advance of the traffic demands of the country, and in the exigencies of war their facilities for moving the wheat and corn of the Mississippi valley were to be taxed to their limit for the first time, although the country's total yield of wheat was less than one-fourth, and of corn less than one-third of the corresponding crops in 1910.

In tapping the rich grain fields of the interior, the Government at Washington had decidedly the advantage over that at Richmond, for the Confederate authorities were served by transportation lines that were even less efficient than those of the North, and, moreover, a large proportion of their tillable land was devoted to cotton growing, and the home-grown food products of the South were unequal to the demands of home consumption. In January, 1862, the Confederate quartermaster-

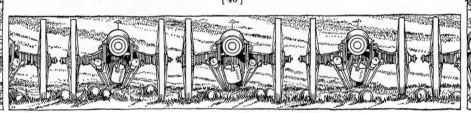

At Belle Plain, at Centerville, Virginia, and at Baton Rouge appear the omnipresent army wagons, which followed the armies from Washington to the Gulf. The dimensions of the box of these useful vehicles were as follows: Length (inside), 120 inches; width (inside), 43 inches; height, 22 inches. Such a wagon could carry a load weighing about 2536 pounds, or 1500 rations of hard bread, coffee, sugar, and salt. Each wagon was drawn by a team of four horses or six mules.

THE BIVOUAC—WAGON-TRAIN AT CUMBERLAND LANDING, PAMUNKEY RIVER

general complained that the railroad lines on which his Government was dependent for transportation, were operating only two trains a day each way, at an average speed of six miles an hour. Before the war, the railroads of the South had been dependent for most of their equipment on the car-shops and locomotive-works of the Northern States. The South had only limited facilities for producing rolling-stock. After communication with the North had ceased, most of the Southern railroads deteriorated rapidly. Quite apart from the ruin caused by the war itself, many of the railroads soon became comparatively useless for lack of equipment and repairs, and the familiar expression "two streaks of rust and a right of way" was applied with peculiar fitness to some of them.

Yet the railroads played an important part in the war from the beginning. This was indeed the first great war in history in which railroads entered, to any important extent, into the plans of campaigns and battles. The Federal quartermaster-general, not being harassed by hostile movements within the territory from which his supplies were drawn, perfected the system of railroad transportation for both troops and supplies, until he had it working with smoothness and a high degree of efficiency. The railroad corporations that remained loyal to the Government at Washington, came together in the early days of the war and agreed on a schedule of rates for army transportation. This was probably the earliest instance of a general railroad agreement in the history of the country. These rates were adhered to throughout the war, and while the prices of almost all commodities rose far above the price-level of 1861, transportation rates, so far as the Government was concerned, remained uniform and constant. The railroads, for the most part, prospered under this arrangement. Never before had their rolling-stock been so steadily employed, and the yearly volume of business, both passenger and freight, was unprecedented. The Government soon found that in the transportation of troops, the two thousand dollars which was paid

WEIGHING BREAD FOR THE UNION ARMY, 1864

The counting of every pound of flour was one of the essentials required of the quartermaster's department. Each pan of baked bread must be weighed. This was systematically done by the commissary-sergeant especially detailed for that purpose. In this photograph the scales stand in front of him, while a colored boy has placed a batch of loaves from the pyramid of bread upon the scales. A soldier is handing out another batch of loaves ready to be weighed. When the Army of the Potomac lay in front of Petersburg in 1864 and 1865, there were a great many inventions brought to the fore for the benefit of the men serving at the front. Among them was the army bake-oven, a regular baker's oven placed on wheels. In the lower picture the bakers are shoving the bread just kneaded into the oven to bake. The bearded man in the foreground at the left is the fireman who keeps the fires going. From this bakery the loaves went out, after each batch was duly weighed, to the various regiments according to the amount requisitioned by their several commissaries. It was always a happy moment for the soldiers when "fresh-bread day" came around. It varied the monotony of "hard-tack," and formed quite a luxury after the hard campaign through the Wilderness and across the James River. Soft bread was obtainable only in permanent camp. There was no time for it on the march.

A GOVERNMENT OVEN ON WHEELS

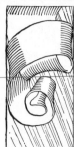

for moving one thousand men one hundred miles by rail was far less than the cost of marching the same number of men an equivalent distance over the roads of the country.

Unfortunately, however, campaign plans, more frequently than otherwise, called for long marches between points not connected by rail. Water transportation was used by General McClellan to good advantage in beginning the Peninsula campaign; after that, the Army of the Potomac, once having made the acquaintance of Virginia mud, retained it to the end. The wagon roads of the Old Dominion were tested in all seasons and by every known form of conveyance. A familiar accompaniment of the marching troops was the inevitable wagon train, carrying subsistence, ammunition, and clothing. Twelve wagons to every thousand men had been Napoleon's rule on the march, but the highways of Europe undoubtedly permitted relatively heavier loads. For the Army of the Potomac, twenty-five wagons per thousand men was not considered an excessive allowance. No wonder these well-laden supply trains aroused the interest of daring bands of Confederate scouts! Such prizes were well worth trying for.

When General Meade, with his army of one hundred and fifty thousand men, left Brandy Station, Virginia, in May, 1864, on his march to Petersburg, each soldier carried six days' rations of hardtack, coffee, sugar, and salt. The supply trains carried ten days' rations of the same articles, and one day's ration of salt pork. For the remainder of the meat ration, a supply of beef cattle on the hoof for thirteen days' rations was driven along with the troops, but over separate roads. General Thomas Wilson, who was Meade's chief commissary, directed the movements of this great herd of beef cattle by brigades and divisions.

The Federal service required an immense number of draft animals. The Quartermaster's Department bought horses for the cavalry and artillery, and horses and mules for the trains. In 1862, the Government owned approximately

GUARDING LUMBER FOR THE GOVERNMENT

Vast quantities of lumber were used by the Union armies during the war. The Federal Government was at that time the largest builder in the world. The Engineer Corps carried interchangeable parts to replace destroyed railroad bridges, and lumber was needed for pontoons, flooring, hospital buildings, and construction of every kind necessary to the welfare of the armies. Often, when no lumber was at hand, neighboring houses had to be wrecked in order to repair a railroad bridge or furnish flooring for the pontoon-bridges. The upper photograph shows a sentry guarding the Government's lumber-yard at Washington. Much of this lumber was doubtless used in repairing the Orange & Alexandria Railroad, so frequently destroyed by both armies as they operated between Richmond and Washington. In the lower photograph a sentry is guarding a Government mill in the field.

SENTRY AT GOVERNMENT MILL

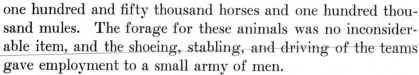

one hundred and fifty thousand horses and one hundred thousand mules. The forage for these animals was no inconsiderable item, and the shoeing, stabling, and driving of the teams gave employment to a small army of men.

The Confederate authorities were never compelled to make such extensive purchases of animals either for transportation or for strictly military uses. Under the system adopted in the Confederate army, the cavalry horses were furnished by the officers and enlisted men themselves; the Quartermaster's Department made no purchases on that account. Furthermore, since the operations were very largely conducted in the home territory, there was less demand for supply-train transportation than in the case of the Federal armies, which repeatedly made expeditions into hostile country and had to be fully provisioned for the march.

The Federal forces seem never to have been for any length of time without abundant food supplies. In the fall of 1863, while the fighting around Chattanooga was in progress, supplies were deficient, but the shortage was soon made up, and the railroads brought great quantities of meat from the West, to feed Sherman's army during its long Atlanta campaign. These commissary stores were obtained at convenient shipping-points, by contracts let after due advertisement by the commissary officers. They were apportioned by the commissary-general at Washington to the respective army commissaries and by them in turn to the corps-, division-, brigade-, and finally the regimental commissaries, who dealt out the rations to the individual soldiers, each officer being held to account for a given quota. Prices fluctuated during the war, but the market for foodstuffs in the North can hardly be said to have been in a condition of panic at any time. The Government had no difficulty in buying all the supplies it needed at prevailing prices.

In the Confederacy, the situation was different. The general system of purchasing supplies that the Richmond Government attempted to follow was essentially the same as that

LOADING SUPPLY–WAGONS FROM TRANSPORTS FOR GRANT'S ARMY—CITY POINT, 1864

PORK, HARD–TACK, SUGAR, AND COFFEE FOR THE REGIMENTAL COMMISSARY AT CEDAR LEVEL

The immense supply and transportation facilities of the North in 1864, contrasted with the situation of the Southern soldiery, recalls Bonaparte's terse speech to his army in Italy: "Soldiers! You need *everything*—the enemy *has* everything." The Confederates often acted upon the same principle. At City Point, Virginia, Grant's wagon-trains received the army supplies landed from the ships.

established at Washington, but, from the very outset, the seceding State Governments were active in provisioning the Confederate armies, and in some instances there was an apparent jealousy of authority, as when Confederate officers began the impressment of needed articles. The inflated currency and soaring prices made such action imperative, in the judgment of the Davis cabinet.

The blockade did not wholly cut off the importation of supplies from abroad. Indeed, considerable quantities were bought in England by the Confederate Subsistence Department and paid for in cotton. Early in the war the South found that its meat supply was short, and the Richmond Government went into the pork-packing business on a rather extensive scale in Tennessee. The Secretary of War made no secret of the fact that, in spite of these expedients, it was still impossible to provision the Confederate army as the Government desired, although it was said that the troops in the field were supplied with coffee long after that luxury had disappeared from the breakfast tables of the " home folks."

In the matter of clothing, the armies of both the Federal and Confederate Governments were relieved of no slight embarrassment at the beginning of the war by the prompt action of States and communities. The Quartermaster's Department at Washington was quite unequal to the task of uniforming the " three-months' men " who responded to Lincoln's first call for volunteers. This work was done by the State Governments. Wisconsin sent its first regiments to the front clad in cadet gray, but the uniforms, apart from the confusion in color, were said to have been of excellent quality, and the men discarded them with regret, after a few weeks' wear, for the flimsy blue that the enterprising contractors foisted on the Washington Government in its mad haste to secure equipment. Those were the days when fortunes were made from shoddy—an era of wholesale cheating that ended only with the accession of Stanton, Lincoln's great war secretary, who numbered

PROVISIONING BURNSIDE'S ARMY—BELLE PLAIN LANDING ON THE POTOMAC

CLOSER VIEWS OF BELLE PLAIN LANDING, LATE IN NOVEMBER, 1862

NEARER STILL—ARRIVAL OF THE WAGON-TRAINS AT BELLE PLAIN LANDING

among the special objects of his hatred the dishonest army contractor.

After the work of the Quartermaster's Department had been systematized and some effort had been made to analyze costs, it appeared that the expense incurred for each soldier's equipment, exclusive of arms, amounted to fifty dollars.

For the purchase and manufacture of clothing for the Federal army, it was necessary to maintain great depots in New York, Philadelphia, Boston, Cincinnati, Louisville, Indianapolis, St. Louis, Detroit, and Springfield, Illinois. Confederate depots for similar purposes were established at Richmond, New Orleans, Memphis, Charleston, Savannah, San Antonio, and Fort Smith. The Confederacy was obliged to import most of its shoes and many articles of clothing. Wool was brought from Texas and Mexico to mills in the service of the Confederate Quartermaster's Department. Harness, tents, and camp and garrison equipage were manufactured for the department in Virginia, Georgia, Louisiana, North Carolina, and Mississippi. The department's estimate to cover contracts made in England for supplies to run the blockade during a single six-months' period amounted to £570,000.

It is the conclusion of James Ford Rhodes, the historian of the Civil War period, that "never had an army been so well equipped with food and clothing as was that of the North; never before were the comfort and welfare of the men so well looked after." The appropriations for the Quartermaster's Department alone, during the war, aggregated more than a billion dollars. Extensive frauds were perpetrated on the Government, not only in the clothing contracts of the first year, to which reference has been made, but in the transport service and in various transactions which were not properly checked under a system of audit and disbursement that broke down altogether in the emergency of real war. In the opinion of Mr. Rhodes, the administrators of the War Department were not only efficient, but aggressively honest public servants.

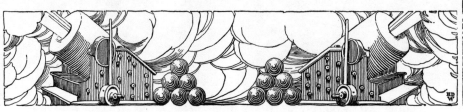

PART I

SOLDIER LIFE

MARSHALLING THE FEDERAL VOLUNTEERS

OFFICER AND SERGEANT IN '61

MEN OF THE SIXTH VERMONT NEAR WASHINGTON

A HOLLOW–SQUARE MANEUVER FOR THE NEW SOLDIERS

This regiment was organized at Bangor, Me., for three months' service, and left the State for Willett's Point, N. Y., May 14, 1861. Such was the enthusiasm of the moment that it was mustered into the United States service, part for two and part for three years, May 28, 1861. It moved to Washington on May 30th. The first camp of the regiment was on Meridian Hill, near Washington, till July 1st. The live-long days were spent in constant "drill, drill, drill" during this period. McClellan was fashioning the new levies into an army. The total population of the Northern States in 1860 was 21,184,305. New England's population was 3,135,283, or about one-seventh of the whole. New England's troops numbered 363,162, over one-tenth of its population, practically one-seventh the total muster of forces raised in the North during the war, namely, 2,778,304. The New England population was distributed as follows: Maine, 628,279; Massachusetts, 1,231,066; Vermont, 315,098; New Hampshire, 326,073; Connecticut, 460,147, and

SECOND MAINE INFANTRY AT CAMP JAMESON, 1861

Rhode Island, 174,620. The number of troops that these States respectively furnished and the losses they incurred were: Maine, 70,107—loss, 9,398; Massachusetts, 146,730—loss, 13,942; Vermont, 33,288—loss, 5,224; New Hampshire, 33,937—loss, 4,882; Connecticut, 55,864—loss, 5,354; and Rhode Island, 23,236—loss, 1,321. The total loss was thus 40,121. Maine's contribution of more than 11 per cent. of its population took the form of two regiments of cavalry, one regiment of heavy artillery, seven batteries of light artillery, one battalion and a company of sharpshooters, with thirty-three regiments, one battalion, and seven companies of infantry. The Second Maine fought with the Army of the Potomac until the battle of Chancellorsville, May 1 to 5, 1863. The regiment was ordered home on the 20th of that month, and the three-years men were transferred to the Twentieth Maine Infantry. The regiment was mustered out June 9, 1863, having lost four officers and 135 enlisted men, killed or mortally wounded, and by disease.

COPYRIGHT, 1911, REVIEW OF REVIEWS CO.

THE FIRST RHODE ISLAND INFANTRY LEAVING PROVIDENCE, APRIL 20, 1861

The sidewalks were filled with cheering throngs, and unbounded enthusiasm greeted the volunteers, as the first division of the First Regiment of Detached Rhode Island Militia left Providence for Washington April 20, 1861. At 10:30 in the morning Colonel Ambrose E. Burnside, in command, had ordered the men of the first division to assemble upon Exchange Place. The band was followed by the National Cadets and the first division was led by Colonel Burnside himself. It contained practically half of each of the ten companies, six of which were recruited in Providence and one each in Pawtucket, Woonsocket, Newport, and Westerly. The second division left four days later. The men in this photograph marched through Exchange Street to Market Square, up North Main Street and through Meeting to Benefit, and down Benefit to Fox Point.

BURNSIDE AND HIS BOYS OF THE FIRST RHODE ISLAND AFTER BULL RUN

The officers of the First Rhode Island Volunteers looked quite martial in their pleated blue blouses and gauntlets at the outset of the war. Colonel Ambrose E. Burnside sits in the center, with folded arms in front of the tree. Above his head to the right is the rude sign: "Welcome home." The little State of Rhode Island contributed three regiments and a battalion of cavalry, three regiments of heavy artillery, ten batteries of light artillery, twelve regiments of infantry, and an independent company of hospital guards to the Union cause. The first Rhode Island was a three-months regiment which was mustered out August 2, 1861. This photograph shows the young officers after the Union disaster at Bull Run. From April, 1861, to August, the regiment lost one officer and sixteen enlisted men killed and mortally wounded, and eight enlisted men by disease.

THIRD CONNECTICUT INFANTRY, CAMP DOUGLAS, 1861

Only one day after the First Regiment of Connecticut Infantry started from Hartford—May 18, 1861—the Second and Third left New Haven for the great camps that encircled Washington. All three of these three-months regiments took part in the battle of Bull Run, and all three were mustered out by the middle of August. This was one of the first steps by which the fighting men of the North were finding themselves. Connecticut sent a regiment of cavalry, two regiments of heavy artillery, three batteries of light artillery, and thirty regiments of infantry to the front in the course of the war. Two of the latter, the Twenty-ninth and the Thirtieth, were colored regiments. The company of the Third in the photograph looks quite natty in its dark blue uniforms. These men have not yet heard the crash of a Confederate volley, but they are soon to do so on the disastrous field of Bull Run. They served almost three months, being mustered in on May 14, 1861, and mustered out August 12th.

OFFICERS OF THE NINTH MASSACHUSETTS INFANTRY AT CAMP CASS, 1861

A little over two months before this regiment left Boston for Washington, the Sixth Massachusetts had been defending itself against the mob in the streets of Baltimore, April 19, 1861. Massachusetts poured regiment after regiment to the front until seventy-one regiments had answered President Lincoln's calls. Besides the infantry, Massachusetts sent five regiments and three battalions of cavalry, four regiments, a battalion, and thirty unassigned companies of heavy artillery, eighteen batteries of light artillery, and two companies of sharpshooters. The Ninth Massachusetts left Boston for Washington on June 27, 1861. At the first and second Bull Run, on the Peninsula, at Antietam, Fredericksburg, Chancellorsville, Gettysburg, the Wilderness, Spotsylvania, and Cold Harbor this regiment fought bravely and well. When it was finally mustered out June 21, 1864, it had lost 15 officers, 194 enlisted men killed and mortally wounded, and 3 officers and 66 enlisted men by disease.

"GREEN MOUNTAIN BOYS" AT DRILL, 1861

"I" AND "D" COMPANIES OF THE SIXTH VERMONT

THE SIXTH VERMONT INFANTRY BEFORE CAMP GRIFFIN, NEAR WASHINGTON, IN 1861

From October 19 and 22, 1861, when the Sixth Vermont Infantry left Montpelier for Washington, until its final corps-review June 8, 1865, nearly two months after Appomattox, this regiment served with the Army of the Potomac and the Army of the Shenandoah. These hardy mountain boys shown in the photograph are drilling in full accouterment, carrying their knapsacks on their sturdy backs. Clad in gray turned up with emerald, as befitted "the Green Mountain Boys," they added one more note of color to the kaleidoscope of uniforms that gathered in Washington that summer and fall.

Vermont sent one regiment of cavalry, a regiment and a company of heavy artillery, three batteries of light artillery, and eighteen regiments of infantry to the front. The Sixth Vermont fought at Yorktown, Antietam, Fredericksburg, Chancellorsville, Gettysburg, Wilderness, Spotsylvania, at Opequon, in the Shenandoah Valley, and at Petersburg, and formed part of the Sixth Corps sent to the relief of Washington when Early threatened it in July, 1864. When mustered out June 26, 1865, the Sixth had lost 12 officers and 191 enlisted men killed and wounded, and 3 officers and 212 men by disease.

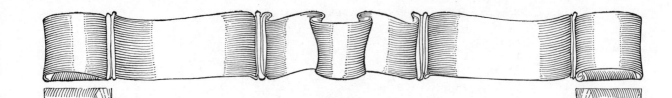

MARSHALING THE FEDERAL ARMY

By Charles King
Brigadier-General, United States Volunteers

UNION men wore anxious faces early in the spring of 1861. For months the newspapers had been filled with accounts of the seizure of Government forts and arsenals all over the South. State after State had seceded, and the *New York Tribune*, edited by Horace Greeley, had bewildered the North and encouraged the South by declaring that if the latter desired to set up a government of its own it had every moral right to do so. The little garrison of Fort Moultrie, in Charleston Harbor, threatened by a superior force and powerless against land attack, had spiked its guns on Christmas night, in 1860, and pulled away for Sumter, perched on its islet of rocks a mile from shore, hoisted the Stars and Stripes, and there, in spite of pitiful numbers, with a Southern-born soldier at its head, practically defied all South Carolina.

The *Star of the West* had been loaded with soldiers and supplies at New York, and sent to Sumter's relief. Then South Carolina, duly warned, had manned the guns of Morris Island and driven her back to sea. Not content with that, South Carolina, the envy of an applauding sisterhood of Southern States, had planted batteries on every point within range of Sumter. All the North could see that its fate was sealed, and no one, when the 1st of April came, could say just how the North would take it.

The second week settled the question. With one accord, on April 12th, the Southern guns opened on the lone fortress and its puny force. The next day, with the flagstaff shot away and the interior of the fort all ablaze, the casemates thick with

THE FAMOUS NEW YORK SEVENTH, JUST AFTER REACHING
WASHINGTON IN APRIL, 1861

The first New York State militia regiment to reach Washington after President Lincoln's call for troops, April 15, 1861, was the Seventh Infantry. The best blood and most honored names in New York City were prominent in its ranks. It eventually supplied no less than 606 officers to the Union army. Veterans now hail it as the highest type of the citizen soldiers who went to the front. The old armory at the foot of Third Avenue could not contain the crowds that gathered. At this writing (1911) it is just being demolished. The Seventh left for Washington April 19, 1861, and as it marched down Broadway passed such a multitude of cheering citizens that its splendid band was almost unheard through the volume of applause. On April 24th the regiment reached Annapolis Junction, Maryland. On that and the day following, with the Eighth Massachusetts for company, it had to patch the railway and open communications with Washington. The men were mustered into service on April 26th, and their camp on Meridian Hill, May 2d to 23d, was pointed out as a model. They took part in the occupation of Arlington Heights, Virginia, May 24th to May 26th, and assisted in building Fort Runyon. They returned to Camp Cameron on the latter date, and were mustered out at New York City, June 3, 1861, but those not immediately commissioned were mustered in again the following year, and in 1863.

blinding smoke, with no hope from friends, the gallant garrison could ask only the mercy of the foes, and it was given willingly—the soldier's privilege of saluting his colors and marching out with the honors of war.

And then the North awoke in earnest. In one day the streets of New York city, all seeming apathy the day before, blazed with a sudden burst of color. The Stars and Stripes were flung to the breeze from every staff and halyard; the hues of the Union flamed on every breast. The transformation was a marvel. There was but one topic on every tongue, but one thought in every heart: The flag had been downed in Charleston Harbor, the long-threatened secession had begun, the very Capitol at Washington was endangered, the President at last had spoken, in a demand for seventy-five thousand men.

It was the first call of many to follow—calls that eventually drew 2,300,000 men into the armies of the Union, but the first was the most thrilling of all, and nowhere was its effect so wonderful as in the city of New York.

Not until aroused by the echo of the guns at Sumter could or would the people believe the South in deadly earnest. The press and the prophets had not half prepared them. Southern sympathizers had been numerous and aggressive, and when the very heads of the Government at Washington were unresentful of repeated violation of Federal rights and authority, what could be expected of a people reared only in the paths of peace? The military spirit had long been dominant in the South and correspondingly dormant in the North. The South was full of men accustomed to the saddle and the use of arms; the North had but a handful. The South had many soldier schools; the North, outside of West Point, had but one worthy the name. Even as late as the winter of 1860 and 1861, young men in New York, taking counsel of far-seeing elders and assembling for drill, were rebuked by visiting pedagogues who bade them waste no time in " silly vanities."

" The days of barbaric battle are dead," said they. " The

OFFICERS OF THE SEVENTY–FIRST NEW YORK INFANTRY

The Seventy-first New York Infantry, or "Second Excelsior," was organized at Camp Scott, Staten Island, New York, as the second regiment of Sickles' brigade in June, 1861. The men left for Washington July 23d. The lower photograph shows a group off duty, lounging in the bright sunshine near their canvas houses—in this case "A" tents. They accompanied McClellan to the Peninsula, and served in all the great battles of the Army of the Potomac until they were mustered out at New York City, July 30, 1864. The regiment lost five officers and eighty-three enlisted men killed and mortally wounded, and two officers and seventy-three enlisted men by disease.

MEN OF THE SEVENTY–FIRST NEW YORK AT CAMP DOUGLAS IN 1861

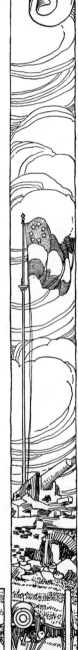

good sense of the American people will ever stand between us and a resort to arms." The ominous rumbles from Pensacola, Augusta, Baton Rouge, and San Antonio meant nothing to these peace proclaimers; it took the thunderclap of Sumter to hush them. It took the sudden and overwhelming uprising of April 15th to bring the hitherto confident backers of the South face to face with an astounding fact.

Seventy-five thousand men needed at once!—the active militia called instantly to the front! Less than fifteen thousand regulars scattered far and wide—many of them in Texas, but mainly on the Indian frontier—could the Nation muster in gathering toils. Many a Southern-born officer had resigned and joined the forces of his native State, but the rank and file, horse, foot, and gunners stood sturdily to their colors. Still, these tried and disciplined men were few and far between.

Utterly unprepared for war of any kind, the Union leaders found themselves forced to improvise an army to defend their seat of Government—itself on Southern soil, and compassed by hostile cities. The new flag of the seceding States was flaunted at Alexandria, in full view of the unfinished dome of the Capitol. The colors of the South were openly and defiantly worn in the streets of Baltimore, barring the way of the would-be rescuers.

The veteran Virginian, General Winfield Scott, at the head of the United States army, had gathered a few light guns in Washington. His soldierly assistant, Colonel Charles P. Stone, had organized, from department clerks and others, the first armed body of volunteers for the defense of the threatened center, and within a few months the first-named was superseded as too old, the second imprisoned as too Southern— an utterly baseless charge. The one hope to save the capital lay in the swift assembling of the Eastern militia, and by the night of April 15th the long roll was thundering from the walls of every city armory. From Boston Common to the Mississippi, loyal States were wiring assurance of support.

THE WEST IN 1861—BOYS OF THE FOURTH MICHIGAN INFANTRY

While the East was pouring its thousands to Washington, the West, an unknown quantity to the Confederacy, was rapidly organizing and sending forward its regiments. In 1860, the population of Michigan was 748,112. In the course of the war Michigan furnished 87,364 soldiers, of which 14,753 gave their lives. At the outbreak of the war the State had a militia strength of only twenty-eight companies, aggregating 1,241 officers and men. The State appropriation for military service was only $3,000 a year. At the President's call for troops on April 15th, Michigan's quota was only one infantry regiment. On May 7th the Legislature met and passed an Act giving the Governor power to raise ten regiments and make a loan of $1,000,000. On May 13th, the first regiment left for the seat of war, fully armed and equipped. Public subscriptions were started at all centers. Detroit raised $50,000 in one day as a loan to the State.

And that night the muster began, Massachusetts promptly rallying her old line-militia in their quaint, high-topped shakos and long gray overcoats—the Sixth and Eighth regiments mustering at once. New York city was alive with eager but untried soldiery. First and foremost stood her famous Seventh, the best blood and most honored names prominent in its ranks. The old armory at the foot of Third Avenue could not contain the crowds that gathered. Close at hand mustered the Seventy-first—the "American Guard" of the ante-bellum days. But a few streets away, with Centre Market as a nucleus, other throngs were cheering about the hall where Michael Corcoran, suspended but the year before because his Irishmen would not parade in honor of the Prince of Wales, was now besieged by fellow countrymen, eager to go with him and his gallant Sixty-ninth. Four blocks further, soon to be led by Cameron, brother to the Pennsylvania Secretary of War, the Highlanders were forming to the skirl of the piper and under the banner of the Seventy-ninth. West of Broadway, Le Gal and DeTrobriand were welcoming the enthusiastic Frenchmen who made up the old "red-legged Fifty-fifth," while, less noisily, yet in strong numbers, the Eighth, the Twelfth, and in Brooklyn the Fourteenth, were flocking to their armories and listening with bated breath to the latest news and orders from Washington.

Orders came soon enough. First to march from the metropolis for the front was New York's soldierly Seventh, striding down Broadway through countless multitudes of cheering citizens, their splendid band almost unheard through the volume of applause. Never before had New York seen its great thoroughfare so thronged; never had it shown such emotion as on that soft April afternoon of the 19th. Prompt as had been the response to marching orders, the gray column of the Seventh was not the first to move. The Massachusetts Sixth had taken the lead one day earlier, and was even now battling its way through the streets of Baltimore. Barely

A YOUNG VOLUNTEER FROM THE WEST

This youthful warrior in his "hickory" shirt looks less enthusiastic than his two comrades of the Fourth Michigan Infantry shown on the previous page. Yet the Fourth Michigan was with the Army of the Potomac from Bull Run to Appomattox. The regiment was organized at Adrian, Mich., and mustered in June 20, 1861. It left the State for Washington on June 26th, and its first service was the advance on Manassas, July 16th to 21, 1861. It participated thereafter in every great battle of the Army of the Potomac until it was relieved from duty in the trenches before Petersburg, June 19, 1864. The veterans and recruits were then transferred to the First Michigan Infantry. The regimental loss was heavy. Twelve officers and 177 enlisted men were killed or mortally wounded, and the loss by disease was one officer and 107 enlisted men.

had the Cortlandt Street Ferry borne the last detachment of the Seventh across the Hudson when the newsboys were shrieking the tidings of the attack on the men of New England by the mob of "blood-tubs" and "plug-uglies" in the Maryland city.

It takes five hours to go from New York to Washington to-day; it took six days that wild week in 1861. The Seventh, with the Massachusetts Eighth for company, had to patch the railway and trudge wearily, yet manfully, from Annapolis to the junction of the old Baltimore and Washington Railroad, before it could again proceed by rail to its great reception on Pennsylvania Avenue in Washington. Then New York's second offering started—another wonderful day in Gotham. In less than a week from the original call, the active militia was under arms in full ranks, and most of it en route for the front.

Farther west the Lake cities—Buffalo, Cleveland, Detroit, Milwaukee, Chicago—each had mustered a regiment with its own favorite companies—Continentals, Grays or Light Guards as a nucleus. Michigan, Wisconsin, Iowa, and Minnesota each had been called upon for a regiment, and the response was almost instantaneous. Ohio, Indiana, and Illinois, more populated, had tendered more than the thousands demanded.

By the 1st of June, there was camped or billeted about Washington the cream of the State soldiery of every commonwealth east of the Ohio and north of the Potomac—except Maryland. Maryland held aloof. Pennsylvania, asked for twelve thousand men, had rushed twenty thousand to the mustering officers. Massachusetts, called on for fifteen hundred, sent more than twice that number within two days. Ohio, taxed for just ten thousand, responded with twelve thousand, and Missouri, where Southern sentiment was rife and St. Louis almost a Southern stronghold, tumultuously raised ten thousand men, unarmed, undrilled, yet sorely needed. But for Nathaniel Lyon of the regular army, and the prompt muster

SOLDIERS FROM THE WEST IN 1861—FOURTH MICHIGAN INFANTRY

No less enthusiastic than the sister State across Lake Michigan was the then far-Western State of Wisconsin. Its population in 1860 was 775,881, and the State furnished during the war 91,327 men, or nearly 13 per cent. of the population. The State's loss in men was 12,301. Within a week after the President's call for 75,000 men, April 15, 1861, Governor Randall, of Wisconsin, had thirty-six companies offered him, although only one regiment was Wisconsin's quota under the Federal Government's apportionment. Within six days the first regiment was enrolled. Wisconsin suffered a financial panic within a fortnight after the fall of Fort Sumter. Thirty-eight banks out of one hundred and nine suspended payment, but the added burden failed to check the enthusiasm of the people. The State contained large and varied groups of settlers of foreign birth. Among its troops at the front, the Ninth, Twenty-sixth, and Forty-sixth Regiments were almost wholly German; the Twelfth Regiment was composed of French Canadians; the Fifteenth of Scandinavians; the Seventeenth of Irish, and the Third, Seventh, and Thirty-seventh contained a large enrollment of Indians. Wisconsin's contribution of troops took the form of four regiments of cavalry, one regiment of heavy artillery, thirteen batteries of light artillery, one company of sharpshooters, and fifty-four regiments of infantry. Such unanimity for the Union cause surprised the Confederacy.

of her Union men, Missouri would early have been lost to the Nation. And as for Kentucky, though in grand numbers and gallant services her sons repudiated his action, Governor Magoffin refused a man for the defense of the general Government, or what he called the "coercion" of the Southern States.

But it was a motley concourse, that which gathered at Washington where all eyes were centered. The call for seventy-five thousand militia for three months was quickly followed by the call for five hundred thousand volunteers for three years, and such was the spirit and enthusiasm of the North that, as fast as they could be uniformed, faster than they could be armed, the great regiments of State volunteers came dustily forth from the troop trains and went trudging along the length of Pennsylvania Avenue, out to the waiting camps in the suburbs. Within the month of its arrival, the Seventh New York, led by engineers and backed by comrade militiamen, had crossed the Potomac, invaded the sacred soil of Virginia, and tossed the red earth into rude fortifications. Then it had been sent home for muster-out as musketmen, but, let this ever be remembered, to furnish almost instantly seven hundred officers for the newly organizing regiments, regular and volunteer.

Two little classes of West Point cadets, graduated in May and June respectively, brave boys just out of their bell-buttoned coatees, were set in saddle and hard at work drilling whole battalions of raw lads from the shops and farms, whose elected officers were to the full as untaught as their men. Local fame as a drillmaster of cadets or Zouaves gave many a young fellow command of a company; some few, indeed, like Ellsworth, even of a regiment. Foreign soldiers of fortune, seeing their chance, had hurried to our shores and tendered their swords, many of them who could barely speak English receiving high commissions, and swaggering splendidly about the camps and streets. Many of the regiments came headed by local politicians, some who, but the year gone by, had been fervent supporters of Southern rights and slavery. A favored

IN THE QUOTA FROM MICHIGAN

WOODSMEN OF THE NORTH WITH THEIR TASSELED CAPS

An officer, privates, and bandsmen of the Fourth Michigan Infantry, who came from the West in their tasseled caps to fight for the Union cause. By the close of the war Michigan had sent eleven regiments and two companies of cavalry, a regiment of heavy artillery, fourteen batteries of light artillery, a regiment and a company of engineers, a regiment and eight companies of sharpshooters, and thirty-five regiments and two companies of infantry to the front. In

face of the fact that the original demand upon the State of Michigan had been for one company of infantry, this shows something of the spirit of the West. This was one of the earliest regiments sent to the front by the State of Michigan. Some of its companies were dressed in a sort of Zouave uniform, as shown above, that is, Canadian caps without visors, and short leggings; while other companies were dressed in the ordinary uniform of the volunteer regiments.

few came under command of soldierly, skilled young officers from the regular service, and most of them led by grave, thoughtful men in the prime of life who realized their responsibility and studied faithfully to meet the task.

Then wonderful was the variety of uniform! It was marked even before McDowell led forth the raw levies to try their mettle at Bull Run. Among the New Yorkers were Highlanders in plaid "trews" (their kilts and bonnets very properly left at home), the blue jackets of the Seventy-first, the gray jackets of the Eighth, and Varian's gunners—some of whom bethought them at Centreville that their time was up and it would be pleasanter "going home than hell-ward," as a grim, red-whiskered colonel, Sherman by name, said they surely would if they didn't quit straggling. There were half-fledged Zouaves, like the Fourteenth New York (Brooklyn), and full-rigged Zouaves, albeit their jackets and "knickers" were gray and only their shirts were red—the First "Fire" of New York, who had lost their martial little colonel—Ellsworth—before Jackson's shotgun in Alexandria. There were Rhode Islanders in pleated blue blouses—Burnside's boys; there were far Westerners from Wisconsin, in fast-fading gray. Michigan and Minnesota each was represented by a strong regiment. Blenker's Germans were there, a reserve division in gray from head to foot. There were a few troops of regular cavalry, their jackets gaudy with yellow braid and brazen shoulder scales. There were the grim regular batteries of Carlisle, Ricketts, and Griffin, their blouses somber, but the cross cannon on their caps gleaming with polish, such being the way of the regular. It was even more marvelous, later, when McClellan had come to organize the vast array into brigades and divisions, and to bring order out of chaos, for chaotic it was after Bull Run.

The States were uniforming their soldiery as best they could in that summer of 1861. New York, Massachusetts, and Pennsylvania usually in blue, the Vermonters in gray, turned-up with emerald, as befitted the Green Mountain boys. The

FIRST MINNESOTA INFANTRY AT CAMP STONE, NEAR POOLES–
VILLE, MARYLAND, IN JANUARY, 1862

The First Minnesota Infantry was the first regiment tendered to the Government, April 14, 1861. It was mustered into the service April 29, 1861, fourteen days after the President's proclamation. The regiment embarked June 22, 1861, for Prairie du Chien, whence it proceeded by rail to Washington. Its first uniforms furnished by the State were black felt hats, black trousers, and red flannel shirts. It served throughout the war. The population of Minnesota in 1860 was 172,023, including 2,369 Indians. It furnished 24,020 soldiers, of whom 2,584 were lost. While the whole people of Minnesota were striving night and day to fill up new regiments to reënforce the national armies, they had to maintain garrisons along the Indian frontiers. One garrison was at Fort Ripley, below Crow Wing, and another at Fort Ridgly, in Nicolett County. Fort Abercrombie and a post on the Red River fifteen miles north of Breckinridge were strongly fortified. In the Sioux war of 1861, from one thousand to fifteen hundred persons were killed, and property to the value of over half a million dollars destroyed. Most of the regiments raised for the war saw some service at home, fighting the Indians within the borders of the State. Thus the First Minnesota sent two companies to Fort Ridgly, one to Fort Ripley, and two to Fort Abercrombie to quell Indian uprisings before they dared to gather at Fort Snelling to leave the State for the struggle with the South. Minnesota sent two regiments and two battalions of cavalry, one regiment of heavy artillery, three batteries of light artillery, two companies of sharpshooters, and eleven infantry regiments to the front during the war.

one Western brigade in the newly formed Army of the Potomac came clad in gray throughout, not to be changed for the blue until late in September.

But for variety, New York city led the country. A second regiment of Fire Zouaves had been quickly formed, as dashing in appearance as the first. Abram Duryée of the old militia (with a black-eyed, solemn-faced little regular as second in command, soon to become famous as a corps leader) marched forth at the head of a magnificent body of men, the color-guard, nearly all seven-footers, all in the scarlet fez and breeches of the favorite troops of France. Zouave rig was by long odds the most pleasing to the popular eye in the streets of the big city—and, less happily, to Southern marksmen later —for all in a day the improvised wooden barracks were thronging with eager lads seeking enlistment in the Zouave regiments. Baxter's in Philadelphia, Farnsworth's (Second Fire), Duryée's (Fifth New York), Bendix's, Hawkins', and "Billy Wilson's" in New York.

To cater still further to the love for the spectacular and the picturesque, still more distinctive regiments were authorized—the Garibaldi Guard—mainly Italians, under Colonel D'Utassy, in a dress that aped the Bersaglieri. The D'Epineul Zouaves, French and would-be Frenchmen, in the costliest costume yet devised, and destined to be abandoned before they were six months older. Still another French battalion, also in Algerian campaign rig—"*Les Enfants Perdus.*" Lost Children, indeed, once they left New York and fell in with the campaigners of Uncle Sam. Then came the Chasseurs, in very natty and attractive dress, worn like the others until worn out in one real campaign, when its wearers, like the others, lost their identity in the universal, most unbecoming, yet eminently serviceable blue-flannel blouse and light-blue kersey trousers, with the utterly ugly forage cap and stout brogans of the Union army.

Fanciful names they took, too, at the start, and bore

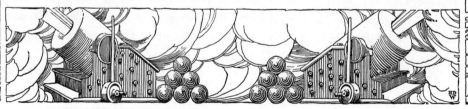

THE GUARD EXAMINING PASSES AT GEORGETOWN FERRY

So expert became the patrols of the provost-guard, and so thorough the precautions at headquarters during the first half-year of drill and picket duty along the Potomac, that straggling from camp to camp, especially from camp to town, became a thing of the past. Guards were stationed at the bridges and ferry-boats to examine all passes. These were granted by the regimental, brigade, or division commanders—or by all three—and prescribed the time of departure and also the time of return. The holder was liable also to be stopped by a patrol of the provost-guard in Washington and required to show it again. Attempts were frequently made by officers and men who had overstayed their leave to tamper with the dates on their passes, but these seldom succeeded. Several officers were dismissed the service, and many a soldier suffered punishment of hard labor for this offense. Among old army men of 1861–62 located near Washington, the signature of Drake de Kay, Adjutant-General of the War Department, became well-known. His signature was considerably larger even than the renowned signature of John Hancock, who made his name under the Declaration of Independence an inscription so enormous that "King George would not have to take off his glasses to read it," and one not easily mistaken.

SERGEANT AND SENTRY ON GUARD AT LONG BRIDGE

proudly at home but meekly enough at the front, where speedily the "Ellsworth Avengers" became the Forty-fourth; the "Brooklyn Phalanx," the Sixty-seventh; the "Engineers," the Thirty-eighth; the "Lancers," the Sixth Pennsylvania. Dick Rush's gallant troopers were soon known as the "Seventh Regulars," and well did they earn the title. So, too, in the West, where the "Guthrie Grays," once Cincinnati's favorite corps, were swallowed up in the Sixth Ohio, and in St. Louis, where the "Fremont Rifles," "Zagonyi Guards," and "Foreign Legions" drew many an alien to the folds of the flag, and later to the dusty blue of the Union soldier.

As for arms, the regiments came to the front with every conceivable kind, and some with none at all. The regular infantry, what there was of it, had but recently given up the old smooth-bore musket for the Springfield rifle, caliber 58, with its paper cartridge and conical, counter-sunk bullet; but Harper's Ferry Arsenal had been burned, Springfield could not begin to turn out the numbers needed; Rock Island Arsenal was not yet built, and so in many a regiment, flank companies, only, received the rifle, the other eight using for months the old smooth-bore with its "buck-and-ball" cartridge, good for something within two hundred yards and for nothing beyond.

Even of these there were enough for only the first few regiments. Vast purchases, therefore, were made abroad, England selling us her Enfields, with which the fine Vermont brigade was first armed, and France and Belgium parting with thousands of the huge, brass-bound, ponderous *"carabines à tige"*—the Belgian guns with a spike at the bottom to expand the soft leaden bullet when "rammed home." With this archaic blunderbus whole regiments were burdened, some foreign-born volunteers receiving it eagerly as "from the old country," and therefore superior to anything of Yankee invention. But their confidence was short lived. One day's march, one

[82]

TASTING THE SOUP
A FORMALITY SOON ABANDONED

One of the formalities soon abandoned after the soldiers took the field was that of tasting the soup. Here it appears as observed at the camp of the 31st Pennsylvania near Washington, in 1861. This duty fell to one of the officers of each company, and its object was to discover whether the soup was sufficiently strong to pass muster with the men, but as the war went on the men themselves became the only "tasters." The officers had too many other pressing duties to perform, and the handling of the soup, when there was any, became the simple matter of ladling it out to men who were only too glad to fill up their cans and devour the contents. The hunting-horn on the hat of the man leaning on his gun just behind the officer betokens the infantry. It was a symbol adopted from European armies, where the hunter became by a natural process of evolution the *chasseur* or light infantryman. In the Union armies the symbol was stretched to cover all the infantry. The presence of the feather in his hat also indicates that this photograph was taken early in the war. After the first campaign such superfluous decorative insignia were generally discarded.

short hour's shooting, and all predilection for such a weapon was gone forever.

And then the shoes with which the Federals reached the front! Not one pair out of four would have borne the test of a ten-mile tramp, not one out of ten would have stood the strain of a ten-days' march, and those that first took their places, the make of contractors, were even worse. Not until the "Iron Secretary," Stanton, got fairly into swing did contractors begin to learn that there was a man to dread in the Department of War, but Stanton had not even been suggested in the fall of 1861. Simon Cameron, the venerable Pennsylvania politician, was still in office. McClellan, the young, commanding general was riding diligently from one review to another, a martial sight, accompanied by his staff, orderlies, and escort.

The weather was perfect along the Potomac that gorgeous early autumn of 1861. The beautiful wooded heights were crowned with camps; the plains and fields were white with snowy tentage; the dust hung lazily over countless drill-grounds and winding roadways; the bands were out in force on every afternoon, filling the soft, sunshiny air with martial melody; the camps were thronged with smile-wreathed visitors, men and women from distant homes; the streets of Washington were crowded, and its famous old caravanseries prospered, as never before, for never had the Nation mustered in such overwhelming strength as here about the sleepy old Southern "city of magnificent distances"—a tawdry, shabby town in all conscience, yet a priceless something to be held against the world in arms, for the sacred flag that floated over the columned White House, for the revered and honored name it bore.

In seven strong divisions, with three or four brigades in each, "Little Mac," as the volunteers rejoiced to call him, had organized his great army as the autumn waned, and the livelong days were spent in the constant drill, drill that was absolutely needed to impart cohesion and discipline to this vast

OFFICERS OF THE FOURTH NEW JERSEY REGIMENT, 1861

This three-months regiment was formed at Trenton, N. J., in April, 1861, and arrived at Washington on May 6th. It was on duty at Meridian Hill until May 24th, when it took part in the occupation of Arlington Heights. It participated in the battle of Bull Run, July 21st, and ten days later was mustered out at the expiration of its term of service. New Jersey contributed three regiments of cavalry, five batteries of light artillery, and forty-one regiments of infantry to the Union armies during the war.

THE FOURTH NEW JERSEY ON THE BANKS OF THE POTOMAC, 1861

array, mostly American bred, and hitherto unschooled in discipline of any kind. When McDowell marched his militiamen forward to attack Beauregard at Bull Run, they swarmed all over the adjacent country, picking berries, and plundering orchards. Orders were things to obey only when they got ready and felt like it, otherwise " Cap "—as the company commander was hailed, or the "orderly," as throughout the war very generally and improperly the first sergeant was called— might shout for them in vain. " Cap," the lieutenant, the sergeant—all, for that matter—were in their opinion creatures of their own selection and, if dissatisfied with their choice, if officer or non-commissioned officer ventured to assert himself, to " put on airs," as our early-day militiamen usually expressed it, the power that made could just as soon, so they supposed, unmake.

It took many weeks to teach them that, once mustered into the service of " Uncle Sam," this was by no means the case. They had come reeling back from Bull Run, a tumultuous mob of fugitives, some of whom halted not even on reaching Washington. It took time and sharp measures to bring them back to their colors and an approximate sense of their duties. One fine regiment, indeed, whose soldierly colonel was left dead, found itself disarmed, deprived of its colors, discredited, and a dozen of its self-selected leaders summarily court-martialed and sentenced for mutiny. It took time and severe measures to bring officers and men back from Washington to camp, thereafter to reappear in town only in their complete uniform, and with the written pass of a brigade commander.

It took more time and many and many a lesson, hardest of all, to teach them that the men whom they had known for years at home as " Squire " or " Jedge," " Bob " or " Billy," could now only be respectfully addressed, if not referred to, as captain, lieutenant, or sergeant. It took still longer for the American man-at-arms to realize that there was good reason why the self-same " Squire " or " Jedge " or even a " Bob "

OFFICERS OF THE EIGHTH NEW YORK STATE MILITIA INFANTRY, ARLINGTON HEIGHTS, VIRGINIA, 1861

There were three organizations from New York State known as the Eighth Infantry—the Eighth Regiment State Militia Infantry, or "Washington Grays"; the Eighth Regiment Infantry, or "First German Rifles"; and the Eighth Regiment National Guard Infantry. The second of these was organized at New York and mustered in April 23, 1861. It left for Washington on May 26th, and served for two years. It served in the defenses of Washington till July 16, 1861; advanced to Manassas, Va., on that date, and took part in the battle of Bull Run July 21st. It did duty in the defenses of Washington, with various scouts and reconnaissances, till April, 1862, and then went to the Shenandoah Valley, where it fought in the battle of Cross Keys. Back to the Rappahannock, and service at Groveton and second Bull Run, and it was mustered out on April 23, 1863. The day before being mustered out, the three-years men were consolidated into a company and transferred to the Sixty-eighth Regiment of New York Infantry, May 5, 1863. The regiment lost ninety men, killed and wounded, and one officer and forty-two enlisted men by disease. The third organization was a three months regiment, organized May 29, 1862, which did duty in the defenses of Washington till September 9th of that year, and was again mustered into service for thirty days in June, 1863, and sent to Harrisburg, Pa. It was mustered out at New York City, July 23, 1863.

or " Billy " of the year agone, could not now be accosted or
even passed without a soldierly straightening-up, and a prompt
lifting of the open hand to the visor of the cap.

All through the months of August and September, the
daily grind of drill by squad, by company, by battalion was
pursued in the " hundred circling camps " about Washington.
Over across the Long Bridge, about the fine old homestead of
the Lees, and down toward Alexandria the engineers had
traced, and the volunteers had thrown up, strong lines of fortification. Then, as other brigades grew in discipline and precision, the lines extended. The Vermonters, backed by the
Western brigade, crossed the Chain Bridge one moonless night,
seized the opposite heights, and within another day staked out
Forts Ethan Allen and Marcy, and ten strong regiments fell
to hacking down trees and throwing up parapets. Still further up the tow-path of the sleepy old Chesapeake and Ohio
Canal, the men of Massachusetts, New York, and Minnesota
made their lodgment opposite Edwards' Ferry, and presently
from Maryland Heights down to where Anacostia Branch joins
the Potomac, the northern shore bristled everywhere with the
bayonets of the Union, and with every sun the relentless drill,
drill, drill went on.

At break of day, the soldier lads were roused from slum-
ber by the shrill rattle of the reveille. Following the methods
of the Mexican War, every regiment had its corps of drummers
and fifers, and stirring music did the youngsters make. The
mists rolled lazily from the placid reaches of the Potomac
until later banished by the sun, and doctors agreed that miasma
lurked in every breath, and that coffee, piping hot, was the
surest antidote. And so each company formed for reveille
roll-call, tin cup in hand, or slung to the haversack in those
regiments whose stern, far-sighted leaders required their men
to appear full panoplied, thereby teaching them the soldier
lesson of keeping arms, equipment, and clothing close at hand,
where they could find them instantly, even in the dark. It

[88]

TWELFTH NEW YORK INFANTRY AT CAMP ANDERSON, 1861

The painfully new uniforms, and the attitudes that show how heavy the gold lace lay on unaccustomed arms, betoken the first year of the war.   This three-months regiment sailed from New York for Fortress Monroe, Virginia, April 21, 1861; it arrived April 23d, and continued to Annapolis and Washington.   It was mustered in on May 2, 1861, and assigned to Mansfield's command.   It took part in the advance into Virginia May 23d, and the occupation of Arlington Heights the following day.   It was there that, under the supervision of the Engineer Corps, its members learned that a soldier must dig as well as fight, and their aching backs and blistered hands soon made them forget their spruce, if awkward, appearance indicated in this photograph.   Ten strong regiments were set to hacking down trees and throwing up parapets for Forts Ethan Allen and Marcy, staked out by the boys from Vermont.   These New York volunteers were ordered to join Patterson's army on July 6th, and were part of the force that failed to detain Johnston in the Shenandoah Valley.   With his fresh troops Johnston was able to turn the tide in favor of the Confederates on the field of Bull Run, July 21st.   They bore themselves well in a skirmish near Martinsburg, Va., on July 12th. On the 5th of August they were mustered out at New York City.   Many, however, reënlisted.

was not the best of coffee the commissaries served in 1861, but never did coffee taste better than in the keen air of those early misty mornings, and from those battered mugs of tin.

Customs varied according to the caprice of brigade or regimental commander, but in many a battalion in that early-day Army of the Potomac, a brief, brisk drill in the manual followed reveille; then "police" and sprucing-up tents and camp, then breakfast call and the much relished, yet often anathematized, bacon, with abundant loaves from Major Beckwith's huge Capitol bakery, and more steaming tins of coffee. Then came guard-mounting, with the band out, and the details in their best blue and brightest brasses, with swarms of men from every company, already keen critics of the soldiership of the adjutant, the sergeants, and rival candidates for orderly, for the colonel and the officer-of-the-day.

Later still, the whole regiment formed on the color line, and with field-officers in saddle—many of them mightily unaccustomed thereto—and ten stalwart companies in line, started forth on a two or three hours' hard battalion drill, field-officers furtively peeping at the drill books, perhaps, yet daily growing more confident and assured, the men speedily becoming more springy and muscular, and companies more and more machine-like.

Back to camp in time for a brush-off, and then "fall to" with vigorous appetite for dinner of beef and potatoes, pork and beans, and huge slabs of white bread, all on one tin plate, or a shingle. Then time came for a "snooze," or a social game, or a stroll along the Potomac shore and a call, perhaps, on a neighboring regiment; then once again a spring to ranks for a sharp, spirited drill by company; and then the band would come marching forth, and the adjutant with his sergeant-major, and "markers," with their little guidons, would appear; the colonel and his field seconds would sally forth from their tents, arrayed in their best uniforms, girt with sash and sword, white-gloved and precise, and again the long line would

EIGHTH NEW YORK, 1861

This regiment was organized for three months' service in April, 1861, and left for Washington on April 20th. It was known as the "Washington Grays." It did duty in the defenses of Washington until July, and took part in the battle of Bull Run on July 21st. It was attached to Porter's first brigade, Hunter's second division, McDowell's Army of Northeast Virginia. On August 2, 1861, it was mustered out at New York City. All of the fanciful regimental names, as well as their variegated uniforms, disappeared soon after the opening of the war, and the "Grays," "Avengers," "Lancers," and "Rifles" became mere numerical units, while the regiments lost their identity in the universal blue flannel blouse and light-blue kersey trousers, with the utterly ugly forage cap and stout brogans of the Union armies—a uniform that was most unbecoming, yet eminently serviceable for rough work and actual warfare. The Eighth New York, for instance, at the battle of Bull Run, was mistaken several times for a Confederate regiment, although the error was always discovered in the nick of time.

MEN OF THE EIGHTH REGIMENT, NEW YORK STATE MILITIA INFANTRY, 1861

form for the closing, stately ceremony of the day—the martial dress-parade.

It was at this hour that the great army, soon to be known as the Army of the Potomac, seemed at its best. Many of the regiments had been able to draw the picturesque black felt hat and feather, the ugly, straight-cut, single-breasted coat of the regular service, and, with trousers of sky blue, and glistening black waist, and shoulder-belt, and spotless white gloves, to pride themselves that they looked like regulars. Many of them did.

Excellent were the bands of some of the Eastern regiments, and throngs of visitors came out from Washington to hear the stirring, spirited music and to view the martial pageant. Often McClellan, always with his staff, would watch the work from saddle, his cap-visor pulled well down over his keen eyes. Occasionally some wandering soldier, on pass from neighboring camp, would shock the military sensibilities of veteran officers by squirming through the guard lines and offering the little general-in-chief a chance to " shake hands with an old Zouave."

Once it happened in front of a whole brigade, and I heard him say "Certainly " before a scandalized aide-de-camp, or corporal of the guard, could hustle the intruder, grinning and triumphant, away from the imposing front of the cavalcade.

Time and again, in open barouche, with not a sign of escort, guard, or secret-service officer, there would come the two foremost statesmen of the day; one of them just rising above his companion and great rival of the East—as he had already overcome his great antagonist, the " Little Giant of the West "—and rising so steadily, rising so far above any and all contemporaries that, within another year, there lived no rival to his place in the hearts of the Nation, and within the compass of the two generations that followed, none has yet approached it. Tall, lank, angular, even awkward, but simple and unpretentious, cordial and kindly and sympathetic alike

SCIENCE IN
THE TRAINING
OF AN ARMY

The stout sergeant in front of the adjutant's tent probably lost some weight during the process used by General George B. McClellan to make an army out of the raw material which flocked to Washington in the summer and fall of 1861. Through constant drill the volunteers speedily became more springy and muscular, and the companies daily more and more machine-like. The routine was much the same throughout the various camps. At break of day the soldier lads were roused by the hurried notes of the reveille. Hot coffee was served to guard against the miasmatic mists, and the regiments were required by their stern, far-sighted leaders to appear full-panoplied, thereby learning the soldier lesson of keeping arms,

A VOLUNTEER ABOUT TO LOSE SOME WEIGHT

THE EIGHTH NEW YORK GETTING INTO SHAPE

equipment, and clothing close at hand, where they could be found instantly, even in the dark. This was a lesson which proved invaluable many a time later in the war. In many a regiment a brief, brisk drill in the manual followed reveille; then "police" and sprucing up tents and camp, then breakfast call. Next came guard mounting, and later still the whole regiment formed on the color line, and started forth on a two or three hours' hard battalion drill. By the time General McClellan was ready to move his army to the Peninsula they had learned much of the lesson that they were to put to practical use. They could march under the burning sun or through the drenching rain with equal indifference, and their outdoor life had inured them to exposure that would have meant sunstroke on one hand, or pneumonia and death on the other, a few months earlier in the war.

to colonel, corporal, or drum-boy, Abraham Lincoln sprawled at his ease, with William H. Seward sitting primly by his side —the President and the Premier—the Commander-in-Chief and the Secretary of State—the latter, his confident opponent for the nomination but the year agone, his indulgent adviser a few months back, but now, with wisdom gained through weeks of mental contact, his admiring and loyal second.

It was characteristic of our people that about the knoll where sat McClellan, in statuesque and soldierly pose, his aides, orderlies, and escort at his back, there should gather an admiring throng, while about the carriage of the dark-featured, black-whiskered, black-coated, tall-hatted civilian there should be but a little group. It was characteristic of McClellan that he should accept this homage quite as his due. It was characteristic of Lincoln that he did not seem to mind it. "I would hold McClellan's horse for him," he was sadly saying, just one year later, "if he would only *do* something."

Only a few days after this scene at Kalorama, all the camps along the Potomac about the Chain Bridge were roused to a sudden thrill of excitement at the roar of cannon in brisk action on the Lewinsville road. General "Baldy" Smith had sent out a reconnaissance. It had stumbled into a hornet's nest of Confederates; it needed help, and Griffin's regulars galloped forward and into battery. For twenty minutes there was a thunderous uproar. A whole division stood to arms. The firing ended as suddenly as it began, but not so the excitement. To all but two regiments within hearing that was the first battle-note their ears had ever known—how fearfully familiar it was soon to be!—and then, toward sunset, who should come riding out from Washington, with a bigger staff and escort than ever, but our hero, "Little Mac," and with enthusiasm unbounded, five thousand strong, the "boys" flung themselves about him, cheering like mad, and, after the American manner, demanding "speech." That was the day he said, "We've had our last defeat; we have made our last retreat," and then

PLEASANT DAYS IN '61 FOR VOLUNTEERS FROM EAST AND WEST

After the various drills through the day in the camps about Washington in the fall of 1861, the men had time for a "snooze" or a social game. They would stroll along the shore of the Potomac, their minds full of the great battles to come—how great and terrible they little knew—or call perhaps on friends in a neighboring regiment to discuss what Mc-Clellan was going to do to the Confederates with his well-disciplined army in the spring. They did not suspect that "Little Mac" was to be deposed for Burnside; and that the command of the Army of the Potomac was to pass on to Hooker and then to Meade. In the meantime, the star of Grant was to rise steadily in the West, and he was finally to guide the Army of the Potomac to victory. All these things were hidden to these men of the Eighth New York State Militia Infantry in their picturesque gray uniforms. They have already some of the rough and ready veteran appearance, as have their Western comrades (Fourth Michigan) in the smaller picture. At the outset of the war there was no regular or prescribed uniform, and in many regiments each company varied from the others. One company might even be clad in red, another in gray, another in blue, and still another in white. Since the South had regiments in gray uniform and many of the men of the North were clad in gray, at the first battle of Bull Run some fatal mistakes occurred, and soldiers fired upon their own friends. Thereafter all the soldiers of the Union army were dressed practically alike in blue, with slight variations in the color of insignia to designate cavalry, artillery, and infantry. Head covering varied, many regiments wearing black hats. During the last years of the war individual soldiers wore hats—usually black—on the march.

followed the confident prediction that the war would be " short, sharp, and decisive." In unbounded faith and fervor, old and young, they yelled their acclamations. Was there ever a commander by whom " the boys " stood more loyally or lovingly?

A few days later still, on the Virginia slopes south of the Chain Bridge, where was stationed a whole brigade of " the boys "—Green Mountain boys principally, though stalwart lads from Maine, Wisconsin, New York, and Pennsylvania, were there also, preparations were in progress for a tragic scene. There had been some few instances of sentries falling asleep. Healthy farm-boys, bred to days of labor in the sunshine, and correspondingly long hours of sleep at night, could not always overcome the drowsiness that stole upon them when left alone on picket. An army might be imperiled—a lesson must be taught. A patrol had come upon a young Vermonter asleep on post. A court martial had tried and sentenced, and to that sentence General Smith had set the seal of his approval. For the soldier-crime of sleeping on guard, Private Scott was to be shot to death in sight of the Vermont brigade.

A grave would be dug; a coffin set beside it; the pale-faced lad would be led forth; the chaplain, with bowed head and quivering lips, would speak his final word of consolation; the firing-party—a dozen of his own brigade—would be marched to the spot, subordinate, sworn to obey, yet dumbly cursing their lot; the provost-marshal would give the last order, while all around, in long, rigid, yet trembling lines, a square of soldiery would witness a comrade's death. But on the eve of the appointed day, the great-hearted Lincoln, appealed to by several of the lad's company, went himself to the Chain Bridge, had a long conversation with the young private and sent him back to his regiment, a free man. The President of the United States could not suffer it that one of his boys should be shot to death for being overcome by sleep. He gave his young soldier life only that the lad might die gloriously a few months later, heading the dash of his comrades upon the Southern line at

OFFICERS OF "THE RED–LEGGED FIFTY–FIFTH" NEW YORK AT FORT GAINES, 1861

Right royally did Washington welcome the Fifty-fifth New York Infantry, surnamed "Garde de Lafayette" in memory of that distinguished Frenchman's services to our country in Revolutionary days, in September, 1861. The "red-legged Fifth-fifth" was organized in New York City by Colonel Philip Regis de Trobriand (who ended the war as a brevet major-general of volunteers, a rank bestowed upon him for highly meritorious services during the Appomattox campaign) and left for Washington August 31st. The French uniforms attracted much attention and elicited frequent bursts of applause as the crowds on Pennsylvania Avenue realized once again how many citizens from different lands had rushed to the defense of their common country. The Fifty-fifth accompanied McClellan to the Peninsula, and took part in the desperate assault on Marye's Heights at Fredericksburg, after which it was consolidated, in four companies, with the Thirty-eighth New York December 21, 1862. The regiment lost during service thirty-three enlisted men killed and mortally wounded, and twenty-nine enlisted men by disease. Its gallant colonel survived until July 15, 1897.

Lee's Mill—sending, with his last breath, a message to the President that he had tried to live up to the advice he had given.

It was indeed a formative period, that first half-year of drill, picket duty, and preparation along the Potomac, and so expert became the patrols of the provost guard, so thorough the precautions at headquarters, that straggling from camp to camp, especially from camp to town, became a thing of the past. Except a favored few, like the mounted orderlies, or messengers, men of one brigade knew next to nothing of those beyond their lines. Barely three miles back from the Potomac, up the valley of Rock Creek, was camped an entire division, the Pennsylvania Reserves, in which the future leader of the Army of the Potomac was modestly commanding a brigade.

Just across the Chain Bridge, he who was destined to become his great second, proclaimed " superb " at Gettysburg, was busily drilling another, yet the men under George G. Meade and those under Winfield S. Hancock saw nothing of each other in the fall of 1861.

Over against Washington, the Jerseymen under dashing Philip Kearny brushed with their outermost sentries the picket lines of " Ike Stevens' Highlanders," camped at Chain Bridge, yet so little were the men about Arlington known to these in front of the bridge, that a night patrol from the one stirred up a lively skirmish with the other. In less than a year those two heroic soldiers, Kearny and Stevens, were to die in the same fight only a few miles farther out, at Chantilly. Only for a day or two did the " Badgers," the " Vermonters," and the " Knickerbockers " of King's, Smith's, and Stevens' brigades compare notes with the so-called " California Regiment," raised in the East, yet led by the great soldier-senator from the Pacific slope, before they, the " Californians," and their vehement colonel marched away along the tow-path to join Stone's great division farther up stream.

Three regiments, already famous for their drill and discipline had preceded them, the First Minnesota, the Fifteenth

A DRESS PARADE OF THE SEVENTEENTH NEW YORK IN 1861

New York's Seventeenth Infantry Volunteers entered the war as the "Westchester Chasseurs." It was organized at New York City and mustered in for two years, Colonel H. Seymour Lansing in command. The regiment left for Washington June 21, 1861, and was stationed near Miner's Hill, just across the District of Columbia line, a mile and a half from Falls Church. It fought on the Peninsula, at the second Bull Run, at Antietam, Fredericksburg, and Chancellorsville, and took part in the famous "mud march" January 20 to 24, 1863. On May 13, 1863, the three-years men were detached and assigned to a battalion of New York volunteers, and on June 23, 1863, were transferred to the 146th New York Infantry. The regiment was mustered out June 2, 1863, having lost during service five officers and thirty-two enlisted men killed and mortally wounded, and three officers and thirty-seven enlisted men by disease.

THE SEVENTEENTH NEW YORK AT MINER'S HILL, NEAR WASHINGTON

It was not often during army life that the advantage of churches or places of religious worship were available to the troops in the field. When chaplains were connected with regiments in active service, any improvised tent or barrel for an altar or pulpit was utilized for the minister's benefit. The question of denomination rarely entered the minds of the men. Where a church edifice was near the camps, or when located near some village or city, services were held within the edifice, but this was very infrequent. The camp at Arlington Heights was located directly opposite Washington and Georgetown, D. C., overlooking the banks of the Potomac River on the Virginia side. The Ninth Massachusetts was a regiment composed of Irish volunteers from the vicinity of Boston. The Catholic chaplains were very assiduous in their attention to the ritual of the Church, even on the tented field. Many of these chaplains have

FATHER SCULLY PREACHING TO THE NINTH
MASSACHUSETTS REGIMENT

since risen to high positions in the Church. Archbishop Ireland was one of these splendid and devoted men. An example of the fearless devotion of the Catholic chaplains was the action of Father Corby, of the Irish Brigade, at the battle of Gettysburg. As the brigade was about to go into the fiercest fighting at the center of the Federal line and shot and shell were already reaching its ranks, at the solicitation of Father Corby it was halted, and knelt; standing upon a projecting rock, the brave father rendered absolution to the soldiers according to the rites of the Catholic Church. A few minutes later the brigade had plunged to the very thick of the fierce fighting at the "Loop."

SERVICE FOR THE RECRUITS AT CAMP CASS,
ARLINGTON HEIGHTS, VIRGINIA, 1861

Attentive and solemn are the faces of these men new to warfare, facing dangers as yet unknown, while they listen to Father Scully's earnest words. Not a few of the regiments in the Union armies were led by ministers who assisted in organizing them, and then accepted the command. When the Fiftieth New York Engineers were stationed in front of Petersburg, Virginia, they made a rustic place of worship, spire and all, after the model of their winter-quarters. A photograph of this soldier-built edifice is shown on page 257. The muskets and glistening bayonets of the soldiers, leaning against the fence in the foreground of the Petersburg picture, contrast vividly with the peaceful aspect of the little church—an oasis in a desert.

BLAIR, OF MISSOURI

Although remaining politically neutral throughout the war, Missouri contributed four hundred and forty-seven separate military organizations to the Federal armies, and over one hundred to the Confederacy. The Union sentiment in the State is said to have been due to Frank P. Blair, who, early in 1861, began organizing home guards. Blair subsequently joined Grant's command and served with that leader until Sherman took the helm in the West. With Sherman Major-General Blair fought in Georgia and through the Carolinas.

BAKER, OF CALIFORNIA

California contributed twelve military organizations to the Federal forces, but none of them took part in the campaigns east of the Mississippi. Its Senator, Edward D. Baker, was in his place in Washington when the war broke out, and, being a close friend of Lincoln, promptly organized a regiment of Pennsylvanians which was best known by its synonym "First California." Colonel Baker was killed at the head of it at the battle of Ball's Bluff, Virginia, October 21, 1861. Baker had been appointed brigadier-general but declined.

KELLEY, OF WEST VIRGINIA

West Virginia counties had already supplied soldiers for the Confederates when the new State was organized in 1861. As early as May, 1861, Colonel B. F. Kelley was in the field with the First West Virginia Infantry marshalled under the Stars and Stripes. He served to the end of the war and was brevetted major-general. West Virginia furnished thirty-seven organizations of all arms to the Federal armies, chiefly for local defense and for service in contiguous territory. General Kelley was prominent in the Shenandoah campaigns.

SMYTH, OF DELAWARE

Little Delaware furnished to the Federal armies fifteen separate military organizations. First in the field was Colonel Thomas A. Smyth, with the First Delaware Infantry. Early promoted to the command of a brigade, he led it at Gettysburg, where it received the full force of Pickett's charge on Cemetery Ridge, July 3, 1863. He was brevetted major-general and fell at Farmville, on Appomattox River, Va., April 7, 1865, two days before the surrender at Appomattox. General Smyth was a noted leader in the Second Corps.

MITCHELL, OF KANSAS

The virgin State of Kansas sent fifty regiments, battalions, and batteries into the Federal camps. Its Second Infantry was organized and led to the field by Colonel R. B. Mitchell, a veteran of the Mexican War. At the first battle in the West, Wilson's Creek, Mo. (August 10, 1861), he was wounded. At the battle of Perryville, Brigadier-General Mitchell commanded a division in Mc-Cook's Corps and fought desperately to hold the Federal left flank against a sudden and desperate assault by General Bragg's Confederates.

CROSS, OF NEW HAMPSHIRE

New Hampshire supplied twenty-nine military organizations to the Federal armies. To the Granite State belongs the grim distinction of furnishing the regiment which had the heaviest mortality roll of any infantry organization in the army. This was the Fifth New Hampshire, commanded by Colonel E. E. Cross. The Fifth served in the Army of the Potomac. At Gettysburg, Colonel Cross commanded a brigade, which included the Fifth New Hampshire, and was killed at the head of it near Devil's Den, on July 2, 1863.

PEARCE, OF ARKANSAS

Arkansas entered into the war with enthusiasm, and had a large contingent of Confederate troops ready for the field in the summer of 1861. At Wilson's Creek, Missouri, August 10, 1861, there were four regiments and two batteries of Arkansans under command of Brigadier-General N. B. Pearce. Arkansas furnished seventy separate military organizations to the Confederate armies and seventeen to the Federals. The State was gallantly represented in the Army of Northern Virginia, notably at Antietam and Gettysburg.

STEUART, OF MARYLAND

Maryland quickly responded to the Southern call to arms, and among its first contribution of soldiers was George H. Steuart, who led a battalion across the Potomac early in 1861. These Marylanders fought at First Bull Run, or Manassas, and Lee's army at Petersburg included Maryland troops under Brigadier-General Steuart. During the war this little border State, politically neutral, sent six separate organizations to the Confederates in Virginia, and mustered thirty-five for the Federal camps and for local defense.

CRITTENDEN, THE CONFEDERATE

Kentucky is notable as a State which sent brothers to both the Federal and Confederate armies. Major-General George B. Crittenden, C. S. A., was the brother of Major-General Thomas L. Crittenden, U. S. A. Although remaining politically neutral throughout the war, the Blue Grass State sent forty-nine regiments, battalions, and batteries across the border to uphold the Stars and Bars, and mustered eighty of all arms to battle around the Stars and Stripes and protect the State from Confederate incursions.

RANSOM, OF NORTH CAROLINA

The last of the Southern States to cast its fortunes in with the Confederacy, North Carolina vied with the pioneers in the spirit with which it entered the war. With the First North Carolina, Lieut.-Col. Matt W. Ransom was on the firing-line early in 1861. Under his leadership as brigadier-general, North Carolinians carried the Stars and Bars on all the great battlefields of the Army of Northern Virginia. The State furnished ninety organizations for the Confederate armies, and sent eight to the Federal camps.

FINEGAN, OF FLORIDA

Florida was one of the first to follow South Carolina's example in dissolving the Federal compact. It furnished twenty-one military organizations to the Confederate forces, and throughout the war maintained a vigorous home defense. Its foremost soldier to take the field when the State was menaced by a strong Federal expedition in February, 1864, was Brigadier-General Joseph Finegan. Hastily gathering scattered detachments, he defeated and checked the expedition at the battle of Olustee, or Ocean Pond, on February 20.

CLEBURNE, OF TENNESSEE

Cleburne was of foreign birth, but before the war was one year old he became the leader of Tennesseeans, fighting heroically on Tennessee soil. At Shiloh, Cleburne's brigade, and at Murfreesboro, Chattanooga, and Franklin, Major-General P. R. Cleburne's division found the post of honor. At Franklin this gallant Irishman "The 'Stonewall' Jackson of the West," led Tennesseeans for the last time and fell close to the breastworks. Tennessee sent the Confederate armies 129 organizations, and the Federal fifty-six,

and Twentieth Massachusetts, followed by longing hearts and admiring eyes, for rumors from Edwards' Ferry told of frequent forays of Virginia horse, and the stories were believed and these noted regiments envied by those held back here for other duty. The Fortieth New York, too, had gone—Tammany Hall's contribution to the Union cause—Tammany that a year back had been all pro-slavery. Something told the fellows that grand opportunity awaited those favored regiments, and something like a pall fell over the stunned and silent camps when late October brought the news of dire disaster at Ball's Bluff. Baker, the brave Union leader, the soldier-senator, the hero of Cerro Gordo, the intimate friend of Abraham Lincoln, shot dead, pierced by many a bullet—Raymond Lee and many of his best officers wounded or captured—the Fifteenth and Twentieth Massachusetts tricked, ambushed, and driven in bewilderment into the Potomac, brave and battling to the last, yet utterly overwhelmed.

No wonder there was talk of treachery! No wonder the young faces in our ranks were grave and sad! Big Bethel, Bull Run, Ball's Bluff—three times had the Federals clashed with these nimble foemen from the South, and every clash had wrought humiliation. No wonder the lessons sank home, for young hearts are impressionable, and far more than half the rank and file of the Army of the Potomac was under twenty-one—far more than a third not then nineteen years of age. With all its fine equipment, its rapidly improving arms, its splendid spirit that later endured through every trial, defeat and disaster, with all its drills, discipline, and preparation, the army East and West—Potomac, Ohio, or Tennessee, had yet to learn the bitter lessons of disastrous battle, had yet to withstand the ordeal by fire. It took all the months of that formative period, and more, to fit that army for the fearful task before it, but well did it learn its lesson, and nobly did it do its final duty.

GLIMPSES OF
THE CONFEDERATE
ARMY

THE FIRST HISTORICAL PUBLICATION OF SCENES PHOTOGRAPHED WITHIN THE CONFEDERATE LINES, DURING THE CIVIL WAR, MAY BE FOUND IN THE ILLUSTRATIONS TO THE CHAPTERS BY ADMIRAL FRENCH E. CHADWICK AND GENERAL MARCUS J. WRIGHT, ON PAGES 86–110 OF VOLUME I. MORE OF SUCH PREVIOUSLY UNPUBLISHED PHOTOGRAPHS APPEAR IN VOLUME III, PAGES 169–171. WITH THE THREE CHAPTERS THAT FOLLOW ARE PRESENTED AN EVEN LARGER NUMBER OF WAR-TIME CONFEDERATE PHOTOGRAPHS. ALL THE SERIES ABOVE REFERRED TO WERE NEVER BEFORE REPRODUCED, OR EVEN COLLECTED; IN FACT, THE VERY EXISTENCE OF SUCH FAITHFUL CONTEMPORARY RECORDS REMAINED UNKNOWN TO MOST VETERANS AND HISTORIANS UNTIL THE PUBLICATION OF THIS "PHOTOGRAPHIC HISTORY." THE OPPORTUNITY THUS FURNISHED TO STUDY THE VOLUNTEERS OF THE CONFEDERACY AS THEY CAMPED AND DRILLED AND PREPARED FOR WAR IS UNIQUE.

A VIVID "GLIMPSE OF THE CONFEDERATE ARMY"—1861

This spirited photograph by Edwards of New Orleans suggests more than volumes of history could tell of the enthusiasm, the hope, with which the young Confederate volunteers, with their queerly variegated equipment, sprang to the defense of their land in '61.   Around this locality in Florida some of the very earliest operations centered.   Fort McRee and the adjacent batteries had passed into Confederate hands on January 12, 1861, when Lieutenant Adam J. Slemmer withdrew with his eighty-two men to Fort Pickens in Pensacola Harbor.   The lack of conventional military uniformity shown above must not be thought exceptional.   Con-

INSIDE THE BATTERY NORTH OF FORT McREE AT PENSACOLA

federate camps and men in general pretended to nothing like the "smartness" of the well-equipped boys in blue. Weapons, however, were cared for. All through the Southern camps, soldiers could be found busily polishing their muskets, swords, and bayonets with wood ashes well moistened. "Bright muskets" and "tattered uniforms" went together in the Army of Northern Virginia. Swords, too, were bright in Florida, judging from the two young volunteers flourishing theirs in the photograph. This is one of the batteries which later bombarded Fort Pickens and the Union fleet. It was held by the Confederates until May 2, 1862.

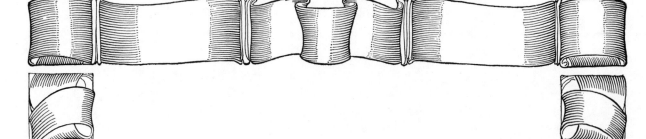

GLIMPSES OF THE CONFEDERATE ARMY

By Randolph H. McKim, D.D.

Late First Lieutenant, and A. D. C. 3d Brigade, Army of Northern Virginia

[This chapter was prepared by Dr. McKim at the request of the Editors of the "Photographic History of the Civil War" to describe the Confederate army from the standpoint of the individual and to bring out conditions under which the war was waged by that army, as well as to show the differences between those conditions and the life and activity of the Union army. The following pages are written under the limitations imposed by these conditions.]

WRITERS on the Civil War frequently speak of the Southern army as "the Secession army." Yet the most illustrious leaders of that army, Robert E. Lee and "Stonewall" Jackson, to name no more, were in fact opposed to secession; though when Virginia at length withdrew from the Union, they felt bound to follow her. I think it likely indeed that a very large proportion of the conspicuous and successful officers, and a like proportion also of the men who fought in the ranks of the Confederate armies were likewise originally Union men—opposed, at any rate, to the exercise of the right of secession, even if they believed that the right existed.

It will be remembered that months elapsed between the secession of the Gulf States and that of the great border States, Virginia, North Carolina, and Tennessee, which furnished so large a proportion of the soldiers who fought for the Southern Confederacy. But, on the 15th of April, 1861, an event occurred which instantly transformed those great States into Secession States—the proclamation of Abraham Lincoln calling

THE DRUM–MAJOR OF THE FIRST VIRGINIA, APRIL, 1861

C. R. M. Pohlé of Richmond, Virginia, drum-major of the crack Richmond regiment, the First Virginia, presented a magnificent sight indeed, when this photograph was taken in April, 1861. The Army of Northern Virginia did not find bands and bearskin hats preferable to food, and both the former soon disappeared, while the supply of the latter became only intermittent. Bands, however, still played their part now and then in the Virginia men's fighting. David Homer Bates records that when Early descended on Washington a scout reported to General Hardin at Fort Stevens: "The enemy are preparing to make a grand assault on this fort to-night. They are tearing down fences and are moving to the right, their bands playing. Can't you hurry up the Sixth Corps?" Many of the regiments raised among men of wealth and culture in the larger cities of the Confederacy were splendidly equipped at the outset of the war. Captain Alexander Duncan of the Georgia Hussars, of Savannah, is authority for the statement that the regiment spent $25,000 on its initial outfit. He also adds that at the close of the war the uniforms of this company would have brought about twenty-five cents.

upon them to furnish their quota of troops to coerce the seceded States back into the Union. Even the strongest Federalists, like Hamilton, had, in the discussions in the Constitutional Convention, utterly repudiated and condemned the coercion of a State. It was not strange, then, that the summons to take up arms and march against their Southern brethren, aroused deep indignation in these States, and instantly transformed them into secession states. But for that proclamation, the Southern army would not have been much more than half its size, and would have missed its greatest leaders.

A glance at its personnel will perhaps be instructive. In its ranks are serving side by side the sons of the plain farmers, and the sons of the great landowners—the Southern aristocrats. Not a few of the men who are carrying muskets or serving as troopers are classical scholars, the flower of the Southern universities. In an interval of the suspension of hostilities at the battle of Cold Harbor, a private soldier lies on the ground poring over an Arabic grammar—it is Crawford H. Toy, who is destined to become the famous professor of Oriental languages at Harvard University. In one of the battles in the Valley of Virginia a volunteer aid of General John B. Gordon is severely wounded—it is Basil L. Gildersleeve, who has left his professor's chair at the University of Virginia to serve in the field. He still lives (1911), wearing the laurel of distinction as the greatest Grecian in the English-speaking world. At the siege of Fort Donelson, in 1862, one of the heroic captains who yields up his life in the trenches is the Reverend Dabney C. Harrison, who raised a company in his own Virginia parish, and entered the army at its head. In the Southwest a lieutenant-general falls in battle—it is General Leonidas Polk, who laid aside his bishop's robes to become a soldier, having been educated to arms at West Point.

It is a striking fact that when Virginia threw in her lot with her Southern sisters in April, 1861, practically the whole body of students at her State University, 515 out of 530 who

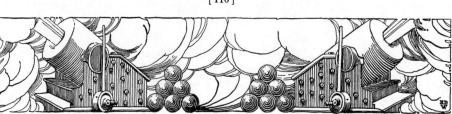

CONFEDERATE VOLUNTEERS OF '61—OFFICERS OF THE "NOTTAWAY GRAYS"

After John Brown's attempt at Harper's Ferry, the people of the border states began to form military companies in almost every county and to uniform, arm, and drill them. In the beginning, each of these companies bore some designation instead of a company letter. There were various "Guards," "Grays," and "Rifles"— the last a ludicrous misnomer, the "rifles" being mostly represented by flint-lock muskets, dating from the War of 1812, resurrected from State arsenals and carrying the old "buck and ball" ammunition, "caliber '69." On this and the following illustration page are shown some members of

CAPTAIN R. CONNALLY

CAPTAIN ARCH. CAMPBELL

Company G, Eighteenth Virginia Regiment, first called Nottaway Rifle Guards and afterward Nottaway Grays. The company was organized on the 12th of January, 1861. Its original roll was signed by fifty men. April 13, 1861, its services were tendered to Governor Letcher "to repel every hostile demonstration, either upon Virginia or the Confederate States." This sentiment of home defense animated the Confederate armies to heroic deeds. The company from Nottaway, for example, was active in every important combat with the Army of Northern Virginia; yet it was composed of citizens who had, with possibly one exception, no military education, and who, but for the exigencies of the time, would never have joined a military company.

were registered from the Southern States, enlisted in the Confederate army. This army thus represented the whole Southern people. It was a self-levy *en masse* of the male population in all save certain mountain regions in Virginia, North Carolina, Tennessee, Alabama, and Georgia.

One gets a perhaps new and surprising conception of the character of the rank and file of the Southern army in such incidents as the following: Here are mock trials going on in the moot-court of a certain artillery company, and the discussions are pronounced by a competent authority "brilliant and powerful." Here is a group of privates in a Maryland infantry regiment in winter-quarter huts near Fairfax, Virginia; and among the subjects discussed are the following: Vattel and Philmore on international law; Humboldt's works and travels; the African explorations of Barth; the influence of climate on the human features; the culture of cotton; the laws relating to property. Here are some Virginia privates in a howitzer company solemnly officiating at the burial of a tame crow; and the exercises include an English speech, a Latin oration, and a Greek ode!

These Confederate armies must present to the historian who accepts the common view that the South was fighting for the perpetuation of the institution of slavery a difficult—in fact, an insoluble—problem. How could such a motive explain the solidarity of the diverse elements that made up those armies? The Southern planter might fight for his slaves; but why the poor white man, who had none? How could slavery generate such devotion, such patient endurance, such splendid heroism, such unconquerable tenacity through four long years of painfully unequal struggle? The world acknowledges the superb valor of the men who fought under the Southern Cross—and the no less superb devotion of the whole people to the cause of the Confederacy.

Colonel Theodore Roosevelt has written, "The world has never seen better soldiers than those who followed Lee."

LIEUTENANT
R. FERGUSON

LIEUTENANT
E. H. MUSE

LIEUTENANT
AL. CAMPBELL

COMPANY G
OF THE
EIGHTEENTH VIRGINIA
"OLD IRONSIDES"

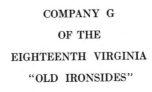

LIEUTENANT
SAMUEL HARDY

A look at these frank, straightforward features conveys at a glance the caliber of the personnel in the Army of Northern Virginia. Good American faces they are, with good old-fashioned Anglo-Saxon names—Campbell, Ferguson, Hardy, Irby, Sydnor. They took part in the first battle of Bull Run, and "tasted powder." In the fall of '61 First-Lieutenant Richard Irby resigned to take his seat in the General Assembly of Virginia, but on April 20, 1862, he was back as captain of the company. He was wounded twice at Second Manassas and died at last of prison fever. Company G took part in Pickett's charge at Gettysburg. Of the men who went into the battle, only six came out unhurt. Eleven were killed or mortally wounded, and nineteen were wounded. The company fought to the bitter end; Captain Campbell (page 111) was killed at Sailor's Creek, only three days before Appomattox.

CAPTAIN
P. F. ROWLETT

CAPTAIN
RICHARD IRBY

LIEUTENANT
A. D. CRENSHAW

LIEUTENANT
J. E. IRVIN

COLOR–SERGEANT
E. G. SYDNOR

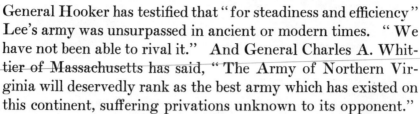

General Hooker has testified that "for steadiness and efficiency" Lee's army was unsurpassed in ancient or modern times. "We have not been able to rival it." And General Charles A. Whittier of Massachusetts has said, "The Army of Northern Virginia will deservedly rank as the best army which has existed on this continent, suffering privations unknown to its opponent."

Nor is it credible that such valor and such devotion were inspired by the desire to hold their fellow men in slavery? Is there any example of such a phenomenon in all the long records of history?

Consider, too, another fact for which the historians must assign a sufficient motive. On the bronze tablets in the rotunda of the University of Virginia, memorializing the students who fell in the great war, there are upwards of five hundred names, and, of these, two hundred and thirty-three were still privates when they fell; so that, considering the number of promotions from the ranks, it is certain that far more than half of those alumni who gave up their lives for the Southern cause, volunteered as private soldiers. They did not wait for place or office, but unhesitatingly entered the ranks, with all the hardships that the service involved.

Probably no army ever contained more young men of high culture among its private soldiers—graduates in arts, in letters, in languages, in the physical sciences, in the higher mathematics, and in the learned professions—as the army that fought under the Southern Cross. And how cheerful—how uncomplaining—how gallant they were! They marched and fought and starved, truly without reward. Eleven dollars a month in Confederate paper was their stipend. Flour and bacon and peanut-coffee made up their bill of fare. The hard earth, or else three fence-rails, tilted up on end, was their bed, their knapsacks their pillows, and a flimsy blanket their covering. The starry firmament was often their only tent. Their clothing—well, I cannot describe it. I can only say it was "a thing of shreds and patches," interspersed with rents.

A FINE-LOOKING GROUP OF CONFEDERATE OFFICERS

The officers in camp at the east end of Sullivan's Island, near Charleston, illustrate forcibly Dr. McKim's description of the personnel of the Confederate army. The preservation of the photograph is due to the care of the Washington Light Infantry of Charleston, S. C., in which these men were officers. To the left stands M. Master, and in front of him are Lieutenant Wilkie, R. Choper, and Lieutenant Lloyd. Facing them is Captain Simmonton, and the soldier shading his eyes with his hand is Gibbs Blackwood. It is easy to see from their fine presence and bearing that these were among the many thousands of Southerners able to distinguish themselves in civil life who nevertheless sprang to bear arms in defense of their native soil. "In an interval of the suspension of hostilities at the battle of Cold Harbor," writes Randolph H. McKim in the text of this volume, "a private soldier lies on the ground poring over an Arabic grammar—it is Crawford H. Toy, who is destined to become the famous professor of Oriental languages at Harvard University. In one of the battles in the Valley of Virginia, a volunteer aid of General John B. Gordon is severely wounded—it is Basil L. Gildersleeve, who has left his professor's chair at the University of Virginia to serve in the field. He still lives (1911), wearing the laurel of distinction as the greatest Grecian in the English-speaking world. At the siege of Fort Donelson, in 1862, one of the heroic captains who yields up his life in the trenches is the Reverend Dabney C. Harrison, who raised a company in his own Virginia parish and entered the army at its head. In the Southwest a lieutenant-general falls in battle—it is General Leonidas Polk, who laid aside his bishop's robes to become a soldier in the field."

[I—8]

But this was not all. They had not even the reward which is naturally dear to a soldier's heart—I mean the due recognition of gallantry in action. By a strange oversight there was no provision in the Confederate army for recognizing either by decoration or by promotion on the field, distinguished acts of gallantry. No "Victoria Cross," or its equivalent, rewarded even the most desperate acts of valor.

Now with these facts before him, the historian will find it impossible to believe that these men drew their swords and did these heroic deeds and bore these incredible hardships for four long years for the sake of the institution of slavery. Everyone who was conversant, as I was during the whole war, with the opinions of the soldiers of the Southern army, knows that they did not wage that tremendous conflict for slavery. That was a subject very little in their thoughts or on their lips. Not one in twenty of those grim veterans, who were so terrible on the battlefield, had any financial interest in slavery. No, they were fighting for liberty, for the right of self-government. They believed the Federal authorities were assailing that right. It was the sacred heritage of Anglo-Saxon freedom, of local self-government, won at Runnymede, which they believed in peril when they flew to arms as one man, from the Potomac to the Rio Grande. They may have been right, or they may have been wrong, but that was the issue they made. On that they stood. For that they died.

Not until this fact is realized by the student of the great war will he have the solution of the problem which is presented by the qualities of the Confederate soldier. The men who made up that army were not soldiers of fortune, but soldiers of duty, who dared all that men can dare, and endured all that man can endure, in obedience to what they believed the sacred call of Country. They loved their States; they loved their homes and their firesides; they were no politicians; many of them knew little of the warring theories of Constitutional interpretation. But one thing they knew—armed legions were

TALENTED YOUNG VOLUNTEERS UNDER THE SOUTHERN CROSS
IN THE FIRST YEAR OF THE WAR

There is an artist among the young Confederate volunteers, judging from the device on the tent, and the musicians are betrayed by the violin and bugle. This photograph of '61 is indicative of the unanimity with which the young men of the South took up the profession of arms. An expensive education, music, art, study abroad, a knowledge of modern and ancient languages—none of these was felt an excuse against enlisting in the ranks, if no better opportunity offered. As the author of the accompanying article recalls: "When Virginia threw in her lot with her Southern sisters in April, 1861, practically the whole body of students at her State University, 515 out of 530 men who were registered from the Southern States, enlisted in the Confederate army. This army thus represented the whole Southern people. It was a self-levy *en masse* of the male population." The four men in the foreground of the photograph are H. H. Williams, Jr., S. B. Woodberry, H. I. Greer, and Sergeant R. W. Greer of the Washington Light Infantry of Charleston, S. C.

marching upon their homes, and it was their duty to hurl them back at any cost!

Such were the private soldiers of the Confederacy as I knew them. Not for fame or for glory, not lured by ambition or goaded by necessity, but, in simple obedience to duty as they understood it, these men suffered all, sacrificed all, dared all—and died! I would like to add a statement which doubtless will appear paradoxical, but which my knowledge of those men, through many campaigns, and on many fields, and in many camps, gives me, I think, the right to make with confidence, viz.: *the dissolution of the Union was not what the Southern soldier had chiefly at heart. The establishment of the Southern Confederacy was not, in his mind, the supreme issue of the conflict. Both the one and the other were secondary to the preservation of the sacred right of self-government. They were means to the end, not the end itself.*

I place these statements here in this explicit manner because I believe they must be well considered by the student of the war, in advance of all questions of strategy, or tactics, or political policy, or racial characteristics, as explanatory of what the Confederate armies achieved in the campaigns and battles of the titanic struggle.

The spirit—the motives—the aims—of the Southern soldier constituted the moral lever that, more than anything else, controlled his actions and accounted for his achievements.

A conspicuous feature of this Southern army is its Americanism. Go from camp to camp, among the infantry, the cavalry, the artillery, and you are impressed with the fact that these men are, with very few exceptions, Americans. Here and there you will encounter one or two Irishmen. Major Stiles tells a story of a most amusing encounter between two gigantic Irishmen at the battle of Gettysburg—the one a Federal Irishman, a prisoner, and the other a Rebel Irishman, private in the Ninth Louisiana—a duel with fists in the midst

OFFICERS OF THE WASHINGTON ARTILLERY OF NEW ORLEANS

This photograph shows officers of the Fifth Company, Washington Artillery of New Orleans, in their panoply of war, shortly before the battle of Shiloh. On the following page is a photograph of members of the same organization as they looked after passing through the four terrible years. Nor were such force and ability as show in the expressions of these officers lacking in the gray-clad ranks. "And how cheerful—how un-complaining—how gallant they were!" Dr. McKim records. "They had not even the reward which is naturally dear to a soldier's heart—I mean the due recognition of gallantry in action. By a strange over-sight there was no provision in the Confederate army for recognizing, either by decoration or by promotion on the field, distinguishing acts of gallantry. No 'Victoria Cross,' or its equivalent, rewarded even the most desperate acts of valor." But brave men need no such artificial incentive to defend their homes.

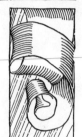

of the roar of the battle! Very, very rarely you will meet a German, like that superb soldier, Major Von Borcke, who so endeared himself to "Jeb" Stuart's cavalry. But these exceptions only accentuate the broad fact that the Confederate army was composed almost exclusively of Americans. That throws some light on its achievements, does it not?

I think the visitor to the Confederate camps would also be struck by the spirit of *bonhommie* which so largely prevailed. These "Johnnie Rebs," in their gray uniforms (which, as the war went on, changed in hue to butternut brown) are a jolly lot. They have a dry, racy humor of their own which breaks out on the least provocation. I have often heard them cracking jokes on the very edge of battle. They were soldier *boys* to the bitter end!

General Rodes, in his report, describing the dark and difficult night-passage of the Potomac on the retreat from Gettysburg, says, "All the circumstances attending this crossing combined to make it an affair not only involving great hardship, but one of great danger to the men and company officers; but, be it said to the honor of these brave fellows, they encountered it not only promptly, but actually with cheers and laughter."

On the other hand, some from the remote country districts were like children away from home. They could not get used to it—and often they drooped, and sickened and died, just from *nostalgia*. In many of the regiments during the first six months or more of the war, there were negro cooks, but as time went on these disappeared, except in the officers' mess. Among the Marylanders, where my service lay, it was quite different. We had to do our own cooking. Once a week, I performed that office for a mess of fifteen hungry men. At first we lived on "slapjacks"—almost as fatal as Federal bullets!—and fried bacon; but by degrees we learned to make biscuits, and on one occasion my colleague in the culinary business and I created an apple pie, which the whole mess

"THESE 'JOHNNIE REBS' ARE A JOLLY LOT"

This quotation from the accompanying text is thoroughly illustrated by the photograph reproduced above. It was taken in 1861 by J. D. Edwards, a pioneer camera-man of New Orleans, within the Barbour sand-batteries, near the lighthouse in Pensacola harbor. Nor was the Confederate good humor merely of the moment. Throughout the war, the men in gray overcame their hardships by a grim gaiety that broke out on the least provocation—at times with none at all as when, marching to their armpits in icy water, for lack of bridges they invented the term "Confederate pontoons" in derision of the Federal engineering apparatus. Or while a Federal brigade magnificently led—and clad—swept on to the charge, the ragged line in gray, braced against the assault, would crackle into amazing laughter with shouts of "Bring on those good breeches!" "Hey, Yank, might as well hand me your coat now as later!

considered a *chef d'œuvre!* May I call your attention to those ramrods wrapped round with dough and set up on end before the fire? The cook turns them from time to time, and, when well browned, he withdraws the ramrod, and, lo! a loaf of bread, three feet long and hollow from end to end.

The general aspect of the Confederate camps compared unfavorably with those of the men in blue. They were not, as a rule, attractive in appearance. The tents and camp equipage were nothing like so "smart," so spick and span—very far from it, indeed! Our engineer corps were far inferior, lacking in proper tools and equipment. The sappers and miners of the Federal army on Cemetery Hill, at Gettysburg, did rapid and effective work during the night following the first day's battle, as they had previously done at Chancellorsville—work which our men could not begin to match. When we had to throw up breastworks in the field, as at Hagerstown, after Gettysburg, it had usually to be done with our bayonets. Spades and axes were luxuries at such times. Bands of music were rare, and generally of inferior quality; but the men made up for it as far as they could by a gay *insouciance,* and by singing in camp and on the march. I have seen the men of the First Maryland Infantry trudging wearily through mud and rain, sadly bedraggled by a long march, strike up with great gusto their favorite song, "Gay and Happy."

> So let the wide world wag as it will,
> We'll be gay and happy still.

The contrast between the sentiment of the song and the environment of the column was sufficiently striking. In one respect, I think, our camps had the advantage of the Union camps—we had no sutlers, and we had no camp-followers.

But though our camp equipage and equipment were so inferior to those of our antagonists, I do not think any experienced soldier, watching our marching columns of infantry or cavalry, or witnessing our brigade drills, could fail to be

CONFEDERATE TYPES—"GAY AND HAPPY STILL"

A conspicuous feature of the Southern army was its Americanism. In every camp, among the infantry, the cavalry and the artillery, the men were, with few exceptions, Americans. In spite of deprivations, the men were light-hearted; given a few days' rest and feeding, they abounded in fun and jocularity and were noted for indulgence in a species of rough humor which found suggestion in the most trivial incidents, and was often present in the midst of the most tragical circumstances. In so representative a body the type varied almost as did the individual; the home sentiment, however, pervaded the mass and was the inspiration of its patriotism—sectional, provincial, call it what you will. This was true even in the ranks of those knight-errants from beyond the border: Missourians, Kentuckians, Marylanders. The last were nameworthy sons of the sires who had rendered the old "Maryland Line" of the Revolution of 1776 illustrious, and, looking toward their homes with the foe arrayed between as a barrier, they always cherished the hope of some day reclaiming those homes—when the war should be over. To many of them the war was over long before Appomattox—when those who had "struck the first blow in Baltimore" also delivered "the last in Virginia." To the very end they never failed to respond to the call of duty, and were—to quote their favorite song, sung around many a camp-fire—"Gay and Happy Still."

thrilled by the spectacle they presented. Here at least, there was no inferiority to the army in blue. The soldierly qualities that tell on the march, and on the field of battle, shone out here conspicuously. A more impressive spectacle has seldom been seen in any war than was presented by "Jeb" Stuart's brigades of cavalry when they passed in review before General Lee at Brandy Station in June, 1863. The pomp and pageantry of gorgeous uniforms and dazzling equipment of horse and riders were indeed absent; but splendid horsemanship, and that superb *esprit de corps* that marks the veteran legion, and which, though not a tangible or a visible thing, yet stamps itself upon a marching column—these were unmistakably here. And I take leave to express my own individual opinion that the blue-gray coat of the Confederate officer, richly adorned with gold lace, and his light-blue trousers, and that rakish slouch-hat he wore made up a uniform of great beauty. Oh, it was a gallant array to look upon—that June day, so many years ago!

When our infantry soldiers came to a river, unless it was a deep one, we had to cross it on "Confederate pontoons," i. e., by marching right through in column of fours. This, I remember, we did twice on one day on the march from Culpeper to Winchester at the opening of the Gettysburg campaign.

Among the amusements in camp, card-playing was of course included; seven-up and vingt-et-un, I believe, were popular. And the pipe was "Johnnie Reb's" frequent solace. His tobacco, at any rate, was the real thing—genuine, no make-believe, like his coffee. Often there were large gatherings of the men, night after night, attending prayer-meetings, always with preaching added, for there was a strong religious tone in the Army of Northern Virginia. One or two remarkable revivals took place, notably in the winter of 1863–64.

It seems to me, as I look back, that one of the characteristics which stood out strongly in the Confederate army was the independence and the initiative of the individual soldier.

THE PRIVATE SOLDIER OF THE CONFEDERACY

This photograph shows the private soldier of the Confederacy "at home" early in 1862. The men are members of the Washington Artillery, the crack New Orleans organization. They were dandies as compared with most of the volunteers. On the mess-tent to the left, the sign announces that Hemming's mess consists of Sergeant Hemming and Privates Knight, Hoerner, and Potthoft. Even at this date there was no such commissary organization as in the North. The individuality of the Southern soldier was shown in the absence of anything like company kitchens, each mess preparing its rations to suit its own fancy, and according to what might be its special re-sources or luck in foraging on the road. And when the fierce struggle had swept down the rivers and closed the ports, the Confederates "marched and fought," to quote Dr. McKim, "and starved truly without reward. Eleven dollars a month in Confederate paper was their stipend. Flour and bacon and peanut coffee made up their bill of fare. The hard earth or else three fence-rails, tilted up on end, was their bed; their knapsacks, their pillows; and a flimsy blanket their covering. The starry firmament was often their only tent. Their clothing—well, I cannot describe it. I can only say it was 'a thing of shreds and patches' interspersed with rents."

It would have been a better army in the field if it had been welded together by a stricter discipline; but this defect was largely atoned for by the strong individuality of the units in the column. It was not easy to demoralize a body composed of men who thought for themselves and acted in a spirit of independence in battle.

It was a characteristic of the Confederate soldier—I do not say he alone possessed it—that he never considered himself discharged of his duty to the colors by any wound, however serious, so long as he could walk, on crutches or otherwise. Look at that private in the Thirty-seventh Virginia Infantry—he has been hit by a rifle-ball, which, striking him full between the eyes, has found its way somehow through and emerged at the back of his head. But there he is in the ranks again, carrying his musket—while a deep depression, big enough to hold a good sized marble, marks the spot where the bullet entered in its futile attempt to make this brave fellow give up his service with the Confederate banner! Look at Captain Randolph Barton, of another Virginia regiment. He is living to-day (1911) with just about one dozen scars on his body. He would be wounded; get well; return to duty, and in the very next battle be shot again! Look at that gallant old soldier, General Ewell. Like his brave foeman, General Sickles, he has lost his leg, but that cannot keep him home; he continues to command one of Lee's corps to the very end at Appomattox. Look at Colonel Snowden Andrews of Maryland. At Cedar Mountain, in August, 1862, a shell literally nearly cut him in two; but by a miracle he did not die; and in June, 1863, there he is again commanding his artillery battalion! He is bowed crooked by that awful wound; he cannot stand upright any more, but still he can fight like a lion.

As you walk through the camps, you will see many of the men busily polishing their muskets and their bayonets with wood ashes well moistened. "Bright muskets" and "tattered uniforms" went together in the Army of Northern Virginia.

CONFEDERATES WHO SERVED THE GUNS
MEMBERS OF THE FAMOUS
"WASHINGTON ARTILLERY" OF NEW ORLEANS

The young men of the cities and towns very generally chose the artillery branch of the service for enlistment; thus, New Orleans sent five batteries, fully equipped, into the field—the famous "Washington Artillery"— besides some other batteries; and the city of Richmond, which furnished but one regiment of infantry and a few separate companies, contributed no less than eight or ten full batteries. Few of the minor towns but claimed at least one. The grade of intelligence of the personnel was rather exceptionally high, so that the artillery came in time to attain quite a respectable degree of efficiency, especially after the objectionable system under which each battery was attached to an infantry brigade, subject to the orders of its commander, was abolished and the battery units became organized into battalions and corps commanded by officers of their own arm. The Confederate artillery arm was less fortunate than the infantry in the matter of equipment, of course. From start to finish it was under handicap by reason of its lack of trained officers, no less than from the inferiority of its material, ordnance, and ammunition alike. The batteries of the regular establishment were, of course, all in the United States service, commanded and served by trained gunners, and were easily distributed among the volunteer "brigades" by way of "stiffening" to the latter. This disparity was fully recognized by the Confederates and had its influence in the selection of more than one battle-ground in order that it might be neutralized by the local conditions, yet the service was very popular in the Southern army.

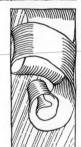

Swinton, the historian of the Army of the Potomac, exclaims, "Who can ever forget, that once looked upon it, that army of tattered uniforms and bright muskets, that body of incomparable infantry, the Army of Northern Virginia, which for four years carried the revolt on their bayonets, opposing a constant front to the mighty concentration of power brought against it; which, receiving terrible blows, did not fail to give the like, and which, vital in all its parts, died only with its annihilation."

Apropos of muskets, you will observe that a large portion of those in the hands of the Confederate soldiers are stamped "U. S. A."; and when you visit the artillery camps you will note that the three-inch rifles, the Napoleons, and the Parrott guns, were most of them "Uncle Sam's" property, captured in battle; and when you inspect the cavalry you will find, after the first year, that the Southern troops are armed with sabers captured from the Federals.* During the first year, before the blockade became stringent, Whitworth guns were brought in from abroad. But that soon stopped, and we had to look largely to "Uncle Sam" for our supply.

We used to say in the Shenandoah Valley campaign, of 1862, that General Banks was General Jackson's quartermaster-general—yes, and his chief ordnance officer, too. General Shields was another officer to whom we were much indebted for artillery and small arms, and later General Pope.† But these sources of equipment sometimes failed us, and so it came to pass that some of our regiments were but poorly armed even in our best brigades. For instance the Third Brigade in Ewell's corps, one of the best-equipped brigades in the army, entered the Gettysburg campaign with 1,941 men present for

*It is estimated by surviving ordnance officers that not less than two-thirds of the artillery in the Army of Northern Virginia was captured, especially the 3-inch rifles and the 10-pound Parrotts.

† General Gorgas, Chief of the Confederate Ordnance Bureau, stated that from July 1, 1861, to Jan. 1, 1865, there were issued from the Richmond arsenal 323,231 infantry arms, 34,067 cavalry arms, 44,877 swords and sabers, and that these were chiefly arms from battlefields, repaired.

"Seven Pines"

THE ONLY KNOWN PHOTOGRAPH OF TEXAS BOYS IN THE ARMY OF NORTHERN VIRGINIA

This group of the sturdy pioneers from Texas, heroes of many a wild charge over the battlefields of Virginia, has adopted as winter-quarters insignia the words "Wigfall Mess," evidently in honor of General Wigfall, who came to Virginia in command of the Texas contingent. The general was fond of relating an experience to illustrate the independence and individuality of his "boys." In company with Major-General Whiting he was walking near the railroad station at Manassas, and, according to wont, had been "cracking up" his "Lone Star" command, when they came upon a homespun-clad soldier comfortably seated with his back against some baled hay, his musket leaned against the same, and contentedly smoking a pipe. The two officers passed with only the recognition of a stare from the sentry, and Whiting satirically asked Wigfall if that was one of his people, adding that he did not seem to have been very well instructed as to his duty. To his surprise the Texan general then addressed the soldier: "What are you doing here, my man?" "Nothin' much," replied the man; "jes' kinder takin' care of this hyar stuff." "Do you know who I am, sir?" asked the general. "Wall, now, 'pears like I know your face, but I can't jes' call your name—who is you?" "I'm General Wigfall," with some emphasis. Without rising from his seat or removing his pipe, the sentry extended his hand: "Gin'ral, I'm pleased to meet you—my name's Jones." Less than a year later, this same man was probably among those who stormed the Federal entrenchments at Gaines' Mill, of whom "Stonewall" Jackson said, on the field after the battle: "The men who carried *this* position were soldiers indeed!"

duty, but only 1,480 muskets and 1,069 bayonets. But this was not all, or the worst. Our artillery ammunition was inferior to that of our antagonists, which was a great handicap to our success.

When General Alexander, Lee's chief of artillery at Gettysburg, was asked why he ceased firing when Pickett's infantry began its charge—why he did not continue shelling the Federal lines over the heads of the advancing Confederate column; he replied that his ammunition was so defective, he could not calculate with any certainty where the shells would explode; they might explode among Pickett's men, and so demoralize rather than support them. It will help the reader to realize the inequality in arms and equipment between the two armies to watch a skirmish between some of Sheridan's cavalry and a regiment of Fitzhugh Lee. Observe that the Federal cavalryman fires his rifle seven times without reloading, while the horseman in gray opposed to him fires but once, and then lowers his piece to reload. One is armed with the Spencer repeating rifle; the other with the old Sharp's rifle.

In another engagement (at Winchester, September 19, 1864), see that regiment of mounted men give way in disorder before the assault of Sheridan's cavalry, and dash back through the infantry. Are these men cowards? No, but they are armed with long cumbrous rifles utterly unfit for mounted men, or with double-barreled shotguns, or old squirrel-rifles. What chance has a regiment thus armed, and also miserably mounted, against those well-armed, well-equipped, well-mounted, and well-disciplined Federal cavalrymen? *

Another feature of the conditions prevailing in the Confederate army may be here noted. Look at Lee's veterans as

*The arms and equipment of the Confederate army will be found fully discussed by Professer J. W. Mallet, late Superintendent of the Ordnance Laboratories of the Confederate States, and Captain O. E. Hunt, U.S.A., in a chapter on the "Organization and Operation of the Ordnance Department of the Confederate Army" in the volume on "Forts and Artillery."

COPYRIGHT, 1911, REVIEW OF REVIEWS CO.

AMUSEMENTS IN A CONFEDERATE CAMP—1864

This camp of Confederate pickets on Stono Inlet near Charleston, S. C., was photographed by George S. Cook, the same artist who risked his life taking photographs of Fort Sumter. It illustrates the soldiers' methods of entertaining themselves when time lay heavy on their hands. Among the amusements in camp, card-playing was of course included. "Seven-up" and "Vingt-et-un" were popular. And the pipe was "Johnnie Reb's" frequent solace. His tobacco, at any rate, was the real thing—genuine, no make-believe, like his coffee. Often one might see large gatherings of the men night after night attending prayer-meetings, always with preaching added, for there was a strong religious tone among Southern soldiers, especially in the Army of Northern Virginia. One or two remarkable revivals took place, notably in the winter of 1863–64. That this photograph was taken early in the war is indicated by the presence of the Negroes. The one with an axe seems about to chop firewood for the use of the cooks. A little later, "Johnnie Reb" considered himself fortunate if he had anything to cook.

[I—9]

they march into Pennsylvania, in June, 1863. See how many of them are barefooted—literally hundreds in a single division. The great battle of Gettysburg was precipitated because General Heth had been informed that he could get shoes in that little town for his barefooted men!

These hardships became more acute as the war advanced, and the resources of the South were gradually exhausted, while at the same time the blockade became so effective that her ports were hermetically sealed against the world. With what grim determination the Confederate soldier endured cold and nakedness and hunger I need not attempt to describe, but there was a trial harder than all these to endure, which came upon him in the fourth year of the war. Letters began to arrive from home telling of food scarcity on his little farm or in the cabin where he had left his wife and children. Brave as the Southern women were, rich and poor alike, they could not conceal altogether from their husbands the sore straits in which they found themselves. Many could not keep back the cry: " What am I to do? Food is hard to get. There is no one to put in the crop. God knows how I am to feed the children!"

So a strain truly terrible was put upon the loyalty of the private soldier. He was almost torn asunder between love for his wife and children and fidelity to the flag under which he was serving. What wonder if hundreds, perhaps thousands, in those early spring months of 1865, gave way under the pressure, slipped out of the Confederate ranks, and went home to put in the crop for their little families, meaning to return to the colors as soon as that was done! Technically, they were deserters, but not in the heart or faith, poor fellows! Still, for Lee's army the result was disastrous. It was seen in the thinning ranks that opposed Grant's mighty host, week after week. This is the South's explanation of the fact, which the records show, that while at the close of the war there were over a million men under arms in the Federal armies, the aggregate of the Confederates was but 133,433.

RUINS OF THE TREDEGAR IRON WORKS IN RICHMOND, APRIL, 1865—THE MAIN FACTORY
FOR HEAVY CANNON IN THE SOUTH

The Tredegar Iron Works in Richmond was practically the only factory for cannon in the South, especially for pieces of heavy caliber. This supplied one of the chief reasons for the Confederate Government's orders to hold Richmond at all hazards. Thus the strategy of Confederate generals was hampered and conditioned, through the circumstance that Richmond contained in the Tredegar Works almost the only means of supplying the South with cannon. Augusta, Georgia, where the great powder factory of the Confederacy was located, was another most important point. Military strategists have debated why Sherman did not turn aside in his march to the sea in order to destroy this factory. Augusta was prepared to make a stout de-

AFTER THE GREAT RICHMOND FIRE

fense, and the Confederacy was already crumbling at this time. The Union armies were fast closing about Richmond, and possibly Sherman regarded such an attempt as a work of supererogation and a useless sacrifice of life. Only a few months more, and Richmond was to fall, with a conflagration that totally demolished the Tredegar Works. Colonel John W. Clarke, of 1103 Greene Street, an old inhabitant of Augusta, who made an excellent record in the Confederate army, tells of a story current in that city that the sparing of Augusta was a matter of sentiment. Sherman recalled his former connection with the local Military Academy for boys, and that here dwelt some of his former sweethearts and valued friends.

How could an army so poorly equipped, so imperfectly armed, so ill fed and ill clothed, win out in a contest with an army so vastly its superior in numbers and so superbly armed and equipped?* How could an agricultural people, unskilled in the mechanical arts, therefore unable to supply properly its armies with munitions and clothing, prevail against a great, rich, manufacturing section like the North, whose foreign and domestic trade had never been so prosperous as during the great war it was waging from 1861 to 1865?

Remember, also, that by May, 1862, the armies of the Union were in permanent occupancy of western and middle Tennessee, of nearly the whole of Louisiana, of parts of Florida, of the coast of North and South Carolina and of southeastern, northern, and western Virginia. Now, the population thus excluded from the support of the Confederacy amounted to not less than 1,200,000. It follows that, for the last three years of the war, the unequal contest was sustained by about 3,800,000 Southern whites with their slaves against the vast power of the Northern States. And yet none of these considerations furnishes the true explanation of the failure of the Confederate armies to establish the Confederacy. It was not superior equipment. It was not alone the iron will of Grant, or the strategy of Sherman. A power mightier than all these held the South by the throat and slowly strangled its army and its people. That power was Sea Power. The Federal navy, not the Federal army, conquered the South.

"In my opinion," said Field-Marshal Viscount Wolseley, in a private letter to me, dated November 12, 1904, "in my opinion, as a student of war, the Confederates must have won,

---

*I do not enter upon the contested question of the numbers serving in the respective armies. Colonel Livermore's Numbers and Losses in the Civil War is the authority relied upon usually by writers on the Northern side; but his conclusions have been strongly, and as many of us think, successfully challenged by Cazenove G. Lee, in a pamphlet entitled Acts of the Republican Party as Seen by History, and published (in Winchester, 1906) under the pseudo "C. Gardiner."

A FUTURE HISTORIAN, WHILE HISTORY WAS IN THE MAKING—1864

In the center of this group, taken before Petersburg, in August, 1864, sits Captain Charles Francis Adams, Jr., then of the First Massachusetts Cavalry, one of the historians referred to in the text accompanying. In his oration on General Lee, delivered October 30, 1901, Captain Adams vigorously maintains that the Union was saved not so much by the victories of its armies as by the material exhaustion of the Confederacy; a view ably elaborated by Hilary A. Herbert, former colonel of the Confederate States Army, in an address delivered while Secretary of the Navy, at the War College in 1896. A quotation from it appears on page 88, of Volume I, of the PHOTOGRAPHIC HISTORY. In the picture above, the officer on Captain Adams' left is Lieutenant G. H. Teague; on his right is Captain E. A. Flint. The fine equipment of these officers illustrates the advantage the Northern armies enjoyed through their splendid and never-failing system of supplies. The First Massachusetts was in active service at the front throughout the war and the conditions that Captain Adams actually witnessed afford a most direct basis for the truth of his conclusions.

had the blockade of the Southern ports been removed by us. . . . It was the blockade of your ports that killed the Southern Confederacy, not the action of the Northern armies." Compare with this mature opinion of the accomplished English soldier the words of Honorable Hugh McCulloch, one of Lincoln's Secretaries of the Treasury. " It was the blockade that isolated the Confederate States and caused their exhaustion. If the markets of Europe had been open to them for the sale of their cotton and tobacco, and the purchase of supplies for their armies, their subjugation would have been impossible. It was not by defeats in the field that the Confederates were overcome, but by the exhaustion resulting from their being shut up within their own domain, and compelled to rely upon themselves and their own production. Such was the devotion of the people to their cause, that the war would have been successfully maintained, if the blockade had not cut off all sources of supply and bankrupted their treasury." Again he says: " It must be admitted that the Union was not saved by the victories of its armies, but by the exhaustion of its enemies." Charles Francis Adams, in his oration on General Lee, vigorously maintains the same view, and Colonel Hilary A. Herbert, while Secretary of the Navy, delivered an elaborate address in 1896, in which he demonstrated the correctness of that interpretation of the true cause of the failure of the South.

In concluding, I may recall the well-known fact that the men in gray and the men in blue, facing each other before Petersburg, fraternized in those closing months of the great struggle. A Confederate officer, aghast at finding one night the trenches on his front deserted, discovered his men were all over in the Federal trenches, playing cards. The rank and file had made a truce till a certain hour!

PART I
SOLDIER LIFE

THE CONFEDERATE
OF '61

BUGLER IN A CONFEDERATE
CAMP—1861

THE CONFEDERATE OF '61

By ALLEN C. REDWOOD

Fifty-fifth Virginia Regiment, Confederate States Army

THE ill-fated attempt of John Brown at Harper's Ferry was significant in more directions than the one voiced in the popular lyric in the Southern States. The militia system had fallen into a condition little less than farcical, but the effect of Brown's undertaking was to awaken the public sense to an appreciation of the defenseless condition of the community, in the event of better planned and more comprehensive demonstrations of the kind in the future.

Rural populations do not tend readily to organization, and the Southerner was essentially rural, but under the impetus above indicated, and with no immediate thought of ulterior service, the people, of the border States especially, began to form military companies in almost every county, and to uniform, arm, and drill them.

The habit and temper of the men, no less than the putative intent of these organizations, gave a strong bias toward the cavalry arm. In the cities and larger towns the other branches were also represented, though by no means in the usual proportion in any regular establishment. In Virginia the mounted troops probably outnumbered the infantry and artillery combined. All were imperfectly armed or equipped for anything like actual campaigning, but at the beginning of hostilities a fair degree of drill and some approach to discipline had been attained, and these bodies formed a nucleus about which the hastily assembled levies, brought into the field by the call to arms, formed themselves, and doubtless received a degree of " stiffening " from such contact.

CONFEDERATES OF '61

THE CLINCH RIFLES ON MAY 10TH

NEXT DAY THEY JOINED A REGIMENT DESTINED TO FAME

On the day before they were mustered in as Company A, Fifth Regiment of Georgia Volunteer Infantry, the Clinch Rifles of Augusta were photographed at their home town. A. K. Clark, the boy in the center with the drum, fortunately preserved a copy of the picture. Just half a century later, he wrote: "I weighed only ninety-five pounds, and was so small that they would only take me as a drummer. Of the seventeen men in this picture, I am the only one living." Hardly two are dressed alike; they did not become "uniform" for many months. With the hard campaigning in the West and East, the weights of the men also became more uniform. The drummer-boy filled out and became a real soldier, and the stout man lying down in front lost much of his superfluous avoirdupois in the furious engagements where it earned its title as a " fighting regiment." The Confederate armies were not clad in the uniform gray till the second year of the war. So variegated were the costumes on both sides at the first battle of Bull Run that both Confederates and Federals frequently fired upon their own men. There are instances recorded where the colonel of a regiment notified his supports to which side he belonged before daring to advance in front of them.

In the beginning, each of these companies bore some designation instead of a company letter; there were various "Guards," "Grays," "Rifles"—the last a ludicrous misnomer —the "rifles" being mostly represented by flint-lock muskets, dating from the War of 1812, brought to light from State arsenals, only serviceable as issued, and carrying the old "buck-and-ball" ammunition, "Cal. .69."

Even this rudimentary armament was not always attainable. When the writer's company was first called into camp, requisition was made upon all the shotguns in the vicinity, these ranging all the way from a piece of ordnance quite six feet long and which chambered four buckshot, through various gages of double-barrels, down to a small single-barrel squirrel-gun. Powder, balls, and buckshot were served out to us in bulk, and each man made cartridges to fit the arm he bore, using a stick whittled to its caliber as a "former."

As the next step in the armament the obsolete flintlocks were converted into percussion as rapidly as the arsenals could turn them out. These difficulties were supplemented, however, by certain formidable weapons of war privately contributed— revolvers, and a most truculent species of double-edged cutlass, fashioned by blacksmiths from farrier's rasps, and carried in wooden scabbards bound with wire, like those affected by the Filipino volunteer. They proved very useful later on for cutting brush, but, so far as known, were quite guiltless of bloodshed, and soon went to the rear when the stress of active campaign developed the need of every possible reduction of *impedimenta*. One or two marches sufficed to convince the soldier that his authorized weapon and other equipment were quite as much as he cared to transport.

The old-pattern musket alone weighed in the neighborhood of ten pounds, which had a way of increasing in direct ratio with the miles covered, until every screw and bolt seemed to weigh a pound at least.

But I anticipate somewhat—we were really in our

COMPANY D, FIRST GEORGIA—OGLETHORPE INFANTRY

The photograph shows sixty-one Southerners who on March 16, 1861, became Company D of the First Georgia. Glowing in their hearts was that rare courage which impelled them to the defense of their homes, and the withstanding through four long years of terrible blows from the better equipped and no less determined Northern armies, which finally outnumbered them hopelessly. As Company D, First Georgia, they served at Pensacola, Fla., in April and May, 1861. The Fifth was then transferred to Western Virginia, serving under Gen. R. E. Lee in the summer and fall of that year, and under "Stonewall" Jackson, in his winter campaign. Mustered out in March, 1862, the men of Company D, organized as Company B, Twelfth Georgia Batt., served for a time in Eastern Tennessee, then on the coast of Georgia and last with the Army of Tennessee under Johnston and Hood in the Dalton and Atlanta campaign, and Hood's dash to Nashville in the winter of '64. Again transferred with the remnant of that army, they fought at Bentonville, N. C., and surrendered with Johnston's army, April 26, 1865, at Greensboro, N. C. Some significant figures pertaining to Georgia volunteers appear in a pamphlet compiled by Captain J. M. Folsom, printed at Macon, in 1864, "Heroes and Martyrs of Georgia." Among 16,000 men considered, 11,000 were original members of the organizations in which they served, and 5,000 were recruits who joined from time to time between 1861 and 1864. Only 100 were conscripts. Of the total number treated of by Captain Folsom, 5,000 died in service during the first three years of the war, 2,000 were permanently disabled by wounds, and 5,000 who were wounded, recovered. These figures represent the individuals wounded, some of them two or three times. It would be quite fair to assume that 11,000 of the Georgians were hit, and that the hits totalled 16,000, or one for every man in the ranks.

novitiate according to the dictum of Napoleon, who rightly believed that the proper school of war is *war*. By a species of *lucus a non lucendo* mode of designation, the uniforming of this inchoate force was not so irregular early in the war. Gray had been adopted as the color most serviceable, but the supply of cloth of that hue was soon exhausted under the influence of the blockade, and so numerous varieties came into use and were accepted as complying with the requirements of the service. Thus, in the writer's regiment, the companies were garbed from dark gray to almost white-kersey " nigger cloth." The facings varied from black, through various shades of blue and rifle-green, to artillery-red.

To revert to the matter of equipment, there was no official attempt in the beginning to do more than to arm the troops and to provide the purely warlike accouterments of cartridge-boxes, belts, and haversacks. Canteens and the like were provided quite as a matter of course, and, in default of blankets and waterproof coverings, requisition was made upon the household stock of the individual and duly honored—bed-quilts and homespun " spreads " were freely contributed, also buggy lap-robes, and pianos and tables were despoiled of their oilcloth covers to fend the rain from the men gone from the homes to do battle for the Cause, which was even dearer to the women left behind, who were steadfast to the end.

The minor courtesies and observances of military life were not readily inculcated in this mass of civilians as yet in process of conversion into soldiers, and this difficulty was present in a peculiar degree, perhaps, in the Confederate ranks. The mode of life, the whole ritual of his civilization, tendered to foster in the Southerner an individuality and independence of character to which the idea of subordination to authority was entirely foreign. He had come to war to fight, and could see no sense in any such "tomfoolery" as saluting his officer, lately " Tom " or " Jack," and his associate on terms of equality, especially when the elevation to the title had been, as it was in

A MILITIA COMPANY IN LOUISIANA AT DRILL

BEFORE ITS ARMORY

1861

During its half-century of oblivion, damage came to this unique photograph of a militia company in Louisiana hopefully drilling in front of its armory as the war began. In many sections, the notions of the hastily organized companies in regard to military discipline and etiquette were crude in the extreme. A certain Virginia regiment, for the first time in its service, held a dress-parade. At the stage of the ceremony when the first-sergeants of the respective companies announce the result of the evening roll-call, one reported thus: "All present in the Rifles, except Captain Jones, who is not feeling well this evening, but hopes to be feeling better to-morrow." Of like tenor was the response of a militia field-officer in the late autumn of 1861, when challenged by a sentry who demanded: "Who comes there?" "We kem from over the river, gwine the grand rounds," was the response of him who presumptuously sported the insignia of a colonel. From such raw material was developed the magnificent Confederate army which supplied the "matchless infantry" of Lee.

the lower grades, at least, procured by the exercise of his own suffrage. For the officers of the volunteers up to and including company commands, were purely elective, and were distinguished more by personal popularity or local prominence than by any consideration of fitness for the position under the use of actual service, yet to be applied. In view of this circumstance, it is fortunate that the early contestants were enlisted generally for the period of one year, that being estimated at the outset as the probable duration of the war.

When the time came for reenlistment " for three years or the war," the experience of that first year had begun to bear fruit, and the reelection showed better discrimination as to the quality of the officers chosen. The soldier had begun to learn his trade and to recognize that the " good fellow " or the county magistrate was by no means therefore the best officer, when it got down to the real business in hand. But all this required time, a test not even yet grasped by the American people, who are prone to confound good raw—excessively " raw "—material with an efficient fighting force, and to ignore the waste of blood and treasure pending the conversion of one into the other.

Naturally, the evolving of an army from this crude personnel, and its organization into an effective body capable of being handled in the field, were matters requiring time and much consideration of the peculiar conditions of the situation—a problem further complicated by the fact that an overwhelming proportion of the officers of the force were quite as devoid of any military experience as the men they commanded, or of any right appreciation of their shortcomings in this regard—all were untrained. The political aspect had to be taken into account—the popular sentiment underlying and sustaining the enterprise. A very large percentage of the force, amounting to a majority perhaps, had been but little in sympathy with secession in the beginning; had only given in their adherence to the movement when actually at the parting

A LIEUTENANT OF THE FOURTH GEORGIA, IN 1861

The ornateness of the uniform of Lieutenant R. A. Mizell, Company A, Fourth Georgia Regiment, would be sufficient proof that his ambrotype was taken early in the war. The epaulets, the towering shako, and the three rows of buttons are all more indicative of pomp and glory than of actual work. Two years later, even the buttons became so rare that the soldiers of the Army of Northern Virginia were driven to sew one or two tough berries on their tunics to serve as fastenings. The war career of this hopeful and earnest-looking young soldier was traced through a clue afforded by the letters "S. R." visible on his shako. This suggested "Southern Rifles," which was found to be the original title of Company A, Fourth Georgia Regiment. From its muster roll it was learned that Robert A. Mizell enlisted as a private April 26, 1861. He was promoted to second-lieutenant in April, 1862. He was wounded in the Wilderness, and at Winchester, Va.; resigned, but re-enlisted in Company A, Second Kentucky Cavalry, of Morgan's command.

of the ways and constrained to make a choice between stay-
ing in the Union their ancestors had helped to establish and
to which they were bound by the traditions of a lifetime, and
taking arms against their fellow countrymen whose institutions and political creed accorded with their own.

It is to be remembered that Virginia steadfastly declined
in its conversion to sever its connection with the Government
of which it had formed so large and so significant a part
from its formation, until called upon to furnish its quota of
troops for the army of invasion, and the final decision was
made with full recognition of what the choice implied, of the
devastation and bitter misery to be visited upon the territory
thus predestined to become the main battle-ground of the contending forces.

And so those wiser in the ways of war had, perforce, to
proceed cautiously, to feel their way in the undertaking of
welding these heterogeneous elements into a tempered weapon
capable of dealing effective and intelligently directed blows,
when the time should arrive for confronting the formidable
adversary assembling his forces just across the border. The
primary policy of the Confederate Government of attempting
to defend its entire frontier, mistaken as it was soon proved to
be, in the purely military sense, was possibly influenced in
large degree by this consideration.

The deficiency of transportation may have also wielded
its influence; indeed, the entire staff administration was, for
quite a year or more, scarcely organized, and any movement
of even a small body of troops could only be effected by the
impressment of teams and wagons from the adjacent country,
if leading away from the railway lines, and these last were
neither numerous nor very efficient in the South at that period.

Yet, in spite of the many incongruities and deficiencies
already indicated, the Southern volunteer was perhaps more
prompt to acquire the ways of war than was his Northern
opponent. The latter indisputably outclassed him in point of

SOUTH CAROLINA SOLDIERS IN '61

A group of Charleston Zouave Cadets—militia organized before the war, hence among the few that had swords and guns to start with in '61. The Zouave Cadets, under command of Captain C. E. Chichester, formed part of the First Regiment of Rifles, Fourth Brigade, South Carolina, at the outset of the war. The Fourth Brigade was the largest organized body of State militia. It was commanded by Brigadier-General James Simons, was well-organized, well-drilled and armed, and was in active service from December 27, 1860, to May, 1861. Some of its companies continued in service until the Confederate regiments, battalions, and batteries were organized and finally absorbed all the effective material of the brigade. One of the first duties of these companies was to guard some of the prisoners from New York regiments who were captured at the first battle of Bull Run, sent to Charleston harbor, and incarcerated at Castle Pinckney.

material, and was, in general, more amenable to discipline, for reasons heretofore stated—having been recruited, in large part, in the cities and large industrial centers. The Northern soldier had already formed the habit of subordination. The company or regimental commander simply replaced the general manager or the "boss"—it was merely a new job, and in one case as in the other what the superior said "went." The country-bred Southerner, on the other hand, was accustomed to the exercise of almost absolute authority over his slaves, few or many, according to his estate. But the simple and more primitive habit of his rural mode of life stood him in good stead when he came into the field. A gun was by no means an unfamiliar implement in his hands; he had known its use from boyhood and could usually hit what he aimed at. And in the mounted service his efficiency in action was in no wise impaired by preoccupation with his mount. He could no more remember when he learned to ride than when he learned to walk, and had graduated from the "school of the trooper" long before he brought himself and his best saddle-horse into the field.

It was in this arm of the service peculiarly that the Southerner, at the outset, held a long lead in advance of his adversary. As has been already stated, there were many organized bodies of horse in existence before the beginning of hostilities, and finer cavalry material has rarely, if ever, been assembled. The service had naturally tended to attract, for the most part, young men of wealth, leisure, and intelligence, forming a species of *corps d'élite*, and the equine part of the force could boast the best blood of Virginia and Kentucky stables. A few battlefields served to make good all deficiencies of equipment, so that by the time the war was well under way there was no distinction between the opposing forces in this respect: arms, saddlery, accouterment, down to blankets, haversacks, and canteens—all bore the stamp of some United States arsenal— "requisition on the spot," without process of Ordnance or

SUPPER WITH SOLDIERS OF THE NINTH MISSISSIPPI—1861

Ignorance of military conventionalities was of course the rule among Confederate volunteers of '61. In the matter of meals especially many amusing instances arose. There was the reply of a soldier of Dreux's Louisiana battalion of Magruder's division, when that force was holding the lines of Yorktown. "Prince John," who was noted for "putting on side," had bespoken dinner for himself and staff at a nearby farmhouse. Meanwhile the "full private" put in a petition to be fed. The good lady of the house, who was no respector of official rank, so long as one wore a gray jacket, and confident of the abundance of her provision, readily acceded to his request. When the somewhat belated staff entered the dining-room, the general was scandalized to find a bob-tail private already putting away the good cheer upon which he considered he held a prior claim. "This dinner was engaged, sir," he said haughtily, in his peculiar lisp. "That's all right," rejoined the private. "Sit down; there's plenty for all of us, I daresay." "Perhaps, young man, you don't know whom you are talking to," said the general, with increased hauteur. "I haven't the honor, but that doesn't matter," was the reply; "sit right down and help yourself." "I'm General Magruder, sir—your commanding officer." "Don't worry about that, general," said the imperturbable youngster; "I used to be particular who I ate with before this war, but now I don't care, so long as the victuals are clean." The Ninth Mississippi men in this photograph appear equally careless in preparing their evening meal. When it came to fighting, however, they could hold up their heads with the "smartest" European troops. Not long after this photograph, their regiment was especially mentioned for conspicuous gallantry at the attack of Price and Van Dorn on Corinth, October 3–4, 1862. The soldiers awaiting their evening meal above, from left to right, are James Pequio, Kinlock Falconer, and John Fennel.

Quartermaster's Department. The discriminating eye could discern from a glance at its equipment whether or not a regiment or brigade had been so engaged. It might, indeed, without straining the point unduly, be asserted that long before the close of the war the Federal Government had fitted out *both* armies.

The artillery arm was less fortunate, and for obvious reasons. This branch of the service is not so readily improvised as either of the other fighting forces. From start to finish it was under handicap by reason of its lack of trained officers, no less than from the marked inferiority of its material, ordnance, and ammunition. The batteries of the regular establishment were, of course, all in the United States service, commanded and served by trained gunners, and were easily distributed among the volunteer brigades by way of " stiffening " to the latter. This disparity was fully recognized by the Confederates and had its influence in the selection of more than one battle-ground, in order that it might be neutralized by local conditions, yet the service was very popular in the Southern army, and it was pervaded by a strong *esprit de corps*.

The young men of the cities and towns very generally chose it for enlistment; thus, New Orleans sent a battalion of five batteries, fully equipped, into the field—the famous " Washington Artillery "—besides some other batteries, and the city of Richmond, which furnished but one regiment of infantry and a few separate companies, contributed no less than eight or ten full batteries. Few of the minor towns but claimed at least one. The grade of intelligence of the personnel was rather exceptionally high, so that in the school of war, already referred to, these came in time to attain quite a respectable degree of efficiency, especially after the abolition of the system under which each battery was attached to an infantry brigade, subject to the orders of its commander, and the battery units became organized into battalions and corps commanded by officers of their own arm.

[150]

MOTLEY CONFEDERATE UNIFORMS—COMPANY B, NINTH MISSISSIPPI, IN '61

"Falstaff's regiment could hardly have exhibited a more motley appearance than did ours at 'dress parade,' at which the feature of 'dress' was progressively and conspicuously absent." This reminiscence is furnished by Allen C. Redwood, of the Fifty-fifth Virginia, from whom other contributions appear in the following pages. "There was no official attempt in the beginning to do more than to arm the troops and to provide the purely warlike accouterments of cartridge-box and belts and haversacks. Canteens and the like were provided quite as a matter of course, and in default of blankets and waterproof coverings, requisition was made upon the household stock of the individual and duly honored—bed-quilts and homespun 'spreads' were freely contributed, and buggy lap-robes and pianos and tables were despoiled of their oilcloth covers to fend the rain from the men gone from the homes to do battle for the cause, which was even dearer to the women left behind, who were steadfast to the end." These conditions applied also in States farther south, as the Mississippi photograph above witnesses. Standing at the left is James Cunningham; on the camp-stool is Thomas W. Falconer, and to his left are James Sims and John I. Smith.

Some of the early organizations were quite erratic; for a while, "legions" were a good deal in favor—mixed bodies comprising the several arms of the service under one command. These were speedily abandoned as unwieldy and inoperative. They probably had their origin in tradition, dating back to the days of Marion and Sumter and "Light Horse Harry" Lee, and may possibly have been effective in the partisan operations of that period. Otherwise, the regiments hurried to the front were thrown together into brigades in the hap-chance order of their arrival; gradually those hailing from the same State were brigaded together as far as practicable, an arrangement significant in its recognition of the State feeling, of the issue pending between the sections. This feature was not generally prevalent in the Federal ranks. As a result, the unit of the brigade persistently maintained its prominence in the estimation of the Confederate soldier throughout the whole term of his service; when vaunting his prowess he was apt to speak of his " brigade "; with his antagonist it was usually the " corps." The rivalry between the respective States had probably no small influence in stimulating his zeal; the men from Georgia or the Carolinas could not hold back when the Alabamans or Texans on right or left were going ahead. It was but the repetition of Butler's rallying cry at Cherabusco, " Palmettos! stand your ground; *remember where you came from!*" when Bee, at Manassas, pointing to the Virginians, " standing like a stone wall," restored his wavering line.

The Confederate soldier of the ranks may be said to have been *sui generis.* In the mass he was almost devoid of military spirit, as the term is popularly applied, and quite indifferent—antagonistic, even—to the " pomp and circumstance of glorious war." As to devotion to his flag, he had scarcely time to cultivate the sentiment which figured so largely in the patriotic fervor of his opponents. No one of the " motley many " national ensigns ever entirely received his approval.

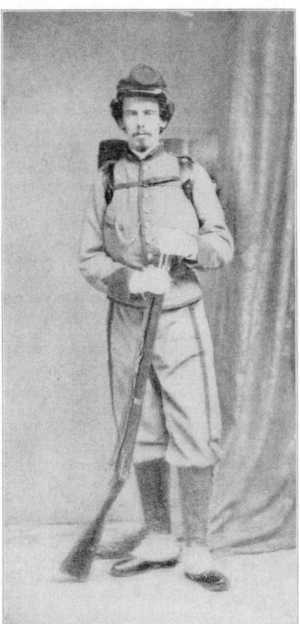

TWO MEMBERS OF THE McCLELLAN ZOUAVES IN 1861

The host of ornately uniformed and armed companies which sprang up at the outset of the war was ultimately merged into the gray monotone of the respective regiments into which they were incorporated. The Confederate soldier on the left is Ellis Green, of the McClellan Zouaves, and his companion on the right belonged to the same company. The photographs were taken at Charleston, S. C., and the spruce appearance and spotless uniforms make it unnecessary to add that they were taken early in the war. The Southern volunteer was perhaps more prompt to acquire the ways of war than was his Northern opponent. The latter was more amenable to discipline, having been recruited, in large part, in the cities and large industrial centers. He had already formed the habit of subordination. The country-bred Southerner, on the other hand, was accustomed to the exercise of almost absolute authority over his slaves, but the simple and more primitive habits of his rural mode of life stood him in good stead when he came into the field.

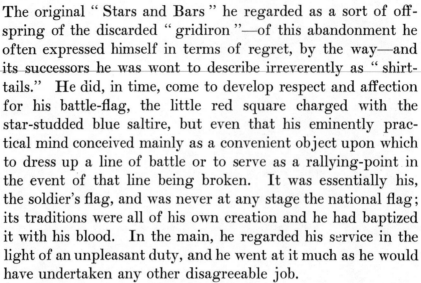

The original " Stars and Bars " he regarded as a sort of off-spring of the discarded " gridiron "—of this abandonment he often expressed himself in terms of regret, by the way—and its successors he was wont to describe irreverently as " shirt-tails." He did, in time, come to develop respect and affection for his battle-flag, the little red square charged with the star-studded blue saltire, but even that his eminently practical mind conceived mainly as a convenient object upon which to dress up a line of battle or to serve as a rallying-point in the event of that line being broken. It was essentially his, the soldier's flag, and was never at any stage the national flag; its traditions were all of his own creation and he had baptized it with his blood. In the main, he regarded his service in the light of an unpleasant duty, and he went at it much as he would have undertaken any other disagreeable job.

General Lord Wolseley—then Colonel Wolseley—relates an interview he had with General Lee, during a visit to the headquarters of the latter, just after the Maryland campaign of 1862. Having intimated a desire to see the troops of whose performance he had heard so much, General Lee took him for a ride through the lines, and upon their return remarked to his distinguished guest:

" Well, Colonel, you have seen my army—how does it impress you, on the whole? "

" They seem a hardy, serviceable looking lot of fellows," Wolseley replied, " but, to be quite frank, General, I must say that one misses the smartness which we in Europe are accustomed to associate with a military establishment—but perhaps it would not be reasonable to look for that so soon after the hard campaign they had just gone through."

" Ho! " replied " Marse Robert," " my men don't show to advantage in camp, and to tell the truth, I am a little ashamed to show them to visitors. But, sir, you should see them when they are fighting—then I would not mind if the whole world were looking on! "

PART I
SOLDIER LIFE

———

THE CONFEDERATE
IN THE FIELD

———

WASHING DISHES
REAL SOLDIERING FOR
A CONFEDERATE OF 1863

WHERE UNIFORMS WERE LACKING, BUT RESOLUTION WAS FIRM

The Confederates who stood in this well-formed line saw active service from the earliest period of the war. The day that Florida seceded from the Union, First-Lieutenant Adam J. Slemmer withdrew with Company G of the First United States Artillery from the shore to Fort Pickens, on the western extremity of Santa Rosa Island. Colonel W. H. Chase was in command of the Southerners and demanded the surrender of Fort Pickens January 13, 1861. It is recorded that his voice shook and his eyes filled with tears when he attempted to read his formal demand for the surrender; he realized, with all true and far-sighted Americans, how terrible a

A CONFEDERATE DRILL IN FORT McREE, PENSACOLA HARBOR

blow was impending in the form of fratricidal strife. Lieutenant Slemmer refused the demand. Colonel Chase had an insufficient force at the time to take the fort by storm. November 22d and 23d, the United States vessels *Niagara* and *Richmond*, together with Fort Pickens and the adjoining batteries, bombarded the Confederate lines. Although Fort McRee was so badly damaged that General Bragg thought of abandoning it, the garrison held firm, and the plan of the Union commanders to "take and destroy it" did not succeed. Forts McRee and Barrancas were bombarded again by the Union warships and batteries January 1, 1862.

THE CONFEDERATE IN THE FIELD

By Allen C. Redwood
Fifty-fifth Virginia Regiment, Confederate States Army

A QUESTION which is often asked of the survivor of the Civil War, when recounting the " battles, sieges, and fortunes he has passed," is, " How does it feel to be in battle?" If he is in the habit of taking account of his sensations and impressions the answer is not so simple as might appear at first sight.

Much of the ground disputed by the contending forces in our Civil War was quite unlike the popular conception of a battlefield, derived from descriptions of European campaigns or from portrayals of the same, usually fanciful. The choice of a battle-ground in actual warfare is not determined by its fitness for the display of imposing lines, as at a review. As often as not, the consideration of concealment of those lines has much to do with the selection, or else there is some highway which it is important to hold or to possess, or again, some vulnerable point of the foe invites attack, in which case the actual *terrain* is such as may happen, and the disposition of the forces is made to conform as far as possible thereto.

The first engagement in which the writer took a modest part had been entirely foreseen, yet its development refuted all preconceived ideas of what a battle was like. It was the beginning of the series which resulted in frustrating McClellan's campaign on the Peninsula and raising the siege of Richmond, in 1862. We had been holding the left of the Confederate line on the Meadow Bridge road, picketing the bridges spanning a fork of the Chickahominy at that point—a Union picket-post being at the crossing of another branch, about a hundred yards distant, and in plain view from our outpost.

[158]

CONFEDERATES AT DRILL—NOT "SMART" BUT FIGHTERS

"One misses the smartness which we in Europe are accustomed to associate with military establishments." The sight of this Confederate officer in his shirt-sleeves, and of his determined-looking company behind, recalls this remark, made by General Lord Wolseley, then Colonel Wolseley and later Governor-General of Canada, after inspecting Lee's army in the lower Shenandoah Valley just after the Maryland campaign of 1862—the year after the Florida photograph above was taken. The look of the men, gaunt and hollow-eyed, worn with marching and lack of proper food, until they did not carry an ounce of superfluous flesh; powdered thick with dust until their clothing and accouterment were all one uniform dirty gray, except where the commingled grime and sweat had streaked and crusted the skin on face and head; the jaded, unkempt horses and dull, mud-bespattered gun-carriages and caissons of the artillery; even trivial details; the nauseating flavor of the unsalted provisions, the pungent smell of the road-dust which filled the nostrils—all these impressions came thronging back across the intervening years which have transformed the beardless young soldier into the grizzled veteran who still "lags superfluous on the stage," and who recalls these things that have passed. And he glories in "Marse Robert's" reply: "No, my men don't show to advantage in camp, and to tell the truth I am a little ashamed to show them to visitors. But, sir," he resumed, his face flushing and his eyes kindling, as sometimes happened when stirred from his habitual poise, "you should see them when they are fighting—then I would not mind if the whole world were looking on!"

At the date of the opening of the battle, June 26, 1862, it was the turn of the regiment for this duty, our company holding the advanced post at the bridges. But we had supposed that we were to receive an attack from the foe, being ignorant of the fact that the Federal force on the north bank was " in the air," owing to the retention of McDowell's corps, before which we had retired from Fredericksburg, and which was to have joined and extended this flank on the Rappahannock. Thus, when the advance began, we were the first to cross the river. For some distance the road was a corduroy through the swamp, which our company traversed at double-quick and without opposition until we came into the open and approached the small hamlet of Mechanicsville, at the intersection of a road leading to Richmond and the Old Cold Harbor road, running almost parallel with the Chickahominy.

Thus far we had seen no Federals except the picket, which had promptly retired before our advance. Nor was the country about us in any way distinctive—just an ordinary eastern Virginia landscape of fields, farmhouses, and commonplace woods, and seeming peaceful enough in the light of a summer's afternoon. Before opening this vista the column, marching in fours, was halted in a shallow cut of the road, and some one ahead called back an order to " clear the road for the artillery!" A wild scramble up the banks ensued, under the apprehension that we were about to be raked by McClellan's guns. But the real intent was to advance a section of our brigade battery traveling in our rear, to " feel " a thin belt of timber intervening between us and the village. This was our first scare; number two was soon to follow.

Meanwhile, we had formed line on the right of the road and approached the wooded camp-site in which, as we supposed, the foe was concealed and awaiting us. When almost up to it, some excited soldier discharged his musket; at once, and without orders, the entire right wing of the regiment blazed away at the numerous collection of tent-poles and cracker-

THE CONFEDERATE SOLDIER AT WORK

The photograph of this garrison at a "sand battery" on the Gulf Coast gives a view of the Confederate at work that will be treasured by veterans. Every one of them knows how eminently unsatisfactory an occupation is war for the private in the ranks. He is ordered, he knows not whither, he knows not why, and, likely as not, has to stay there to die. "I wondered if they were deliberately planning my death," recalled an old soldier who was invariably chosen for the skirmish line. "First, we had to go out there to see if anyone could be induced to shoot at us; and if they did, and we got back alive, we had to take our places in the ranks and go forward with the other fellows, taking an equal risk with them after the other fellows were entirely through shooting at us individually. Somehow it didn't seem quite fair."

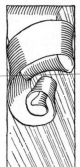

boxes, reminders of its late occupation. At that time there probably was not a Federal soldier nearer than the further side of Beaver Dam Creek, nearly a mile distant. But we were to hear from them before long.

Having passed through the straggling little village we were halted again just beyond, in a dip of the ground through which coursed a small rivulet, and some of us took the opportunity to fill canteens. It was while waiting there that we received the first hostile shots from the guns beyond the creek. They soon got our range and it began to look like real war at last.

It was at this point that, for the first time, I saw a man killed in battle. We were standing to arms awaiting orders to advance; another regiment of the brigade was supporting us a short distance in the rear—the Sixtieth Virginia, under Colonel Starke, who was killed later while commanding a Louisiana brigade at Sharpsburg, in September, 1862. A shell plowed the crest of the elevation in front, and our line made a profound obeisance as it passed over; it seemed as if it must clear us but about reach the Sixtieth, and as I ducked I glanced back that way and witnessed its effect in their ranks. The body of a stalwart young fellow suddenly disappeared, and on the ground where he had stood was a confused mass of quivering limbs which presently lay still—the same shell, as I learned afterward, carried away the top of a man's head in our own regiment.

Another took effect soon after, as we were moving out by the left flank, knocking over several men and killing one of them. By this time the fire had grown quite brisk, and we lost more men as we lay in the open field before entering some woods still more to the left, where the regiment commenced firing, against an imaginary foe, I have cause to believe. Yet, these same skittish troops, under fire for the first time, just four days later charged and captured a regular battery of 12-pounder guns and were complimented on the field by

THE WORK OF WAR WITH COASTWISE GARRISON—INSIDE SUMTER, 1864

The soldiers of the Army of Northern Virginia, with the Confederate troops who struggled over the Western mountains and swamps, were wont to allude to coast "garrison" duty as an easy berth, but this Confederate photograph of the interior of Fort Sumter, taken in 1864, does not indicate any degree of superfluous ease and convenience. The garrison drawn up in the background, in front of the ruined barracks, could point to the devastation wrought by the bombardment, visible in the foreground and on the parapets, with just pride. In spite of the hundreds of shells that crashed into the fort from the belching guns of the Federal fleets, the Stars and Bars still floated defiant throughout the four years of the war. The Southern heart may well glow with pride at the thought of the little fort.

General Longstreet—such progress had they made within that brief period in the " school of the soldier."

We are coming to the period in this narration when we might fairly claim to have been soldiers indeed; when the disjointed fragments had at last been welded together into an army. We had been " shooted over " and even " blooded "; had heard the screech of shell and the hiss of minie balls, and had learned to discount their deadliness in some measure; had learned how to make ourselves snug and comfortable in camp, even though our wagons still might be miles in the rear; had learned to cook without utensils and to improvise a shelter without tents or, failing that, to take the weather as it came and say no more about it. We knew that a march meant much fatigue —agony, even—and accepted both as a matter of course and part of the work on which we were engaged. Blistered feet, we had come to learn, were indeed serious, and as a corollary, that it was wise to get a foot-bath, and to put on dry socks upon going into camp for the night, even if one were tired out, and felt more disposed just to lie down and rest. There was to-morrow's march to be considered, and we had come to recognize that to-day's exertion was by no means exceptional.

We knew how to make a fire which would last all night; that it was well to start out before daylight with just a bite, if no more, rather than upon an empty stomach, and to confine the consumption of water while on the road to what was in the canteen, though that might be lukewarm, instead of going out of ranks at a spring or well—the canteen's contents were just as *wet*—and one was not tempted to drink too much when overheated, and most important of all, he did not have to overfatigue himself in trying to catch up with his command in a road full of other troops, who had " troubles of their own " and were by no means disposed to get out of the way.

The soldier could find water in a perfectly unfamiliar country just by the lay of the land, and by a kind of prescience almost amounting to instinct, and, at a glance, could estimate

THE CHANGE FROM THEORY TO PRACTICE

Wall-tents, such as appear in this photograph of 1861, were not seen for long in the Confederate army. At the beginning, no less than three wagons conveyed the *impedimenta* of a company of the Fifty-fifth Virginia—one having been provided by private subscription to transport the knapsacks! The rest of the transportation was in proportion. The regimental train, as it left the Rappahannock, would have sufficed amply for the use of at least a brigade. But a few months later, just after the "Seven Days," all this was changed and the soldiers began for the first time to realize what actual soldiering meant and to find out how very few were the articles one needed in his kit when he had to transport them on his person. An inkling of this had been gained before, however, when the brigade retained as an outpost at Fredericksburg, after Johnston's army went to Yorktown, evacuated that position before the advance of McDowell's Corps, which was moving overland to join McClellan north of the Chickahominy and complete the investment of Richmond on that side. This movement relegated to the rear the capacious mess-chests and wall-tents which had hitherto been regarded as requisite or necessary paraphernalia for field service. The soldiers in the field were permitted to retain only the "flies" belonging to the tents.

the merits or demerits of a camp-site, at the end of a day's march. Also, we had grown weather-wise in forecasting the final events to which all the preliminaries tended, from indications whose significance the experience of service enabled us to read with a fair approach to certainty, however these might vary, as they did, with the outward conditions—accidents of locality, the immediate object in view, and the like.

Many of the early engagements, from the point of view of the man in the ranks and the officers of the lower grades, seemed quite impromptu. Of one of the most stupendous of these— that of Gettysburg—a Confederate officer of high grade has said, "We accidentally stumbled into this fight."

It seemed so to the writer, then serving in Heth's division of the Third Army Corps, and which opened the engagement on the morning of July 1, 1863. Usually we knew there must be trouble ahead, but not always how imminent it might be. The column would be marching as it had been doing for perhaps some days preceding, the fatigue, heat, dust, and general discomfort being far more insistent upon the thought of the men than any consideration of its military objective. Perhaps the pace may have been rather more hurried than usual for some miles, and a halt, for any reason, was most welcome to the foot-sore troops, who promptly proceeded to profit by every minute of it—lying down on the dusty grass by the roadside, easing knapsack straps and belts, and perhaps snatching the opportunity for a short smoke (for which there had been no breath to spare previously) or for a moistening of parched throats from the canteen.

This might be of longer or shorter duration, often it was aggravatingly cut up into a series of advances or stops, more fatiguing than the regular marching swing. Getting up and down is rather tiresome when one is carrying the regular campaigning kit of a soldier and when muscles have been taxed until there is no spring left in them—quite another affair from the same process when fresh and unencumbered. It is then that

WALL–TENTS

COMPARATIVE COMFORT ON THE CONFEDERATE COAST

Although most comforts had disappeared from the Army of Northern Virginia by 1862, as well as from the armies in the West, the port garrisons like those around Charleston were able to keep their wall-tents. So great is the "luxury" among this mess of the Washington Light Infantry in garrison at Charleston, that they even have initials painted upon their water-bucket; and, wonder of wonders! there hangs a towel. One who inquired of a veteran as to the opportunities for toilet-making was answered thus: "On the march we generally had water enough to wash our hands and faces, but sometimes, especially when there was brisk skirmishing every day, the men didn't get a chance to wash their bodies for weeks together. It was fun in a country comparatively free from the enemy to see a column strike a river. Hundreds of the boys would be stripped in an instant, and the river banks would reëcho with their shouts and splashing. It was only on garrison duty or in winter-quarters that the supreme luxury, laundry from home, could ever be attained." The men in this photograph from left to right are Sergeant W. A. Courtney, Privates H. B. Olney, V. W. Adams, and Sergeant R. A. Blum. The organization still existed, half a century after the scene above.

the voice of a man with a " grouch " is heard in the land. There is sure to be one in every company, and his incessant jeremiads by no means tend to alleviate the discomforts of his fellows, and so receive small sympathy from them.

A mounted orderly comes riding back, picking his way through the recumbent ranks, and pretending indifference to the rough chaffing prescribed by custom in the infantry as the appropriate greeting for the man on horseback—good-natured on the whole, even if a little tinged with envy—or some general officer with his staff is seen going forward at a brisk trot through the fields bordering the road, or maybe a battery of guns directing its course toward some eminence. It becomes apparent that the check ahead is not due to such ordinary causes as a stalled wagon or caisson or to the delay occasioned by some stream to be forded; the objective aspect of the situation begins to assert itself; the thought of present personal discomfort gives place to that of prospective peril, and a certain nervous tension pervades the ranks.

Soldiers are but human, and the veterans who have been in battle before know what is implied in the work ahead and that some—and it may be one as well as another—will probably not answer at next roll-call. The " eagerness for the fray " of which we read so often, rarely survives the first battle; in all that follows, it is conspicuously absent, however the men may have gained in steadiness and have acquired self-possession under fire.

The troops in front are moving now, filing off to right or left, to take their allotted position in the line, or possibly beginning a flank movement; there may be no fight to-day after all—these things have happened before, without anything serious coming of it. The hostile force may be only a small one and we daresay will not give battle, but retire on its main body. For, in the field we live merely from day to day anyhow and " sufficient unto the day is the evil thereof." We are not in the confidence of the powers that be and know nothing of their

CONFEDERATES IN CAMP

This photograph of Confederate troops in camp was taken at Camp Moore, Louisiana, in 1861. The man writing the letter home on the box is Emil Vaquin, and Arthur Roman is the man completing the washing. Thomas Russel is gleaning the latest news from the paper, and Amos Russel is grinding coffee. The fifth man is Octave Babin. Names of French extraction, these, appropriate to Louisiana. The soldiers are facing their period of "breaking-in." A veteran of the eastern army describes this transition period: "Our breaking-in was rather rough—it was the beginning of a prolonged spell of wet, raw weather, which is so often mentioned in McClellan's reports of his operations on the Peninsula—and, with little notion of how to adapt ourselves to the situation, we suffered much discomfort at first. After the experience of a few months and with half the equipage we then possessed, we would have been entirely comfortable, by campaigning standards. As yet we were drawing the full army ration, including the minor items of coffee, sugar, rice, and beans, and were abundantly supplied with the necessary utensils for their preparation whenever we were in contact with our wagons, but we simply did not know how to use this bountiful provision and had yet to learn that the situation was not exceptional or ephemeral but would be just the same in the future months of war, and must be met and faced in permanent fashion—that it was 'all in the day's work,' and that any departure from these hard times, as they then seemed, would be in the direction of 'worse a-comin'.'"

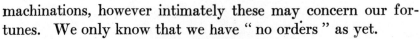

machinations, however intimately these may concern our fortunes. We only know that we have " no orders " as yet.

This condition of affairs may continue for hours or for minutes. Meanwhile, the best thing to do is to make ourselves as comfortable as possible—the philosophy of the seasoned soldier, in all circumstances—and take the chance of being permitted to remain so, and we shall be all the better prepared for the work if it *does* come. But, hello! look yonder! the battery-men, who have been lounging about, are standing to their pieces now, and immediately become busy executing mysterious movements about the same, in the methodical fashion distinctive of their arm. Those about the nearest gun suddenly break away to right and left. A dense white stream of smoke leaps from the muzzle, and the crashing report strikes our ears a few seconds later, as the gunners step forward again, lay hold of handspike and spokes, and run the gun back into position. Another shot and another, and yet another, and the smoke thickens and we discern only vaguely the movements at the cannon —but the war-music has begun and we know the battle has opened.

From somewhere in front comes another and fainter report, and possibly in mid-air above our battery a round cloud jumps into view, snowy white against the blue sky; another remote, jarring growl, followed by a fluttering sound but too familiar to our ears and growing louder each moment, and a spurt of earth is projected into the air not far from the road we occupy. One finds the foe does not propose that the argument shall be all on one side and is rising " to a point of information."

Evidently it is this road which is the object of their curiosity; just now we also are interested, but in the sense of wishing we were somewhere else before their aim shall have become more accurate with practice—we don't like the talk to be too one-sided either, and they are beyond the range of our ordnance, while the ground in front which conceals from view what is beyond affords slight protection. Ah! there is a staff-

"IMPEDIMENTA" DID NOT HARASS THE CONFEDERATES

AN UNUSUALLY LUXURIOUS CAMP

This is an unusually luxurious Confederate camp for the second year of the war. The photograph was taken by Scheier of Nashville, Tenn., and the scene is indicated as on the Harding road. The shining muskets stacked in front of the tents contrast with the soldiers' nondescript costumes. The boxes and barrels have rather the appearance of plunder than that of a steady supply from the commissary department. Conspicuous are the skillet on the barrel-head, and the shirt hung up to dry. The Confederate soldier traveled light. Indeed, a long train would have impeded, perhaps frustrated, the swift movements which were so great an element of his strength. The old Romans rightly termed their baggage "*impedimenta*," when put upon their mettle. However, the size of their wagon-train was seldom a cause of anxiety to the Confederates. Jackson's "Foot Cavalry" could always outstrip the wagons, and the size of the Union wagon-train was apt to interest them more frequently. For the rank and file of the Army of Northern Virginia, there were no more tents after the middle of the war. The camping site was almost always in the woods, as giving ready access to fuel and being as near as possible to some stream of water. Each company selected ground in the rear of its stacks of arms, but beyond that there was little semblance of order in the arrangement. The consideration of level ground, free from stubs or roots, usually determined the selection.

officer talking in an animated tone to the brigade commander, motioning with his hand, while the other closely studies a folding map which has just been handed to him and which he presently returns, nodding the while to signify that he understands what he is expected to do. "Attention!"—but we are already on our feet in advance of the order, and most willingly leave the road, now growing momentarily more insalubrious, following the head of the column through fields of stubble or fallow or standing corn, the blades of which cut and the pollen irritates the moist skin. Or it may be through dense woodland, where nothing is visible a few yards distant, in which furious fighting may occur and many men fall with the opposing lines in close contact, yet entirely concealed from each other, the position of either being only conjectured by the smoke and the direction of the firing, as the bullets from the opposite side come rapping against the tree trunks and cutting twigs and leaves overhead.

Before this stage is reached, however, there may be numerous changes of direction, countermarching and the like to attain the position; long lines of battle require a good deal of space for their deployment, and in the woods, especially, it is not easy to determine in advance just how much ground any command will occupy. In each case, however, at some stage, the troops are in line, and we may suppose them there, awaiting the attack or about to deliver it, as may be.

It is perhaps the most ominous moment of all when the command is heard, "Load at will—load!" followed by the ringing of rammers in the barrels and the clicking of gun-locks —neither of which sounds, with the arms of to-day, has any significance, but it was otherwise when we loaded "in nine times," as the manual prescribed. The modern soldier fails utterly to grasp the meaning of biting cartridges; a cartridge to him is essentially a brass shell with the fulminate enclosed in its base, requiring only to be taken from his belt and put in the chamber of his rifle—nowadays, indeed, they go in in

FIELD AND FOREST—TWO CONTRASTING BUT FAMOUS SCENES OF CONFLICT

The two photographs are eloquent of the two distinct styles of warfare that Captain Redwood contrasts. Over the wide fields near Gettysburg, across the trampled stubble where lie the bodies of Confederates fallen in the battle, ten, fifteen, twenty thousand men could be maneuvered intelligently. But in the dense woodland conflicts were waged blindly, in total ignorance of the strength and location of the foe—yet sanguinary, as the photograph of the battlefield of the Wilderness below attests.

"clips" of five. But we veterans managed to fight through the big war with the old muzzle-loaders, and they seem to have done some execution, too. It has "a strange, quick jar upon the ear," the dry metallic snapping running along the line when it came to "prime," and each man realized that when next heard it will be with no uncertain sound and closely followed by the command, "Fire!"

Once engaged, the soldier's attention is too much taken up with delivering his fire effectively to give heed to much else —it is hard work and hot work, in the literal, no less than in the figurative, sense, and extremely dirty work withal. The lips become caked with powder-grime from biting the twist of cartridges, and after one or two rounds the hands are blackened and smeared from handling the rammer; the sweat streams down and has to be cleared from the eyes in order to see the sights of the rifle, and the grime is transferred from hands to face.

Think you of a gang of coal-heavers who have just finished putting in a winter's supply ordered by some provident householder in midsummer, and you get a fair impression of troops at the end of a day's fighting. The line soon loses all semblance of regular formation; the companies have become merely groups of men, loading and firing and taking advantage of any accident of ground—natural depression, tree, rock, or even a pile of fence rails that will give protection. But if the soldier is about where he belongs—to right or left of the regimental colors, according to the normal place of his company in line—he feels reasonably sure of resuming formation whenever the command may come to "cease firing" and to "dress on colors" preparatory to an advance or a charge. If the latter, though the move next may begin in perfect order, it is almost immediately lost.

The charge delivered by our brigade at Frayser's Farm —to which allusion has been made earlier in this chapter— was, as seen by a Federal general who was captured there, "in V-shape, without order and in perfect recklessness." This

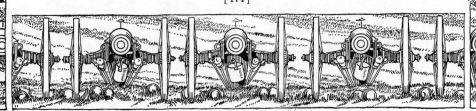

WHERE THE COURAGE TO FIGHT IN THE DARK WAS NEEDED

Old soldiers say that it takes more courage to fight with an unseen foe than it does to sweep in long lines through the open fields to the mouths of the roaring batteries. A veteran cavalryman has stated that he thought a cavalry charge took less bravery than any other kind of action. There is the dash, the emulation, the "thunder of the captains and the shouting" all stimulating the participant to supreme effort. Such are the famous European battles of song and story— usually waged in open fields; but the American soldier soon became an adept at fighting an unseen enemy. These dense woodlands of the Wilder- ness are not the European idea of a battlefield, but the ghastly ruins of the human frame, and the trees clipped and broken by the fearful hail of shot and shell, attest that here was a battle where they fought in the darkness of the woods, instead of on the open plain. These photographs convey wonderful mute tributes to the courage of every American participant, from the South or from the North. The forest-trees are pitted and scored and hacked and gnawed by the galling fire of musketry—in some instances, entirely felled from this cause alone, for the country afforded but little scope for the employment of artillery by either side. The underbrush, withered and reddened by the summer's sun, lies at all angles as the bullets have cut it down along the battlefield.

formation was in no wise intentional, the apex of the V in question being simply the brigade commander, General Field, who personally conducted the attack upon the battery and the slope of the sides, as the individual prowess of his followers might determine. Even more characteristic of a Confederate infantry onset was the description of an officer of high rank on that side, "A tumultuous rush of men, each aligning on himself, and yelling like a demon, on his own hook." The "yell" which has become historical, was merely another expression of the individuality of the Southern soldier, though as its moral force came to be recognized, it was rather fostered officially, and grew into an institution—it was the peculiar slogan of the Gray people. A gallant, accomplished staff-officer of General Meade's household, in a recent work on the battle of the Wilderness, pays the thrilling yell this tribute, "I never heard that yell that the country in the rear did not become intensely interesting!" And more than one Federal soldier has borne similar testimony.

This allusion recalls to mind a visit of two days' duration, made to that historic field in the summer of 1910, after an interval of forty-six years, which served to illustrate forcibly what has already been recorded in these recollections as to the absence of distinction in the features of a battle-ground *per se*. When last seen the blighting breath of war had but lately passed over those dense and tangled woodlands and the signs of strife, deadly and determined, were manifest everywhere. The forest trees were pitted and scored and hacked and gnawed by the galling fire of musketry, in some instances, entirely felled from this cause alone, for the country afforded but little scope for the employment of artillery by either side. The underbrush, withered and reddened by the summer's sun, lay at all angles as the bullets had cut it down, as if some one had gone over the ground with a *machete* and given each little bush or sapling a stroke. In all directions, one came upon the rude breastworks hastily thrown up, of earth, logs, rails—anything that might serve to stop a bullet. They had failed to stop a

IN THE WILDERNESS

In these photographs reappears the dreadful Wilderness as it looked in 1864—the shambles in the thickets, with the forest trees pitted and scarred and hacked and gnawed by the galling musketry fire, where the dead still outnumbered the living, where the woods bordering the Orange Plank Road were thickly strewn with the bodies of Hancock's men who had so furiously assailed Hill and Longstreet on that line. The underbrush, withered and reddened by the summer's sun, lay at all angles as the bullets had cut it down, as if someone had gone over the ground with a *machete* and given each little bush or sapling a stroke. In all

directions one came upon the rude breastworks, hastily thrown up, of earth, logs, rails—anything that might serve to stop a bullet. But nearly half a century later, a visitor could find here the deep significance of peace; as Captain Redwood records in his accompanying reminiscence: "The bark has closed over the bullet scars on the trees; a new growth has sprung up to replace that leveled by the musketry; goodly trees, even, are standing upon the diminished earthworks. The others have long since rotted into mould. The traveler might easily pass along that quaint road, so hotly contested, with never a suspicion of what befell there—'grim-visaged war has smoothed his wrinkled front' indeed."

THE ORANGE PLANK ROAD
AS IT LOOKED IN 1864

"THE GRIM HARVEST" OF THE WILDERNESS—SOLDIERS' GRAVES
AFTER THE BATTLE

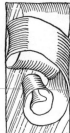

good many, and all the failures were not recorded upon the natural growth.

In this sparsely settled region, but lately so populous, the dead occupants still outnumbered the living. The woods bordering the Orange plank road were thickly strewn with the mouldering bodies of Hancock's men who had furiously assailed Hill and Longstreet on that line. Here gallant old Webb, for whom " taps " have sounded, led his staunch brigade against Gregg's Texans and Low's Alabamans, almost up to the works, and the trefoil badges—the " clover-leaves " on the cap-fronts of the fallen covered the ground on the edge of the Widow Tapp's field where Lee attempted to lead the Texans' charge, and the men refused to go forward until he consented to go back. Cattle were quietly browsing the herbage in a little grass glade at this point, their pasture the aftermath of the grim harvest reaped there on that May morning long ago.

To-day scarcely a trace remains of all that. In the intervening years beneficent Nature has been silently but unremittingly at work effacing the marks of man's devastation of her domain. The bark has closed over the bullet-scars on the trees, so that diligent search is required to detect them now; a new growth has sprung up to replace that leveled by the musketry; goodly trees, even, are standing upon the diminished earthworks. The others have long since rotted into mold. The traveler might easily pass along that quaint road, so hotly contested, with never a suspicion of what befell there—" grim visaged war has smoothed his wrinkled front," indeed.

The war is definitely over. In its time it ravaged our fair land almost beyond recognition, put our young manhood to the uttermost proof, and left in its track many deeper and more poignant wounds than those in the Wilderness woods, but it ended at last. And time has been closing over the scars ever since and new growth springing into life all the while. Who was right; who was wrong?—the God above us " who doth all things aright " alone knows surely.

THE SCHOOL OF THE SOLDIER

VETERANS ALREADY IN '61

These drummer-boys of the Eighth Regiment of the National Guard of the State of New York were photographed in the '50s, wearing their Mexican War uniforms. The boys of this regiment went to the front in these same uniforms and marched throughout the war.

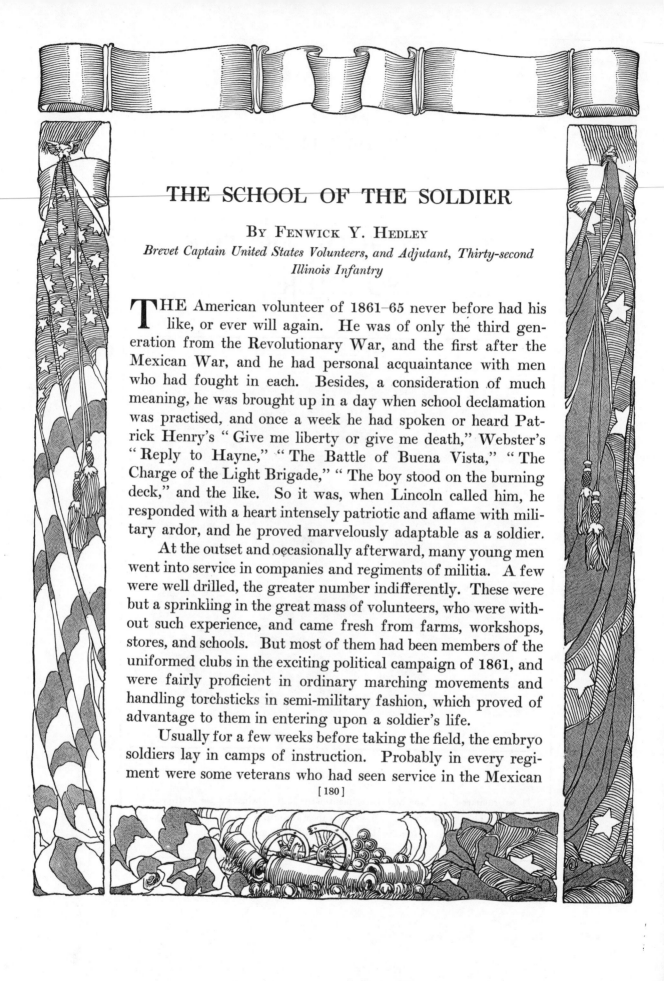

THE SCHOOL OF THE SOLDIER

By Fenwick Y. Hedley
Brevet Captain United States Volunteers, and Adjutant, Thirty-second Illinois Infantry

THE American volunteer of 1861–65 never before had his like, or ever will again. He was of only the third generation from the Revolutionary War, and the first after the Mexican War, and he had personal acquaintance with men who had fought in each. Besides, a consideration of much meaning, he was brought up in a day when school declamation was practised, and once a week he had spoken or heard Patrick Henry's "Give me liberty or give me death," Webster's "Reply to Hayne," "The Battle of Buena Vista," "The Charge of the Light Brigade," "The boy stood on the burning deck," and the like. So it was, when Lincoln called him, he responded with a heart intensely patriotic and aflame with military ardor, and he proved marvelously adaptable as a soldier.

At the outset and occasionally afterward, many young men went into service in companies and regiments of militia. A few were well drilled, the greater number indifferently. These were but a sprinkling in the great mass of volunteers, who were without such experience, and came fresh from farms, workshops, stores, and schools. But most of them had been members of the uniformed clubs in the exciting political campaign of 1861, and were fairly proficient in ordinary marching movements and handling torchsticks in semi-military fashion, which proved of advantage to them in entering upon a soldier's life.

Usually for a few weeks before taking the field, the embryo soldiers lay in camps of instruction. Probably in every regiment were some veterans who had seen service in the Mexican

A TIME–STAINED PHOTOGRAPH OF THE 'FIFTIES

OFFICERS AND NON–COMMISSIONED OFFICERS

COMPANY "F," EIGHTH NEW YORK

These officers of the Eighth New York are garbed in the same uniforms that they wore to the Mexican War. This and the hotly contested political campaign of 1861 served as the two great "drill-masters" of the Federal recruits at the outset of the war. A few of them were indifferently drilled through their connection with regiments of militia, but these were but a sprinkling in the great mass that thronged from the farms, the workshops, and the schools. Most of these had marched as members of the uniformed clubs in the exciting political campaign of 1861, and were fairly proficient in ordinary movements and in handling torch-sticks instead of rifles. Probably in every quota there were some men who had seen service in the Mexican War or in the militia. They had become accustomed to military systems now obsolete, but their training enabled them to speedily put off the old and put on the new, and they often proved highly capable drill-masters.

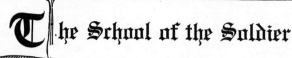

War or in the militia. They had been accustomed to military systems now obsolete, but their training enabled them to speedily put off the old and put on the new, and they proved fairly capable drillmasters.

It was days, often weeks, before uniforms were provided, and entire battalions performed their evolutions in their civilian clothes, of all cuts and hues. Longer were they without arms. The sentries, or camp guards, walked their beats day or night with clubs. At the regimental headquarters were a score or two of " condemned " muskets which were utilized all day long by alternating squads of non-commissioned officers, practising the manual of arms in preparation for instructing the men.

Now armed and equipped, the men were industriously drilled, by squads, by companies, and by battalions, six to eight hours a day. There were awkwardness and blundering; sergeants would march their platoons, and captains, their companies, by the right instead of by the left flank, or *vice versa* to the destruction of a column or square, necessitating re-formation and repetition of the movement, sometimes again and again. But, on the whole, the men progressed well, and soon performed ordinary evolutions with creditable approach to soldierlike exactness.

The greatest stress was laid upon the use of the musket, and this was the young soldier's severest experience. To begin with, the arms were old muzzle-loaders—muskets of Mexican War days, altered from flint-lock to percussion, or obsolete Austrian or Belgian guns, heavy and clumsy. The manual of arms, as laid down in the text-book of the time, Hardee's " School of the Soldier," was complicated and wearisome. In particular, the operation of loading and firing involved numerous counted " motions "—handling the cartridge (from the cartridge-box), biting off its end, inserting it in the gun-barrel, drawing the ramrod, ramming the cartridge home, returning the ramrod, and placing the percussion cap upon the

"THE SCHOOL OF THE SOLDIER"—BAYONET DRILL OF THE FORTIETH MASSACHUSETTS, 1863

The center photograph shows one of the lessons that had to be learned by the soldiers of both sides. This mock battery at Seabrook Point, South Carolina—logs of wood to represent guns—was Federal; but the Confederates, at Centerville, Port Hudson, and elsewhere, used "dummy" guns effectively. Before the soldiers met these problems, however, they had to conquer the manual of arms, and were diligently drilled in firing, by file and by company, to the right oblique, to the left oblique, and to the rear. But most awkward and wearisome of all was the bayonet experience, as shown in the upper photograph of the Forti-

"WHEN IS A GUN NOT A GUN?"—WHEN IT IS A DUMMY, LIKE THESE AT SEABROOK POINT, S. C., 1862

eth Massachusetts Infantry at bayonet drill. The men were drilled in open order so as to admit of free movement and give the instructing officer an opportunity to see the performance and action of each individual man, and correct his mistakes. Less arduous than bayonet drill was morning guard-mount. The men detailed to this duty were assembled about nine o'clock, drilled in a few of the movements of the manual of arms, and inspected by the officer of the day, distinguished by a scarf across the shoulder. Then they were marched out to relieve the guards on duty, and their full tour of this duty was twenty-four hours.

GUARD-MOUNT OF A SMART REGIMENT—THE ONE HUNDRED AND SIXTY-FOURTH NEW YORK

gun-nipple. This feat (or series of feats) required much practice. The musket was to rest upon the ground, immediately in front of the soldier, and exactly perpendicular. Its excessive length made it impossible for a short man to draw and return his ramrod in precise manner, and, in either act, he frequently interfered with the man upon his right, breaking the symmetry of the movement, and provoking language forbidden by the "Articles of War."

Further, the men were diligently drilled in firing—by file and by company, to the front, to the right oblique, to the left oblique, and to the rear. But most awkward and wearisome of all was the bayonet exercise, requiring acrobatic agility, while the great length of the musket and fixed bayonet rendered the weapon almost impracticable except in the hands of one above the average stature. As a matter of fact, all of the accomplishments thus particularized—methods of loading and firing, and bayonet exercise—fell into disuse with entrance upon actual field-service, as having no practical worth.

With such preparation and such equipment, the soldiers marched to their first battle. The experience of a single regiment was that of thousands. The drums sound the "long roll," or the bugle "the assembly," and companies form and march to the regimental color-line. A few moments later the regiment marches forward until the first scattering fire of the foe is received. Sometimes the antagonists are visible; often but few are seen, but their presence is known by the outburst of flame and smoke from a fringe of forest. The regiment forms in line of battle, and at the word of command from the colonel, passed from company to company, opens fire. No thought now of manual of arms, but only of celerity of movement and rapidity of fire. Shouted a gallant officer who at home (as he was in the field, the war through) an exemplary Christian gentleman, "Load as fast as you can, and give them the devil!" The battle is now on in earnest, and the discharge of thousands of muskets becomes a roar. The range is not more than two hundred

THE VOLUNTEER'S TEACHERS—CLASS OF 1860, UNITED STATES MILITARY ACADEMY
IN THE FIELD, 1862

The men who founded the United States Military Academy in 1802 little thought that, three-score years later, hundreds of the best-trained military men in America would go forth from its portals to take up the sword against one another.   Nine of the forty-one men who were graduated from West Point in 1860 joined the Confederate army.   The men of this class and that of 1861 became the drill-masters, and in many cases the famous leaders, of the Federal and Confederate armies.   The cadet who stood third at graduation in 1860 was Horace Porter.   He became second-lieutenant, lieutenant-colonel three years later, and brigadier-general at the close of the war.   He received the Congressional medal of honor for gallantry at Chickamauga, and later gained great honor as ambassador to France.   Two other members, James H. Wilson and Wesley Merritt, fought their way to the top as cavalry leaders.   Both again were found at the front in the Spanish-American War.   The former was chief of the Cavalry Bureau in 1864 and commanded the assault and capture of Selma and Montgomery, Ala.   He was major-general of volunteers in the Spanish-American War, commanded the column of British and American troops in the advance on Peking, and represented the United States army at the coronation of King Edward VII of England.   General Wesley Merritt earned six successive promotions for gallantry as a cavalry leader—at Gettysburg, Yellow Tavern, Hawe's Shop, Five Forks, and other engagements—and was one of the three Union leaders to arrange for the surrender at Appomattox.   He participated in several Indian campaigns, commanded the American troops in the Philippines, and was summoned from there to the aid of the American Peace Commission, in session in Paris.

yards—sufficient for antiquated weapons carrying a nearly three-quarter-inch ball and three buckshot.

It may be here remarked that early in 1862 practically all the obsolete muskets were replaced with Springfield or En-field rifles, the former of American, the latter of English make, and the best of their day. They were shorter and lighter than the discarded arms, well balanced, and of greater efficiency, carrying an elongated ball of the minie pattern, caliber .58, with a range of a thousand yards.

At times the regiment shifts its position, to right or left, sometimes diminishing the distance. During much of the time the men experience heavy artillery as well as musketry fire. At the outset a lad threw away a pack of cards, saying, "I don't know they would bring me any bad luck, but I wouldn't want to be killed and have them found in my pocket, and mother hear of it." He lived the war through, but never again so disburdened himself.

A grape-shot tore off the end of a lad's gun as he was cap-ping it. He finished the operation, discharged his weapon, and recovered it for reloading, to find that, while the ragged muzzle would receive the powder, it would not admit the ball. "Don't that beat the devil," he exclaimed—his very first use of language he was taught to abhor. On the instant he had grasped another gun from the hands of a comrade by his side.

A youth, in a regiment which had lost nearly half its men, his ammunition exhausted, fell back into a ravine where the wounded had crawled, to replenish from their cartridge boxes. Returning, he saw so few of his comrades that he thought the regiment gone, and started for the rear. He came face to face with the colonel, who called out, "Where are you go-ing?" "To find the regiment!" "Well, go to the front! All that are left are there," said the colonel. "All right," responded the lad, and he again went into action.

The first battle was a great commencement which grad-uated both heroes and cowards. A few, under the first fire,

THE "BEEF-KILLERS" OF THE ARMY

OFFICERS' "STRIKERS" AT HEADQUARTERS

WASHDAY IN WINTER-QUARTERS

RUSHING UP A CAMP

The recruit soon learned that slaughtering cattle, cooking, cleaning and washing accouterments, chopping wood, and laundry work all come within the province of the soldier. The upper left-hand photograph was taken at Yorktown in May, 1862. In the upper right-hand view we see cooking, washing, and the vigorous polishing of a scabbard. Enlisted men who were discovered to be efficient artisans were taken from the ranks and transferred to the repair department. A group of these "veterans" is shown in the lowest photograph.

MECHANICS OF THE FIRST DIVISION, NINTH ARMY CORPS, NEAR PETERSBURG, 1864

ran away, and are only known on their company rolls as deserters. An elbow comrade of the lad whose gun was shot away, as told of above, ran from the field, and died the next day, from sheer fright. Men were known to fire their muskets into the ground, or skyward. In various battles scores of muskets were found to contain a half-dozen or more charges, the soldier having loaded his gun again and again without discharging it, and many a tree in Southern forests held a ramrod which had been fired into it by some nervous soldier. A great majority of those who had demonstrated their worthlessness, soon left the service, usually under a surgeon's certificate of disability, for they were generally so lacking in pride as to be unconformable to health-preserving habits. There were, however, some who fell short at first, but eventually proved themselves good soldiers, and the great majority of volunteers were pluck personified.

A soldier who saw the war through from beginning to end has said that he knew only two men who actually enjoyed a battle. The majority held to their place in the line from duty and pride. Except among the sharpshooters, charged with such a duty as picking off artillerists or signalmen, few soldiers have knowledge that they ever actually killed a man in battle, and are well satisfied with their ignorance.

More than thirty years after the war, an Illinoisan went into the heart of Arkansas to bury a favorite sister. After the funeral service, in personal conversation with the attending minister, Northerner and Southerner discovered that, in one of the fiercest battles of the first war year, their respective regiments had fought each other all day long; that they were similarly engaged in the severest battle of the Atlanta campaign, and finally in the last battle in North Carolina, in 1865; also that, in the first of these, as determined by landmarks recognized by each, the two men had probably been firing directly at each other. These past incidents, with the pathos of the present meeting, cemented a lasting friendship.

BOYS WHO MADE
GOOD SOLDIERS

"Jimmy" Dugan was a bugler-boy in the band at Carlisle barracks, the cavalry depot in Pennsylvania, as the Civil War opened. One who knew him writes: "He was about three feet six high, could ride anything on four legs, sound all the calls, and marched behind the band at guard-mounting at the regulation twenty-eight-inch step at the risk of splitting himself in two." "Jimmy" was heard of later when the serious work began, and, like many another daring youngster in the field-music contingent, did his duty under fire.

BOYS OF THE WAR DAYS

By Charles King
Brigadier-General, United States Volunteers

TIME and again of late years Grand Army men have made this criticism of the organized militia, "They look like mere boys." But it is a singular fact that, man for man, the militia of to-day are older than were the "old boys" when they entered service for the Civil War. In point of fact, the war was fought to a finish by a grand army of boys. Of 2,778,304 Union soldiers enlisted, over two million were not twenty-two years of age—1,151,438 were not even nineteen.*

So long as the recruit appeared to be eighteen years old and could pass a not very rigid physical examination, he was accepted without question; but it happened, in the early days of the war, that young lads came eagerly forward, begging to be taken—lads who looked less than eighteen and could be accepted only on bringing proof, or swearing that they were eighteen. It has since been shown that over eight hundred thousand lads of seventeen or less were found in the ranks of the Union army, that over two hundred thousand were no more than sixteen, that there were even one hundred thousand on the Union rolls who were no more than fifteen.

Boys of sixteen or less could be enlisted as "musicians." Every company was entitled to two field musicians; that made twenty to the average war-time regiment. There were 1981 regiments—infantry, cavalry, and artillery—organized during the war, and in addition there were separate companies sufficient in number to make nearly seventy more, or two thousand and fifty regiments. This would account for over forty thousand

*Abercrombie, Paper before Military Order of the Loyal Legion, Illinois Commandery.

A YOUNG OFFICER OF THE CONFEDERACY—WILLIAM H. STEWART

The subject of this war-time portrait, William H. Stewart, might well have been a college lad from his looks, but he was actually in command of Confederate troops throughout the entire war. His case is typical. He was born in Norfolk County, Virginia, of fighting stock; his grandfather, Alexander Stewart, had been a soldier of 1812, and his great-grandfather, Charles Stewart, member of a Virginia regiment (the Eleventh) during the Revolution. It was no uncommon thing to find regularly enlisted men of eighteen, seventeen, or even sixteen. And numerous officers won distinction, though even younger than Stewart. His first command, at the age of twenty-one, was the lieutenancy of the Wise Light Dragoons, two years before the war. After hostilities began, he soon won the confidence of his superiors in spite of his boyish face. During the Antietam advance, September, 1862, he was left in command of the force at Bristoe's Station. In the Wilderness campaign he commanded a regiment in General R. H. Anderson's division. In the battle of the Wilderness, May 6th, he took part in the flank movement which General Longstreet planned to precede his own assault on the Federal lines. Colonel Stewart served also at Spotsylvania and Cold Harbor, and helped to repel the assaults on the Petersburg entrenchments. On the evacuation of Petersburg the next April, he marched with the advance guard to Amelia Court House, and took part in the battle of Sailor's Creek on April 6th. Thus, like many another youth of the South, Colonel Stewart did not give up as long as there was any army with which to fight.

boy musicians. Here, at least, the supply far exceeded the demand; there were mere lads of twelve to fourteen all over the land vainly seeking means of enlistment. There were three hundred boys of thirteen or under who actually succeeded in being mustered into the Federal military service.

Many of the fine regiments that took the field early in 1861 had famous drum-and-fife corps made up entirely of boys. In those days, too, each regiment had two or more "markers," who, with the adjutant and sergeant-major, established the alignment on battalion drill or parade, and these were generally mere lads who carried a light staff and fluttering guidon instead of the rifle. There were little scamps of buglers in some of the old regular cavalry regiments and field-batteries, who sometimes had to be hoisted into the saddle, but once there could stick to the pigskin like monkeys, and with reckless daring followed at the heels of the squadron leader in many a wild saber charge.

There were others, too, that were so short-legged they could not take the service stride of twenty-eight inches and were put to other duties. One of the most famous of these was little Johnny Clem, who at the age of eleven went out as drummer in the Twenty-second Michigan, and before long was made a mounted orderly with the staff of Major-General George H. Thomas and decorated with a pair of chevrons and the title of lance-sergeant.

Another Western boy who saw stirring service, though never formally enlisted, was the eldest son of General Grant, a year older than little Clem, when he rode with his father through the Jackson campaign and the siege of Vicksburg. There were other sons who rode with commanding generals, as did young George Meade at Gettysburg, as did the sons of Generals Humphreys, Abercrombie, and Heintzelman, as did "Win" and Sam Sumner, both generals in their own right to-day, as did Francis Vinton Greene, who had to be locked up to keep him from following his gallant father into the

[192]

ADELBERT AMES AS BRIGADIER–GENERAL WITH HIS STAFF

"THE FIRST OF THE BOY GENERALS"

Surrounded by his staff, some of whom are older than he, sits Adelbert Ames (third from the left), a brigadier-general at twenty-eight. He graduated fifth in his class at West Point on May 6, 1861, and was assigned to the artillery service. It was while serving as first-lieutenant in the Fifth Artillery that he distinguished himself at Bull Run and was brevetted major for gallant and meritorious service. He remained upon the field in command of a section of Griffin's battery, directing its fire after being severely wounded, and refusing to leave the field until too weak to sit upon the caisson, where he had been placed by the men of this command. For this he was awarded a medal of honor. About a year later he again distinguished himself, at the battle of Malvern Hill. He then became colonel of the Twentieth Maine Infantry, from his native State, and on the twentieth of May, 1863, was made brigadier-general of volunteers. He had a distinguished part in the first day's battle at Gettysburg, July 1, 1863, and in the capture of Fort Fisher, North Carolina, January 15, 1865. For this he was promoted to major-general of volunteers. In the class of '61 with Ames at West Point was Judson Kilpatrick, who

JUDSON KILPATRICK
AS
BRIGADIER–GENERAL

stood seventeenth, and who became a general at twenty-seven. He, too, was assigned to the artillery, but after a short transfer to the infantry, in the fall of 1861, was made lieutenant-colonel of the Second New York Cavalry, rising to the rank of brigadier-general of volunteers on June 18, 1865. It was in the cavalry service that he became a picturesque figure, distinguishing himself at the battle of Aldie, in the third day's battle at Gettysburg, and in the engagement at Resaca, Georgia. In June, 1865, he was made major-general of volunteers and later brevetted major-general in the United States Army.

The third of these youthful leaders, a general at twenty-seven, was Wesley Merritt. He graduated from West Point the year before Kilpatrick and Ames. He was made brigadier-general of volunteers on June 29, 1863, distinguished himself two days later at Gettysburg, but won his chief fame as one of Sheridan's leaders of cavalry. He was conspicuous at Yellow Tavern and at Hawe's Shop, was made major-general of volunteers for gallant service in the battles of Winchester and Fisher's Hill, and brigadier-general in the United States Army for Five Forks. The boy generals won more than their share of glory on the grim "foughten field."

MAJOR–GENERAL WESLEY MERRITT AND STAFF

thick of the fray at Gettysburg, but "lived to fight another day" and win his own double stars at Manila.

And while the regulations forbade carrying the musket before reaching one's eighteenth birthday, they were oddly silent as to the age at which one might wield the sword, and so it resulted that boys of sixteen and seventeen were found at the front wearing the shoulder-straps of lieutenants, and some of them becoming famous in an army of famous men.

Two instances were those of two of the foremost major-generals of later years—Henry W. Lawton, of Indiana, and Arthur MacArthur, of Wisconsin. Lawton, tall, sinewy, and strong, was chosen first sergeant, promoted lieutenant, and was commanding a regiment as lieutenant-colonel at the close of the war and when barely twenty. MacArthur's case was even more remarkable. Too young to enlist, and crowded out of the chance of entering West Point in 1861, he received the appointment of adjutant of the Twenty-fourth Wisconsin when barely seventeen, was promoted major and lieutenant-colonel while still eighteen, and commanded his regiment, though thrice wounded, in the bloody battles of Resaca and Franklin. The "gallant boy colonel," as he was styled by General Stanley in his report, entered the regular army after the war, and in 1909, full of honors, reached the retiring age (sixty-four) as the last of its lieutenant-generals.

The East, too, had boy colonels, but not so young as MacArthur. The first, probably, was brave, soldierly little Ellsworth, who went out at the head of the Fire Zouaves in the spring of 1861, and was shot dead at Alexandria, after tearing down the Confederate flag. As a rule, however, the regiments, East and West, came to the front headed by grave, earnest men over forty years of age. Barlow, Sixty-first New York, looked like a beardless boy even in 1864 when he was commanding a division. The McCooks, coming from a famous family, were colonels almost from the start—Alexander, of the First Ohio, later major-general and corps commander;

BOYS WHO FOUGHT AND PLAYED WITH MEN

The boys in the lower photograph have qualified as men; they are playing cards with the grown-up soldiers in the quiet of camp life, during the winter of 1862-3. They are the two drummers or "field musicians," to which each company was entitled. Many stories were told of drummer-boys' bravery. A poem popular during the war centered around an incident at Vicksburg. A general assault was made on the town on May 19, 1863, but repulsed with severe loss. During its progress a boy came limping back from the front and stopped in front of General Sherman, while the blood formed a little pool by his foot. Unmindful of his own condition, he shouted, "Let our soldiers have some more cartridges, sir—caliber fifty-four," and trudged off to the rear. Another poem is based on an incident in the first year of the war. A drummer-boy had beat his *rat-tat-too* for the soldiers until he had been struck on the ankle by a flying bullet. He would not fall out, but, mounted on the shoulders of a grown comrade, he continued to beat his drum as the company charged to victory, and at the end of the day's fighting he rode to camp sitting in front on the general's horse, sound asleep. The drummer-boy was the inspiration of many a soldierly deed and ballad both North and South. The little chaps in the photograph are not as long as the guns of their comrades.

A DRUMMER IN "FULL DRESS"

DRUMMER-BOYS OFF DUTY—PLAYING CARDS IN CAMP, WINTER OF '62

Dan, of the Fifty-second Ohio; Edward, of the Second Indiana Cavalry; and gallant " Bob," of the Ninth Ohio, named brigadier-general before he was killed in August, 1862.

With the close of the second twelve months of the war came the first of the little crop of " boy generals," as they were called, nearly all of them young graduates of West Point. The first of the " boy generals " was Adelbert Ames, of the class of '61, colonel of the Twentieth Maine, closely followed by Judson Kilpatrick, colonel of the Second New York Cavalry, and by Wesley Merritt, whose star was given him just before Gettysburg, when only twenty-seven.

With Merritt, too, came Custer, only twenty-three when he donned the silver stars, and first charged at the head of the Wolverine Brigade on Stuart's gray squadrons at the far right flank at Gettysburg. A few months later and James H. Wilson, Emory Upton, and Ranald Mackenzie, all young, gifted, and most soldierly West Pointers, were also promoted to the stars, as surely would have been gallant Patrick O'Rorke, but for the bullet that laid him low at Gettysburg. That battle was the only one missed by another boy colonel, who proved so fine a soldier that New York captured him from his company in the Twenty-second Massachusetts and made him lieutenant-colonel of their own Sixty-first. Severe wounds kept him out of Gettysburg, but May, 1864, found him among the new brigadiers. Major-general when only twenty-six, he gave thirty-eight years more to the service of his country, and then, as lieutenant-general, Nelson A. Miles passed to the retired list when apparently in the prime of life.

The South chose her greatest generals from men who were beyond middle life—Lee, Jackson, Sidney Johnston, Joseph E. Johnston, Bragg, Beauregard, and Hardee. Longstreet and A. P. Hill were younger. Hood and Stuart were barely thirty. The North found its most successful leaders, save Sherman and Thomas, among those who were about forty or younger.

PART I

SOLDIER LIFE

MARCHING AND FORAGING
EAST AND WEST

A WESTERN BAND—FIELD—MUSIC
OF THE FIRST INDIANA HEAVY
ARTILLERY AT BATON ROUGE

GRANT'S SOLDIERS DIGGING POTATOES—ON THE MARCH TO COLD HARBOR, MAY 28, 1864

These boys of the Sixth Corps have cast aside their heavy accouterments, blankets, pieces of shelter-tent, and rubber blankets, and set cheerfully to digging potatoes from a roadside "garden patch." One week later their corps will form part of the blue line that will rush toward the Confederate works—then stagger to cover, with ten thousand men killed, wounded, or missing in a period computed less than fifteen minutes. When Grant found that he had been out-generaled by Lee on the North Anna River, he immediately executed a flank movement past Lee's right, his weakest point. The Sixth Corps and the Second Corps, together with Sheridan's cavalry, were used in the flank movement and secured a more favorable position thirty-five miles nearer Richmond. It was while Sedgwick's

FORAGING A WEEK BEFORE THE BLOODIEST ASSAULT OF THE WAR

Sixth Corps was passing over the canvas pontoon-bridges across the Pamunkey at Hanovertown, May 28, 1864, that this photograph was taken. When the foragers in the foreground have exhausted this particular potato-field, one of the wagons of the quartermaster's train now crossing on the pontoon will halt and take aboard the prize, carrying it forward to the next regular halt, when the potatoes will be duly distributed. Not alone potatoes, but wheat and melons and turnips, or any other class of eatables apparent to the soldiers' eye above ground, were thus ruthlessly appropriated. This incongruous episode formed one of the many anomalies of the life of the soldier on the march. Especially when he was approaching an enemy, he relaxed and endeavored to secure as much comfort as possible.

THE BUSY ENGINEERS STOP TO EAT

This is the camp of an engineer or pontonier company. The pontoons resting on their wagon bases are ready to be launched. But before work comes a pause for an important ceremony—dinner. In the eyes of the rank and file the company cook was more important than most officers. The soldiers in the upper photograph are located near the headquarters' wagons, while the cook himself is standing proudly near the center, "monarch of all he surveys." To his left is seen one of the beeves that is soon to be sacrificed to the soldiers' appetites. Of the two lower photographs on the left-hand page, one shows cooks of the Army of the Potomac in the winter

PREPARING A MEAL IN WINTER–QUARTERS

COOKING OUT–OF–DOORS

THE COMPANY COOK WITH HIS OUTFIT "IN ACTION"—BEEF ON THE HOOF AT HAND

of 1864, snug in their winter-quarters, and the next illustrates cooking in progress outdoors. The two lower photographs on the right-hand page draw a contrast between dining in a permanent camp and on the march. On the left is a mess of some of the officers of the Ninety-third New York Infantry, dining very much at ease, with their folding tables and their colored servants, at Bealton, Virginia, the month after Gettysburg. But in the last photograph a soldier is cowering apprehensively over the fire at Culpeper, Virginia, in August, 1862, while the baffled Army of Virginia under Pope was retreating before Lee's victorious northward sweep.

OFFICERS' LUXURY AT BEALTON—AUGUST, 1863   A MOUTHFUL DURING POPE'S RETREAT

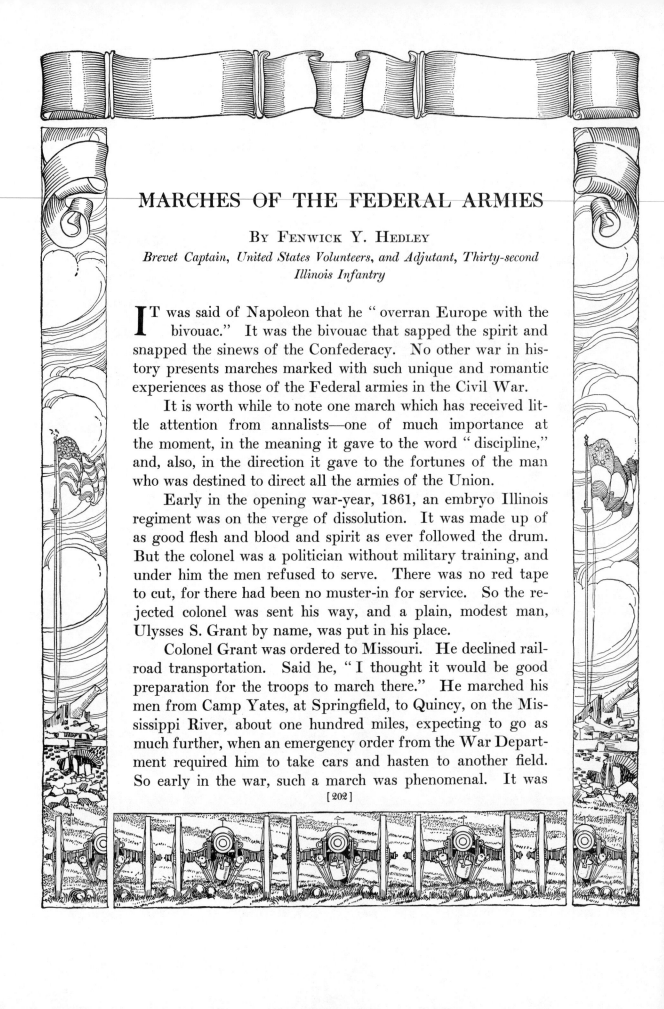

MARCHES OF THE FEDERAL ARMIES

By Fenwick Y. Hedley

Brevet Captain, United States Volunteers, and Adjutant, Thirty-second Illinois Infantry

IT was said of Napoleon that he "overran Europe with the bivouac." It was the bivouac that sapped the spirit and snapped the sinews of the Confederacy. No other war in history presents marches marked with such unique and romantic experiences as those of the Federal armies in the Civil War.

It is worth while to note one march which has received little attention from annalists—one of much importance at the moment, in the meaning it gave to the word "discipline," and, also, in the direction it gave to the fortunes of the man who was destined to direct all the armies of the Union.

Early in the opening war-year, 1861, an embryo Illinois regiment was on the verge of dissolution. It was made up of as good flesh and blood and spirit as ever followed the drum. But the colonel was a politician without military training, and under him the men refused to serve. There was no red tape to cut, for there had been no muster-in for service. So the rejected colonel was sent his way, and a plain, modest man, Ulysses S. Grant by name, was put in his place.

Colonel Grant was ordered to Missouri. He declined railroad transportation. Said he, "I thought it would be good preparation for the troops to march there." He marched his men from Camp Yates, at Springfield, to Quincy, on the Mississippi River, about one hundred miles, expecting to go as much further, when an emergency order from the War Department required him to take cars and hasten to another field. So early in the war, such a march was phenomenal. It was

THE CIVIL WAR SOLDIER AS HE REALLY LOOKED AND MARCHED

There is nothing to suggest military brilliancy about this squad. Attitudes are as prosaic as uniforms are unpicturesque. The only man standing with military correctness is the officer at the left-hand end. But this was the material out of which was developed the soldier who could average sixteen miles a day for weeks on end, and do, on occasion, his thirty miles through Virginia mud and his forty miles over a hard Pennsylvania highway. Sixteen miles a day does not seem far to a single pedestrian, but marching with a regiment bears but little relation to a solitary stroll along a sunny road. It is a far different matter to trudge along carrying a heavy burden, choked by the dust kicked up by hundreds of men tramping along in front, and sweltering in the sun—or trudge still more drearily along in a pelting rain which added pounds to a soaked and clinging uniform, and caused the soldiers to slip and stagger in the mud.

"RIGHT SHOULDER SHIFT"—COLUMN OF FOURS—THE TWENTY-SECOND NEW YORK ON THE ROAD

midsummer, and the men, fresh from school, workshop, and farm, suffered severely. From the day Grant assumed command of the Twenty-first Illinois, it gave as good an account of itself as did any in the service.

In the East, throughout the war, the principal military movements were restricted to a comparatively small territory —the region about the Confederate capital, Richmond, and the approaches thereto. The chief exception was the Gettysburg campaign, in 1863, involving a march of somewhat more than two hundred miles. The famous marches in this part of the country were forced ones, short in duration, but involving intense fatigue and hardship, and often compelling troops to go into battle without much-needed rest. In the hasty concentration at Gettysburg there were some very noteworthy performances by Meade's army. The Sixth Corps started from Manchester, Maryland, at dark, on July 1st. "Without halting," says General Wright, "except for a few moments each hour to breathe the men, and one halt of about half an hour to enable the men to make coffee, the corps was pushed on to Gettysburg, where it arrived about 4 P.M. after a march variously estimated at from thirty-two to thirty-five miles."

Early in the afternoon of May 4, 1864, Grant telegraphed Burnside to bring the Ninth Corps immediately to the Wilderness. The divisions were stationed along the Orange and Alexandria Railroad, but by the morning of the 6th all were on the battlefield. Some of the troops had marched over thirty miles. General Grant says, "Considering that a large proportion, probably two-thirds, of the corps was composed of new troops, unaccustomed to marches, and carrying the accouterments of a soldier, this was a remarkable march." For hardships and exhaustion few marches exceeded the race from the North Anna to the Pamunkey in May, 1864. Hundreds of men dropped dead from lack of proper precaution in the intense heat.

In the West, unlike the East, the principal Union armies were almost constantly in motion, and on long extended lines.

OVER THE CUMBERLAND MOUNTAINS ON THE MARCH TO CHATTANOOGA—SEPTEMBER, 1863

A FOURTH ARMY CORPS DIVISION AT SHAM BATTLE NEAR MISSIONARY RIDGE, 1863

The peculiarity of the drill in the Western armies was their long swinging stride. The regulation army step was twenty-eight inches, and the men in the East were held rigidly to this requirement. But the Westerners swung forward with a long sweep of the leg which enabled them to cover great distances at a rapid pace. In November, 1863, Sherman marched his Fifteenth Corps four hundred miles over almost impassable roads from Memphis to Chattanooga; yet his sturdy soldier boys were ready to go into action next day.

A SENTRY ON THE RAMPARTS AT KNOXVILLE, TENNESSEE, 1864

Their field operations, from beginning to end, extended through seven States—Kentucky, Tennessee, Mississippi, Alabama, Georgia, South Carolina, and North Carolina, in all of which they fought important battles. Some of their divisions and brigades operated in Missouri, Arkansas, Louisiana, and Texas.

Operations in the West opened early in 1861, with St. Louis and the Ohio River as primary bases. By the summer of 1862, armies under Halleck in Missouri, under Grant in Tennessee, and under Buell in Kentucky had pushed their way hundreds of miles southward. These operations involved much marching, but, in view of later experiences, were not marked with such peculiar incidents as to claim attention here.

In September, 1862, occurred a march which alarmed the North much as did Lee's invasion of Pennsylvania the following year. General Don Carlos Buell's troops occupied points in Tennessee. The Confederates, under General Bragg, so threatened his rear that he was obliged to abandon his position. Then ensued a veritable foot-race between the two armies, on practically parallel roads, with Louisville as the goal. Buell reached the city just in advance of his opponent—both armies footsore and jaded from constant marching and frequent skirmishing.

An early march, and one well worthy of remark, was that ordered and directed by General Grant, in the fall of 1862. The objective point was the rear of Vicksburg. His army moved in two columns—one from La Grange, Tennessee, under his own personal command; the other from Memphis, Tennessee, under General Sherman. Their advance reached the neighborhood of Grenada, Mississippi, having marched a distance of one hundred miles. Further progress was stayed by the capture of Holly Springs, Mississippi, in their rear, with all its ammunition stores and commissary supplies, by the Confederate general, Forrest. As a consequence, a retrograde march was inevitable.

PROTECTING THE REAR FOR THE MARCH TO THE SEA—A TYPICAL ARMY SCENE—1864

The armed guard indicates that the pick-and-shovel detail is made up of delinquent soldiers serving petty sentences. It seems strange that the throwing up of entrenchments about a city should form an essential part of marching, but so it was in the case of the greatest march of the Civil War, which covered a total distance of a thousand miles in less than six months. Sherman did not dare to leave Atlanta with his 62,000 veterans until his rear was properly fortified against the attacks of Hood. The upper photograph shows some of Sherman's men digging the inner line of entrenchments at Decatur, Alabama, a task in vivid contrast to the comfortable quarters of the officers at the Decatur Hotel shown in the cut below. Their military appear-

OFFICERS' QUARTERS AT DECATUR HOTEL, 1864

PONTOON–BRIDGE AT DECATUR

ance suffers somewhat from their occupation, but digging was often more important than fighting, for the soldier. Having despatched Thomas to Nashville, and having left strongly entrenched garrisons at Allatoona and Resaca, as well as at Decatur, Sherman launched his army from Atlanta, November 15, 1864. He cherished the hope that Hood would attack one of the fortified places he had left behind, and that is precisely what occurred. Hood and Beauregard believed that Sherman's army was doomed, and turned toward Tennessee. Sherman believed that his march would be the culminating blow to the Confederacy. The lower photograph shows the pontoon-bridge built by Sherman at Decatur at the time his army marched swiftly to the relief of Chattanooga.

While southward bound, the Union troops found just sufficient opposition by the Confederates under General Pemberton to keep them engaged, without impeding their progress. The conditions were now changed. They were greatly harassed, and at times were obliged to march with the utmost speed to avoid being cut off at an intersecting road in their rear. Their unusual and protracted privations were experiences such as had been heretofore unknown. They had set out in the lightest marching order known at that time. Wagon trains were reduced to carry only ammunition and indispensable food. No tents were carried except a few for officers.

When Grant advanced upon Vicksburg in May, 1863, the army again "marched light," and it has been said that the general's only baggage was a package of cigars and a toothbrush. Vicksburg surrendered on July 4th, and the same day, without entering the city, a large portion of the army marched rapidly away to attack General Johnston, at Jackson. The distance was little more than fifty miles, but never did troops suffer more severely. It was a forced march, under an intense, burning sun; the dust was stifling, and the only water was that from sluggish brooks and fetid ponds.

In November, 1863, General Sherman marched his Fifteenth Corps from Memphis to Chattanooga, a distance of nearly four hundred miles, over almost impassable roads. When he arrived his men were in a most exhausted condition, yet they were ready to go into action the next day.

Following almost immediately after the march above mentioned, Sherman moved his men from Chattanooga to the relief of Burnside at Knoxville. The distance was not great, about one hundred and twenty-five miles, but the troops were utterly worn out by their forced march in the intensely cold mountain atmosphere.

In February, 1864, General Sherman marched a force of twenty thousand men from Memphis and Vicksburg to Meridian, Mississippi, a distance of one hundred and fifty miles.

[208]

ON THE MARCH—WATER FOR THE OUTER AND INNER MAN

It was a hot and dusty tramp after Spotsylvania in May, 1864, as Grant strove to outflank Lee. When Grant's men reached the North Anna River, they found that the bridge had been burned. Ignorant of the fighting before them at Cold Harbor, where ten thousand men were to be shot down in a few minutes, they enjoyed a refreshing swim and bath. The lower photograph will bring memories to every veteran of the Virginia campaigns—the eager rush of the men on the march for the deep dark well of the Virginia plantations. This one has been covered and a guard placed over it to prevent waste of water; for a well soon runs dry when an army commences to drink.

The troops moved in light marching order. The expedition entailed severe labor upon the men in the destruction of the arsenal and supply depots at Meridian, and the practical demolition of the railroad almost the entire distance.

Sherman's "march to the sea" is unique among marches. The army had good training for its undertaking. Its commander had led it from Chattanooga to the capture of Atlanta, and had followed the Confederate general, Hood, northward. Shortly after Sherman abandoned the pursuit of Hood, he detached Stanley's Fourth Corps and Schofield's Twenty-third Corps to the assistance of Thomas, in Tennessee. This march of nearly three hundred miles was one of the most arduous of the war, though lacking in the picturesqueness of that to the sea; it included the severe battle of Franklin, and had victorious ending at Nashville.

Sherman's army marched from Atlanta and vicinity on November 15, 1864. The men set forward, lifting their voices in jubilant song. As to their destination, they neither knew nor cared. That they were heading south was told them by the stars, and their confidence in their leader was unbounded.

It was a remarkable body of men—an army of veterans who had seen three years of constant field-service. Through battle, disease, and death, nearly every regiment had been greatly reduced. He was a fortunate colonel who could muster three hundred of the thousand men he brought into service. Thirty men made more than an average company; there were those which numbered less than a score. It was also an army of youngsters. Most of the older men and the big men had been worn down and sent home.

To each company was allowed a pack-mule for cooking utensils (frying-pans and coffee-pots), but frequently these were dispensed with, each soldier doing his own cooking after even more primitive fashion than in his earlier campaigns. All dispensable items of the army ration had been stricken out, the supply being limited to hard bread, bacon, coffee, sugar, and

THE EXTREMITIES OF THE THOUSAND–MILE FEDERAL LINE ON THE MISSISSIPPI

It was from Cairo that the Federals in 1862 cautiously began to operate with large forces in Confederate territory. And it was in New Orleans, the same spring, that the Federal Military Department of the Gulf established its headquarters. Farragut had forced the forts, and the city had fallen. The lower photograph shows the Federal Headquarters at New Or-

leans, a thousand miles from Cairo. The orderlies on the porch and the flag floating in front of the delicate "banquettes" of the building, the iron tracery that came over from France, show that the city has passed into Union hands and become the headquarters of the Military Department of the Gulf. The flag can be dimly descried opposite the corner of the building just below the roof. There was evidently enough wind to make it flap in the breeze.

CAIRO, WHEN THE ADVANCE BEGAN

THE BUILDING USED AS NEW ORLEANS HEADQUARTERS OF THE FEDERAL MILITARY
DEPARTMENT OF THE GULF

salt. A three days' supply of bread and bacon was issued at intervals to last the soldier ten days, the " foragers," of whom more anon, being his dependence for all else. Coffee, the greatest of all necessities to the soldier, was liberally provided, and the supply seldom failed. The soldier's personal effects were generally limited to his blanket, a pair of socks, and a piece of shelter tent, though many discarded the latter with contempt. In addition to his gun and cartridge-box with its forty rounds, the soldier carried his haversack, which with his food contained one hundred and sixty rounds of cartridges. After every occasion calling for expenditure of ammunition, his first concern was to restock, so as constantly to have two hundred rounds upon his person.

The train with each corps had been reduced to the lowest possible number of wagons. Nothing was transported but ammunition, commissary supplies, and grain for the animals —the latter only to be used when the country would not afford animal subsistence. In addition, to each regiment was allowed a single wagon to carry ammunition, a single tent-fly to shelter the field-desks of the adjutant and quartermaster, a small mess-kit for the officers in common, and an ordinary valise for each of them. In case of necessity (not an uncommon occurrence on account of crippled horses and bad roads), some or all of these personal belongings were thrown out and destroyed.

The army marched in four columns, usually ten to fifteen miles apart, on practically parallel roads. The skirmishers and flankers of each corps extended right and left until they met those of the next corps, thus giving a frontage of forty to fifty miles. As a consequence, the widely dispersed forces were soon ready for handling as a unit. At a river, two or more corps met, to utilize a pontoon train in common.

The day's itinerary was much the same throughout the march. Soon after daybreak the bugle sounded the reveille, and the men rolled their blankets and prepared their meal. An

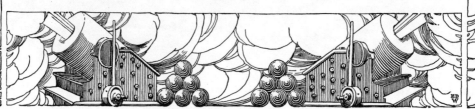

COMMISSARY DEPARTMENT AT ARMY OF THE POTOMAC HEADQUARTERS, APRIL, 1864

The big barracks of a mess-hall with such food as would make a soldier grumble in times of peace, would have seemed a veritable Mecca to a soldier of 1864 in camp or on the march. The accompanying photographs show how the commissary department of the Army of the Potomac supplied the individual soldier with meat and water. Above is displayed a commissary at the front in full swing

WAITING FOR SUPPER
ON A CHILLY AUTUMN
EVENING OF '63

with a sentry to guard its precious stores. Below, soldiers can be seen filling their water cart at a well, and waiting while an attaché of the commissary department cuts off rounds of beef and issues portions to the various messes. The photograph in the center shows the final result, witnessed by the savory-looking steam blown from the kettle on top of the charred timbers.

THE SOLDIERS' WATER CART

SERVING OUT RATIONS

hour later, at the call of the assembly, they fell in, and soon took up the line of march, reaching the end for the day in the middle of the afternoon or early evening. The rear brigade awaited the movement of the wagon train and fell in behind. It frequently did not reach the halting-place until midnight, and sometimes much later. The average distance covered daily was something more than sixteen miles.

The men marched "at will," with little semblance of military order, yet each knew his place. Good-natured badinage, songs, school-day recitations, discussions as to destination—these served to pass the time. Seldom was halt made for a noon-time meal, the men eating as they marched. At an occasional halt, some gathered over their cards; some put a few stitches in a dilapidated garment; some beat the sand and dust out of their shoes, and nursed their blistered, travel-worn feet. The evening was pleasantly passed around the camp-fire.

But a day seldom passed without its trials. Frequently a Confederate force appeared in front; the cavalry advance was driven back, while a regiment or brigade, and a few pieces of artillery, moved rapidly to the front. A half-hour later the foe had vanished; a grave or two was dug beneath the shadow of the trees; an ambulance received a few wounded men, and the march was resumed.

Again, the rain fell in torrents the day long, and, sometimes, for days. The men marched in soaked clothing. The roads were quagmires, and thousands of men labored for hours tearing down fences and felling saplings to make a corduroy road, over which the artillery and wagon trains might pass.

At another time the march lay across or near a railway which could be of much use to the Confederates. The soldiers lined up along its length and, lifting the ends of the ties, literally overturned the iron way. The ties were piled together and fired; the iron rails were thrown upon them, and, after they were well heated in the middle, they were wrapped around trees, or twisted with cant-hooks.

[214]

PICKETS SEVEN HUN- DRED MILES APART

The two picket stations shown in these photographs illustrate the extended area over which the Federal soldiers marched out to picket duty. European wars, with the exception of Napoleon's Russian campaign, have rarely involved such widely separated points simultaneously. Picketing was considered by the soldiers a pleasant detail. It relieved them of all other camp requirements, such as drills and parades. The soldiers in the photographs are lolling at ease with no apparent apprehension of any enemy, but it must not be assumed from their relaxation that they are not vigilant. Beyond these little camps

VIRGINIA—FEDERAL PICKET STATION NEAR BULL RUN, 1862

GEORGIA—PICKETS JUST BEFORE THE BATTLE OF ATLANTA, JULY 22, 1864

regular sentinels are on duty with keenly observant eyes. When their tour of duty has been completed they will be relieved by some of the men who are so much at ease. The pickets retreated before any advance in face of the Confederates, and rejoined the main body of troops. In the Atlanta photograph, the "reserve post" is slightly in the rear of the outer line of pickets. Judging from the rough earthworks, the dilapidated house, and the smashed window-frame in the foreground, there has evidently been fighting at this point. Nearly all of the men have on high-crowned hats, which afforded better protection against the sun than the forage cap.

General Sherman reduced foraging to a system in the West, and, more especially during his rapid and extended marches, foraging became a necessary means of subsistence for men and animals. As the general expressed it, " No army could carry food and forage for a march of three hundred miles, and there being no civil authorities to respond to requisition, this source of supply was indispensable to success."

In preparing for his march to the sea, he issued specific instructions for foraging "liberally upon the country," and these were reasonable in the interest of his men, and humane as regarding the people who were to be foraged upon. Each brigade commander was to send out a foraging party under a discreet commissioned officer, to gather in from the region adjacent to the route traveled whatever might serve as subsistence for man and beast, also wagons, horses, and mules for conveying the supplies to the troops; the animals were then to be utilized in the artillery and wagon trains to replace those worn out. Entering dwelling-houses was forbidden. With each family was to be left a reasonable portion of food, and discrimination was to be made in favor of the poor. As a matter of fact, few soldiers saw or heard of these regulations until after the march was ended. But, with the remarkable adaptability of the American soldier, they became on the instant " a law unto themselves," and in spirit and deed carried out the provisions of their commander, of which they had not heard. These foraging parties numbered twenty-five to fifty men each. They set out usually before the troops broke camp, and extended their expeditions three to five miles on either flank. They brought in their supplies in every manner of vehicle— wagons, carts, and carriages, drawn indiscriminately by horses, mules, oxen, or cows, strung together with harness, rope, or chains; a complete set of harness was seldom found.

The supplies thus obtained were turned over to the brigade commissary for issue in the regular way to the various regiments. The result was general dissatisfaction. At no time

PREPARATIONS FOR THE MARCH TO THE SEA—ATLANTA, 1864

The soldiers sprawling on the freight-cars are one of the bodies of troops that Sherman was shifting—changing garrisons, and establishing guards, in preparation for his famous march to the sea. Below appears a wagon-train leaving Atlanta; but comparatively few wagons accompanied the troops on this movement. Everything possible was discarded and sent back over Sherman's strong line of communications. The soldier's personal effects were generally limited to his blanket, a pair of socks, and a piece of shelter-tent, although many discarded even the latter. Nothing was transported but ammunition, absolutely necessary commissary supplies, and grain for the animals. All invalids and those incapacitated for hard marching were sent back, and the average company was less than thirty men.

ONE OF SHERMAN'S WAGON–TRAINS

was there a sufficiency for all. The men provided a remedy. Probably every regiment in the army sent out its independent foragers—a class known in history as "Sherman's Bummers," and there were no more venturesome men. They had no official being, but were known to all, from commanding general down, and their conduct was overlooked unless flagrant.

The forager or "bummer" at first was usually afoot; sometimes he rode a horse or mule which had been "condemned" and turned out of the wagon train. His search at the first farm was for a fresh mount; with this, success was assured. The forager frequently found a willing ally in the plantation negro, who would guide him to a swamp where animals had been taken, or to a spot where provisions had been buried. In some instances what appeared to be a grave was pointed out, which would yield treasures of preserves, choice beverages, and jewelry.

Nearly all the inhabitants had gone farther into the interior, taking with them what of their possessions they could; in such cases, the deserted buildings were utterly despoiled. The few people who remained were old men, women, and children. To these the forager was usually respectful, even sympathetic, and in some instances he laid the foundations for a personal friendship which exists to this day. But with all his good nature, the forager was diplomatic, and he so skilfully directed his conversation that he frequently acquired knowledge of sources of supply at the next plantation, and even of movements of the Confederate soldiery, which was esteemed of value at headquarters.

If the foragers were fortunate, the meal of their squad or company was incomparable—turkeys, chickens, smoked meats, sweet potatoes, preserves, sorghum, and not infrequently a jug or keg of whisky. The cellars of some abandoned mansions yielded even richer store—cobwebbed wine-bottles dating back to the '30's.

Thus lived Sherman's army for eighteen days on its march

AT CHATTANOOGA, WHERE THE MARCH BEGAN—TROOPS AT THE "INDIAN MOUND"

SCENES AT THE BEGINNING, MIDDLE, AND END OF SHERMAN'S MARCH TO THE SEA

In these three photographs appear sturdy Western troops at the beginning, middle, and end of Sherman's march to the sea. Between Chattanooga and Atlanta he was busy strengthening the rear. At Atlanta he gathered his resources and made his final depositions for the great march. His was a remarkable body of men, the majority veterans who had seen three years of constant field service, yet in considerable proportion not yet old

HALF–WAY—SHERMAN'S MEN
RESTING AT ATLANTA

enough to vote. Many of the staff and company officers were as young as the men in the ranks. The army marched in four columns usually ten to fifteen miles apart, and the skirmishes and flankers of the various corps extended over a frontage of forty or fifty miles. The day's itinerary was much the same throughout—reveille soon after daybreak, breakfast, assembly, and "forward march." The end of the day's march was reached in the middle of the afternoon or early evening, and the average distance was something more than sixteen miles. The sea was finally sighted at Savannah, Georgia, on the 10th of December.

THE SEA AT LAST—FEDERAL TROOPS IN FORT McALLISTER JUST AFTER ITS CAPTURE

through Georgia. But this season of feasting was followed by a dismal fortnight of almost famine on the outskirts of Savannah, before entrance to the city was obtained. In the subsequent march through the Carolinas, foraging was resumed as in the interior of Georgia, but, except in a few favored localities, the provisions were neither so plentiful nor so choice.

The forager experienced a startling transformation in April of 1865. The war was over. Sherman's men were marching from Raleigh, North Carolina, for the national capital to be disbanded. The citizens no longer fled at their approach, but flocked to the road to see them pass. Among them were scores of Lee's or Johnston's men, still clad in their " butternut " uniforms. The forager's occupation was gone, and he was now in his place in the ranks, and he stepped out, now and again, to buy eatables, paying out " Uncle Sam's greenbacks."

Sherman's last two campaigns may be called a march in three acts. The march to the sea began at Atlanta and ended at Savannah, a distance of three hundred miles, consuming eighteen days. After a period of rest began the march through the Carolinas, ending at Goldsboro, four hundred and twenty-five miles, in the words of Sherman, " concluding one of the longest and most important marches ever made by an organized army," and culminating in the close of hostilities with the surrender of General Johnston.

After a few days the march to Washington was begun, a further distance of three hundred and fifty miles, and May 24, 1865, the troops marched down Pennsylvania Avenue in presence of applauding thousands, then to be at once disbanded and never to assemble again.

The total distance marched between Atlanta and Washington, in less than six months, was about one thousand miles. General Sherman claimed for his army, in its various marches, beginning at Vicksburg and ending at Washington, a total of twenty-eight hundred miles, including the many detours.

PART I
SOLDIER LIFE

———

WITH THE VETERAN ARMIES

———

THE

WELL–DISCIPLINED

"REGULARS"—A SCENE OF APRIL 3, 1864

MEN WHO DEMONSTRATED THE VALUE OF TRAINING AT GAINES' MILL

They stand up very straight, these regulars who formed the tiny nucleus of the vast Union armies. Even in the distance they bear the stamp of the trained soldier. At Bull Run the disciplined soldiers showed a solid front amid the throng of fugitives. At Gaines' Mill, again, they kept together against an over-whelming advance. It was not long, however, before the American volunteers on both sides were drilled and disciplined, furnishing to Grant and Lee the finest soldiery that ever trod the field of battle. There were surprisingly few regulars when '61 came. The United States regular army could furnish only six regi-ments of cavalry, sixty batteries of artillery, a battalion of engineers, and nineteen regiments of infantry.

THE

ELEVENTH "U. S."

IN THEIR TRIM CAMP AT ALEXANDRIA

THE AMERICAN VOLUNTEERS, HOWEVER, SOON ACQUIRED THE SOLDIERLY BEARING

Of the 3,559 organizations in all branches of the service in the Union armies, the States furnished 3,473. The Eleventh Infantry in the regular army was organized at Fort Independence, Boston Harbor, by direction of the President, May 4, 1861, and confirmed by Act of Congress, July 29, 1861. It fought throughout the war with the Army of the Potomac. This photograph was taken at Alexandria, Va., a month before the Wilderness. The regiment participated in every important battle of the Army of the Potomac, and was on provost duty at Richmond, Va., from May to October, 1865. The regiment lost during service eight officers, 117 enlisted men killed and mortally wounded, and two officers and eighty-six enlisted men by disease.

VETERANS IN CAMP—THE 114TH PENNSYLVANIA AT BRANDY STATION, WINTER OF 1863

A vivid illustration of the daily camp life of the Army of the Potomac in the winter of 1863–64 is supplied by these two photographs of the same scene a few moments apart. On the left-hand page the men are playing cards, loafing, strolling about, and two of them are engaged in a boxing match. On the right the horse in the foreground is dragging a man seated on a barrel over the snow on a sled, another man is fetching water, and the groups in front of the huts are reading newspapers. In the lower photograph the card-playing,

BELOW, THE SAME AS IT HAD SHIFTED A FEW MOMENTS LATER

lounging, and boxing continue, the horses have been ridden, led, and driven out of the picture, and the man with the bucket has turned away. During the war Pennsylvania furnished to the service twenty-eight regiments, three battalions and twenty-two companies of cavalry, five regiments, two battalions, and three companies of heavy artillery, one battalion and twenty-nine batteries of light artillery, a company of engineers, one of sharpshooters, and 258 regiments, five battalions, and twenty-five companies of infantry.

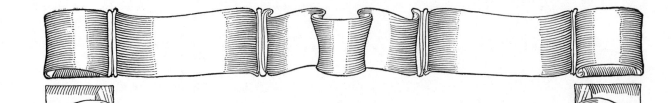

WITH THE VETERAN ARMIES

By Charles King
Brigadier-General, United States Volunteers

IT was a fine, enthusiastic army that General McClellan finally marched forward on Manassas in the early spring of 1862. So far as dress and " style " were concerned it far surpassed that with which, two years later, General Grant crossed the Rapidan southward, and, unlike all preceding commanders in that field, took no backward step until he had crushed his foe.

But in point of discipline, efficiency, and experience—the essentials of modern military craft—it is doubtful if the world contained, man for man, anything to equal the two armies confronting each other in May, 1864, the matchless soldiery of Grant and Lee. Three years had they marched and maneuvered, fenced and fought—three tremendous years—and now it seemed as though every man realized that this would be the final struggle, that the question of the supremacy of the Union or of the South was to be settled forever.

Beautiful and bright had been the colors that fluttered over each proud battalion as it took the road for Manassas— gay and vivid the uniforms of the " foreign legions " and the Zouaves, spick and span the blue battalions, all with gleaming belts and brasses, many with white gloves, and some even with white gaiters. In spite of the clerical cut of his uniform, the average officer had a soldierly look about him, enhanced by a trimly buttoned coat well set off by the crimson sash. Those were the days of the dandy, encouraged by the example of many a general like McClellan, Porter, " Phil " Kearny, and Hooker, who believed in fine accouterments and glittering

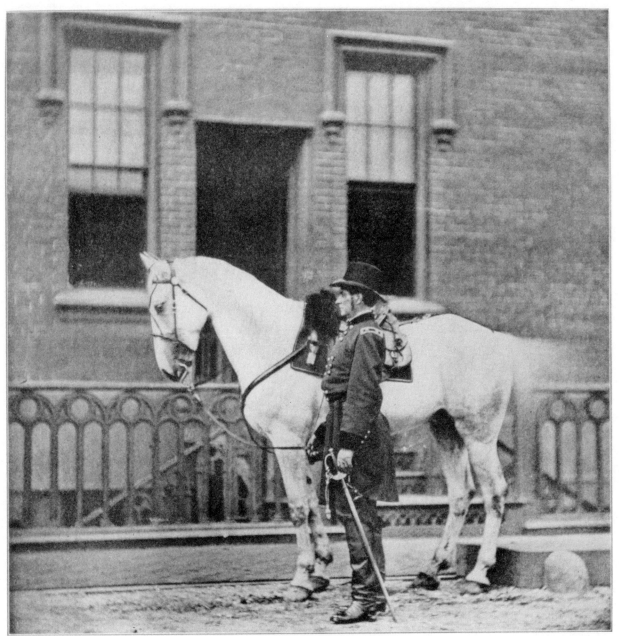

HOOKER—HANDSOME IN PERSON AND EQUIPMENT

General Joseph Hooker, whose photograph appears above, was one of many able generals, such as McClellan, Porter, "Phil" Kearny, and others, who believed in fine accouterments and glittering trappings. These leaders used the costliest of housings and horse equipments, and expected their staff officers to follow suit. The latter were nothing loth; much money was spent at the outset of the war in giving the army as trig and smart an appearance as a European host. But there were no military roads in the United States, and the pageantry of a European army is not adapted to the swamps and morasses, the mountain heights, and rocky roads over which the war was fought. By the end of the second year the red sash which set off the trimly buttoned coat had turned to purple or disappeared entirely, and in many instances the coat was gone as well. The costly shoulder-straps of gold embroidery had given place to metal substitutes, and the "hundred-dollar housings" of the grand review in the fall of 1861 were left in the swamps or lost in battle.

trappings, used the finest of housings and horse equipments, and expected their staff officers to follow suit. Those were the days when each regiment still had its band, some of them strong in numbers and splendid in effect, when each band still had its spectacular drum-major, and some few of them even a prettily dressed *vivandière*. By common consent, the glittering epaulet had been abandoned, but the plumed felt hat, the yellow sash and gantlets still decked the martial persons of the corps, division, and brigade commanders, and the regimental officers in many an instance made the most of the regulations as to uniform.

Much of the picturesque remained with the army when McClellan floated it around to the Peninsula and lost priceless weeks at Yorktown. But the few *vivandières* seemed to wilt after Williamsburg. Many a bandsman balked at having to care for the wounded under fire. Quite a few chaplains decided that their calling was with the hospitals at the rear rather than with the fighters at the front. Then the humid heat of a Chickahominy June had taken the starch out of the last collar, and utterly killed the buttoned-up coat. Officers and men by thousands shed the stiff and cumbersome garment, marched and fought in their flannel shirt-sleeves until they could get the uncouth but unbothersome " blouse." Regiments that long had paraded in leggings or gaiters kicked themselves loose and left the relics strung out from Mechanicsville to Malvern. When next they came trudging out toward Manassas, to join John Pope and his hard-hammered army, many men had learned the trick of rolling the trousers snug at the ankle, and hauling the gray woolen sock, legging-wise, round them. *There* was a fashion that endured to the last, and spread westward and southward to the ends of the lines.

But with the second summer of the war the hooked standing collar and buttoned-up coat were almost gone. Men had learned wisdom, and wore the blue blouse and gray-flannel shirt—open at the throat in warm weather, snug-fastened in

ONE FOREIGN UNIFORM RETAINED THROUGHOUT THE WAR—A "RUSH HAWKINS' ZOUAVE" AT GENERAL GILLMORE'S HEADQUARTERS, 1863

The vivid sunlight in this photograph makes the grass and roof look almost like snow, but the place is Folly Island before Charleston in July, 1863. In the foreground to the left stands one of Rush Hawkins' Zouaves, from the Ninth New York Infantry. He adheres to his foreign uniform, although most of the white gaiters and other fancy trappings of the Union army had disappeared early in '62. But his regiment did good service. It fought at South Mountain, at Antietam, and Fredericksburg, with much scouting and several forced marches before it was mustered out May 20, 1863. The three-years men, after they were assigned to the Third New York Infantry, which was ordered to Folly Island in July, 1863, retained their uniforms when in entire companies. The scene is the headquarters of General Quincy Adams Gillmore, who was promoted to lieutenant-colonel April 11, 1862, for gallant and meritorious service in the capture of Fort Pulaski, Ga., and to colonel, March 30, 1863, for gallant and meritorious service in the battle of Somerset, Ky. He became major-general of volunteers in July, 1863. Note the black shadows cast by the soldier and the tree.

cold—and so lived and marched in comfort. Almost everything that was conspicuous or glittering had disappeared from the dress of horse or man. The army that came back from Fair Oaks and Gaines' Mill plodded on through the heart of Maryland in quest of Lee, bronzed, bearded in many cases, but destitute of ornament of any kind. The red sash had turned to purple or faded away entirely; the costly shoulder-straps of gold embroidery, so speedily ruined by dust and rain, had given place to creations of metal, warranted to keep their shape, nor rust or fade—no matter what the weather.

Officers who proudly bestrode " hundred-dollar housings " at the grand review in the fall of 1861, had left them in the swamps or lost them in battle, and were now using the cavalry blanket instead of the shabrack, and the raw hogshide, rough stitched to wooden saddle-tree, instead of the stuffed seat of the Jenifer—and speedily learning that what they lost in style they gained in comfort. So, too, had the polished brass or steel stirrup given way to the black-hooded, broad-stepped, wooden frame wherein the foot kept warm and dry whatever the weather.

Only generals were wearing, with the second and third years, the heavily frogged and braided overcoats of dark blue. Capes, ponchos, and cavalry surtouts were the choice of the line-officer, and the men of the ranks had no choice. By the time they had finished the second summer of the war, had later crossed the icy Rappahannock and vainly stormed the heights at Fredericksburg, and later still had followed " Fighting Joe " to Chancellorsville—and back—the pomps and vanities of soldier life had become things of the remote past; they had settled down to the stern realities of campaigning. It was a seasoned, a veteran army that marched to Gettysburg and for the first time fairly drove the Southern lines from the field. Long before this the treasured colors were stained, faded, rent, and torn. Some had been riven to shreds in the storm of shot and shell along the Chickahominy, in front of the

UNION SOLDIERS AT WORK TO PRESERVE THEIR HEALTH

The soldier in the field had to learn to take care of his health between battles as well as to save his skin while the bullets were flying. In these two photographs, separated by only a few moments, Union men appear at the work of sanitation. Huts are being erected and ditches dug for drainage near the headquarters of General George W. Getty, Sixth Army Corps. In the upper photograph the man with the wheelbarrow is just starting away from the tent with a load. In the lower, he has reached the unfinished hut. The men standing upright in the upper picture have bent to their work and the sentry has paced a little farther along on his beat.

unfinished railway at Second Bull Run, in the cornfields of the Antietam, on the frozen slopes of Marye's Hill, or among the murky woods of Chancellorsville. Now, in many a regiment, by the spring of 1864, half the original names had gone from the muster-rolls, the fearful cost of such battling as had been theirs—theirs, the home-loving lads who came flocking in the flush of youth and the fervor of patriotism to offer their brave lives at the earliest call, in 1861.

It was a veteran army of campaigners with which Meade, Hancock, and Reynolds, those three gallant Pennsylvanians, overthrew at Gettysburg the hard-fighting army of the South —Reynolds laying down his life in the fierce grapple of the first day—veterans, yet more than half of them beardless boys. Few people to-day who see the bent forms and snowy heads of our few remaining " comrades " of the Civil War, begin to know, and fewer still can realize, the real facts as to the ages of our volunteers. It is something worthy of being recorded here and remembered for all time, that the " old boys," as they love to speak of themselves, were young boys, very young, when first they raised their ungloved right hands to swear allegiance to the flag, and obedience to the officers appointed over them.

It is something to be inscribed on the tablets of memory —the fact that over one million of the soldiers who fought for the preservation of the Union were but eighteen years of age or less at date of enlistment—that over two millions were not over twenty-one. It is a matter of record that of a total of 1,012,273 enlistments statistically examined it was found that only 46,626 were twenty-five years of age—only 16,070 were forty-four. It is something for mothers to know to-day that three hundred boys of thirteen years or less (twenty-five were but ten or under) were actually accepted and enlisted, generally as drummers or fifers, but, all the same, regularly enrolled and sworn in by the recruiting officers of the United States. Many a time those little fellows were

MILITARY MUSIC OF THE BEGINNING

Many of the Union regiments started the war with complete and magnificent bands, but when active campaigning began they proved too great a luxury. Every man was needed then to fight. It was the bandsman's duty during an engagement to attend to the wounded on the field, a painful and dangerous task which discour-

aged many a musician. The topmost photograph shows one of the bands that remained in permanent headquarters, in camp near Arlington, Virginia. In the next appears the field music of the 164th New York. In the next photograph the post musicians of Fortress Monroe stand imposingly beneath their bearskins. The bottom picture shows a band at winter headquarters—Camp Stoneman, near Washington.

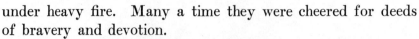

under heavy fire. Many a time they were cheered for deeds of bravery and devotion.

But with the coming of the spring of 1864 such a thing as a boyish face was hard to find among them. Young faces there were by hundreds, but the boyish look was gone. The days of battle and peril, the scenes of bloodshed and carnage, the sounds of agony or warning—all had left indelible impress. Eyes that have looked three years upon death in every horrible shape, upon gaping wounds and battle-torn bodies, lose gradually and never regain the laughing light of youth. The correspondents of the press filled many a column with description of the boy-faced generals—men like Barlow, Merritt, and curly-haired Custer; but a closer study of the young faces thus pictured would have told a very different story—a story of hours of anxious thought and planning, of long nights of care and vigil, of thrilling days of headlong battle wherein a single error in word or action might instantly bring on disaster.

In both East and West, by this time, there were regiments commanded by lads barely twenty years of age, brave boys who, having been leaders among their schoolfellows, on enlistment had been elected or appointed lieutenants at seventeen, and who within two years had shown in many a battle such self-control, such self-confidence, such capacity for command that they rose by leaps and bounds to the head of their regiments. Of such were the boy colonels of the Western armies—Lawton of Indiana, MacArthur of Wisconsin. There were but few young colonels in the camps of the Army of the Potomac, as the buds began to burst and the sap to bubble in the groves along the swirling Rappahannock—the last springtide in which those scarred and ravaged shores were ever to hear the old familiar thunder of shotted cannon, or the rallying cries of the battling Blue and Gray.

Three winters had the men of McClellan, of Hooker, and of Meade dwelt in their guarded lines south of the Potomac, three winters in which the lightest hearted of their number

EVENING MUSIC AT PLEASONTON'S HEADQUARTERS, AUBURN, 1863

FIELD MUSIC

The fife and drum corps became the chief dependence of the regimental commanders for music as the fighting wore on. They remained with the army to the end, and sounded all the "calls." They served under the surgeon. A cheerful bit of music is an inspiring thing to a tired column of soldiers on a long day's march or before a danger-

THE MUSIC THAT STAYED WITH THE SOLDIERS—TALTY'S FIFERS AND DRUMMERS

ous foe. General Sheridan recognized the value of this stimulus to the men, and General Horace Porter records that as late as March 30, 1865, he encountered one of Sheridan's bands under heavy fire at Five Forks, playing "Nellie Bly" as cheerfully as if it were furnishing music for a country picnic. The top photograph shows one of the cavalry bands at Auburn, in the fall of 1863. The frayed trousers of the band below show hard service.

A BAND THAT HAD SEEN SERVICE, NEAR FAIRFAX, 1863

must have matured ten years. What sights had they seen,
what miles had they marched, what furious battles had they
fought, yet to what end? In spite of all their struggles and all
their sacrifices, here they lay along the same familiar slopes
and fields, with the same turbid stream still barring the southward way. Once had the grand Army of the Potomac, led by
McClellan, turned the opposing line, tried the water route,
marched up the Peninsula, and after a few weeks of fighting,
drifted back again. Twice had the gallant Army of Northern
Virginia, led by Robert E. Lee, turned the opposing lines,
tramped up to the Cumberland valley, and after the stirring
days of Antietam and Gettysburg, fallen back, fearfully crippled, yet defiant. Now, nearly two to one in point of numbers, and with a silent, simple-mannered Westerner in command of a great array made up mainly of Eastern men, the
Army of the Potomac was to begin its final essay. In size
it was about what it had been when it set forth in the spring
of 1862. In discipline, in experience, in knowledge of the war-
game, it was immeasurably greater.

The winter had been long and dull. The novelty had long
since worn off; the camps and cantonments had been made
as snug and comfortable as so many homes; rations were abundant and fairly good; the sutler shops were full of tempting
provender; the paymaster's visits had been regular; currency,
in greenbacks, "shinplasters," and postal notes was plentiful.
Drills, except for recruits, were well-nigh done away with. Reviews and parades were few and far between. Guard and
sentry, patrol and picket, were about the only duties ordered,
so time hung heavily on the hands of all. Writing home was
one relaxation; cards, checkers, or dice supplied another, but in
almost every regiment after nightfall and before tattoo, men
gathered together and talked of those they had lost, of those
that remained in high command, and sang or crooned their
soldier songs. Across the Rapidan—where all day long silent,
statuesque, yet undeniably shabby, sat in saddle those gray

DRUMMER–BOYS OF THE WAR DAYS

IDENTIFIED BY COMRADES HALF A CENTURY LATER

The rub-a-dub-dub of the drums and the tootle-te-toot of the fifes inspired the Union armies long after there remained in the service but a few of the bands which marched to the front in '61. All the calls from "reveille" to "taps," "assembly," breakfast call, sick call, were rendered by the brave little boys who were as ready to go under fire as the stoutest hearted veteran. Many a time a boy would drop his drum or fife to grab up the gun of a wounded soldier and go in on the firing-line. Fifty years afterward, members of this group were recognized by one of their companions during the war. The one standing immediately below the right-hand star in the flag, beating the long roll on his drum, is Newton Peters. He enlisted at fifteen, in the fall of 1861, and served throughout the four years, not being mustered out until June 29, 1865. The boy standing in the front line at his left is Samuel Scott, aged sixteen when he entered the army as a drummer in August of 1862. He, too, was faithful to the end, receiving his discharge on June 1, 1865. The leader, standing forward with staff in his right hand, is Patrick Yard, who served from November 14, 1861, to July 1, 1865, having been principal musician or drum-major from July 1, 1862. These are only a few of the forty thousand boy musicians who succeeded in securing enlistment in the Union armies, and followed the flag.

vedettes—the widely dispersed army of Lee had been undergoing a great religious revival, until they entered upon their final and fateful campaign with fervent hope and prayer and self-devotion.

Along the north bank, the spirit of the Union host, as compared with the lightsome heart of 1861, had become tinged with sadness. It was manifest in their songs. The joyous, spirited, or frolicsome lays of the earlier months of the war had been well nigh forgotten. Men no longer chorused "Cheer Boys Cheer," or "Gay and Happy," for the songs of 1864 were pitched in mournful, minor chord. The soldiers sang of home and mother and of comrades gone before—"Just Before the Battle," "We Shall Meet, but We Shall Miss Him" were in constant demand. Only rarely did the camps resound with "The Battle Cry of Freedom" and "The Red, White, and Blue." They had seen so much of the sadness, they had thus far known so little of the joy of soldier life. In the West it had been different. There they had humbled the foe at Forts Henry and Donelson. They had fought him to a draw, winning finally the field, if not the fight, at Shiloh and Stone's River. Brilliantly led by Grant, they had triumphed at Jackson and Champion's Hill, and then besieged and captured Vicksburg, setting free the Mississippi. They had suffered fearful defeat at Chickamauga where, aided by Longstreet and his fighting divisions from Virginia, their old antagonist, Bragg, had been able to overwhelm the Union lines.

Yet within three months the Army of the Cumberland, led by George H. Thomas, and under the eyes of Grant, had taken the bit in their teeth, refused to wait longer for Sherman's columns to their left, or Hooker's divisions sweeping from Lookout to their rear, and in one tumultuous rush had carried the heights of Missionary Ridge, sweeping Bragg and his veterans back across the scene of their September triumph, winning glorious victory in sight of those who had declared they could not fight at all. They of the West had more than

AN INTERLUDE OF WARFARE — SERENADING THE COLONEL

The colonel of the regiment is sitting upon a chair fronting the house, holding his baby on his lap. His family has joined him at his headquarters, which he is fortunate to have established in a comfortable farm-house near Union Mills, Virginia, early in 1862. A veteran, examining this photograph, found it to represent a rare event in soldier life—the serenading of an officer by the regimental band. These organizations, which entered the service with the regiments of 1861 and 1862, did not retain their organization very long. Their duty during action was to care for the wounded on the field and carry them to the rear, but it was soon found that those with sufficient courage for this service were needed on the firing-line with muskets in their hands, and they either became soldiers in the ranks or were mustered out of service. Thereafter the regiments depended for music upon their own fife and drum corps and buglers, or upon brigade bands.

held their own, and now as the spring released them from their winter quarters along the Tennessee, they were eager to be marched onward to Atlanta, even to Mobile. They had with them still many of the leaders whom they had known from their formative period—notably Sherman, Thomas, McPherson, Stanley, and by them they enthusiastically swore.

They had lost Halleck, Pope, Grant, and Sheridan, as they proudly said, " sent to the East to teach them Western ways of winning battles," but Halleck and Pope had hardly succeeded, and Grant and Sheridan were yet to try. They had as yet lost no generals of high degree in battle, though they mourned Lytle, Sill, Terrill, W. H. L. Wallace, and " Bob " McCook, who had been beloved and honored. They were destined to see no more of two great leaders who had done much to make them the indomitable soldiers they became—Buell and Rosecrans. They had parted with Crittenden, McCook, and McClernand, corps commanders much in favor with the rank and file, though not so fortunate with those higher in authority. They were soon to be rejoined by Blair and Logan, generals in whom they gloried, and all the camps about Chattanooga were full of fight.

But here along the open fields in desolated Virginia there was far different retrospect; there was far less to cheer. With all its thorough organization, armament, equipment; with all its months of preparation, its acknowledged superiority in drill and its vaunted superiority in discipline, the Army of the Potomac had been humbled time and again, and it was not the fault of the rank and file—the sturdy soldiery that made up those famous *corps d'armée*. At First Bull Run they had been pitted from the very start against forces supposed to be beyond the Blue Ridge, and overthrown at the eleventh hour by arriving brigades that a militia general was to have held fast on the Shenandoah. At Ball's Bluff they had been slowly surrounded by concentrating battalions, no precaution having been taken for their extrication or

PASTIMES
OF OFFICERS
AND MEN

Occasionally in permanent camps, officers were able to receive visits from members of their families or friends. This photograph shows an earnest game of chess between Colonel (afterward Major-General) Martin T. McMahon, assistant adjutant-general of the Sixth Corps, Army of the Potomac, and a brother officer, in the spring of 1864 just preceding the Wilderness campaign. Colonel McMahon, who sits near the tent-pole, is evidently studying his move with care. The young officer clasping the tent-pole is one of the colonel's military aides. Chess was also fashionable in the Confederate army, and it is recorded that General Lee frequently played chess with his aide, Colonel Charles Marshall, on a three-pronged pine stick surmounted by a pine slab upon which the squares had been roughly cut and the black ones inked in. Napoleon Bonaparte is said to have been another earnest student of chess.

A GAME OF CHESS AT COLONEL McMAHON'S CAMP

WHEN THE ARMY RELAXED

With the first break of spring the soldiers would seize the opportunity to decorate their winter huts with green branches, as this photograph shows. Care has been cast aside for the moment, and with their arms stacked on the parade ground the men are lounging comfortably in the soft spring air, while the more enterprising indulge in a game of cards. From the intentness of their comrades who are looking over their shoulders, it may be imagined that there is a little money at stake, as was frequently the case.

support. In front of Washington, long months they had been held inert by much less than half their number. At Yorktown, one hundred thousand strong, they had been halted by a lone division and held a fatal month. At Williamsburg they had been stopped by a much smaller force. At Fair Oaks their left had been crushed while the right and center were "refused."

At Gaines' Mill their right had been ruined while the center and left, under McClellan's own eye, had been held passive in front of a skeleton line. At Second Bull Run they had been hurled against an army secure behind embankments, while another, supposed to be miles away, circled their left flank and crushed it. At Antietam, bloodiest day of the story thus far, they had been sent in, a corps at a time, to try conclusions with an army in position, to the end that, when Lee slipped away with his battered divisions, even with superior numbers McClellan dare not follow. Twice within six months had Stuart, with a handful of light horsemen, ridden entirely around them, and with abundant cavalry had failed to stop him. In November they had mournfully parted with their idol of the year before, never to look again on "Little Mac," realizing that something must have been wrong, though it was not theirs to ask or to reason why. Obedient to Burnside's orders, they had stormed the heights of Fredericksburg in the face of Lee's veterans, laying down their lives in what they knew was hopeless battle.

Confident in their numbers, in their valor, in their comrades, and hopeful of their new and buoyant commander, they had crossed above Fredericksburg, while Sedgwick menaced from the north, and then, worst fate of all, had found themselves tricked and turned, their right wing sent whirling before "Stonewall" Jackson, whom Hooker and Howard had thought to be in full retreat for the mountains, their far superior force huddled in helpless confusion and then sent back, sore-hearted, to the camps from which they had come. They

THE THIRTEENTH NEW YORK ARTILLERY PLAYING FOOTBALL DURING THE SIEGE OF PETERSBURG

THE BIRTH OF BASE-BALL

Some of the men who went home on furlough in 1862 returned to their regiments with tales of a marvelous new game which was spreading through the Northern States. In camp at White Oak Church near Falmouth, Va., Kearny's Jersey brigade and Bartlett's brigade played this "baseball," as it was known. Bartlett's boys won this historic ball-game.

BOXING AT THE CAMP OF THE THIRTEENTH NEW YORK AT CITY POINT, 1864

AN ARMY OF BOYS

It is hard to remember when one reads of the bloody battles, the manly sacrifices, the stern, exhausting work of the Union armies, that over one million of the soldiers who fought for the Union were not over twenty-one. It was an army of boys, and in camp they acted as such. They boxed and wrestled and played tricks on each other like boys in school.

A DIVERSION AT GENERAL O. B. WILCOX'S HEADQUARTERS, IN FRONT OF PETERSBURG, AUGUST, 1864

had taken full measure of recompense for this humiliation in the three tremendous days at Gettysburg, had triumphed at last over the skilled and valiant foemen who for two long years had beaten them at every point, but even now they could not make it decisive, for, just as after Antietam, they had to look on while Lee and his legions were permitted to saunter easily back to the old lines along the Rapidan. They had served in succession five different masters. They had seen the stars of McDowell, McClellan, Pope, Burnside, and Hooker, one after another, effaced. They had seen such corps commanders as Sumner, Heintzelman, Keyes, Fitz John Porter, Sigel, Franklin, and Stoneman relieved and sent elsewhere. They had lost, killed in battle, such valiant generals as Philip Kearny, Stevens, Reno, Richardson, Mansfield, Whipple, Bayard, Berry, Weed, Zook, Vincent, and the great right arm of their latest and last commander—John F. Reynolds, head of the First Corps, since he would not be head of the army.

They had inflicted nothing like such loss upon the Army of Northern Virginia, for "Stonewall" Jackson had fallen, seriously wounded, before the rifles of his own men, bewildered in the thickets and darkness of Chancellorsville. They had been hard hit time and again—misled, misdirected, mishandled —yet through it all and in spite of all had maintained their high courage and dauntless spirit. Tried again and again in adversity and disaster, saddened, sobered, but resolute and indomitable, they asked only the chance to try it again under a leader who would *stay,* and that chance they were now to have—that test which was destined to be the most deadly and desperate of all; for though Meade was commander of the Army of the Potomac, Grant had come, supreme in command of all, and Grant had brought with him that black-eyed little division commander from the Army of the Cumberland whose men had broken loose and swept the field at Missionary Ridge. The cavalry corps of the Army of the Potomac was to take the field under, and soon to learn to swear by, Philip Sheridan.

WHEN WAR HAD LOST ITS GLAMOUR—PROVOST-MARSHAL'S OFFICE IN ALEXANDRIA, 1863

The novelty had departed from "the pomp and pageantry of war" by the fall of 1863. The Army of the Potomac had lost its thousands on the Peninsula, at Cedar Mountain, at Second Bull Run, Antietam, Fredericksburg, Chancellorsville, and Gettysburg. The soldiers were sated with war; they had forgotten a host of things taught to them as essential in McClellan's training camps that first winter around Washington. The paraphernalia of war had become familiar, and they yearned for the now unfamiliar paraphernalia of peace. This photograph shows the provost-marshal's office in Alexandria, Virginia, in the fall of 1863. The provost-marshal's men had long since learned to perform their duties with all the languid dignity of a city policeman. Attached to the flag-pole is a sign which heralds the fact that Dick Parker's Music Hall is open every night. Two years before the soldiers might have disdained to seek such entertainment in the face of impending battles. Now war was commonplace, and the "gentle arts of peace" seemed strange and new.

And they had need of all their discipline and determination, for over against them, along the southern shores of the Rapidan, Lee's widely dispersed army was girding up its loins for the last supreme struggle, sustained and strengthened as never before. There had always been a devout and prayerful spirit among their chieftains, notably in Lee, Jackson, and "Jeb" Stuart.

And so as the soft springtide flooded with sunshine the Virginia woods and fields, and all the trees were blossoming, and the river banks were green, the note of preparation was sounding in the camps of Meade, from Culpeper over to Kelly's Ford, and one still May morning, long before the dawn —their only reveille the plaintive call of the whippoorwill— the Army of the Potomac stole from its blankets, soaked the smouldering fires, silently formed ranks and filed away southeastward, heading for the old familiar crossings of the Rapidan. Three strong corps were there, with Hancock, Warren, and Sedgwick as their commanders, while away toward the Potomac stood Burnside, leading still another.

It was the beginning of the end, for the strong and disciplined array that marched onward into the tangled Wilderness nearly doubled the number of Lee's tried and trusted soldiery. It was the last stand of the Confederacy along that historic line, but was a stand never to be forgotten. Away to the southwest were the cheerless camps of the Southern corps, led by grim, one-legged old Ewell (he had lost the other in front of the Western brigade at the opening fight of Second Bull Run), by courtly A. P. Hill, by Grant's old comrade in the army, now Lee's "best bower," Longstreet. It was an easy march for the Army of the Potomac—Sheridan's troopers picking the way. It was far longer and harder for those ragged fellows, the Army of Northern Virginia, but the Northerners reeled and fell by hundreds under the terrific blows of Longstreet, when, with the second day, he came crashing in through the tangled shrubbery. It cost the North

SHIFTING GROUPS BEFORE THE SUTLER'S TENT—1864

In the early days, when there were delays in paying the troops, the sutlers discounted their pay-checks at ruinous rates. Sometimes when the paymaster arrived the sutler would be on hand and absorb all the money due to some of the soldiers. Before the end of the war the term "sutler" came to have no very honorable meaning, and an overturned wagon filled with his stores found plenty of volunteers to send it on its way, somewhat lighter as to load. Sometimes, however, a popular and honest vendor of the store supplies contributed by his industry and daring to smooth the corners of a hard campaign and break the monotony of camp fare.

FIRST WISCONSIN LIGHT ARTILLERY AT BATON ROUGE, LOUISIANA, IN AUGUST, 1864

This and the facing page show the first light artillery sent to the Union armies from what were then far-Western States. This battery was commanded by Captain Jacob T. Foster, and consisted of six 20-pounder Parrott guns. On April 3, 1862, they accompanied an expedition under General Morgan to Cumberland Gap, hauling their heavy guns by hand over the steep passes of the mountains. After the retreat from Cumberland Gap they joined the forces of General Cox at Red House Landing, Virginia, and December 21, 1862, they proceeded down the Mississippi to take part in Sherman's movement against Vicksburg. On the first of January, 1863, Sherman withdrew the army and moved to Arkansas Post. During Grant's campaign in Mississippi the battery fired over twelve thousand rounds. Their guns were condemned at Vicksburg, being so badly worn as to be unserviceable. They were then furnished with 30-pounder Parrotts, and ordered with the Thirteenth Army Corps to the Department of the Gulf. In December the Wisconsin men were ordered to New Orleans, and assigned to a position in the defenses of that city. There they were equipped as horse artillery and armed with three-inch rifled guns. By this time they were seasoned artillerists; the report of a commission appointed to inspect the quarters of all troops in New Orleans closes thus: "A more self-sustaining, self-reliant body of men cannot be found in the United States army." On April 22, 1864, they went to the aid of Banks' columns on their retreat from the Red River expedition, and in August took part in an expedition to Clinton, Louisiana. The battery lost during service five enlisted men killed and mortally wounded, and one officer and twenty-two enlisted men by disease.

[248]

COMPANY I, FIRST OHIO LIGHT ARTILLERY, AT CHATTANOOGA, NOVEMBER, 1863

This company was organized at Cincinnati, Ohio, and mustered in December 3, 1861. This photograph shows it in charge of some hundred-pounder Parrott guns on Signal Hill at Chattanooga where it was encamped in November, 1863. The guns had just been placed and the battery was not yet finished. Company I served at Gainesville, Groveton, and Second Bull Run in August, 1862, fought at Chancellorsville and Gettysburg, and took part in the Chattanooga-Ringgold campaign, and remained on garrison duty at Chattanooga till April 23, 1864. Thereafter it took part in Sherman's Atlanta campaign, fought at Kenesaw Mountain and Jonesboro and in many lesser engagements, and was mustered out June 13, 1865. The battery lost during service one officer and thirteen enlisted men killed and mortally wounded, and fifteen enlisted men by disease. Ohio furnished to the Federal armies thirteen regiments, five battalions, and ten companies of cavalry, two regiments of heavy artillery, forty-two batteries of light artillery, ten companies of sharpshooters, and 227 regiments, one battalion, and five companies of infantry—a grand total during the war of 313,180 soldiers out of a military population of 459,534 in 1860.

the lives of two great leaders—Hays and Wadsworth, and hosts of gallant officers and men, did that battle of the Wilderness. Fearful was the toll taken by Lee in his initial grapple of the last campaign, for no less than eighteen thousand men, killed, wounded, and missing, were lost to Grant. It would have cost very much more but for one potent fact that, in the hour of success, triumph, and victory, even as Lee's greatest corps commander had been stricken just the year before and almost within bugle-call of the very spot, Lee's next greatest corps commander, Longstreet, was here shot down and borne desperately wounded from the field.

And when another morning dawned, and through the misty light the wearied eyes of the Southern pickets descried long columns in the Union blue marching, apparently, away from the scene of their fearful struggle, away to the barrier river, the woods rang with frantic cheers of exultation. Small wonder they thought that Grant, too, had given it up and gone. They had yet to know him. They had barely time to spring to arms and dart away, full tilt by the right flank, on the eastward race for Spotsylvania, there once again to clinch in furious battle—to kill and maim almost as many of Grant's indomitable host as three days at Gettysburg had cost them, and still, with an added eighteen thousand shot out of his ranks, that grim, silent, stubborn leader forced his onward way. On to the North Anna, and another sharp encounter; on to Cold Harbor and the dread assault upon entrenched and sheltered lines, where in two hours' fighting the Southern army, suffering heavily in spite of its screen, none the less took ten times its loss out of the assailing lines, and still had to fall back, amazed at the persistence of the foe. Sixty-one thousand effectives in round numbers, could Lee muster at the first gun of the campaign. Fifty-five thousand effectives in round numbers at the last gun had they shot from the ranks of Grant—nearly their own weight in foes. But even Cold Harbor could not turn that inflexible Westerner from his purpose. With nearly half

FOURTEENTH IOWA VETERANS
AT LIBBY PRISON, RICHMOND, IN 1862, ON THEIR WAY TO FREEDOM

In the battle of Shiloh the Fourteenth Iowa Infantry formed part of that self-constituted forlorn hope which made the victory of April 7, 1862, possible. It held the center at the "Hornet's Nest," fighting the live-long day against fearful odds. Just as the sun was setting, Colonel William T. Shaw, seeing that he was surrounded and further resistance useless, surrendered the regiment. These officers and men were held as prisoners of war until October 12, 1862, when, moving by Richmond, Virginia, and Annapolis, Maryland, they went to Benton Barracks, Missouri, being released on parole, and were declared exchanged on the 19th of November. This photograph was taken while they were held at Richmond, opposite the cook-houses of Libby Prison. The third man from the left in the front row, standing with his hand grasping the lapel of his coat, is George Marion Smith, a descendant of General Marion of Revolutionary fame. It is through the courtesy of his son, N. H. Smith, that this photograph appears here. The Fourteenth Iowa Infantry was organized at Davenport and mustered in November 6, 1861. At Shiloh the men were already veterans of Forts Henry and Donelson. Those who were not captured fought in the battle of Corinth, and after the prisoners were exchanged they took part in the Red River expedition and several minor engagements. They were mustered out November 16, 1864, when the veterans and recruits were consolidated in two companies and assigned to duty in Springfield, Illinois, till August, 1865. These two companies were mustered out on August 8th. The regiment lost during service five officers and fifty-nine enlisted men killed and mortally wounded, and one officer and 138 enlisted men by disease. Iowa sent nine regiments of cavalry, four batteries of light artillery and fifty-one regiments of infantry to the Union armies, a grand total of 76,242 soldiers.

his army strewn from the Rapidan to the lines of Richmond, Grant flung his pontoons across the James, and marched to Petersburg.

And there at last he had to pause, refit, reorganize, for Sedgwick and Hancock were lost to him—Sedgwick killed at the head of the Sixth Corps, still mourning for their beloved "Uncle John"; Hancock disabled by wounds. New men, but good, were now leading the Second and Sixth corps— Humphreys, and Wright of the Engineers, while Warren still was heading the Fifth. And now came the details of Sherman's victorious march from Chattanooga to Atlanta, and later of the start to the sea. Here the waiting soldiers shouted loud acclaim of Thomas' great victory at Nashville, of the pursuit and ruin of the army under Hood. Here they had to lounge in camp and read with envy of Sheridan and the Sixth Corps playing havoc with Early in the Shenandoah, and now with occasional heavy fighting on the flanks, here they heard of Sherman at Savannah, and a little later of his marching northward to meet them.

And then it seemed as though the very earth were crumbling at Petersburg, the Government at Richmond. With Thomas, free now to march eastward up the Tennessee and through the Virginia mountains at the west; with Sherman coming steadily from the south, with Grant forever hammering from the east, and with formidable reserves always menacing at the north, what could be the future of that heroic, hard-pounded army of Lee! Long since the last call had been made upon their devoted people. The aged and the immature were side by side in the thinned and starving ranks. Food and supplies were well nigh exhausted. The sturdy, hard-marching, hard-fighting Southern infantry had learned to live on parched corn; their comrades, the gaunt cavalry, on next to nothing. With the end of March, Sheridan came again, riding buoyantly down from the Shenandoah, singing trooper songs along the James River Canal, rounding the Richmond

SOLDIER LIFE UNDERGROUND—BOMB-PROOFS ON THE LINES IN FRONT OF PETERSBURG, 1864

There were places on the advanced line around Petersburg where it was almost certain death to look over the side of the trench. There pickets had to be changed at night. The constant hail of shot and shell made life underground, such as the soldiers in these photographs are leading, not only welcome but necessary. There are two distinct kinds of physical courage. The story is told of a burly camp-bully who threatened to thrash a wiry little veteran half his size for some trivial or fancied slight. "No," said the veteran, "I won't fight you now, but come out on picket where you can be alone after dark with me to-night." They crept out silently to relieve the picket in the outer trench that night, but a dislodged stone attracted the Confederates' attention and the shots whistled about their ears. "Oh!" whined the camp-bully, as he crouched in the bottom of the trench, "they're trying to kill me!" "Of course they are," replied the little veteran quietly: "They've been trying to kill me for the last six nights." But there was no fight left in the camp-bully when he was required to face bullets.

BOMB-PROOFS NEAR ATLANTA, GEORGIA

fortifications, and rejoining Grant at Petersburg. Within a week he bored a way into the dim, dripping forests about Dinwiddie, found and overwhelmed Pickett at Five Forks, and, with thirty thousand men, turned Lee's right and cut the South Side Railroad.

That meant the fall of Petersburg—the fall of Richmond. There was barely time to fire the last volleys over the third of Lee's great corps commanders, A. P. Hill; to send hurried warning to Jefferson Davis at Richmond; to summon Longstreet, and then began the seven days' struggle to escape the toils by which the army was enmeshed. There had been no Sheridan in command of the cavalry when the Southern army fell back from the Antietam in 1862, or from Gettysburg in 1863, but now, on their moving flanks, ever leaping ahead and dogging their advance, ever cutting in and out among the weary and straggling columns, lopping off a train here, a brigade there, but never for a moment, day or night, ceasing to worry and wear and tear, Sheridan and his troopers rode vengefully, and there was no " Jeb " Stuart to lead the Southern horse—Stuart had gone down before his great foeman in sight of the spires of Richmond, long months before—and at last, with their wagon-loads of waiting rations cut off and captured before the eyes of their advance, with every hour bringing tidings of new losses and disasters at the rear, worn out with hunger, fatigue, and loss of sleep, their clothing in shreds, their horses barely able to stagger, the men who never yet had failed " Marse Robert," as they loved to call him, found their further way blocked at Appomattox; the road to Lynchburg held by long lines of Union cavalry, screening the swift coming of longer lines of infantry in blue. And then their great-hearted leader bowed his head in submission to the inevitable.

" Not a drum was heard, not a funeral note " when the British buried Sir John Moore at Corunna. Not a shot was heard, not a single cheer, not a symptom of triumph or

WHEN TIME SEEMED LONG, BUT HOME WAS NEAR—ON DUTY AT FORT WHIPPLE IN JUNE, '65

The war is over and the great machine of the Union armies which has been whirring at breakneck speed for full four years is now moving more and more slowly. But it cannot be stopped all at once, and the men who form its component parts are going through motions now become mechanical. The scene is Fort Whipple, Va., part of the vast system of defenses erected for the protection of Washington. The time is June, 1865. With the sash across his breast stands the Officer of the Day, whose duty it is during his tour of twenty-four hours to inspect all portions of the camp and to see that proper order is preserved. Just at the moment when this picture was taken, the adjutant of the regiment was giving some information to the Officer of the Day from his general order book. It is safe to assume that the thoughts of the three other officers, as well as those of the sentry pacing to and fro, are all tinged with alluring pictures of home and the comforts that have been so long denied to them. The sturdy bugler below will need no urging to sound taps for the last time. He is a soldier of the 26th Michigan. It was his regiment that issued the paroles to Lee's soldiers at Appomattox. In a few weeks he may rest his eyes on the long undulations of the inland prairies. In his western home he will often find echoing in his memory the mournful dying notes of the bugle as it sounded "taps" and will recall the words soldiers have fitted to the music: "Go to sleep. Go to sleep. The day is done." One of the marvels of our war to the belligerent nations of Europe was that, having raised and trained such gigantic armies, we should disperse them so quietly when the fighting was over. There is an apocryphal story of a mad scheme to combine the armies of the North and South and proceed to intervene in Mexico.

A BUGLER OF THE 26TH MICHIGAN

rejoicing when the Army of the Potomac leaned at last upon their rifles, and from under the peaked visors of their worn forage-caps watched the sad surrender of the men of Lee. Four long years they had fought and toiled and suffered; four long years they had everywhere encountered those grim gray lines, and always at fearful cost; four long years had they been cut off from home and loved ones, to face at any moment death, desperate wounds, the prison stockade, hardship, and privation, all that the great Union might be maintained—that even these, their skilled and valiant opponents, might prosper in future peace and unity under the rescued and resistless flag. All the peril, privation, and suffering were ended now. All the joys of home-coming were soon and surely to be theirs. Glad, glorious thanksgiving welled in every heart and would have burst forth in shout and song and maddening cheers, but for the sight of the sorrow in those thinned and tattered ranks, the unutterable grief in the gaunt, haggard faces of these, their brethren, as they stacked in silence the battle-dinted arms and bent to kiss, as many did, the sacred remnants of the battle-flags that had waved in triumph time and again, only to be borne down at the last, when further struggle was hopeless, useless, impossible. It was but the remnant, too, of his once indomitable array that was left to Lee for the final rally at Appomattox. The South had fought until between the cradle and the grave there were no more left to muster—fought as never a people fought before, and suffered as few in the North-land ever yet knew or dreamed.

Without a sound of exultation, without a single cheer, we have said, yet there *was* a sound—the murmur of pity and sympathy along the serried lines in blue, as there slowly passed before their eyes the wearied column of disarmed, dejected soldiery, weak from wounds, from hardship, from hunger. There *was* a cheer—a sudden spontaneous outburst from the nearest division, when, almost the last of all, the little remnant of the old Stonewall brigade stacked the arms they had borne

THE 69TH NEW YORK AT MASS IN THE FIELD

CHAPLAINS OF THE NINTH ARMY CORPS—OCTOBER, 1864

Nearly every regiment that went into the Civil War from the Northern cities had a chaplain as a member of its staff. Many of these peaceful warriors kept on through the campaigns. They worked in the field-hospitals, often under fire on the field itself where the wounded lay. More than one was carried away by patriotic ardor and, grasping the musket and cartridge-box of a wounded soldier, was seen to sally out on the firing-line, and bear himself as courageously as any veteran—after the battle returning to the duty of ministering to the wounded. And in several instances, chaplains asked for a command after a few months in the field. The church shown below was built by the Fiftieth New York Engineers at Petersburg.

SPIRE AND BAYONETS

FEDERAL VETERANS IN WEST AND EAST, 1863—TWO ENTIRE REGIMENTS IN LINE

These two photographs are unusual as showing each an entire regiment in line on parade. Here stands the type of soldier developed West and East by the far-flung Union armies. The Fifty-seventh Illinois were already veterans of Forts Donelson and Henry and the bloody field of Shiloh when this photograph was taken, and had seen hard service at the siege of Corinth. Their camp is near the Corinth battlefield, May, 1863. The Forty-fourth New York, known as the "People's Ellsworth Regiment," was a graduate of Bull Run, the Peninsula, Antietam, Second Bull Run, Fredericksburg, Chancellorsville, and Gettysburg. It took part in even

ABOVE, THE FIFTY–SEVENTH ILLINOIS; THE FORTY–FOURTH NEW YORK BELOW

more pitched battles than the Illinois regiment and its loss was proportionately larger. Both were known as "fighting regiments." The Fifty-seventh Illinois lost during service three officers and sixty-five enlisted men killed and mortally wounded, and four officers and 118 enlisted men by disease. The Forty-fourth New York lost four officers and 178 enlisted men killed and mortally wounded, and two officers and 145 enlisted men by disease. The long lines of soldiers shown in these photographs have already looked death in the face, and will do so again; the Westerners at Atlanta and Kenesaw, the New Yorkers in the Wilderness and before Petersburg.

on every field from First Bull Run, but the cheer was for the gallant fellows who had fought so bravely and so well. It was the tribute of innate chivalry to a conquered foe, and many an officer, listening a moment in mute appreciation, suddenly swung his cap on high and joined the cheer, or, too much moved to speak, unsheathed the sword that so long had flashed in defiance of the Southern cause, and in silence lowered the battle-worn blade in salute to Southern valor.

For that was the lesson learned by these men who had borne the brunt of so many a desperate battle; for this army was the finished product of four long years of the sternest discipline, the hardest fighting, the heaviest losses known to modern warfare. The beardless boys of the farm, school, and shop had been trained by the hand of masters in the art to the highest duties of the soldier of the Nation; and now, their stern task ended, their victory won, it was theirs to be the first to take this foeman by the hand, comfort him with food and drink, and words of soldier cheer and sympathy, and then, turning back from the trampled fields of Virginia, to march yet once again through the echoing avenues of Washington, to drape their colors and to droop their war-worn crests in mourning for their martyred, yet immortal President, to place their battle-flags under the dome of the Capitol of their States, and then, unobtrusively to melt away and become absorbed in the throng of their fellow citizens, conscious of duty faithfully performed, and intent now only on reverent observance of the last lesson of him who had been through all their patient, prayerful, heaven-inspired leader. "To bind up the Nation's wounds; to care for him who shall have borne the battle, and for his widow and his orphan—to do all which may achieve and cherish a just and lasting peace among ourselves, and with all nations."

THE SECRET SERVICE
OF THE
FEDERAL ARMIES

WILLIAM WILSON—A SCOUT
WITH THE ARMY OF THE POTOMAC

THE FAMOUS ALLAN PINKERTON—THE MONTH OF THE BATTLE OF ANTIETAM

The name of Allan Pinkerton became one of the most famous in secret-service work, the world over. This keen-witted detective came to America from Scotland about twenty years before the opening of the Civil War. He was conducting a successful agency in Chicago when his friend, George B. McClellan, sent for him to be chief detective in the Department of the Ohio. Shortly after, he went to Washington and under General McClellan directed the secret-service operations in the Army of the Potomac, besides doing extensive detective work for the provost-marshal at the Capital. As a stanch admirer of McClellan, Pinkerton refused to continue in the military end of the service after the general's removal in November, 1862. He remained, however, in Government service, investigating cotton claims in New Orleans, with other detective work, until the close of the war, when he returned to his agency in Chicago.

AT THE TENT OF McCLELLAN'S CHIEF DETECTIVE, 1862

Only a handful of people, in North and South together, knew the identity of "Major Allen," as, cigar in hand, he sat before his tent in 1862. His real name was Allan Pinkerton. As the head of his famous detective agency, he had been known by General McClellan before the war. He was chosen as the head of "Little Mac's" secret service, and remained until McClellan himself retired in November, 1862, only a month after this picture was made. Directly behind "Major Allen" stands young Babcock (in the same costume that he wears with his beautiful horse in the frontispiece), between George H. Bangs and Augustus K. Littlefield, two operatives. The man seated at Pinkerton's right is William Moore, private secretary to Edwin M. Stanton, the Secretary of War, down from the Capital to consult Pinkerton.

A NEW SECRET SERVICE—THE "MILITARY INFORMATION BUREAU"

After Pinkerton's departure from the Army of the Potomac, the secret-service department was allowed to fall into hopeless neglect. All organization vanished. When General Hooker assumed command there was hardly a record or document of any kind at headquarters to give information of what the Confederates were doing. Hooker was as ignorant of what was going on just across the Rappahannock as if his opponents had been in China. With the energy that marked his entire course of organization, he put Colonel George H. Sharpe, of the 120th New York regiment, in charge of a special and separate bureau, known as Military Information. Sharpe was appointed deputy provost-marshal-general. From March 30, 1863, until the close of the war, the Bureau of Military Information, Army of the Potomac, had no other head. Gathering a staff of keen-witted men, chiefly from the ranks, Sharpe never let his com-

RESTING AFTER THE HARD WORK OF THE GETTYSBURG CAMPAIGN

manding general suffer for lack of proper information as to the strength and movements of Lee's army. The Confederate advance into Pennsylvania, in June, taxed the resources of the bureau greatly. Scouts and special agents, as well as signal-men, were kept in incessant action, locating and following the various detachments of the invading force. It was a difficult matter to estimate, from the numerous reports and accounts received daily, just what Lee was trying to do. The return to Virginia brought some relief to the secret-service men. In August, while Lee hastened back to the old line of the Rapidan, Colonel Sharpe lay at Bealeton, and here the army photographer took his picture, as above, on the extreme left. Next to him sits John C. Babcock; the right-hand figure is that of John McEntee, detailed from the 80th New York Infantry. These men were little known, but immensely useful.

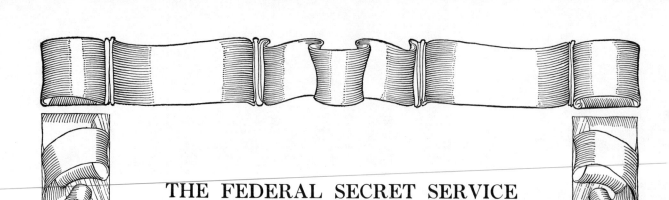

THE FEDERAL SECRET SERVICE

By George H. Casamajor

THERE was one fact that became evident with startling emphasis to the American people the moment secession was established, and this was that it was not political ties alone that had held the Union together. Financial, commercial, and domestic bonds had, in seventy years, so stretched from North to South that to divide and disrupt the social organism was a much more difficult feat to accomplish than mere political separation upon a point of Constitutional interpretation. An unparalleled state of public confusion developed in the early months of 1861, which was all the worse because there was little or no uncertainty in the individual mind. Probably every citizen of the country capable of reason had reached conviction upon the points at issue.

Not only the Government at Washington but the whole world was astounded that the new Confederacy could bring at once into the field a military force superior in numbers to the standing army of the United States. Every department at the capital was disorganized by the defection of employees whose opinions and ties bound them to the cause of the South. Legislators in both houses, cabinet officers, and judges volunteered their services in the making of the new nation. Ministers and consuls hastened from foreign countries to enter its councils or fight for its existence. Army and navy officers left their posts and resigned their commissions for commands under another standard. The Episcopal bishop of Louisiana exchanged the surplice for the uniform and rode at the head of an army corps.

Opinion was positive, but it did not separate along

SCOUTS AND GUIDES IN THE ARMY OF THE POTOMAC

The individuals in the group were attached to the secret-service department of the Army of the Potomac when it was directed by Allan Pinkerton. Many of these men who were gathered for service on the Peninsula were known as Pamunkey Indians, relics of a small Virginia tribe which had intermarried considerably with the Negroes. They were very loyal to the Union, and their services were invaluable to McClellan during the spring and summer of 1862. After Pinkerton left the army, the whole secret-service department was reorganized by Colonel Sharpe, and he drew more largely from the ranks for the composition of his force. Whenever these men were captured they were hanged as spies.

geographic lines. Thousands in the North believed sincerely in the justice of the Southern cause. Business men dealing largely with the South realized that hostilities would reduce them to poverty. Northern men established in Southern territory, solicitous for their fortunes and their families, found that an oath of allegiance would mean the confiscation of their property and the ruin of their hopes. Political combinations and secret societies in the most loyal parts of the Union were aiding the new Government to establish itself on a firm basis. Individuals, for reasons more or less advantageous to themselves, were supplying men, money, materials of war, and supplies to the Confederacy.

This review of existing conditions is necessary to understand the full scope of the secret service which was necessary in order that the Federal Government might comprehend and grapple with the situation. Congress had not anticipated the emergency and made no provisions for it, but the Constitution gives the President extraordinary powers to suppress insurrection, and these were employed at once and with energy. Most important was the organization of that branch of the military service whose function it is to obtain information as to the adversary's resources and plans, and to prevent like news from reaching the opponents. But the work of fighting was only a portion of the task. All communication between the North and South was carefully watched. The statutes of the post-office were arbitrarily changed and its sacredness violated, in order to prevent its use as a means of conveying information. Passengers to and from foreign countries were subjected to new passport regulations. A trade blockade was instituted. The writ of habeas corpus was suspended in many places, and all persons who were believed to be aiding the South in any way were arrested by special civil and military agents and placed in military custody for examination. Most of this, it will be evident, had to be accomplished by means of detection known as "secret service."

IN THE HEART OF THE HOSTILE COUNTRY—MAY, 1862

As the secret-service men sit at Follen's house, near Cumberland Landing, all is ready for the advance to the Chickahominy and to Richmond. The scouts and guides are aware that there is hard and dangerous work before them. Their skilful leader, whom they know as Major Allen, sits apart from the group at the table, smoking his pipe and thinking hard. He must send his men into the Confederate lines to find out how strong is the opposing army. Probably some of them will never come back. The men were new to the work, and had not yet learned to approximate the numbers of large masses of troops. Thus it happened that Pinkerton greatly overestimated the size of the Army of Northern Virginia, and McClellan acted as if dealing with an overwhelming opponent. Had he discovered that he greatly outnumbered the Confederates, the war in the East might have been ended by the 1st of July, 1862.

The Federal Government was, in the beginning, lacking in any organized secret service. The Department of State, the Department of War, and the Department of the Navy each took a hand in early attempts to define the line between loyalty and disloyalty to the Union cause, but upon that of State fell the greater share of the effort. Secretary Seward engaged a force of detectives, and sent them to Canada and frontier places to intercept all communication between the British dominion and the South. He assigned other secret agents to the specific task of stopping the sale of shoes for the Confederate army. The police chiefs of Northern cities were requested to trail and arrest suspected persons. No newspaper editorial that might be construed as containing sentiments disloyal to the Union appeared in print but some one sent a copy to Washington, and, if necessary, the offending journal was suppressed.

The police commissioners of Baltimore were arrested, as was also a portion of the Maryland legislature. So active was the multifarious work of the secret service that the prisons at Forts Warren, Lafayette, and McHenry were soon over-flowing with prisoners of state and war. Distracted wardens pleaded that there was no room for more, but it was not until the middle of February, 1862, that relief was afforded. By this time the Government felt that the extent of all forms of activity in the Southern cause within the existing Union were well understood and under control. The President was anxious to return to a more normal course of administration and issued an order for the release on parole of all political and state prisoners, except such detained as spies or otherwise inimicable to public safety. Henceforth, important arrests were made under the direction of the military authorities alone.

These, meanwhile, had not been idle, since detective work in regard to the plans and movements of the foe has always been one of the most important departments of warfare. The organization of the Federal military secret service involved no complicated machinery. In every military department the

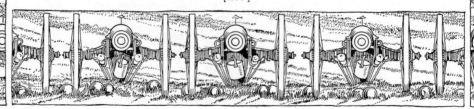

PINKERTON ENTERTAINS VISITORS FROM WASHINGTON

DETECTIVE WORK FOR THE
FEDERAL ADMINISTRATION

The proximity ot the headquarters cf the Army of the Potomac to the National Capital, after the battle of Antietam, drew many visitors from Washington during the pleasant October days of 1862. Naturally they spent some time with Allan Pinkerton, whom they knew as Major Allen, for he had come to be a prominent figure in the city. There he made his headquarters, and could be found when not in the field with the commanding-general. In the Capital city there was much work to do of a kind for which Pinkerton was already famous. When he arrived from

A CHARACTERISTIC POSE

Chicago shortly after the first battle of Bull Run, he brought his entire force with him and began to investigate people suspected of assisting the Confederate cause by sending information secretly to Richmond and the Southern armies in the field. He made a number of important arrests, both in Washington and in Baltimore, acting under orders from Provost-Marshal Andrew Porter, as well as General McClellan and the heads of the Departments of State and War. Several of his most skilful operatives, both men and women, were constantly traveling between Richmond and Washington, bringing valuable information of the plans of President Davis and his advisers, military and civil.

commander appointed a chief detective who gathered about him such a force of soldiers and civilians as he required to perform the work of espionage and investigation. These detectives were responsible to the heads of the military departments. Besides these the War Department employed special agents who reported directly to the secretary.

The imagination is apt to enwrap the character of the detective or spy in an atmosphere of mystery and excitement, against which these individuals are generally the first to protest. An aptitude for the work naturally implies an amount of fearlessness and daring which deadens the feeling of danger and affords real pleasure in situations involving great risk. We must picture the successful secret-service agent as keen-witted, observant, resourceful, and possessing a small degree of fear, yet realizing the danger and consequences of detection.

His work, difficult as it is to describe precisely, lay, in general, along three lines. In the first place, all suspected persons must be found, their sentiments investigated and ascertained. The members of the secret service obtained access to houses, clubs, and places of resort, sometimes in the guise of guests, sometimes as domestics, as the needs of the case seemed to warrant. As the well-known and time-honored shadow detectives, they tracked footsteps and noted every action. Agents, by one means or another, gained membership in hostile secret societies and reported their meetings, by which means many plans of the Southern leaders were ascertained. The most dangerous service was naturally that of entering the Confederate ranks for information as to the nature and strength of defenses and numbers of troops. Constant vigilance was maintained for the detection of the Confederate spies, the interception of mail-carriers, and the discovery of contraband goods. All spies, "contrabands," deserters, refugees, and prisoners of war found in or brought into Federal territory were subjected to a searching examination and reports upon their testimony forwarded to the various authorities.

"MAJOR" PAULINE CUSHMAN, THE FEDERAL SPY WHO BARELY ESCAPED HANGING

Pauline Cushman was a clever actress, and her art fitted her well to play the part of a spy. Although a native of New Orleans, she spent much of her girlhood in the North, and was so devoted to the Union that she risked her life in its secret service. The Federal Government employed her first in the hunt for Southern sympathizers and spies in Louisville, and the discovery of how they managed to convey information and supplies into the territory of the Confederacy. She performed the same work in Nashville. In May, 1863, as Rosecrans was getting ready to drive Bragg across the Tennessee River, Miss Cushman was sent into the Confederate lines to obtain information as to the strength and location of the Army of Tennessee. She was captured, tried by court-martial, and sentenced to be hanged. In the hasty evacuation of Shelbyville, in the last days of June, she was overlooked and managed to regain the Union lines. It was impossible to describe the joy of the soldiers when they found the brave spy, whom they had thought of as dead, once more in their midst. Her fame after this spread all over the land. The soldiers called her "Major" and she wore the accouterments of that rank. Her accurate knowledge of the roads of Tennessee, Georgia, Alabama, and Mississippi was of great value to the commander of the Army of the Cumberland.

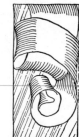

As the conflict progressed the activities of the baser elements of society placed further burdens upon the secret service. Smuggling, horse-stealing, and an illicit trade in liquor with the army were only the lesser of the many crimes that inevitably arise from a state of war. Government employees and contractors conspired to perpetrate frauds. The practice of bounty-jumping assumed alarming proportions. Soldiers' discharges were forged and large sums collected upon them. Corrupt political organizations attempted to tamper with the soldiers' vote. The suppression of all this was added to the already heavy labors of the secret agents.

There were, from the very beginning, several strongly concentrated centers of suspicion, and of these probably the most important and dangerous was located within the higher social circles of the city of Washington itself. In the spring of 1861, the capital was filled with people suspected of supplying information to the Confederate authorities. These Southern men and women did not forget the cause which their friends and families in the home-land were preparing valiantly to defend. Aristocratic people still opened their doors to those high in office, and who could tell what fatal secrets might be dropped by the guests, or inadvertently imparted, to be sent to the leaders of the South? Nor were the activities confined entirely to homes. At office doors in the department buildings the secret agents watched and waited to learn some scrap of information; military maps and plans were often missing after the exit of some visitor.

Such vital information as this was constantly sent across the Potomac: "In a day or two, twelve hundred cavalry supported by four batteries of artillery will cross the river above to get behind Manassas and cut off railroad and other communications with our army whilst an attack is made in front. For God's sake heed this. It is positive." And again: "To-day I have it in my power to say that Kelley is to advance on Winchester. Stone and Banks are to cross and go to

GUERRILLA AND SCOUT—"TINKER DAVE" BEATTY WITH DR. HALE

General Crook, writing to General James A. Garfield, chief of staff, Army of the Cumberland, in March, 1863, asked, "Who is 'Tinker Dave' Beatty?" One would like to learn what Crook had heard about the tinker. There is no record that Garfield ever replied to the question, and perhaps he, too, knew very little of this famous character. David Beatty was the leader of an irregular band of guerrillas working in the Federal cause throughout middle Tennessee. The Confederate officers, to whom they gave constant trouble, refer to them as "bushwhackers" and "tories." Especially annoying were Beatty and his men to Captain John M. Hughs, commanding a small detachment from Bragg's army. Hughs attempted to stop Beatty's marauding expeditions. On September 8, 1863, he attacked Beatty, killing eight of his men and putting the rest to rout. Again on February 14, 1864, Hughs fell upon Beatty, who this time had a band of about one hundred. The Confederate troops killed seventeen and captured two of the band, and the remainder disappeared. Beatty continued his irregular activities from time to time. He often worked in connection with Dr. Jonathan P. Hale, who was the chief of scouts of the Army of the Cumberland under Rosecrans and Thomas. Both leaders valued Hale's services highly. He kept special watch on Morgan, Forrest, and Wheeler when they were in his neighborhood, making constant reports as to their strength and location.

Leesburg. Burnside's fleet is to engage the batteries on the Potomac, and McClellan and Company will move on Centreville and Manassas next week. This information comes from one of McClellan's aides."

In the secret-service work at Washington the famous name of Allan Pinkerton is conspicuous, but it is not on the records, as during his entire connection with the war he was known as E. J. Allen, and some years elapsed before his identity was revealed. Pinkerton, a Scotchman by birth, had emigrated to the United States about twenty years before, and had met with considerable success in the conduct of a detective agency in Chicago. He was summoned to grapple with the difficult situation in Washington as early as April, 1861. He was willing to lay aside his important business and put his services at the disposal of the Government. But just here he found his efforts hampered by department routine, and he soon left to become chief detective to General McClellan, then in charge of the Department of the Ohio.

When this secret service was well established, Pinkerton went to Washington, shortly after the first battle of Bull Run. He immediately pressed his entire staff of both sexes into the work, but even that was insufficient for the demands upon it. Applications came in on all sides and not the least of the problems was the selection of new members.

Pinkerton was in daily contact with and made reports to the President, Secretary of War, the provost-marshal-general and the general-in-chief of the armies. But his connection with the military concerns of the Government was brief. In November, 1862, McClellan, to whom Pinkerton was sincerely attached, was removed. Indignant at this treatment, the detective refused to continue longer at Washington. He was, however, afterward employed in claim investigations, and at the close of the war returned to Chicago.

Later on, when Hooker took command of the Army of the Potomac, Colonel George H. Sharpe was placed at the

In April, 1862, **J. J.** Andrews, a citizen of Kentucky and a spy in General Buell's employment, proposed seizing a locomotive on the Western and Atlantic Railroad at some point below Chattanooga and running it back to that place, cutting telegraph wires and burning bridges on the way. General O. **M.**

Mitchel authorized the plan and twenty-two men volunteered to carry it out. On the morning of April 12th, the train they were on stopped at Big Shanty station for breakfast. The bridge-burners (who were in citizens' clothes) detached the locomotive and three box-cars and started at full speed for Chattanooga, but after a run of about a hundred miles their fuel was exhausted and their pursuers were in sight. The whole party was captured. Andrews was condemned as a spy and hanged at Atlanta, July 7th. The others were confined at Chattanooga, Knoxville, and afterward at Atlanta, where seven were executed as spies. Of the fourteen survivors, eight escaped from prison; and of these, six eventually reached the Union lines. Six were removed to Richmond and confined in Castle Thunder until they were exchanged in 1863. The Confederates attempted to destroy the locomotive when they evacuated Atlanta.

head of the Bureau of Military Information and supervised all its secret-service work until the close of the war. He brought the bureau to a state of great efficiency. Lieutenant H. B. Smith was chief detective of the Middle Department, which comprised Maryland, Delaware, and part of Virginia. His headquarters was at Baltimore, one of the most fertile fields for the work of the secret service. This city, of all that remained within the Union, was probably the most occupied in aiding and abetting the cause of the South.

Smith gathered about him a staff of about forty soldiers and civilians, and an immense amount of significant information as to the plans and movements of the citizens, some of them of great prominence, began to pour into the provost-marshal's office. Many schemes were frustrated and the offenders arrested. The numerous coves and bays of the Chesapeake offered secure harbors and secluded landing-places for contraband vessels. On one occasion, Smith and two of his assistants came upon a fleet of a dozen schooners riding at anchor in an isolated spot. The crews were unarmed and the three agents succeeded in capturing the entire lot of blockade-runners with their rich cargoes.

Spies and mail-carriers were constantly apprehended and their activities interrupted. Deserters were pursued and brought to justice. In March, 1865, one Lewis Payne was arrested in Baltimore on a criminal charge. Smith believed the man to be a spy, but a searching examination failed to procure any definite evidence. The cautious detective, however, made him take the oath of allegiance, and recommended his release on condition that he would go to some point north of Philadelphia and remain there until the close of the war. A month later Payne committed the attack on William H. Seward and others at the secretary's Washington home.

During the presidential campaign of 1864, certain party powers at Albany were striving for the election. They sent their political agents to various voting-agencies of the New

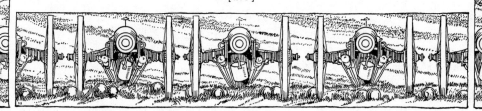

COLONEL SHARPE GETTING READY FOR THE LAST GRAND MOVE—1864

In the spring of 1864, the headquarters of the Army of the Potomac was near Brandy Station, Virginia. One of the busiest spots is shown in this picture—the headquarters of Colonel Sharpe, deputy provost-marshal-general, who was organizing his scouts and secret-service men for the coming campaign. It is April, and although no one knows yet what the new General-in-Chief purposes doing, he has announced his intention of making his headquarters with the Army of the Potomac. Many scouting parties have been sent southward beyond the Rapidan, where the Army of Northern Virginia lies entrenched. Sutlers and their employees have been ordered to leave the army. General Patrick, the provost-marshal-general, has recalled all permits granted citizens to remain within the lines; leaves of absence and furloughs have been revoked; army-lists have been called for. The secret-service men around Colonel Sharpe's quarters know that they will soon be off on their many dangerous missions, as the eyes and ears of the moving army.

York troops with instructions to forge the officers' affidavits that accompanied the votes and turn in illegal ballots for their candidate. The keen eye of Smith detected an unknown abbreviation of the word "Cavalry" on one of the signatures, and this led to the exposure of the plot and the arrest of three of the corrupt agents. The detective also did much work in western Maryland and West Virginia in observing and locating the homes of Mosby's famous raiders who were a source of great trouble to the Federal army.

Other missions often took Smith outside the boundaries of his department. In the guise of a New York merchant he took into custody in Washington a Confederate agent who was endeavoring to dispose of bonds and scrip. Many visits to New York and Philadelphia were made in connection with bounty-jumping and other frauds, and he once arrested in New York an agent of the Confederacy who was assisting in the smuggling of a valuable consignment of tobacco. All this was combined with various and hazardous trips south of the Potomac, when necessary, in search of information concerning the strength and position of Confederate defenses and troops. It all denotes a life of ceaseless activity, but it is very typical of the secret agents' work during the Civil War.

In addition to the various detective forces in the field, the War Department had its special agents directly under the control of the President and the Secretary of War. These, too, were employed in the multiform duties previously outlined. One of the most noted of the special agents, Colonel Lafayette C. Baker, was a New Yorker by birth who had removed to California, but was in the East when the conflict opened. He hastened to put his services at the command of the Union, and on account of his work on the Vigilance Committee in the stormy days of 1856, was engaged as a detective in the Department of State.

The authorities at Washington were most anxious to obtain information as to the Confederate force at Manassas.

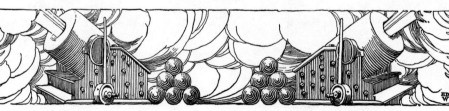

LATER SCOUTS AND GUIDES
ARMY OF THE POTOMAC

As the Federal secret service developed under experience, a great change came over the personnel of its members. Less and less were civilians employed. Instead, capable scouts were drafted from the army. Much had been learned through the excellent results obtained by the Confederate scouts, who were chiefly the daring cavalrymen of Ashby, Morgan, Wheeler, and Forrest. In this picture appears a group of scouts and guides headed by Lieutenant Robert Klein, Third Indiana Cavalry, who spent some time with the Army of the Potomac. On the ground by his side is his young son. Many of the men here depicted were among the most noted of the army's secret-service men. Standing at the back are James Doughty, James Cammock, and Henry W. Dodd. On the ground are Dan Plue, W. J. Lee, — Wood, Sanford Magee, and John W. Landegon. Seated at the left is John Irving, and on the right is Daniel Cole, seen again on page 289.

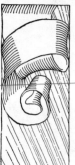

Five men had been sent to Richmond; of these two had been killed, and the others were thought to be prisoners. In July, 1861, Baker started for the Confederate capital. He was promptly arrested but managed to convince both General Beauregard and President Davis that he belonged in Tennessee. So cleverly was the part played that he was sent North as a Confederate agent, and before the end of three weeks was able to give General Scott a vast amount of valuable information regarding Manassas, Fredericksburg, and Richmond, together with the plans of the Confederate leaders, and the scheme for blockade-running on the Potomac. After that he reported on suspected persons in Baltimore, and was sent to Niagara Falls to watch and arrest the Southern agents there.

When in February, 1862, the secret service came directly under the control of the War Department, Baker was employed as special agent. He was given a commission as colonel and organized the First District of Columbia Cavalry, a regiment chiefly employed in the defense and regulation of the National capital, although it saw some service in the field.

Baker's concerns were chiefly with matters that had little to do with the active conduct of the war. He took charge of all abandoned Confederate property; he investigated the fraudulent practices of contractors; he assisted the Treasury Department in unearthing counterfeiters; he was the terror of the bounty-jumper, and probably did more than anyone else to suppress the activities of that vicious citizen. His last notable achievement in the secret service was the pursuit and capture of the assassin of Abraham Lincoln.

Another valuable agent in the War Department was William P. Wood, superintendent of the Old Capitol Prison, at Washington. In pursuit of his duties Mr. Wood was in daily contact with the most important of the military prisoners who fell into the clutches of the Federal Government. He lost no opportunity of gaining any sort of information in regard to the workings of the Confederacy and the plans of its armies,

SECRET–SERVICE HEADQUARTERS IN THE LAST MONTHS OF THE WAR

During the winter of 1864–65, General Grant had his headquarters at City Point, Virginia, and the building occupied by the secret-service men is shown here, as well as a group of scouts who are as idle as the two armies in the Petersburg trenches. But a few weeks' work in the opening spring, as Grant maneuvers to starve Lee out of Petersburg, and the scouts' duties will be over. Sheridan will come, too, from the Shenandoah with his cavalry scouts, the finest body of information seekers developed by the war. General Grant was in a constant state of uneasiness during the winter, fearing that Lee would leave his strong lines around Petersburg and unite with Johnston. Consequently he depended on his secret-service men to keep him informed as to any signs of movement on the part of Lee.

and his reports to the Secretary were looked upon as among the most helpful that reached the department.

The maintenance of the secret service was a large item in the conduct of the war. The expenses of the provost-marshal's office at Washington alone, covering a period of nearly three years, were nearly $175,000 for detective service and incidental expense. This, of course, was only a small portion of the total outlay.

In dealing with the secret service the words " spies " and " scouts " are constantly used. A clear and definite distinction between the two is indeed difficult to make. By far the greater number of persons described as spies in an account of the war would be classed as scouts by a military man. To such a one the word " spy " would most often mean a person who was located permanently within the lines or territory of the opponent and applied himself to the collection of all information that would be valuable to his military chief. The latter communicated with his spies by means of his scouts, who took messages to and fro. The real spies seldom came out. Scouts were organized under a chief who directed their movements. Their duties were various—bearing despatches, locating the foe, and getting precise information about roads, bridges, and fords that would facilitate the march of the army. Thus many opportunities for genuine spy work came to the scout and hence the confusion in the use of the terms, which is increased by the fact that an arrested scout is usually referred to as a spy.

The use and number of Federal spies were greatly increased as the war went on and in the last year the system reached a high degree of efficiency, with spies constantly at work in all the Confederate armies and in all the cities of the South. In the very anonymity of these men lay a large part of their usefulness. The names of a few, who occupied high places or met with tragic ends, have been rescued from obscurity. Those of the remainder are not to be found on any rolls of honor. They remain among the unknown heroes of history.

PART II

MILITARY INFORMATION

THE SECRET SERVICE
OF THE
CONFEDERACY

UNCONSCIOUS ALLIES OF THE CONFEDERACY—
NEWSPAPER CORRESPONDENTS IN THE FIELD WITH
THE UNION ARMY, WHOSE MOVEMENTS WERE MANY
TIMES REVEALED BY NEWSPAPER DESPATCHES
SUPPLYING INFORMATION TO THE SOUTHERNERS.

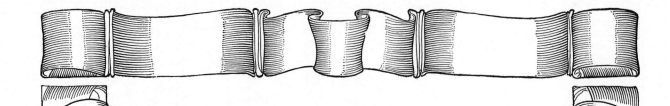

THE CONFEDERATE SECRET SERVICE

By John W. Headley
Captain, Confederate States Army

THE Confederate States had no such secret-service organization as was developed and used by the Federal Government during the Civil War, and yet it is probably true that, in the matter of obtaining needed military information, the Confederacy was, on the whole, better served than was the North. Of course, many uses of the Federal secret service were not necessary in the South. The Government at Washington had to face at once the tremendous problem of separating in the non-seceding States loyalty from disloyalty to the idea that the Union formed under the Constitution was a unit and could not be divided. Thousands of citizens in the North not only denied the right of the Federal Government to invade and coerce the South, but in this belief many stood ready to aid the Confederate cause.

From such conditions as these the Southern States were practically free. They contained nothing that the North needed for the coming conflict, while the latter had much to give. The prevention of assistance to the North was not one of the problems of existence. So, while a certain class of spies and detectives for the Union and the Confederacy operated on both sides of the dividing line, the Confederacy needed none of these in its own territory. Capable devotees of the South readily volunteered for secret service within the Federal military lines or territory, while the United States Government was compelled to organize and employ several classes of spies and detectives all over the North, for the purpose of suppressing bounty-jumpers, fraudulent discharges, trade in contra-

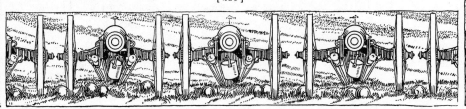

NANCY HART

THE CONFEDERATE GUIDE AND SPY

The women of the mountain districts of Virginia were as ready to do scout and spy work for the Confederate leaders as were their men-folk. Famous among these fearless girls who knew every inch of the regions in which they lived was Nancy Hart. So valuable was her work as a guide, so cleverly and often had she led Jackson's cavalry upon the Federal outposts in West Virginia, that the Northern Government offered a large reward for her capture. Lieutenant-Colonel Starr of the Ninth West Virginia finally caught her at Summerville in July, 1862. While in a temporary prison, she faced the camera for the first time in her life, displaying more alarm in front of the innocent contrivance than if it had been a body of Federal soldiery. She posed for an itinerant photographer, and her captors placed the hat decorated with a military feather upon her head. Nancy managed to get hold of her guard's musket, shot him dead, and escaped on Colonel Starr's horse to the nearest Confederate detachment. A few days later, July 25th, she led two hundred troopers under Major Bailey to Summerville. They reached the town at four in the morning, completely surprising two companies of the Ninth West Virginia. They fired three houses, captured Colonel Starr, Lieutenant Stivers and other officers, and a large number of the men, and disappeared immediately over the Sutton road. The Federals made no resistance.

band goods, and contract frauds, thus maintaining a large force which was prevented from doing any kind of secret service within the Southern lines or territory.

The personality, the adventures, and the exploits of the Confederate scouts and spies are seldom noted in the annals of the war, and yet these unknown patriots were often a controlling factor in the hostilities. Generals depended largely on the information they brought, in planning attack and in accepting or avoiding battle. It is indeed a notable fact that a Confederate army was never surprised in an important engagement of the war.

Apart from the military service in the field, the State Department at Richmond maintained a regular line of couriers at all periods between the capital and Maryland, and thus kept familiar with every phase of the war situation at Washington and in the North. The operations of these skilful secret agents gave constant employment to the detective force of the Federal Middle Department. One efficient means of securing information was through agents at Washington, Baltimore, New York, and other Northern points, who used the cipher and inserted personals in friendly newspapers, such as the New York *News, Express,* and *Day Book.* These journals were hurried through to Richmond. At the opening of the war many well-known people of Baltimore and Washington were as hostile to the Federal Government as were the inhabitants of Richmond and New Orleans, and these were of great service to the Southern armies.

Colonel Thomas Jordan, adjutant-general of the Confederate forces under General Beauregard at Manassas, made arrangements with several Southern sympathizers at Washington for the transmission of war information, which in almost every instance proved to be extremely accurate. On July 4, 1861, some Confederate pickets captured a Union soldier who was carrying on his person the returns of McDowell's army. "His statement of the strength and composition of

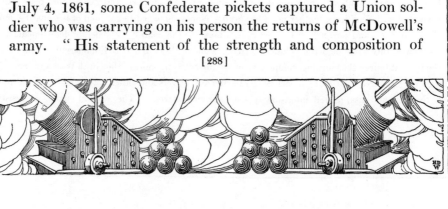

OLD CAPITOL PRISON, WASHINGTON, IN THE EARLY DAYS OF THE WAR

This historic building once the temporary Capitol of the United States, played a large part in the workings of the Federal secret service; its superintendent, William P. Wood, was a special secret agent of the War Department. It was used for the incarceration of many Confederate prisoners of war, suspects and political offenders. Mr. Wood frequently subjected his wards to searching examination. Information thus gained was immediately forwarded to the Secretary of War. Mrs. Greenhow, Belle Boyd, Mrs. Morris, M. T. Walworth, Josiah E. Bailey, Pliny Bryan, and other famous Confederate spies spent some time within its walls. The advantage gained by the Confederate secret agents was often nullified through the counter information secured by the Federal scouts. The photograph shows one of Colonel Sharpe's trusted men, a private of the Third Indiana Cavalry, who would often lead out a party of scouts to get information as to the location and strength of the various parts of the Army of Northern Virginia. These men would go forward until they discovered the line of Confederate pickets, and then use all their trained powers of observation to find out what was behind it. Citizens in the neighborhood were closely questioned, and all the information procurable was turned in to Colonel Sharpe.

DANIEL COLE, A FEDERAL SCOUT

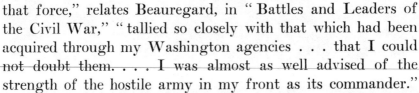

that force," relates Beauregard, in "Battles and Leaders of the Civil War," "tallied so closely with that which had been acquired through my Washington agencies . . . that I could not doubt them. . . . I was almost as well advised of the strength of the hostile army in my front as its commander."

Not only that, but Beauregard had timely and accurate knowledge of McDowell's advance to Manassas. A former government clerk was sent to Mrs. Rose O'Neal Greenhow, at Washington, who was one of the trusted friends of the Confederacy and most loyal to its cause. She returned word in cipher immediately, "Order issued for McDowell to march upon Manassas to-night," and the vitally important despatch was in Beauregard's hands between eight and nine o'clock on that same night, July 16, 1861. Every outpost commander was immediately notified to fall back to the positions designated for this contingency, and Johnston in the Valley, who had likewise been informed by careful scouting parties that Patterson was making no move upon him, was able to exercise the option permitted by the Richmond authorities in favor of a swift march to Beauregard's assistance.

Thus "opportunely informed," the Confederate leader prepared for battle without orders or advice from Richmond. The whole of these momentous Confederate activities were carried out through the services of couriers, spies, and scouts. In the opening of the war, at least, the Confederate spy and scout system was far better developed than was the Federal.

As the war went on, each commanding general relied upon his own spies and the scouts of his cavalry leader. Colonel J. Stoddard Johnston was a nephew of Albert Sidney Johnston and served on General Bragg's staff from Stone's River to Chattanooga. All through this important campaign he had charge of the secret-service orders and reports. He has related how he always utilized soldiers of known intelligence, honor, and daring as spies, without extra compensation, and employed the cavalrymen of Wheeler, Morgan, and Forrest

BELLE BOYD—A FAMOUS SECRET AGENT OF THE CONFEDERACY

This ardent daughter of Virginia ran many hazards in her zeal to aid the Confederate cause. Back and forth she went from her home at Martinsburg, in the Valley, through the Federal lines, while Banks, Frémont, and Shields were trying in vain to crush "Stonewall" Jackson and relieve Washington from the bugbear of attack. Early in 1862 she was sent as a prisoner to Baltimore. However, General Dix, for lack of evidence, decided to send her home. This first adventure did not dampen her ardor or stop her activities. Since she was now well known to the Federals, her every movement was watched. In May she started to visit relatives in Richmond, but at Winchester happened to overhear some plans of General Shields. With this knowledge she rushed to General Ashby with information that assisted Jackson in planning his brilliant charge on Front Royal. On May 21st she was arrested at the Federal picket-line. A search showed that she had been entrusted with important letters to the Confederate army. About the 1st of August Miss Boyd was taken to Washington by order of the Secretary of War, incarcerated in the Old Capitol Prison and was afterward sent South.

as scouts. It was the same with Lee and the commanders in the Trans-Mississippi Department.

In "Stonewall" Jackson's 1862 campaign against Banks, Fremont, and Shields in the Valley of Virginia, the Federal forces were defeated, within a month, in five battles by an army that aggregated one-fifth their total, though divided, numbers. This great achievement must not be attributed entirely to the genius of Jackson and the valor of his army. A part of the glory must be given to the unknown daring spies and faithful scouts of Ashby's cavalry, who were darting, day and night, in all directions. Their unerring information enabled Jackson to strike and invariably escape. On the other hand, the Federal generals had no such means of gathering information, and they seem never to have been protected from surprise or advised of Jackson's movements.

Among the most noted bands of Confederate scouts was one organized by General Cheatham, over which one Henry B. Shaw was put in command. Shaw, who had been a clerk on a steamboat plying between Nashville and New Orleans, had an accurate knowledge of middle Tennessee, which in the summer of 1863 was in the hands of the Federal army, owing to Bragg's retreat from Tullahoma. He assumed the disguise of an itinerant doctor while in the Federal lines, and called himself Dr. C. E. Coleman. In the Confederate army he was known as Captain C. E. Coleman, commander of General Bragg's private scouts. The scouts dressed as Confederate soldiers, so that in case of capture they would not be treated as spies. Nevertheless, the information they carried was usually put into cipher.

Shaw was finally captured and sent to Johnson's Island. The command of the famous scouts devolved upon Alexander Gregg, who continued to sign despatches "C. E. Coleman," and the Federal authorities never knew that the original leader of the daring band was in safe-keeping in Sandusky Bay.

On April 7, 1864, President Davis, at Richmond, sent the

NEW YORK HERALD HEADQUARTERS IN THE FIELD, 1863

The Confederate secret service worked through the Northern newspapers to an extent little appreciated. Without any disloyalty on the part of the newspaper men, this was necessarily the case. The North swarmed with spies, special correspondents, paid agents, Southern sympathizers by the score, and "copperheads" innumerable. It followed that Richmond often knew pretty much everything worth knowing of the disposition and preparation of the Union forces, and even of their carefully guarded plans. The Northern newspaper correspondent with the armies incurred practically all the perils that fell upon the soldier himself, and the more enterprising and successful he became, the less he ingratiated himself with the commanding generals, whose plans he predicted and whose conduct he criticised in newspaper leaders. But it was necessary that the people at home, whose money was paying for the armies in the field, should be kept informed how those armies fared, and it is safe to contend that a great debt was due to the American war-correspondents. While they were a source of information to the South on occasions, they were also active and indefatigable allies of the Northern Government, in that they persuaded the people at home to submit to the extraordinarily heavy taxation necessary to support the large and costly armies and prosecute the war to the end.

following telegram to the Honorable Jacob Thompson, in Mississippi, "If your engagements permit you to accept service abroad for the next six months, please come here immediately." Thompson was a citizen of Oxford, Mississippi, and said to be one of the wealthiest men in the South. He was, besides, a lawyer and a statesman, had served in Congress, and in the cabinet of President Buchanan as Secretary of the Interior.

The reason of the sending for Thompson was that the Confederate Government had decided to inaugurate certain hostile movements in Northern territory. Clement C. Clay, Jr., of Alabama, was selected as Mr. Thompson's fellow commissioner to head the Department of the North. Both were among the foremost public men of the Confederacy. Their mission was one of great secrecy, and if one of their projects could be successfully accomplished there was no doubt, in the opinion of the Southern Government, that the war would be brought to a speedy conclusion. Negotiations looking toward peace were opened with men like Horace Greeley and Judge Black, but the correspondence with Greeley was made public, and the matter reached an untimely end.

There existed in the Northern States an essentially military organization known as the Sons of Liberty, whose principle was that the States were sovereign and that there was no authority in the central Government to coerce a seceding State. It was estimated that the total membership of this society was fully three hundred thousand, of whom eighty-five thousand resided in Illinois, fifty thousand in Indiana, and forty thousand in Ohio. The feeling was general among the members that it would be useless to hold the coming presidential election, since Mr. Lincoln held the power and would undoubtedly be reelected. Therefore it was planned to resort to force. Plans for a revolution and a new Confederacy were promoted, in all of which the Southern commissioners took a most active interest.

The grand commander of the Sons of Liberty was C. L.

VESPASIAN CHANCELLOR

ONE OF "JEB" STUART'S KEENEST SCOUTS

The scouts were the real eyes and ears of the army. From the very beginning of the war the Confederate cavalry was much used for scouting purposes, even at the time when Federal commanders were still chiefly dependent upon civilian spies, detectives, and deserters for information as to their opponents' strength and movements. They saw the folly of this, after much disastrous experience, and came to rely like the Confederates on keen-witted cavalrymen. The true scout must be an innate lover of adventure, with the sharpest of eyesight and undaunted courage. Such was Vespasian Chancellor, one of the most successful scouts in General J. E. B. Stuart's cavalry command. He was directly attached to the general's headquarters.

Vallandigham, a sympathizer with the South, who in 1863 had been expelled from Federal territory to the Confederacy. He managed, however, to make his way to Canada, and now resided at Windsor. The prominence of his attitude against the further prosecution of the war led to his receiving the Democratic gubernatorial nomination in Ohio, and, braving rearrest, he returned home in June, 1864, ostensibly to begin the campaign, but with a far deeper purpose in view.

In brief, Vallandigham purposed by a bold, vigorous, and concerted action, engineered by the Sons of Liberty, to detach the States of Illinois, Indiana, and Ohio from the Union, if the Confederate authorities would, at the same time, move sufficient forces into Kentucky and Missouri to hold those lukewarm Federal States. The five commonwealths would thereupon organize the Northwestern Confederacy upon the basis of State sovereignty, and the former Federal Union would now be in three parts, and compelled, perforce, to end the contest with the South. The date for the general uprising was several times postponed, but finally settled for the 16th of August. Confederate officers were sent to various cities to direct the movement. Escaped Confederate prisoners were enlisted in the cause. Thompson furnished funds for perfecting county organizations. Arms were purchased in New York and secreted in Chicago.

Peace meetings were announced in various cities to prepare the public mind for the coming revolution. The first one, held in Peoria, was a decided success, but the interest it aroused had barely subsided when the publication of the Greeley correspondence marked the new Confederacy as doomed to stillbirth. The peace party in the Union was won over to the idea of letting the ballot-box in the coming presidential election decide the question of war or peace. The Sons of Liberty, none too careful as to who were admitted to membership, inadvertently elected a number of Federal spies to their ranks. Prominent members were arrested. The garrison at Camp

FEDERAL PRECAUTIONS AGAINST SURPRISE, AS PHOTOGRAPHED BY A SECRET–SERVICE ADVERSARY

The Confederates, kept out of their former stronghold at Baton Rouge, Louisiana, by the Union army of occupation, still obtained knowledge of the state of affairs there through Lytle, the photographer, who sent pictorial evidence of the Federal occupation in secrecy to the Southern leaders. The industrious and accommodating photographer, who was willing to photograph batteries, regiments, camps, headquarters, fortifications, every detail, in fact, of the Union army, did not limit himself to sending this exact knowledge through to the Confederate secret service. With flag and lantern he used to signal from the observation tower on the top of the ruins of the Baton Rouge capitol to Scott's Bluff, whence the messages were relayed to the Confederates at New Orleans. Here is pictured the wreckage of private houses torn down by Colonel Halbert E. Paine, in order that the Federal batteries might command the approaches to the town and prevent a surprise. In August, 1862, General Butler, fearing an attack on New Orleans, had decided to concentrate all the forces in his department there and ordered Colonel Paine to bring troops from Baton Rouge. The capital of Louisiana accordingly was evacuated, August 21st. Paine left the *Essex* and *Gunboat No. 7* in the Mississippi with instructions to bombard the city in case the Confederate army, then in the neighborhood, should make any attempt to enter. The citizens promised that Breckinridge's troops would not do so, and thus the town was spared.

Douglas, Chicago, was increased to seven thousand. The strength of the allies was deemed insufficient to contend with such a force, and the project was abandoned. The Confederates returned to Canada.

Before the prospects of the Northwestern Confederacy had begun to wane, Captain Charles H. Cole, one of Forrest's cavalrymen, confined as a prisoner on Johnson's Island in Sandusky Bay, made his escape. Reporting in Canada to Mr. Thompson, plans were made at once for the seizure of the United States gunboat *Michigan,* which was guarding Johnson's Island, and the release of the prisoners. The plot developed rapidly, and the services of Captain John Y. Beall of the Confederate navy were added in carrying out the scheme. The Confederates on the island were ready to overpower their guards as soon as the *Michigan* and her fourteen guns were in Beall's hands. The 19th of December was decided on for the date of the seizure. Cole, who had become very friendly with the *Michigan's* officers, was to go on board and give the signal for Beall and a boat-load of Confederates to approach and surprise the vessel. Beall, who had mustered some twenty Confederates at Windsor, was approaching Sandusky Bay in the steamer *Philo Parsons,* which he had seized, when seventeen of his men mutinied, and he was obliged to turn back. To make the failure complete, Cole fell under suspicion and was arrested even while waiting for Beall to appear.

The latter was arrested at the Suspension Bridge railway station, about the middle of December, while working on a plan to rescue seven captured Confederate generals, as they were being transferred from Johnson's Island to Fort Lafayette. He was hanged in New York, February 24, 1865, by order of a military court, for the seizure of the steamer *Philo Parsons.*

The active commissioners were also attempting to carry out an economic policy which had been suggested by Secretary of State Benjamin and developed by a Nashville banker, John

THE FIRST INDIANA HEAVY ARTILLERY AT BATON ROUGE

PHOTOGRAPHS THAT FURNISHED VALUABLE SECRET–SERVICE INFORMATION TO THE
CONFEDERATES

The clearest and most trustworthy evidence of an opponent's strength is of course an actual photograph. Such evidence, in spite of the early stage of the art and the difficulty of "running in" chemical supplies on "orders to trade," was supplied the Confederate leaders in the Southwest by Lytle, the Baton Rouge photographer—really a member of the Confederate secret service. Here are photographs of the First Indiana Heavy Artillery (formerly the Twenty-first Indiana Infantry), showing its strength and position on the arsenal grounds at Baton Rouge. As the Twenty-first Indiana, the regiment had been at Baton Rouge during the first Federal occupation, and after the fall of Port Hudson it returned there for garrison duty. Little did its officers suspect that the quiet man photographing the batteries at drill was about to convey the "information" beyond their lines to their opponents.

Porterfield by name. It was hoped thereby to work great damage to, and bring much distrust upon, the Federal finances. The Southern sympathizers in the North had, in obedience to request, converted much paper money into gold and withdrawn it from circulation. This, however, caused the price of gold to rise until it reached 290, which great figure naturally caused a change of policy. When the precious metal had fallen as low as 180, Mr. Porterfield went from Montreal, his temporary residence, to New York and began purchasing and exporting gold, selling it for sterling bills of exchange, and reconverting this into gold, the amount lost in trans-shipment being met out of the funds placed at his disposal by the commissioners. About two million dollars was thus exported, but before any perceptible disaster had been wrought upon the national finances, General Butler, in New York, arrested a former partner of Porterfield, and the latter prudently returned to Montreal.

About the 1st of September, Thompson's force of secret workers in the Southern cause had been joined by Colonel Robert M. Martin, who had been a brigade commander in Morgan's cavalry, and myself, who had served on Martin's staff. We had been detached for this service by the Secretary of War. We expected to take an active part in an attempt by the Sons of Liberty to inaugurate a revolution in New York city, to be made on the day of the presidential election, November 8th. Thompson sent Martin with seven selected Confederate officers, myself included, to report for duty to the leaders. Martin was in charge of the whole thing. The plot was exposed by Northern secret-service agents, and General Butler with ten thousand troops arrived, which so disconcerted the Sons of Liberty that the attempt was postponed. We remained in the city awaiting events, but the situation being chaotic we had nothing to do.

When Sherman burned Atlanta, November 15th, Martin proposed to fire New York city. This was agreed to by

HOW THE FEDERAL CAMP LAY BY THE ROAD OF APPROACH

A RECONNAISSANCE

BY MEANS OF THE CAMERA

Lytle, the Confederate secret agent at Baton Rouge, sent photographs of the Federal occupation from time to time to his generals. Thus they could determine just where the invading troops were located. The position of the large camps north of the State House, behind the penitentiary and near the Methodist Church, their relation to the avenues of approach, could be noted through the photographs. One of General Banks' first acts on assuming command of the Department of

THE CAMP NEAR THE PENITENTIARY

the Gulf had been to order the reoccupation of Baton Rouge. On December 17, 1862, General Grover arrived with forty-five hundred men. About five hundred Confederates who were in the town immediately departed, and Grover prepared for an attack which did not come. Baton Rouge suffered less than might have been expected during the war. Butler gave orders for its destruction in August, 1862, but on account of the many institutions it contained these were rescinded. The State House was burned December 28, 1862, but this was due to a defective flue and not to an incendiary's vandal torch.

THE CAMP IN FRONT OF THE METHODIST CHURCH

Thompson, and the project was finally undertaken by Martin and five others, including myself.

On the evening of November 25th, I went to my room in the Astor House, at twenty minutes after seven. I hung the bedclothes over the foot-board, piled chairs, drawers, and other material on the bed, stuffed newspapers into the heap, and poured a bottle of turpentine over the whole mass. I then opened a bottle of " Greek fire " and quickly spilled it on top. It blazed instantly. I locked the door and went downstairs. Leaving the key at the office, as usual, I passed out. I did likewise at the City Hotel, Everett House, and United States Hotel. At the same time Martin operated at the Hoffman House, Fifth Avenue, St. Denis, and others. Altogether our little band fired nineteen hotels. Captain Kennedy went to Barnum's Museum and broke a bottle on the stairway, creating a panic. Lieutenant Harrington did the same at the Metropolitan Theater, and Lieutenant Ashbrook at Niblo's Garden. I threw several bottles into barges of hay, and caused the only fires, for, strange to say, nothing serious resulted from any of the hotel fires. It was not discovered until the next day, at the Astor House, that my room had been set on fire. Our reliance on " Greek fire " was the cause of the failure. We found that it could not be depended upon as an agent for incendiary work. Kennedy was hanged in New York, March 25, 1865.

We left New York on the following Saturday over the Hudson River Railroad, spent Sunday at Albany, and arrived in Toronto on Monday afternoon.

Every Confederate plot in the North was fated to fail. The Federal secret service proved to be more than a match for the Sons of Liberty and the Confederates. Captain T. H. Hines, another daring officer of Morgan's command, had undertaken an even more extensive plot in Chicago for November 8th, election night. He had to assist him many escaped prisoners of war, Confederate soldiers, and members of the

THE FATE OF A CONFEDERATE SPY
BEFORE PETERSBURG
1864

The photograph gives an excellent idea of a military execution of a Confederate spy within the Federal lines. The place was in front of Petersburg; the time August, 1864. It is all terribly impressive: the double line of troops around the lonely gallows waiting for the unfortunate victim who is about to suffer an ignominious death. Many devoted sons of the South met their fate by accepting duty in the secret service and performing the work of a spy. The penalty of capture was certain death on the gallows, for the real spy wore civilian clothes and consequently could not claim the protection of the uniform. Many men refused to do most kinds of secret-service work, scouting and gathering information, unless they were permitted to wear the insignia of their calling, but sometimes it was absolutely impossible to appear in uniform, and then the worst penalty was risked. Many men, Federals and Southerners too, actuated by the most patriotic and self-denying motives, thus met death not only in shame, but also completely severed from all that was dear to them; for in their anonymity had lain the large part of their usefulness. Their names will not be found on any roll of honor. Their place is among the unknown heroes of history.

Sons of Liberty. The plot involved not only the overpowering of the little garrison at Camp Douglas, and the release of over eight thousand military prisoners, but the cutting of telegraph wires, the seizure of banks, the burning of the railroad stations, the appropriation of arms and ammunition within the city, in fact, the preparation for a general uprising in favor of terminating the war.

The Federal secret service, however, forestalled the conspirators' plans, and one hundred and six of them were arrested on November 7th. They were subsequently tried by a military court at Cincinnati, and many were sent to penitentiaries for terms ranging from three years to life.

Such were the last of the Confederate operations from Canada. The considerable force collected there gradually returned to the Confederacy. Martin and I left during the first week of February, 1865. We went from Toronto to Cincinnati and Louisville, where we attempted to kidnap the Vice President elect, Andrew Johnson, on his way to the inauguration. This failing, about ten o'clock on the morning of March 1st we went to a stable where Major Fossee of General Palmer's staff kept three fine horses. Two of these we seized, locked the surprised attendants in the stable and rode away to the South. We were at Lynchburg when Lee surrendered at Appomattox, eighteen miles away.

As we came to Salisbury, North Carolina, we met two gentlemen strolling alone in the outskirts. Martin recognized them as President Davis and Secretary of State Benjamin. We halted, and Mr. Benjamin remembered Martin. He enquired for Colonel Thompson. Continuing south, we fell in at Chester, South Carolina, with Morgan's old brigade under General Basil W. Duke, and marched in President Davis' escort as far as Washington, Georgia, where he left us all behind, and the Confederacy perished from the earth.

PART II
MILITARY
INFORMATION

THE
SIGNAL
SERVICE

CENTRAL STATION,
WASHINGTON,
SIGNALING
ACROSS THE
POTOMAC

A QUIET EVENING, BEFORE THE DANGEROUS WORK BEGAN

Fashionable folks from Washington have come to the signal camp to look at what seems a strange new pastime of the soldiers, playing with little sticks and flags and entertaining themselves at night with fireworks. But now the shadows lengthen, and the visitors are mounting their horses and about to take their places in the waiting barouche to depart. In the foreground the signal-men are lounging comfortably, feet in the air, or drowsing against the sides of their tents. Their work is done, unless practice is ordered with the rockets and lights after the nightfall. A few months from now they will be in a place where the patronizing visitors will be loth to follow. With Confederate shells shrieking about them on the Peninsula,

SIGNAL CAMP OF INSTRUCTION, AT RED HILL, GEORGETOWN, 1861

the men with the flags will dip and wave and dip again, conveying sure information to "Little Mac" more speedily than the swiftest courier. Who would grudge them these few moments of peaceful comfort at twilight when he learns that the ratio of killed to wounded in the Signal Corps was one hundred and fifty per cent., as against the usual ratio of twenty per cent. in other branches of the service? Many found their fate in Confederate prisons. Sense of duty, necessity of exposure to fire, and importance of mission were conditions frequently incompatible with personal safety—and the Signal Corps paid the price. In no other corps can be found greater devotion to duty without reward.

EXPERTS OF THE UNITED STATES SIGNAL SERVICE
PHOTOGRAPHED IN 1861

General (then Major) Myer is distinguishable, leaning against the table on the right-hand page, by the double row of buttons on his field-officer's coat. The group comprises Lieutenant Samuel T. Cushing, Second United States Infantry, with seventeen officers selected for signal duty from the noted Pennsylvania Reserve Corps. Most of the enlisted men were from the same volunteer organization. It is interesting to examine the field paraphernalia with which the corps was provided. Every man has a collapsible telescope, or a powerful field-glass. Leaning against the table is a bunch of staffs, to which the flags were attached, for wig-wagging signals. One of the signal flags is lying in front of the group, and another is extended in the breeze behind. White flags with a red center were most frequent. In case of snow, a

CHIEF SIGNAL OFFICER A. J. MYER, WITH A GROUP OF HIS SUBORDINATES
AT RED HILL

black flag was used.   Against a variegated background the red color was seen farther.   In every important campaign and on every bloody ground, these men risked their lives at the forefront of the battle, speeding stirring orders of advance, warnings of impending danger, and sullen admissions of defeat.   They were on the advanced lines of Yorktown, and the saps and trenches at Charleston, Vicksburg, and Port Hudson, near the battle-lines at Chickamauga and Chancellorsville, before the fort-crowned crest of Fredericksburg, amid the frightful carnage of Antietam, on Kenesaw Mountain deciding the fate of Allatoona, in Sherman's march to the sea, and with Grant's victorious army at Appomattox and Richmond.   They signaled to Porter clearing the central Mississippi River, and aided Farragut when forcing the passage of Mobile Bay.

"THREE"—SIGNALING FROM THE COBB'S HILL TOWER
BY THE APPOMATTOX—1864

In this second view of the Cobb's Hill signal tower, appearing in full length on the opposite page, the signal-man has dipped his flag forward in front of him—signifying "Three." Signal messages were sent by means of flags, torches, or lights, by combinations of three separate motions. With the flag or torch initially held upright, "one" was indicated by waving the flag to the left and returning it to an upright position; "two" by a similar motion to the right; and "three" by a wave or dip to the front. One or more figures constituted a letter of the alphabet, and a few combinations were used for phrases. Thus 11 indicated "A," 1221 "B," 212 "C," and so on. 12221 meant "Wait a moment"; 21112 "Are you ready?" And 3 meant the end of a word, 33 the end of a sentence, and 333 the end of a message. Where a letter was composed of several figures, the motions were made in rapid succession without any pause. Letters were separated by a very brief pause, and words or sentences were distinguished by one or more dip motions to the front; one, signifying the end of a word; two, the end of a sentence; and three, the end of a message. The tower shown in this photograph, 125 feet high, was first occupied June 14, 1864. It commanded a view of Petersburg, sections of the Petersburg and Richmond Railway, and extended reaches of the James and Appomattox Rivers. Its importance was such that the Confederates constructed a two-gun battery within a mile of it for its destruction, but it remained in use until the fall of Petersburg.

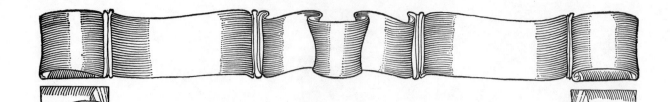

THE SIGNAL CORPS

By A. W. Greely
Major-General, United States Army

NO other arm of the military services during the Civil War excited a tithe of the curiosity and interest which surrounded the Signal Corps. To the onlooker, the messages of its waving flags, its winking lights and its rushing rockets were always mystic in their language, while their tenor was often fraught with thrilling import and productive of far-reaching effects.

The signal system, an American device, was tested first in border warfare against hostile Navajos; afterward the quick-witted soldiers of both the Federal and Confederate armies developed portable signaling to great advantage. The invention of a non-combatant, Surgeon A. J. Myer, it met with indifferent reception and evoked hostility in its early stages. When the stern actualities of war were realized, its evolution proceeded in the Federal army in face of corporation and departmental opposition, yet despite all adverse attacks it ultimately demonstrated its intrinsic merits. Denied a separate organization until the war neared its end, the corps suffered constantly from strife and dissension in Washington, its misfortunes culminating in the arbitrary removal of its first two chiefs. Thus its very existence was threatened. Nevertheless, the gallant, efficient services of its patriotic men and officers in the face of the foe were of such striking military value as to gain the confidence and win the commendation of the most distinguished generals.

Major Myer began work in 1861, at Georgetown, District of Columbia, with small details from the volunteers, though the

CONFEDERATE SIGNALMEN IN '61

The Confederate signal service was first in the field. Beauregard's report acknowledges the aid rendered his army at Bull Run by Captain (afterwards General) E. P. Alexander, a former pupil of Major A. J. Myer. McDowell was then without signalmen, and so could not communicate regularly with Washington. While Major Myer was establishing a Federal signal training-school at Red Hill, such towers were rising along the already beleaguered Confederate coast. This one at Charleston, South Carolina, is swarming with young Confederate volunteers gazing out to sea in anticipation of the advent of the foe. They had not long to wait. During nearly four years the Union fleet locked them in their harbor. For all that time Fort Sumter and its neighbors defied the Union power.

corps eventually numbered about three hundred officers and twenty-five hundred men. Authorized as a separate corps by the act of Congress, approved March 3, 1863, its organization was not completed until August, 1864. The outcome was an embodiment of the army aphorism that "one campaign in Washington is worth two in the field." More than two thousand signalmen served at the front, of whom only nine were commissioned in the new corps, while seventeen were appointed from civil life. As a result of degradation in rank, eleven detailed officers declined commissions or resigned after acceptance. Colonel Myer, the inventor and organizer of the service, had his commission vacated in July, 1864, and his successor, Colonel Nicodemus, was summarily dismissed six months later, the command then devolving on Colonel B. F. Fisher, who was never confirmed by the Senate. That a corps so harassed should constantly distinguish itself in the field is one of the many marvels of patriotism displayed by the American soldier.

Signal messages were sent by means of flags, torches, or lights, by combinations of three separate motions. The flag (or torch) was initially held upright: "one" was indicated by waving the flag to the left and returning it from the ground to the upright position; "two" by a similar motion to the right, and "three" by a wave (or dip) to the front. Where a letter was composed of several figures, the motions were made in rapid succession without any pause. Letters were separated by a very brief pause, and words or sentences were distinguished by one or more dip motions to the front.

SIGNAL ALPHABET, AS USED LATE IN THE WAR

A— 11	G—1122	M—2112	S— 121	Y— 222
B—1221	H— 211	N— 22	T— 1	Z—1111
C— 212	I— 2	O— 12	U— 221	&—2222
D— 111	J—2211	P—2121	V—2111	tion—2221
E— 21	K—1212	Q—2122	W—2212	ing—1121
F—1112	L— 112	R— 122	X—1211	ed—1222

GENERAL MORELL'S LOOKOUT TOWARD THE CONFEDERATE LINES—1861

When General McClellan was rapidly organizing his army from the mass of troops, distinguished only by regimental numerals, into brigades, divisions, and corps, in the fall and winter of 1861, General George W. Morell was placed in command of the first brigade of the Army of the Potomac and stationed at the extreme front of Minor's Hill, Virginia, just south of Washington. The city was distraught with apprehension, and the lookout, or tower, in the foreground was erected especially for the purpose of observations toward the Confederate lines, then in the direction of Manassas. At the particular moment when this picture was taken, the lookout has undoubtedly shouted some observation to General Morell, who stands with his finger pointing toward the south, the Confederate position. That the army has not yet advanced is made evident by the fact that a lady is present, dressed in the fashion of the day.

NUMERALS

1—12221 = Wait a moment.
2—21112 = Are you ready?
3—11211 = I am ready.
4—11121 = Use short pole and small flag.
5—11112 = Use long pole and large flag.
6—21111 = Work faster.
7—22111 = Did you understand?
8—22221 = Use white flag.
9—22122 = Use black flag.
0—11111 = Use red flag.

CODE SIGNALS

3 = " End of word." 33 = " End of sentence." 333 = " End of message." 121212 = " Error." 11, 11, 11, 3 = " Message received (or understood)." 11, 11, 11, 3 = " Cease signaling." Constant and unbroken waving = " Attention, look for signals."

To hasten work there were many abbreviations, such as: A = " After "; B = " Before "; C = " Can "; Imy = " Immediately "; N = " Not "; Q = " Quiet "; R = " Are "; U = " You " and Y = " Why."

When using Coston signals there were more than twenty combinations of colored lights which permitted an extended system of prearranged signals. White rockets (or bombs) = one; red = two, and green = three. White flags with a square red center were most frequently employed for signaling purposes, though when snow was on the ground a black flag was used, and with varying backgrounds the red flag with a white center could be seen at greater distances than the white.

To secure secrecy all important messages were enciphered by means of a cipher disk. Two concentric disks, of unequal size and revolving on a central pivot, were divided along their outer edges into thirty equal compartments. The inner and smaller disk contained in its compartments letters, terminations, and word-pauses, while the outer, larger disk contained

AT YORKTOWN

Skilled Union signal parties were available for the Peninsular campaign of 1862, where they rendered invaluable service to McClellan. Work strictly for the army was supplemented by placing signal officers with the navy, and thus ensuring that coöperation so vitally essential to success. The victory of Franklin's command at West Point, after the evacuation of Yorktown, was largely due to the efficiency of the Signal Corps. Vigorously attacked by an unknown force, Franklin ordered his signal officer to call up the fleet just appearing down the river. A keen-sighted signal officer was alert on the gunboat, and in a few minutes Franklin's request that the woods be shelled was thoroughly carried out. This photograph shows the location of Union Battery No. 1 on the left, in the peach-orchard, at Yorktown, and the York River lies at hand, to the right of the house.

A LOOKOUT ON THE ROOF OF FARENHOLT'S HOUSE, YORKTOWN

SIGNAL CORPS HEADQUARTERS IN AUGUST, 1862

ARMY AND NAVY

These quarters were established near Harrison's Landing, Virginia, in July, 1862, after the "Seven Days" battles during McClellan's retreat. Colonel (then Lieutenant) Benjamin F. Fisher, of the Signal Corps, then in command, opened a local station on the famous Berkely mansion. The Signal Corps had proved indispensable to the success of McClellan in changing his base from York River to James River. When the vigorous Confederate attack at Malvern Hill threatened the rout of the army, McClellan was aboard the gunboat *Galena*, whose army signal officer informed him of the situation through messages flagged from the shore. Through information from the signal officers directing the fire of the fleet, he was aided in repelling the advances of the Confederates. The messages ran like this: "Fire one mile to the right. Fire low into the woods near the shore."

groups of signal numbers to be sent. Sometimes this arrangement was changed and letters were on the outer disks and the numbers on the inner. By the use of prearranged keys, and through their frequent interchange, the secrecy of messages thus enciphered was almost absolutely ensured.

In every important campaign and on every bloody ground, the red flags of the Signal Corps flaunted defiantly at the forefront, speeding stirring orders of advance, conveying warnings of impending danger, and sending sullen suggestions of defeat. They were seen on the advanced lines of Yorktown, Petersburg, and Richmond, in the saps and trenches at Charleston, Vicksburg, and Port Hudson, at the fierce battles of Chickamauga and Chancellorsville, before the fort-crowned crest of Fredericksburg, amid the frightful carnage of Antietam, on Kenesaw Mountain deciding the fate of Allatoona, in Sherman's march to the sea, and with Grant's victorious army at Appomattox and Richmond. They spoke silently to Du Pont along the dunes and sounds of the Carolinas, sent word to Porter clearing the central Mississippi River, and aided Farragut when forcing the passage of Mobile Bay.

Did a non-combatant corps ever before suffer such disproportionate casualties—killed, wounded, and captured? Sense of duty, necessity of exposure to fire, and importance of mission were conditions incompatible with personal safety—and the Signal Corps paid the price. While many found their fate in Confederate prisons, the extreme danger of signal work, when conjoined with stubborn adherence to outposts of duty, is forcefully evidenced by the fact that the killed of the Signal Corps were one hundred and fifty per cent. of the wounded, as against the usual ratio of twenty per cent.

The Confederates were first in the field, for Beauregard's report acknowledges the aid rendered his army at Bull Run by Captain E. P. Alexander, a former pupil of Myer. McDowell was then without signalmen, and so could neither communicate regularly with Washington nor receive word of the

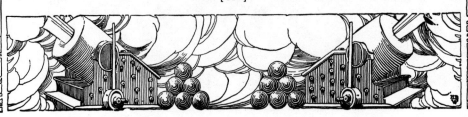

OCTOBER, 1862—WHERE THE CONFEDERATE INVASION OF MARYLAND WAS
DISCOVERED

The signal officer is on outlook duty near the Point of Rocks station, in Maryland. This station was opened and operated by First-Lieutenant John H. Fralick for purposes of observation. It completely dominated Pleasant Valley. On the twelfth of the month Fra'ick had detected and reported General J. E. B. Stuart's raiding cavalry crossing the Potomac on their way back from Maryland and Pennsylvania. The Confederate cavalry leader had crossed the Potomac at Williamsport on the 10th of October, ridden completely around the rear of the Army of the Potomac, and eluded the vigorous pursuit of General Pleasonton and his Union cavalry. Within twenty hours he had marched sixty-five miles and kept up his artillery. Lieutenant-Colonel Edwin R. Biles, with the Ninety-ninth Pennsylvania, opposed Stuart's crossing at Monocacy Ford, but was unable to detain him. This was one of the combination of events which finally cost McClellan the command of the Army of the Potomac. Lee's invasion of Maryland in 1862 would have been a complete surprise, except for the watchful vigilance of Lieutenant Miner of the Signal Corps, who occupied Sugar Loaf, the highest point in Maryland. From this lofty station were visible the more important fords of the Potomac, with their approaches on both sides of the river. Miner detected the Confederate advance-guard, then the wagon-train movements, and finally the objective points of their march. Although unprotected, he held his station to the last and was finally captured by the Southern troops.

SIGNAL OFFICER PIERCE
RECEIVING A MESSAGE FROM
GENERAL McCLELLAN
AT THE ELK MOUNTAIN STATION
AFTER THE BATTLE OF ANTIETAM

Elk Mountain is in the South Mountain Range of the Blue Ridge; its summit here shown commanded a view of almost the entire Antietam battlefield during September 17th, 1862, the bloodiest single day of the Civil War. The Elk Mountain Signal Station was operated after the battle by Lieutenants Pierce and Jerome. As the photograph above was taken, the former officer was receiving a dispatch from General McClellan, presumably requesting further information in regard to some reported movement of General Lee. The Union loss in this terrific battle was twelve thousand five hundred, and the Confederate loss over ten thousand. The correspondent of a Richmond paper, describing his part as an eye-witness of the engagement, wrote on the succeeding day: "Their signal stations on the Blue Ridge commanded a view of every movement. We could not make a maneuver in front or rear that was not instantly revealed by keen lookouts; and as soon as the intelligence could be communicated to their batteries below, shot and shell were launched against the moving columns. It was this information, conveyed by the little flags upon the mountain-top, that no doubt enabled the enemy to concentrate his force against our weakest points and counteract the effect of whatever similar movements may have been attempted by us." Captain Joseph Gloskoski, who had received commendation for bravery at Gaines' Mill, sent many important messages to Burnside as a result of the telescopic reconnoitering of Lieutenants N. H. Camp and C. Herzog. It was the message received from this station, "Look well to your left," which enabled Burnside to guard his left against A. P. Hill's advance from Harper's Ferry.

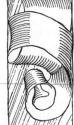

vitally important despatch from Patterson at Harper's Ferry telling of Johnston's departure to reenforce Beauregard at Manassas, which should have obviated the battle. Major Myer was quick, however, to establish a signal training-school at Red Hill, Georgetown, District of Columbia.

In view of modern knowledge and practice, it seems almost incredible to note that the Secretary of War disapproved, in 1861, the recommendation made by Major Myer, signal officer of the army, for an appropriation for field-telegraph lines. While efforts to obtain, operate, and improve such lines were measurably successful on the part of the army, they were strenuously opposed by the civilian telegraph corporations so potent at the War Department.

Active protests proved unavailing and injurious. Colonel Myer's circular, in 1863, describing the systematic attempts of the civilian organization to deprive the Signal Corps of such lines " as an interference with a part of the Signal Corps' legitimate duties," caused him to be placed on waiting orders, while all field-trains were ordered to be turned over to the civilian force. It may be added that both organizations in the field cooperated with a degree of harmony and good-fellowship that was often lacking in Washington.

Skilled parties were thus available for the Peninsula campaign of 1862, where McClellan utilized them, strictly army work being supplemented by placing signal officers with the navy, and thus ensuring that cooperation vitally essential to success. Not only was military information efficiently collected and distributed, but at critical junctures McClellan was able to control the fire-direction of both the field-artillery of the army and the heavy guns of the navy.

At Yorktown, coigns of vantage were occupied in high trees and on lofty towers, whence messages were sent to and fro, especially those containing information of the position and movements of the foe, which were discerned by high-power telescopes—an important duty not always known or

SIGNAL CORPS RECONNOITERING AT FREDERICKSBURG, VIRGINIA

From December 11 to 13, 1862, four signal stations were engaged in observing and reporting the operations of the Confederates on the south side of the Rappahannock River at Fredericksburg. The flag station at headquarters kept General Burnside in constant touch with the Federal attacking force on the right, under Couch and Hooker, through their signalmen in the courthouse steeple. This is prominent in the center of the lower photograph. One station near a field hospital came under a fire that killed about twenty men and wounded many others nearby. Finally the surgeons requested a suspension of flagging, that the lives of the wounded might be spared.

FREDERICKSBURG—THE COURTHOUSE STEEPLE IN THE CENTER CONTAINED FEDERAL SIGNALMEN

appreciated. Often their work drew the Confederate artillery and sharpshooters' fire, of unpleasant accuracy. The saving of Franklin's command at West Point, after the evacuation of Yorktown, was in large part due to the efficiency of the Signal Corps.

Valuable as was the work before Richmond, under fire, in reconnoitering and in cooperation with the military telegraph service, it proved to be indispensable to the success of McClellan in changing his base from York River to James River —its importance culminating at Malvern Hill. It will be recalled that the Seven Days' Battles ended with the bloody struggle on the banks of the James, where the use of the Signal Corps enabled McClellan to transform impending defeat into successful defense. When the vigorous Confederate attack at Malvern Hill threatened the flank of the army, McClellan was aboard the United States steamship *Galena,* whose army signal officer informed him of the situation through messages flagged from the army. McClellan was thus enabled not only to give general orders to the army then in action, but also to direct the fire of the fleet, which had moved up the James for cooperation, most efficiently.

Lee's invasion of Maryland in 1862 would have been a complete surprise, except for the watchful vigilance of an officer of the Signal Corps, Lieutenant Miner, who occupied Sugar Loaf, the highest point in Maryland. From this lofty station were visible the more important fords of the Potomac, with their approaches on both sides of the river. Miner detected the Confederate advance guard, the train movements, and noted the objective points of their march. Notifying Washington of the invasion, although unprotected he held his station to the last and was finally captured by the Southern troops. The reoccupancy of Sugar Loaf a week later enabled McClellan to establish a network of stations, whose activities contributed to the victory of South Mountain.

As Elk Mountain dominated the valley of the Antietam,

After the surrender of Vicksburg, July 4, 1863, the Signal Corps of Grant's army was under the command of Lieutenant John W. Deford, a recently exchanged prisoner of war. Its location was on the southern continuation of Cherry Street near the A. & V. railway. From the balcony of the house are hanging two red flags with square white centers, indicating the headquarters of the Signal Corps. Many times before the fall were orders flashed by night by means of waving torches to commands widely separated; and in the daytime the signal-men standing drew on themselves the attention of the Confederate sharpshooters. A message begun by one signal-man was often finished by another who picked up the flag his fallen companion had dropped. The tower at Jacksonville, Florida, over a hundred feet high, kept in communication with the signal tower at Yellow Bluff, at the mouth of the St. John's River. Note the two men with the Signal Corps flag on its summit. Just below them is an enclosure to which they could retire when the efforts of the Confederate sharpshooters became too threatening.

HEADQUARTERS OF THE UNION SIGNAL
CORPS AT VICKSBURG
1864

SIGNAL STATIONS

FROM

THE MISSISSIPPI

TO

THE ATLANTIC

TOWER AT JACKSONVILLE

EVIDENCE OF THE

SIGNAL–MAN'S ACTIVITY

THROUGHOUT

THE

THEATER OF WAR

LOOKOUT MOUNTAIN—THE ANTICIPATED SIGNALS

After Grant arrived and occupied Chattanooga, Bragg retired up the Cumberland Mountains and took up two strong positions—one upon the top of Lookout Mountain, overlooking Chattanooga from the south, and the other on Missionary Ridge, a somewhat lower elevation to the east. His object was to hold the passes of the mountain against any advance upon his base at Dalton, Georgia, at which point supplies arrived from Atlanta. Grant, about the middle of November, 1863, advanced with 80,000 men for the purpose of dislodging the Confederates from these positions. At the very summit of Lookout Mountain, "The Hawk's Nest" of the Cherokees, the Confederates had established a signal station from which every movement of the Federal Army was flashed to the Confederate headquarters on Missionary Ridge. The Federals had possessed themselves of this signal code, and could read all of Bragg's messages. Hence an attempt to surprise Hooker when he advanced, on November 23d, failed.

it was occupied only to find that the dense woods on its summit cut off all view. However, energetic action soon cleared a vista, known to the soldiers as "McClellan's Gap," through which systematic telescopic search revealed all extended movements of the foe. The busy ax furnished material for a rude log structure, from the summit of which messages of great importance, on which were based the general disposition of the Federal troops, were sent.

At Fredericksburg flag-work and telescopic·reconnoitering were supplemented by the establishment of a field-telegraph line connecting army headquarters with Franklin's Grand Division on the extreme left. The flag station at headquarters kept Burnside in constant touch with the Federal attacking force on the right, under Couch and Hooker, through their signalmen in the court-house steeple. One station near a field-hospital was under a fire, which killed about twenty men and wounded many others near by, until the surgeons asked suspension of flagging to save the lives of the wounded.

A most important part of the Signal Corps' duty was the interception and translation of messages interchanged between the Confederate signalmen. Perhaps the most notable of such achievements occurred in the Shenandoah valley, in 1864. On Massanutten, or Three Top Mountain, was a signal station which kept Early in touch with Lee's army to the southeastward, near Richmond, and which the Federals had under close watch. Late in the evening of October 15th, a keen-eyed lieutenant noted that "Three Top" was swinging his signal torch with an unwonted persistency that betokened a message of urgency. The time seemed interminable to the Union officer until the message began, which he read with suppressed excitement as follows: "To Lieutenant-General Early. Be ready to move as soon as my forces join you, and we will crush Sheridan. Longstreet, Lieutenant-General."

Sheridan was then at Front Royal, en route to Washington. The message was handed to General Wright, in

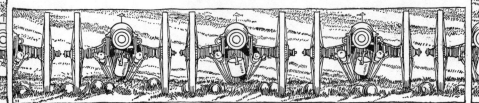

THE SIGNAL CORPS AT GETTYSBURG

In the battle of Gettysburg the Confederates established their chief signal station in the cupola of the Lutheran Seminary, which commanded an extended field of operations. From here came much of Lee's information about the battle which surged and thundered to and fro until the gigantic wave of Pickett's charge was dashed to pieces against the immovable rock of Meade's defense on the third culminating day. The Union Signal Corps was equally active in gathering information and transmitting orders. Altogether, for perhaps the first time in military history, the generals-in-chief of two large armies were kept in constant communication during active operations with their corps and division commanders. It was the Union Signal Corps with its deceptive flags that enabled General Warren to hold alone the strangely neglected eminence of Little Round Top, the key to the Federal left, until troops could be sent to occupy it.

HEADQUARTERS, CONFEDERATE SIGNAL CORPS
AT GETTYSBURG, PENNSYLVANIA

SIGNAL CORPS OFFICERS, HEADQUARTERS ARMY OF THE POTOMAC, OCTOBER, 1863

Standing are Lieutenant F. E. Beardsley, Lieutenant Neal, Lieutenant George J. Clarke, [unknown], and General (then Captain) Charles L. Davis (leaning on peach-tree). Seated are Captain Charles J. Clarke, Lieutenant W. S. Stryker, and Lieutenant A. B. Capron (afterwards Member of Congress).

temporary command, at once, and was forwarded by him to Sheridan at midnight. The importance of this information is apparent, yet Early took the Union army completely by surprise three days later, at daybreak of October 19th, although the tide of morning defeat was turned to evening victory under the inspiration of Sheridan's matchless personality.

In the battles at Gettysburg the Confederates established their chief signal station in the cupola of the Lutheran seminary, which commanded an extended field of operations. The Union Signal Corps was extremely active in gathering information and transmitting orders, and for perhaps the first time in military history the commanding general of a large army was kept in communication during active operations with his corps and division commanders.

The most important Union signal station, on the second day of this titanic struggle, was at Little Round Top on the Federal left flank, which commanded a view of the country occupied by the right of Lee's army. Heavy was the price paid for flag-work at this point, where the men were exposed to the fierce shrapnel of artillery and the deadly bullet of Confederate sharpshooters in Devil's Den. On or beside this signal station, on a bare rock about ten feet square, seven men were killed or seriously wounded. With rash gallantry, Captain James A. Hall held his ground, and on July 2d, at the most critical phase of the struggle signaled to Meade's headquarters, "A heavy column of enemy's infantry, about ten thousand, is moving from opposite our extreme left toward our right."

General Warren had hastened by Meade's order to Little Round Top to investigate. He says: "There were no troops on it [Little Round Top] and it was used as a signal station. I saw that this was the key of the whole position, and that our troops in the woods in front of it could not see the ground in front of them, so that the enemy could come upon them unawares." A shot was fired into these woods by Warren's

SIGNALING ORDERS FROM GENERAL MEADE'S HEADQUARTERS, JUST BEFORE THE WILDERNESS

In April, 1864, General Meade's headquarters lay north of the Rapidan. The Signal Corps was kept busy transmitting the orders preliminary to the Wilderness campaign, which was to begin May 5th. The headquarters are below the brow of the hill. A most important part of the Signal Corps' duty was the interception and translation of messages interchanged between the Confederate signal-men. A veteran of Sheridan's army tells of his impressions as follows: "On the evening of the 18th of October, 1864, the soldiers of Sheridan's army lay in their lines at Cedar Creek. Our attention was suddenly directed to the ridge of Massanutten, or Three Top Mountain, the slope of which covered the left wing of the army—the Eighth Corps. A lively series of signals was being flashed out from the peak, and it was evident that messages were being sent both eastward and westward of the ridge. I can recall now the feeling with which we looked up at those flashes going over our heads, knowing that they must be Confederate messages. It was only later that we learned that a keen-eyed Union officer had been able to read the message: 'To Lieutenant-General Early. Be ready to move as soon as my forces join you, and we will crush Sheridan. Longstreet, Lieutenant-General.' The sturdiness of Sheridan's veterans and the fresh spirit put into the hearts of the men by the return of Sheridan himself from 'Winchester, twenty miles away,' a ride rendered immortal by Read's poem, proved too much at last for the pluck and persistency of Early's worn-out troops."

orders. He continues: " This motion revealed to me the ene-my's line of battle, already formed and far outflanking our troops. . . . The discovery was intensely thrilling and almost appalling." After narrating how he asked Meade for troops, Warren continues, " While I was still alone with the signal officer, the musket balls began to fly around us, and he was about to fold up his flags and withdraw, but remained, at my request, and kept them waving in defiance." This action saved the day for the Federals, as Warren declares.

The system around Vicksburg was such as to keep Grant fully informed of the efforts of the Confederates to disturb his communications in the rear, and also ensured the fullest coop-eration between the Mississippi flotilla and his army. Judi-cious in praise, Grant's commendation of his signal officer speaks best for the service. Messages were constantly ex-changed with the fleet, the final one of the siege being flagged as follows on the morning of July 4th: " 4.30 A. M. 4: 1863. Admiral Porter: The enemy has accepted in the main my terms of capitulation and will surrender the city, works and garrison at 10 A. M. . . . U. S. Grant, Major-General, Commanding."

The fleets of Farragut and Porter, while keeping the Mis-sissippi open, carried signal officers to enable them to commu-nicate with the army, their high masts and lofty trees enabling signals to be exchanged great distances. Doubtless the loftiest perch thus used during the war was that on the United States steamship *Richmond,* one of Farragut's fleet at Port Hudson. The *Richmond* was completely disabled by the central Con-federate batteries while attempting to run past Port Hudson, her signal officer, working, meanwhile, in the maintop. As the running of the batteries was thus found to be too dangerous, the vessel dropped back and the signal officer suggested that he occupy the very tip of the highest mast for his working perch, which was fitted up, one hundred and sixty feet above the water. From this great height it was barely possible to signal over the highland occupied by the foe, and thus maintain

"CROW'S NEST"—SIGNAL TOWER TO THE RIGHT
OF BERMUDA HUNDRED

AT HEADQUARTERS OF 14TH N. Y. HEAVY
ARTILLERY NEAR PETERSBURG

THE PEEBLE'S FARM SIGNAL TOWER
NEAR PETERSBURG

THE SIGNAL TOWER
NEAR POINT OF ROCKS

uninterrupted communication and essential cooperation between the fleets of the central and lower Mississippi.

The most dramatic use of the Signal Corps was connected with the successful defense of Allatoona, Sherman's reserve depot in which were stored three millions of rations, practically undefended, as it was a distance in the rear of the army. Realizing the utmost importance of the railroad north of Marietta and of the supplies to Sherman, Hood threw Stewart's corps in the rear of the Union army, and French's division of about sixty-five hundred men was detached to capture Allatoona. With the Confederates intervening and telegraph lines destroyed, all would have been lost but for the Signal Corps station on Kenesaw Mountain. Corse was at Rome, thirty-six miles beyond Allatoona. From Vining's Station, the message was flagged over the heads of the foe to Allatoona by way of Kenesaw, and thence telegraphed to Corse, as follows: "General Corse: Sherman directs that you move forward and join Smith's division with your entire command, using cars if to be had, and burn provisions rather than lose them. General Vandever." At the same time a message was sent to Allatoona: "Sherman is moving with force. Hold out." And again: "Hold on. General Sherman says he is working hard for you."

Sherman was at Kenesaw all day, October 5th, having learned of the arrival of Corse that morning, and anxiously watched the progress of the battle. That afternoon came a despatch from Allatoona, sent during the engagement: "We are all right so far. General Corse is wounded." Next morning Dayton, Sherman's assistant adjutant-general, asked how Corse was and he answered, "I am short a cheekbone and one ear, but am able to whip all h—l yet." That the fight was desperate is shown by Corse's losses, seven hundred and five killed and wounded, and two hundred captured, out of an effective force of about fifteen hundred.

An unusual application of signal stores was made at the

COLONEL BENJAMIN F. FISHER AND HIS ASSISTANTS AT SIGNAL CORPS HEAD-
QUARTERS, WASHINGTON

Although authorized as a separate corps by the Act of Congress approved March 3, 1863, the Signal Corps did not complete its organization until August, 1864. More than two thousand signal-men served at the front, of whom only nine were commissioned in the new corps, while seventeen officers were appointed from civil life. Colonel A. J. Myer, the inventor and organizer of the service, had his commission vacated in July, 1864. On December 26th of that year Colonel Benjamin F. Fisher was placed in command of the Signal Corps, but his appointment was never confirmed by the Senate. Note the curious wording of the sign by the door: "Office of the Signal Officer of the Army," as if there were but one. That a corps so harassed should constantly distinguish itself in the field is one of the many marvels of American patriotism.

SIGNALING FROM FORT McALLISTER, GEORGIA—THE END OF THE MARCH
TO THE SEA

General Sherman's flag message with Hazen's soldierly answer upon their arrival at Savannah, December 13, 1864, has become historic. Sherman's message was an order for Hazen's Division of the Fifteenth Army Corps to make an assault upon the fort. Hazen's terse answer was: "I am ready and will assault at once." The fort was carried at the first rush. A flag station was immediately established on the parapet. It wigwagged to Dahlgren's expectant fleet the news that Sherman had completed the famous march to the sea with his army in excellent condition. Only a week later General Hardee evacuated Savannah with his troops.

HOW SHERMAN WAS WELCOMED UPON HIS ARRIVAL AT THE SEA

This photograph shows a party of Admiral John A. Dahlgren's signal-men on board ship receiving a message from the Georgia shore. The two flagmen are standing at attention, ready to send Dahlgren's answering message, and the officer with the telescope is prepared to read the signals from the shore. Thus Sherman's message from the parapet of Fort McAllister was read. Commander C. P. R. Rodgers and Admiral Dupont had been prompt to recognize the value of the Army Signal Corps system and to introduce it in the navy. This concert between the North's gigantic armies on shore and her powerful South Atlantic fleet was bound to crush the Confederacy sooner or later. Without food for her decimated armies she could not last.

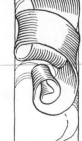

siege of Knoxville, when Longstreet attacked at dawn. Sending up a signal by Roman candles to indicate the point of attack, the signal officer followed it by discharging the candles toward the advancing Confederates, which not only disconcerted some of them, but made visible the approaching lines and made possible more accurate fire on the part of the Union artillery.

While at Missionary Ridge, the following message was flagged at a critical point: "Sherman: Thomas has carried the hill and lot in his immediate front. Now is your time to attack with vigor. Do so. Grant." Other signal work of value intervened between Missionary Ridge and Allatoona, so that the Signal Corps was placed even more to the front in the Atlanta campaign and during the march to the sea.

The Confederates had changed their cipher key, but Sherman's indefatigable officers ascertained the new key from intercepted messages, thus giving the general much important information.

Several stations for observation were established in high trees, some more than a hundred feet from the ground, from which were noted the movements of the various commands, of wagon trains, and railroad cars. Hood's gallant sortie from Atlanta was detected at its very start, and despite the severity of the fight, during which one flagman was killed, messages were sent throughout the battle—even over the heads of the foe.

Of importance, though devoid of danger, among the final messages on arrival at Savannah was one ordering, by flag, the immediate assault on Fort McAllister by Hazen, with the soldierly answer, "I am ready and will assault at once," and the other announcing to the expectant fleet that Sherman had completed the famous march to the sea with his army in excellent condition.

In the approaches and siege of Petersburg, the work of the Signal Corps was almost entirely telescopic reconnoitering.

SIGNALING   THE WHITE FLAG

BY   WITH

THE SEA   THE RED CENTER

This station was established by Lieutenant E. J. Keenan on the roof of the mansion of a planter at the extreme northern point of Hilton Head Island, Port Royal Bay. Through this station were exchanged many messages between General W. T. Sherman and Admiral S. F. Dupont. Sherman had been forced by Savannah's stubborn resistance to prepare for siege operations against the city, and perfect coöperation between the army and navy became imperative. The signal station adjoining the one portrayed above was erected on the house formerly owned by John C. Calhoun, lying within sight of Fort Pulaski, at the mouth of the Savannah River. Late in December, General Hardee and his Confederate troops evacuated the city. Sherman was enabled to make President Lincoln a present of one of the last of the Southern strongholds.

FROM SHORE TO SHIP—HILTON HEAD SIGNAL STATION

While an occasional high tree was used for a perch, yet the country was so heavily timbered that signal towers were necessary. There were nearly a dozen lines of communication and a hundred separate stations. The most notable towers were Cobb's Hill, one hundred and twenty-five feet; Crow's Nest, one hundred and twenty-six feet, and Peebles Farm, one hundred and forty-five feet, which commanded views of Petersburg, its approaches, railways, the camps and fortifications. Cobb's Hill, on the Appomattox, was particularly irritating and caused the construction of an advance Confederate earthwork a mile distant, from which fully two hundred and fifty shot and shell were fired against the tower in a single day—with slight damage, however. Similar futile efforts were made to destroy Crow's Nest.

At General Meade's headquarters a signal party had a unique experience—fortunately not fatal though thrilling in the extreme. A signal platform was built in a tree where, from a height of seventy-five feet the Confederate right flank position could be seen far to the rear. Whenever important movements were in progress this station naturally drew a heavy fire, to prevent signal work. As the men were charged to hold fast at all hazards, descending only after two successive shots at them, they became accustomed in time to sharpshooting, but the shriek of shell was more nerve-racking. On one occasion several shots whistled harmlessly by, and then came a violent shock which nearly dislodged platform, men, and instruments. A solid shot, partly spent, striking fairly, had buried itself in the tree half-way between the platform and the ground.

When Petersburg fell, field flag-work began again, and the first Union messages from Richmond were sent from the roof of the Confederate Capitol. In the field the final order of importance flagged by the corps was as follows: " Farmville, April 7, 1865. General Meade: Order Fifth Corps to follow the Twenty-fourth at 6 A. M. up the Lynchburg road.

STRIKING THE SIGNAL CORPS FLAG FOR THE LAST TIME—AUGUST, 1865

THE SIGNAL CAMP OF INSTRUCTION ON RED HILL

In this camp all signal parties were trained before taking the field. In the center is the signal tower, from which messages could be sent to all stations in Virginia not more than twenty miles distant. The farthest camps were reached from the Crow's Nest; nearer ones from the base of the tower. Here General A. J. Myer, then a civilian, appeared after the muster out of his old comrades to witness the dissolution of the corps which owed its inception, organization, and efficiency to his inventive genius and administrative ability.

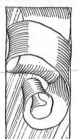

The Second and Sixth to follow the enemy north of the river. U. S. Grant, Lieutenant-General."

It must not be inferred that all distinguished signal work was confined to the Union army, for the Confederates were first in the field, and ever after held their own. Captain (afterward General) E. P. Alexander, a former pupil in the Union army under Myer, was the first signal officer of an army, that of Northern Virginia. He greatly distinguished himself in the first battle of Bull Run, where he worked for several hours under fire, communicating to his commanding general the movements of opposing forces, for which he was highly commended. At a critical moment he detected a hostile advance, and saved a Confederate division from being flanked by a signal message, "Look out for your left. Your position is turned."

Alexander's assignment as chief of artillery left the corps under Captain (later Colonel) William Norris. Attached to the Adjutant-General's Department, under the act of April 19, 1862, the corps consisted of one major, ten each of captains, first and second lieutenants, and twenty sergeants, the field-force being supplemented by details from the line of the army. Signaling, telegraphy, and secret-service work were all done by the corps, which proved to be a potent factor in the efficient operations of the various armies.

It was at Island No. 10; it was active with Early in the Valley; it was with Kirby Smith in the Trans-Mississippi, and aided Sidney Johnston at Shiloh. It kept pace with wondrous "Stonewall" Jackson in the Valley, withdrew defiantly with Johnston toward Atlanta, and followed impetuous Hood in the Nashville campaign. It served ably in the trenches of beleaguered Vicksburg, and clung fast to the dismantled battlements of Fort Sumter. Jackson clamored for it until Lee gave a corps to him, Jackson saying, "The enemy's signals give him a great advantage over me."

TELEGRAPHING
FOR THE ARMIES

" NO ORDERS EVER HAD TO BE GIVEN TO ESTABLISH
THE TELEGRAPH." THUS WROTE GENERAL GRANT
IN HIS MEMOIRS. "THE MOMENT TROOPS WERE
IN POSITION TO GO INTO CAMP, THE MEN WOULD
PUT UP THEIR WIRES." GRANT PAYS A GLOWING
TRIBUTE TO " THE ORGANIZATION AND DISCIPLINE
OF THIS BODY OF BRAVE AND INTELLIGENT MEN."

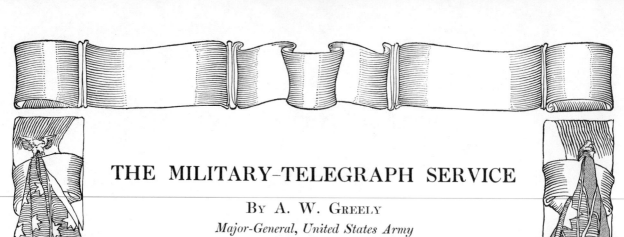

THE MILITARY-TELEGRAPH SERVICE

By A. W. Greely
Major-General, United States Army

[The Editors express their grateful acknowledgment to David Homer Bates, of the United States Military-Telegraph Corps, manager of the War Department Telegraph Office and cipher-operator, 1861–1866, and author of "Lincoln in the Telegraph Office," etc., for valued personal assistance in the preparation of the photographic descriptions, and for many of the incidents described in the following pages, which are recorded in fuller detail in his book.]

THE exigencies and experiences of the Civil War demonstrated, among other theorems, the vast utility and indispensable importance of the electric telegraph, both as an administrative agent and as a tactical factor in military operations. In addition to the utilization of existing commercial systems, there were built and operated more than fifteen thousand miles of lines for military purposes only.

Serving under the anomalous status of quartermaster's employees, often under conditions of personal danger, and with no definite official standing, the operators of the military-telegraph service performed work of most vital import to the army in particular and to the country in general. They fully merited the gratitude of the Nation for their efficiency, fidelity, and patriotism, yet their services have never been practically recognized by the Government or appreciated by the people.

For instance, during the war there occurred in the line of duty more than three hundred casualties among the operators —from disease, death in battle, wounds, or capture. Scores of these unfortunate victims left families dependent upon charity, as the United States neither extended aid to their destitute families nor admitted needy survivors to a pensionable status.

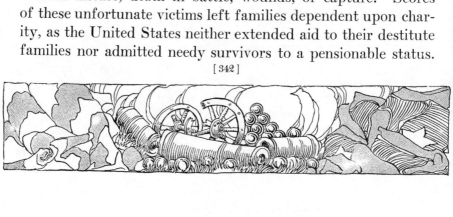

AT THE TELEGRAPHERS' TENT, YORKTOWN—MAY, 1862

These operators with their friends at dinner look quite contented, with their coffee in tin cups, their hard-tack, and the bountiful appearing kettle at their feet. Yet their lot, as McClellan's army advanced toward Richmond and later, was to be far from enviable. "The telegraph service," writes General A. W. Greely, "had neither definite personnel nor corps organization. It was simply a civilian bureau attached to the quartermaster's department, in which a few of its favored members received commissions. The men who performed the dangerous work in the field were mere employees—mostly underpaid and often treated with scant consideration. During the war there occurred in the line of duty more than three hundred casualties among the operators—by disease, killed in battle, wounded, or made prisoners. Scores of these unfortunate victims left families dependent on charity, for the Government of the United States neither extended aid to their destitute families nor admitted needy survivors to a pensionable status."

The telegraph service had neither definite personnel nor corps organization. It was simply a civilian bureau attached to the Quartermaster's Department, in which a few of its favored members received commissions. The men who performed the dangerous work in the field were mere employees—mostly underpaid, and often treated with scant consideration. The inherent defects of such a nondescript organization made it impossible for it to adjust and adapt itself to the varying demands and imperative needs of great and independent armies such as were employed in the Civil War.

Moreover, the chief, Colonel Anson Stager, was stationed in Cleveland, Ohio, while an active subordinate, Major Thomas T. Eckert, was associated with the great war secretary, who held the service in his iron grasp. Not only were its commissioned officers free from other authority than that of the Secretary of War, but operators, engaged in active campaigning thousands of miles from Washington, were independent of the generals under whom they were serving. As will appear later, operators suffered from the natural impatience of military commanders, who resented the abnormal relations which inevitably led to distrust and contention. While such irritations and distrusts were rarely justified, none the less they proved detrimental to the best interests of the United States.

On the one hand, the operators were ordered to report to, and obey only, the corporation representatives who dominated the War Department, while on the other their lot was cast with military associates, who frequently regarded them with a certain contempt or hostility. Thus, the life of the field-operator was hard, indeed, and it is to the lasting credit of the men, as a class, that their intelligence and patriotism were equal to the situation and won final confidence.

Emergent conditions in 1861 caused the seizure of the commercial systems around Washington, and Assistant Secretary of War Thomas A. Scott was made general manager of all such lines. He secured the cooperation of E. S. Sanford,

TELEGRAPHERS AFTER GETTYSBURG

The efficient-looking man leaning against the tent-pole in the rear is A. H. Caldwell, chief cipher operator for McClellan, Burnside, Hooker, Meade, and Grant. To him, just at the time this photograph was made, Lincoln addressed the famous despatch sent to Simon Cameron at Gettysburg. After being deciphered by Caldwell and delivered, the message ran: "I would give much to be relieved of the impression that Meade, Couch, Smith, and all, since the battle of Gettysburg, have striven only to get the enemy over the river without another fight. Please tell me if you know who was the one corps commander who was for fighting, in the council of war on Sunday night." It was customary for cipher messages to be addressed to and signed by the cipher operators. All of the group are mere boys, yet they coolly kept open their telegraph lines, sending important orders, while under fire and amid the utmost confusion.

of the American Telegraph Company, who imposed much-needed restrictions as to cipher messages, information, and so forth on all operators. The scope of the work was much increased by an act of Congress, in 1862, authorizing the seizure of any or all lines, in connection with which Sanford was appointed censor.

Through Andrew Carnegie was obtained the force which opened the War Department Telegraph Office; which speedily attained national importance by its remarkable work, and with which the memory of Abraham Lincoln must be inseparably associated. It was fortunate for the success of the telegraphic policy of the Government that it was entrusted to men of such administrative ability as Colonel Anson Stager, E. S. Sanford, and Major Thomas T. Eckert. The selection of operators for the War Office was surprisingly fortunate, including, as it did, three cipher-operators—D. H. Bates, A. B. Chandler, and C. A. Tinker—of high character, rare skill, and unusual discretion.

The military exigencies brought Sanford as censor and Eckert as assistant general manager, who otherwise performed their difficult duties with great efficiency; it must be added that at times they were inclined to display a striking disregard of proprieties and most unwarrantedly to enlarge the scope of their already extended authority. An interesting instance of the conflict of telegraphic and military authority was shown when Sanford mutilated McClellan's passionate despatch to Stanton, dated Savage's Station, June 29, 1862, in the midst of the Seven Days' Battles.*

Eckert also withheld from President Lincoln the despatch announcing the Federal defeat at Ball's Bluff. The suppression by Eckert of Grant's order for the removal of Thomas

* By cutting out of the message the last two sentences, reading: "If I save this army now, I tell you plainly that I owe no thanks to you or to any other person in Washington. You have done your best to sacrifice this army."

QUARTERS OF TELEGRAPHERS AND PHOTOGRAPHERS AT ARMY OF THE POTOMAC HEADQUARTERS, BRANDY STATION, APRIL, 1864

It was probably lack of military status that caused these pioneer corps in science to bunk together here. The photographers were under the protection of the secret service, and the telegraphers performed a similar function in the field of "military information."

THE TELEGRAPHER'S BOMB–PROOF BEFORE SUMTER

It is a comfort to contemplate the solidity of the bomb-proof where dwelt this telegraph operator; he carried no insurance for his family such as a regular soldier can look forward to in the possibility of a pension. This photograph was taken in 1863, while General Quincy A. Gillmore was covering the marshes before Charleston with breaching batteries, in the attempt to silence the Confederate forts. These replied with vigor, however, and the telegrapher needed all the protection possible while he kept the general in touch with his forts.

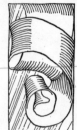

finds support only in the splendid victory of that great soldier at Nashville, and that only under the maxim that the end justifies the means. Eckert's narrow escape from summary dismissal by Stanton shows that, equally with the President and the commanding general, the war secretary was sometimes treated disrespectfully by his own subordinates.

One phase of life in the telegraph-room of the War Department—it is surprising that the White House had no telegraph office during the war—was Lincoln's daily visit thereto, and the long hours spent by him in the cipher-room, whose quiet seclusion made it a favorite retreat both for rest and also for important work requiring undisturbed thought and undivided attention.

There Lincoln turned over with methodical exactness and anxious expectation the office-file of recent messages. There he awaited patiently the translation of ciphers which forecasted promising plans for coming campaigns, told tales of unexpected defeat, recited the story of victorious battles, conveyed impossible demands, or suggested inexpedient policies. Masking anxiety by quaint phrases, impassively accepting criticism, harmonizing conflicting conditions, he patiently pondered over situations—both political and military—swayed in his solutions only by considerations of public good. For in this room were held conferences of vital national interest, with cabinet officers, generals, congressmen, and others. But his greatest task done here was that which required many days, during which was written the original draft of the memorable proclamation of emancipation.

Especially important was the technical work of Bates, Chandler, and Tinker enciphering and deciphering important messages to and from the great contending armies, which was done by code. Stager devised the first cipher, which was so improved by the cipher-operators that it remained untranslatable by the Confederates to the end of the war. An example of the method in general use, given by Plum in his " History of

TELEGRAPH CONSTRUCTION CORPS—STRINGING WIRE IN THE FIELD

This corps was composed of about one hundred and fifty men, with an outfit of wagons, tents, pack-mules, and paraphernalia. During the first two years of the war the common wire was used; but when Grant set out in his Wilderness campaign, a flexible insulated wire was substituted. The large wire was wound on reels and placed in wagons, which drove along the route where the line was to be erected. The men followed, putting up the wire as rapidly as it was unreeled. So expert were the linemen that the work seldom became disarranged. The first lines were constructed around Washington and to Alexandria, Virginia, in May. On the Peninsula the next year, the telegraph followed the troops in all directions. During the Fredericksburg and Chancellorsville campaigns it

proved an unfailing means of communication between the army and Washington. As it was intended only for temporary use, the poles were not required to be very substantial, and could usually be found in the wooded Virginia country near any proposed route. The immense labor required in such construction led to the adoption of insulated wire, which could be strung very quickly. A coil of the latter was placed on a mule's back and the animal led straight forward without halting. While the wire was unreeled, two men followed and hung up the line on the fences and bushes, where it would not be run over. When the telegraph extended through a section unoccupied by Federal forces in strength, cavalry patrols watched it, frequently holding the inhabitants responsible for its safety.

the Military Telegraph," is Lincoln's despatch to ex-Secretary Cameron when with Meade south of Gettysburg. As will be seen, messages were addressed to and signed by the cipher-operators. The message written out for sending is as follows:

Washington, D. C.	July	15th	18	60	3	for
Sigh	man	Cammer	on	period	I	would
give	much	to be	relieved	of the	impression	that
Meade	comma	Couch	comma	Smith	and	all
comma	since	the	battle	of	get	ties
burg	comma	have	striven	only	to	get
the enemy	over	the river	without	another	fight	period
please	tell	me	if	you	know	who
was	the	one	corps	commander	who	was
for	fighting	comma	in the	council	of	war
on	Sunday	night	signature	A. Lincoln	Bless	him

In the message as sent the first word (blonde) indicated the number of columns and lines in which the message was to be arranged, and the route for reading. Arbitrary words indicated names and persons, and certain blind (or useless) words were added, which can be easily detected. The message was sent as follows:

"WASHINGTON, D. C., July 15, 1863.
"A. H. Caldwell, Cipher-operator, General Meade's Headquarters:

"Blonde bless of who no optic to get an impression 1 madison-square Brown cammer Toby ax the have turnip me Harry bitch rustle silk adrian counsel locust you another only of children serenade flea Knox county for wood that awl ties get hound who was war him suicide on for was please village large bat Bunyan give sigh incubus heavy Norris on trammeled cat knit striven without if Madrid quail upright martyr Stewart man much bear since ass skeleton tell the oppressing Tyler monkey.
                                                    "BATES."

Brilliant and conspicuous service was rendered by the cipher-operators of the War Department in translating Con-

ONE OF GRANT'S FIELD–TELEGRAPH STATIONS IN 1864

This photograph, taken at Wilcox Landing, near City Point, gives an excellent idea of the difficulties under which telegraphing was done at the front or on the march. With a tent-fly for shelter and a hard-tack box for a table, the resourceful operator mounted his "relay," tested his wire, and brought the commanding general into direct communication with separated brigades or divisions. The U. S. Military Telegraph Corps, through its Superintendent of Construction, Dennis Doren, kept Meade and both wings of his army in communication from the crossing of the Rapidan in May, 1864, till the siege of Petersburg. Over this field-line Grant received daily reports from four separate armies, numbering a quarter of a million men, and replied with daily directions for their operations over an area of seven hundred and fifty thousand square miles. Though every corps of Meade's army moved daily, Doren kept them in touch with headquarters. The field-line was built of seven twisted, rubber-coated wires which were hastily strung on trees or fences.

federate cipher messages which fell into Union hands. A notable incident in the field was the translation of General Joseph E. Johnston's cipher message to Pemberton, captured by Grant before Vicksburg and forwarded to Washington. More important were the two cipher despatches from the Secretary of War at Richmond, in December, 1863, which led to a cabinet meeting and culminated in the arrest of Confederate conspirators in New York city, and to the capture of contraband shipments of arms and ammunition. Other intercepted and translated ciphers revealed plans of Confederate agents for raiding Northern towns near the border. Most important of all were the cipher messages disclosing the plot for the wholesale incendiarism of leading hotels in New York, which barely failed of success on November 25, 1864.

Beneficial and desirable as were the civil cooperation and management of the telegraph service in Washington, its forced extension to armies in the field was a mistaken policy. Patterson, in the Valley of Virginia, was five days without word from the War Department, and when he sent a despatch, July 20th, that Johnston had started to reenforce Beauregard with 35,200 men, this vital message was not sent to McDowell with whom touch was kept by a service half-telegraphic and half-courier.

The necessity of efficient field-telegraphs at once impressed military commanders. In the West, Fremont immediately acted, and in August, 1861, ordered the formation of a telegraph battalion of three companies along lines in accord with modern military practice. Major Myer had already made similar suggestions in Washington, without success. While the commercial companies placed their personnel and material freely at the Government's disposal, they viewed with marked disfavor any military organization, and their recommendations were potent with Secretary of War Cameron. Fremont was ordered to disband his battalion, and a purely civil bureau was substituted, though legal authority and funds were equally lack-

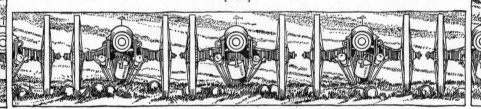

A TELEGRAPH BATTERY–WAGON NEAR PETERSBURG, JUNE, 1864

The operator in this photograph is receiving a telegraphic message, writing at his little table in the wagon as the machine clicks off the dots and dashes. Each battery-wagon was equipped with such an operator's table and attached instruments. A portable battery of one hundred cells furnished the electric current. No feature of the Army of the Potomac contributed more to its success than the field telegraph. Guided by its young chief, A. H. Caldwell, its lines bound the corps together like a perfect nervous system, and kept the great controlling head in touch with all its parts. Not until Grant cut loose from Washington and started from Brandy Station for Richmond was its full power tested. Two operators and a few orderlies accompanied each wagon, and the army crossed the Rapidan with the telegraph line going up at the rate of two miles an hour. At no time after that did any corps lose direct communication with the commanding general. At Spotsylvania the Second Corps, at sundown, swung round from the extreme right in the rear of the main body to the left. Ewell saw the movement, and advanced toward the exposed position; but the telegraph signaled the danger, and troops on the double-quick covered the gap before the alert Confederate general could assault the Union lines.

ing. Efforts to transfer quartermaster's funds and property to this bureau were successfully resisted, owing to the manifest illegality of such action.

Indirect methods were then adopted, and Stager was commissioned as a captain in the Quartermaster's Department, and his operators given the status of employees. He was appointed general manager of United States telegraph lines, November 25, 1861, and six days later, through some unknown influence, the Secretary of War reported (incorrectly, be it known), "that under an appropriation for that purpose at the last session of Congress, a telegraph bureau was established." Stager was later made a colonel, Eckert a major, and a few others captains, and so eligible for pensions, but the men in lesser positions remained employees, non-pensionable and subject to draft.

Repeated efforts by petitions and recommendations for giving a military status were made by the men in the field later in the war. The Secretary of War disapproved, saying that such a course would place them under the orders of superior officers, which he was most anxious to avoid.

With corporation influence and corps rivalries so rampant in Washington, there existed a spirit of patriotic solidarity in the face of the foe in the field that ensured hearty cooperation and efficient service. While the operators began with a sense of individual independence that caused them often to resent any control by commanding officers, from which they were free under the secretary's orders, yet their common sense speedily led them to comply with every request from commanders that was not absolutely incompatible with loyalty to their chief.

Especially in the public eye was the work connected with the operations in the armies which covered Washington and attacked Richmond, where McClellan first used the telegraph for tactical purposes. Illustrative of the courage and resourcefulness of operators was the action of Jesse Bunnell, attached to General Porter's headquarters. Finding himself on the fight-

HEADQUARTERS FIELD–TELEGRAPH PARTY AT PETERSBURG, VIRGINIA, JUNE 22, 1864

A battery-wagon in "action"; the operator has opened his office and is working his instrument. Important despatches were sent in cipher which only a chosen few operators could read. The latter were frequently under fire but calmly sat at their instruments, with the shells flying thick about them, and performed their duty with a faithfulness that won them an enviable reputation. At the Petersburg mine fiasco, in the vicinity of where this photograph was taken, an operator sat close at hand with an instrument and kept General Meade informed of the progress of affairs. The triumph of the field telegraph exceeded the most sanguine expectations. From the opening of Grant's campaign in the Wilderness to the close of the war, an aggregate of over two hundred miles of wire was put up and taken down from day to day; yet its efficiency as a constant means of communication between the several commands was not interfered with. The Army of the Potomac was the first great military body to demonstrate the advantages of the field telegraph for conducting military operations. The later campaigns of all civilized nations benefited much by these experiments. The field telegraph was in constant use during the Russian-Japanese War. Wireless stations are now an integral part of the United States army organization.

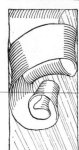

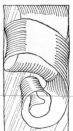

ing line, with the Federal troops hard pressed, Bunnell, without orders, cut the wire and opened communication with McClellan's headquarters. Superior Confederate forces were then threatening defeat to the invaders, but this battle-office enabled McClellan to keep in touch with the situation and ensure Porter's position by sending the commands of French, Meagher, and Slocum to his relief. Operator Nichols opened an emergency office at Savage's Station on Sumner's request, maintaining it under fire as long as it was needed.

One of the great feats of the war was the transfer, under the supervision of Thomas A. Scott, of two Federal army corps from Virginia to Tennessee, consequent on the Chickamauga disaster to the Union arms. By this phenomenal transfer, which would have been impossible without the military telegraph, twenty-three thousand soldiers, with provisions and baggage, were transported a distance of 1,233 miles in eleven and a half days, from Bristoe Station, Virginia, to Chattanooga, Tennessee. The troops had completed half their journey before the news of the proposed movement reached Richmond.

While most valuable elsewhere, the military telegraph was absolutely essential to successful operations in the valleys of the Cumberland and of the Tennessee, where very long lines of communication obtained, with consequent great distances between its separate armies. Apart from train-despatching, which was absolutely essential to transporting army supplies for hundreds of thousands of men over a single-track railway of several hundred of miles in length, an enormous number of messages for the control and cooperation of separate armies and detached commands were sent over the wires. Skill and patience were necessary for efficient telegraph work, especially when lines were frequently destroyed by Confederate incursions or through hostile inhabitants of the country.

Of great importance and of intense interest are many of the cipher despatches sent over these lines. Few, however, ex-

MEN WHO WORKED THE WIRES BEFORE PETERSBURG

These photographs of August, 1864, show some of the men who were operating their telegraph instruments in the midst of the cannonading and sharpshooting before Petersburg. Nerve-racking were the sounds and uncomfortably dangerous the situation, yet the operators held their posts. Amidst the terrible confusion of the night assault, the last despairing attempt of the Confederates to break through the encircling Federal forces, hurried orders and urgent appeals were sent. At dawn of March 25, 1865, General Gordon carried Fort Stedman with desperate gallantry and cut the wire to City Point. The Federals speedily sent the message of disaster: "The enemy has broken our right, taken Stedman, and are moving on City Point." Assuming command, General Parke ordered a counter-attack and recaptured the fort. The City Point wire was promptly restored and Meade, controlling the whole army by telegraph, made a combined and successful attack by several corps, capturing the entrenched picket-line of the Confederates.

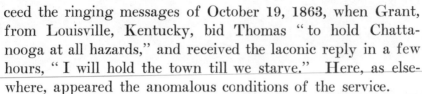

ceed the ringing messages of October 19, 1863, when Grant, from Louisville, Kentucky, bid Thomas "to hold Chattanooga at all hazards," and received the laconic reply in a few hours, "I will hold the town till we starve." Here, as elsewhere, appeared the anomalous conditions of the service.

While telegraph duties were performed with efficiency, troubles were often precipitated by divided authority. When Superintendent Stager ordered a civilian, who was engaged in building lines, out of Halleck's department, the general ordered him back, saying, "There must be one good head of telegraph lines in my department, not two, and that head must be under me." Though Stager protested to Secretary of War Stanton, the latter thought it best to yield in that case.

When General Grant found it expedient to appoint an aide as general manager of lines in his army, the civilian chief, J. C. Van Duzer, reported it to Stager, who had Grant called to account by the War Department. Grant promptly put Van Duzer under close confinement in the guardhouse, and later sent him out of the department, under guard. As an outcome, the operators planned a strike, which Grant quelled by telegraphic orders to confine closely every man resigning or guilty of contumacious conduct. Stager's efforts to dominate Grant failed through Stanton's fear that pressure would cause Grant to ask for relief from his command.

Stager's administration culminated in an order by his assistant, dated Cleveland, November 4, 1862, strictly requiring the operators to retain "the original copy of every telegram sent by any military or other Government officer . . . and mailed to the War Department." Grant answered, "Colonel Stager has no authority to demand the original of military despatches, and cannot have them." The order was never enforced, at least with Grant.

If similar experiences did not change the policy in Washington, it produced better conditions in the field and ensured harmonious cooperation. Of Van Duzer, it is to be said that

FRIENDS OF LINCOLN IN HIS LAST DAYS—MILITARY TELEGRAPH OPERATORS AT
CITY POINT, 1864

When Lincoln went to City Point at the request of General Grant, March 23, 1865, Grant directed his cipher
operator to report to the President and keep him in touch by telegraph with the army in its advance on
Richmond and with the War Department at Washington. For the last two or three weeks of his life Lincoln virtually lived in the telegraph office in company with the men in this photograph. He and Samuel
H. Beckwith, Grant's cipher operator, were almost inseparable and the wires were kept busy with despatches
to and from the President. Beckwith's tent adjoined the larger tent of Colonel Bowers, which Lincoln
made his headquarters, and where he received the translations of his numerous cipher despatches.

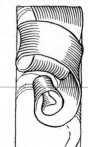

he later returned to the army and performed conspicuous service. At the battle of Chattanooga, he installed and operated lines on or near the firing-line during the two fateful days, November 24–25, 1863, often under heavy fire. Always sharing the dangers of his men, Van Duzer, through his coolness and activity under fire, has been mentioned as the only fighting officer of the Federal telegraph service.

Other than telegraphic espionage, the most dangerous service was the repair of lines, which often was done under fire and more frequently in a guerilla-infested country. Many men were captured or shot from ambush while thus engaged. Two of Clowry's men in Arkansas were not only murdered, but were frightfully mutilated. In Tennessee, conditions were sometimes so bad that no lineman would venture out save under heavy escort. Three repair men were killed on the Fort Donelson line alone. W. R. Plum, in his "Military Telegraph," says that "about one in twelve of the operators engaged in the service were killed, wounded, captured, or died in the service from exposure."

Telegraphic duties at military headquarters yielded little in brilliancy and interest compared to those of desperate daring associated with tapping the opponent's wires. At times, offices were seized so quickly as to prevent telegraphic warnings. General Mitchel captured two large Confederate railway trains by sending false messages from the Huntsville, Alabama, office, and General Seymour similarly seized a train near Jacksonville, Florida.

While scouting, Operator William Forster obtained valuable despatches by tapping the line along the Charleston-Savannah railway for two days. Discovered, he was pursued by bloodhounds into a swamp, where he was captured up to his armpits in mire. Later, the telegrapher died in prison.

In 1863, General Rosecrans deemed it most important to learn whether Bragg was detaching troops to reenforce the garrison at Vicksburg or for other purposes. The only cer-

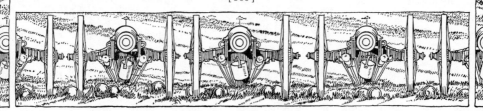

MILITARY TELEGRAPH OPERATORS AT CITY POINT, AUGUST, 1864

The men in this photograph, from left to right, are Dennis Doren, Superintendent of Construction; A. H. Caldwell, who was for four years cipher clerk at the headquarters of the Army of the Potomac; James A. Murray, who as wire-tapper of Confederate telegraph lines accompanied Kilpatrick in his raid toward Richmond and down the Peninsula in February, 1864, when the Union cavalry leader made his desperate attempt to liberate the Union prisoners in Libby prison. The fourth is J. H. Emerick, who was complimented for distinguished services in reporting Pleasonton's cavalry operations in 1863, and became cipher operator in Richmond in 1865. Through Emerick's foresight and activity the Union telegraph lines were carried into Richmond the night after its capture. Samuel H. Beckwith was the faithful cipher operator who accompanied Lincoln from City Point on his visit to Richmond April 4, 1865. In his account of this visit, published in "Lincoln in the Telegraph Office," by David Homer Bates, he tells how the President immediately repaired to his accustomed desk in Colonel Bowers' tent, next to the telegraph office, upon his return to City Point. Beckwith found a number of cipher messages for the President awaiting translation, doubtless in regard to Grant's closing in about the exhausted forces of Lee.

tain method seemed to be by tapping the wires along the Chattanooga railroad, near Knoxville, Tennessee. For this most dangerous duty, two daring members of the telegraph service volunteered—F. S. Van Valkenbergh and Patrick Mullarkey. The latter afterward was captured by Morgan, in Ohio. With four Tennesseeans, they entered the hostile country and, selecting a wooded eminence, tapped the line fifteen miles from Knoxville, and for a week listened to all passing despatches. Twice escaping detection, they heard a message going over the wire which ordered the scouring of the district to capture Union spies. They at once decamped, barely in time to escape the patrol. Hunted by cavalry, attacked by guerillas, approached by Confederate spies, they found aid from Union mountaineers, to whom they owed their safety. Struggling on, with capture and death in daily prospect, they finally fell in with Union pickets—being then half starved, clothed in rags, and with naked, bleeding feet. They had been thirty-three days within the Confederate lines, and their stirring adventures make a story rarely equaled in thrilling interest.

Confederate wires were often tapped during Sherman's march to the sea, a warning of General Wheeler's coming raid being thus obtained. Operator Lonergan copied important despatches from Hardee, in Savannah, giving Bragg's movements in the rear of Sherman, with reports on cavalry and rations.

Wiretapping was also practised by the Confederates, who usually worked in a sympathetic community. Despite their daring skill the net results were often small, owing to the Union system of enciphering all important messages. Their most audacious and persistent telegraphic scout was Ellsworth, Morgan's operator, whose skill, courage, and resourcefulness contributed largely to the success of his daring commander. Ellsworth was an expert in obtaining despatches, and especially in disseminating misleading information by bogus messages.

In the East, an interloper from Lee's army tapped the

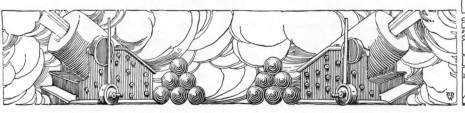

WAR SERVICE OVER—MILITARY TELEGRAPH OPERATORS IN RICHMOND, JUNE, 1865

"The cipher operators with the various armies were men of rare skill, unswerving integrity, and unfailing loyalty," General Greeley pronounces from personal knowledge. Caldwell, as chief operator, accompanied the Army of the Potomac on every march and in every siege, contributing also to the efficiency of the field telegraphers. Beckwith remained Grant's cipher operator to the end of the war. He it was who tapped a wire and reported the hiding-place of Wilkes Booth. The youngest boy operator, O'Brien, began by refusing a princely bribe to forge a telegraphic reprieve, and later won distinction with Butler on the James and with Schofield in North Carolina. W. R. Plum, who wrote a "History of the Military Telegraph in the Civil War," also rendered efficient service as chief operator to Thomas, and at Atlanta. The members of the group are, from left to right: 1, Dennis Doren, Superintendent of Construction; 2, L. D. McCandless; 3, Charles Bart; 4, Thomas Morrison; 5, James B. Norris; 6, James Caldwell; 7, A. Harper Caldwell, chief cipher operator, and in charge; 8, Maynard A. Huyck; 9, Dennis Palmer; 10, J. H. Emerick; 11, James H. Nichols. Those surviving in June, 1911, were Morrison, Norris, and Nichols.

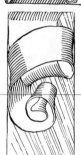

wire between the War Department and Burnside's headquarters at Aquia Creek, and remained undetected for probably several days. With fraternal frankness, the Union operators advised him to leave.

The most prolonged and successful wiretapping was that by C. A. Gaston, Lee's confidential operator. Gaston entered the Union lines near City Point, while Richmond and Petersburg were besieged, with several men to keep watch for him, and for six weeks he remained undisturbed in the woods, reading all messages which passed over Grant's wire. Though unable to read the ciphers, he gained much from the despatches in plain text. One message reported that 2,586 beeves were to be landed at Coggins' Point on a certain day. This information enabled Wade Hampton to make a timely raid and capture the entire herd.

It seems astounding that Grant, Sherman, Thomas, and Meade, commanding armies of hundreds of thousands and working out the destiny of the Republic, should have been debarred from the control of their own ciphers and the keys thereto. Yet, in 1864, the Secretary of War issued an order forbidding commanding generals to interfere with even their own cipher-operators and absolutely restricting the use of cipher-books to civilian " telegraph experts, approved and appointed by the Secretary of War." One mortifying experience with a despatch untranslatable for lack of facilities constrained Grant to order his cipher-operator, Beckwith, to reveal the key to Colonel Comstock, his aide, which was done under protest. Stager at once dismissed Beckwith, but on Grant's request and insistence of his own responsibility, Beckwith was restored.

The cipher-operators with the various armies were men of rare skill, unswerving integrity, and unfailing loyalty. Caldwell, as chief operator, accompanied the Army of the Potomac on every march and in every siege, contributing also to the efficiency of the field-telegraphs. Beckwith was Grant's cipher-

COPYRIGHT 1911. PATRIOT PUB. CO.

A TELEGRAPH OFFICE IN THE TRENCHES

In this photograph are more of the "minute men" who helped the Northern leaders to draw the coils closer about Petersburg with their wonderful system of instantaneous intercommunication. They brought the commanding generals actually within seconds of each other, though miles of fortifications might intervene. There has evidently been a lull in affairs, and they have been dining at their ease. Two of them in the background are toasting each other, it may be for the last time. The mortality among those men who risked their lives, with no hope or possibility of such distinction and recognition as come to the soldier who wins promotion, was exceedingly high.

operator to the end of the war, and was the man who tapped a wire and reported the hiding-place of Wilkes Booth. Another operator, Richard O'Brien, in 1863 refused a princely bribe to forge a telegraphic reprieve, and later won distinction with Butler on the James and with Schofield in North Carolina. W. R. Plum, who wrote "History of the Military Telegraph in the Civil War," also rendered efficient service as chief operator to Thomas, and at Atlanta. It is regrettable that such men were denied the glory and benefits of a military service, which they actually, though not officially, gave.

The bitter contest, which lasted several years, over field-telegraphs ended in March, 1864, when the Signal Corps transferred its field-trains to the civilian bureau. In Sherman's advance on Atlanta, Van Duzer distinguished himself by bringing up the field-line from the rear nearly every night. At Big Shanty, Georgia, the whole battle-front was covered by working field-lines which enabled Sherman to communicate at all times with his fighting and reserve commands. Hamley considers the constant use of field-telegraphs in the flanking operations by Sherman in Georgia as showing the overwhelming value of the service. This duty was often done under fire and other dangerous conditions.

In Virginia, in 1864–65, Major Eckert made great and successful efforts to provide Meade's army with ample facilities. A well-equipped train of thirty or more battery-wagons, wire-reels, and construction carts were brought together under Doren, a skilled builder and energetic man. While offices were occasionally located in battery-wagons, they were usually under tent-flies next to the headquarters of Meade or Grant. Through the efforts of Doren and Caldwell, all important commands were kept within control of either Meade or Grant— even during engagements. Operators were often under fire, and at Spotsylvania Court House telegraphers, telegraph-cable, and battery-wagons were temporarily within the Confederate lines. From these trains was sent the ringing des-

THE TELEGRAPH CONSTRUCTION TRAIN, IN RICHMOND AT LAST

This train, under the direction of Mr. A. Harper Caldwell, Chief Operator of the Army of the Potomac, was used in the construction of field-telegraph lines during the Wilderness campaign and in operations before Petersburg. After the capture of Richmond it was used by Superintendent Dennis Doren to restore the important telegraph routes of which that city was the center. In Virginia in 1864–5, Major Eckert made great and successful efforts to provide Meade's army with ample facilities. A well-equipped train of thirty or more battery wagons, wire-reels, and construction carts was brought together under the skilful and energetic Doren.

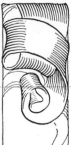

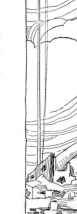

patch from the Wilderness, by which Grant inspired the North, " I propose to fight it out on this line if it takes all summer."

During siege operations at Petersburg, a system of lines connected the various headquarters, depots, entrenchments, and even some picket lines. Cannonading and sharpshooting were so insistent that operators were often driven to bomb-proof offices—especially during artillery duels and impending assaults. Nerve-racking were the sounds and uncomfortably dangerous the situations, yet the operators held their posts. Under the terrible conditions of a night assault, the last despairing attempt to break through the encircling Federal forces at Petersburg, hurried orders and urgent appeals were sent. At dawn of March 25, 1865, General Gordon carried Fort Stedman with desperate gallantry, and cut the wire to City Point. The Federals speedily sent the message of disaster, " The enemy has broken our right, taken Stedman, and are moving on City Point." Assuming command, General Parke ordered a counter-attack and recaptured the fort. Promptly the City Point wire was restored, and Meade, controlling the whole army by telegraph, made a combined attack by several corps, capturing the entrenched picket line of the Confederates.

First of all of the great commanders, Grant used the military telegraph both for grand tactics and for strategy in its broadest sense. From his headquarters with Meade's army in Virginia, May, 1864, he daily gave orders and received reports regarding the operations of Meade in Virginia, Sherman in Georgia, Sigel in West Virginia, and Butler on the James River. Later he kept under direct control military forces exceeding half a million of soldiers, operating over a territory of eight hundred thousand square miles in area. Through concerted action and timely movements, Grant prevented the re-enforcement of Lee's army and so shortened the war. Sherman said, " The value of the telegraph cannot be exaggerated, as illustrated by the perfect accord of action of the armies of Virginia and Georgia."

PART II
MILITARY INFORMATION

ARMY
BALLOONS

OBSERVING THE BATTLE OF FAIR OAKS, MAY, 1862
PROFESSOR LOWE IN HIS BALLOON

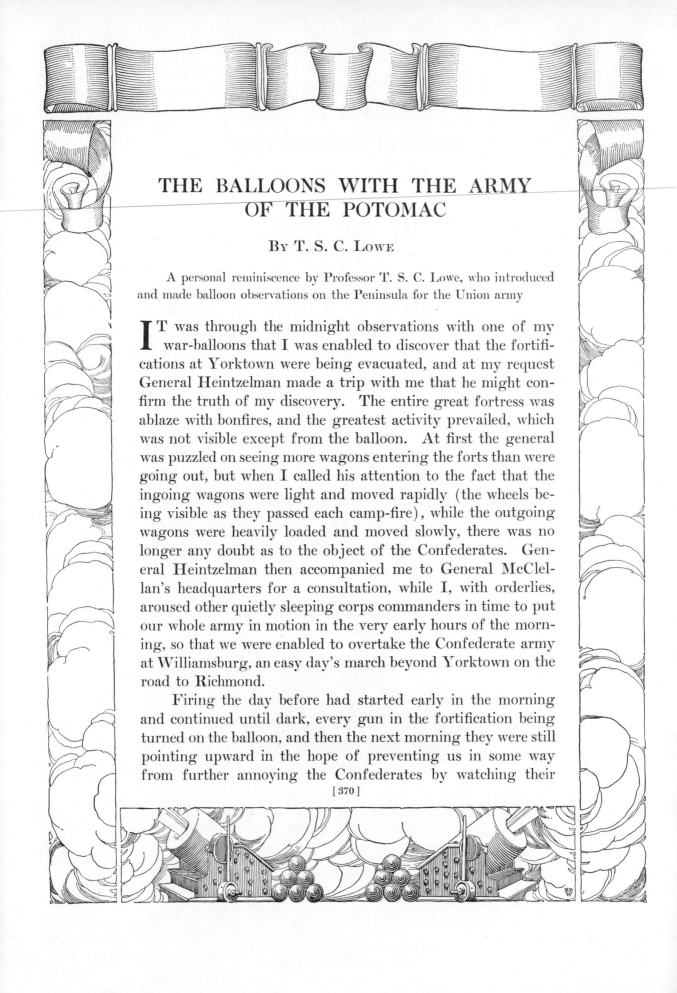

THE BALLOONS WITH THE ARMY
OF THE POTOMAC

By T. S. C. Lowe

A personal reminiscence by Professor T. S. C. Lowe, who introduced
and made balloon observations on the Peninsula for the Union army

IT was through the midnight observations with one of my
war-balloons that I was enabled to discover that the fortifications at Yorktown were being evacuated, and at my request
General Heintzelman made a trip with me that he might confirm the truth of my discovery. The entire great fortress was
ablaze with bonfires, and the greatest activity prevailed, which
was not visible except from the balloon. At first the general
was puzzled on seeing more wagons entering the forts than were
going out, but when I called his attention to the fact that the
ingoing wagons were light and moved rapidly (the wheels being visible as they passed each camp-fire), while the outgoing
wagons were heavily loaded and moved slowly, there was no
longer any doubt as to the object of the Confederates. General Heintzelman then accompanied me to General McClellan's headquarters for a consultation, while I, with orderlies,
aroused other quietly sleeping corps commanders in time to put
our whole army in motion in the very early hours of the morning, so that we were enabled to overtake the Confederate army
at Williamsburg, an easy day's march beyond Yorktown on the
road to Richmond.

Firing the day before had started early in the morning
and continued until dark, every gun in the fortification being
turned on the balloon, and then the next morning they were still
pointing upward in the hope of preventing us in some way
from further annoying the Confederates by watching their

CONFEDERATE BATTERY AT YORKTOWN WHICH FIRED UPON THE FEDERAL BALLOONIST AND UPON
WHICH "BALLOON BRYAN" LOOKED DOWN

Captain John Randolph Bryan, aide-de-camp to General J. B. Magruder, then commanding the Army of the Peninsula near York-town, Virginia, made three balloon trips in all above the wonderful panorama of the Chesapeake Bay, the York and the James Rivers, Old Point Comfort and Hampton, the fleets lying in both the York and the James, and the two opposing armies facing each other across the Peninsula. General Johnston complimented him upon the detailed information which he secured in this fashion, braving the shells and shrapnel of the Union batteries, and his fellow-soldiers nicknamed the young aeronaut "Balloon Bryan." On his final trip, made just before Williamsburg, May 5, 1862, the rope which held him to the earth entangled a soldier. It was cut. The balloon bounded two miles into the air. First it drifted out over the Union lines, then was blown back toward the Confederate lines near Yorktown. The Confederates, seeing it coming from that direction, promptly opened fire. Finally it skimmed the surface of the York River, its guide-rope splashing in the water, and landed in an orchard. On this trip the balloon made a half-moon circuit of about fifteen miles, about four miles of which was over the York River. The information which Captain Bryan was able to give General Johnston as to the roads upon which the Federals were moving enabled him to prepare for an attack the following morning

movements. The last shot, fired after dark, came into General Heintzelman's camp and completely destroyed his telegraph tent and instruments, the operator having just gone out to deliver a despatch. The general and I were sitting together, discussing the probable reasons for the unusual effort to destroy the balloon, when we were both covered with what appeared to be tons of earth, which a great 12-inch shell had thrown up. Fortunately, it did not explode. I suggested that the next morning we should move the balloon so as to draw the foe's fire in another direction, but the general said that he could stand it if I could. Besides, he would like to have me near by, as he enjoyed going up occasionally himself. He told me that, while I saw a grand spectacle by watching the discharge of all those great guns that were paying their entire compliments to a single man, it was nothing as compared with the sight I would look down upon the next day when our great mortar batteries would open their siege-guns on the fortifications, which General McClellan expected to do.

I could see readily that I could be of no service at Williamsburg, both armies being hidden in a great forest. Therefore, General McClellan at the close of the battle sent orders to me to proceed with my outfit, including all the balloons, gas-generators, the balloon-inflating boat, gunboat, and tug up the Pamunkey River, until I reached White House and the bridge crossing the historic river, and join the army which would be there as soon as myself.

This I did, starting early the next morning, passing by the great cotton-bale fortifications on the York River, and soon into the little winding but easily navigated stream of the Pamunkey. Every now and then I would let the balloon go up to view the surrounding country, and over the bridge beyond the Pamunkey River valley, I saw the rear of the retreating Confederates, which showed me that our army had not gotten along as fast as it was expected, and I could occasionally see a few scouts on horseback on the hills beyond. I saw my helpless

Professor T. S. C. Lowe appears here standing by his father in camp before the battle of Fair Oaks, explaining by means of an engineers' map the service he proposed to render the Union army. Below is the balloon from which General George Stoneman, McClellan's cavalry leader on the Peninsula, and Professor Lowe were able to look into the windows of Richmond. In this balloon also Professor Lowe was telegraphing, reporting, and sketching during the battle of May 31–June 1st, and it was from his night observations at this time that came knowledge on which McClellan acted in saving his army. On arriving in sight of Richmond, Lowe took observations to ascertain the best location for crossing the Chickahominy River and sketched the place where the

"Grapevine" or Sumner Bridge was afterward built across that stream. His main station and personal camp lay on Gaines' Hill, four miles from Mechanicsville, overlooking the bridge where the army was to cross. Desperate efforts were made by the Confederates at Mechanicsville to destroy the observation balloon in order to conceal their movements. At one point they masked twelve of their best rifled cannon; while Professor Lowe was taking an early morning observation, the whole twelve guns were simultaneously discharged at short range, some of the shells passing through the rigging of the balloon and nearly all bursting not more than two hundred feet beyond it. Professor Lowe immediately changed his base of operations, and escaped the imminent danger.

PROFESSOR LOWE AND HIS FATHER

AT "BALLOON CAMP," GAINES' HILL, WHILE THE TWO ARMIES WAITED

condition without my gunboat, the *Cœur de Lion,* which had served me for the past year so well on the Potomac, Chesapeake, and York, and which I had sent to Commodore Wilkes to aid him in the bombardment of Fort Darling, on the James River, thinking I would have no further use for it. Therefore, all I had was the balloon-boat and the steam-tug and one hundred and fifty men with muskets, a large number of wagons and gas-generators for three independent balloon outfits. My balloon-boat was almost a facsimile of our first little *Monitor* and about its size, and with the flag which I kept at the stern it had the appearance of an armed craft, which I think is all that saved me and my command, for the *Monitor* was what the Confederates dreaded at that time more than anything else.

After General Stoneman had left me at White House, I soon had a gas-generating apparatus beside a little pool of water, and from it extracted hydrogen enough in an hour to take both the general and myself to an altitude that enabled us to look into the windows of the city of Richmond and view its surroundings, and we saw what was left of the troops that had left Yorktown encamped about the city.

While my illness at Malvern Hill prevented me from reporting to headquarters until the army reached Antietam, those in charge of transportation in Washington took all my wagons and horses and left my command without transportation. Consequently I could render no service there, but the moment General McClellan saw me he expressed his regret that I had been so ill, and that he did not have the benefit of my services; for if he had he could have gotten the proper information, he could have prevented a great amount of stores and artillery from recrossing the Potomac and thus depleted the Confederate army that much more. I explained to him why he had been deprived of my services, which did not surprise him, because he stated that everything had been done to annoy him, but that he must still perform his duty regardless of

SAVING "A MILLION DOLLARS A MINUTE" IN 1862

This is a photograph of a feat that would be noteworthy in the twentieth century, and in 1862 was revolutionary—actually being performed on the field of battle. At Fair Oaks, May 31, 1862, the lifting force of the balloon *Constitution* proved too weak to carry up the telegraph apparatus, its wires, and cables to a height sufficient to overlook the forests and hills. "I was at my wit's end," writes Professor Lowe, "as to how I could best save an hour's time—the most precious and important hour of all my experience in the army. As I saw the two armies coming nearer and nearer together, there was no time to be lost. It flashed through my mind that if I could only get the gas which was in the smaller balloon *Constitution* into the balloon *Intrepid*, which was then half filled, I would save an hour's time, and to us that hour's time would be worth a million dollars a minute." By the ingenious use of a 10-inch camp kettle with the bottom cut out, a connection was made and the gas in the *Constitution* was transferred to the *Intrepid*.

annoyances. When I asked him if I should accompany him across the river in pursuit of Lee, he replied that he would see that I had my supply trains immediately, but that the troops after so long a march were nearly all barefoot, and in no condition to proceed until they had been properly shod and clothed.

Without the time and knowledge gained by the midnight observations referred to at the beginning of this chapter, there would have been no battle of Williamsburg, and McClellan would have lost the opportunity of gaining a victory, the importance of which has never been properly appreciated. The Confederates would have gotten away with all their stores and ammunition without injury. It was also my night observations that gave the primary knowledge which saved the Federal army at the battle of Fair Oaks.

On arriving in sight of Richmond, I took observations to ascertain the best location for crossing the Chickahominy River. The one selected was where the Grapevine, or Sumner, Bridge was afterward built across that stream. Mechanicsville was the point nearest to Richmond, being only about four miles from the capital, but there we would have had to face the gathering army of the Confederacy, at the only point properly provided with trenches and earthworks. Here I established one of my aeronautic stations, where I could better estimate the increase of the Confederate army and observe their various movements. My main station and personal camp was on Gaines' Hill, overlooking the bridge where our army was to cross.

When this bridge was completed, about half of our army crossed over on the Richmond side of the river, the remainder delaying for a while to protect our transportation supplies and railway facilities. In the mean time, the Confederate camp in and about Richmond grew larger every day.

My night-and-day observations convinced me that with the great army then assembled in and about Richmond we were too late to gain a victory, which a short time before was within our grasp. In the mean time, desperate efforts were made by

PROFESSOR LOWE IN HIS BALLOON AT A CRITICAL MOMENT

As soon as Professor Lowe's balloon soars above the top of the trees the Confederate batteries will open upon him, and for the next few moments shells and bullets from the shrapnels will be bursting and whistling about his ears. Then he will pass out of the danger-zone to an altitude beyond the reach of the Confederate artillery. After the evacuation of Yorktown, May 4, 1862, Professor Lowe, who had been making daily observations from his balloon, followed McClellan's divisions, which was to meet Longstreet next day at Williamsburg. On reaching the fortifications of the abandoned city, Lowe directed the men who were towing the still inflated balloon in which he was riding to scale the corner of the fort nearest to his old camp, where the last gun had been fired the night before. This fort had devoted a great deal of effort to attempting to damage the too inquisitive balloon, and a short time previously one of the best Confederate guns had burst, owing to over-charging and too great an elevation to reach the high altitude. The balloonist had witnessed the explosion and a number of gunners had been killed and wounded within his sight. His present visit was in order to touch and examine the pieces and bid farewell to what he then looked upon as a departed friend. This is indicated as the same gun on page 371.

the Confederates to destroy my balloon at Mechanicsville, in order to prevent my observing their movements.

At one point they masked twelve of their best rifle-cannon, and while taking an early morning observation, all the twelve guns were simultaneously discharged at short range, some of the shells passing through the rigging of the balloon and nearly all bursting not more than two hundred feet beyond me, showing that through spies they had gotten my base of operations and range perfectly. I changed my base, and they never came so near destroying the balloon or capturing me after that.

I felt that it was important to take thorough observations that very night at that point, which I did. The great camps about Richmond were ablaze with fires. I had then experience enough to know what this meant, that they were cooking rations preparatory to moving. I knew that this movement must be against that portion of the army then across the river. At daylight the next morning, May 31st, I took another observation, continuing the same until the sun lighted up the roads. The atmosphere was perfectly clear. I knew exactly where to look for their line of march, and soon discovered one, then two, and then three columns of troops with artillery and ammunition wagons moving toward the position occupied by General Heintzelman's command.

All this information was conveyed to the commanding general, who, on hearing my report that the force at both ends of the bridge was too slim to finish it that morning, immediately sent more men to work on it.

I used the balloon *Washington* at Mechanicsville for observations, until the Confederate army was within four or five miles of our lines. I then telegraphed my assistants to inflate the large balloon, *Intrepid,* in case anything should happen to either of the other two. This order was quickly carried out, and I then took a six-mile ride on horseback to my camp on Gaines' Hill, and made another observation from the balloon

THE PHOTOGRAPH THE BALLOONIST RECOGNIZED FORTY-EIGHT YEARS AFTER

"When I saw the photograph showing my inflation of the balloon *Intrepid* to reconnoiter the battle of Fair Oaks," wrote Professor T. S. C. Lowe in the *American Review of Reviews* for February, 1911, "it surprised me very much indeed. Any one examining the picture will see my hand at the extreme right, resting on the network, where I was measuring the amount of gas already in the balloon, preparatory to completing the inflation from gas in the smaller balloon in order that I might ascent to a greater height. This I did within a space of five minutes, saving a whole hour at the most vital point of the battle." A close examination of this photograph will reveal Professor Lowe's hand resting on the network of the balloon, although his body is not in the photograph. It truly is remarkable that Professor Lowe should have seen and recognized, nearly half a century afterward, this photograph taken at one of the most critical moments of his life.

Constitution. I found it necessary to double the altitude usually sufficient for observations in order to overlook forests and hills, and thus better to observe the movements of both our army and that of the Confederates.

To carry my telegraph apparatus, wires, and cables to this higher elevation, the lifting force of the *Constitution* proved to be too weak. It was then that I was put to my wits' end as to how I could best save an hour's time, which was the most important and precious hour of all my experience in the army. As I saw the two armies coming nearer and nearer together, there was no time to be lost. It flashed through my mind that if I could only get the gas that was in the smaller balloon, *Constitution,* into the *Intrepid,* which was then half filled, I would save an hour's time, and to us that hour's time would be worth a million dollars a minute. But how was I to rig up the proper connection between the balloons? To do this within the space of time necessary puzzled me until I glanced down and saw a 10-inch camp-kettle, which instantly gave me the key to the situation. I ordered the bottom cut out of the kettle, the *Intrepid* disconnected with the gas-generating apparatus, and the *Constitution* brought down the hill. In the course of five or six minutes connection was made between both balloons and the gas in the *Constitution* was transferred into the *Intrepid.*

I immediately took a high-altitude observation as rapidly as possible, wrote my most important despatch to the commanding general on my way down, and I dictated it to my expert telegraph operator. Then with the telegraph cable and instruments, I ascended to the height desired and remained there almost constantly during the battle, keeping the wires hot with information.

The Confederate skirmish line soon came in contact with our outposts, and I saw their whole well-laid plan. They had massed the bulk of their artillery and troops, not only with the intention of cutting off our ammunition supplies, but of

COMPLETING A DESPATCH AT FAIR OAKS BEFORE THE ASCENSION
DURING THE BATTLE OF FAIR OAKS

MAY 31, 1862

It was during the American Civil War that war information was first telegraphed from the sky. This photograph shows Professor Lowe during the battle of Fair Oaks, completing a despatch just before ascending with telegraph apparatus and wire. "It was one of the greatest strains upon my nerves that I have ever experienced," he writes in regard to this ascension, "to observe for many hours an almost drawn battle, while the Union forces were waiting to complete the bridge to connect their separated army. This fortunately was accomplished, and our first troops under Sumner's command were able to cross at four o'clock in the afternoon, followed by wagons of ammunition for those who needed it. Earlier in the day many brigades and regiments had entirely exhausted their ammunition. Brave Heintzelman rode along the line giving orders for the men to shout in order to deceive the Confederates as to their real situation. When Sumner's troops swung into line, I could hear a real shout, which sounded entirely different from the former response."

preventing the main portion of the army from crossing the bridge to join Heintzelman.

As I reported the movements and maneuvers of the Confederates, I could see, in a very few moments, that our army was maneuvering to offset their plans.

At about twelve o'clock, the whole lines of both armies were in deadly conflict. Ours not only held its line firmly, but repulsed the foe at all his weaker points.

It was one of the greatest strains upon my nerves that I ever have experienced, to observe for many hours a fierce battle, while waiting for the bridge connecting the two armies to be completed. This fortunately was accomplished and our first reenforcements, under Sumner, were able to cross at four o'clock in the afternoon, followed by ammunition wagons.

It was at that time that the first and only Confederate balloon was used during the war. This balloon, which I afterward captured, was described by General Longstreet as follows:*

It may be of interest at the outset to relate an incident which illustrates the pinched condition of the Confederacy even as early as 1862.

The Federals had been using balloons in examining our positions, and we watched with envious eyes their beautiful observations as they floated high up in the air, well out of range of our guns. While we were longing for the balloons that poverty denied us, a genius arose for the occasion and suggested that we send out and gather silk dresses in the Confederacy and make a balloon. It was done, and we soon had a great patchwork ship of many varied hues which was ready for use in the Seven Days' campaign.

We had no gas except in Richmond, and it was the custom to inflate the balloon there, tie it securely to an engine, and run it down the York River Railroad to any point at which we desired to send it up. One day it was on a steamer down on the James River, when the tide went out and left the vessel and balloon high and dry on a bar. The Federals gathered it in, and with it the last silk dress in the Confederacy. This capture was the meanest trick of the war and one that I have never yet forgiven.

*Battles and Leaders of the Civil War. (New York.)

ONE OF THE BOY SOLDIERS

CHARLES F. MOSBY, A CONFEDERATE DRUMMER-BOY
WHO ENLISTED AT THE AGE OF THIRTEEN AND SERVED
FROM '61 TO '65 THROUGHOUT THE WAR, FIRST WITH
THE "ELLIOTT GRAYS" OF THE SIXTH VIRGINIA INFAN-
TRY AND LATER WITH HENDERSON'S HEAVY ARTILLERY.

The Photographic History
of The Civil War

TWO VOLUMES IN ONE.
Prisons and Hospitals

CONFEDERATE BOY–SOLDIERS GUARDING UNION CAPTIVES, 1861—PRISONERS FROM BULL RUN IN
CASTLE PINCKNEY—ABOVE, THE CHARLESTON ZOUAVE CADETS

The Union prisoners shown in this remarkable photograph are members of the Seventy-ninth (Highlanders) Regiment of New York City and the Eighth Michigan Regiment, captured at the first battle of Bull Run, July 21, 1861. Guarding them on the parapet are a number of the Charleston Zouave Cadets. The bearded officer resting his head on his hand, next to the civilian, is Captain C. E. Chichester, of the Cadets. Next to him is Private T. G. Boag, and sitting in front of him with his coat in his hands is Lieutenant E. John White. The head and shoulders of W. H. Welch, orderly-sergeant, appear behind the mouth of the cannon. The center figure of the three cadets sitting at his left, with his sword-point on the ground, is Sergeant (later Captain) Joseph F. Burke. The uniform of the Seventy-ninth New York was dark blue with a small red stripe on trousers and jackets. The latter had small brass buttons. On their caps was the number "79" in brass figures. Many of the other men shown without coats belonged to the Eighth Michigan Infantry. This photograph and the two others of Castle Pinckney shown on subsequent pages were taken in August, 1861.

The Photographic History
of The Civil War

Complete and Unabridged

TWO VOLUMES IN ONE.

Volume 4
Soldier Life and Secret Service
*Prisons and Hospitals

EDITOR

HOLLAND THOMPSON, Ph.D.

Assistant Professor of History, College of the
City of New York
Sometime Secretary of the North Carolina Historical Society

Contributors

HOLLAND THOMPSON

EDWARD L. MUNSON, M.D.
Major, Medical Department, U. S. Army

DEERING J. ROBERTS, M.D.
Late Surgeon, Confederate States Army

THE BLUE & GREY PRESS

CONTENTS

Part I—Prisons

Holland Thompson

Part II—Hospitals

Contents

PHOTOGRAPHIC DESCRIPTIONS THROUGHOUT THE VOLUME
  Roy Mason

PREFACE

AMBULANCES OF
THE UNION ARMY
TAKING PART IN
THE GRAND REVIEW
1865

WHEN MUSKETS AND BAYONETS WERE TURNED INTO TENT-POLES

CARING FOR THE ANTIETAM WOUNDED

IN SEPTEMBER, 1862, JUST AFTER

THE BLOODIEST DAY OF THE WAR

Erect, to the right of the center, stands Dr. A. Hurd, of the Fourteenth Indiana Volunteers, caring for Confederate wounded near the battlefield of Antietam. Around him the twisted forms of sufferers lie under temporary coverings, made of blankets or flaps from shelter-tents suspended upon guns for tent-poles. Swords are not yet "beaten into plowshares," but bayonets are thrust into the ground for the merci-ful purpose of protecting the feverish patients from the burning sun. Use has been made of the hay from Smith's farm nearby to form soft beds for the wounded limbs. Further shelter has been improvised by laying fence-rails against supporting poles. Below appear the straw huts for wounded on Smith's farm, erected a day or two later. The surgeon on the field of battle knew neither friend nor foe in his treatment of the wounded. On June 6, 1862, a week after the battles of Seven Pines or Fair Oaks, a general order was issued from Washington that surgeons should be considered non-combatants and not sent to prison. It was a result of "Stonewall" Jackson's previous action, and was accepted by Lee at Richmond on the 17th.

PREFACE

THE pages of this volume tell little of war's pomp and pageantry. Their subject is, and must be, grim and terrible. Though prisoners of war were not criminals, but often men whose courage was their only fault, and though their detention must not be considered as deserved punishment, but as a military necessity, nevertheless all prisons are unlovely. The groans of men, one moment vigorous, the next shattered and broken, or the sight of strength visibly ebbing away from disease, are awful. It is the dark and cruel side of war that must here be told.

The reader who finds nothing more than this is, however, careless and superficial, seeing only the object immediately before his eyes, and neglecting relations and perspective. One may hold a dime so that it shuts out the sun. A fact out of its relations to other facts is no better than a lie. Just so far as history enables us to see any particular epoch in its relation to those before, and as the portent of those coming after, to that extent history is true. The failure of the sentimentalist and the social reformer often grows out of myopia. They see only what is near their eyes.

That men must be judged by the standard of their times is a platitude, but it is well to emphasize platitudes, for the obvious is often forgotten. We are prone to judge the past by the standards of the present, and some of our standards are rising.

Unpleasant as is the story of the prisons of the Civil War, however great their shortcomings, the treatment of prisoners, taken as a whole, marks a decided advance over the general practice of the world before that time. Instances of theatrical generosity have always been plentiful, but never before had the dictates of humanity so profoundly influenced the action of so many. We must believe that the greatest horrors—for there were horrors— arose from ignorance or apparent necessity, rather than from intention.

During our own Revolution, the treatment of prisoners is a subject upon which both we and the English must prefer not to dwell. Less than three score years separated the Civil War from the War of 1812 and from the

CAMPBELL HOSPITAL NEAR WASHINGTON—FLOWERS AND FEMALE NURSES HERE

HOSPITAL AND CAMP NEAR WASHINGTON

STANTON HOSPITAL IN WASHINGTON

TWO-STORY BUILDINGS IN WASHINGTON

CARVER HOSPITAL IN WASHINGTON

SIGHTS IN WAR-TIME WASHINGTON, AFTER IT HAD BECOME A CITY OF WOUNDED SOLDIERS, BUSY ARMY SURGEONS, AND CROWDED HOSPITALS

THE QUARTERMASTER'S DEPARTMENT EMPLOYED SUCH A HUGE FORCE OF MEN THAT IT WAS NECESSARY TO FURNISH THEM A SEPARATE HOSPITAL

Preface

Napoleonic wars, which shook the foundations of Europe. The whole story of the prisoners whom fortune threw at the mercy of the contending forces in the first years of the nineteenth century has not been told—perhaps wisely —though even here it was indifference or low standards rather than deliberate intent which made life in Dartmoor a living death to the French and American captives confined there.

Never in history were money and effort so lavishly expended upon the cure of disease and the care of the wounded as during the Civil War; and never before was effort so well rewarded. A few years before, great captains had repudiated any obligations to their sick or wounded. These were no more than the dead on the field. Only the man able to carry a musket, a lance, or a saber had their attention. That effort was misdirected during our great contest is true. Only supernatural wisdom and more than mortal strength could have brought the surgeon, the sufferer, and the relief together at precisely the right moment on every occasion, but the effort to accomplish this impossible task was made.

The echoes of the guns in the Crimea had hardly died away when the Civil War began. Yet during that terrible winter of 1854–55 the mortality from sickness in the English camps, was so great that, had it continued, the whole English army would have been wiped out in less than a year. Compare this record with that of the United States army as told in the following pages and see what advance a few years had brought. While the medical records of the Confederate Armies do not exist, we know that in that service, also, extraordinary results were accomplished.

The picture which introduces these paragraphs has a significance which cannot be over-emphasized. It is a section of the line of march of the grand review of the armies of the United States, held in Washington May 23–24, 1865. Occupying a place of honor among the marching thousands are ambulances. When before could an army have dared to boast of the provision made for those incapacitated by disease or wounds?

In the preparation of the prison sections, the author has consulted a large number of the published accounts of experiences, has talked with dozens of one-time prisoners, and has corresponded with many more. The conflicting accounts have been checked by the contemporary documents contained in the eight prison volumes of the "Official Records of the Union and

AID FOR THE MEN AT THE FRONT—CHRISTIAN COMMISSION

The Christian Commission was second as a civilian agency of relief only to the Sanitary Commission. The scene above tells its own story. The box numbered 1103 and addressed to the United States Christian Commission suggests how numerous were its consignments to the front. The veteran who has lost a leg is leaning on crutches furnished by the organization. He need have no fear for his pension. They have helped him to keep his papers straight. The basket on the man's arm suggests the charitable nature of the enterprise, the women in the doorway and on the porch indicate the feminine interest in it, and the ecclesiastical garb of one or two of the crowd suggests its religious nature. True heroes, some of these men who labored for the Sanitary Commission and Christian Commission to counteract the awful effects of the madness which sets men to killing one another. In March, 1865, General Terry had instituted a contraband camp where the colored refugees were gathered, about a mile outside of New Berne, North Carolina. There they were maintained with army rations and some measure of official supervision. In this camp an epidemic of smallpox broke out. The camp was quarantined, but word came to the authorities that it was in bad shape. The dead were not being buried, the sick were not being cared for, and the food was being appropriated by the stronger. Vincent Colyer and an associate, representative of the Sanitary

JOHN WANAMAKER IN '61

One of the wartime merchants who raised many millions for the relief of the soldiers at the front, through the Christian Commission and other civilian agencies.

Commission, volunteered to take charge of matters and restore order. Their action probably saved the town and the entire command from an epidemic of smallpox. In other countries they would have received decorations. Never before in the history of warfare did so many lawyers, merchants, ministers, and thousands of the people who stayed at home, combine to bring friendship and comfort to the sufferers in the field. It is recorded in the "Annals of the United States Christian Commission" by the Reverend Lemuel Moss, its Home Secretary, that its business committee collected no less than $5,478,280.31 for the soldiers.

On October 28, 1861, the Central Committee of the Young Men's Christian Association in Philadelphia addressed a circular letter to all the associations in the Union, inviting them to send delegates to a convention at the rooms of the Young Men's Christian Association of New York, on the 14th of the following month. This letter was signed by George H. Stuart, Chairman, John Wanamaker, Corresponding Secretary, James Grant, John W. Sexton, and George Cookman. The letter met with immediate response, and at the convention George H. Stuart was chosen President, Edward S. Tobey, Vice-President, Cephas Brainard and William Ballantyne, Secretaries. Messrs. Desmond, Vernon, Wanamaker, Masiurre, Baird, Colyer, and Stuart were appointed on the Business Committee. Thus was organized the Christian Commission.

Preface

Confederate Armies," an invaluable mine of material, heretofore little worked. His earnest effort has been to be absolutely just and impartial.

Whether or not he has succeeded, the pictures here published, absolutely without change or retouching, must be accepted as truthful. They have come from every section, and there has been no selection to prove a theory. Many Confederate pictures, the very existence of which was unknown, have been unearthed and are here given to the world. Here are the prisoners, their prisons, and their guards, the hospitals, and the surgeons, the whole machinery of relief.

The list of those who have given their time to answer the almost numberless questions of the author regarding both facts and their interpretation is so long that separate acknowledgment is impracticable. Especial thanks for courtesies are due, however, to George Haven Putnam, Esq., Doctor John A. Wyeth, and Thomas Sturgis, Esq., of New York, John Read, Esq., of Cambridge, Massachusetts, Doctor W. J. W. Kerr, of Corsicana, Texas, and the late Doctor Stanford E. Chaillé, of New Orleans. None of these, however, may be held responsible for any sections not specifically quoted on his authority.

HOLLAND THOMPSON.

July 4, 1911.

PRISONERS
OF
WAR

A UNION SENTRY AT LIBBY IN 1865—CONFEDERATE PRISONERS

PRISONERS

OF WAR IN FORT

DELAWARE, MAY, 1864

Captain Hart Gibson (No. 4) was serving at the time of his capture as assistant adjutant-general on General John H. Morgan's staff. Colonel R. C. Morgan (No. 11) and Captain C. H. Morgan (No. 13) were brothers of General Morgan. The former served on the staff of General A. P. Hill in the Army of Northern Virginia, and subsequently commanded the Fourteenth Kentucky Cavalry. The latter served as aide-de-camp on his brother's staff. Lieutenant Henry H. Brogden (No. 1), of Maryland, later held an official position under President Cleveland. Lieut.-Colonel Joseph T. Tucker (No. 2) served with the Eleventh Kentucky Cavalry. Brigadier-General R. B. Vance (No. 6) was a brother of the distinguished Zebulon B. Vance, who was three times Governor

11.   13.   14.   15

10.

12.

BRAVE AND DISTIN-

GUISHED SOUTHERNERS

IN A UNION PRISON

of North Carolina, and afterwards United States Senator from that State.   Lieut.-Colonel Cicero Coleman (No. 7) served with the Eighth Kentucky Cavalry.   The Rev. I. W. K. Handy (No. 8) was a Presbyterian minister.   B. P. Key (No. 9), "Little Billy," was a lad of about sixteen, a private in a Tennessee regiment.   Brigadier-General M. Jeff Thompson (No. 10) was a native of Virginia but a citizen of Missouri.   Colonel W. W. Ward (No. 12) commanded the Ninth Tennessee Cavalry.   After the close of the war he was elected Chancellor in a Judicial District of Tennessee.   Colonel (later General) Basil W. Duke (No. 14) was a daring cavalry leader.   No. 3 was Lieutenant H. H. Smith, of North Carolina; 5, Lieutenant J. J. Andrews, of Alabama; and 15, J. A. Tomlinson, of Kentucky.

CAMP DOUGLAS, NEAR CHICAGO

In the foreground stands a Confederate sergeant with rolls of the prisoners in his hands. It was the custom of the captives to choose a mess-sergeant from among their own number. These hundreds of men are a part of the thousands confined at Camp Douglas. The barracks were enclosed by a fence to confine the Confederate prisoners taken at Forts Donelson and Henry, and new barracks were afterward built. The barracks were wooden buildings ninety by twenty-four feet, of which twenty feet was cut off for the kitchen.

WHERE CONFEDERATE PRISONERS FROM THE WEST WERE CONFINED

In the remaining seventy feet an average of one hundred and seventy men slept in tiers of bunks. Camp Douglas was located on land belonging to the Stephen A. Douglas estate, and was bounded by Cottage Grove Avenue on the east, Forest Avenue on the west, Thirty-first Street on the north, and Thirty-third Street on the south. In 1911 the Cottage Grove Avenue electric cars were running past the old front, and the Thirty-first Street cross-town cars past the north boundary; the "Camp" was a residence district.

PRISONERS OF WAR

By Holland Thompson, Ph.D.

Assistant Professor of History in the College of the City of New York

In this mass of material the man with a preconceived notion can find facts to his liking. . . . In no part of the history of the Civil War is a wholesome skepticism more desirable, and nowhere is more applicable a fundamental tenet of historical criticism that all the right is never on one side and all the wrong on the other.—*James Ford Rhodes in " History of the United States."*

FROM first to last, omitting the armies surrendered during April and May, 1865, more than four hundred thousand prisoners were confined for periods ranging from days to years. At the beginning of the war no suitable provision was made on either side. Naturally, a South which did not believe that there would be a war and therefore did not adequately provide for the contest, made no advance preparation for the care of prisoners. A North which believed that the South would be subjugated within ninety days, saw little need of making provision for captives. When the war began in earnest, the task of organizing and equipping the fighting men so engrossed the attention of the authorities that no time to think of possible prisoners was found.

A majority of the people, North and South, believed that an army might spring, full-armed, from the soil at the word of command, and that training in the duties and obligations of the soldier was not only unnecessary but in some way inconsistent with the dignity of a free-born American citizen. The thousands of volunteers, officers and men, who made up the armies in the years 1861–65, brought with them varying ideas and ideals, diverse standards of courtesy and justice.

MEN OF NEW YORK'S "FIGHTING SIXTY–NINTH," PRISONERS IN CHARLESTON

The prisoners shown in this photograph are members of Colonel Michael Corcoran's Irish Regiment, the Sixty-ninth New York. They were captured at the first battle of Bull Run, July 21, 1861. Colonel Corcoran (shown on a previous page) and his men were taken first to Richmond, and then in September to Castle Pinckney in Charleston Harbor. These prisoners have light-heartedly decorated their casemate with a sign reading: "Musical Hall, 444 Broadway." One of their number, nicknamed "Scottie," had been formerly with Christy's minstrels, who played at 444 Broadway, New York, during the war. According to the recollections of Sergeant Joseph F. Burke, of the Cadets, the prisoners and their youthful guards indulged in good-natured banter about the outcome of the war, the prisoners predicting that their friends would soon come to the rescue—that the positions would be reversed, so that they, not the Cadets, would be "on guard." Four terrible years elapsed before their prediction as to the outcome of the war came true.

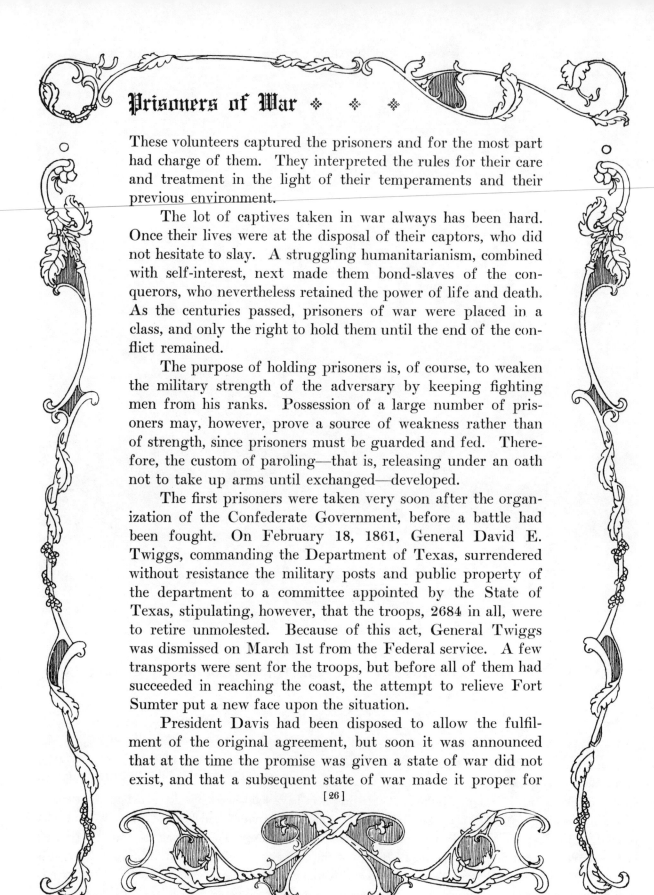

These volunteers captured the prisoners and for the most part had charge of them. They interpreted the rules for their care and treatment in the light of their temperaments and their previous environment.

The lot of captives taken in war always has been hard. Once their lives were at the disposal of their captors, who did not hesitate to slay. A struggling humanitarianism, combined with self-interest, next made them bond-slaves of the conquerors, who nevertheless retained the power of life and death. As the centuries passed, prisoners of war were placed in a class, and only the right to hold them until the end of the conflict remained.

The purpose of holding prisoners is, of course, to weaken the military strength of the adversary by keeping fighting men from his ranks. Possession of a large number of prisoners may, however, prove a source of weakness rather than of strength, since prisoners must be guarded and fed. Therefore, the custom of paroling—that is, releasing under an oath not to take up arms until exchanged—developed.

The first prisoners were taken very soon after the organization of the Confederate Government, before a battle had been fought. On February 18, 1861, General David E. Twiggs, commanding the Department of Texas, surrendered without resistance the military posts and public property of the department to a committee appointed by the State of Texas, stipulating, however, that the troops, 2684 in all, were to retire unmolested. Because of this act, General Twiggs was dismissed on March 1st from the Federal service. A few transports were sent for the troops, but before all of them had succeeded in reaching the coast, the attempt to relieve Fort Sumter put a new face upon the situation.

President Davis had been disposed to allow the fulfilment of the original agreement, but soon it was announced that at the time the promise was given a state of war did not exist, and that a subsequent state of war made it proper for

IN CASEMATE No. 2

UNION PRISONERS, CASTLE PINCKNEY

Among the Union prisoners taken at the first battle of Bull Run and transferred to Castle Pinckney, besides the Seventy-ninth New York (Scotch) Regiment, the Sixty-ninth New York (Irish) Regiment, and the Eighth Michigan Infantry, were some of the Eleventh Fire Zouaves, recruited from the New York Fire Department. These prisoners were an extremely intelligent lot of men, and adapted themselves to the situation. They willingly performed police duty. Their casemates were kept in excellent condition. They shared the same fare as their guards, and taught them the army method of softening "hard-tack" so that they could eat it with less violent exercise of their jaws and danger to their molars. The Charleston Zouave Cadets was a company of very young men, residents of Charleston, full of patriotic ardor and well disciplined. The State of South Carolina seceded from the Union at three o'clock in the afternoon of December 20, 1860, and at four o'clock the young company was on duty. Their uniform was gray with a red stripe and trimmings, red fatigue-caps, and white cross-belts. Later in the war they saw service at the front.

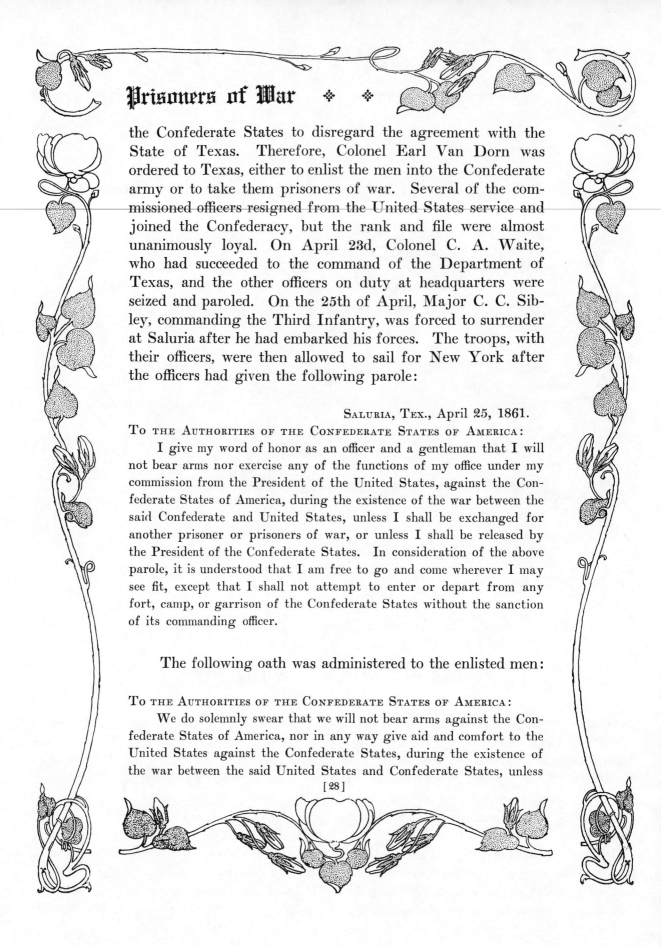

the Confederate States to disregard the agreement with the State of Texas. Therefore, Colonel Earl Van Dorn was ordered to Texas, either to enlist the men into the Confederate army or to take them prisoners of war. Several of the commissioned officers resigned from the United States service and joined the Confederacy, but the rank and file were almost unanimously loyal. On April 23d, Colonel C. A. Waite, who had succeeded to the command of the Department of Texas, and the other officers on duty at headquarters were seized and paroled. On the 25th of April, Major C. C. Sibley, commanding the Third Infantry, was forced to surrender at Saluria after he had embarked his forces. The troops, with their officers, were then allowed to sail for New York after the officers had given the following parole:

SALURIA, TEX., April 25, 1861.

To THE AUTHORITIES OF THE CONFEDERATE STATES OF AMERICA:

I give my word of honor as an officer and a gentleman that I will not bear arms nor exercise any of the functions of my office under my commission from the President of the United States, against the Confederate States of America, during the existence of the war between the said Confederate and United States, unless I shall be exchanged for another prisoner or prisoners of war, or unless I shall be released by the President of the Confederate States. In consideration of the above parole, it is understood that I am free to go and come wherever I may see fit, except that I shall not attempt to enter or depart from any fort, camp, or garrison of the Confederate States without the sanction of its commanding officer.

The following oath was administered to the enlisted men:

To THE AUTHORITIES OF THE CONFEDERATE STATES OF AMERICA:

We do solemnly swear that we will not bear arms against the Confederate States of America, nor in any way give aid and comfort to the United States against the Confederate States, during the existence of the war between the said United States and Confederate States, unless

[28]

COLONEL CORCORAN, WHO WAS CHOSEN BY LOT FOR DEATH

Around the tall, commanding figure of Colonel Michael Corcoran, of the New York "Fighting Sixty-ninth," a storm raged in the summer of 1861. Corcoran had been chosen by lot to meet the same fate as Walter W. Smith, prize-master of the schooner *Enchantress*, with a prize-crew from the Confederate privateer *Jeff. Davis*, who was captured July 22, 1861, tried for piracy in the United States Court in Philadelphia, October 22d–28th, and convicted of the charge. Soon after the news of his conviction reached Richmond, Acting Secretary of War J. P. Benjamin issued an order to Brigadier-General John H. Winder to choose by lot, from among the Federal prisoners of war, of the highest rank, one who was to receive exactly the same treatment as prize-master Walter W. Smith. He also ordered that thirteen other prisoners of war, the highest in rank of those captured by the Confederate forces, should be served as the crew of the *Savannah*. It fell to Colonel Corcoran to become the hostage for Smith. Since only ten other Federal field-officers were held as prisoners, three captains were chosen by lot to complete the quota, and all were placed in close confinement. The United States was forced to recede from its position, which was untenable. Judge Grier, one of the bench who tried Smith in Philadelphia, aptly remarked that he could not understand why men taken on the sea were to be hanged, while those captured on land were to be held as prisoners or released.

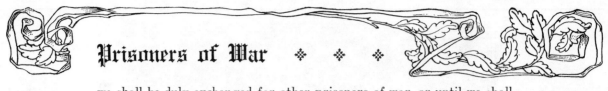

we shall be duly exchanged for other prisoners of war, or until we shall be released by the President of the Confederate States. In consideration of this oath, it is understood that we are free to go wherever we may see fit.

On the 9th of May, Lieutenant-Colonel I. V. D. Reeve, who was on his way to the coast from the forts in New Mexico, surrendered ten officers and two hundred and seventy men at San Lucas Spring, near San Antonio. Meanwhile, President Lincoln had issued his proclamation threatening to treat privateers as pirates. Therefore, Colonel Van Dorn restricted the limits of these men to Bexar County, Texas, and the officers to the Confederate States, though the officers were later limited to the State of Texas. Because of the death of his daughter, Colonel Van Dorn gave Lieutenant-Colonel Reeve the privilege of going North.

On May 10th, a brigade of Missouri State Militia at Camp Jackson, near St. Louis, Missouri, was taken by Captain Nathaniel Lyon, U. S. A., and the officers and men were paroled not to serve again during the war. Several hundred prisoners were taken by General George B. McClellan at Rich Mountain, Virginia, in July, and all were paroled, except two who had previously served in the United States army. These the War Department ordered General McClellan to retain. Then, on July 21, 1861, came the battle of Bull Run, or Manassas, when the Confederates took more than a thousand prisoners. The war was on in earnest.

The Federal government was inclined to refuse to recognize the validity of the Texas paroles, and was only prevented from such action by the firmness of the officers themselves. Secretary of War Cameron, for example, ordered Lieutenant-Colonel Reeve to disregard his parole or else leave the army by resignation or dismissal. Colonel Reeve appealed to President Lincoln, who overruled the secretary. Other paroled officers were ordered to duty before exchange, but all declined.

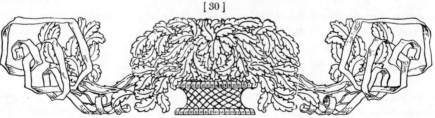

MRS. GREENHOW, THE CONFEDERATE SPY, WITH HER DAUGHTER, IN THE OLD CAPITOL PRISON

Mrs. Rose O'Neal Greenhow, a zealous and trusted friend of the Confederacy, lived in Washington at the opening of the war. It was she who, on July 16, 1861, sent the famous cipher message to Beauregard, "Order issued for McDowell to move on Manassas to-night." Acting on this, Beauregard promptly arranged his army for the expected attack, while Johnston and "Stonewall" Jackson hastened from the Valley to aid in repelling the Federal advance. Mrs. Greenhow's secret-service work was cut short on August 26th, when Allan Pinkerton, the Federal detective, arrested her and put her under military guard at her home, 398 Sixteenth Street. Afterward she was transferred to the Old Capitol Prison. She remained there until April, 1862. On June 2d, after pledging her word not to come north of the Potomac until the war was over, Mrs. Greenhow was escorted beyond the lines of the Union army and set at liberty. It was later discovered that she had, even while in prison, corresponded extensively with Colonel Thomas Jordan, of General Beauregard's staff.

According to the laws of war, prisoners taken in an armed contest between two belligerents must be protected, are entitled to quarters, to proper food and clothing, to medical attendance, and to a reasonable amount of fuel, bedding, and camp equipage. They may be required to labor, except upon military works, and in attempting to escape they commit no crime. In fact, it is the duty of a prisoner to escape if he can, and he should not be punished therefor, though he may be confined with greater strictness. Prisoners may be exchanged as the captor wills, though no obligation rests upon him to enter into such an agreement. A captor also may allow his prisoner, if he so wills, to sign a written parole, or may accept a parole in an oral form. Generally, only an officer is given the privilege of a parole, while an oath is administered to an enlisted man. If a prisoner's government refuses to recognize the instrument, the prisoner is bound in honor to return to captivity.

Some of these provisions are the ordinary dictates of humanity. Others are conventions which have been accepted by the common consent of nations. In previous wars they had been generally violated, and the same thing happened during the Civil War. Sometimes the violation was unintentional; at other times, because some apparent advantage was gained. Some officers in charge of prisoners looked upon them as felons and acted as the warden of a penitentiary might. Others seemed to feel that " all is fair in war."

If the contest had been between two independent nations, the captives upon each side would naturally have been exchanged, but it was the theory of the United States that the contest was an insurrection, not a war, and therefore the authorities were at first inclined to treat their prisoners as civil delinquents, guilty of treason. It was feared that an agreement to exchange prisoners would be regarded as a recognition of the Confederacy as a nation, and it was determined to avoid such action. After the battles of Bull Run and Ball's Bluff,

[32]

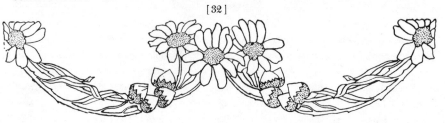

CONFEDERATES CAPTURED AT CEDAR MOUNTAIN, IN CULPEPER COURT HOUSE, AUGUST, 1862

The Confederate prisoners on the balcony seem to be taking their situation very placidly. They have evidently been doing some family laundry, and have hung the results out to dry. The sentries lounging beneath the colonnade below, and the two languid individuals leaning up against the porch and tree, add to the peacefulness of the scene. At the battle of Cedar Mountain, August 9, 1861, the above with other Confederates were captured and temporarily confined in this county town of Culpeper. Like several other Virginia towns, it does not boast a name of its own, but is universally known as Culpeper Court House. A settlement had grown up in the neighborhood of the courthouse, and the scene was enlivened during the sessions of court by visitors from miles around.

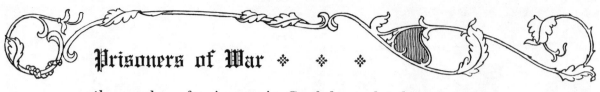

the number of prisoners in Confederate hands was so large
and their political influence so great, that commanders were
authorized to make special exchanges, and many were made
both in the East and in the West.

This denial of belligerent rights could not be maintained,
since the Government was forced to take warlike measures
for the suppression of the so-called insurrection, and no real
attempt was made to carry this theory to its logical conclusion, except in the case of the first privateers captured. Learning that the Confederacy had issued commissions for privateers
to prey upon the commerce of the United States, President
Lincoln issued a proclamation on April 19, 1861, declaring
that these would be treated as pirates.

An opportunity to enforce the proclamation soon arose.
The privateer *Savannah*, with thirteen men on board, was captured off Charleston Harbor on June 3d. The prisoners were
taken to New York and placed in the "Tombs" (the city
prison), where they remained until turned over to the War
Department and transferred to Fort Lafayette, on February 3,
1862. They were brought to trial on the charge of piracy
on October 23, 1861, but they had excellent counsel and their
case was presented with such skill and vigor that the jury dis-
agreed. Before another trial could be had, it had been decided
to treat them as prisoners of war. Undoubtedly this decision
was hastened by the attitude of Great Britain, which was decidedly unfriendly to the claim of the United States, but the
principal cause was the action of the Confederate Government,
to be mentioned hereafter.

The day after the battle of Bull Run (or Manassas),
July 22d, the schooner *Enchantress*, under charge of a prize
crew from the privateer *Jeff Davis*, was captured and the
crew was taken to Philadelphia. There, Walter W. Smith,
prize-master, was tried for piracy in the United States Court,
October 22–28th, and was convicted. Soon after the news
reached Richmond, the following order was issued:

AWAITING TRANSPORTATION TO A NORTHERN PRISON, 1863

In this photograph appear more of the prisoners represented on the previous page, captured at the battle of Chattanooga, November 23, 24, and 25, 1863. In the background rises Lookout Mountain, where Hooker fought his sensational battle above the clouds, driving his opponents from every position. Their work is over for the present; in a few days more these prisoners will be shivering in the unaccustomed climate of the North. Shelter was provided for such unfortunates in Federal prisons, but fuel was often scanty and in some cases wholly lacking. The Northern winters destroyed many Southern lives. The medical and surgical attendance of the prisoners was unsatisfactory on both sides; 10,000 of the flower of the Northern medical profession were at the front. To say that abundant bedding and clothing was issued to Confederate prisoners in the North is too sweeping. Report after report of Federal medical inspectors states that prisoners were frequently without blankets or straw. The problem of caring for them was a tremendous one.

[H—3]

Prisoners of War ❖ ❖

WAR DEPARTMENT, Richmond, Nov. 9, 1861.

SIR: You are hereby instructed to choose, by lot, from among the prisoners of war, of highest rank, one who is to be confined in a cell appropriated to convicted felons, and who is to be treated in all respects as if such convict, and to be held for execution in the same manner as may be adopted by the enemy for the execution of the prisoner of war Smith, recently condemned to death in Philadelphia.

You will also select thirteen other prisoners of war, the highest in rank of those captured by our forces, to be confined in the cells reserved for prisoners accused of infamous crimes, and will treat them as such so long as the enemy shall continue so to treat the like number of prisoners of war captured by them at sea, and now held for trial in New York as pirates.

As these measures are intended to repress the infamous attempt now made by the enemy to commit judicial murder on prisoners of war, you will execute them strictly, as the mode best calculated to prevent the commission of so heinous a crime.

Your obedient servant,

(Signed) J. P. BENJAMIN,
Acting Secretary of War.

To Brig.-Gen. John H. Winder.

The order was obeyed the next day, and Colonel Michael Corcoran of the Sixty-ninth New York was chosen by lot as the hostage for Smith. As only eleven Federal field-officers were held as prisoners, three captains were chosen by lot to complete the quota, and all were placed in close confinement.

This move caused intense excitement in the North. The friends of the officers bombarded the War Department with letters pleading for exchange, and finally the United States Government receded from its position, which was untenable. Judge Grier, one of the bench who tried Smith in Philadelphia, aptly said that he could not understand why men taken on the sea were to be hanged while those captured on land were to be held as prisoners, or released.

At first buildings already constructed were used for the confinement of prisoners. The abandoned penitentiary at Alton,

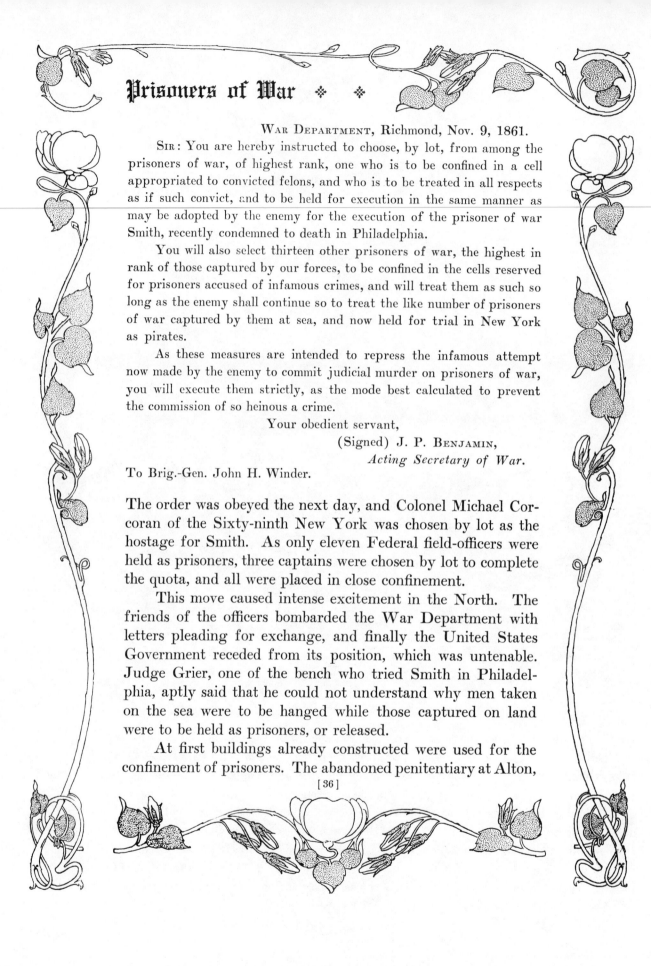

CONFEDERATE PRISONERS WAITING FOR THE RAILROAD TRAIN

CHATTANOOGA, TENNESSEE

1864

At the battle of Chattanooga the Army of the Cumberland under General Thomas assailed the field-works at the foot of Mission Ridge, November 25, 1863, and captured them at the point of the bayonet. Then, without orders, the troops, eager to wipe out the memory of Chickamauga, pressed gallantly on up the ridge, heedless of the deadly fire belched into their very faces, and overran the works at the summit like a torrent, capturing thirty-five guns and prisoners wholesale. As this photograph was taken, some of the Confederate prisoners were standing at the railroad depot awaiting transportation to the prisons in the North. There such bodies were usually guarded by partially disabled soldiers organized as the Veteran Reserve Corps. They had more to eat than the Northern prisoners in the South, yet often less than the amount to which they were entitled by the army regulations. In the South, during the last years of the war, prisoners almost starved, while their guards fared little better. With all the resources of the North, Confederate prisoners often went hungry, because of the difficulty of organizing such a tremendous task and finding suitable officers to take charge. The Northern soldiers in the field frequently suffered from hunger for days at a time.

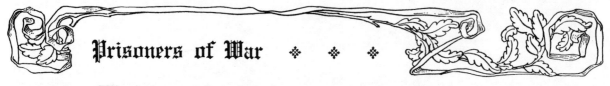

Illinois, was taken for the accommodation of Confederate prisoners in the West, while in the East the forts along the seaboard, including Fort Warren in Boston Harbor, Forts Lafayette and Columbus at New York, Fort McHenry in Chesapeake Bay, Fort Delaware in the Delaware River, and the Old Capitol at Washington, were converted into prisons. In Richmond, tobacco-factories which could be transformed with comparatively little work into places for the detention of prisoners, were leased. Among these were Liggon's, Crew's, Castle Thunder, Pemberton, and others. Later Libby, which had been an old warehouse, became the chief officers' prison. Castle Pinckney in Charleston Harbor, and some empty buildings in Tuscaloosa, Alabama, were also used.

As the war went on, it was found that such accommodations were entirely inadequate. The capacity of the forts along the seaboard was limited, with the exception of Fort Delaware, and besides they were soon full of political prisoners. Fort Warren, in Boston Harbor, sheltered a number of Confederate privates during the first year of the war, but later was used chiefly for the confinement of political prisoners and general officers. Likewise, the Old Capitol at Washington, which had been built after the destruction of the Capitol during the War of 1812, and in which for several years the sessions of Congress had been held, while the present Capitol was building, was very seldom used for prisoners of war, but was devoted to the detention of citizens suspected of disloyalty to the Union. The pressure upon the accommodations at Richmond led to the transfer of the private soldiers to an enclosure on Belle Isle in the James River.

For the purpose of better administration, the government at Washington, in October, 1861, appointed Lieutenant-Colonel William Hoffman, one of the officers who had been surrendered in Texas, commissary-general of prisoners. Colonel Hoffman, for he was soon promoted, served to the end of the war, though for a few months he was transferred west of the

DISTANT VIEW OF BELLE PLAIN CAMP OF CONFEDERATE PRISONERS, MAY, 1864

This photograph was taken just after the Spotsylvania campaign, in the course of which Grant lost thirty-six thousand men in casualties but captured several thousand Confederates, part of whom appear crowding this prison camp. A tiny tortuous stream runs through the cleft in the hills. Near the center of the picture a small bridge spanning it can be descried. Farther to the right is a group of Union soldiers. The scene is on the line of communication from Belle Plain, the base of supplies, to the army at the front. Exchanges had been stopped by order of General Grant on the 17th of the previous month, when he started the hammering process by which he ultimately exhausted the Confederacy, but at the price of terrible losses to the Union. The prisons in the North became populated to suffocation, yet Grant held firm until it was certain that exchanges could have little influence on the final result.

Mississippi. All correspondence in regard to prisoners passed through his hands, and whatever uniformity there was in the conditions in Federal prisons was largely due to this fact, as he established rules for the guidance of the commandants, and provided for an elaborate system of inspections and reports. The rules, unfortunately, were not interpreted uniformly by the officers in charge, and he was hampered in administration by political influences.

The Confederacy created no such office until November 21, 1864, when General Winder was appointed. After his death in February, 1865, General G. J. Pillow served for a few days, and was then succeeded by General Daniel Ruggles. In the last days of the Confederacy it was too late to reduce chaotic conditions to order. When prisoners were kept chiefly in Richmond, General Winder had command, and had an undefined supervision over those outside. When the greater number of prisoners was sent South, he was placed in command of the prisons in Georgia and Alabama, July 26, 1864, while General W. M. Gardner was given charge of prisons in Virginia and the Carolinas. The latter officer was partially disabled and was never able to assert his authority, on account of friction with local military commanders.

Citizens suspected of disloyalty to the Confederacy were confined in Richmond chiefly in the " Negro Jail," so called, usually known as Castle Godwin, and after this building was given up, were transferred to Castle Thunder. The prison at Salisbury, North Carolina, sheltered a number of this class, though later it was filled to overflowing with prisoners of war. The provost-marshals kept others under this charge in prisons scattered over the Confederacy.

Citizens charged with disloyalty in the North were confined in various places. The Old Capitol, Fort Lafayette, Fort Warren, and dozens of other places were used for this purpose. At the end of the war, Jefferson Davis was confined in Fortress Monroe, but this had been too near the lines during

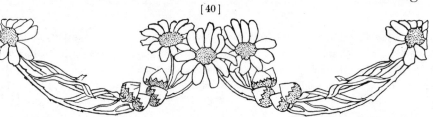

A CLOSER VIEW OF THE CONFEDERATE PRISONERS AT BELLE PLAIN

The photographer had worked up the valley nearer to the camp of Confederate prisoners at Belle Plain when this view was taken. The bed of the little stream is now visible, with the group of soldiers lounging by its banks. It was on May 23–26, 1864, that Lee had checkmated Grant at the North Anna River in the latter's advance toward Richmond. While the army was at Spotsylvania, its water base had been at Belle Plain, on Potomac Creek, but when Grant moved to the North Anna the base was transferred to Port Royal, on the Rappahannock, and the Confederates at Belle Plain were sent on to Northern prisons. The burden placed upon the South in feeding and guarding its prisoners was overwhelming, and Colonel Robert Ould, agent of exchange, offered, later in the year, to deliver the sick and wounded at Savannah without equivalent. Transportation was sent late in November, and here and at Charleston, when the delivery was completed after the railroad leading to Savannah was cut, about thirteen thousand men were delivered. More than three thousand Confederates were delivered at the same time. After January 24, 1865, exchanges were recommenced and continued with little interruption to the end of hostilities in April.

WHERE FIVE THOUSAND CONFEDERATE PRISONERS LAY ENCAMPED

On the heights above the hollow the Union sentries can be descried against the sky-line. The cluster of huts on the right-hand page is part of the Federal camp. From December, 1862, to June, 1863, the gloomiest half-year of the war for the North, the Federal army was encamped near Falmouth, Virginia, a little town on the Rappahannock River opposite Fredericksburg. The winter-quarters stretched back for miles toward Belle Plain and Aquia Creek, the bases of supplies. Continuous scouting and skirmishing went on throughout the winter, and the Confederate prisoners captured during this time were confined at Belle Plain until arrangements could be made to send them to Northern prisons. Here also was the great quartermaster's supply depot, and these prisoners at least never lacked ample rations. They were but a

A SCENE AFTER THE BATTLE OF SPOTSYLVANIA—May, 1864

few of the 462,634 Confederate soldiers who were captured during the war. This figure is that of General F. C. Ainsworth, of the United States Record and Pension Office. Of this number 247,769 were paroled on the field, and 25,796 died while in captivity. The Union soldiers captured during the war numbered 211,411, according to the same authority, and of these 16,668 were paroled on the field, and 30,218 died while in captivity. The difference between the number of Union and Confederate prisoners is due to the inclusion in the Confederate number of the armies surrendered by Lee, Johnston, Taylor, and Kirby Smith during the months of April and May, 1865. There are other estimates which differ very widely from this, which is probably as nearly correct as possible, owing to the partial destruction of the records.

the war to risk the placing of prisoners of importance there. Provost-marshals arrested thousands in the North, who were often held for months and frequently dismissed without being informed of the charges against them. The number thus arrested in the South was large, but much smaller than in the North. Military commanders attempted to play the despot both North and South.

As the war went on and prisoners were taken in larger and larger numbers, it was seen on both sides that greater provision must be made for them. In the North, some prisons were constructed especially for this purpose. In other cases camps of instruction were surrounded by fences and the enclosed barracks were filled with captives. The most important of the first class were Johnson's Island, in Sandusky Bay, Ohio; Point Lookout, Maryland, and Rock Island, in the Mississippi River. Among the second were Camp Douglas, at Chicago, Illinois; Camp Butler, at Springfield, Illinois; Camp Morton, at Indianapolis, Indiana; Camp Chase, at Columbus, Ohio; and the Barracks, at Elmira, New York.

The Gratiot Street Prison in St. Louis had been an old medical college, and Myrtle Street Prison had been used as a negro market. Fort Delaware, on an island in the Delaware River, had been constructed by General McClellan while a member of the Engineer Corps. A dike kept out the tide which would otherwise have washed over the island, and barracks were constructed within the enclosure. At various times and for short periods, prisoners were held in other places, but those mentioned were the most important.

The principal Confederate prisons besides those already mentioned were Camp Sumter at Anderson, Georgia; Camp Lawton, at Millen, Georgia, established late in 1864, to relieve Andersonville; Camp Asylum, at Columbia, South Carolina; Macon, Georgia; Florence, South Carolina; and Charleston, South Carolina. Large numbers of prisoners were also confined for short periods at Raleigh, Charlotte, and Savannah.

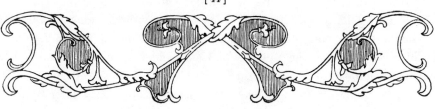

BREVET MAJOR-GENERAL CHARLES K. GRAHAM

BREVET MAJOR-GENERAL JOSEPH HAYES

LIEUTENANT-COLONEL JAMES M. SANDERSON

FOUR CONSPICUOUS UNION INMATES OF LIBBY PRISON

General Graham was wounded and taken prisoner at Gettysburg, after having distinguished himself at Glendale and Malvern Hill. He was confined for several months in Libby Prison, and after his exchange he had command of the gunboat flotilla and took part in the attack on Fort Fisher. General Hayes was taken prisoner in the operations around Richmond and held in Libby almost to the end of the war. He was appointed to distribute the supplies sent to the Federal prisoners in Richmond by the United States Government and the Sanitary Commission. While Col-

BRIGADIER-GENERAL NEAL DOW

onel Sanderson was confined in Libby Prison he issued a statement sustaining the contention of the Confederate authorities regarding the rations issued the prisoners, for which he was denounced by a mass-meeting of officers held in the prison, who declared that their food was insufficient to sustain life. General Dow was wounded and captured in the attack on Port Hudson in July, 1863. For more than eight months he was confined in Libby Prison, but was afterward sent South. He was exchanged for W. H. F. Lee, nephew of Robert E. Lee.

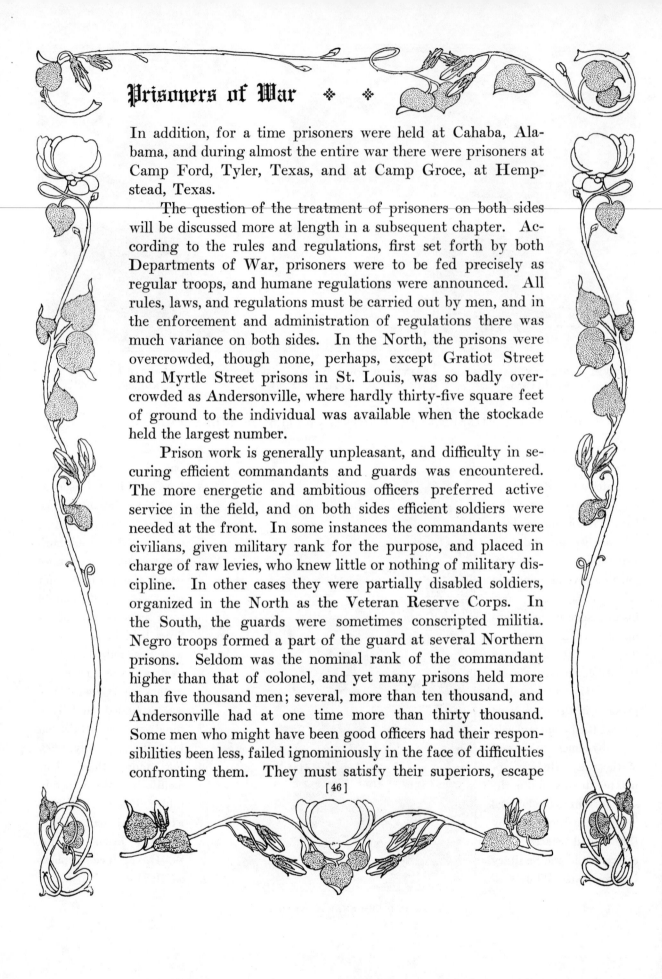

Prisoners of War ❖ ❖

In addition, for a time prisoners were held at Cahaba, Alabama, and during almost the entire war there were prisoners at Camp Ford, Tyler, Texas, and at Camp Groce, at Hempstead, Texas.

The question of the treatment of prisoners on both sides will be discussed more at length in a subsequent chapter. According to the rules and regulations, first set forth by both Departments of War, prisoners were to be fed precisely as regular troops, and humane regulations were announced. All rules, laws, and regulations must be carried out by men, and in the enforcement and administration of regulations there was much variance on both sides. In the North, the prisons were overcrowded, though none, perhaps, except Gratiot Street and Myrtle Street prisons in St. Louis, was so badly overcrowded as Andersonville, where hardly thirty-five square feet of ground to the individual was available when the stockade held the largest number.

Prison work is generally unpleasant, and difficulty in securing efficient commandants and guards was encountered. The more energetic and ambitious officers preferred active service in the field, and on both sides efficient soldiers were needed at the front. In some instances the commandants were civilians, given military rank for the purpose, and placed in charge of raw levies, who knew little or nothing of military discipline. In other cases they were partially disabled soldiers, organized in the North as the Veteran Reserve Corps. In the South, the guards were sometimes conscripted militia. Negro troops formed a part of the guard at several Northern prisons. Seldom was the nominal rank of the commandant higher than that of colonel, and yet many prisons held more than five thousand men; several, more than ten thousand, and Andersonville had at one time more than thirty thousand. Some men who might have been good officers had their responsibilities been less, failed ignominiously in the face of difficulties confronting them. They must satisfy their superiors, escape

BREVET BRIGADIER-GENERAL
G. W. NEFF

BREVET BRIGADIER-GENERAL
P. J. REVERE

BRIGADIER-GENERAL
I. VOGDES

As Colonel Michael Corcoran was held as hostage for Walter W. Smith, prize-master of the schooner *Enchantress*, who was convicted of piracy in the United States Court in October, 1861, so the officers shown on this page were held as hostages for the privateers taken aboard the *Savannah*. They were to receive exactly the same treatment as that meted out to the privateers. General Neff was lieutenant-colonel of the Second Kentucky at that time, General Revere major of the Twentieth Massachusetts, General Vogdes a major in the regular artillery, and General Lee was colonel of the Twentieth Massachusetts.

COLONEL W. E. WOODRUFF   BREVET BRIGADIER-GENERAL W. R. LEE   COLONEL A. M. WOOD

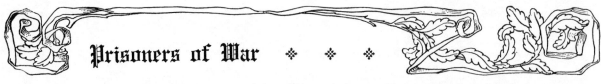

the unreasoning censure of public opinion, and at the same time keep their prisoners.

Prisoners in the North got more to eat than in the South, after 1862, at least, yet they often got less than the amount to which they were entitled by the army regulations. In the South during the last year of the war, prisoners starved, while their guards fared little better. With all the resources of the North, prisoners were often hungry, frequently because of the inefficiency of their commanders. Commissaries in collusion with contractors sometimes reduced the rations of the prisoners both in quality and quantity. In one case, at least, a commissary was dismissed from service, but because of his political friends was restored. The reports of the Federal inspectors are set forth in the " Official Records."

Shelter was provided in the North, but fuel was often scanty, and in some cases lacking. In some of the Southern prisons no shelter was provided, and fuel was likewise scanty, though fortunately not so much needed for comfort. The medical and surgical attendance was very often unsatisfactory. For, as in the case of the commanding officers, surgeons preferred service among their own people to that of attending prisoners. Even where the intentions of the surgeon were the best, they had lately come, in most cases, from civil life. Many were not commissioned, but were hired by the month. Of the management of hospitals many knew almost nothing. Some rose to their responsibilities, others did not. Where they did not the prisoners suffered.

Nor must the influence of climate be neglected. To many of the Northern prisoners the prolonged heat of the Southern prison-camps during the summer caused disease regardless of other factors. It is no less true that, if the Southern sun was disastrous to the Northerner, so the Northern winter destroyed many Southern lives. The men taken to Elmira or Johnson's Island in the summer-time, wearing thin summer clothes, often without blankets or overcoats, suffered during the winter. The

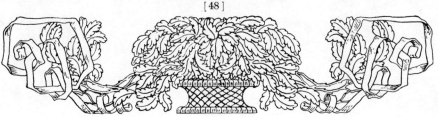

COMMISSIONED OFFICERS OF THE NINETEENTH IOWA INFANTRY AS PRISONERS OF WAR

These pictures represent some of the ragged non-commissioned officers and commissioned officers of the Nineteenth Iowa Infantry after they reached New Orleans for exchange. Razors and scissors had evidently been held at a premium in Camp Ford, from which they had come. During almost the entire war this Confederate prison was maintained near Tyler, Texas. For a time it seemed forgotten. Up to the spring of 1864, conditions here were better than in many other prisons. The stockade included a number of noble trees, several springs, and a stream of some size. Abundant opportunities for bathing were afforded. Drinking water was excellent. Wood was plentiful and an abundant supply of fresh meat was furnished. Prisoners at first built themselves log huts. Later any simple shelter was a luxury. Many of the captives were forced to burrow into the sides of the hill. The supply of wood became scanty. Meat grew scarcer until at last corn-meal was the staple article of diet. Clothes wore out and were not replaced.

NON-COMMISSIONED OFFICERS OF THE NINETEENTH IOWA AT NEW ORLEANS

statement an abundance of clothing and bedding was issued to Confederate prisoners in the North is too sweeping. Large quantities of cast-off and rejected clothing were issued, but report after report of Union medical inspectors states that prisoners were frequently without blankets or straw. This was usually because the quartermaster was inefficient or careless.

The number of prisoners held during the war can, perhaps, never be accurately known. General F. C. Ainsworth, when chief of the United States Record and Pension Office, is quoted by Rhodes as follows: " According to the best information now obtainable from both Union and Confederate records, it appears that 211,411 Union soldiers were captured during the Civil War, of which number 16,668 were paroled on the field and 30,218 died while in captivity; and that 462,634 Confederate soldiers were captured during that war, of which number 247,769 were paroled on the field and 25,976 died while in captivity." A letter under date of March 9, 1911, says that he has no further information justifying a change in these figures. Of course, this large number of Confederates captured includes the armies of Lee, Johnston, Taylor, and Kirby Smith surrendered during the months of April and May, 1865.

This report is probably as nearly correct as can be made, owing to the partial destruction of records, though it differs very widely from two other reports which are often quoted: one by partisan historians of the North, attempting to prove inhumanity on the part of the South, and the other by Southerners who have attempted by it to show that conditions in Northern prisons were more fatal than those in the Southern. The first contention is based upon a report of Secretary Stanton, from information furnished by the commissary-general of prisoners. This says that "220,000 rebel prisoners were held in the North and about 126,950 Union prisoners in the South," and that 26,436 deaths of Confederate prisoners occurred, while 22,576 Union prisoners are reported to have died in Southern prisons.

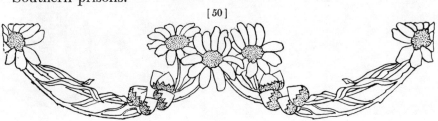

DILAPIDATED UNION PRISONERS AFTER EIGHTEEN MONTHS AT TYLER, TEXAS

The prison near Tyler, Texas, known as Camp Ford, was always an interesting place, even when food and clothing were most scanty. The prisoners here were an ingenious lot, who apparently spent their time in unmilitary but natural fraternizing with their guards, with whom their relations were nearly always pleasant. In spite of all the efforts of the officers, the guards could not be prevented from trading with the prisoners. The latter slaughtered the cattle for their own food; and from the hoofs and horns they made effective combs, and carved beautiful sets of checkers and chessmen. Conditions in this prison were not hard until 1864, when the concurrent increase in numbers and exhaustion of supplies and wood in the neighborhood brought much suffering. It is reported that when the guards learned of the capture of Richmond, they went to their homes, leaving the prisoners almost without supervision to make their way to New Orleans. With continued confinement, clothes wore out, as is evident in the photographs, which represent officers and enlisted men of the Nineteenth Iowa. With their bare feet they were evidently not in a condition to be presented in "society."

ENLISTED MEN OF THE NINETEENTH IOWA AFTER THEIR CAPTIVITY

The second estimate, used by Alexander H. Stephens, Senator Benjamin H. Hill, and President Davis, cites an alleged report of J. K. Barnes, Surgeon-General, U. S. A., which purports to give the number of Confederate prisoners as 220,000, and the number of Union prisoners in the South as 270,000. The authority quoted is an editorial in the *National Intelligencer,* of Washington, which seems not to have been contradicted, though General Barnes lived for many years afterward. The report, however, is not to be found in the Federal archives; it is claimed that there is no evidence that it was ever made, and further that there is no way in which Surgeon-General Barnes could have secured these figures. This, however, does not seem an impossibility, as the surgeons naturally made reports of the sick to him, and these reports always included the number in prison quarters as well as the number in hospital. Whether or not such a report was ever made, it does not now seem to be in existence.

Absolute accuracy cannot now be secured, if indeed such accuracy was ever possible. During the last six months of the war, the Federal prisoners were transferred hither and thither, sometimes stopping for a week or less in one place, in the attempts to avoid the raids of Sherman's cavalry and the constantly tightening coils which were closing around the Confederates. In these changes, as the prisoners were handed from commander to commander, were unloaded from one train into another, and transferred from one set of inefficient guards to another, hundreds escaped.

Furthermore, since a Confederate commissary-general of prisoners was not appointed until the war was almost over, many commandants of prisons in the South made reports only to the commanders of departments, who often failed to forward them to Richmond. Any statement of the number of Federal prisoners held in the South is, therefore, only an estimate. The relative mortality growing out of prison life will be discussed in another chapter.

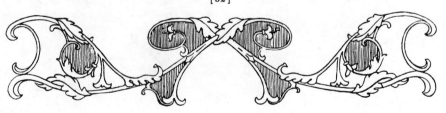

PART I
PRISONS

NORTHERN AND
SOUTHERN
PRISONS

BRIGADIER-GENERAL WILLIAM HOFFMAN, FEDERAL COMMIS-
SARY-GENERAL OF PRISONERS. TO HIM WAS DUE WHATEVER
OF UNIFORMITY THERE WAS IN THE CARE OF PRISONERS.

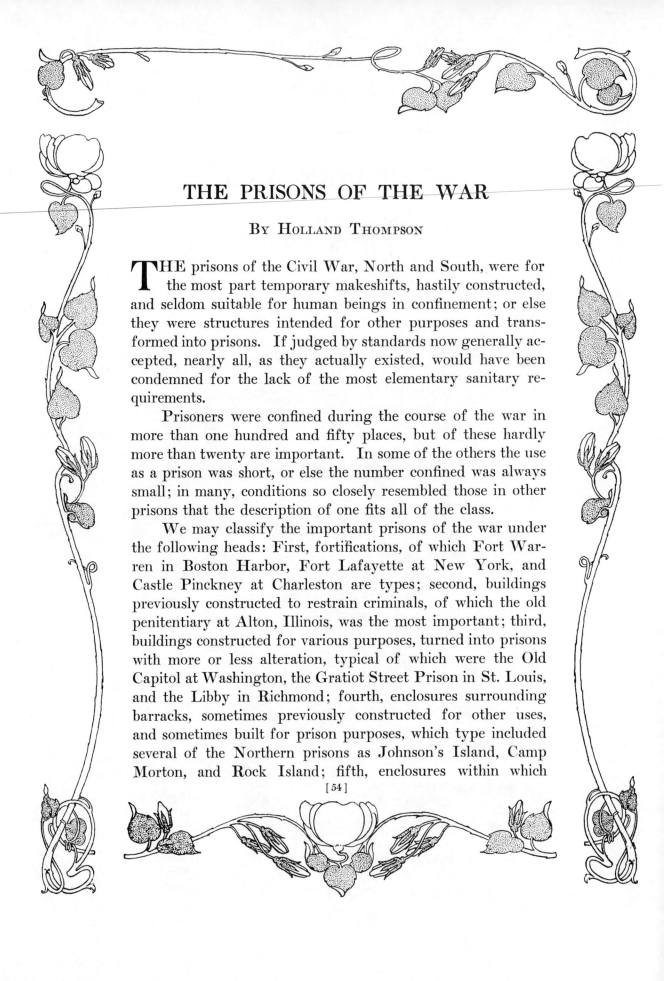

THE PRISONS OF THE WAR

By Holland Thompson

THE prisons of the Civil War, North and South, were for the most part temporary makeshifts, hastily constructed, and seldom suitable for human beings in confinement; or else they were structures intended for other purposes and transformed into prisons. If judged by standards now generally accepted, nearly all, as they actually existed, would have been condemned for the lack of the most elementary sanitary requirements.

Prisoners were confined during the course of the war in more than one hundred and fifty places, but of these hardly more than twenty are important. In some of the others the use as a prison was short, or else the number confined was always small; in many, conditions so closely resembled those in other prisons that the description of one fits all of the class.

We may classify the important prisons of the war under the following heads: First, fortifications, of which Fort Warren in Boston Harbor, Fort Lafayette at New York, and Castle Pinckney at Charleston are types; second, buildings previously constructed to restrain criminals, of which the old penitentiary at Alton, Illinois, was the most important; third, buildings constructed for various purposes, turned into prisons with more or less alteration, typical of which were the Old Capitol at Washington, the Gratiot Street Prison in St. Louis, and the Libby in Richmond; fourth, enclosures surrounding barracks, sometimes previously constructed for other uses, and sometimes built for prison purposes, which type included several of the Northern prisons as Johnson's Island, Camp Morton, and Rock Island; fifth, enclosures within which

LIBBY PRISON

A UNIQUE PHOTOGRAPH

Several views of Libby Prison were taken from the land side, but this picture is unique in that it shows the building as it appeared from the river. The boat at the landing is loaded with provisions which have been brought from the mills of the upper James River for the prisoners and garrison. The view is taken from the south side of the dock. This photograph, with those on the three following pages, were taken inside the Confederate lines during the war by Confederate photographers. The officers in Libby Prison were not satisfied with their food, with the exception of Major James M. Sanderson, who had served in the Union commissary department and who issued a statement confirming the claims of the Confederate officials, thereby exciting the ire of his fellow-prisoners, who held a mass-meeting to condemn him.

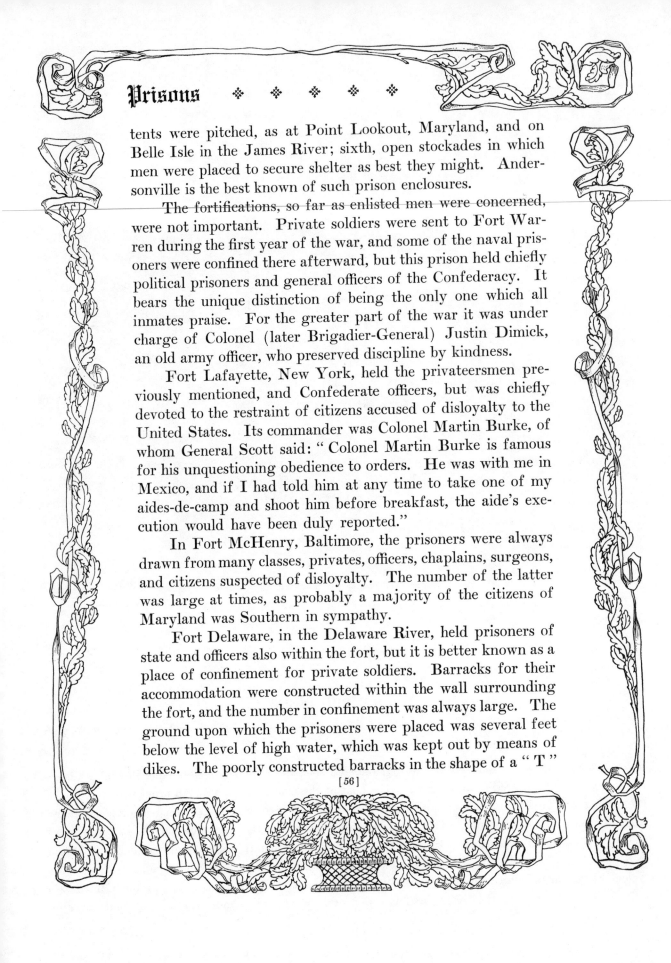

tents were pitched, as at Point Lookout, Maryland, and on Belle Isle in the James River; sixth, open stockades in which men were placed to secure shelter as best they might. Andersonville is the best known of such prison enclosures.

The fortifications, so far as enlisted men were concerned, were not important. Private soldiers were sent to Fort Warren during the first year of the war, and some of the naval prisoners were confined there afterward, but this prison held chiefly political prisoners and general officers of the Confederacy. It bears the unique distinction of being the only one which all inmates praise. For the greater part of the war it was under charge of Colonel (later Brigadier-General) Justin Dimick, an old army officer, who preserved discipline by kindness.

Fort Lafayette, New York, held the privateersmen previously mentioned, and Confederate officers, but was chiefly devoted to the restraint of citizens accused of disloyalty to the United States. Its commander was Colonel Martin Burke, of whom General Scott said: " Colonel Martin Burke is famous for his unquestioning obedience to orders. He was with me in Mexico, and if I had told him at any time to take one of my aides-de-camp and shoot him before breakfast, the aide's execution would have been duly reported."

In Fort McHenry, Baltimore, the prisoners were always drawn from many classes, privates, officers, chaplains, surgeons, and citizens suspected of disloyalty. The number of the latter was large at times, as probably a majority of the citizens of Maryland was Southern in sympathy.

Fort Delaware, in the Delaware River, held prisoners of state and officers also within the fort, but it is better known as a place of confinement for private soldiers. Barracks for their accommodation were constructed within the wall surrounding the fort, and the number in confinement was always large. The ground upon which the prisoners were placed was several feet below the level of high water, which was kept out by means of dikes. The poorly constructed barracks in the shape of a " T "

LIBBY

THE FIRST REPRODUCTION OF A PHOTOGRAPH SHOWING THIS MOST FAMOUS OF ALL PRISONS WHILE IN
CONFEDERATE HANDS

The negative of this war-time photograph of Libby Prison was destroyed in the Richmond conflagration of 1865. Positives from this negative, taken by Rees of Richmond inside the Confederate lines during the war, were never sold. Its publication in this HISTORY is its first appearance. Remarkable also is the fact that the central figure in the group of three in the foreground is Major Thomas P. Turner, commandant of Libby Prison and of Belle Isle. Major Turner was prominent in prison work almost from the beginning to the end of the war. He excited the enmity of a number of his prisoners, and it was expected that he would be tried after the surrender. No charges, however, were brought against him, and he was released. The whole number of Union prisoners confined in Libby Prison from the outbreak of the war to its close is estimated in round figures at 125,000. The books used in the office of Libby Prison and containing names, regiment, date of capture, etc., of every Federal officer and private that ever passed its doors, were deposited in Washington. The books were found to be carefully and accurately kept by the chief-clerk, E. W. Ross.

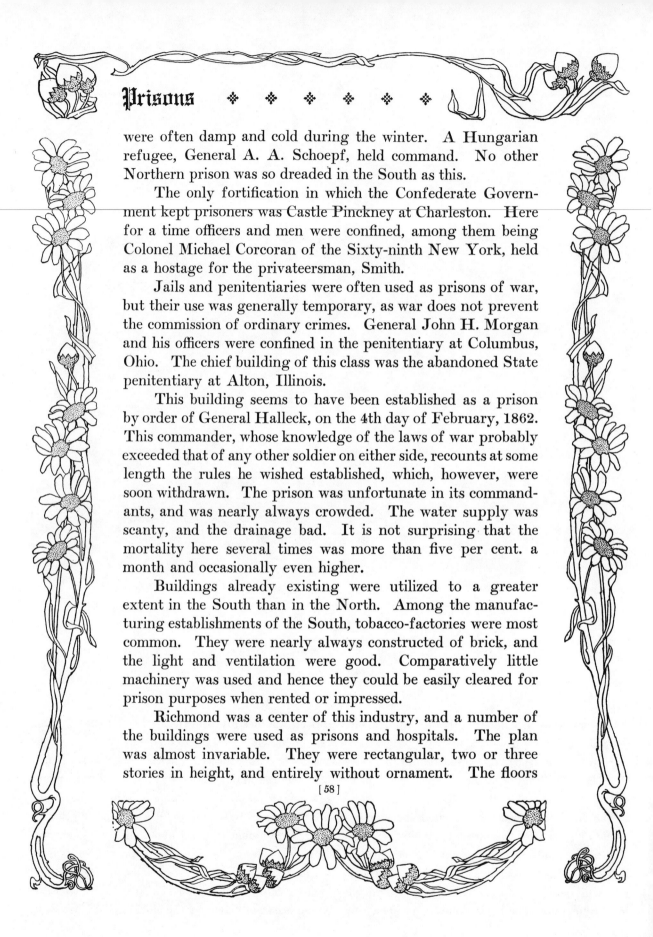

were often damp and cold during the winter. A Hungarian refugee, General A. A. Schoepf, held command. No other Northern prison was so dreaded in the South as this.

The only fortification in which the Confederate Government kept prisoners was Castle Pinckney at Charleston. Here for a time officers and men were confined, among them being Colonel Michael Corcoran of the Sixty-ninth New York, held as a hostage for the privateersman, Smith.

Jails and penitentiaries were often used as prisons of war, but their use was generally temporary, as war does not prevent the commission of ordinary crimes. General John H. Morgan and his officers were confined in the penitentiary at Columbus, Ohio. The chief building of this class was the abandoned State penitentiary at Alton, Illinois.

This building seems to have been established as a prison by order of General Halleck, on the 4th day of February, 1862. This commander, whose knowledge of the laws of war probably exceeded that of any other soldier on either side, recounts at some length the rules he wished established, which, however, were soon withdrawn. The prison was unfortunate in its commandants, and was nearly always crowded. The water supply was scanty, and the drainage bad. It is not surprising that the mortality here several times was more than five per cent. a month and occasionally even higher.

Buildings already existing were utilized to a greater extent in the South than in the North. Among the manufacturing establishments of the South, tobacco-factories were most common. They were nearly always constructed of brick, and the light and ventilation were good. Comparatively little machinery was used and hence they could be easily cleared for prison purposes when rented or impressed.

Richmond was a center of this industry, and a number of the buildings were used as prisons and hospitals. The plan was almost invariable. They were rectangular, two or three stories in height, and entirely without ornament. The floors

WHERE THE FIRST FEDERAL PRISONERS WERE SENT—YOUNG SOUTH CAROLINIANS AT DRILL

Again the reader penetrates inside the Confederate lines in war-time, gazing here at the grim prison barriers of Castle Pinckney, in Charleston Harbor, where some of the Union prisoners captured at the first battle of Bull Run, July 21, 1861, had been sent. The thick stone walls frown down upon the boys of the Charleston Zouave Cadets, assigned to guard these prisoners. Here they are drilling within the prison under the command of Lieutenants E. John White (in front at the right) and B. M. Walpole, just behind him. The cadet kneeling upon the extreme right is Sergeant (later Captain) Joseph F. Burke. The responsibility was a heavy one, but the "Cadets" were a well-drilled body of youngsters and proved quite equal to their duties. This was early in the war before there were brigadier-generals scarcely of age, and youth had been found not to preclude soldierly qualities. No escapes from this fortress have been chronicled.

were of heavy planks and were sometimes divided by partitions, but oftener the entire area of the floor was in one large room.

Among these factory prisons was Liggon's, where the Bull Run and Ball's Bluff officers and a part of the privates were confined. This was next used as a hospital, then closed for a time, and again opened to receive Federal sick. Castle Thunder, where Confederate soldiers undergoing punishment, deserters, and citizens who were accused of disloyalty were confined, was another of this sort. Perhaps a half-dozen other factories in Richmond were used for prison purposes at different times during the war. Warehouses were also used for prison purposes in Danville, Lynchburg, Shreveport, and other towns. Castle Thunder was perhaps the worst of these, but it was a penitentiary rather than a prison of war.

Libby Prison is often incorrectly called a tobacco-factory. It was the warehouse of Libby and Sons, ship-chandlers, situated on the James River at the corner of Twentieth and Cary streets. It was a large four-story building, containing eight rooms. No furniture was ever placed in it, and the men slept upon the floor. From it, Colonel Rose and his companions escaped, in 1864, by tunneling from the basement floor under the street, but escapes were generally few. This prison was under command of Major Thomas P. Turner, though a subordinate, Richard Turner, had more direct control.

For a time an attempt to preserve reasonable sanitary precautions was made. The floors were washed; a rude bathroom was installed, and the walls were frequently whitewashed. As the months went on, conditions gradually grew worse, as it was generally crowded, even after some of the officers were sent to Macon, Danville, and Salisbury.

The prison at Cahaba, Alabama, was an old cotton-shed, partially unroofed, with bunks for five hundred men. A few hundred prisoners were confined here early in 1864, but were transferred to Andersonville soon after that prison was opened. In the summer of 1864 prisoners were again sent here, and in

BELLE ISLE

THE CONFEDERATE COMMANDANT IN THE FOREGROUND

THE CAPITOL OF THE CONFEDERACY

IN THE DISTANCE

Prominent in the foreground is Major Thomas P. Turner, commandant of Belle Isle and Libby Prison. He is clad in Confederate gray, with a soft felt hat, and his orderly stands behind him. Before him are some tents of the Union prisoners—a trifle nearer the Capitol at Richmond seen across the river than they care to be at the present juncture. The fact that this noble edifice was erected under the direction of Thomas Jefferson, on the plan of the Maison-Carrée at Nîmes, could do little to alleviate their mental distress. The crest of the hill on which Major Turner is standing is one hundred and twelve feet above tidewater, overlooking the encampment. The guard and guard-tents appear in the distance at the edge of the river. This is the fourth successive war-time photograph taken inside the Confederate lines shown in this chapter. The original negative was destroyed by fire on the memorable morning of the 3rd of April, 1865.

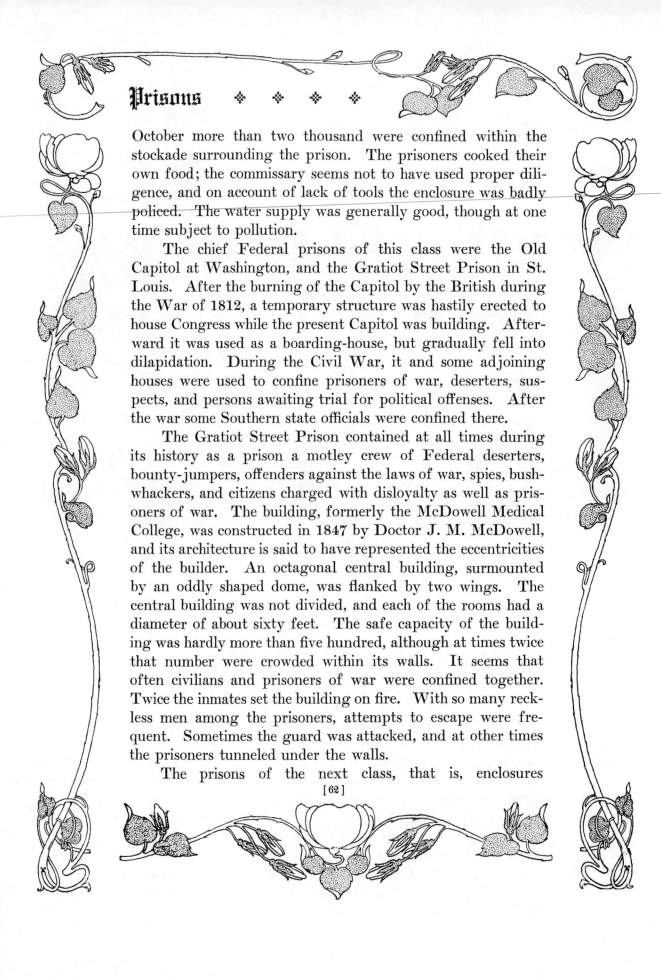

October more than two thousand were confined within the stockade surrounding the prison. The prisoners cooked their own food; the commissary seems not to have used proper diligence, and on account of lack of tools the enclosure was badly policed. The water supply was generally good, though at one time subject to pollution.

The chief Federal prisons of this class were the Old Capitol at Washington, and the Gratiot Street Prison in St. Louis. After the burning of the Capitol by the British during the War of 1812, a temporary structure was hastily erected to house Congress while the present Capitol was building. Afterward it was used as a boarding-house, but gradually fell into dilapidation. During the Civil War, it and some adjoining houses were used to confine prisoners of war, deserters, suspects, and persons awaiting trial for political offenses. After the war some Southern state officials were confined there.

The Gratiot Street Prison contained at all times during its history as a prison a motley crew of Federal deserters, bounty-jumpers, offenders against the laws of war, spies, bushwhackers, and citizens charged with disloyalty as well as prisoners of war. The building, formerly the McDowell Medical College, was constructed in 1847 by Doctor J. M. McDowell, and its architecture is said to have represented the eccentricities of the builder. An octagonal central building, surmounted by an oddly shaped dome, was flanked by two wings. The central building was not divided, and each of the rooms had a diameter of about sixty feet. The safe capacity of the building was hardly more than five hundred, although at times twice that number were crowded within its walls. It seems that often civilians and prisoners of war were confined together. Twice the inmates set the building on fire. With so many reckless men among the prisoners, attempts to escape were frequent. Sometimes the guard was attacked, and at other times the prisoners tunneled under the walls.

The prisons of the next class, that is, enclosures

THE KEEPERS OF POINT LOOKOUT PRISON

BRIGADIER–GENERAL JAMES BARNES AND STAFF AT POINT LOOKOUT, MD.

Brigadier-General James Barnes was in command of the district of St. Mary's, with headquarters at Point Lookout, Md., during the latter part of the war. Here the largest prison of the North was established August 1, 1863, on the low peninsula where the Potomac joins the Chesapeake Bay. No barracks were erected within the enclosure; tents were used instead. There was at all times a sufficiency of these for shelter, though at times nearly twenty thousand Confederate prisoners were in confinement here, and they were occasionally overcrowded. Negro troops formed part of the guard, and such a vast number of prisoners naturally required a large organization to take care of them. In this photograph are shown all the officers in connection with the prison. From left to right, not counting the two soldiers holding the flags, they are: Dr. A. Heger, medical director; Captain C. H. Drew, assistant adjutant-general; Captain H. E. Goodwin, assistant quartermaster; Lieutenant H. C. Strong, assistant quartermaster; Brigadier-General James Barnes; Major A. G. Brady, provost-marshal; Dr. T. H. Thompson, surgeon; Captain J. W. Welch, ordnance officer; Lieutenant Wilson, aide-de-camp; and the last is Lieutenant J. T. Cantwell, engineer.

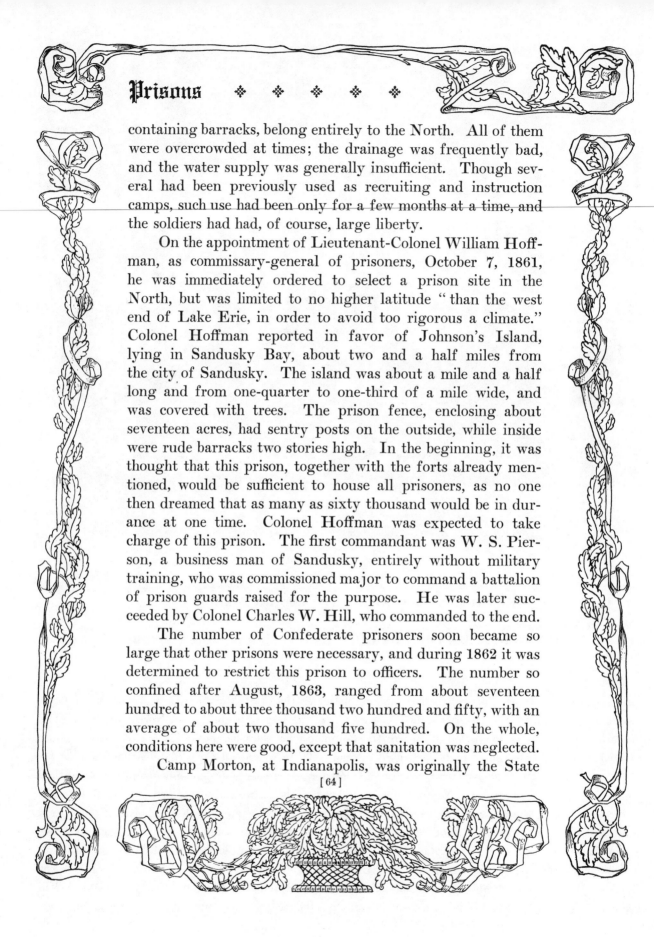

containing barracks, belong entirely to the North. All of them were overcrowded at times; the drainage was frequently bad, and the water supply was generally insufficient. Though several had been previously used as recruiting and instruction camps, such use had been only for a few months at a time, and the soldiers had had, of course, large liberty.

On the appointment of Lieutenant-Colonel William Hoffman, as commissary-general of prisoners, October 7, 1861, he was immediately ordered to select a prison site in the North, but was limited to no higher latitude " than the west end of Lake Erie, in order to avoid too rigorous a climate." Colonel Hoffman reported in favor of Johnson's Island, lying in Sandusky Bay, about two and a half miles from the city of Sandusky. The island was about a mile and a half long and from one-quarter to one-third of a mile wide, and was covered with trees. The prison fence, enclosing about seventeen acres, had sentry posts on the outside, while inside were rude barracks two stories high. In the beginning, it was thought that this prison, together with the forts already mentioned, would be sufficient to house all prisoners, as no one then dreamed that as many as sixty thousand would be in durance at one time. Colonel Hoffman was expected to take charge of this prison. The first commandant was W. S. Pierson, a business man of Sandusky, entirely without military training, who was commissioned major to command a battalion of prison guards raised for the purpose. He was later succeeded by Colonel Charles W. Hill, who commanded to the end.

The number of Confederate prisoners soon became so large that other prisons were necessary, and during 1862 it was determined to restrict this prison to officers. The number so confined after August, 1863, ranged from about seventeen hundred to about three thousand two hundred and fifty, with an average of about two thousand five hundred. On the whole, conditions here were good, except that sanitation was neglected.

Camp Morton, at Indianapolis, was originally the State

BREVET BRIGADIER-GENERAL
B. F. TRACY

BRIGADIER-GENERAL
ALBIN SCHOEPF

BREVET BRIGADIER-GENERAL
JUSTIN DIMICK

THREE COMMANDANTS OF FEDERAL PRISONS

Above are the officers in charge of three Federal prisons, the first two of which were a terror to the captured Confederates. Students of physiognomy will be interested in comparing the faces of the three men. B. F. Tracy entered the war as colonel of the 109th New York Infantry, August 28, 1862. He was honorably discharged May 10, 1864, and on September 10th of that year he was made colonel of the 127th United States Colored Infantry, and placed in charge of Elmira Prison, where the mortality was very high. He was appointed brevet brigadier-general of volunteers March 13, 1865. Brigadier-General Albin Schoepf, a Hungarian refugee, held the command of Fort Delaware until he was mustered out, January 15, 1866. No prison was so dreaded in the South as this, where the poorly constructed barracks, several feet below the level of high water, were always damp and cold. Fort Warren, for the greater part of the war, was under charge of Colonel (later Brigadier-General) Justin Dimick, an officer who graduated from the Military Academy October 18, 1814, served in the war against the Florida Indians and in the Mexican War, and received promotions for gallant and meritorious conduct in both. This kind-hearted veteran was able to preserve discipline by kindness, and Fort Warren bears the unique distinction of being the only one which all inmates praised. The Gratiot Street Prison in St. Louis, shown below, was commanded during the last year of the war by an able officer, Captain R. C. Allen.

GRATIOT STREET PRISON, ST. LOUIS, MISSOURI

Fair Ground, which had been used during the fall and winter of 1861 and 1862 as barracks for a few Indiana troops. The camp was turned into a prison to accommodate those captured in Forts Henry and Donelson, and what had formerly been sheds for horses and cattle or exhibition halls became barracks for prisoners. Apparently some of these barracks had no floors and during the winter could not be kept clean. The buildings were cheaply built, and the snow, wind, and rain came through. A part of the time fuel was insufficient. The enclosure was large, contained a number of trees, and the possibilities of drainage were good. During the first year the camp was under control of the governor of Indiana, but afterward came under the supervision of Colonel Hoffman, the commissary-general of prisoners. In 1863, Colonel A. A. Stevens of the Invalid Corps became commandant of the prison, and under him conditions improved.

The prison at Rock Island stood on an island in the Mississippi River between the cities of Rock Island, Illinois, and Davenport, Iowa. The island itself was about three miles long and half a mile wide. The construction of the prison was ordered in July, 1863, and on August 12th, the quartermaster-general instructed the builder that "the barracks for prisoners on Rock Island should be put up in the roughest and cheapest manner, mere shanties, with no fine work about them." A high fence enclosed eighty-four barracks arranged in six rows of fourteen each. The barracks were eighty-two by twenty-two by twelve feet, with a cook-house at the end of each. The ventilation was poor, and only two stoves were placed in each of the barracks. The water supply was partly secured from an artesian well and partly from the river by means of a steam-pump, which frequently gave out for days at a time. Though the prison was not quite completed, over five thousand prisoners were sent during the month of December, 1863, and from that time on the prison usually contained from five thousand to eight thousand prisoners until the end of the war.

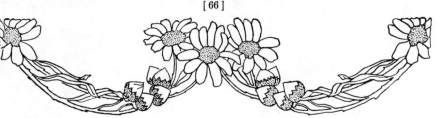

THE OLD CAPITOL PRISON—SHOWING THE ADDITIONS BUILT AFTER 1861

At the outset of the war, the only tenant of the Old Capitol—where once the United States Congress had been housed—was an humble German, who managed to subsist himself and his family as a cobbler. Six months later the place was full of military offenders, prisoners of state, and captured Confederates, and the guards allowed no one to stop even for a minute on the other side of the street. Many prominent Confederate generals were confined in it, with scores of citizens suspected of disloyalty to the Union. Captain Wirz, the keeper of Andersonville Prison, was imprisoned here, and was executed on a gallows in the yard. These views show the extensions built upon each side of the prison to contain mess-halls, and also to shelter prisoners of war. Iron bars have been placed in all the windows, and sentries and soldiers stand upon the sidewalk. Here Mrs. Rose O'Neal Greenhow, the Confederate spy, was incarcerated.

SOLDIERS OUTSIDE THE PRISON

During the first months the medical staff was inexperienced, and the camp was scourged by smallpox which was, in fact, seldom absent for any length of time. Later, a new medical officer brought order out of confusion, but the staff here was never so efficient as at some other prisons. A very expensive hospital was erected, paid for from the "prison fund," which amounted to one hundred and seventy-five thousand dollars in 1865.

Camp Douglas, in Chicago, was a large instruction and recruiting camp, of which the prison formed a comparatively small part. The camp was on low ground, which was flooded with every rain, and during a considerable part of the winter was a sea of mud. The barracks were poor and conditions generally were unsanitary. President H. W. Bellows of the Sanitary Commission says, June 30, 1862, speaking of the barracks, "Nothing but fire can cleanse them," and urges the abandonment of the camp as a prison. The place was not abandoned, however; and in February, 1863, out of 3884 prisoners, 387 died. This mortality rate, almost exactly ten per cent. for the month, was not reached in any month, in any other large prison during the war, so far as the "Official Records" indicate.

Camp Chase, at Columbus, Ohio, was another instruction camp turned into a prison to accommodate the prisoners captured at Forts Henry and Donelson, in February, 1862, and used as such until the end of the war. Conditions here were similar to those at Camp Morton in general features, as were also those at Camp Butler, near Springfield, Illinois, which was, however, abandoned for prison purposes in 1862.

After the suspension of the agreement to exchange prisoners, May 25, 1863, the numbers in confinement began to exceed the provision made for them, and in May, 1864, some barracks on the Chemung River near Elmira, New York, were enclosed for prison purposes. Before the end of August, the number of prisoners reached almost ten thousand. Conditions

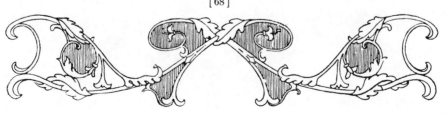

FORT JOHNSON IN SANDUSKY BAY, LAKE ERIE

This photograph shows one of the forts used to guard the prisoners at Johnson's Island, Lake Erie. The prison here was expected to be sufficient to accommodate the whole number of prisoners taken during the war, in which, however, Quartermaster-General Meigs was much disappointed. When Lieutenant-Colonel William Hoffman, commissary-general of prisoners, had been ordered to Lake Erie in the fall of 1861 to select a prison-site, with the limitation that it must be in no higher latitude "than the west end of Lake Erie, in order to avoid too rigorous a climate," he reported in favor of Johnson's Island, lying in Sandusky Bay, about two and a half miles from the city of Sandusky. The prison fence, enclosing about seventeen acres, had sentry posts upon the outside, while inside were rude barracks about two stories high. This prison was first commanded by Major W. S. Pierson, and was then under charge of Colonel Charles W. Hill. After the first year of its existence it was occupied exclusively as an officers' prison. Sometimes more than three thousand were confined here at the same time. The average was about two thousand five hundred. Conditions in this prison were generally good, although the prisoners from the Gulf States suffered intensely from the cold winds from Lake Erie. Some of them froze on the terrible New Year's Day of 1864.

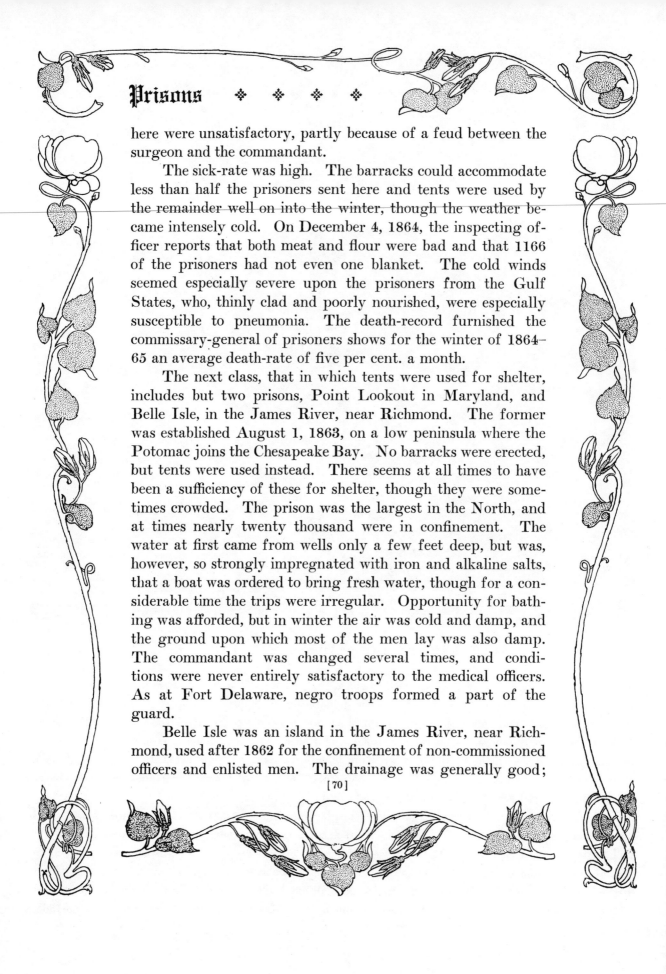

here were unsatisfactory, partly because of a feud between the surgeon and the commandant.

The sick-rate was high. The barracks could accommodate less than half the prisoners sent here and tents were used by the remainder well on into the winter, though the weather became intensely cold. On December 4, 1864, the inspecting officer reports that both meat and flour were bad and that 1166 of the prisoners had not even one blanket. The cold winds seemed especially severe upon the prisoners from the Gulf States, who, thinly clad and poorly nourished, were especially susceptible to pneumonia. The death-record furnished the commissary-general of prisoners shows for the winter of 1864–65 an average death-rate of five per cent. a month.

The next class, that in which tents were used for shelter, includes but two prisons, Point Lookout in Maryland, and Belle Isle, in the James River, near Richmond. The former was established August 1, 1863, on a low peninsula where the Potomac joins the Chesapeake Bay. No barracks were erected, but tents were used instead. There seems at all times to have been a sufficiency of these for shelter, though they were sometimes crowded. The prison was the largest in the North, and at times nearly twenty thousand were in confinement. The water at first came from wells only a few feet deep, but was, however, so strongly impregnated with iron and alkaline salts, that a boat was ordered to bring fresh water, though for a considerable time the trips were irregular. Opportunity for bathing was afforded, but in winter the air was cold and damp, and the ground upon which most of the men lay was also damp. The commandant was changed several times, and conditions were never entirely satisfactory to the medical officers. As at Fort Delaware, negro troops formed a part of the guard.

Belle Isle was an island in the James River, near Richmond, used after 1862 for the confinement of non-commissioned officers and enlisted men. The drainage was generally good;

THE GUARD AT THE GATE—CAMP MORTON

CAMP MORTON, THE INDIANAPOLIS PRISON

The people who entered this enclosure before the war were required to pay for the privilege. It was originally the State Fair-grounds which had been used during the fall and winter of 1861 and 1862 as barracks for Indiana troops. The camp was turned into a prison to accommodate the Confederates taken at Forts Henry and Donelson. The sheds where horses and cattle had been shown and the halls where agricultural products had been exhibited were turned into barracks for prisoners. The buildings, originally of cheap construction, were penetrated by the

BLANKETS OF THE PRISONERS, CAMP MORTON

snow and wind and rain. A part of the time fuel was insufficient. However, as seen in the middle photograph, all of the prisoners had blankets. In 1863, Colonel A. A. Stevens, of the invalid corps, became commandant of the prison and under him conditions improved. It is curious to examine the ornate gateway through which the throng is so eager to pass, in the upper photograph. The crowd shown inside was even more eager to pass through this gate, but in the opposite direction after this became a prison. The sanitary conditions were bad. This was as much due to the ignorance of proper sanitation in those times as to neglect. No one would dream in the twentieth century of allowing sewage to flow through an open ditch.

PRIMITIVE DRAINAGE AT CAMP MORTON

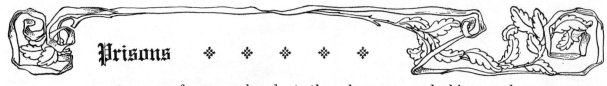

water was of course abundant, though soap was lacking, and at first rations were sufficient to preserve the strength of the prisoners. During the summer of 1863 conditions were endurable, but as larger numbers were sent thither, food became scarcer, and as the weather grew colder, much suffering ensued. On November 18, 1863, according to the report of the Confederate inspector, there were sixty-three hundred in confinement, though the encampment had been intended for about three thousand, and tents for only that number had been provided. An effort to provide more was made, but tents to shelter all the prisoners were never furnished. Many prisoners lay on the damp ground without protection of any sort and there was much suffering during the winter.

Little seems to have been done to better conditions except to hurry along the completion of the stockade at Andersonville, and on March 6, 1864, the medical inspector reported that one-fourth the prisoners were sick. As captives were sent further south there were fewer complaints for a time, but in September, 1864, conditions were evidently as bad as ever. The efforts of the officers in charge show how strained were the resources of the Confederacy. Only seventy-five tents could be found in Richmond, and lumber could not be had at all.

The last class of prisons, open stockades without shelter, was found only in the South. It included Camp Sumter at Anderson, and Camp Lawton at Millen, Georgia; Camp Ford, near Tyler, and Camp Groce near Hempstead, Texas, and the stockades at Savannah, Charleston, Florence, and Columbia. Though there were several buildings within the fence at Salisbury, they could accommodate only a small proportion of the prisoners confined there, so that this prison belongs, in part at least, to this class also.

As early as 1862, the Confederate Commissary Department broke down under the strain of feeding both the Army of Northern Virginia and a considerable number of prisoners in Virginia. The exchange of prisoners following the agreement

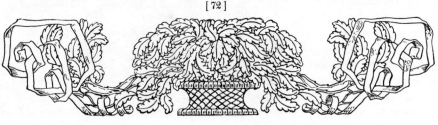

CAMP DOUGLAS, WHERE TEN PER CENT. OF THE PRISONERS DIED ONE MONTH

In February, 1863, out of 3,884 prisoners, 387 died at Camp Douglas in Chicago, or almost exactly ten per cent., a mortality rate for one month not reached by any other large prison during the war. The camp was on low ground, the drainage bad, and conditions generally were unsanitary. Its abandonment as a prison was urged by President H. W. Bellows of the Sanitary Commission. It is hard for us to realize, as we look at this group of apparently hale and hearty young men, how great a toll death took by reason of the ignorance or indifference of their keepers. It was no contemplated part of the war to allow such things to happen, but those in charge of the prisoners were often hampered by lack of appropriations and delay in delivering supplies. The question of the proper feeding and adequate housing of prisoners in sanitary surroundings remained unsolved by either side until the close of the protracted conflict.

of July, 1862, lessened the pressure somewhat, but subsequent captures made further provision necessary. In 1863, it was determined to build a large prison further south, in territory which was not tributary to Virginia as far as food was concerned. After much investigation, Anderson, then a railroad station twelve miles north of Americus, Georgia, was chosen. Here was constructed in 1863–64 the structure which acquired notoriety equal to that of the Bastile or Newgate. The locality was selected by Captain W. S. Winder, a son of General John H. Winder, then commanding the Department of Henrico. The plan of the post allowed both for offense and defense, and showed engineering ability of no mean order.

The prison was a stockade, within which it was intended to build barracks for from eight to ten thousand men. This stockade was constructed of squared trunks of trees, about twenty feet long, set five feet into the ground, enclosing an area, first of about seventeen acres, afterward enlarged to about twenty-seven acres, though several acres were swamp. An outer stockade surrounded the prison, and a third was begun but never completed. The ground sloped down on both sides to a small stream, a branch of Sweet Water Creek, which ran from west to east through the stockade. This stream was about fifty feet below the highest point within the enclosure and the stream itself was about three hundred feet above the sea level. The hills were covered with pine trees which were cut down to furnish material for the stockade, and no trees of any considerable size were left, though the stumps, the branches, and the underbrush covered the ground when the first prisoners entered. The soil was sandy with small admixture of vegetable mold or of clay. Water sank readily into the soil or was drained off. The stream flowing through the stockade was clear, the water naturally pure, and the locality seems not to have been unsuitable for a prison for the number of inmates for which it was originally designed.

Though orders had been given to construct the prison in

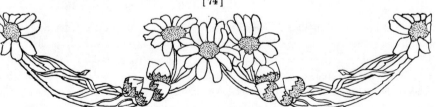

ANDERSONVILLE EXACTLY AS IT LOOKED FROM THE STOCKADE, AUGUST 17, 1864

The taking of these remarkable photographs was witnessed by C. W. Reynolds, Ninety-second Illinois Infantry. Describing himself as a former "star boarder at Andersonville," he writes to the editors of this HISTORY: "I was a prisoner of war in that place during the whole summer of '64, and I well remember seeing a photographer with his camera in one of the sentinel-boxes near the south gate during July or August, trying to take a picture of the interior of the prison. I have often wondered in later years what success this photographer had and why the public had never had an opportunity to see a genuine photograph of Andersonville Prison."

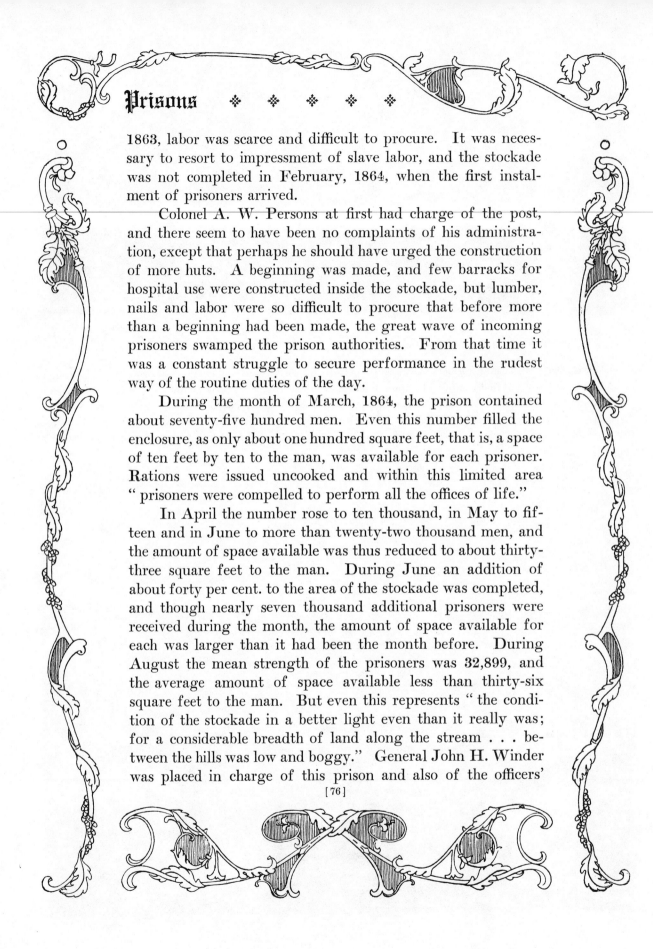

1863, labor was scarce and difficult to procure. It was necessary to resort to impressment of slave labor, and the stockade was not completed in February, 1864, when the first instalment of prisoners arrived.

Colonel A. W. Persons at first had charge of the post, and there seem to have been no complaints of his administration, except that perhaps he should have urged the construction of more huts. A beginning was made, and few barracks for hospital use were constructed inside the stockade, but lumber, nails and labor were so difficult to procure that before more than a beginning had been made, the great wave of incoming prisoners swamped the prison authorities. From that time it was a constant struggle to secure performance in the rudest way of the routine duties of the day.

During the month of March, 1864, the prison contained about seventy-five hundred men. Even this number filled the enclosure, as only about one hundred square feet, that is, a space of ten feet by ten to the man, was available for each prisoner. Rations were issued uncooked and within this limited area " prisoners were compelled to perform all the offices of life."

In April the number rose to ten thousand, in May to fifteen and in June to more than twenty-two thousand men, and the amount of space available was thus reduced to about thirty-three square feet to the man. During June an addition of about forty per cent. to the area of the stockade was completed, and though nearly seven thousand additional prisoners were received during the month, the amount of space available for each was larger than it had been the month before. During August the mean strength of the prisoners was 32,899, and the average amount of space available less than thirty-six square feet to the man. But even this represents " the condition of the stockade in a better light even than it really was; for a considerable breadth of land along the stream . . . between the hills was low and boggy." General John H. Winder was placed in charge of this prison and also of the officers'

ELMIRA PRISON BEFORE THE ADDITIONAL BARRACKS WERE BUILT

This is an early picture of Elmira Prison before additional barracks had been constructed. The old barracks are visible in the middle distance, while almost the entire space in front is covered with tents under which a considerable part of the Confederate prisoners were accommodated until the winter. The Elmira Prison was opened in May, 1864. Before the end of August the prisoners there numbered almost ten thousand. Conditions here were always bad, partly on account of the insufficient shelter, and partly because of a feud between the commandant and surgeon. The latter, E. F. Sanger, wrote under date of November 1, 1864, to Brigadier-General J. K. Barnes, Surgeon-General of the United States Army: "Since August there have been 2,011 patients admitted to the hospital, 775 deaths out of a mean strength of 8,347 prisoners of war, or twenty-four per cent. admitted and nine per cent. died. Have averaged daily 451 in hospital and 601 in quarters, an aggregate of 1,052 per day sick. At this rate the entire command will be admitted to hospital in less than a year and thirty-six per cent. die." This was due to the delay in filling his requisitions.

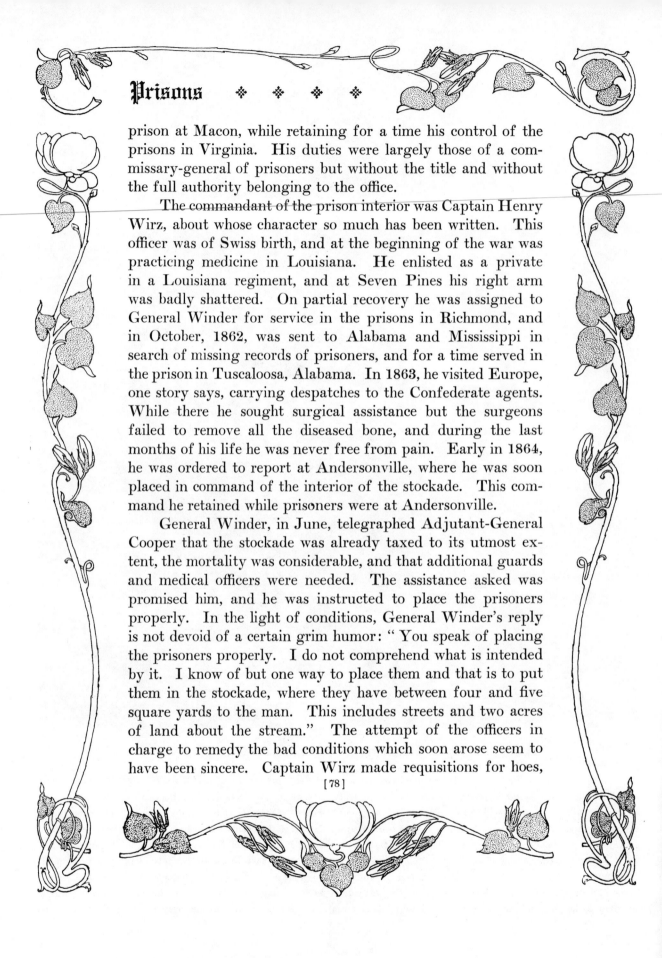

prison at Macon, while retaining for a time his control of the prisons in Virginia. His duties were largely those of a commissary-general of prisoners but without the title and without the full authority belonging to the office.

The commandant of the prison interior was Captain Henry Wirz, about whose character so much has been written. This officer was of Swiss birth, and at the beginning of the war was practicing medicine in Louisiana. He enlisted as a private in a Louisiana regiment, and at Seven Pines his right arm was badly shattered. On partial recovery he was assigned to General Winder for service in the prisons in Richmond, and in October, 1862, was sent to Alabama and Mississippi in search of missing records of prisoners, and for a time served in the prison in Tuscaloosa, Alabama. In 1863, he visited Europe, one story says, carrying despatches to the Confederate agents. While there he sought surgical assistance but the surgeons failed to remove all the diseased bone, and during the last months of his life he was never free from pain. Early in 1864, he was ordered to report at Andersonville, where he was soon placed in command of the interior of the stockade. This command he retained while prisoners were at Andersonville.

General Winder, in June, telegraphed Adjutant-General Cooper that the stockade was already taxed to its utmost extent, the mortality was considerable, and that additional guards and medical officers were needed. The assistance asked was promised him, and he was instructed to place the prisoners properly. In the light of conditions, General Winder's reply is not devoid of a certain grim humor: " You speak of placing the prisoners properly. I do not comprehend what is intended by it. I know of but one way to place them and that is to put them in the stockade, where they have between four and five square yards to the man. This includes streets and two acres of land about the stream." The attempt of the officers in charge to remedy the bad conditions which soon arose seem to have been sincere. Captain Wirz made requisitions for hoes,

EVENING ROLL–CALL FOR THE ELMIRA PRISONERS—1864

This photograph was cherished through half a century by Berry Benson, of the First South Carolina Volunteer Infantry, who escaped from Elmira by digging a tunnel sixty-six feet long under the tents and stockade. It shows the prisoners at evening roll-call for dinner in the winter of 1864. The sergeants in front of the long line of prisoners are calling the roll. There were both Federal and Confederate sergeants. Elmira prison contained from the time of its establishment several thousand Confederate prisoners. The barracks in the foreground had been completed only a few days when this picture was made, and up to that time a large number of prisoners had occupied tents. The leaves are gone from the trees, and it is obvious that the winter frosts have set in. The tents were unheated, and the inmates suffered severely from the cold. The sentry in the foreground is not paying strict attention to the prisoners. The men grouped around the tree are indicated by Mr. Benson as Federal officers. The rate cf mortality in this prison was very high.

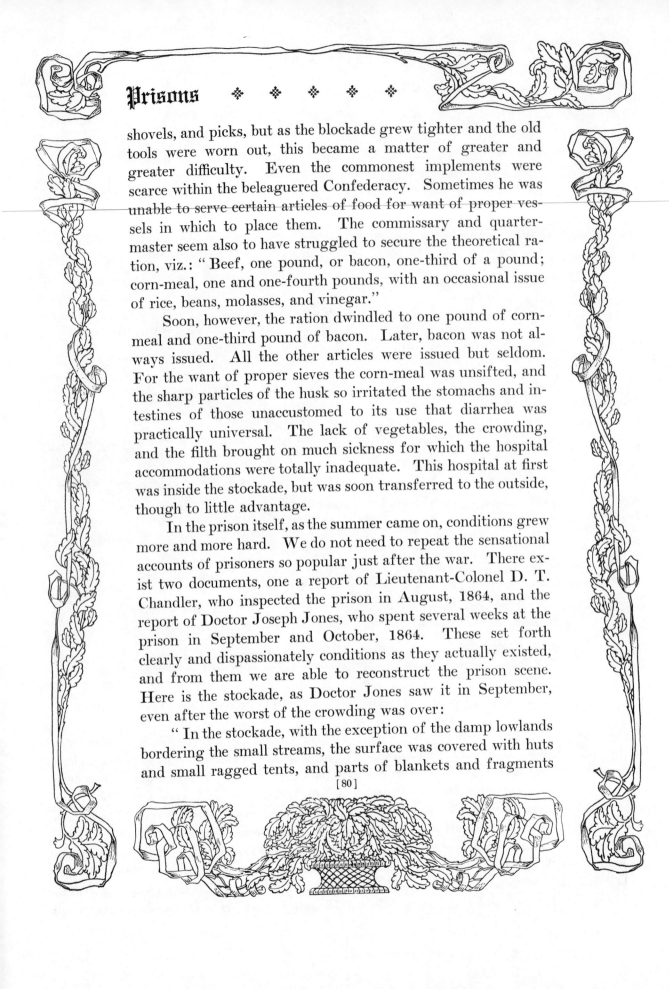

shovels, and picks, but as the blockade grew tighter and the old tools were worn out, this became a matter of greater and greater difficulty. Even the commonest implements were scarce within the beleaguered Confederacy. Sometimes he was unable to serve certain articles of food for want of proper vessels in which to place them. The commissary and quartermaster seem also to have struggled to secure the theoretical ration, viz.: "Beef, one pound, or bacon, one-third of a pound; corn-meal, one and one-fourth pounds, with an occasional issue of rice, beans, molasses, and vinegar."

Soon, however, the ration dwindled to one pound of corn-meal and one-third pound of bacon. Later, bacon was not always issued. All the other articles were issued but seldom. For the want of proper sieves the corn-meal was unsifted, and the sharp particles of the husk so irritated the stomachs and intestines of those unaccustomed to its use that diarrhea was practically universal. The lack of vegetables, the crowding, and the filth brought on much sickness for which the hospital accommodations were totally inadequate. This hospital at first was inside the stockade, but was soon transferred to the outside, though to little advantage.

In the prison itself, as the summer came on, conditions grew more and more hard. We do not need to repeat the sensational accounts of prisoners so popular just after the war. There exist two documents, one a report of Lieutenant-Colonel D. T. Chandler, who inspected the prison in August, 1864, and the report of Doctor Joseph Jones, who spent several weeks at the prison in September and October, 1864. These set forth clearly and dispassionately conditions as they actually existed, and from them we are able to reconstruct the prison scene. Here is the stockade, as Doctor Jones saw it in September, even after the worst of the crowding was over:

" In the stockade, with the exception of the damp lowlands bordering the small streams, the surface was covered with huts and small ragged tents, and parts of blankets and fragments

THE ONLY PHOTOGRAPH SHOWING THE WHOLE OF ELMIRA PRISON CAMP

This photograph, reproduced one-half above and one-half below, is the only one showing the whole prison, which takes in an area of forty acres. Early in the war a rendezvous camp had been established at Elmira, New York. After exchange of prisoners ceased in 1863, though battles continued to be fought, the number of Confederate prisoners increased very rapidly and further accommodation was necessary. These barracks were chosen to serve as a prison in May, 1864. The first detachment of Confederate prisoners arrived there July 6th, 649 in number. During the month of July, 1864, 4,424 more were brought; during August, 5,195; and from September 1, 1864, to May 12, 1865, 2,503 additional, making a total of 12,122 prisoners of war. For a considerable time a large proportion of these were accommodated in tents, though barracks were completed in the early part of the winter. The site of the prison was badly chosen; it was below the level of the Chemung River, and a lagoon of stagnant water caused much sickness. The severity of the winter also brought much suffering to the prisoners, may of whom came from the warm Gulf States. The number of deaths to July 1, 1865, was 2,917; the number of escapes 17; those in the hospital, July 1, 1865, 218; and the number released, 8,970; total, 12,122. These figures were taken from the books of the officer in charge. The high fence was built when prisoners were ordered to this point.

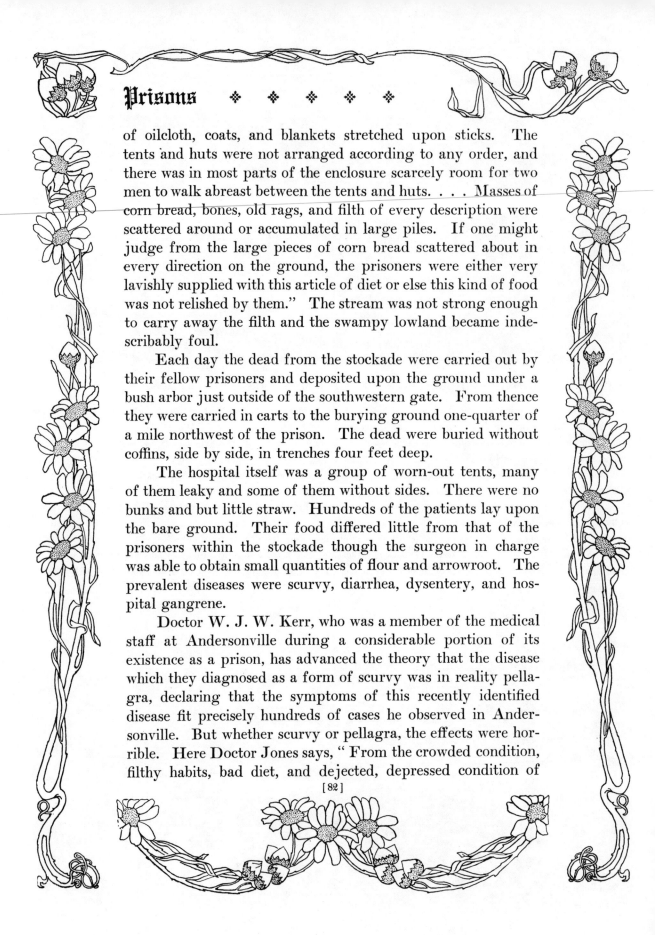

of oilcloth, coats, and blankets stretched upon sticks. The tents and huts were not arranged according to any order, and there was in most parts of the enclosure scarcely room for two men to walk abreast between the tents and huts. . . . Masses of corn bread, bones, old rags, and filth of every description were scattered around or accumulated in large piles. If one might judge from the large pieces of corn bread scattered about in every direction on the ground, the prisoners were either very lavishly supplied with this article of diet or else this kind of food was not relished by them." The stream was not strong enough to carry away the filth and the swampy lowland became indescribably foul.

Each day the dead from the stockade were carried out by their fellow prisoners and deposited upon the ground under a bush arbor just outside of the southwestern gate. From thence they were carried in carts to the burying ground one-quarter of a mile northwest of the prison. The dead were buried without coffins, side by side, in trenches four feet deep.

The hospital itself was a group of worn-out tents, many of them leaky and some of them without sides. There were no bunks and but little straw. Hundreds of the patients lay upon the bare ground. Their food differed little from that of the prisoners within the stockade though the surgeon in charge was able to obtain small quantities of flour and arrowroot. The prevalent diseases were scurvy, diarrhea, dysentery, and hospital gangrene.

Doctor W. J. W. Kerr, who was a member of the medical staff at Andersonville during a considerable portion of its existence as a prison, has advanced the theory that the disease which they diagnosed as a form of scurvy was in reality pellagra, declaring that the symptoms of this recently identified disease fit precisely hundreds of cases he observed in Andersonville. But whether scurvy or pellagra, the effects were horrible. Here Doctor Jones says, " From the crowded condition, filthy habits, bad diet, and dejected, depressed condition of

BEFORE THE OFFICE OF THE COMMISSARY–GENERAL OF PRISONERS—1864

The work in the office of the commissary-general of prisoners was arduous and important.   The reports of all prisons, the requisitions for extraordinary supplies, and every detail of the handling of prisoners passed through his hands.   Guided by these records and statistics, he indicated to the provost-marshals of the various armies where the prisoners should be sent.   He issued his orders directly to the commanding officers regardless of the departmental commanders; he determined how the prisoners should be clothed and fed, and what accommodations in the way of new buildings and stockades should be prepared for them.   Through this systematic method the whereabouts of almost every prisoner taken by the United States troops was at all times a matter of record at headquarters.

[H—6]

the prisoners, their systems became so disordered that the smallest abrasion of the skin from the rubbing of a shoe, or from the effects of the hot sun, or from the prick of a splinter, or from scratching a mosquito bite, in some cases took on rapid and frightful ulceration and gangrene."

From this description of prison and hospital, one cannot wonder that nearly one-third of the total number of prisoners confined died within the space of eleven months. The crowding, the poor food, the lack of medicine, the hospital infected with gangrene, the lack of the simplest hygienic appliances, homesickness, and last, but not least, the hot Southern sun altogether took fearful toll of those confined within the stockade. With the approach of Sherman's army all prisoners, except about five thousand sick, were transferred to Savannah and Charleston during the months of September and October. Colonel G. C. Gibbs, who now commanded at the post, took energetic proceedings to renovate the command. It was possible to secure sufficient vegetable food for a few thousand men, and the death-rate fell considerably during December. Hospital sheds were built, and though a small number of prisoners was returned after General Sherman had passed, conditions were never so horrible.

Camp Lawton, at Millen, Georgia, had been planned by General Winder early in the summer of 1864, after he had seen that the number of prisoners sent to Andersonville would exceed the capacity of that prison. The prison was larger than Andersonville; the stream of water was stronger, and better hospital accommodation was planned.

It was a stockade resembling that at Andersonville, but was square, and contained about forty-two acres. The interior was laid off by streets into thirty-two divisions, each of which in turn was subdivided into ten parts. The branches of the trees used in making the stockade were left on the ground, and the prisoners were able to make huts of them. The question of shelter was never serious here.

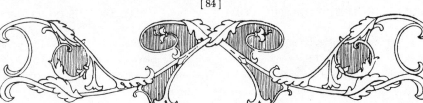

FOREST HALL MILITARY PRISON, AT GEORGETOWN

This was one of the military prisons utilized by the provost-marshal. The activities of these officials first brought to the consciousness of the non-combatant citizen the fact that a state of war actually existed. As a result of the widespread suspicion and broadcast accusations that persons not in sympathy with the Federal Government were spies, the arrest of hundreds in and about Washington and in the other larger cities of the Union States was ordered without warrants on a simple order from the State or War Department, but chiefly the former.   President Lincoln had claimed the right to suspend the writ of *habeas corpus*. Commanders of such prisons as the above were instructed to refuse to allow themselves to be served with writs; or either to decline to appear or to appear and courteously refuse to carry out the instruction of the court.

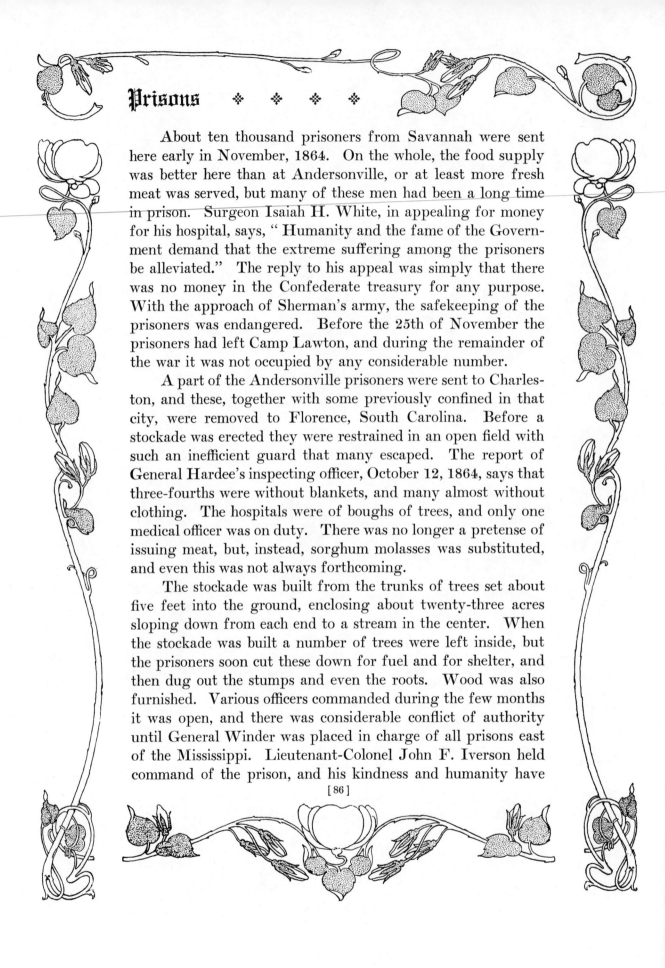

Prisons ❖ ❖ ❖ ❖

About ten thousand prisoners from Savannah were sent here early in November, 1864. On the whole, the food supply was better here than at Andersonville, or at least more fresh meat was served, but many of these men had been a long time in prison. Surgeon Isaiah H. White, in appealing for money for his hospital, says, " Humanity and the fame of the Government demand that the extreme suffering among the prisoners be alleviated." The reply to his appeal was simply that there was no money in the Confederate treasury for any purpose. With the approach of Sherman's army, the safekeeping of the prisoners was endangered. Before the 25th of November the prisoners had left Camp Lawton, and during the remainder of the war it was not occupied by any considerable number.

A part of the Andersonville prisoners were sent to Charleston, and these, together with some previously confined in that city, were removed to Florence, South Carolina. Before a stockade was erected they were restrained in an open field with such an inefficient guard that many escaped. The report of General Hardee's inspecting officer, October 12, 1864, says that three-fourths were without blankets, and many almost without clothing. The hospitals were of boughs of trees, and only one medical officer was on duty. There was no longer a pretense of issuing meat, but, instead, sorghum molasses was substituted, and even this was not always forthcoming.

The stockade was built from the trunks of trees set about five feet into the ground, enclosing about twenty-three acres sloping down from each end to a stream in the center. When the stockade was built a number of trees were left inside, but the prisoners soon cut these down for fuel and for shelter, and then dug out the stumps and even the roots. Wood was also furnished. Various officers commanded during the few months it was open, and there was considerable conflict of authority until General Winder was placed in charge of all prisons east of the Mississippi. Lieutenant-Colonel John F. Iverson held command of the prison, and his kindness and humanity have

A CONFEDERATE PRISON IN PETERSBURG, APRIL, 1865

This prison in Petersburg was known as "Castle Thunder." When this photograph was taken, in April, 1865, for many months Confederate sentries had been pacing up and down where the Union sentry now stands with his gun at "support arms." For months a succession of Union prisoners had gazed out longingly through the bars, listening to the Union guns which day after day roared out the approaching doom of the Confederacy. The investment of Petersburg was the last great task demanded cf the Army of the Potomac. During the night of April 2d, Lee retreated from Petersburg and Richmond, and a week later he surrendered at Appomattox. On the following page are some views of the interior courtyards of this great tobacco warehouse converted into a prison, where the incessant sound of the surge and thunder of battle and the increasing scarcity of food were the only indications to the prisoners of the fortunes of the armies.

been praised by some of his charges, and the adjutant, Lieutenant Cheatham, was also liked by the prisoners. The medical staff seems to have been unusually efficient, though as the prisoners sent to this place had been long in captivity, the mortality rate was heavy.

An abandoned cotton-factory at Salisbury, North Carolina, was purchased for prison purposes by the Confederate Government, November 2, 1861. From the beginning it was designed to contain Confederates under sentence of court martial, disloyal citizens, and deserters suspected of being spies, as well as prisoners of war.

The first prisoners of war reached the town on December 12, 1861, and were the object of much curiosity to the people from the town and country around, many of whom had never seen " a real live Yankee " before. Other prisoners of war soon arrived, and during the month of March, 1862, they numbered nearly fifteen hundred. At this time, conditions were exceedingly favorable. Food was abundant, quarters were ample, weather was pleasant, and the prisoners frequently engaged in athletic sports. According to the report of the surgeon, only one died during the month of March, and the report for the quarter ending in April is also marvelous. The favorable conditions lasted through 1863.

During the early months of 1864, the capacity of the prison began to be reached, but additions to the number were constantly made. During the month of October, about ten thousand arrived. Some of these were desperate men who had long been in prison. Cases of robbery, and even murder, among the prisoners were not uncommon, according to Junius Henri Browne and other prisoners there.

For a considerable time the shelter remained inadequate, though an insufficient supply of old tents was finally provided. Those prisoners who could not be furnished with shelter burrowed in the earth or else built little mud huts, partly above and partly below the surface of the ground. The quartermaster

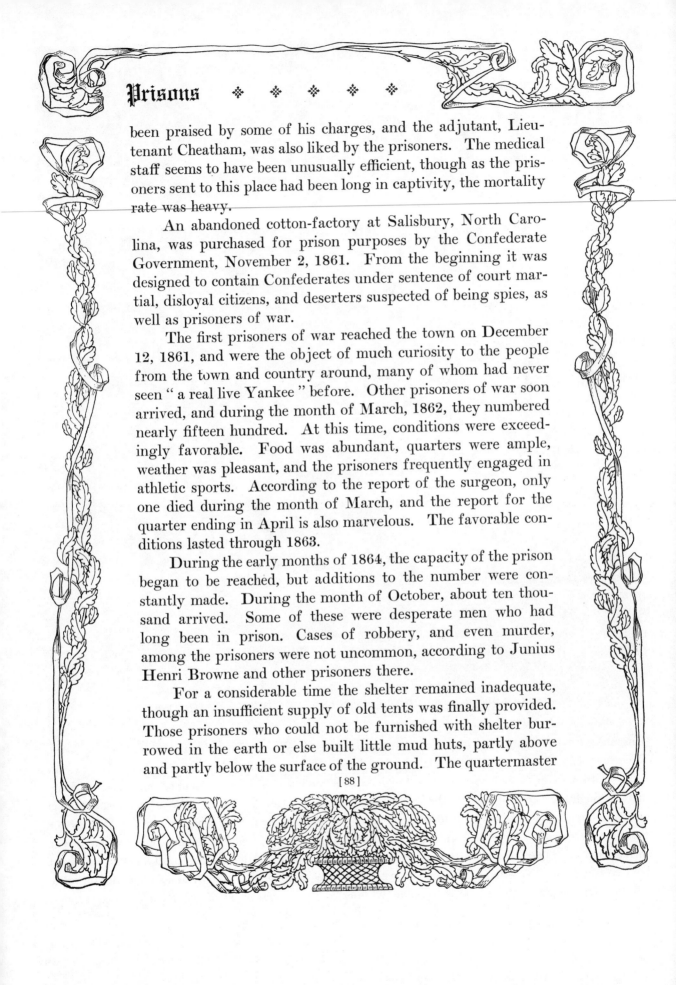

WITHIN THE BOMBARDED TOWN

These buildings in Petersburg, formerly tobacco warehouses, had been used, when this photograph was made, for the temporary confinement of Union soldiers captured during the numerous sorties of the winter of 1864–65. On account of the continual bombardment on both sides and the number of shots which fell within the town, the prisoners who languished within these walls called them "Castle Thunder." In the South commercial buildings that already existed were transformed to a large extent to serve for the detention of

"CASTLE THUNDER" ON APRIL 4, 1865 — A PETERSBURG TOBACCO FACTORY USED AS A PRISON

INSIDE THE PRISON YARD

prisoners. Tobacco factories were often used for this purpose; the light and ventilation were good, and comparatively little machinery was used, so that they could be easily cleared. At "Castle Thunder" there was but little besides tobacco with which to feed either the prisoners or their captors. When the Federal troops finally occupied the city, they found the warehouses full of tobacco and gleefully helped themselves to it. Not a single source of supply of food was to be found within the town. Rations from the Federal stores were issued to a large number of the needy and hungry inhabitants.

set to work to build frame barracks which would be adequate to shelter the multitude, but General Winder, after inspection, pronounced the place unfit for a prison and declared that the prisoners should shortly be moved. All work was thereupon suspended, though the prisoners were not moved, and the greatest suffering occurred after this time.

An organization and a tributary territory sufficient for two thousand prisoners failed utterly when ten thousand were confined. The food supply became scanty in spite of the energetic commissary. With the necessity of providing thirteen thousand rations every day, the commissary very often did not have one day's rations on hand. Mills were impressed and forced to grind wheat and corn, and agents to secure provisions were also sent. Rain or shine, hot or cold, Major Myers might have been seen seeking for supplies, but in spite of all his efforts, days upon which no meat could be procured became more frequent. The hospital was badly placed and poorly supplied. It was too small, and hundreds of prisoners died in their quarters. Sometimes, where one lived alone in a burrow, his body might not be discovered for several days. Probably the quartermaster, Captain Goodman, was inefficient. He might have been able to procure a larger supply of straw for the bunks, and probably could have furnished a larger quantity of wood than he actually did. As a result of these deficiencies, whether arising from necessity or inefficiency, conditions in the prison were bad and constantly grew worse.

Prisoners ate with avidity acorns from the great oaks in the yard, for want of better food. The soil was a stiff, red clay, which under the rain and the tramp of thousands of feet became tenacious mortar. The mortality was fearful, as from October, 1864, to February, 1865, inclusive, there were 3419 deaths. The burial place near by was an abandoned field in which long pits about four feet deep, six feet wide, and sixty yards long were dug. No coffins could be furnished, as it was impossible to secure enough lumber for the ordinary needs of

LIBBY PRISON AT THE CLOSE OF THE WAR

The Stars and Stripes are floating at last over the big brick building where so many men who owed them allegiance have wearied through the monotonous days, months, and years watching the sluggish flow of the James. The crowd in front is largely composed of Negroes who have come to draw rations. This building has often been incorrectly called a tobacco warehouse. As a matter of fact, it was originally the establishment of William Libby & Son, ship chandlers, 20th and Cary Streets. The sign had been removed before this photograph was taken, but it may be plainly deciphered in the picture on page 57 showing Libby Prison early in the war.

the prisoners, and so great was the scarcity of clothes that the living were often allowed to take the garments of their dead companions. The place of burial to-day is a national cemetery. As at all the prisons, North and South, attempts were made to induce prisoners to desert their flag. About eighteen hundred of these "galvanized Yankees" were enlisted, but were not worth the pains or the money they cost. The enlistment of "galvanized Rebs" in various Northern prisons was no more successful. Men who would desert once would desert again.

The guards for the greater part of the time were the State Junior and Senior Reserves, that is to say, boys under seventeen and men over forty-five, and later fifty, as all between those ages were supposed to be in the army. Some of the boys were almost infants and could hardly carry their heavy guns.

Finally, in February, 1865, the commandant, Major Gee, was notified to send his prisoners to Wilmington for exchange. As it was impossible to procure transportation for all, those who were able started to march. Of twenty-eight hundred who began the journey only about eighteen hundred reached the point of destination in a body. Some fell by the wayside and died. Others were sheltered by the kindness of people along the road until they were able to move again. After this time about five hundred prisoners were confined for a time, but were hastily removed to Charlotte to escape Stoneman's cavalry. When Salisbury was taken by that officer, he confined his prisoners in the same stockade which had held the Federal captives, and when he left the town, he burned the stockade and everything that was within it. After the collapse of the Confederacy, Major Gee was tried by a military commission similar to that which tried Wirz, on the charge of cruelty and conspiracy, but after a careful investigation the commission found a verdict of not guilty, declaring that he was censurable only because he remained in command after it had appeared that the simplest dictates of humanity could not be carried out.

LIBBY PRISON AFTER THE WAR—RUINS IN THE FOREGROUND

This photograph was taken in April, 1865, after the city had passed into the hands of the Federals. The near-by buildings had been destroyed, and the foreground is strewn with débris and bricks. The prison was purchased as a speculation some time after the war and transported to Chicago. The enterprise, like every other monument of bitterness, failed and has since been destroyed. While it was still standing, among its exhibits were some ghastly drawings of the horrors of Andersonville, under the charge of an old soldier whose duty it was to dilate upon them. One day his account of the unspeakable misery there so inflamed the mind of a young man belonging to the generation after the war that he broke into cursing and reviling of the Confederacy. The Union veteran listened quietly for a moment, and then said: "That's all over now, and both sides are glad of it. If the truth were known, I guess we did pretty nearly as bad in some of our prisons, especially considering our superior resources. Just stow away that cussing, young man. If there's any cussing to be done, we old soldiers will do it—and we don't want to." Happily, the above furnishes no hint of the dark side of war.

LIBBY PRISON AFTER THE TABLES WERE TURNED

In this dramatic record by the camera of April, 1865, appear Confederate captives pressing their faces against the bars through which one hundred and twenty-five thousand Federal prisoners had gazed from the inside during the war. Union sentinels are guarding the prison. Major Thomas P. Turner, who had been commandant of the prison, though a subordinate, Richard Turner, had more direct authority, was confined here at this time. Strenuous efforts were made to secure evidence on which to prefer charges against

CONFEDERATE PRISONERS CONFINED IN THE SOUTHERN STRONGHOLD

him.   The attempts proved unsuccessful and he was released.   During the war this building was occupied almost entirely as a prison for Federal officers.   The privates were confined elsewhere in the city, or in Belle Isle in the James River.   After the war a quarter-master, Major Morfit, in whose charge money had been placed, was examined by a military commission, but his accounts were found correct, and he was exonerated from all blame.   The group of men gathered on the outside are mostly Union soldiers.

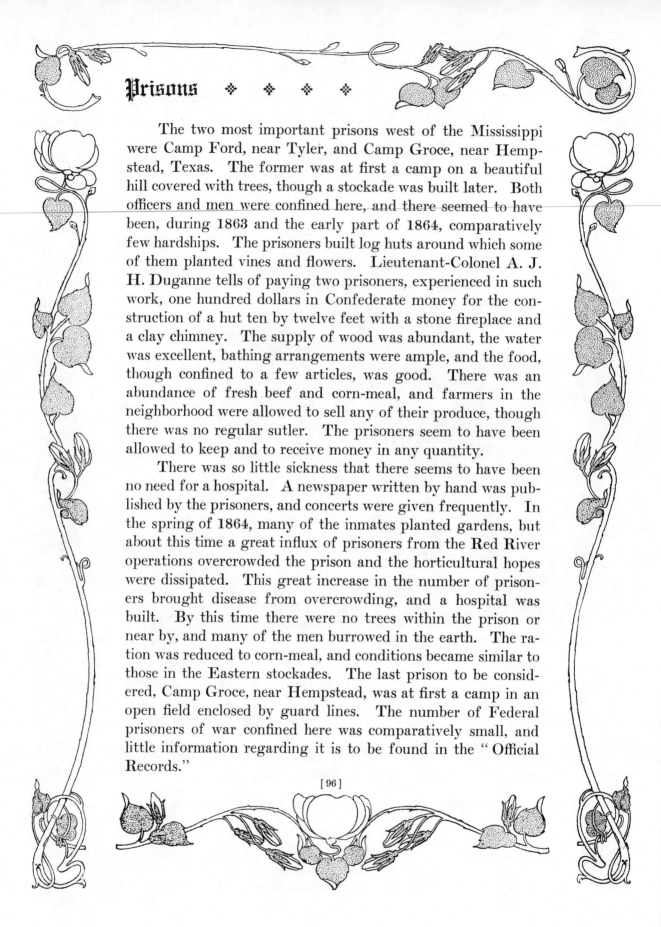

Prisons ❖ ❖ ❖ ❖

The two most important prisons west of the Mississippi were Camp Ford, near Tyler, and Camp Groce, near Hempstead, Texas. The former was at first a camp on a beautiful hill covered with trees, though a stockade was built later. Both officers and men were confined here, and there seemed to have been, during 1863 and the early part of 1864, comparatively few hardships. The prisoners built log huts around which some of them planted vines and flowers. Lieutenant-Colonel A. J. H. Duganne tells of paying two prisoners, experienced in such work, one hundred dollars in Confederate money for the construction of a hut ten by twelve feet with a stone fireplace and a clay chimney. The supply of wood was abundant, the water was excellent, bathing arrangements were ample, and the food, though confined to a few articles, was good. There was an abundance of fresh beef and corn-meal, and farmers in the neighborhood were allowed to sell any of their produce, though there was no regular sutler. The prisoners seem to have been allowed to keep and to receive money in any quantity.

There was so little sickness that there seems to have been no need for a hospital. A newspaper written by hand was published by the prisoners, and concerts were given frequently. In the spring of 1864, many of the inmates planted gardens, but about this time a great influx of prisoners from the Red River operations overcrowded the prison and the horticultural hopes were dissipated. This great increase in the number of prisoners brought disease from overcrowding, and a hospital was built. By this time there were no trees within the prison or near by, and many of the men burrowed in the earth. The ration was reduced to corn-meal, and conditions became similar to those in the Eastern stockades. The last prison to be considered, Camp Groce, near Hempstead, was at first a camp in an open field enclosed by guard lines. The number of Federal prisoners of war confined here was comparatively small, and little information regarding it is to be found in the " Official Records."

PART I
PRISONS

———

EXCHANGE OF PRISONERS

———

AT COX'S LANDING
WAITING FOR THE
FLAG-OF-TRUCE BOAT

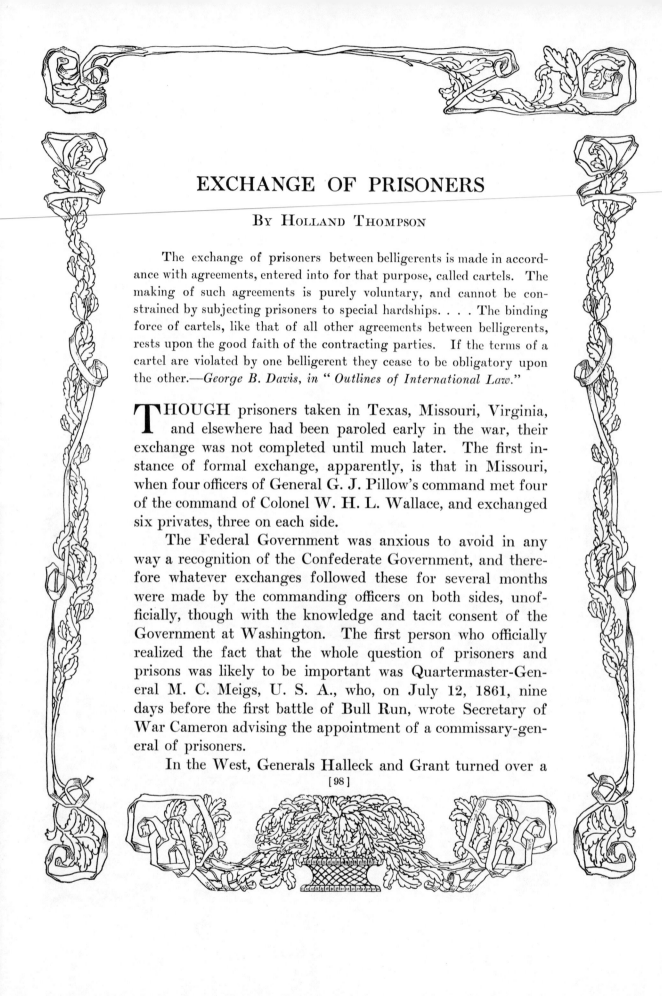

EXCHANGE OF PRISONERS

By Holland Thompson

The exchange of prisoners between belligerents is made in accordance with agreements, entered into for that purpose, called cartels. The making of such agreements is purely voluntary, and cannot be constrained by subjecting prisoners to special hardships. . . . The binding force of cartels, like that of all other agreements between belligerents, rests upon the good faith of the contracting parties. If the terms of a cartel are violated by one belligerent they cease to be obligatory upon the other.—*George B. Davis, in " Outlines of International Law."*

THOUGH prisoners taken in Texas, Missouri, Virginia, and elsewhere had been paroled early in the war, their exchange was not completed until much later. The first instance of formal exchange, apparently, is that in Missouri, when four officers of General G. J. Pillow's command met four of the command of Colonel W. H. L. Wallace, and exchanged six privates, three on each side.

The Federal Government was anxious to avoid in any way a recognition of the Confederate Government, and therefore whatever exchanges followed these for several months were made by the commanding officers on both sides, unofficially, though with the knowledge and tacit consent of the Government at Washington. The first person who officially realized the fact that the whole question of prisoners and prisons was likely to be important was Quartermaster-General M. C. Meigs, U. S. A., who, on July 12, 1861, nine days before the first battle of Bull Run, wrote Secretary of War Cameron advising the appointment of a commissary-general of prisoners.

In the West, Generals Halleck and Grant turned over a

ON THE WAY TO FREEDOM—EXCHANGED CONFEDERATE PRISONERS BOUND FOR COX'S LANDING UNDER GUARD, SEPTEMBER 20, 1864

At a slight distance, this might seem a picture of a caravan in the Sahara Desert, but as a matter of fact the men in the far-stretching line are Confederate prisoners escorted by cavalry on their way from the Federal lines to Cox's Landing. The moral courage to surrender is held by all true soldiers to be greater than the physical courage that it requires to die. Sometimes the words are spoken for the soldier by one in authority whose sense of responsibility for the lives of those he leads causes him to sink personal pride. Before the surrendered soldier there rise two hopes, parole or exchange, and one dreaded alternative—long imprisonment. Parole embraces the assumption that the man with the courage to fight for his country is a man of honor who will keep his word. A signature to a bit of paper, and the soldier may walk forth a free man to return to his home and family, bound to abstain from any further warfare until "regularly exchanged." Grant took the words of twenty-nine thousand men at Vicksburg and let them go. As the war progressed there grew to be a regular barter and exchange in human flesh and military utility—a pawn for a pawn, a knight for a knight, a king for a king, sick men for sick men, and well men for well. Still the prisons of both North and South were filled with the unfortunate. There were specified places, such as Cox's Landing and City Point, where these transfers took place. Grant's later policy was to allow as few as possible. A glance at this hardy band of captured Confederate veterans here tells the reason why. There are a hundred fights in these men yet. Why let them return to the firing-line to combat Union soldiers anew? The only reason was to release Union prisoners from confinement and hasten their return to duty.

number of prisoners to Generals Polk and Jeff. Thompson and received their own men in return. In the East, General Benjamin Huger, the Confederate commander at Norfolk, and General John E. Wool, U. S. A., made a number of special exchanges. As the number of prisoners grew, much of the time of the commanding officers was required for this business. A large amount of political pressure was brought to bear upon the officials at Washington, urging them to arrange for an exchange, and on December 3, 1861, General Halleck wrote that the prisoners ought to be exchanged, as it was simply a convention, and the fact that they had been exchanged would not prevent their being tried for treason, if desired, after the war.

The Confederate officials, conscious of their deficient resources, were eager to escape the care of prisoners, and welcomed the announcement of General Wool, February 13, 1862, that he had been empowered to arrange a general exchange. General Wool met General Howell Cobb, on February 23d, and an agreement, except upon the point of delivery at the " frontier of their own country," was reached for the delivery of all prisoners, the excess to be on parole. At a subsequent meeting, General Wool announced that his instructions had been changed and that he could exchange man for man only. This offer was refused by General Cobb, who charged that the reason for the unwillingness to complete the agreement was the capture of Forts Henry and Donelson, which gave the Federal Government an excess of prisoners which it was unwilling to release on parole.

As the next move on the chess-board, the Confederate Government refused longer to make individual exchanges on the ground that, as political pressure in many cases caused the Federal Government to ask for the exchange of certain individuals, those who had no influential friends would be left in prison. On a letter of General McClellan proposing an exchange, the Confederate Secretary of War, G. W. Randolph,

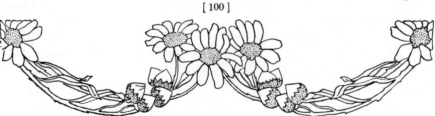

COLONEL ROBERT OULD
CONFEDERATE AGENT FOR THE EXCHANGE OF PRISONERS

The most important person in the exchange of prisoners in the South was Colonel Robert Ould. His appointment as Confederate agent for exchange came immediately after the signing of the agreement to exchange prisoners, July 22, 1862. When Virginia left the Union, Colonel Ould followed his State. He served for a short time as Assistant Secretary of War. His relations with Colonel William H. Ludlow, the Federal agent of exchange, were always pleasant. Though they frequently clashed, it was as lawyers seeking to gain advantages for their clients, and without personal animosity. With General S. A. Meredith, who succeeded Colonel Ludlow, Colonel Ould was at odds; he preferred to deal with Major Mulford, the assistant agent. He refused to treat with General Butler at first, but finally opened negotiations with him. Colonel Ould had one advantage over the Federal agents in that he was seldom hampered by interference by other officials of the War Department. He remained in charge of all questions relating to exchange to the end of the war.

endorsed June 14, 1862: "No arrangement of any sort has been made, and individual exchanges are declined. We will exchange generally or according to some principle, but not by arbitrary selections."

An interesting correspondence, marked by perfect courtesy on both sides, took place during the summer of 1862 between General Lee and General McClellan. On the 6th of June, a week after the battle of Seven Pines, or Fair Oaks, a general order that surgeons should be considered non-combatants and not sent to prison was issued from Washington, and was accepted by General Lee on the 17th. On the 9th of July, General Lee proposed to release General McClellan's wounded on parole, and the offer was accepted by General McClellan.

Finally, on the 12th of July, General John A. Dix was authorized by Secretary Stanton to negotiate for the exchange, but was cautioned in every possible way to avoid any recognition of the Confederate Government. The cartel in force between the United States and Great Britain during the War of 1812 was suggested as a basis. General Lee was informed of General Dix's appointment on July 13th, and the next day announced that he had appointed General D. H. Hill as commissioner on the part of the Confederacy. The commissioners met on the 17th of July and adjourned on the following day for further instructions from their Governments, and finally, July 22d, came to an agreement. The cartel, which is interesting in view of the subsequent disputes, is to be found in Appendix A.

All prisoners in the East were to be delivered at Aiken's Landing on the James River (soon changed to City Point), and in the West at Vicksburg, with the provision that the fortunes of war might render it necessary to change these places and substitute others bearing the same general relation to the contending armies. Each party agreed to appoint two agents, one in the East and one in the West, to carry out the stipulations of the contract. General Lorenzo Thomas was temporarily detached from his position as adjutant-general to

THE ACTIVE FEDERAL EXCHANGE AGENT

BRIGADIER–GENERAL JOHN ELMER MULFORD, U.S.A. (TO THE RIGHT)

As assistant agent of exchange, Major Mulford occupied a most difficult position. For a time Colonel Robert Ould refused to deal with General Butler, when the latter was the Federal agent of exchange, on the ground that he had been proclaimed an outlaw by President Davis, and instead addressed all of his communications to Major Mulford. After General Grant stopped all exchanges, April 17, 1864, both General Butler and Major Mulford were bombarded with hysterical letters of appeal, abuse, and criticism. A few special exchanges were arranged after this time, and Major Mulford was ordered to Savannah to receive the thirteen thousand Federal sick and wounded delivered without full equivalent by Colonel Ould in the latter part of 1864. On July 4th of that year Major Mulford was advanced to brevet brigadier-general of volunteers for special service and highly meritorious conduct. He entered the war as captain in the Third New York Infantry May 14, 1861, and was promoted to major June 10, 1863, to lieutenant-colonel December 8, 1864, and to colonel April 9, 1865. He was honorably mustered out June 30, 1866.

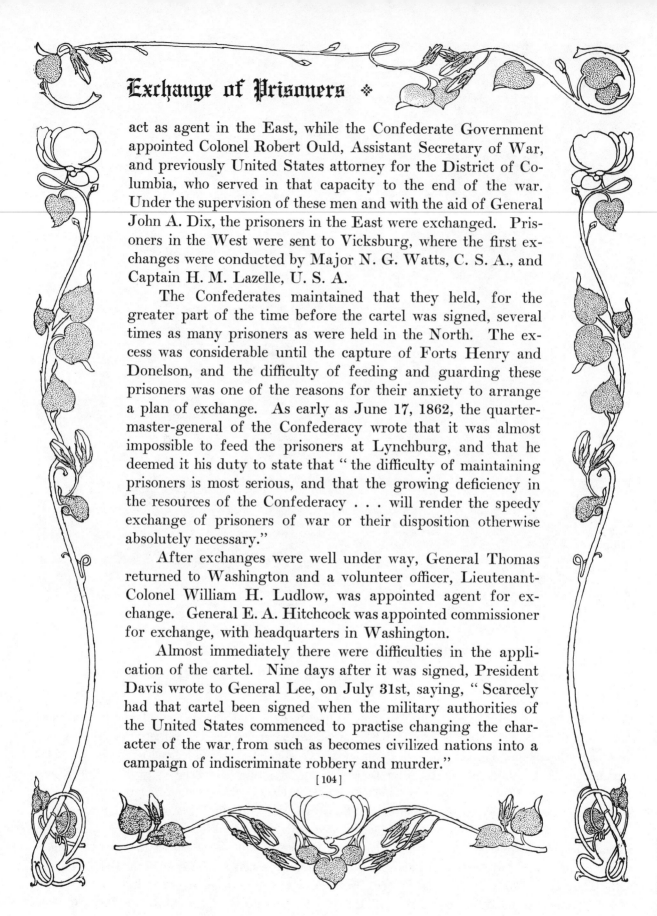

act as agent in the East, while the Confederate Government appointed Colonel Robert Ould, Assistant Secretary of War, and previously United States attorney for the District of Columbia, who served in that capacity to the end of the war. Under the supervision of these men and with the aid of General John A. Dix, the prisoners in the East were exchanged. Prisoners in the West were sent to Vicksburg, where the first exchanges were conducted by Major N. G. Watts, C. S. A., and Captain H. M. Lazelle, U. S. A.

The Confederates maintained that they held, for the greater part of the time before the cartel was signed, several times as many prisoners as were held in the North. The excess was considerable until the capture of Forts Henry and Donelson, and the difficulty of feeding and guarding these prisoners was one of the reasons for their anxiety to arrange a plan of exchange. As early as June 17, 1862, the quartermaster-general of the Confederacy wrote that it was almost impossible to feed the prisoners at Lynchburg, and that he deemed it his duty to state that "the difficulty of maintaining prisoners is most serious, and that the growing deficiency in the resources of the Confederacy . . . will render the speedy exchange of prisoners of war or their disposition otherwise absolutely necessary."

After exchanges were well under way, General Thomas returned to Washington and a volunteer officer, Lieutenant-Colonel William H. Ludlow, was appointed agent for exchange. General E. A. Hitchcock was appointed commissioner for exchange, with headquarters in Washington.

Almost immediately there were difficulties in the application of the cartel. Nine days after it was signed, President Davis wrote to General Lee, on July 31st, saying, "Scarcely had that cartel been signed when the military authorities of the United States commenced to practise changing the character of the war from such as becomes civilized nations into a campaign of indiscriminate robbery and murder."

COLONEL C. C. DWIGHT

GENERAL LEW WALLACE

FOUR UNION OFFICERS PROMINENT IN THE ARRANGEMENTS FOR EXCHANGE

Colonel C. C. Dwight, of New York, was the Federal agent of exchange in the West. General Lew Wallace, the author of "Ben Hur" and "A Prince of India," was the officer assigned to take command of Camp Chase in Ohio, where he found 3,000 paroled Union soldiers who had not yet been exchanged and refused to do even police duty, claiming that they would perform no soldiers' work until they were formally exchanged. General E. A. Hitchcock was the Federal commissioner of exchange in the East. It was due largely to the efforts of General Lorenzo Thomas that exchange arrangements were perfected. He was temporarily detached from his position as adjutant-general to act as agent in the East.

GENERAL E. A. HITCHCOCK

GENERAL LORENZO THOMAS

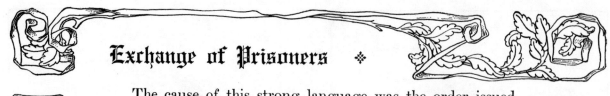

The cause of this strong language was the order issued by Secretary Stanton, on July 22d, which, as interpreted by President Davis, directed " the military authorities of the United States to take the private property of our people for the convenience and use of their armies without compensation." The general order issued by Major-General Pope, July 23d, the day after the signing of the cartel, was also mentioned. The first paragraph of this order reads as follows, " Commanders of army corps, divisions, brigades, and detached commands will proceed immediately to arrest all disloyal male citizens within their lines or within their reach in the rear of their respective stations." Those unwilling to take an oath of allegiance and furnish bond were to be sent to the Confederate lines.

Two days after the letter of President Davis, therefore, General Samuel Cooper, adjutant-general of the Confederacy, issued General Orders No. 54, on August 1, 1862. After referring to Secretary Stanton's order, and General Pope's order already mentioned, together with the action of General Steinwehr, who, it was asserted, had arrested private citizens in Virginia with the threat that they would be put to death if any of his soldiers were killed, the order declares that all these things taken together show a disposition " to violate all the rules and usages of war and to convert the hostilities waged against armed forces into a campaign of robbery and murder against unarmed citizens and peaceful tillers of the soil." It was therefore announced that General Pope and General Steinwehr, and all commissioned officers serving under them, " are hereby specially declared to be not entitled to be considered as soldiers, and therefore not entitled to the benefit of the cartel for the parole of future prisoners of war."

General Lee, apparently against his will, was instructed to convey copies of President Davis' letter and the general orders to General Halleck. These were returned by General Halleck as being couched in insulting language, and were never put into force, as General Pope's authority in Virginia

THE WHITE FLAG BOAT THAT CARRIED PRISONERS TO FREEDOM

Lying at the wharf is the Federal "flag-of-truce boat" *New York*, which carried exchanged prisoners to Aiken's Landing, and later to City Point, in 1862, for the exchange to be completed. Whatever their enthusiasm for the Stars and Stripes or the Stars and Bars, the white flag floating from the mast of the *New York* was greeted with equal joy by Federals and Confederates. It signified liberty and home. The Federal prisoners were usually taken from the point of exchange first to Fortress Monroe, and then to the parole camp at Annapolis. There they awaited payment for their services, which accrued during the time they were imprisoned just as if they had been in active service. This was a formality which the Confederate soldiers overlooked, especially in the last year of the war. By 1865 Confederate currency had depreciated to such an extent that a man paid $400 to have a horse curried, as related by a Confederate veteran, and the exchanged Confederates returned whenever possible directly to their regiments in the field.

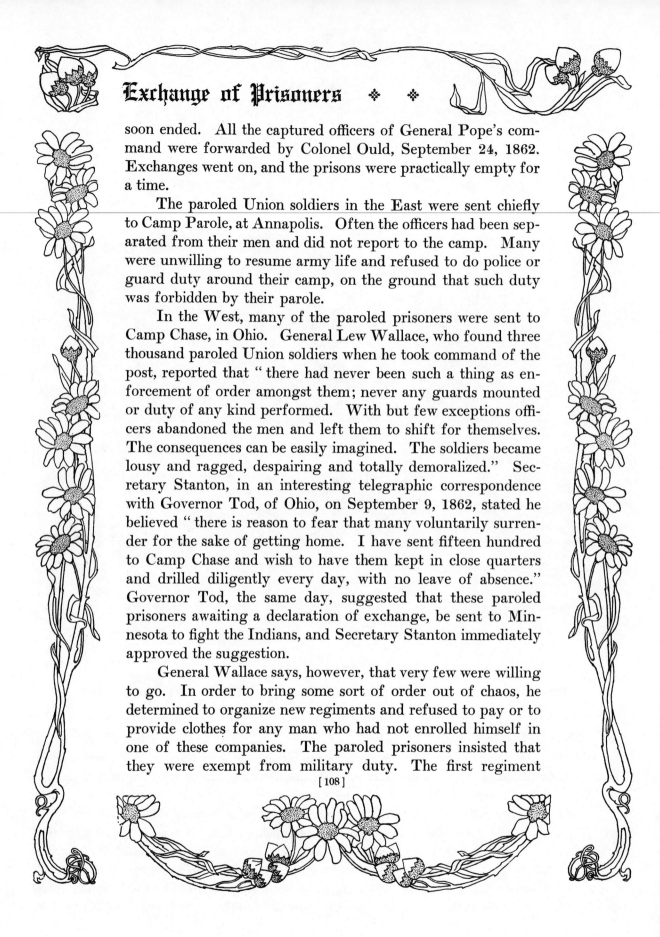

soon ended. All the captured officers of General Pope's command were forwarded by Colonel Ould, September 24, 1862. Exchanges went on, and the prisons were practically empty for a time.

The paroled Union soldiers in the East were sent chiefly to Camp Parole, at Annapolis. Often the officers had been separated from their men and did not report to the camp. Many were unwilling to resume army life and refused to do police or guard duty around their camp, on the ground that such duty was forbidden by their parole.

In the West, many of the paroled prisoners were sent to Camp Chase, in Ohio. General Lew Wallace, who found three thousand paroled Union soldiers when he took command of the post, reported that " there had never been such a thing as enforcement of order amongst them; never any guards mounted or duty of any kind performed. With but few exceptions officers abandoned the men and left them to shift for themselves. The consequences can be easily imagined. The soldiers became lousy and ragged, despairing and totally demoralized." Secretary Stanton, in an interesting telegraphic correspondence with Governor Tod, of Ohio, on September 9, 1862, stated he believed " there is reason to fear that many voluntarily surrender for the sake of getting home. I have sent fifteen hundred to Camp Chase and wish to have them kept in close quarters and drilled diligently every day, with no leave of absence." Governor Tod, the same day, suggested that these paroled prisoners awaiting a declaration of exchange, be sent to Minnesota to fight the Indians, and Secretary Stanton immediately approved the suggestion.

General Wallace says, however, that very few were willing to go. In order to bring some sort of order out of chaos, he determined to organize new regiments and refused to pay or to provide clothes for any man who had not enrolled himself in one of these companies. The paroled prisoners insisted that they were exempt from military duty. The first regiment

WHERE THE VALUE OF A MAN WAS CALCULATED

After a cartel of exchange had been agreed upon between the Federal General John A. Dix and General D. H. Hill of the Confederate army, July 22, 1862, Aiken's Landing on the James River was made a point for exchange of prisoners in the East. These were brought from Richmond or from Fortress Monroe by boats bearing a white flag. The two commissioners met, exchanged rolls, and worked out their exchanges. They had a regular table of equivalents in which the private was a unit. A non-commissioned officer was equivalent to two privates; a lieutenant to four; a captain to six; a major to eight; a lieutenant-colonel to ten; a colonel to fifteen; a brigadier-general to twenty; a major-general to forty; and a general commanding to sixty. A similar table of equivalents was worked out for the navy. Therefore, though one side might have an officer of higher rank than the other, it was easy to work out his value in officers of a lower rank or in privates, according to the tables. Aiken's Landing had served for this purpose only a few weeks when the meeting-place was changed to City Point. The exchange table is in an appendix.

organized deserted almost in a mass. The officer of the guard one morning found three muskets leaning against a tree, left there by sentinels who had deserted.

Since so few of the released Federal prisoners were willing to reenlist, while the majority of the Confederates by this time were in the ranks "for the whole war," it is perhaps natural that doubts of the wisdom of further exchange should become convictions in the minds of some of the Northern leaders. Meanwhile, General Benjamin F. Butler had begun his military government in New Orleans, and William B. Mumford, a citizen, had been hanged for pulling down the United States flag. The Confederacy charged that this was done before the city had been formally occupied by Federal troops. On December 23, 1862, President Davis issued a proclamation denouncing General Butler as "a felon deserving of capital punishment," and the commissioned officers serving under him "robbers and criminals," not entitled to be considered as soldiers engaged in honorable warfare and deserving of execution.

Negro troops also had been enrolled in the Union army, and President Lincoln had issued his preliminary proclamation of emancipation. In answer, President Davis decreed that all negro slaves captured in arms and their white officers should not be treated as prisoners of war but should be delivered to the States to be punished according to their laws. If carried out, these officers would be put to death on the charge of inciting negro insurrection.

Secretary Stanton, December 28, 1862, answered by suspending the exchange of commissioned officers, but the exchange of enlisted men went on as usual, though marked by much mutual recrimination between Colonel Ludlow and Colonel Ould. Special exchanges were sometimes effected, although Colonel Ould attempted to prevent all such. President Davis' proclamation was practically endorsed by the Confederate Congress, and on May 25, 1863, General Halleck ordered all exchanges stopped.

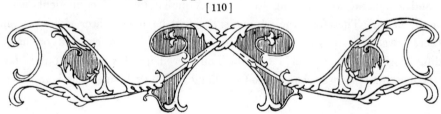

THE DOUBLE–TURRETED MONITOR *ONONDAGA* OFF THE
EXCHANGE LANDING

In the year 1864 the scene was no longer so peaceful at Aiken's Landing, once used as a place of exchange. Union vessels occasionally steamed as far up the river as this point. The queer-looking craft in the center of the river is the double-turreted monitor *Onondaga*. It was no longer safe for women and children to stay in A. M. Aiken's dwelling on the hill; shells from the warship might come hurtling ashore at the slightest sign of Confederates. After the success of the first monitor, several other ironclads were built after the same pattern. They were suitable for river service and harbor defense. The *Onondaga* rendered valuable aid to the army while Grant centered his operations against Richmond at City Point.

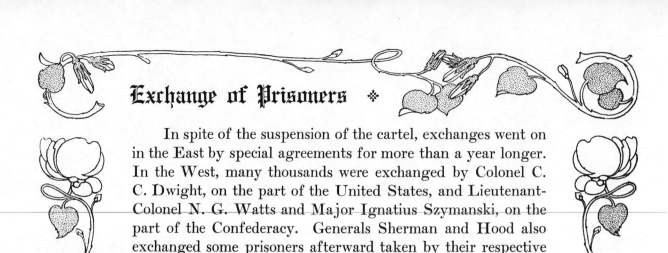

Exchange of Prisoners ❖

In spite of the suspension of the cartel, exchanges went on in the East by special agreements for more than a year longer. In the West, many thousands were exchanged by Colonel C. C. Dwight, on the part of the United States, and Lieutenant-Colonel N. G. Watts and Major Ignatius Szymanski, on the part of the Confederacy. Generals Sherman and Hood also exchanged some prisoners afterward taken by their respective commands, and other special agreements between commanders in the field were made.

Meanwhile, though the cartel of 1862 declared that all captures must be reduced to actual possession, and that all prisoners of war must be delivered at designated places for exchange or parole, unless by agreement of commanders of opposing armies, the custom of paroling prisoners at the point of capture had grown up by common consent. On the last day of the battle of Gettysburg, July 3, 1863, Secretary Stanton issued General Orders No. 207, declaring that all such paroles were in violation of general orders, and therefore null and void; declaring further that any soldier accepting such parole would be returned to duty and punished for disobedience of orders. Some provisions of General Orders No. 100 served upon Colonel Ould on May 23d also forbade parole without delivery. The reasons for the issuance of this order were probably to put an end to the accumulation of paroles by the irregular or guerilla Confederate forces in the West, which picked up prisoners here and there.

The capture of Vicksburg and Port Hudson, together with the battle of Gettysburg, threw the excess of prisoners very largely in favor of the Federals, and from this time on the number of Confederates in Northern prisons was larger than that of Federals in Southern prisons. It was next determined by the War Department to make no exchanges except for those actually held in confinement. This rendered useless, of course, a large number of paroles which Colonel Ould claimed to have, and if accepted would have

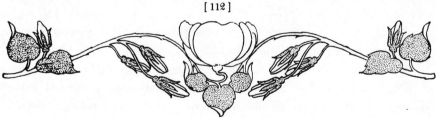

COLORED CONVALESCENT TROOPS AT AIKEN'S LANDING, JAMES RIVER

These convalescent colored troops are resting at Aiken's Landing after a march. On the right is A. M. Aiken's house, on the brow of the hill overlooking the river. The scene was much the same when this was a point of exchange in 1862, but there were no colored troops in the Union armies until the following year. These men are evidently exhausted; they sit or lie upon the ground without taking the trouble to remove their knapsacks. This appears to be only a temporary halt; the wayfarers will shortly march out on the pier to a boat waiting to take them down the James. The opposite shore can dimly be seen on the left of the picture. Here as on the following page, in front of Aiken's mill, appears a martin-box.

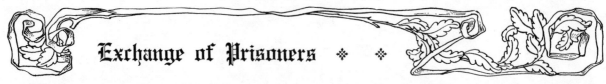

Exchange of Prisoners ❖ ❖

released every Federal prisoner in the South, while leaving thousands of Confederates in confinement. With the practical cessation of exchanges came much complaint upon both sides. The hardships of Salisbury, Libby, and Belle Isle are, of course, better known by the North than those of Fort Delaware, Alton, and Camp Morton. But in Southern experiences and reminiscences, perhaps as many complaints of insufficient food and clothing and of cruel treatment can be found as on the other side up to the summer of 1863.

The Federal officials in control of the matter refused to complete the exchange of those whose paroles had been given, or to exchange the Vicksburg and Port Hudson prisoners. Colonel Ould, however, finally declared them exchanged, regardless of the approval of the Federal commissioner. The question as to whether the consent of both agents or commissioners was necessary to make a valid declaration of exchange, had been discussed before by Generals Buell and Bragg, on October 1, 1862, when General Buell declared that it was not. His version had been accepted in the West, though in the East a mutual declaration had been the rule.

The trouble arose from the lack of clearness in the supplementary articles of the cartel giving permission to " commanders of two opposing armies " for paroling or exchanging prisoners by mutual consent. Colonel Ould claimed that General Gardner, in command at Port Hudson, was a subordinate officer and therefore was not authorized to accept paroles. The Federal commissioner protested vigorously, and a lengthy correspondence ensued, in which Colonel Ould declared that mutual consent was not necessary and that Colonel Ludlow had made similar declarations. Colonel Ould furnished a schedule of captures, some of which were pronounced legitimate while the validity of others was denied. When his paroles were exhausted all further exchanges ceased for a time. Brigadier-General S. A. Meredith succeeded Colonel Ludlow as agent

[114]

AIKEN'S HOUSE IN 1864

A GLAD SIGHT FOR
THE PRISONERS

On top of the gentle slope rising from the river at Aiken's Landing stands the dwelling of A. M. Aiken, who gave the locality his name. For a short time in 1862 Aiken's Landing, on the James River just below Dutch Gap, was used as a point of exchange for soldiers captured in the East. Many prisoners from the Eastern armies in 1862 lifted their tired eyes to this comfortable place, which aroused thoughts of home. There was not likely to be any fighting in a locality selected for the exchange of prisoners, and in this photograph at least

there are women and children. At the top of the steps stands a woman with a child leaning against her voluminous skirts, and a Negro "mammy" with a large white apron stands on the other side of the pillar. Some Union officers are lounging at the near end of the porch. The mill shown in the lower photograph was owned by Mr. Aiken. His rude wharf stretching out into the river enabled the neighboring farmers to land their corn, which they brought to be ground. The structure in the front is a martin-box, a sight common in the South to-day. Martins are known to be useful in driving hawks away from poultry-yards.

THE MILL NEAR AIKEN'S LANDING

[H—8]

for exchange, and soon was involved in acrimonious controversy with Colonel Ould.

General Butler, who had been appointed to command at Fortress Monroe, was, at his own suggestion, created a special agent for exchange, and from that time onward made no reports to General Hitchcock, commissioner for exchange, but assumed the title and duties of commissioner. At first, the Confederate authorities refused to treat with General Butler, but finally Secretary Seddon, on April 28, 1864, wrote: " It may well excite surprise and indignation that the Government of the United States should select for any position of dignity and command a man so notoriously stigmatized by the common sentiment of enlightened nations. But it is not for us to deny their right to appreciate and select one whom they may not inappropriately, perhaps, deem a fitting type and representative of their power and characteristics." After this, Colonel Ould opened negotiations. Previously, General Butler had written many letters to Colonel Ould which the latter answered in detail but addressed his replies to Major Mulford, the assistant agent for exchange. With the natural shrewdness of an astute lawyer, General Butler saw that too many questions were involved for the public to gain a clear idea of the matters in question. Therefore, he was willing to grant to Colonel Ould what the previous commissioners for exchange had refused to do, setting forth in his confidential communication to Secretary Stanton that his great object was to get exchanges started again, and even to exchange a considerable number of prisoners.

The Union authorities held so much larger numbers that they could afford to do this and still retain a number large enough to guard against cruel treatment of negro troops. Butler wrote that it was his object, after exchanges had continued for some time, to bring the matter of negro troops sharply and clearly into view, and to make further exchanges depend absolutely upon the treatment of negro troops as prisoners

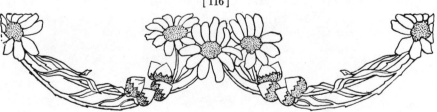

MEN WHO FACED DEATH IF CAPTURED
OFFICERS OF THE NINETY–SECOND UNITED STATES COLORED INFANTRY

When Negro troops were enrolled in the Union army and President Lincoln issued his preliminary proclamation of emancipation, President Davis decreed that slaves captured in arms against the Confederacy (and their white officers) should not be treated as prisoners of war but should be delivered to the States to be punished according to State laws. If this decree had been carried out, these officers might have suffered the penalty of death on the charge of inciting Negro insurrection. The Ninety-second United States Colored Infantry was organized April 4, 1864, from the Twenty-second Corps d'Afrique Infantry of New Orleans. These photographs were taken by Lytle at Baton Rouge, Louisiana, just before the disastrous Red River campaign in which the regiment took part.

of war. The voluminous correspondence between himself and Colonel Ould is interesting. Both were able lawyers, both had a fondness for disputation, and sometimes one is tempted to believe that to both of them the subject of discussion was not really so important as the discussion itself, and that overwhelming the adversary was more vital than securing the objects of the discussion. All of this was stopped by the positive order of General Grant, April 17, 1864, who, after consultation with Secretary Stanton, forbade any exchange until the questions of the Vicksburg and Port Hudson paroles and the matter of exchanges of negro troops were arranged. The Confederacy, despairing of forcing a complete exchange according to the cartel, yielded to the inevitable, and on August 10, Colonel Ould offered a man-for-man exchange so far as the Confederate prisoners would go.

On August 18th, however, General Grant wrote to General Butler, who was still corresponding with Colonel Ould, saying: " It is hard on our men held in Southern prisons not to exchange them, but it is humanity to those left in the ranks to fight our battles. Every man we hold, when released on parole or otherwise, becomes an active soldier against us at once either directly or indirectly. If we commence a system of exchange which liberates all prisoners taken, we will have to fight on until the whole South is exterminated. If we hold those caught, they amount to no more than dead men. At this particular time to release all rebel prisoners in the North would insure Sherman's defeat and would compromise our safety here."

The next day a letter to Secretary Seward closes with the following sentence, " We have got to fight until the military power of the South is exhausted, and if we release or exchange prisoners captured, it simply becomes a war of extermination."

To this determination General Grant held fast against pressure to which a weaker man would have yielded. Conditions in Andersonville and other Southern prisons were, by this time, well known. The Confederate authorities, finding it more

COPYRIGHT, 1911, REVIEW OF REVIEWS CO.

WHERE THE PRISONERS LONGED TO BE EXCHANGED

This view of Andersonville, though not taken at the time when the prison was most crowded, gives some idea of the conditions. Practically no room was left for streets, though there was an opening for the wagons carrying rations. This was ironically called "Broadway."

COPYRIGHT, 1911, REVIEW OF REVIEWS CO.

THE CEMETERY AT ANDERSONVILLE PRISON

The failure of negotiations for exchange of prisoners in 1864 was responsible for many of these rows of prisoners' graves.

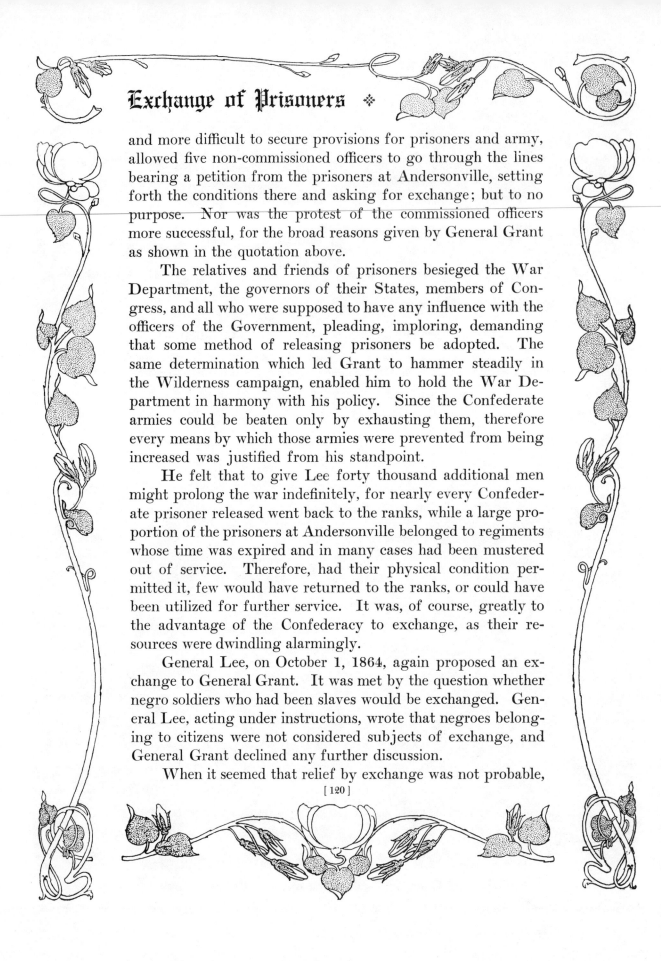

and more difficult to secure provisions for prisoners and army, allowed five non-commissioned officers to go through the lines bearing a petition from the prisoners at Andersonville, setting forth the conditions there and asking for exchange; but to no purpose. Nor was the protest of the commissioned officers more successful, for the broad reasons given by General Grant as shown in the quotation above.

The relatives and friends of prisoners besieged the War Department, the governors of their States, members of Congress, and all who were supposed to have any influence with the officers of the Government, pleading, imploring, demanding that some method of releasing prisoners be adopted. The same determination which led Grant to hammer steadily in the Wilderness campaign, enabled him to hold the War Department in harmony with his policy. Since the Confederate armies could be beaten only by exhausting them, therefore every means by which those armies were prevented from being increased was justified from his standpoint.

He felt that to give Lee forty thousand additional men might prolong the war indefinitely, for nearly every Confederate prisoner released went back to the ranks, while a large proportion of the prisoners at Andersonville belonged to regiments whose time was expired and in many cases had been mustered out of service. Therefore, had their physical condition permitted it, few would have returned to the ranks, or could have been utilized for further service. It was, of course, greatly to the advantage of the Confederacy to exchange, as their resources were dwindling alarmingly.

General Lee, on October 1, 1864, again proposed an exchange to General Grant. It was met by the question whether negro soldiers who had been slaves would be exchanged. General Lee, acting under instructions, wrote that negroes belonging to citizens were not considered subjects of exchange, and General Grant declined any further discussion.

When it seemed that relief by exchange was not probable,

THREE VIEWS OF LIBBY PRISON
AFTER THE FALL
OF RICHMOND

AN IMPORTANT SOURCE OF EXCHANGE
125,000 PRISONERS—MOSTLY OFFICERS—
WERE CONFINED HERE

several Southerners advised that prisoners in South Carolina and Georgia, or a part of them, be released on parole, even without equivalents. It was suggested that all opposed to the administration be sent home in time to vote, and also that all whose time had expired be released. The Confederacy would thus be relieved of the burden of their support. Secretary Seddon evidently considered the matter seriously, for he writes, " It presents a great embarrassment, but I see no remedy which is not worse than the evil," and did not issue the order.

This endorsement was made upon a letter from a citizen of South Carolina, dated September 21, 1864, and forwarded to Secretary Seddon with the tacit approval at least, of Governor Bonham. Previously, on September 9th, Alexander H. Stephens had suggested the release of the Andersonville prisoners, to General Howell Cobb, who was responsible for the suggestion already mentioned that those opposed to the administration be sent home.

The burden upon the South became overwhelming. Colonel Ould offered to deliver the sick and wounded at Savannah, without equivalent. Transportation was sent late in November, and there and at Charleston, where the delivery was completed after the railroad leading to Savannah was cut, about thirteen thousand men were released. More than three thousand Confederates were delivered at the same time. Another proposition for exchange was made on January 24, 1865, and as it was then certain that the action could have little influence on the final result, exchanges were begun and continued with little interruption to the end, though much confusion was caused by the refusal of subordinates who had not been informed of the arrangements to receive the prisoners. In February, for example, General Schofield's orders from General Grant were delayed, and for several days he declined to receive, much to the dismay of the Confederate commander, a large number of prisoners ordered to Wilmington from Salisbury and Florence.

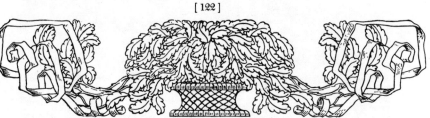

THE LIFE OF
THE
CAPTURED

CONFEDERATES IN
A NORTHERN KEEP.
FORT WARREN, 1864

Nine of the prisoners in this photograph were officers of the Confederate States ironclad "Atlanta," captured at Savannah, June 17, 1863: (1) Master T. L. Wragg, (3) Gunner T. B. Travers, (4) First Assistant Engineer Morrill, (5) Second Assistant Engineer L. G. King, (6) Master Mate J. B. Beville, (7) Pilot Hernandez, (8) Midshipman Peters, (12) Third Assistant Engineer J. S. West, (13) Master Alldridge. The others were: (2) Lieutenant Moses, C. S. A., (9) Captain Underwood, C. S. A., (10) Major Boland, C. S. A., (11) Second Assistant E. H. Browne, (14) Master Mate John Billups of the privateer "Tacony," and (15) Captain Sanders, C. S. A.

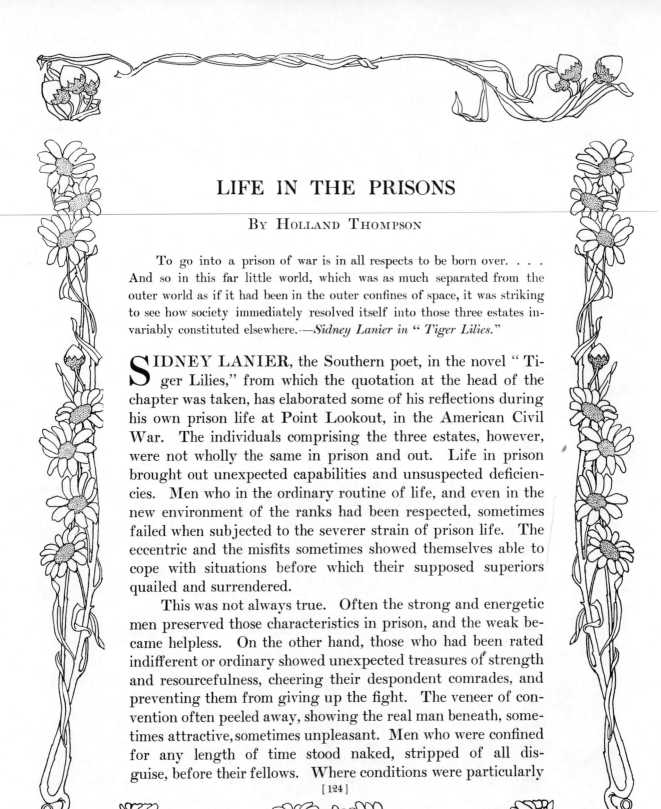

LIFE IN THE PRISONS

By Holland Thompson

To go into a prison of war is in all respects to be born over. . . . And so in this far little world, which was as much separated from the outer world as if it had been in the outer confines of space, it was striking to see how society immediately resolved itself into those three estates invariably constituted elsewhere.—*Sidney Lanier in " Tiger Lilies."*

SIDNEY LANIER, the Southern poet, in the novel " Tiger Lilies," from which the quotation at the head of the chapter was taken, has elaborated some of his reflections during his own prison life at Point Lookout, in the American Civil War. The individuals comprising the three estates, however, were not wholly the same in prison and out. Life in prison brought out unexpected capabilities and unsuspected deficiencies. Men who in the ordinary routine of life, and even in the new environment of the ranks had been respected, sometimes failed when subjected to the severer strain of prison life. The eccentric and the misfits sometimes showed themselves able to cope with situations before which their supposed superiors quailed and surrendered.

This was not always true. Often the strong and energetic men preserved those characteristics in prison, and the weak became helpless. On the other hand, those who had been rated indifferent or ordinary showed unexpected treasures of strength and resourcefulness, cheering their despondent comrades, and preventing them from giving up the fight. The veneer of convention often peeled away, showing the real man beneath, sometimes attractive, sometimes unpleasant. Men who were confined for any length of time stood naked, stripped of all disguise, before their fellows. Where conditions were particularly

"LES MISERABLES DE POINT LOOKOUT"—CONFEDERATES FACING THEIR SECOND FIGHT, 1865

The above caption written on this photograph by a Confederate prisoner's hand speaks eloquently for itself. This was the only Federal prison without any barracks. Only 'tents stood upon the low, narrow sand-spit. Prisoners were sent here from the West for exchange at City Point; at times as many as twenty thousand were crowded within the limits of the stockade. But from the faded photograph on this page there is reflected the spirit of the Confederate army—devotion to duty. As the ex-soldiers stood in line, a task awaited them calling for the truest bravery—the rebuilding of their shattered communities. How well they fought, how gallantly they conquered in that new and more arduous struggle, the following half-century witnessed. On this page is represented David Kilpatrick (third from left), who became mayor *pro tem.* of New Orleans, and G. W. Dupré (tenth), later clerk of the Louisiana Supreme Court. Others well known later as citizens of their home communities and of the United States, can be picked out from the complete roster from left to right as it was written on the photograph: "J. F. Stone, First Maryland Cavalry; H. C. Florance, First W. Artillery; D. Kilpatrick, First W. Artillery; William Byrne, Cit. Maryland; D. W. Slye, Cit. Maryland; Van Vinson, First W. Artillery; J. Black, Louisiana Guard; F. F. Case, First W. Artillery; G. W. Dupré, First W. Artillery; C. E. Inloes, First Maryland Cavalry; Edwin Harris, Company H., Seventh Louisiana; W. D. DuBarry, Twenty-seventh South Carolina; H. L. Allan, First W. Artillery; G. R. Cooke, First Maryland Cavalry; J. Bozant, First W. Artillery; C. Rossiter, First W. Artillery, and S. M. E. Clark, First W. Artillery" (abbreviation for Washington Artillery).

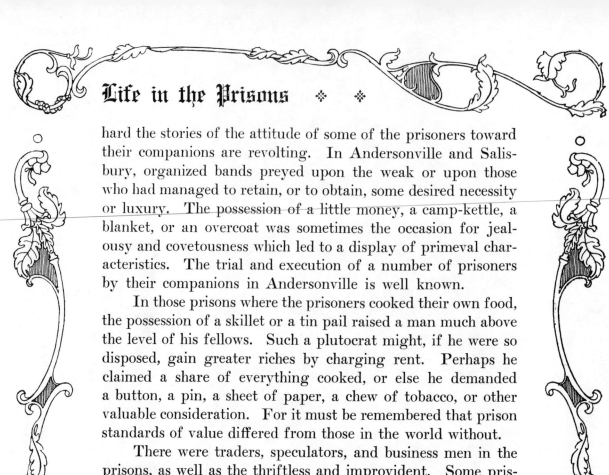

hard the stories of the attitude of some of the prisoners toward their companions are revolting. In Andersonville and Salisbury, organized bands preyed upon the weak or upon those who had managed to retain, or to obtain, some desired necessity or luxury. The possession of a little money, a camp-kettle, a blanket, or an overcoat was sometimes the occasion for jealousy and covetousness which led to a display of primeval characteristics. The trial and execution of a number of prisoners by their companions in Andersonville is well known.

In those prisons where the prisoners cooked their own food, the possession of a skillet or a tin pail raised a man much above the level of his fellows. Such a plutocrat might, if he were so disposed, gain greater riches by charging rent. Perhaps he claimed a share of everything cooked, or else he demanded a button, a pin, a sheet of paper, a chew of tobacco, or other valuable consideration. For it must be remembered that prison standards of value differed from those in the world without.

There were traders, speculators, and business men in the prisons, as well as the thriftless and improvident. Some prisoners always had money, and bought the belongings of the spendthrifts. Even in Andersonville, prisoners kept restaurants and wood-yards, and hundreds peddled articles of food or drink they had managed to procure. " The venders, sitting with their legs under them like tailors, proclaimed loudly the quantity and quality of beans or mush they could sell for a stated price."

The great difficulty in all prisons was the necessity of getting through the twenty-four hours. With nothing to do these hours dragged slowly. Some were able to pass a great number in sleeping. Those of lymphatic temperament slept fifteen or more hours, but others found such indulgence impossible and were forced to seek other methods of enduring the tiresome days. The nervous, mercurial men devised games, laying out checker- or chess-boards on pieces of plank of which they somehow managed to get possession. These boards were never idle,

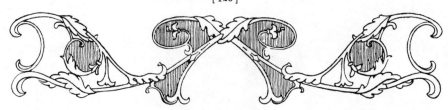

SOUTH CAROLINIANS AND NEW YORKERS

A MEETING THAT WAS AS AGREEABLE AS POSSIBLE

The two facing sentries formally parleying upon the parapet belong to the Charleston Zouave Cadets, under Captain C. E. Chichester.   Below them, past the flag fluttering to the left of the picture, are the prisoners taken at the first battle of Bull Run, July 21, 1861, and placed under their care in Castle Pinckney.   The meeting was as agreeable as possible under the circumstances, to all parties concerned.   The prisoners, chiefly from New York regiments, behaved themselves like gentlemen and kept their quarters clean.   The Cadets treated them as such, and picked up a few useful hints, such as the method of softening "hard-tack" to make it more edible.   The Cadets were well drilled and kept strict discipline.

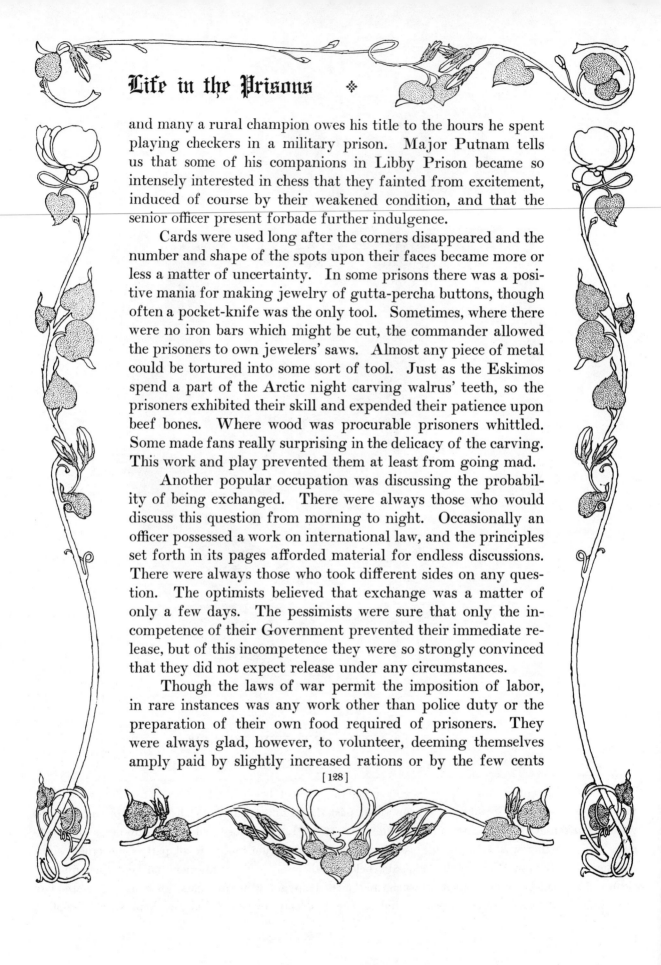

and many a rural champion owes his title to the hours he spent playing checkers in a military prison. Major Putnam tells us that some of his companions in Libby Prison became so intensely interested in chess that they fainted from excitement, induced of course by their weakened condition, and that the senior officer present forbade further indulgence.

Cards were used long after the corners disappeared and the number and shape of the spots upon their faces became more or less a matter of uncertainty. In some prisons there was a positive mania for making jewelry of gutta-percha buttons, though often a pocket-knife was the only tool. Sometimes, where there were no iron bars which might be cut, the commander allowed the prisoners to own jewelers' saws. Almost any piece of metal could be tortured into some sort of tool. Just as the Eskimos spend a part of the Arctic night carving walrus' teeth, so the prisoners exhibited their skill and expended their patience upon beef bones. Where wood was procurable prisoners whittled. Some made fans really surprising in the delicacy of the carving. This work and play prevented them at least from going mad.

Another popular occupation was discussing the probability of being exchanged. There were always those who would discuss this question from morning to night. Occasionally an officer possessed a work on international law, and the principles set forth in its pages afforded material for endless discussions. There were always those who took different sides on any question. The optimists believed that exchange was a matter of only a few days. The pessimists were sure that only the incompetence of their Government prevented their immediate release, but of this incompetence they were so strongly convinced that they did not expect release under any circumstances.

Though the laws of war permit the imposition of labor, in rare instances was any work other than police duty or the preparation of their own food required of prisoners. They were always glad, however, to volunteer, deeming themselves amply paid by slightly increased rations or by the few cents

HUNTING ROOTS FOR FIREWOOD—ANDERSONVILLE PRISONERS IN 1864

In this photograph of Andersonville Prison, the prisoners are searching along the bank of the sluggish stream for roots with which to boil "coffee." Here, as at Salisbury and other prisons, organized bands preyed upon the weak and wealthy. Wealth in this connection implies the possession of a little money, a camp kettle, a blanket, or an overcoat, which led to displays of extreme cupidity. The plutocrat owning a skillet or a tin pail might gain greater riches by charging rent. Perhaps he claimed a share of everything cooked, or else might demand a button, a pin, a sheet of paper, a chew of tobacco, or other valuable consideration. These were some of the prison standards of value. There were traders, speculators, and business men in the prisons, as well as the improvident. Even in Andersonville, there were prisoners who kept restaurants and wood-yards. Hundreds peddled articles of food and drink that they had managed to procure. Another diversion was tunneling, an occupation which served to pass the time even when it was discovered by the guards, which was true of the majority of such attempts to escape. The great difficulty in all prisons was the necessity of getting through the twenty-four hours without yielding to fatal despair.

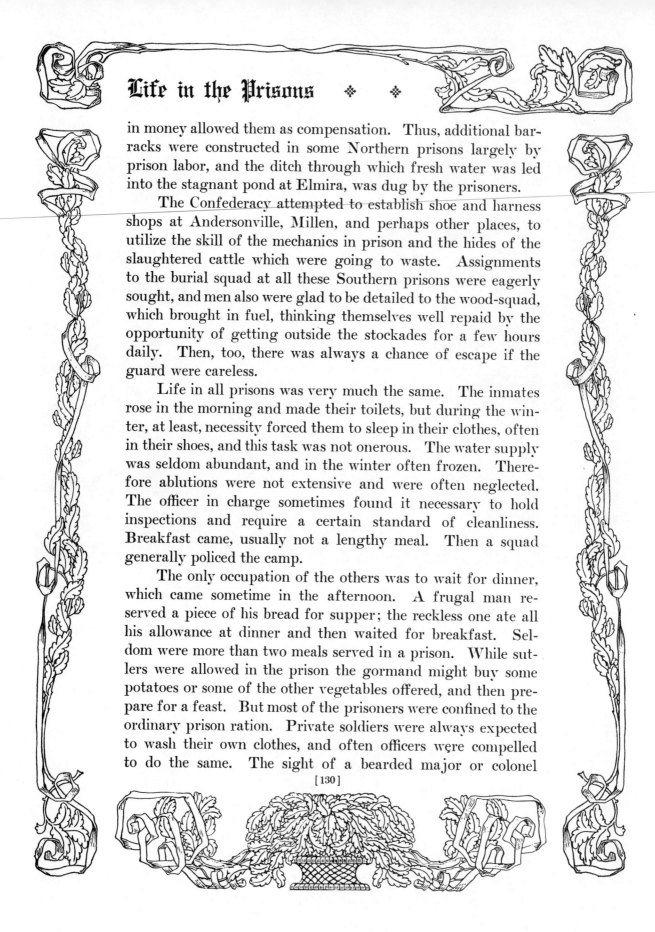

in money allowed them as compensation. Thus, additional barracks were constructed in some Northern prisons largely by prison labor, and the ditch through which fresh water was led into the stagnant pond at Elmira, was dug by the prisoners.

The Confederacy attempted to establish shoe and harness shops at Andersonville, Millen, and perhaps other places, to utilize the skill of the mechanics in prison and the hides of the slaughtered cattle which were going to waste. Assignments to the burial squad at all these Southern prisons were eagerly sought, and men also were glad to be detailed to the wood-squad, which brought in fuel, thinking themselves well repaid by the opportunity of getting outside the stockades for a few hours daily. Then, too, there was always a chance of escape if the guard were careless.

Life in all prisons was very much the same. The inmates rose in the morning and made their toilets, but during the winter, at least, necessity forced them to sleep in their clothes, often in their shoes, and this task was not onerous. The water supply was seldom abundant, and in the winter often frozen. Therefore ablutions were not extensive and were often neglected. The officer in charge sometimes found it necessary to hold inspections and require a certain standard of cleanliness. Breakfast came, usually not a lengthy meal. Then a squad generally policed the camp.

The only occupation of the others was to wait for dinner, which came sometime in the afternoon. A frugal man reserved a piece of his bread for supper; the reckless one ate all his allowance at dinner and then waited for breakfast. Seldom were more than two meals served in a prison. While sutlers were allowed in the prison the gormand might buy some potatoes or some of the other vegetables offered, and then prepare for a feast. But most of the prisoners were confined to the ordinary prison ration. Private soldiers were always expected to wash their own clothes, and often officers were compelled to do the same. The sight of a bearded major or colonel

ISSUING RATIONS IN ANDERSONVILLE PRISON

AUGUST, 1864

Rations actually were issued in Andersonville Prison, as attested by this photograph, in spite of a popular impression to the contrary. The distribution of rations was practically the only event in the prisoner's life, save for the temporary excitement of attempted escapes. Even death itself was often regarded with indifference. Life became one monotonous routine. Breakfast over, the prisoners waited for dinner; dinner rapidly disposed of, they began to wait for breakfast again. Seldom were more than two meals served in any prison. The determination to escape held first place with thousands. Like the man with a "system" at Monte Carlo, such visionaries were always devising fantastic plans which "could not fail" to give them their liberty. The passion for gambling was even stronger in prison. Even at Andersonville captives staked their food, their clothing, their blankets, their most precious belongings. To many, some such excitement was a necessary stimulant, without which they might have died of monotony and despair.

[H—9]

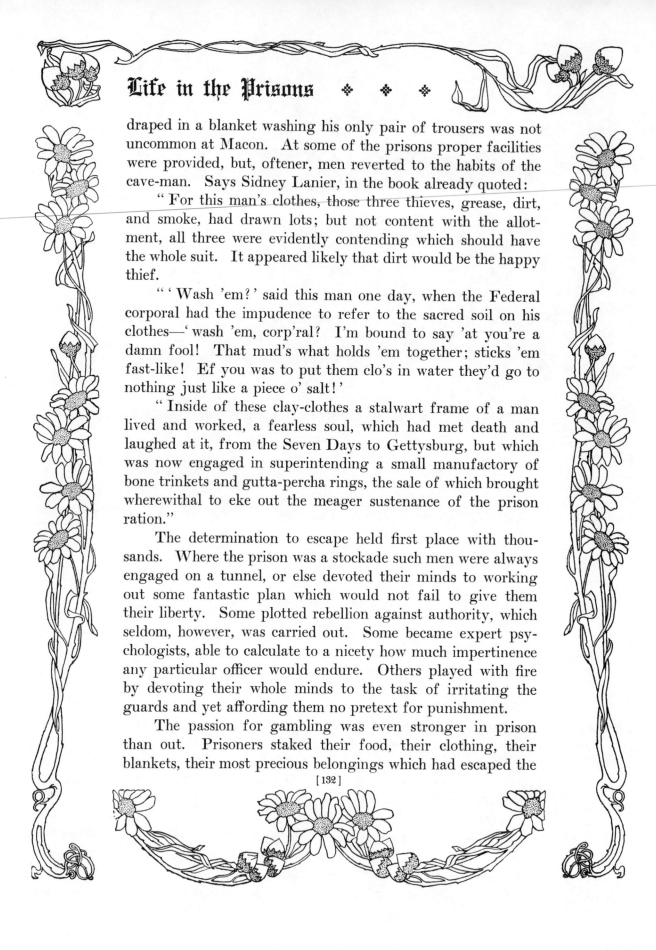

draped in a blanket washing his only pair of trousers was not uncommon at Macon. At some of the prisons proper facilities were provided, but, oftener, men reverted to the habits of the cave-man. Says Sidney Lanier, in the book already quoted:

"For this man's clothes, those three thieves, grease, dirt, and smoke, had drawn lots; but not content with the allotment, all three were evidently contending which should have the whole suit. It appeared likely that dirt would be the happy thief.

"'Wash 'em?' said this man one day, when the Federal corporal had the impudence to refer to the sacred soil on his clothes—'wash 'em, corp'ral? I'm bound to say 'at you're a damn fool! That mud's what holds 'em together; sticks 'em fast-like! Ef you was to put them clo's in water they'd go to nothing just like a piece o' salt!'

"Inside of these clay-clothes a stalwart frame of a man lived and worked, a fearless soul, which had met death and laughed at it, from the Seven Days to Gettysburg, but which was now engaged in superintending a small manufactory of bone trinkets and gutta-percha rings, the sale of which brought wherewithal to eke out the meager sustenance of the prison ration."

The determination to escape held first place with thousands. Where the prison was a stockade such men were always engaged on a tunnel, or else devoted their minds to working out some fantastic plan which would not fail to give them their liberty. Some plotted rebellion against authority, which seldom, however, was carried out. Some became expert psychologists, able to calculate to a nicety how much impertinence any particular officer would endure. Others played with fire by devoting their whole minds to the task of irritating the guards and yet affording them no pretext for punishment.

The passion for gambling was even stronger in prison than out. Prisoners staked their food, their clothing, their blankets, their most precious belongings which had escaped the

SOUTHERNERS UNDER GUARD BY THE PRISON–BOLTS AND WALLS OF FORT WARREN

Perhaps the Confederate prisoner with the shawl in this photograph feels the Northern atmosphere somewhat uncongenial, but his companions are evidently at ease. Not every man is a Mark Tapley who can "keep cheerful under creditable circumstances." But where the prisoners were men of some mentality they adopted many plans to mitigate the monotony. The Confederate officers at Johnson's Island had debating societies, classes in French, dancing, and music, and a miniature government. From left to right the men standing, exclusive of the two corporals on guard, are C. W. Ringgold, F. U. Benneau, S. DeForrest, J. T. Hespin, J. P. Hambleton, and M. A. Hardin; and the four men seated are J. E. Frescott, N. C. Trobridge, Major S. Cabot, and R. D. Crittenden.

vigilance of the prison guard. Some prisoners were often cold and hungry because of their flirtation with the goddess of chance. To many of the prisoners with a limited outlook on life, some excitement was a necessary stimulus, and this was most easily obtained by a game of chance or, if facilities for a game were lacking, by making wagers upon every conceivable event.

At times even some of the poorly clothed prisoners on Belle Isle and in Andersonville and Florence gambled away the clothing and blankets sent by the Sanitary Commission or by the Federal Government. Others, North and South, would wager their rations and then go hungry for days, if chance proved unkind, unless some good Samaritan took pity and stinted himself that the hungry might be fed.

There was little indulgence in athletic sports even where the physical condition of the prisoners would have allowed such exertion. Generally, the prisons North and South were too crowded to afford the necessary room. We hear, however, of balls where half the participants in blanket skirts provided themselves with dance-cards, which were filled out with great formality. Wrestling-matches sometimes occurred, and occasionally boxing-matches. Some of the commanders, however, were chronic alarmists, always expecting a break for liberty, and such always forbade anything which would tend to collect a crowd. In some prisons personal encounters were frequent, and wherever conditions were hardest, then fights naturally were most frequent. Tempers flashed up in times of strain and stress over incidents which would ordinarily have been passed without notice.

Thousands found no pleasure in any of these amusements. Prison life to them was a disaster, appalling and overwhelming. This was particularly true with raw recruits from the country, captured before they had become seasoned by life in the camps. Some relapsed almost at once into helpless and hopeless apathy, caring for nothing, thinking of nothing except the homes and friends they had left. Huddled in corners they sat for hours

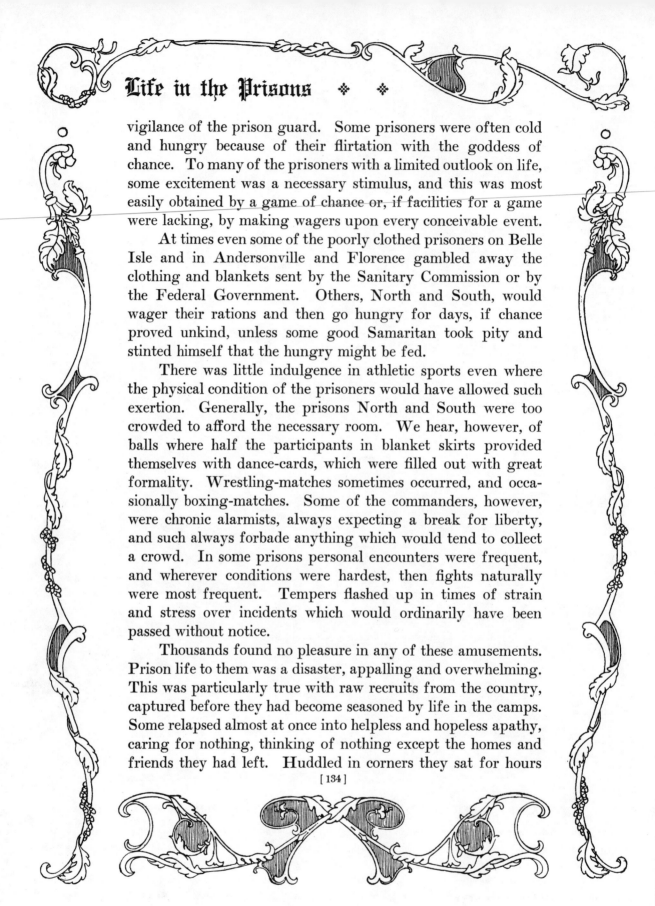

COMFORTABLE CON-FEDERATES IN FORT WARREN—1864

Books and reading matter were evidently available to these Confederates in Fort Warren, 1864. The men in this photograph are C. T. Jenkins, seated on the left; W. W. Helm, standing behind him; R. H. Gayle, in the center with the pipe, and I. Kensfick, seated, with a paper in his hand. Behind him stands Orderly Carey. The only signs of prison are the massive walls and the sergeant on guard with his gun. Many Confederate civilians as well as prominent officers were confined in this stronghold, one of the forts guarding the port of Boston, during

the course of the war. Martial law reigned supreme in those days so far as regarded men with Southern sentiments, but once in Fort Warren the prisoners were treated with the utmost respect, well-fed, and placed in comfortable quarters. Beyond the fact that they were under guard as prisoners of war, they had little to complain of as to their treatment by their captors. Many of these men were taken in the North while traveling from city to city. When they were recognized as Southerners who had uttered secession sentiments, they were quietly taken from the trains, put in charge of a provost-guard, and transported to Fort Warren or some similar Federal prison.

WRITTEN BY A
CONFEDERATE
CAPTIVE, AND
DECORATED
IN COLOR

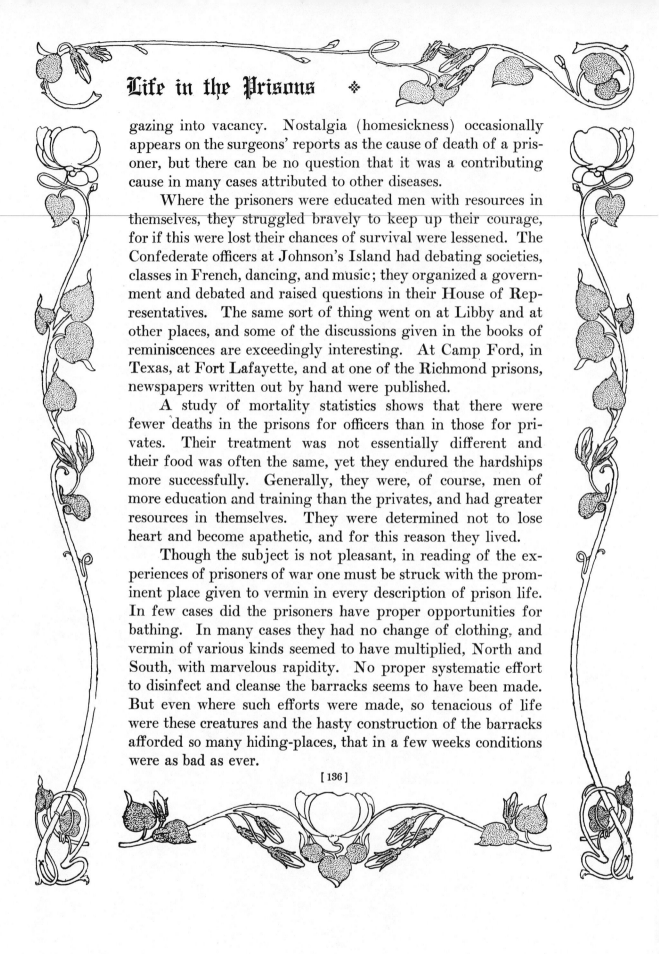

gazing into vacancy. Nostalgia (homesickness) occasionally appears on the surgeons' reports as the cause of death of a prisoner, but there can be no question that it was a contributing cause in many cases attributed to other diseases.

Where the prisoners were educated men with resources in themselves, they struggled bravely to keep up their courage, for if this were lost their chances of survival were lessened. The Confederate officers at Johnson's Island had debating societies, classes in French, dancing, and music; they organized a government and debated and raised questions in their House of Representatives. The same sort of thing went on at Libby and at other places, and some of the discussions given in the books of reminiscences are exceedingly interesting. At Camp Ford, in Texas, at Fort Lafayette, and at one of the Richmond prisons, newspapers written out by hand were published.

A study of mortality statistics shows that there were fewer deaths in the prisons for officers than in those for privates. Their treatment was not essentially different and their food was often the same, yet they endured the hardships more successfully. Generally, they were, of course, men of more education and training than the privates, and had greater resources in themselves. They were determined not to lose heart and become apathetic, and for this reason they lived.

Though the subject is not pleasant, in reading of the experiences of prisoners of war one must be struck with the prominent place given to vermin in every description of prison life. In few cases did the prisoners have proper opportunities for bathing. In many cases they had no change of clothing, and vermin of various kinds seemed to have multiplied, North and South, with marvelous rapidity. No proper systematic effort to disinfect and cleanse the barracks seems to have been made. But even where such efforts were made, so tenacious of life were these creatures and the hasty construction of the barracks afforded so many hiding-places, that in a few weeks conditions were as bad as ever.

PART 1
PRISONS

SOLDIERS WHO
ESCAPED

THOMAS E. ROSE
THE FEDERAL COLONEL
WHO TUNNELED OUT OF LIBBY
IN 1864

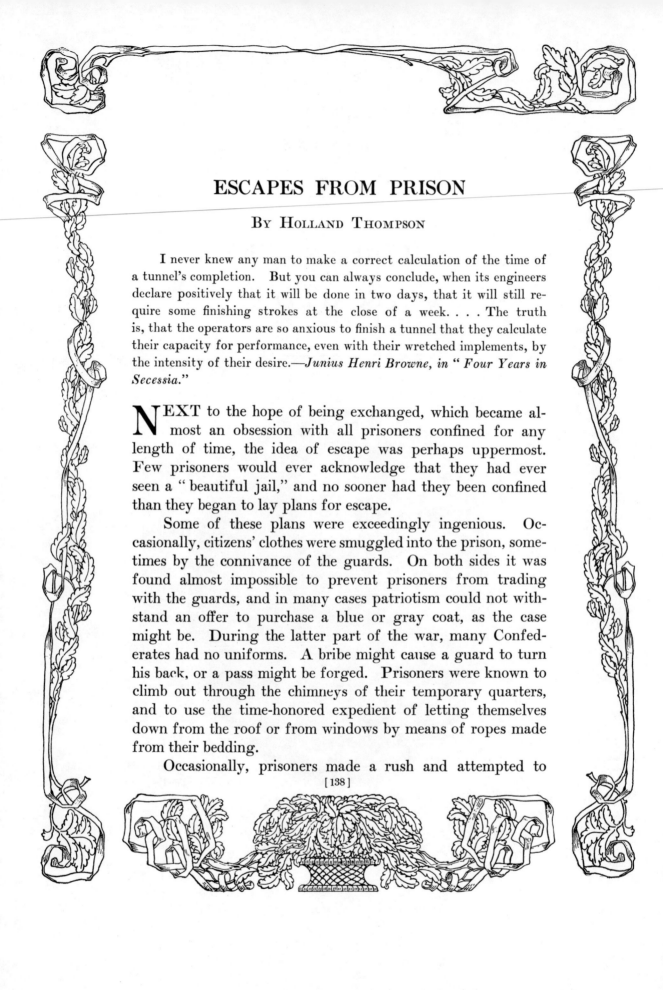

ESCAPES FROM PRISON

By Holland Thompson

I never knew any man to make a correct calculation of the time of a tunnel's completion. But you can always conclude, when its engineers declare positively that it will be done in two days, that it will still require some finishing strokes at the close of a week. . . . The truth is, that the operators are so anxious to finish a tunnel that they calculate their capacity for performance, even with their wretched implements, by the intensity of their desire.—*Junius Henri Browne, in " Four Years in Secessia."*

NEXT to the hope of being exchanged, which became almost an obsession with all prisoners confined for any length of time, the idea of escape was perhaps uppermost. Few prisoners would ever acknowledge that they had ever seen a " beautiful jail," and no sooner had they been confined than they began to lay plans for escape.

Some of these plans were exceedingly ingenious. Occasionally, citizens' clothes were smuggled into the prison, sometimes by the connivance of the guards. On both sides it was found almost impossible to prevent prisoners from trading with the guards, and in many cases patriotism could not withstand an offer to purchase a blue or gray coat, as the case might be. During the latter part of the war, many Confederates had no uniforms. A bribe might cause a guard to turn his back, or a pass might be forged. Prisoners were known to climb out through the chimneys of their temporary quarters, and to use the time-honored expedient of letting themselves down from the roof or from windows by means of ropes made from their bedding.

Occasionally, prisoners made a rush and attempted to

BEFORE HE SWAM TO LIBERTY—ALEXANDER AND HIS FELLOW-CAPTIVES IN FORT WARREN

The boyish-looking prisoner with the big buttons on the right—number "24"—is Lieutenant Joseph W. Alexander, who was captured at Savannah when the iron steamer "Atlanta" was taken on June 17, 1863, and sent to the stronghold near Boston. This slender youth squeezed himself through a loophole a little over eight inches wide, and succeeded in swimming to a small island, after a narrow escape from recapture. Three of his friends and two sailors accompanied him. Before he left the shore with Lieutenant Thurston two sentinels came along. One thought that he saw something lying in the water, and extended his gun till the point of his bayonet rested upon Thurston's chest. The latter lay still, and the sentinel concluded it was a log. Lieutenants Alexander and Thurston escaped in a fishing-smack, but were recaptured and sent back to Fort Warren after a short confinement in Portland. The other captives in this photograph, as numbered are: 16, Pilot Fleetwood; 17, Master-mate N. McBlair, both of the "Atlanta"; 18, Reid Saunders, C. S. A.; 19, Lieutenant A. Bobot; 20, Pilot Austin, both of the "Atlanta"; 21, Lieutenant C. W. Read, of the privateer "Tacony"; 22, Samuel Sterritt, C. S. A.; 23, Midshipman Williamson, and 25, Commander W. A. Webb, both of the "Atlanta."

overcome their guards by force, but this required a better organization and more confidence in the good faith of their companions, to say nothing of more physical courage, than was possessed by the larger proportion of the prisoners. If a large number of men should simultaneously attempt to overcome the guards or throw themselves against the flimsy barriers which enclosed so many prisons, undoubtedly a large number would escape, but it was almost certain that the foremost would be wounded, if not killed. So only the most reckless or the most despairing usually attempted to break their confinement in this manner. Since the prisons were in many cases only enclosures surrounded by a fence or a stockade, and since the only tools easily procured were knives, pieces of tin, or sheet iron, unequal to the task of cutting through stone or iron, but entirely adequate for removing earth, tunneling was the means of escape to which prisoners most often resorted.

Sometimes these tunnels were of great length, and the fact that they could be constructed in the short time given to them is astonishing, particularly when the simple tools are considered. The usual plan was to begin in some concealed spot, preferably under a bunk, sink a shaft three or four feet and then run out horizontally beyond the stockade or fence. Where an outer ring of sentinels was stationed at some distance from the fence, the attempt was always made to run the tunnel beyond them. Seldom was the diameter of the tunnel greater than would accommodate one person on all fours. The loosened earth was either carried back by the operator, thrown into a well, a sewer, a sink, or a stove, or concealed in any one of a dozen other ingenious ways. Sometimes two cords were attached to a box or a haversack. When the vessel was filled, some one at the end would draw it back when the signal was given, and empty it.

The seekers for liberty were sometimes successful in carrying their tunnels under the fence without discovery. A dark night was usually chosen for the attempted escape. The earth

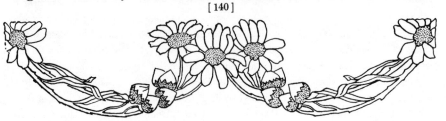

JOHN H. MORGAN

THE CONFEDERATE WHOM PRISON COULD NOT HOLD

In the summer of 1863 General John H. Morgan made his famous cavalry raid across the Ohio River, ending after a hot pursuit in the capture of himself and command on July 26th. General Morgan with about thirty of his officers was confined in the State penitentiary at Columbus. With knives abstracted from the dining-room a hole was cut through the cement floor—about two solid feet of masonry. From the vaulted air-chamber beneath, a hole was continued through the earth underneath the prison until the outer wall was reached. This wall proved too thick to pierce, and a rope of bedding was prepared. On the night of November 27, 1863, the attempt to escape was made. General Morgan's cell was on an upper tier, but that night he exchanged cells with his brother so as to be among the fugitives. The attempt was successful, and General Morgan and six of his companions escaped, leaving a polite note to explain the details of their work. Only two of the prisoners were recaptured.

above the end would be broken through, and the prisoners might emerge like the head of a turtle from its shell. However, in comparison with the number who attempted to escape in this manner, few succeeded, as the odds against their success were too great. Only a few could be entrusted with the secret of an attempt, as any considerable gathering of the prisoners in one particular place was almost sure to arouse the suspicion of the guards. Frequent inspections were made to discover these underground passages, and some of the guards became quite skilful in thwarting such plans. Then, too, in almost every prison there were spies in the guise of prisoners, who reported any suspicious circumstances to the authorities. But if all these dangers were avoided, others remained. Since the prisoners had no means of discovering whether or not they were proceeding horizontally, passages often came to the surface too soon, as it seems to be a tendency of those burrowing underground to work upward. Sometimes the passage of a team caused the roof to fall. At Salisbury, a Confederate officer, making his rounds, broke through the thin crust and sank to his waist.

Attempts to escape in this manner were not always treated with severity. In some prisons the guards appear to have regarded it as a game, at which each side was trying to thwart the other. A prisoner at Andersonville tells of starting a tunnel from the little hut which he occupied. The attempt was betrayed, possibly by a spy, and the sergeant of the guard came and investigated. Plunging a steel ramrod into the ground in various places, he discovered the excavation and sent a negro down to find how far the work had been completed. The negro brought back a box by which the dirt had been removed. "Hello," said the sergeant, "that is the third time I have caught that box. Take it and go to work somewhere else, boys."

Comparatively imperfect tools sometimes accomplished wonderful results. With a small jeweler's saw procured for the making of bone or metal jewelry—a common occupation in

THE CORNER OF LIBBY WHERE FEDERAL OFFICERS TUNNELED UNDER THE STREET

About a hundred Union officers escaped from Libby Prison, chiefly by crawling through a tunnel bored under the street shown in this photograph. Libby was used exclusively for officers after the first year of the war. A few of them banded together, kept the secret from even their fellow-prisoners, and dug a tunnel from a storeroom in the basement under the wall and the adjoining street. The tendency of the human mole is to bore upward; the tunnel came to the top too soon on the near side of the fence. It was finally completed into the lot. But on the very night that the prisoners planned to escape, the news became known to their fellows. Men fought like demons in the close, dark cellar to be the next to crawl into the narrow hole. About a hundred of them got away before the noise attracted the attention of the guards. The fence was immediately destroyed, as appears by this photograph of April, 1865.

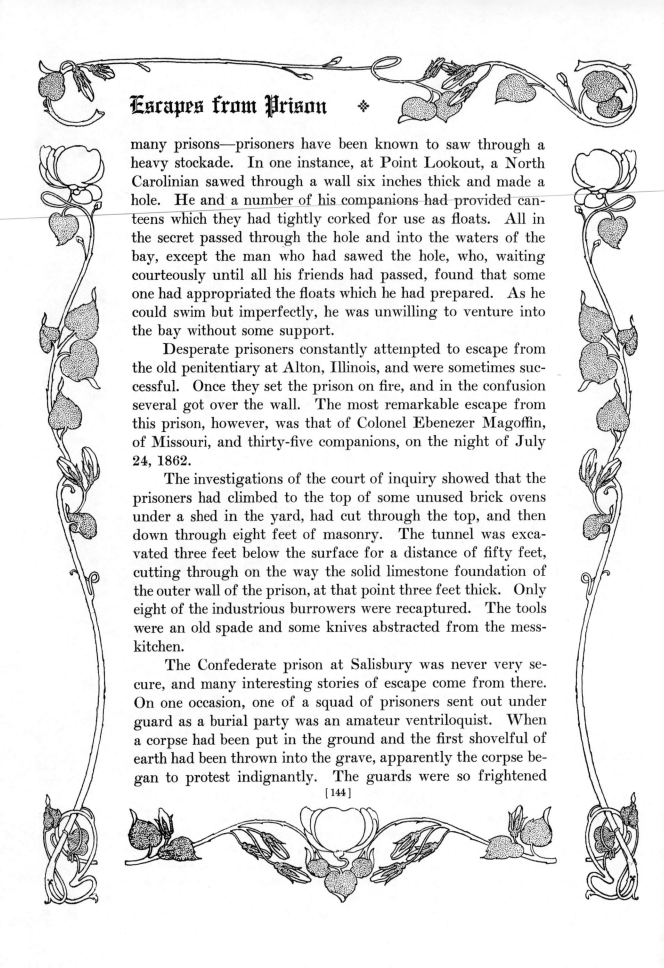

many prisons—prisoners have been known to saw through a heavy stockade. In one instance, at Point Lookout, a North Carolinian sawed through a wall six inches thick and made a hole. He and a number of his companions had provided canteens which they had tightly corked for use as floats. All in the secret passed through the hole and into the waters of the bay, except the man who had sawed the hole, who, waiting courteously until all his friends had passed, found that some one had appropriated the floats which he had prepared. As he could swim but imperfectly, he was unwilling to venture into the bay without some support.

Desperate prisoners constantly attempted to escape from the old penitentiary at Alton, Illinois, and were sometimes successful. Once they set the prison on fire, and in the confusion several got over the wall. The most remarkable escape from this prison, however, was that of Colonel Ebenezer Magoffin, of Missouri, and thirty-five companions, on the night of July 24, 1862.

The investigations of the court of inquiry showed that the prisoners had climbed to the top of some unused brick ovens under a shed in the yard, had cut through the top, and then down through eight feet of masonry. The tunnel was excavated three feet below the surface for a distance of fifty feet, cutting through on the way the solid limestone foundation of the outer wall of the prison, at that point three feet thick. Only eight of the industrious burrowers were recaptured. The tools were an old spade and some knives abstracted from the messkitchen.

The Confederate prison at Salisbury was never very secure, and many interesting stories of escape come from there. On one occasion, one of a squad of prisoners sent out under guard as a burial party was an amateur ventriloquist. When a corpse had been put in the ground and the first shovelful of earth had been thrown into the grave, apparently the corpse began to protest indignantly. The guards were so frightened

AN OFFICER WHO ESCAPED FROM LIBBY
BREVET BRIGADIER–GENERAL A. D. STREIGHT

General Forrest received the thanks of the Confederate Congress when he captured General A. D. Streight, at that time colonel of the Fifty-first Indiana and commanding a provisional brigade, near Rome, Georgia, May 3, 1863. Colonel Streight had been ordered to make a raid into the interior of Alabama and Georgia to destroy railroads and supplies. He started from Nashville April 10th, proceeded to Eastport, Mississippi, and reached Tuscumbia, Alabama, April 24th. General Dodge was to have detained General Forrest, but failed. Streight's command was mounted on mules borrowed from the wagon-trains or impressed from the country, and many of his men were unused to riding. From Tuscumbia he went to Moulton and then to Dug's Gap, where he ambushed some of Forrest's men, wounded his brother, W. H. Forrest, and captured two pieces of artillery. After another skirmish on Hog Mountain, in which the Confederates were repulsed, he proceeded to Blountsville, Alabama, and then toward Gadsden. All of this time there was continuous skirmishing in the rain, and much of his powder became worthless. He attempted to reach Rome, Georgia, but Forrest overtook him and the force was surrendered May 3, 1863. There was much excitement in the South over this raid into the interior of the Confederacy, which was one of the earliest made, and also much indignation over the capture of Negroes for enlistment. The command was charged by the Confederates with many atrocities. The men were soon exchanged, but the officers were kept in prison at Richmond. Colonel Streight and four of his officers escaped from Libby Prison with 105 other Union officers by means of a tunnel dug by Colonel Thomas E. Rose and a few associates, on February 8, 1864.

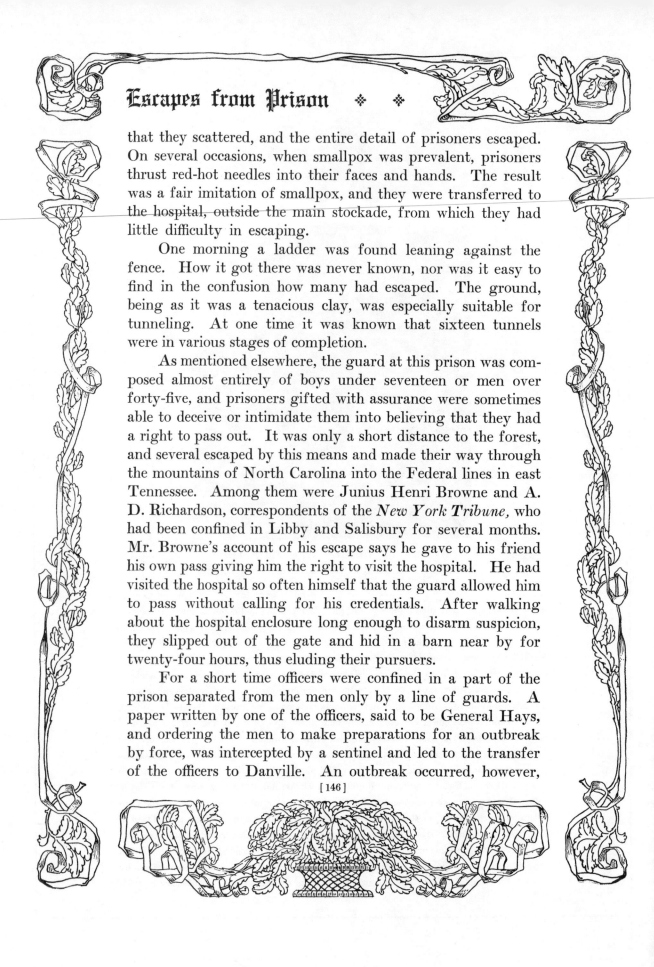

that they scattered, and the entire detail of prisoners escaped. On several occasions, when smallpox was prevalent, prisoners thrust red-hot needles into their faces and hands. The result was a fair imitation of smallpox, and they were transferred to the hospital, outside the main stockade, from which they had little difficulty in escaping.

One morning a ladder was found leaning against the fence. How it got there was never known, nor was it easy to find in the confusion how many had escaped. The ground, being as it was a tenacious clay, was especially suitable for tunneling. At one time it was known that sixteen tunnels were in various stages of completion.

As mentioned elsewhere, the guard at this prison was composed almost entirely of boys under seventeen or men over forty-five, and prisoners gifted with assurance were sometimes able to deceive or intimidate them into believing that they had a right to pass out. It was only a short distance to the forest, and several escaped by this means and made their way through the mountains of North Carolina into the Federal lines in east Tennessee. Among them were Junius Henri Browne and A. D. Richardson, correspondents of the *New York Tribune,* who had been confined in Libby and Salisbury for several months. Mr. Browne's account of his escape says he gave to his friend his own pass giving him the right to visit the hospital. He had visited the hospital so often himself that the guard allowed him to pass without calling for his credentials. After walking about the hospital enclosure long enough to disarm suspicion, they slipped out of the gate and hid in a barn near by for twenty-four hours, thus eluding their pursuers.

For a short time officers were confined in a part of the prison separated from the men only by a line of guards. A paper written by one of the officers, said to be General Hays, and ordering the men to make preparations for an outbreak by force, was intercepted by a sentinel and led to the transfer of the officers to Danville. An outbreak occurred, however,

THE CONFEDERATE SERGEANT BERRY BENSON, WHO TUNNELED OUT OF
ELMIRA PRISON

Sergeant Berry Benson, of Company H, First South Carolina Infantry, was a prisoner at Elmira from July 25 to October 7, 1864. At four o'clock in the morning on the latter date, he and nine companions entered a tunnel sixty-six feet long which they had been digging for about two months. The earth extracted had been carried away in their haversacks and disposed of. On reaching the outside of the stockade the prisoners scattered in parties of two and three, Sergeant Benson going alone, since the companion he had intended to take with him failed to escape. None of them were recaptured. Sergeant Benson, half a century later, still preserved the passes given him from Newmarket, Virginia, where he first reached Early's army, to Richmond. He wrote in 1911 that the men who thus effected their escape were Washington B. Trawick, of the Jeff. Davis Artillery, Alabama, then living at Cold Springs, Texas; John Fox Maull, of the Jeff. Davis Artillery, deceased; J. P. Putegnat, deceased; G. G. Jackson of Wetumpka, Alabama; William Templin, of Faunsdale, Alabama; J. P. Scruggs, of Limestone Springs, South Carolina; Cecrops Malone, of Company F, Ninth Alabama Infantry, then living at Waldron, Ark.; Crawford of the Sixth Virginia Cavalry, and Glenn. Most of them were present at Appomattox.

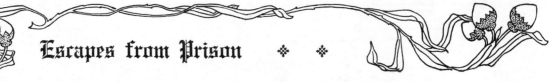

on October 20, 1864. As the relief of the guard entered the prison in the afternoon, the prisoners by a concerted rush disarmed and killed some of them. Sentinels on the parapet raised the alarm and began to fire into the mass, and the cannon at one of the angles discharged grape and canister and did considerable execution. About fifty of the prisoners were killed and wounded.

Escapes from Andersonville were not frequent. The triple stockade required such a long tunnel that many grew tired before it was completed, and many of the prisoners were too weak to do much vigorous work. Then, too, the pack of hounds kept outside the stockade was successful in running down some of the fugitives, though the stories of their ferocity have been much exaggerated. Usually they surrounded the escaping prisoner and prevented his further progress, but did not injure him appreciably.

Warren Lee Goss tells of extending a tunnel from the side of a well abandoned because of lack of water. By night the men worked away, digging the tunnel and throwing the dirt into the well. By day they removed the dirt from the well amid the jeers of their companions, who did not believe that they would ever reach water. The tunnel was finally opened up, and about twenty passed through and scattered into small parties to increase the probability of escape. Living upon fruit and the flesh of a calf they killed, and aided to some extent by negroes, Goss succeeded in getting seventy-five miles away but was finally captured.

Another story from Andersonville says that a tunnel once came to the surface in the middle of a camp-fire which the guards around the stockade had built. The prisoners sprang up through the fire, nevertheless, much to the alarm of the guards, who took to their heels, apparently thinking that the door of the infernal regions had opened. For a time, escapes from Camp Douglas, at Chicago, were frequent. Prisoners were sent to that point before a fence had been constructed

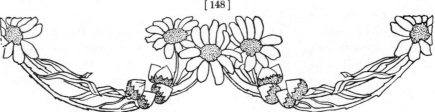

ARTILLERY ON GUARD OVER THE PRISONERS AT ELMIRA

This is part of the military guard in the face of which ten prisoners escaped by tunneling from Elmira Prison. The incentive to get free from the conditions inside the stockade was so compelling that a battery of artillery was deemed necessary to forestall any sudden rush of the prisoners, who numbered at times as many as 10,000. In a report to Surgeon-General J. K. Barnes, dated November 1, 1864, Surgeon E. F. Sanger, assigned to duty at the prison, says: "On the 13th of August I commenced making written reports calling attention to the pond, vaults, and their deadly poison, the existence of scurvy to an alarming extent (reporting 2,000 scorbutic cases at one time), etc. . . . How does the matter stand to-day? The pond remains green with putrescence, filling the air with its messengers of disease and death; the vaults give out their sickly odors, and the hospitals are crowded with victims for the grave." In the face of conditions like these, men become desperate, for there was little choice between death by bullets and death by disease. Later on barracks were erected instead of the tents, and conditions were materially bettered. Correspondingly, Northern prisoners under the hot sun at Andersonville and on an unaccustomed corn-meal diet were contracting dysentery and other diseases more rapidly than would have been the case if they had been acclimated.

around their barracks, and many slipped through the inefficient guard. When the prison was again occupied in 1863, after serving as a detention point for paroled Federal soldiers, it was much dilapidated and extensive repairs were authorized. The commanding officer complained that many prisoners had passed out as workmen, and that once outside the enclosure Southern sympathizers often effectually concealed their friends.

One of the most celebrated escapes was that of General John H. Morgan. In the summer of 1863, his cavalry made a famous raid across the Ohio River, which is described in another volume of this work. The command was captured on the 30th of July, and as General Burnside, commander of the department, declared that he had no safe place in which to keep these dreaded raiders, General Morgan with about thirty of his officers was confined in the State penitentiary at Columbus. It was announced that they were kept in close confinement in retaliation for the treatment of Colonel Streight and his officers at Richmond. Though they did not receive prison fare and were separated from ordinary convicts, they were for three months under the entire charge of the warden in the penitentiary. On the 4th of November, Sergeant J. W. Moon was appointed prison steward by General John S. Mason, military commander at Columbus. His duties were not clearly defined, and the warden understood that the immediate care of the prisoners was no longer one of them.

From this time on, the cells were not inspected and the prisoners were expected to clean them themselves. Some of the resourceful prisoners had discovered that beneath the floor of the cells was a large vaulted air chamber. With knives abstracted from the dining-room a hole was cut through the cement floor and the brick arch—about two feet of solid masonry—into the air chamber beneath. This hole was concealed by a carpet bag from the eyes of the warden, but the slightest inspection inside the cell would have revealed the secret.

A few officers were let into the secret, and each took his

ELMIRA

A DAY SENTRY ON GUARD AFTER BENSON'S ESCAPE

Talking over the possibilities of escape or exchange was one of the chief diversions of the prisoners, both North and South. Sergeant Berry Benson, who escaped with nine other Confederates from Elmira Prison, writes in regard to this photograph: "The sentry on the ground outside the stockade, near the sentry-box, makes me think that this was taken after the 7th of October, 1864, when we ten escaped by the tunnel, for we felt sure that there were no day sentries outside near the fence." This observation is typical of the minuteness with which prisoners of war planning to escape observed every disposition of their guards and speculated about every detail of their surroundings. The photograph was taken about noon, and the river bank distinguishable in the left background is that of the Chemung.

turn at digging. The mortar of the cement was picked from the stones forming the side of the arch, then a hole eighteen inches wide and thirty inches high was continued through the earth underneath the prison until the outer wall was reached. The thickness of this wall made it impracticable to pierce it, and the tunnel was continued under the wall, then upward until it reached within a few inches of the surface of the prison yard. The prisoners next cut away the brick and mortar from beneath a point in the floors of six cells, until only a thin shell was left. A rope of bedding was prepared, and on the night of November 27, 1863, the attempt to escape was made. General Morgan's cell was on an upper tier, but that night he exchanged cells with his brother, who regularly occupied one of the six cells already mentioned. The seven men prepared dummies in their beds to deceive the night watch, broke through the weakened floor into the archway, followed the tunnel to the end, and emerged into the prison yard. By means of a rope they scaled the wall and sought safety in flight, leaving for the warden the following note:

> Commenced work November 4th; number of hours worked per day, 3; completed work November 8th; tools, two small knives. *Patience est amère, mais son fruit est doux.* By order of my six confederates.

Two of the prisoners were recaptured, but Morgan and the others made their escape.

Because of its importance as the chief prison at which officers were confined in the Confederacy, Libby Prison, Richmond, was guarded with especial vigilance, but nevertheless many officers escaped from here. In February, 1864, by the efforts of Colonel Rose, a tunnel was dug from the storeroom in the basement of the building, under the wall and the adjoining street, beneath the feet of the guards.

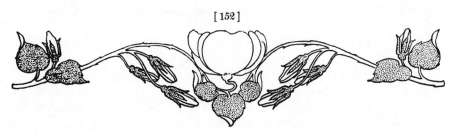

PART I
PRISONS

TREATMENT OF
PRISONERS

A PRISONER OF '64

SIGNAL-OFFICER PRESTON, OF
THE CONFEDERACY, CONFINED
IN FORT WARREN, MASSACHU-
SETTS—ONE OF THE BEST-
MANAGED FEDERAL PRISONS

LINING UP FOR RATIONS FROM THE CONQUERORS

Capture was not an unmixed evil for the Confederate soldiers in the Wilderness campaign. The Army of Northern Virginia had already taken up a hole in its belt on account of the failure of supplies; but the Union troops were plentifully supplied with wagon-trains, and the men in gray who were captured near their base of supplies at Belle Plain were sure at least of a good meal. The Confederate prisoners here shown were captured at Spotsylvania, May 12, 1864, by the Second Corps under General Hancock. They were taken to Belle Plain, where they found not only a Union brigade left to guard them but a brigade

CONFEDERATE PRISONERS AT BELLE PLAIN, CAPTURED AT SPOTSYLVANIA, MAY 12, 1864

commissary and his wagons ready to feed them. Some of the wagons can be seen in this photograph on the left-hand page, unloading supplies for the Confederate prisoners. The camp at Belle Plain was only temporary; the prisoners were taken thence by transports in the direction of Baltimore or Washington, sometimes even New York, and forwarded to the great Union prisons at Elmira, Johnson's Island, Lake Erie, or Camp Douglas, Illinois. On the brow of the hill to the right stands a Union field-piece pointing directly at the mass of prisoners. Behind it are the tents of the guard stretching up over the hill.

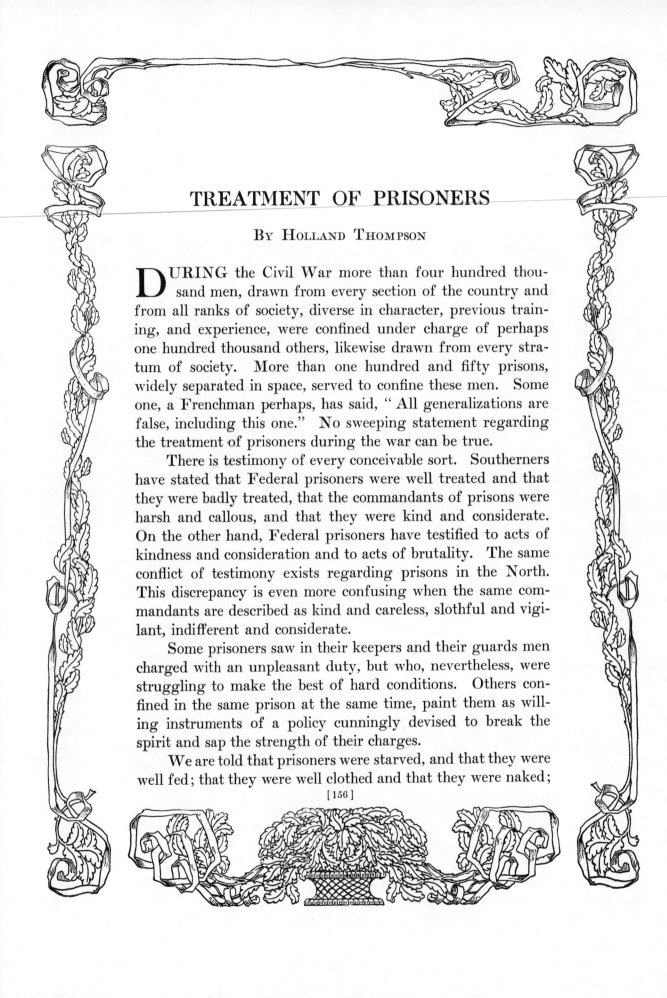

TREATMENT OF PRISONERS

By Holland Thompson

DURING the Civil War more than four hundred thousand men, drawn from every section of the country and from all ranks of society, diverse in character, previous training, and experience, were confined under charge of perhaps one hundred thousand others, likewise drawn from every stratum of society. More than one hundred and fifty prisons, widely separated in space, served to confine these men. Some one, a Frenchman perhaps, has said, " All generalizations are false, including this one." No sweeping statement regarding the treatment of prisoners during the war can be true.

There is testimony of every conceivable sort. Southerners have stated that Federal prisoners were well treated and that they were badly treated, that the commandants of prisons were harsh and callous, and that they were kind and considerate. On the other hand, Federal prisoners have testified to acts of kindness and consideration and to acts of brutality. The same conflict of testimony exists regarding prisons in the North. This discrepancy is even more confusing when the same commandants are described as kind and careless, slothful and vigilant, indifferent and considerate.

Some prisoners saw in their keepers and their guards men charged with an unpleasant duty, but who, nevertheless, were struggling to make the best of hard conditions. Others confined in the same prison at the same time, paint them as willing instruments of a policy cunningly devised to break the spirit and sap the strength of their charges.

We are told that prisoners were starved, and that they were well fed; that they were well clothed and that they were naked;

THE BRIGHT SIDE OF PRISON LIFE—1861

These are some of the Union prisoners taken at the first battle of Bull Run, July 21, 1861, at Castle Pinckney, in Charleston Harbor, where they were placed in charge of the Charleston Zouave Cadets under Captain C. E. Chichester. They received the same rations as their guardians, and were good-enough soldiers to make themselves quite comfortable. Later in the war, when rations grew short in all the Southern armies, prisoners suffered along with the rest. During 1863 the number of prisoners on both sides had increased so largely that their care began to be a serious matter—both on account of the expense of feeding them, and because of the number of soldiers withdrawn from service at the front in order to guard them. The cost of caring for prisoners by the tens of thousands was felt in the North as well as in the South, but in the latter section it finally came to be physically and economically impossible to keep the prisoners' rations up to standard. The South had nothing wherewith to feed its own soldiers and even went to the extreme of liberating 13,000 sick prisoners. Its resources were exhausted. It was lack of food quite as much as the exhaustion of military strength which caused the ultimate downfall of the Confederate States.

that the guards, though efficient, were considerate and kind, and that they were careless but despotic. We are told that the hospital service was efficient and skilful, and that it was careless and neglectful. Probably all of these statements have something of truth in them, and yet they do not tell the whole truth. They may represent the attitude of a commandant before a particular emergency, which did not truly represent his character, for few men are thoroughly consistent; or they may indicate conditions in a prison at a particular time when it was at its best or at its worst.

There is little formal Congressional legislation on the prison question. The policies of the Governments were fixed very largely, as might be expected, by the Department of War, which issued orders for the care of prisoners. The army regulations provided, in a general way, for the prisoners taken by the Federals, but the circulars of instruction issued from the office of the commissary-general of prisoners formed the basis for most of the rules of the separate prisons. Later, the distinguished publicist, Francis Lieber, was selected to draw up rules for the conduct of armies in the field. These were published as General Orders No. 100, April 24, 1863, and constitute a long and minute code, including regulations for prisoners.

The only general legislation of the Confederate Congress during the whole period of the war was an act approved May 21, 1861. It reads as follows:

AN ACT RELATIVE TO PRISONERS OF WAR APPROVED MAY 21, 1861

The Congress of the Confederate States of America do enact, That all prisoners of war taken, whether on land or at sea, during the pending hostilities with the United States shall be transferred by the captors from time to time, and as often as convenient, to the Department of War; and it shall be the duty of the Secretary of War with the approval of the President to issue such instructions to the quartermaster-general and his subordinates as shall provide for the safe custody and sustenance

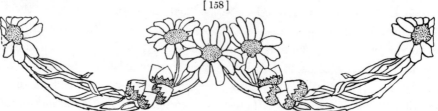

A WET DAY AT CAMP DOUGLAS, NEAR CHICAGO, ILLINOIS

At any period the sanitary conditions at Camp Douglas were not satisfactory. The ground was low and always flooded after a rain, as seen in this photograph, and stagnant pools of water stood there with no means of draining them off. The highest rate of mortality for any one prison during one month of the war was reached at Camp Douglas in February, 1863. Unused to the rigors of the Northern climate, the Southern prisoners died like flies in their unsanitary surroundings. The mortality rate for this one month was ten per cent. Judging from the men shown in this photograph, some of the prisoners were fairly comfortable. The Confederate gray of some of the uniforms can be plainly discerned. The pipes show that they were not denied the luxury of tobacco.

of prisoners of war; and the rations furnished prisoners of war shall be the same in quantity and quality as those furnished to enlisted men in the army of the Confederacy.

A few special acts were passed: one authorizing the close confinement of the higher Federal officers in Richmond and Charleston as hostages for the privateers; one declaring that the men of Butler's command would not be treated as prisoners of war; one declaring that the officers of Pope's command were also to be treated as criminals, and the famous act in regard to negro troops. This is the sum of Confederate Congressional legislation upon the treatment of prisoners.

There are three distinct periods to be recognized while writing of the Civil War prisoners and the treatment they received: one, extending from the beginning of the war to the adoption of the cartel for exchange, July 22, 1862; a transition period, covering the operations of that instrument until its suspension, May 25, 1863, and the third, extending to the end of the war.

During the first period, there is comparatively little complaint which the same men, three years afterward, would not have considered unjustifiable. The prisoners sometimes complained that their rations and accommodations were not elaborate enough to suit their fancy; but for that matter, complaints of food and quarters in their own camps were common. Soldiers cannot be made in a day. A Confederate officer at Alton complained that his breakfast bacon was too salty and that the coffee was too weak. One of the officers in charge of a Richmond prison was disliked because his voice was harsh, and another inmate of the same prison complained that a woman visitor looked scornful. This does not mean that conditions were ideal, even for prisons; few of them were clean, for neither army had learned to live in crowds.

In the first Confederate prison in Richmond, where the officers and part of the privates taken at Manassas and Ball's

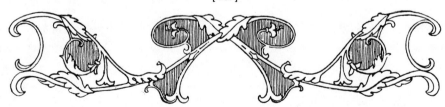

THE PRISONERS HERE BORE NO MALICE

Among the prisoners confined at Charleston during the latter months of the war was Major Orlando J. Smith, of the Sixth Indiana Cavalry, who bore testimony all his life to the fair treatment of young officers like himself. "We were treated," he said, "exactly as well as the Confederates. We were hungry sometimes and so were they." The prisoners were kept, among other places, in the Roper Hospital shown on this page, and the O'Connor House shown on the

MAJOR ORLANDO J. SMITH

page following. Major Smith was confined in the latter place. The battle of Nashville had been fought, and Sherman was on his way from the sea. The investment of Petersburg was drawing closer every day, and the Confederacy was slowly crumbling. Victory and release were at hand, and in the meantime the shady porches of the Roper Hospital shown below were not an unpleasant place to lounge. Undoubtedly many of the prisoners yearned with fierce eagerness to be free again, but their incarceration here was not to be for long.

ROPER HOSPITAL, CHARLESTON, SOUTH CAROLINA

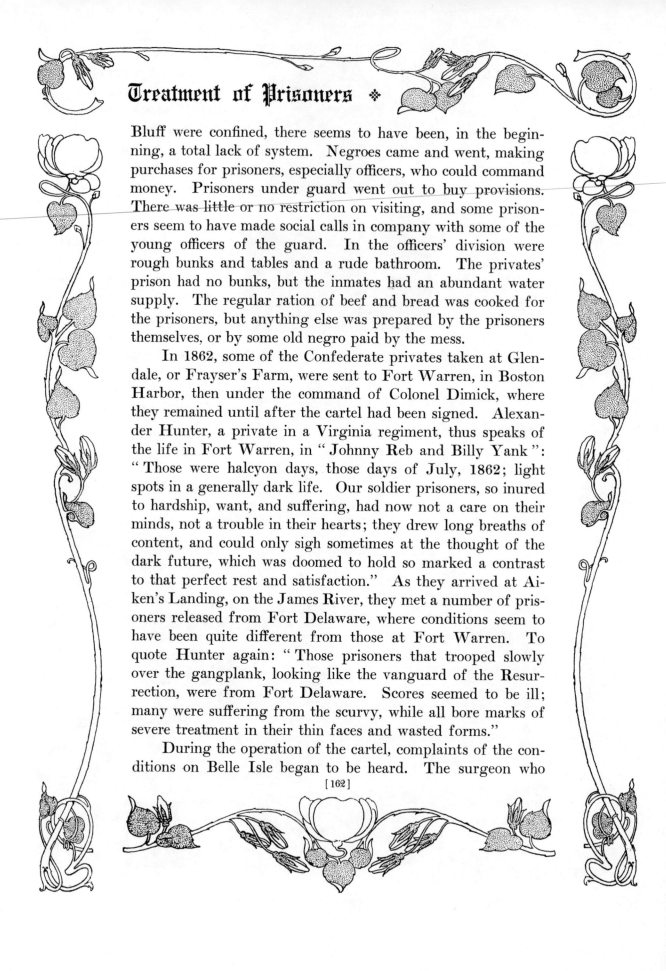

Treatment of Prisoners ❖

Bluff were confined, there seems to have been, in the beginning, a total lack of system. Negroes came and went, making purchases for prisoners, especially officers, who could command money. Prisoners under guard went out to buy provisions. There was little or no restriction on visiting, and some prisoners seem to have made social calls in company with some of the young officers of the guard. In the officers' division were rough bunks and tables and a rude bathroom. The privates' prison had no bunks, but the inmates had an abundant water supply. The regular ration of beef and bread was cooked for the prisoners, but anything else was prepared by the prisoners themselves, or by some old negro paid by the mess.

In 1862, some of the Confederate privates taken at Glendale, or Frayser's Farm, were sent to Fort Warren, in Boston Harbor, then under the command of Colonel Dimick, where they remained until after the cartel had been signed. Alexander Hunter, a private in a Virginia regiment, thus speaks of the life in Fort Warren, in " Johnny Reb and Billy Yank ": " Those were halcyon days, those days of July, 1862; light spots in a generally dark life. Our soldier prisoners, so inured to hardship, want, and suffering, had now not a care on their minds, not a trouble in their hearts; they drew long breaths of content, and could only sigh sometimes at the thought of the dark future, which was doomed to hold so marked a contrast to that perfect rest and satisfaction." As they arrived at Aiken's Landing, on the James River, they met a number of prisoners released from Fort Delaware, where conditions seem to have been quite different from those at Fort Warren. To quote Hunter again: " Those prisoners that trooped slowly over the gangplank, looking like the vanguard of the Resurrection, were from Fort Delaware. Scores seemed to be ill; many were suffering from the scurvy, while all bore marks of severe treatment in their thin faces and wasted forms."

During the operation of the cartel, complaints of the conditions on Belle Isle began to be heard. The surgeon who

THE O'CONNOR HOUSE IN CHARLESTON, WHERE FEDERAL OFFICERS WERE KEPT

During the last months of the war a number of Federal prisoners were confined in Charleston while the town was being bombarded by the Federals from their stronghold on Morris Island. In retaliation, six hundred Confederate officers were sent from Fort Delaware and placed in a stockade on Morris Island under the fire of the Confederate guns. Little or no damage was done on either side. This is a photograph of the O'Connor house in Charleston, used as an officers' prison. It was taken in April, 1865, after the occupation of the city by the Federal forces. The building in front of the O'Connor house is in ruins, but there are no marks of shells visible on the O'Connor house itself. Now that the fierce heat of war has passed, it has been admitted that it would have been impossible to keep prisoners anywhere in Charleston without exposing them to the bombardment, since that covered the entire city.

attended a number of exchanged Federal prisoners confined upon Belle Isle reported that "every case wore upon it the visage of hunger, the expression of despair. . . . Their frames were, in the most cases, all that was left of them." On the other side, we find charges of inhumanity against keepers.

After the suspension of exchanges under the order of May 25, 1863, these complaints increased both in volume and in bitterness, and attempts were made on both sides to send provisions to their men. The boxes sent by relatives or friends were generally delivered. In the fall of 1862, considerable quantities of clothing were sent to Richmond to be distributed by Federal officers, and also a number of boxes of food, so that certain tents in Belle Isle were declared to present the "appearance of a first-class grocery store." The boxes, some sent by the Sanitary Commission and others by private parties, were not examined until a letter, dated November 7, 1863, from General Neal Dow, himself a prisoner, was intercepted. In this he made the suggestion that, as the boxes were not examined, money be sent in cans labeled "Preserved Fruit," which money might be used for bribing the guards and thus effecting escapes. After this, all boxes were opened and carefully examined. Much food was spoiled from delay, or was eaten by hungry Confederates.

It was believed widely in the North that much of the food sent to Richmond was appropriated for the Confederate army, but there seems to be no evidence to sustain such a conclusion. The report had its origin, apparently, in the statement made to a prisoner by a carpenter employed about one of the prisons in Richmond. Without investigation, this was at once accepted as the truth, and blazoned abroad. An interesting feature of the study of the "Official Records" is the discovery of the origin of many of the almost universally accepted beliefs of the day. Beginning as mere camp rumors reported to a superior officer, they are quoted "on reliable authority," which soon becomes "unquestionable," and are spread broadcast.

ONE OF THE FEW SCENES OF RETALIATION
STOCKADE FOR CONFEDERATE PRISONERS ON MORRIS ISLAND

Many threats of retaliation for the alleged mistreatment of prisoners were made during the war, but the photograph above is the scene of one of the few which were carried out. In 1864, while Sherman was pushing everything before him in Georgia, a number of Union prisoners were sent to Charleston and confined within the city limits, actually under fire of the Union batteries, although the city was still inhabited. In retaliation, six hundred Confederate officers were placed on the steamer *Crescent*, August 20, 1864, and started for Charleston from Fort Delaware. When they arrived, the stockade built for their prison on Morris Island under fire of the Confederate batteries was not ready, and the prisoners were not landed till September 7th. The food furnished them was identical with that which rumor had it was furnished the prisoners in the city. The Confederates, however, were careful to fire high. The guard in the stockade was as much exposed as the prisoners. The Federal prisoners in the city were finally withdrawn; the stockade was then abandoned, and its inmates sent to Fort Pulaski, Savannah, on October 23, 1864.

Meanwhile, the first reporter had, perhaps, repudiated the rumor the following day. For a time the issue of boxes was suspended, though we are told by General Butler that this arose from the fact that they were addressed by zealous persons in the North to "Our Brave Defenders in Richmond," or to "Our Starving Soldiers in Richmond." Colonel Ould, the Confederate agent of exchange, says that persistent misrepresentation of the action of the Confederate authorities caused the withdrawal of the privilege.

During 1863, the number of prisoners had increased so largely that their care began to be a serious matter upon both sides, both because of the expense of feeding them, and on account of the number of guards withdrawn from service. From the south and west, only a few lines of rickety, single-track railway ran toward Richmond, by which supplies of every sort might be brought. The expense of feeding and guarding prisoners by the tens of thousands began to be felt in the North, and it was impossible for the commandants to maintain longer their personal acquaintance with individuals.

The statement that the Confederate prisoner in the North was given the same food and the same clothing as his guard has been often made and has been generally believed. A study of the "Official Records" shows that such was not the case. The Confederate prisoner did not in fact receive the same clothes as his captor, or the same quantity of food, except for a few months at the beginning of the war. It was announced, in 1862, that the regular soldier's ration had been found too large for men living lives of absolute idleness, and therefore on July 7, 1862, the commissary-general of prisoners issued a circular authorizing its reduction at the discretion of the commandants.

The difference between the cost of this reduced ration and the regular soldier's ration was to constitute a prison fund, out of which articles for the comfort and health of the prisoners were to be bought. This prison fund was in some cases very large, and, while used to buy articles of food for the prisoners,

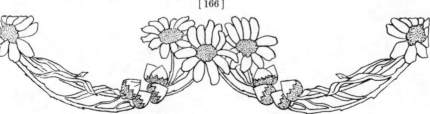

CHANGING THE GUARD AT ELMIRA PRISON, 1864

This photograph of the quarters of the guards who kept watch of the thousands of Confederate prisoners confined at Elmira shows that conditions were much better outside the camp than in. The long shadows of the regular lines of tents indicate plainly that it was taken late in the afternoon. The leafage on the trees fixes the season as summer. The men are apparently engaged in changing guard. Dr. E. F. Sanger, the surgeon attached to Elmira, had great difficulty in getting his requisitions filled. In the midst of plenty in the rich State of New York the prisoners were attacked by scurvy on account of lack of fresh vegetables.

was converted largely into permanent improvements which more properly might have been charged to the Quartermaster's Department. For example, at Rock Island, a hospital costing more than thirty thousand dollars was paid for out of the prisoners' rations, while in some prisons, for months at a time, no vegetables were issued. The accumulation of a large prison fund was a matter of much pride to some officers.

During the latter part of 1863 and the beginning of 1864, the reports of suffering in Southern prisons multiplied, and the belief that it was intentionally inflicted grew to be almost universal in the North. Many suggestions of retaliation were made, and, influenced by this sentiment, the prisoner's ration was reduced, first by a circular dated April 20, 1864, and this was soon superseded by another issued June 1, 1864. Tea and coffee were cut off, and the other items were reduced.

The ration as reduced was then as follows:

Pork or bacon	10	ounces, in lieu of fresh beef.
Fresh beef	14	ounces.
Flour or soft bread	16	ounces.
Hard bread	14	ounces, in lieu of flour or soft bread.
Corn-meal	16	ounces, in lieu of flour or soft bread.
Beans or peas	$12\frac{1}{2}$	pounds
Or rice or hominy	8	pounds
Soap	4	pounds to 100 rations.
Vinegar	3	quarts
Salt	$3\frac{3}{4}$	pounds

As will be seen, this ration is bread, meat, and either beans, peas, rice, or hominy. The manner in which these articles were to be served was left to the discretion of the commandant. This ration, even though reduced, should have been enough to prevent serious suffering, but the testimony of men whose reputation for veracity cannot be questioned, indicates that, after this order went into effect, in some prisons the men were often hungry; and the zest with which prisoners ate articles which

FEDERAL GUARDS WITH CONFEDERATE CAVALRYMEN CAPTURED AT ALDIE, VIRGINIA, JUNE 17, 1863

Firm but considerate treatment seems to be given these Confederates, about to pay the penalty of the loser in a fair fight. On the right- and left-hand sides of the photograph can be seen the strong guard of Union soldiers in charge. The Union forces had a wholesome respect for the Confederate cavalryman, but by the middle of 1863 the Union cavalry had also become a factor. The cavalry fight in which these prisoners were taken occurred at the foot of the upper end of the Bull Run range of hills, in Loudoun County, in and around the village of Aldie. The Confederates were driven from the field by General Pleasonton and his men, but not without serious loss to the latter. Fifty Union cavalrymen were killed outright, 131 wounded, and 124 captured and missing. In return they took heavy toll from the Confederates, as this picture indicates. The Union cavalry regiments engaged in this action were the First Maine, First Maryland, the Purnell Legion of Maryland, First Massachusetts, the Second, Fourth, and Tenth New York, the Sixth Ohio, and the First, Third, Fourth, Eighth and Sixteenth Pennsylvania; also Battery C of the Third United States Artillery. The prisoners were conducted to the North.

a man normally fed would refuse can hardly be explained by their innate perversity. The inspectors' reports show several cases of collusion between commissary and contractor, or else lax supervision which allowed the contractor to do his own weighing and to furnish inferior qualities. Large prison funds continued to accumulate, and the attitude of some of the commandants seems to have been influenced by the idea of retaliation.

The site, the organization, and the history of Andersonville have already been described, and the story of that " gigantic mass of human misery " need not be retold. To many, Andersonville connotes all of prison life in the South. Yet only about twenty per cent. of the total number of prisoners taken by the Confederate forces was sent there. A large proportion of these had been previously confined elsewhere, and later were transferred to other prisons. The mortality rate in some other Confederate stockades was quite as heavy, perhaps heavier, though the records of the others are very incomplete. In several prisons, North and South, the percentage of mortality was higher for short periods, but in none was it so uniformly high for its whole existence.

The charge often made that the site of Andersonville was essentially unhealthful seems to be met by the report of Doctor Jones, who, after analyses of the soil and water of the immediate vicinity, claims that there was nothing in either to have caused excessive mortality. The fearful crowding, insufficient and improper food, lack of clothing, shelter, and fuel, lack of medicines and medical attendance, and the effects of the hot Southern sun, together with the depressed condition of the spirits of the inmates of all prisons, are enough. The hospital arrangements were insufficient, medicines were lacking, the country was thinly populated, and proper food for the sick was unobtainable. Milk and eggs could not be had.

The officers of Andersonville were charged with not providing a sufficient quantity of wood, since raw rations were issued

WHERE BLUE AND GRAY WERE CARED FOR ALIKE—AFTER SPOTSYLVANIA

In the battle of Spotsylvania, May 12, 1864, General Edward Johnson's division of seven thousand men were taken prisoners at the salient known as "Bloody Angle." Some of the wounded prisoners were placed in the same field hospitals as the Federals, and treated by the Union surgeons. They were left on the field as the army moved on, and a small Confederate cavalry force under Colonel Rosser rescued all who could be identified as Confederates, and took all of the hospital attendants not wearing a distinctive badge. The surgeons and other attendants were left unmolested. Owing to the hard fighting and frequent changes of position in this campaign, both medical supplies and medical officers were scarcer than had generally been the case; but owing to the help of the Sanitary Commission and other outside agencies, the prisoners fared better than they would have done inside their own lines, and had one good meal before their rescue.

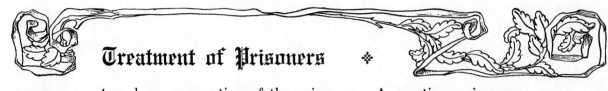

to a large proportion of the prisoners. A one-time prisoner, in a private letter, dated January 16, 1910, says: "If I had been able to cook what I had after it was properly bolted, I should not have been so hungry, and the ration would have sufficed. A man can eat heartily and then die from starvation if he does not digest what he eats, and this was just exactly our condition." Again he says: "I, who drew raw rations for more than one hundred days, ate corn-meal which had just barely been boiled, and which was by no means cooked, or the pea-bean which was not at all softened. . . . I venture the statement that not one-third of the food I ate was digested, or could be digested, and this was true with all those around me."

The officers at this prison lived in constant dread of an uprising. At a time when there were thirty-two thousand prisoners, the guard amounted to less than twenty-three hundred effectives, all except two hundred and nineteen of whom were raw militia, and generally inefficient. In Georgia, practically all the able-bodied men were in the army, leaving only the aged and the youths at home. In many families no white man was left, and while, on the whole, the negroes were loyal to their white mistresses, it was, of course, known that many of them were torn by conflicting emotions—that of regard for the white people they had known, and that of gratitude toward the Federals who were to set them free. These facts, perhaps, may explain—not excuse—the famous order of General Winder ordering the battery of artillery on duty at Andersonville to open on the stockade when notice had been received that the approaching Federals were within seven miles of Andersonville.

During a large part of 1864, prisoners on neither side were permitted to receive supplies from outside. As the complaints of hardships grew more frequent, the relatives and friends of prisoners demanded that some arrangement be made to supply them. After some preliminary correspondence with Major John E. Mulford, the Federal agent for exchange, Colonel Robert Ould, the Confederate agent, asked General Grant, on

BRIGADIER–GENERAL JOHN H. WINDER, C. S. A.

John H. Winder was born in Maryland, where his family had been prominent for many years. He was a son of General W. H. Winder, commanding the American forces at the battle of Bladensburg during the war of 1812. General Winder was graduated at West Point in 1820 and assigned to the artillery; he resigned in 1823 but returned to the army in 1827. For a time he served as instructor at West Point, and entered the Mexican War as captain. He was brevetted major for gallantry at Contreras and Churubusco, and lieutenant-colonel for gallantry in the attack upon the City of Mexico. He reached the rank of major in the regular army in 1860 but resigned April 27, 1861. He was soon appointed brigadier-general in the Confederate army and made inspector-general of the camps around Richmond, which included for the first few months supervision of the prisons. He afterward commanded the Department of Henrico, which is the county in which Richmond is situated, and was also provost-marshal-general of Richmond, where his strictness created considerable feeling against him. In 1864, after the largest number of enlisted men had been transferred to Andersonville and many of the officers to Macon, he was placed in charge of all the prisons in Alabama and Georgia. Finally, November 21, 1864, he was made commissary-general of prisoners east of the Mississippi River. He died February 7, 1865, it is said from disease contracted while visiting the prison stockade at Florence. General Winder's character has been the subject of much dispute. To the last, President Davis, Secretary Seddon, and Adjutant Cooper declared that he was a much-maligned man. He was set to perform a task made impossible by the inadequacy of supplies of men, food, clothing, and medicines.

Treatment of Prisoners ❖ ❖

October 30, 1864, whether he would permit a cargo of cotton to pass through the blockade, for the purpose of securing money to furnish necessities to the prisoners in the North. The agreement was reached November 12th, but, through various delays, the cotton did not leave Mobile, Alabama, until January 15, 1865. A large part of it was sold in New York for eighty-two cents a pound, and from the proceeds General W. N. R. Beall, a prisoner of war paroled for the purpose, sent to Confederate prisoners in seventeen hospitals or prisons, 17,199 blankets, 18,872 coats, 21,669 pairs of trousers, 21,809 shirts, 22,509 pairs of shoes, besides considerable quantities of underclothing. He distributed 2218 boxes from the South.

Reciprocally, the Federal commanders were permitted to send large quantities of clothing and supplies to the prisoners confined in various parts of the Confederacy. The resumption of the exchange of prisoners, however, soon made further action of this sort unnecessary. Since the action of General Halleck, May 25, 1863, regarding exchange of prisoners was based to a considerable extent on the attitude of the Confederate Government toward the negro troops and their white officers, it may be worth while to mention that there seems to be little evidence that any white officer, after he had surrendered, was ever put to death because he had commanded negro troops, though there is testimony that quarter sometimes was refused. A few captured negroes claimed by citizens of South Carolina were put to death on the ground that they were in armed insurrection, but this action was unusual and was soon forbidden. Generally, slaves were restored to their owners, or else were held to work on the fortifications.

Free negroes taken were held as ordinary prisoners of war, though two, at least, were sold into slavery in Texas. That on some occasions no quarter was given to negro soldiers seems certain. Generally speaking, as was clearly set forth by the memorial of the Federal officers confined at Charleston, the lot of the captured negroes was easier than that

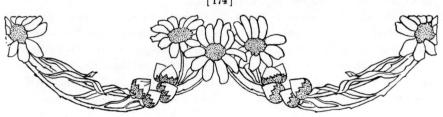

CLOSE TO THE "DEAD–LINE" AT ANDERSONVILLE

The officers in charge of this prison lived in constant dread of an uprising among the prisoners. At one time less than twenty-three hundred effectives, almost all of them raw militia and generally inefficient, were guarding thirty-two thousand prisoners. The order to shoot without hesitation any prisoner crossing the "dead-line," which was maintained in all stockade prisons North and South, was a matter of vital necessity here when the prisoners so far outnumbered the guards. This condition of affairs is what gave rise to the famous order of General J. H. Winder for the battery of artillery on duty at Andersonville to open on the stockade should notice be received that any approaching Federal forces from Sherman's army were within seven miles.

of the whites, since they were "distributed among the citizens or employed upon Government works. Under these circumstances they receive enough to eat and are worked no harder than accustomed to."

Stories of placing prisoners under the fire of their own batteries occasionally occur. On the evidence of two deserters that certain captured negroes had been ordered to work on fortifications under fire, General Butler put a number of Confederate prisoners to work upon the Dutch Gap canal. On the denial of General Lee that it was intended to place prisoners under fire, and the statement of his position in regard to negro soldiers, General Grant ordered the squad withdrawn. During the bombardment of Charleston, Federal prisoners were confined there under fire, though the city was still inhabited. In retaliation, six hundred Confederate officers were sent from Fort Delaware to Morris Island, and there confined in a stockade in front of the Federal lines, where the projectiles from the Confederate artillery passed over them. Little or no damage was done. There are hundreds of other threats to be found in the correspondence contained in the "Official Records." Prisoners were often designated as hostages for the safety of particular persons, but the extreme penalty was visited on few. Many of the threats on both sides were not intended to be executed.

The most prominent figures at Andersonville, and hence in the prison history of the Confederacy, were General John H. Winder and Captain Henry Wirz. The former officer, who was a son of General William H. Winder of the War of 1812, had been graduated at West Point in 1820, and with the exception of four years, had served continuously in the army of the United States, being twice brevetted for gallantry during the Mexican War. As a resident of Maryland he had much to lose and little to gain in following the cause of the South, but, it is alleged, through the personal friendship of President Davis, was promoted early in the war to the rank

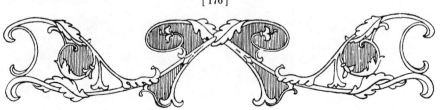

ANDERSONVILLE

1864

HUTS BUILT UPON THE "DEAD–LINE" ITSELF

This view of Andersonville Prison, taken from the northeast angle of the stockade in the summer of 1864, gives some idea of its crowding and discomfort. The photographer had reached a sentry-box on the stockade near the stream, from which the ground sloped in both directions. On the right perches another sentry-box from which a rifle may flash at any instant—for the rail supported by posts in the foreground is the famous "dead-line," across which it was death to pass. So accustomed to all this had the prisoners become, in the filth and squalor and misery engendered by congestion, which finally left but thirty-five square feet of room (a space seven feet by five) to every man, that even the dead-line itself is used as a support for some of the prisoners' tents. Since plenty of room appears farther back in this picture, it would seem that the guards here were reasonably careful not to shoot without provocation—which, as official orders of the time complained, they sometimes were not in Point Lookout, Camp Douglas, and other prisons. General John H. Winder and Captain Henry Wirz were in constant terror of an uprising in force of maddened prisoners, and the rule was inexorable. Inside the line are huts of every description. Some few are built of boughs of trees, but for the most part they are strips of cloth or canvas, old blankets, even a ragged coat to keep off the fierce rays of the ruthless sun. The shelters in front are partly underground, since the blanket was not large enough to cover the greater space. Some in the middle are simply strips of cloth upon poles.

of brigadier-general, and made inspector-general of camps around Richmond with charge of prisons. He soon became commander of the Department of Henrico, which is the county including the city of Richmond. Later he was placed in charge of all the prisons of Richmond, with a shadowy authority over those outside. After the prisoners were sent South, he was assigned to command the prisons in Alabama and Georgia. Finally, November 21, 1864, he was made commissary-general of prisoners east of the Mississippi.

Evidence shown by his official papers is contradictory. Congressman Ely, who had been a prisoner in Liggon's factory, calls him " the kind-hearted general," but Colonel Chandler, in the supplement to his famous report, in words that sting and burn, holds him largely responsible for conditions at Andersonville, while other charges against his character were made. A wounded Federal officer writes of the tenderness with which General Winder carried him in his arms, and yet Richmond drew a sigh of relief when he was ordered away.

We find that he quarreled with Lucius B. Northrop, the Confederate commissary-general of subsistence, insisting that the latter did not furnish sufficient food for the prisoners, and he constantly urges the construction of new prisons to relieve the crowding at Andersonville, and to enable the officers in charge to get food more easily for their prisoners. He many times makes requisitions for food and tools and, finally, when conditions had become intolerable, twice recommended that the prisoners be paroled, even without equivalents, declaring that it was better that they should go than that they should starve. On the other hand, he disputed with some of the surgeons whose reports upon hospitals and prisons had seemed to reflect upon his administration, and denounced Colonel Chandler, making a defense of the Andersonville prison not warranted by his own reports. His death, in February, 1865, did not end the controversy.

The life of Wirz has been mentioned. At the close of the

BURYING THE DEAD AT ANDERSONVILLE, SUMMER OF 1864

The highest death-rate at Andersonville Prison, Georgia, from disease, insufficient food, and the shooting of prisoners who crossed the "dead-line" was one hundred and twenty-seven in a day, or one every eleven minutes. The dead men were hastily packed in carts and hurried out to the burial ground by burial squads composed of prisoners who volunteered gladly for this work, since it enabled them to get out into the fresh air. Trenches four feet deep were waiting, and the bodies were interred side by side without coffins. This haste was necessary to protect the living from the pollution of the air by rapidly decomposing bodies under the hot Southern sun.

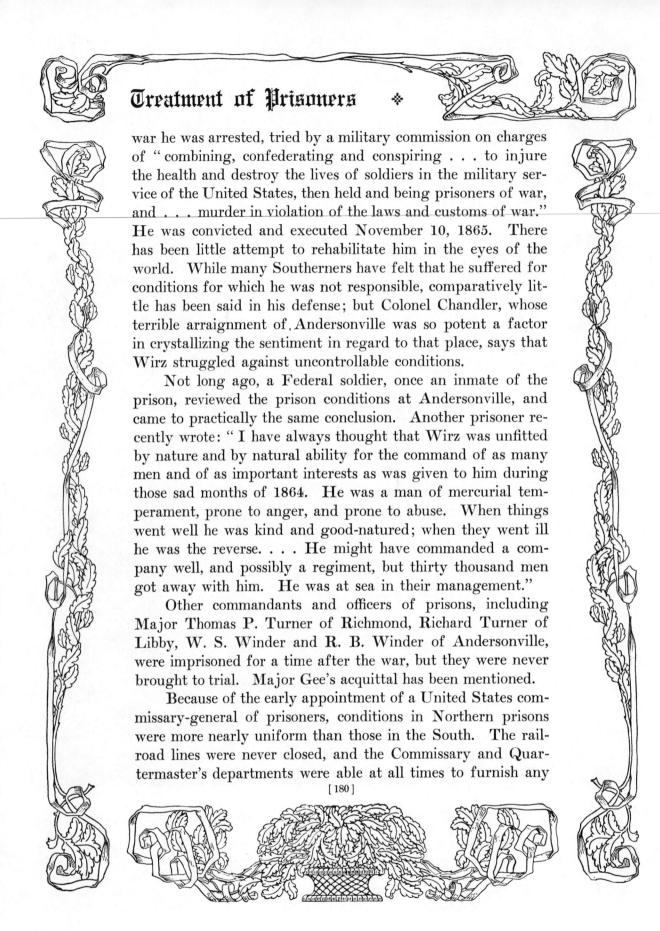

war he was arrested, tried by a military commission on charges of " combining, confederating and conspiring . . . to injure the health and destroy the lives of soldiers in the military service of the United States, then held and being prisoners of war, and . . . murder in violation of the laws and customs of war." He was convicted and executed November 10, 1865. There has been little attempt to rehabilitate him in the eyes of the world. While many Southerners have felt that he suffered for conditions for which he was not responsible, comparatively little has been said in his defense; but Colonel Chandler, whose terrible arraignment of Andersonville was so potent a factor in crystallizing the sentiment in regard to that place, says that Wirz struggled against uncontrollable conditions.

Not long ago, a Federal soldier, once an inmate of the prison, reviewed the prison conditions at Andersonville, and came to practically the same conclusion. Another prisoner recently wrote: " I have always thought that Wirz was unfitted by nature and by natural ability for the command of as many men and of as important interests as was given to him during those sad months of 1864. He was a man of mercurial temperament, prone to anger, and prone to abuse. When things went well he was kind and good-natured; when they went ill he was the reverse. . . . He might have commanded a company well, and possibly a regiment, but thirty thousand men got away with him. He was at sea in their management."

Other commandants and officers of prisons, including Major Thomas P. Turner of Richmond, Richard Turner of Libby, W. S. Winder and R. B. Winder of Andersonville, were imprisoned for a time after the war, but they were never brought to trial. Major Gee's acquittal has been mentioned.

Because of the early appointment of a United States commissary-general of prisoners, conditions in Northern prisons were more nearly uniform than those in the South. The railroad lines were never closed, and the Commissary and Quartermaster's departments were able at all times to furnish any

A FEDERAL COURT–MARTIAL AFTER GETTYSBURG

The court-martial here pictured is that of the second division, Twelfth Army Corps. It was convened at Ellis Ford, Va., in July, 1863. Such officers were especially detailed from various regiments of a division of their corps, for the purpose of judging all classes of cases, crimes, and misdemeanors against the general regulations of the army. The officers above tried a large number of cases of desertion, insubordination, and disobedience to orders, sentencing in this particular court-martial three deserters to be shot. Two of these men were executed in the presence of the whole division, at Morton's Ford on the Rapidan, in September following. The idea of a court-martial in the service was somewhat similar to that of a civil jury. The judge-advocate of a general court-martial stood in the relationship of a prosecuting district-attorney, except for the fact that he had to protect the prisoner's interest when the latter was unable to employ counsel. Privates were seldom able to employ counsel, but officers on trial were generally able to do so. The officers composing this court were, from left to right, Captain Elliott, Sixtieth New York; Captain Stegman, One Hundred and Second New York (judge-advocate); Captain Zarracher, Twenty-ninth Pennsylvania; Captain Fitzpatrick, Twenty-eighth Pennsylvania; Captain Pierson, One Hundred and Thirty-seventh New York, and Captain Greenwalt, One Hundred and Eleventh Pennsylvania.

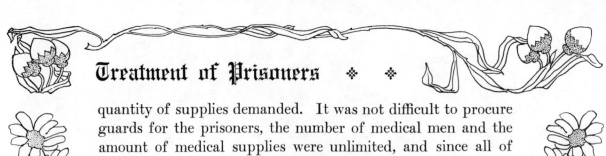

quantity of supplies demanded. It was not difficult to procure guards for the prisoners, the number of medical men and the amount of medical supplies were unlimited, and since all of these could be transferred easily from one locality to another, there was no physical reason why a prison in one State or section might not be as good as that in another.

The prisoner in the North got more to eat, and yet, during 1864, there can be no doubt that he often went hungry. The evidence seems to show that the claim so vigorously made by the Confederates that the prisoners received practically the same rations as the troops in the field was, broadly speaking, true, but the soldier had always the opportunity of picking an apple from a tree, or a turnip from a field. Stray chickens, sheep, or pigs occasionally disappeared mysteriously, and there were sometimes rabbits in the fields, squirrels in the woods, birds in the trees, and fish in the streams. A box from home came, to be shared, of course, with all his friends, who in turn would share theirs. If all these failed the citizens were expected, as a matter of course, to give food to hungry soldiers. And yet we are told that many of the Confederate prisoners captured during the last year of the war were so worn out by hardships and short rations that they fell an easy prey to disease in the Northern prisons.

Students of the war almost universally agree that the commissary-general of the Confederacy was unequal to his responsibilities, though the difficulties with which he had to contend were enormous. Even to the end there was food in the South, but it was in the wrong place. While citizen, soldier, and prisoner were starving in Richmond, Sherman was destroying millions of dollars' worth of supplies in Georgia. If the soldiers were hungry, it is not to be expected, perhaps, of human nature that the prisoners would be fed luxuriously. After 1863, the prisoners held by the Confederates were, generally speaking, hungry all the time. The same fact is true, however, of the armies of the Confederacy.

PROVOST–MARSHAL'S OFFICE, DEPARTMENT OF THE CUMBERLAND

Wherever soldiers congregate there are sure to be found sharpers and thieves. In the ranks of both armies were men who would not behave. In his report of November 12, 1870, the Federal surgeon-general states that 103 men died of homicide and there were 121 military executions during the Civil War. The sentry in this photograph standing in the shade of the doorway of the provost-marshal's headquarters, Department of the Cumberland, gives a hint of the mailed hand that was necessary to govern the soldiery. In front of the house two ropes are stretched between two posts. Here the guard tied its horses when it clattered up with a prisoner.

Treatment of Prisoners ❖

That some of the suffering in Southern prisons might have been prevented if men of greater energy had been charged with the care of prisoners, is doubtless true. The almost superhuman efforts requisite for success were not always made, and for this the feeling of despair, which began to creep over the spirits of many men during 1864, was partly responsible. That any considerable amount of the suffering was due to deliberate intention cannot be maintained, but the result was the same.

The prisoner in the North was better clothed than in the South, where, during the last eighteen months of the war, even soldiers depended to a large extent upon the clothes they captured from the Federals, but the statement that all Confederate prisoners were always well clothed is by no means accurate. Large quantities of condemned and cast-off clothing were issued, but in the bitter winter climate of northern New York or in the Lake region, prisoners from the Gulf States found it almost impossible to keep warm. In the particular of clothing, much depended upon the attitude of the prison commandant, who made requisitions for clothing at his discretion.

In the Southern stockades, there was little shelter except what the prisoners improvised, and wood was often insufficient in quantity. Shelter was always furnished in the North, and fuel in somewhat variable quantities. Where the barracks were new and tight there was generally sufficient warmth; in other cases, the number of stoves allowed did hardly more than temper the air, and as a result every window and door was kept tightly closed.

The attitude of the guards was variable, North and South. Generally speaking, they were not cruel, though they were sometimes callous. It is the unanimous testimony that soldiers who had seen actual service were more considerate than raw recruits or conscripted or drafted militia. Undoubtedly, the negroes who formed a part of the guard at several prisons were disposed to be strict and to magnify their authority, sometimes to the humiliation of their charges.

THE "BULL–RING" AT CITY POINT, A DREADED PROVOST PRISON

The exigencies of war differed so widely from those of peace that at times the prisoners held by their own side had quite as much to complain of as if they had been captured in battle. The "Bull-Ring" at City Point was composed of three large barracks of one story which opened into separate enclosures surrounded by high wooden fences. All this was enclosed in a single railing, between which and the high fence a patrol was constantly in motion. The inner sentry stood guard upon a raised platform built out from the fence, which gave him a view of all the prisoners in the three pens. This is where the provost-marshal's prisoners were confined. The sanitary conditions were indescribably bad. William Howell Reed, in "Hospital Life," published in 1866, quotes an officer recently liberated from Libby Prison as saying that he would rather be confined in Libby for six months than in the "Bull-Ring" for one.

Treatment of Prisoners ❖

In all the prisons, Northern or Southern, enclosed by a fence or a stockade, there was a "dead-line," or what corresponded to it. Its necessity, from the standpoint of the guard, was obvious. If the inmates were allowed to approach the fence, a concerted rush would result in many escapes. Prisoners were shot on both sides for crossing this danger line, and for approaching or leaning out of the prison windows.

Correspondence was restricted as to length and frequency in all prisons, and both incoming and outgoing letters were read by some one detailed for the purpose. Money sent in letters was occasionally abstracted, and not placed to the prisoner's account. After the first year, money was always taken from the prisoners on entering, as it was found that a guard was not always above temptation. When a sutler was allowed in a prison, a prisoner with a balance to his credit was allowed to give orders on his account, or else he was furnished with checks good for purchases. The amount remaining to his credit was supposed to be returned to the prisoner on his release, or to be transferred with him when sent to another prison.

The relative mortality in prisons, North and South, has been much discussed, and very varying results have been reached. The adjutant-general of the United States, in 1908, published a memorandum summarizing the results of his investigations.

According to the best information now obtainable from both Union and Confederate records, it appears that 211,411 Union soldiers were captured during the Civil War, of which number 16,668 were paroled on the field and 30,218 died while in captivity; and that 462,634 Confederate soldiers were captured during that war, of which number 247,-769 were paroled on the field and 25,976 died while in captivity.

From this it would appear that the mortality in Federal prisons was twelve per cent., while in Confederate prisons it was fifteen and one-half per cent. of the total number confined.

[186]

PROVOST MARSHALS
THE ARMY'S
POLICE

AT AQUIA CREEK
WINTER OF '62

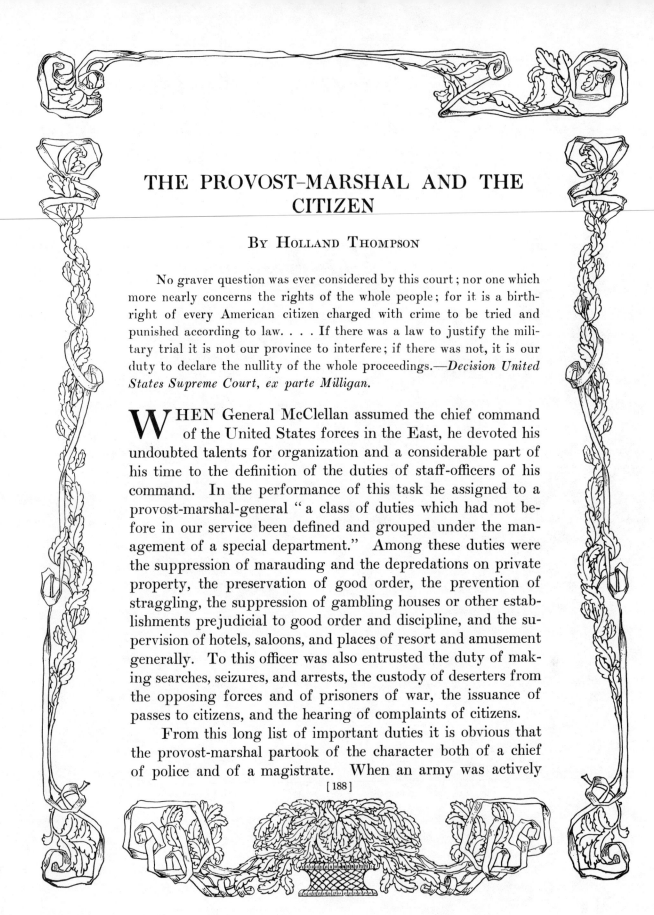

THE PROVOST–MARSHAL AND THE CITIZEN

By Holland Thompson

No graver question was ever considered by this court; nor one which more nearly concerns the rights of the whole people; for it is a birthright of every American citizen charged with crime to be tried and punished according to law. . . . If there was a law to justify the military trial it is not our province to interfere; if there was not, it is our duty to declare the nullity of the whole proceedings.—*Decision United States Supreme Court, ex parte Milligan.*

W HEN General McClellan assumed the chief command of the United States forces in the East, he devoted his undoubted talents for organization and a considerable part of his time to the definition of the duties of staff-officers of his command. In the performance of this task he assigned to a provost-marshal-general " a class of duties which had not before in our service been defined and grouped under the management of a special department." Among these duties were the suppression of marauding and the depredations on private property, the preservation of good order, the prevention of straggling, the suppression of gambling houses or other establishments prejudicial to good order and discipline, and the supervision of hotels, saloons, and places of resort and amusement generally. To this officer was also entrusted the duty of making searches, seizures, and arrests, the custody of deserters from the opposing forces and of prisoners of war, the issuance of passes to citizens, and the hearing of complaints of citizens.

From this long list of important duties it is obvious that the provost-marshal partook of the character both of a chief of police and of a magistrate. When an army was actively

THE PROVOST–MARSHAL AT WORK
DESTROYING HOUSES FROM WHICH LIQUOR HAD BEEN SOLD TO SOLDIERS
ALEXANDRIA, 1863

During the year 1863, while troops of the Union army were located in and around Alexandria, it was frequently the case that both officers and soldiers who visited the city would enter huts and houses in which liquor of the worst quality was sold to them. It was discovered in the course of an examination made by chemists that much of this liquor was made from pure spirits and was inflammable to the highest degree. The soldier, upon entering one of these shops, would have offered to him a large drink at a cheap price, and before many minutes he would become stupefied. In several cases deaths from alcoholism and delirium tremens ensued. After becoming very drunk, the officer or soldier would be robbed by the men and women associated with these groggeries, and thrown unconscious into the street at some distance from the scene of the crime. These places became so obnoxious and created so much trouble that it was finally determined by General Slough to destroy them absolutely as the only hope of abatement. The scene of the photograph shows how thoroughly his men performed this task.

ON GUARD AT THE PROVOST–MARSHAL'S TENT

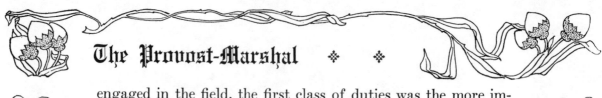

engaged in the field, the first class of duties was the more important. But since provost-marshals were appointed for every military department, though no active warfare was in progress within its limits and they assumed the right to arrest citizens on suspicion and confine them without trial, very often the magisterial side of the office was uppermost.

Not all the military commanders viewed the activity of these officers with satisfaction. General Schofield, while commanding in Missouri, quotes with approval the statement of General S. R. Curtis that the " creation of the so-called provost-marshal invented a spurious military officer which has embarrassed the service. . . . Everybody appoints provost-marshals and these officers seem to exercise plenary powers." General Schofield goes on to say that these officers are " entirely independent of all commanders except the commander of the department, and hence of necessity pretty much independent of them."

The provost-marshals in a department had, or assumed, powers depending in extent somewhat upon the character of the commander. No position in the service demanded greater discretion and sounder judgment. Some of the officers appointed, both civilian and soldier, displayed unusual tact and decision, while others were both obstinate and arbitrary. Perhaps it was too much to expect that all of the hundreds of deputies appointed should be men able to impress their personality and enforce the laws without friction.

While all of the duties mentioned above were important, it is chiefly with the provost-marshal acting under his authority to make searches, seizures, and arrests of the premises, property, and persons of citizens that we are chiefly concerned in this chapter. The action of the provost-marshal brought to a consciousness of the citizen the fact that war existed as did that of no other officer. Later, the supervision of the draft was placed in charge of the provost-marshal-general at Washington, who had no other duties, and the incidents and events

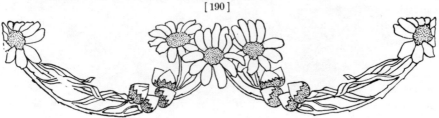

MEN WHO POLICED THE FEDERALS—PROVOST-MARSHALS OF THE THIRD ARMY CORPS,
DECEMBER, 1863

It was not until 1863 that Negro troops were enlisted in the Union army. Properly led, they made excellent soldiers, but there were times, like that shown in this photograph, when they were difficult to handle. In idleness they always deteriorated in discipline. The accompanying photograph, taken after the fall of Vicksburg, shows one of the punishments inflicted on soldiers who had committed breaches of disci-

"RIDING THE SAWBUCK" AT THE
VICKSBURG GUARD-HOUSE

pline. They were set astride of a plank six inches wide and forced to remain in this position, which was neither comfortable nor dignified, for two or three hours under guard. The Negro guard, clothed with a little temporary authority over his fellows, is apparently swelling with importance. The two Negro soldiers "riding the sawbuck" look apathetic, but it is doubtful if they are enjoying themselves to any great extent.

occurring in the discharge of this duty were interesting and exciting, though they do not fall within the scope of this volume.

During the month of April, 1861, all was in confusion in Washington. Senators and representatives in Congress had left their seats, and others were expected to follow their States; occupants of the bench were leaving their court rooms; officers of the army and navy were daily offering their resignations; several members of the diplomatic corps were reported to be on their way home to cast their lot with the Confederacy; many subordinate officials of the Government were resigning, and others were suspected of holding their positions more that they might effectively serve the new Government than because of the sentiment of loyalty. Public sentiment in Washington was inclined to be pro-Southern in the early days of Lincoln's administration. The passage of troops through Baltimore for the defense of Washington was resisted by force. Maryland and Kentucky were hoping to preserve neutrality during the coming contest. No one knew what a day might bring forth.

To add to the confusion, thousands who had no sympathy with secession doubted the Constitutional right of coercion and openly expressed their opposition to such a course. Suspicion and ill-feeling were prevalent, since the attitude of many thousands toward the Union was a matter of uncertainty. Spies and informers developed in such numbers as to remind one of the days of later Rome. Into the ears of the Government officials a constant stream of suspicion was poured. As a result the arrest of hundreds was ordered without warrants on the simple order from the State or War Department, chiefly the former. Some typical orders read as follows:

" Arrest W. H. Winder and send him to Fort Lafayette, New York.
" W. H. Seward, Secretary of State."

" Arrest man referred to in your letter of the 11th and send him to Fort Lafayette.
" Simon Cameron, Secretary of War."

PROVOST OFFICE, DEPARTMENT OF THE CUMBERLAND, AT NASHVILLE, TENNESSEE

The provost-marshals in a department had (or assumed) powers depending in extent somewhat upon the character of the commander. Their position required sound judgment and great discretion. Some of the officers appointed, both civilian and soldier, displayed unusual tact and decision, while others were rash, obstinate, and arbitrary. In a general way the duties of a provost-marshal were similar to those of the chief of police for a certain district, town, or camp. He saw that order was preserved, and arrested all offenders against military discipline under his authority, and was responsible for their safe-keeping. All prisoners taken in a battle were turned over to the provost-marshal and by him later transferred to special guards, who delivered them at prisons farther North.

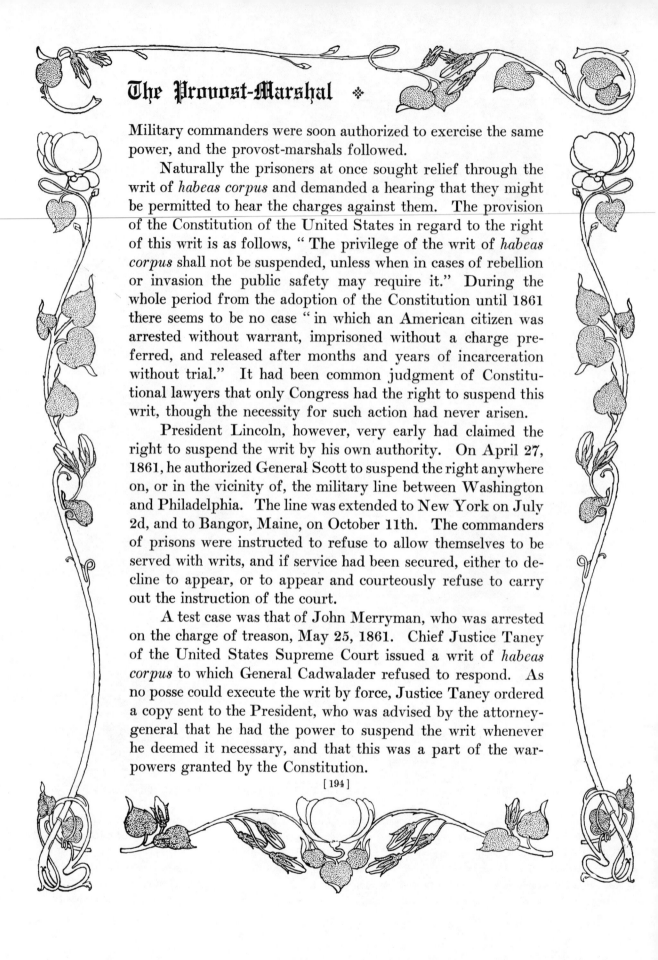

Military commanders were soon authorized to exercise the same power, and the provost-marshals followed.

Naturally the prisoners at once sought relief through the writ of *habeas corpus* and demanded a hearing that they might be permitted to hear the charges against them. The provision of the Constitution of the United States in regard to the right of this writ is as follows, " The privilege of the writ of *habeas corpus* shall not be suspended, unless when in cases of rebellion or invasion the public safety may require it." During the whole period from the adoption of the Constitution until 1861 there seems to be no case " in which an American citizen was arrested without warrant, imprisoned without a charge preferred, and released after months and years of incarceration without trial." It had been common judgment of Constitutional lawyers that only Congress had the right to suspend this writ, though the necessity for such action had never arisen.

President Lincoln, however, very early had claimed the right to suspend the writ by his own authority. On April 27, 1861, he authorized General Scott to suspend the right anywhere on, or in the vicinity of, the military line between Washington and Philadelphia. The line was extended to New York on July 2d, and to Bangor, Maine, on October 11th. The commanders of prisons were instructed to refuse to allow themselves to be served with writs, and if service had been secured, either to decline to appear, or to appear and courteously refuse to carry out the instruction of the court.

A test case was that of John Merryman, who was arrested on the charge of treason, May 25, 1861. Chief Justice Taney of the United States Supreme Court issued a writ of *habeas corpus* to which General Cadwalader refused to respond. As no posse could execute the writ by force, Justice Taney ordered a copy sent to the President, who was advised by the attorney-general that he had the power to suspend the writ whenever he deemed it necessary, and that this was a part of the war-powers granted by the Constitution.

THE VIRGINIA HOME OF JOHN MINOR BOTTS

This beautiful old Virginia mansion was the abiding-place in Culpeper County of John Minor Botts. The most conspicuous arrest made under the suspension of the writ of *habeas corpus* was that of this citizen, who had been prominent in the political life of Virginia for thirty years, having served as a member of the State Legislature and in the United States House of Representatives. He had been a determined opponent of secession, declaring that the State had no right to secede, and that the leaders in the South were "conspirators." After the suspension of the writ of *habeas corpus*, he was arrested March 2, 1862, in his home in Richmond, and confined for several weeks. Through a personal interview with Secretary of War George W. Randolph, he finally obtained permission to remain in his own home in Richmond, upon taking an oath to say nothing "prejudicial to the Confederacy." Tiring of confinement in his house, he purchased a farm in Culpeper County and removed there in January, 1863, where he denounced and criticised secession and the seceders to the Confederate officers who often were his guests. His home was always full of visitors, and Confederate officers and Union generals often sat at his table. He was arrested once again by order of General J. E. B. Stuart, October 12, 1863, but was released the same day and was not further molested.

[H—13]

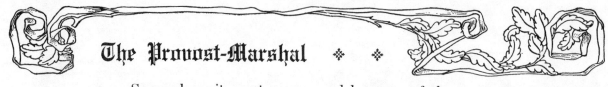

So much excitement was caused by some of these arrests that the House of Representatives in special session, July 12, 1861, asked for information regarding them, and for a copy of the opinion of the attorney-general sustaining the right of the President or his subordinates to order such arrests. No action was taken, however, at this time. From the frequency with which these arrests were made on the order of the State Department grew the alleged statement of Secretary Seward to Lord Lyons, the British minister: "My Lord, I can touch a bell on my right hand and order the arrest of a citizen of Ohio. I can touch a bell again and order the imprisonment of a citizen in New York. And no power on earth except that of the President can release them. Can the Queen of England do so much?"

This statement, though often quoted, does not appear in any of the published correspondence or papers of Secretary Seward, and it is improbable that it was ever made in these precise words. However, it does express definitely and clearly the actual condition of affairs during the first year of the war. On February 14, 1862, according to the proclamation of President Lincoln, the custody of all prisoners of state was transferred from the Department of State to that of War, and only the latter department was thereafter authorized to make arrests. Secretary Stanton, on the same day, issued an order directing that "all political prisoners or state prisoners now held in military custody be released on their subscribing a parole engaging them to render no aid or comfort to the enemies in hostility to the United States. The Secretary of War will, however, in his discretion except . . . others whose release at the present moment may be deemed incompatible with the public safety. . . . Extraordinary arrests will hereafter be made under the direction of the military authorities alone."

In some cases commissions of two, one a soldier the other a civilian, were authorized to hear the cases *ex parte* and report. General John A. Dix and Edwards Pierrepont examined the

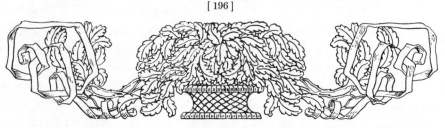

JOHN MINOR BOTTS AND HIS FAMILY—1863

A peaceful scene for Culpeper County, Virginia, whose fair acres were ploughed with shot and shell, and whose soil was reddened with the blood of its sons, during the year 1863. The firm chin and close-set mouth of John Minor Botts stamp him a man of determination. He disbelieved in the right of secession and loudly proclaimed his disbelief until he landed in a Richmond jail. When he was finally convinced that he would not be allowed to attack the Confederacy, verbally or otherwise, in the city of Richmond, he betook himself and his family to Culpeper County, where he talked pretty much as he pleased. Even in Richmond his detention was only temporary. Though it was evident that under war conditions many sudden arrests must be made, a resolution authorizing the President to suspend the writ of *habeas corpus* was not passed until February 27, 1862. It was a month after this when John Minor Botts was arrested. The President's authority to suspend the writ was extended on October 13, 1862, to February 12, 1863. The writ was not again suspended until February, 1864, when Congress suspended it in the case of prisoners whose arrest was authorized by the President or the Secretary of War. This act expired on the 2d of August, 1864, and was never renewed, even at the President's request, so jealous of personal liberty were the Southerners.

prisoners in Forts Lafayette and Warren in the early part of 1862 and recommended the discharge of a considerable number, as no charges whatever had been made against them. These were generally discharged upon taking the oath of allegiance to the United States. Many, however, refused to take the oath, saying that though no charges had been brought against them, such action would be in effect a confession of guilt. For example, Charles Howard; his son, Francis Key Howard, Henry M. Warfield, and other Baltimore prisoners remained in confinement until they were released without conditions, though release on taking an oath had been previously offered.

The policy of arbitrary arrests was extensively employed to crush out secession sentiment in Maryland. The mayor of Baltimore, the chief of police, and the entire board of police commissioners of the city were arrested, not as a result of their action in the Baltimore riots of April 19, 1861, where they seem to have done their best to protect the Sixth Massachusetts regiment, but because their opposition to the passage of further troops through Baltimore was deemed seditious, and their sympathies were supposed to be with the South. Many members of the Maryland legislature were also arrested on and after September 20, 1861, and confined first in Fort McHenry, then in Fort Lafayette, and finally in Fort Warren, in order to forestall the passage of an act of secession. Some of these were soon released after taking the oath of allegiance, but several were confined for months. A number of arrests were also made through the rural counties of Maryland, and out of these grew one of the most interesting cases of the war.

Richard B. Carmichael, a judge of the State court, was a man of courage, devoted to his profession, and almost fanatical in his belief in the supremacy of the law and the strict construction of the Constitution. In 1861, he charged the grand juries of his circuit that these arrests were unlawful and that it was the duty of that body to return indictments against those responsible. His charge, which followed closely the

CASTLE THUNDER IN RICHMOND—THE CHIEF PROVOST PRISON IN THE SOUTH

This ancient tobacco-factory, with the platform for drying the leaf suspended in front, and the bedding hanging from an unbarred window, looked far from warlike as its picture was taken in 1865. Aside from the soldiers, there is no indication that this was the penitentiary of the Confederacy. In it were confined Confederates under sentence of military court, deserters, and only rarely Union soldiers. The commander, Captain G. W. Alexander, was a disabled soldier, a man of great vigor and determination. He enforced discipline, but his motley crew sometimes required vigorous measures. The management of the prison was investigated in 1863 by a committee of the Confederate Congress. The majority of the committee acquitted Captain Alexander, though two minority reports were submitted. The most difficult prisoners with whom he had to deal were said to be "plug-uglies," of Baltimore and the "wharf-rats" of New Orleans. Among his charges were many who thought nothing of murdering. Arbitrary arrests

PHOTOGRAPHER AND PRISON

were less frequent in the South than in the North. President Davis did not assume the right to suspend the writ of *habeas corpus*, and this privilege was grudgingly granted him by the Confederate Congress for only limited periods. The larger number of arrests were made at first under what was known as the "Alien Enemies Act," approved by the President August 8, 1861. On August 30th a commission was appointed on the suggestion of General J. H. Winder, who wrote to the Secretary of War that he believed that many of the prisoners who had been arrested should be discharged. A general jail delivery followed. The jealousy of arbitrary power common to the Southerner was shown by the attitude of the Confederate Congress, the Governors, and Legislatures, who viewed with alarm any curtailment of the power of the courts. Military officers were instructed to obey the writ of *habeas corpus* and, if the judge ordered the discharge of the prisoner, to obey. Afterward, they might then appeal to the Confederate district judge.

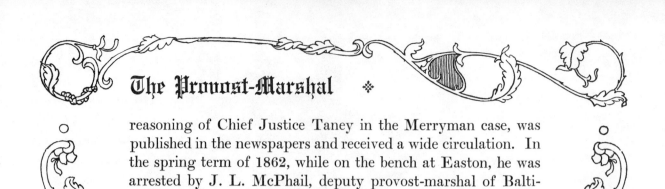

reasoning of Chief Justice Taney in the Merryman case, was published in the newspapers and received a wide circulation. In the spring term of 1862, while on the bench at Easton, he was arrested by J. L. McPhail, deputy provost-marshal of Baltimore.

Refusing to recognize the authority of the provost-marshal, and resisting arrest, he was taken by force and beaten about the head and face. After confinement for a time in Fort McHenry, he was transferred to Fort Lafayette, and then to Fort Delaware. He constantly demanded that he be furnished with a copy of the charges against him or be brought to trial. Neither was ever done, but he was unconditionally released on December 4, 1862, and as his place on the bench had not been filled, he returned to his duties. Undaunted by his experiences, he again charged the grand jury to bring indictments against the instruments of these arrests, but the vigorous action of the United States authorities had convinced the people that opposition was useless, and the grand jury returned no indictments. Judge Carmichael, disappointed at this lack of spirit, resigned his position and retired to his farm.

Another case of interest was that of Mrs. Rose O'Neal Greenhow, the charming widow of Robert Greenhow, who was arrested on the 23d of August, 1861, on the charge of being a spy, confined for a time in her own house, and then transferred to the Old Capitol. After being confined until June 2, 1862, she was released and sent within the Confederate lines, after taking an oath that she would not return. With her were sent Mrs. Augusta Morris and Mrs. C. V. Baxley, against whom similar charges had been brought.

In 1862, a partisan character began to be attached to the arrests. It was charged that many were arrested purely on account of politics. In some of the Western States these arrests influenced the elections of the year. In Ohio, an old man of seventy, Dr. Edson B. Olds, formerly a member of the United States House of Representatives for six years,

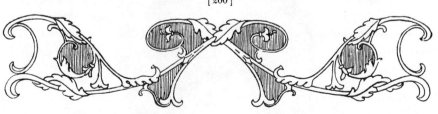

HEADQUARTERS OF PROVOST–MARSHAL–GENERAL, DEFENSES SOUTH OF THE POTOMAC

Provost-marshals were appointed for every military department, even if no active warfare was in progress within its limits. They assumed the right to arrest citizens on suspicion and confine them without trial. Not all the military commanders viewed the activity of these officers with satisfaction. General S. R. Curtis stated that the "creation of the so-called provost-marshal invented a spurious military officer which has embarrassed the service. . . . Everybody appoints provost-marshals and these officers seem to exercise plenary powers." General Schofield quoted this statement with approval, and said that these officers were "entirely independent of all commanders except the commander of the department, and hence of necessity pretty much independent of them." The provost-marshals continued, nevertheless, to exercise large authority.

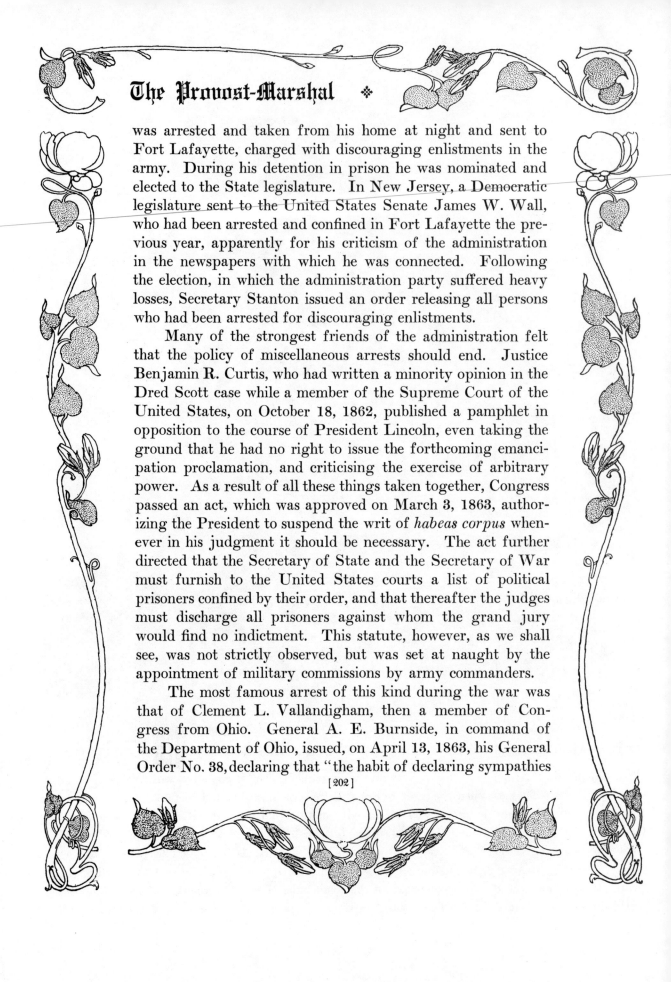

was arrested and taken from his home at night and sent to Fort Lafayette, charged with discouraging enlistments in the army. During his detention in prison he was nominated and elected to the State legislature. In New Jersey, a Democratic legislature sent to the United States Senate James W. Wall, who had been arrested and confined in Fort Lafayette the previous year, apparently for his criticism of the administration in the newspapers with which he was connected. Following the election, in which the administration party suffered heavy losses, Secretary Stanton issued an order releasing all persons who had been arrested for discouraging enlistments.

Many of the strongest friends of the administration felt that the policy of miscellaneous arrests should end. Justice Benjamin R. Curtis, who had written a minority opinion in the Dred Scott case while a member of the Supreme Court of the United States, on October 18, 1862, published a pamphlet in opposition to the course of President Lincoln, even taking the ground that he had no right to issue the forthcoming emancipation proclamation, and criticising the exercise of arbitrary power. As a result of all these things taken together, Congress passed an act, which was approved on March 3, 1863, authorizing the President to suspend the writ of *habeas corpus* whenever in his judgment it should be necessary. The act further directed that the Secretary of State and the Secretary of War must furnish to the United States courts a list of political prisoners confined by their order, and that thereafter the judges must discharge all prisoners against whom the grand jury would find no indictment. This statute, however, as we shall see, was not strictly observed, but was set at naught by the appointment of military commissions by army commanders.

The most famous arrest of this kind during the war was that of Clement L. Vallandigham, then a member of Congress from Ohio. General A. E. Burnside, in command of the Department of Ohio, issued, on April 13, 1863, his General Order No. 38, declaring that "the habit of declaring sympathies

FORD'S THEATER IN WASHINGTON, WHERE LINCOLN WAS SHOT

Within this building the shot rang out that struck a fearful blow to the South as well as to the North. On the night of Friday, April 14, 1865, President Lincoln went to Ford's Theater. About ten o'clock he was shot by John Wilkes Booth. The next morning about seven the President died. As General Sherman was entering a car three days later at Durham Station, N. C., to meet General Johnston and negotiate terms of surrender, he received a telegram telling him of Lincoln's death. None of the Confederate officers had heard of Lincoln's assassination, and when Sherman made this fact known to Generals Johnston and Wade Hampton and a number of their staff officers, they were sincerely affected by the news and shared the grief and indignation of the Union officers.

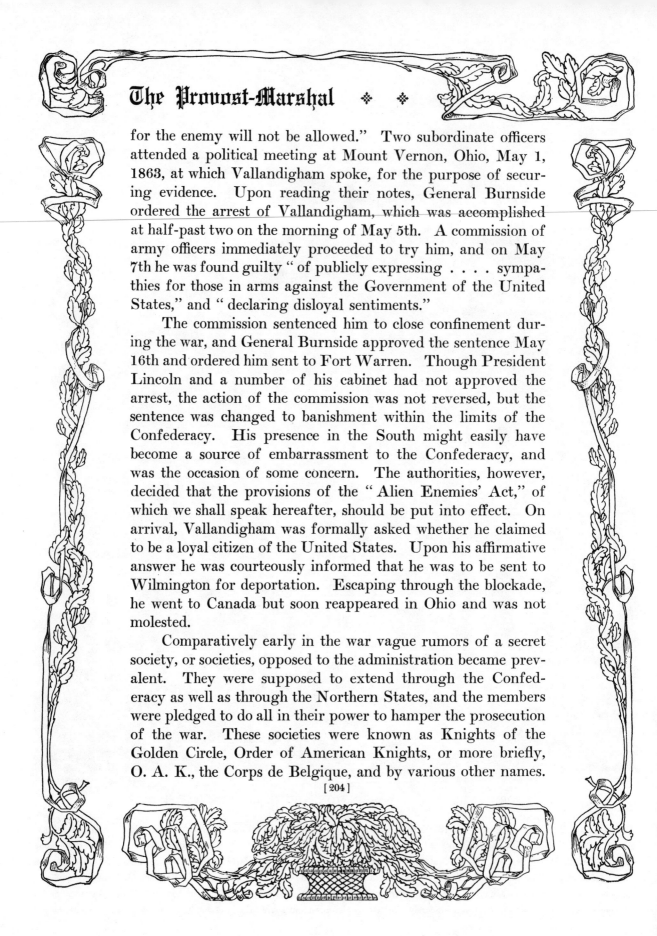

for the enemy will not be allowed." Two subordinate officers attended a political meeting at Mount Vernon, Ohio, May 1, 1863, at which Vallandigham spoke, for the purpose of securing evidence. Upon reading their notes, General Burnside ordered the arrest of Vallandigham, which was accomplished at half-past two on the morning of May 5th. A commission of army officers immediately proceeded to try him, and on May 7th he was found guilty " of publicly expressing . . . . sympathies for those in arms against the Government of the United States," and " declaring disloyal sentiments."

The commission sentenced him to close confinement during the war, and General Burnside approved the sentence May 16th and ordered him sent to Fort Warren. Though President Lincoln and a number of his cabinet had not approved the arrest, the action of the commission was not reversed, but the sentence was changed to banishment within the limits of the Confederacy. His presence in the South might easily have become a source of embarrassment to the Confederacy, and was the occasion of some concern. The authorities, however, decided that the provisions of the " Alien Enemies' Act," of which we shall speak hereafter, should be put into effect. On arrival, Vallandigham was formally asked whether he claimed to be a loyal citizen of the United States. Upon his affirmative answer he was courteously informed that he was to be sent to Wilmington for deportation. Escaping through the blockade, he went to Canada but soon reappeared in Ohio and was not molested.

Comparatively early in the war vague rumors of a secret society, or societies, opposed to the administration became prevalent. They were supposed to extend through the Confederacy as well as through the Northern States, and the members were pledged to do all in their power to hamper the prosecution of the war. These societies were known as Knights of the Golden Circle, Order of American Knights, or more briefly, O. A. K., the Corps de Belgique, and by various other names.

WASHINGTON LIVERY STABLE, 1865

WHERE BOOTH BOUGHT A HORSE AFTER LINCOLN'S ASSASSINATION

After shooting President Lincoln in a box at Ford's Theater in Washington, April 14, 1865, Wilkes Booth escaped from the city. Guided by sympathizers, he crossed the Potomac near Port Tobacco, Md., to Mathias Point, Va., on the night of Saturday, April 22d. The following Monday he crossed the Rappahannock from Port Conway to Port Royal and took refuge in a barn. Here he was discovered two days later by a detachment of Company L, Sixteenth New York Cavalry, and killed. The assassination of the President was the result of a conspiracy. William H. Seward, Secretary of State, was attacked on the same evening by Lewis Payne, a fellow-conspirator of Booth, and was severely injured. Those suspected of being involved in the conspiracy were tried before a military commission convened at Washington May 9, 1865. Their names were David E. Herold, G. A. Atzerodt, Lewis Payne, Michael O'Laughlin, Edward Spangler, Samuel Arnold, Mary E. Surratt, and Dr. Samuel A. Mudd. Herold, Atzerodt, Payne, and Mrs. Surratt were hanged; O'Laughlin, Arnold, and Mudd were sentenced to be imprisoned for life, and Spangler for six years. O'Laughlin died in the bleak prison on the Dry Tortugas in 1867. Arnold, Mudd, and Spangler were pardoned by President Johnson in February, 1869.

The Provost-Marshal ❖ ❖

Many detectives were set to work to discover the secrets of the organizations and the names of the members. Numerous reports were made, some of them based upon the evidence of informers in the order, some of them upon rumors.

All of these organizations late in 1863 or early in 1864 were apparently consolidated under the name, Sons of Liberty, though in some sections the old names continued. The membership in the Middle West, particularly in the States of Ohio, Indiana, Illinois, Kentucky, and Missouri, was quite large, and some of the members undoubtedly contemplated secession from the Union and the formation of a Northwestern Confederacy. A plot to assist the Confederate officials in Canada to release the Confederate prisoners held at Johnson's Island, Camp Chase, Camp Morton, and Camp Douglas had among its principals some members of the Sons of Liberty. The leaders of the Democratic party, to which, naturally, the larger portion of the membership belonged, discountenanced all violence or active disloyalty, though Vallandigham was supposed to be the supreme commander of the order in 1864. The influence of this organization in discouraging enlistments and creating resistance to the draft was considerable.

The most important arrest in connection with the Sons of Liberty was that of Colonel Lambdin P. Milligan, whose case is important also in that it settled definitely certain disputed questions in Constitutional law. This individual was a lawyer and politician in Indiana, who was arrested October 5, 1864, by order of General A. P. Hovey, commanding the District of Indiana, and taken to Indianapolis, where he was confined. A military commission composed of army officers was appointed by General Hovey for trial of Milligan and several associates, under the charges of conspiring against the Government of the United States, inciting insurrection, and otherwise violating the law, but the chief specification in all the charges was their membership in the Sons of Liberty. The commission found the prisoners guilty as charged, December 18th, and sentenced

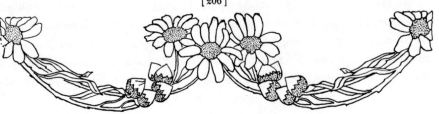

MILITARY COMMISSIONERS WHO TRIED THE LINCOLN CONSPIRATORS

On this and the following page are shown the members of the Military Commission appointed by President Johnson who tried the Lincoln conspirators. All except John Wilkes Booth (who was shot by Sergeant Boston Corbett) and John H. Surratt were tried by this body in Washington. The charges included the allegation that they were incited to their crime by Jefferson Davis and the Confederacy's emissaries in Canada. No proof of encouragement from high officers in the Confederate Government was forthcoming. The assumption of Davis' guilt was widespread, but evidence pointing in that direction was found to be untrustworthy, and the inquiry of a Congressional Committee in the following year was so convincing that the Confederate President was never brought to trial on the conspiracy charge. The commission was composed of officers of high rank and distinction. The members in this photograph, from left to right, are Generals Thomas M. Harris, David Hunter, August V. Kautz, James A. Elkins, Lew Wallace; and the man in civilian costume is the Honorable John A. Brigham, who assisted Judge Advocate Joseph Holt.

them to death. The findings were approved by the district and department commanders, but President Lincoln did not issue the order, without which sentence could not be carried into effect.

After President Lincoln's assassination, however, President Johnson approved the sentence and May 19, 1865, was designated as the date of execution. The sentence of one of the prisoners, Horsey, was, however, commuted to imprisonment for life, and Milligan and Bowles were reprieved until the 2d of June. Just before this day, through the influence of Governor Morton, the sentences were commuted to imprisonment for life. Meanwhile, Colonel Milligan had appealed to the Supreme Court of the United States, which took up the case and finally decided April 3, 1866, that "a military commission in a State not invaded . . . in which the Federal courts were open . . . . had no jurisdiction to try, convict, or sentence for any criminal offense a citizen who was neither a resident of a rebellious State, nor a prisoner of war, nor a person not in the military or naval service." Among the other points decided was that the suspension of the privilege of the writ of *habeas corpus* did not suspend the writ itself. This case was important, as according to it hundreds of trials by military commission in the loyal States were invalid.

How many persons were thus arrested and imprisoned without warrant during the course of the war cannot now be settled with any degree of accuracy, according to the statement of General F. C. Ainsworth, when chief of the Record and Pension Office. The records of the Federal commissary-general of prisoners from February, 1862, until the close of the war show that 13,535 citizens were arrested and confined under various charges. General Ainsworth is certain, however, that many arrests, possibly several thousand, were made by military commanders or provost-marshals, and were not reported to the commissary-general of prisoners.

Contrary to the usual opinion, arrests without warrant

MEMBERS OF THE MILITARY COMMISSION FOR THE TRIAL OF THE LINCOLN
CONSPIRATORS

Here are two more members of President Johnson's court of nine army officers appointed for the trial of the Lincoln conspirators, the Judge advocate, and one of his assistants. From left to right, they are: the Honorable Joseph Holt, Judge advocate; General Robert S. Foster; Colonel H. L. Burnett, who assisted Judge Holt; and Colonel C. R. Clendenin. The two members of the court not shown on this and a preceding page were General Albion P. Howe and Colonel C. H. Tompkins. The military trial in Washington before this court was as extraordinary, as were the methods of treating the prisoners, the chief of whom were kept chained and with heavy bags over their heads. Looking back, the whole affair seems more like a mediæval proceeding than a legal prosecution in the last century; but the nation was in a state of fever, and it was not to be expected that calmness would prevail in dealing with the conspirators. When the Lincoln memorial monument was dedicated at Springfield, October 15, 1874, the reticent Grant closed his eulogy with this tribute to Lincoln: "In his death the nation lost its greatest hero; in his death the South lost its most just friend."

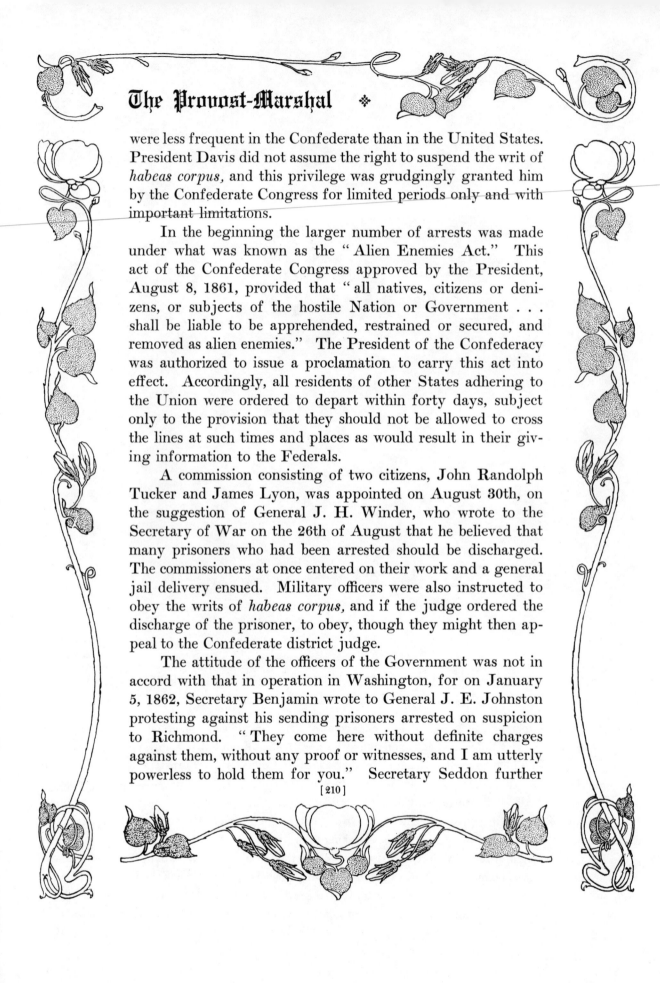

were less frequent in the Confederate than in the United States. President Davis did not assume the right to suspend the writ of *habeas corpus,* and this privilege was grudgingly granted him by the Confederate Congress for limited periods only and with important limitations.

In the beginning the larger number of arrests was made under what was known as the "Alien Enemies Act." This act of the Confederate Congress approved by the President, August 8, 1861, provided that "all natives, citizens or denizens, or subjects of the hostile Nation or Government . . . shall be liable to be apprehended, restrained or secured, and removed as alien enemies." The President of the Confederacy was authorized to issue a proclamation to carry this act into effect. Accordingly, all residents of other States adhering to the Union were ordered to depart within forty days, subject only to the provision that they should not be allowed to cross the lines at such times and places as would result in their giving information to the Federals.

A commission consisting of two citizens, John Randolph Tucker and James Lyon, was appointed on August 30th, on the suggestion of General J. H. Winder, who wrote to the Secretary of War on the 26th of August that he believed that many prisoners who had been arrested should be discharged. The commissioners at once entered on their work and a general jail delivery ensued. Military officers were also instructed to obey the writs of *habeas corpus,* and if the judge ordered the discharge of the prisoner, to obey, though they might then appeal to the Confederate district judge.

The attitude of the officers of the Government was not in accord with that in operation in Washington, for on January 5, 1862, Secretary Benjamin wrote to General J. E. Johnston protesting against his sending prisoners arrested on suspicion to Richmond. "They come here without definite charges against them, without any proof or witnesses, and I am utterly powerless to hold them for you." Secretary Seddon further

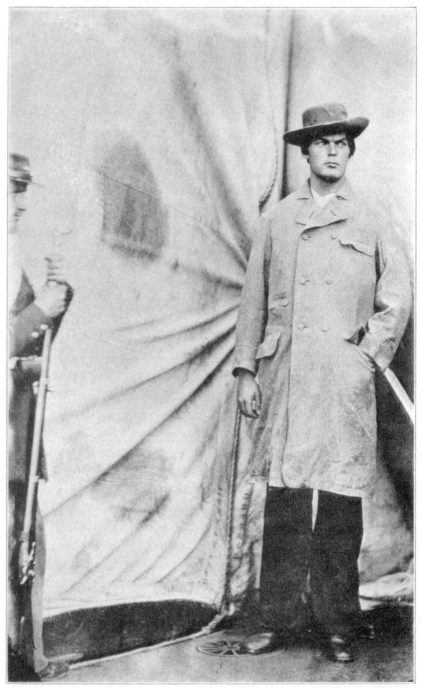

LEWIS POWELL, OR "PAYNE," SHORTLY BEFORE HE WAS HANGED FOR CONSPIRING
AGAINST PRESIDENT LINCOLN'S LIFE

This simple-witted but determined lad, with his sullen, defiant look, has just been captured for a crime that meant death. With the impulse of a maniac, he had attacked with a knife a sick man lying in his bed. On the night of April 14, 1865, the day of Lincoln's assassination, Payne secured admission to the house of William H. Seward, Secretary of State, and attempted to take his life. Secretary Seward had been thrown from his carriage and was lying in bed with his jaws encased in a metallic frame-work. This probably saved his life. The evil written on Payne's countenance tells its own story of the nature of the man.

says, in 1863, in response to a Congressional resolution: " No arrests have been made at any time by any specific order or direction of this department. The persons arrested have been taken either by officers of the army commanding in the field or by provost-marshals exercising authority of a similar nature, and the ground for arrest is, or ought to be, founded upon some necessity, or be justified as a proper precaution against an apparent danger."

The jealousy of arbitrary power characteristic of the Southerner was shown by the attitude of the Confederate Congress, the governors, and legislatures, which opposed any curtailment of the power of the courts. Though it was evident that a more expeditious method was desirable in certain cases, a resolution authorizing the President to suspend the writ was not passed until February 27, 1862.

This action was limited the following April, and it was provided that the act should expire thirty days after the beginning of the session of the next Congress. The act was renewed on the 13th of October, 1862, and the period was extended until the 12th of February, 1863. The writ was not again suspended until February, 1864, when the Confederate Congress did so in the case of prisoners whose arrest was authorized by the President or the Secretary of War. This act expired on the 2d of August, 1864, and was never reenacted, though President Davis recommended its continuance.

No complete lists of arbitrary arrests in the Confederacy are in existence, and we are able only to find a name here and there in the records. From the excitement caused by the arrests under the act for the suspension of the writ of *habeas corpus,* it would appear that they were comparatively few. Some of the governors, as Governor Vance, of North Carolina, and Governor Brown, of Georgia, were much aroused over the arrest and detention of some of their citizens, and, in heated correspondence with the War Department, claimed that the rights of the States were in peril.

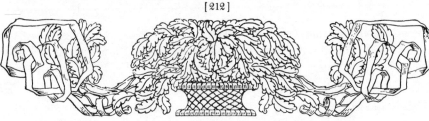

MEDICAL AND SURGICAL SUPPLIES

GUARDING SUPPLIES
FOR THE SURGEONS
WITH THE ARMIES.
WASHINGTON, 1865

UNITED STATES GENERAL HOSPITAL BY THE RIVER AT JEFFERSONVILLE, INDIANA

This type of hospital was highly recommended by the United States medical department, though it was not often built complete as shown here. The wards radiate like the spokes of a wheel from a covered passageway which extends completely around the hospitals. Inside this circle was a bakery, laundry, offices, and rooms for the surgeons. Notable are the roof ventilation and the large number of windows. Camp Nelson, shown below, was originally organized by Major-General George H. Thomas in 1861, for the purpose of bringing together the first Kentucky troops to go to the war. It was an open question that year whether Kentucky would espouse the cause of the North or the South. The Southern sympathizers, led by Simon B. Buckner, organized a State Guard, and the Union

A MOUNTAIN CONVALESCENT CAMP AT CAMP NELSON, KENTUCKY

A GOOD TYPE OF HOSPITAL CONSTRUCTION DEVELOPED DURING THE WAR

sympathizers organized an opposition force to which they gave the name of the Home Guard. When Fort Sumter was fired on, the Home Guard organized itself into Union regiments under such leaders as Thomas L. Crittenden and Lovell H. Rousseau. In 1861 Ohio and Indiana regiments crossed the State to Camp Nelson, and the men gathered there were the men that fought the famous battle of Mill Springs, one of the first Union victories. One of the reasons for the location of Camp Nelson was its proximity to the water. A large pumping-station was erected there on the banks of the Kentucky River. It was always a busy place during the war. No old soldier connected with the camp will ever forget the charming view of the old-style wood-covered Hickman Bridge.

WHERE THE KENTUCKY RECRUITS OF 1861 WERE GATHERED

MEDICAL DIRECTORS, ARMY OF THE CUMBERLAND, JUNE, 1863

The hardest task for a soldier is to remain quiet under fire without replying. Add to this the concentrated thought and delicate nicety of touch necessary to the treatment of mortal and agonizing wounds, and you have the task which confronted the army surgeon on the field of battle. During the first year of the war, before General Jackson had established a precedent to the contrary, they were also liable to capture and imprisonment. In war-time, army medical officers have many things to do beyond the mere treatment of the sick and wounded. Far-reaching health measures are in their hands. Vast hospitals must be organized, equipped, supplied, and administered, to which sick and wounded by the hundreds of thousands must be transported and distributed. There are subordinates to be enlisted, equipped, cared for, trained, and disciplined. No less than ten thousand medical men gave direct assistance to the Northern forces during the war. Under the agreement of the Geneva Convention, medical officers are now officially neutralized. This status cannot free them from the dangers of battle, but it exempts them from retention as prisoners of war.

DR. BLACKWOOD

(CENTER)

AND MEDICAL

OFFICERS

IN 1864

FIRST

DIVISION,

NINTH CORPS,

ARMY OF

THE POTOMAC

During the war forty surgeons were killed and seventy-three wounded while attending to their duties on the battlefield. Without the excitement of actually taking part in the fight, with no hope of high promotion, seeking no approval but that of their own consciences, these men performed their task actuated and sustained by no other impulse than the sense of duty. William James Hamilton White, of the District of Columbia, became assistant-surgeon in the regular army March 12, 1850. He was appointed major-surgeon April 16, 1862, and met

**WILLIAM JAMES HAMILTON WHITE
FEDERAL MAJOR–SURGEON**

KILLED AT THE BATTLE OF ANTIETAM

his fate five months later on the battlefield of Antietam. On this same day E. H. R. Revere, assistant-surgeon of the Twentieth Massachusetts Infantry, was killed on the battlefield. Other surgeons became ill from the excessive labor which they conscientiously and skilfully performed. Surgeon-General Hammond, accompanied by Brigadier-General Muir, deputy medical-inspector-general of the British army, visited the field, inspected the hospitals, and gave the sufferers the benefit of their professional skill soon after the close of the long and terrific battle.

SURGEONS AND HOSPITAL STEWARDS IN WASHINGTON

THE MERCURIAN DOUBLE-SNAKE ON THE SLEEVE IDENTIFIES THE LATTER

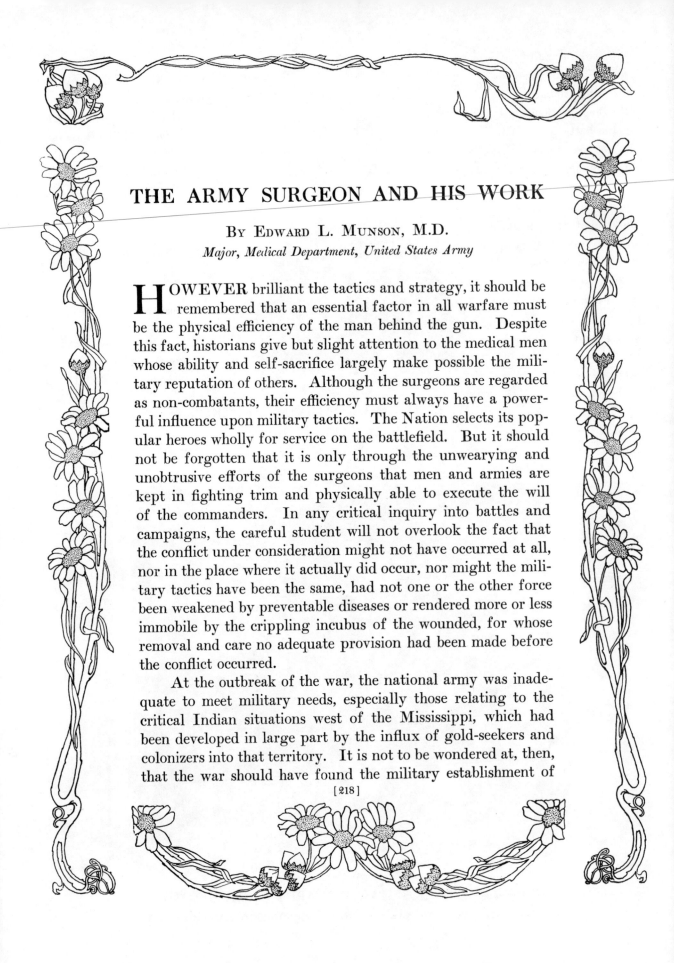

THE ARMY SURGEON AND HIS WORK

BY EDWARD L. MUNSON, M.D.

Major, Medical Department, United States Army

HOWEVER brilliant the tactics and strategy, it should be remembered that an essential factor in all warfare must be the physical efficiency of the man behind the gun. Despite this fact, historians give but slight attention to the medical men whose ability and self-sacrifice largely make possible the military reputation of others. Although the surgeons are regarded as non-combatants, their efficiency must always have a powerful influence upon military tactics. The Nation selects its popular heroes wholly for service on the battlefield. But it should not be forgotten that it is only through the unwearying and unobtrusive efforts of the surgeons that men and armies are kept in fighting trim and physically able to execute the will of the commanders. In any critical inquiry into battles and campaigns, the careful student will not overlook the fact that the conflict under consideration might not have occurred at all, nor in the place where it actually did occur, nor might the military tactics have been the same, had not one or the other force been weakened by preventable diseases or rendered more or less immobile by the crippling incubus of the wounded, for whose removal and care no adequate provision had been made before the conflict occurred.

At the outbreak of the war, the national army was inadequate to meet military needs, especially those relating to the critical Indian situations west of the Mississippi, which had been developed in large part by the influx of gold-seekers and colonizers into that territory. It is not to be wondered at, then, that the war should have found the military establishment of

Dr. Charles S. Tripler was General Mc-Clellan's first medical director. Although he had accomplished an immense amount of work, his machinery was not flexible enough to care for 100,000 men, and during the Peninsula campaign there was much confusion and an immense amount of suffering. But for the Sanitary Commission, which had charge of the hospital-boats near White House Landing and which cared for many thousands wounded and carried away hundreds, the distress might have been much greater. Dr. Jonathan Letterman became medical director of the Army of the Potomac July 1, 1862, succeeding Dr. Tripler. Dr. Letterman was a man of great ability; he organized the ambulance corps, improved the field-hospital service, and instituted a method of furnishing medical supplies by brigades instead of by regiments. Many of his innovations continued throughout the war. After the larger part of the Army of the Potomac had returned with General

DR. CHARLES S. TRIPLER
FIRST MEDICAL DIRECTOR
FOR
GENERAL McCLELLAN

Pope, Dr. Letterman found much difficulty in again organizing it properly. He was successful, however, and the care of the wounded after Antietam marks a distinct advance on anything before this time. During the first year of the Civil War it became evident that many of the forms then in use, especially the report of sick and wounded, were highly defective and unsatisfactory when applied to the new and broader conditions of war; and on May 21, 1862, measures were taken by the surgeon-general to secure much more detailed information in regard to cases of illness and injury, and in respect to other matters of record controlled by the medical department. Some years after the Civil War, however, the mass of records in the surgeon-general's and other offices became so great as to bring about the organization of a record division to take them over and provide for their preservation and care. On these records is founded the national pension system.

DR. JONATHAN LETTERMAN WITH HIS STAFF
DR. LETTERMAN SUCCEEDED DR. TRIPLER AS MEDICAL DIRECTOR OF THE ARMY OF THE POTOMAC,
NOVEMBER, 1862

the United States deficient as regards its medical organization and equipment.

At the opening of hostilities between the States the personnel of the Medical Department of the regular army was composed of one surgeon-general with the rank of colonel, thirty surgeons with the rank of major, and eighty-four assistant surgeons with the rank of first lieutenant for the first five years of service, and thereafter with the rank of captain, until promoted to the grade of major. There was no hospital corps, but the necessary nursing and other hospital assistance were performed by soldiers temporarily detailed to hospital duty from organizations of the line of the army, and here it may be parenthetically remarked that the qualifications and character of the soldiers so detailed were usually far from satisfactory.

The Medical Department, with the above personnel, formed one of the coordinate branches of the general staff of the army as it existed in 1861. Its members were not permanently attached to any regiment or command, but their services were utilized whenever required. Although a separate regimental medical service still existed in many foreign armies, as it did in our militia, experience had demonstrated that our national system of a separate department was better adapted to the needs of troops when scattered over an immense area, and usually serving in small and isolated commands. The latter requirements explained the unusually large proportion of surgeons necessary at the time, amounting to about one per cent. of the total strength.

This little force of one hundred and fifteen trained medical officers theoretically available at the beginning of the war was, however, materially depleted. Many of its members were of Southern birth and sympathy, and no less than twenty-seven resigned from the army at the outbreak of hostilities. Three who so resigned entered into the practice of their profession, declining to assist either against their Southern kindred or

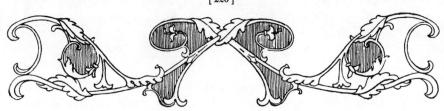

SURGEONS OF THE UNION ARMIES

The upper photograph shows the surgeons' headquarters of the third division hospital, Ninth Army Corps, in front of Petersburg in August, 1864. Not all of the ten thousand medical officers in the service of the Union armies were regularly enlisted, but some were civilians whose services were engaged for a limited time. The middle photograph shows the sur-

THIRD DIVISION, NINTH CORPS, AUGUST, 1864

geons of the second division, Ninth Corps, in front of Petersburg in October, 1864. The actual extent of the work of transportation of sick and wounded of which the surgeons of the Civil War had charge is sufficiently indicated by the fact that, as shown by the official records, the general hospitals alone contained at one time, on December 17, 1864, a total of no less than 83,409 patients, practically all of whom had been returned sick from the front.

SURGEONS OF THE SECOND DIVISION, NINTH CORPS, OCTOBER, 1864

MONOTONOUS HEROISM
THE ARMY DOCTOR IN THE REAR

The men in these photographs can represent only faintly the extent of the gigantic medical organization of which they were merely a small part. Many of the surgeons never got to the front, but served their country faithfully at the rear, watching the slow progress of typhoid and malaria cases. There was much typhoid at City Point on account of the difficulty of obtaining pure water. Nothing except the barest necessities could be brought to the front where large armies were contending. All finally came to realize that the nature and degree of sanitary relief must partake of a compromise except in the well-equipped hospitals in the rear. Besides medical, surgical,

AN ARMY SURGEON AT
CITY POINT
DR. J. M. GILL

and sanitary work, the army surgeon had another important duty of a generally professional nature. Every man who applied for enlistment as a soldier was given a medical examination. During the Civil War a total of 2,859,132 enlistments were credited to the several States and Territories; this number included men who enlisted twice or even a greater number of times. To give the number of individuals who served during the war is not practicable; nor is it important in this connection, since a physical examination was made by the surgeons for each reënlistment as well as enlistment. Besides the above total, some 67,000 men enlisted in the regular army, of whom probably one-third was not credited to any State. All this meant additional work.

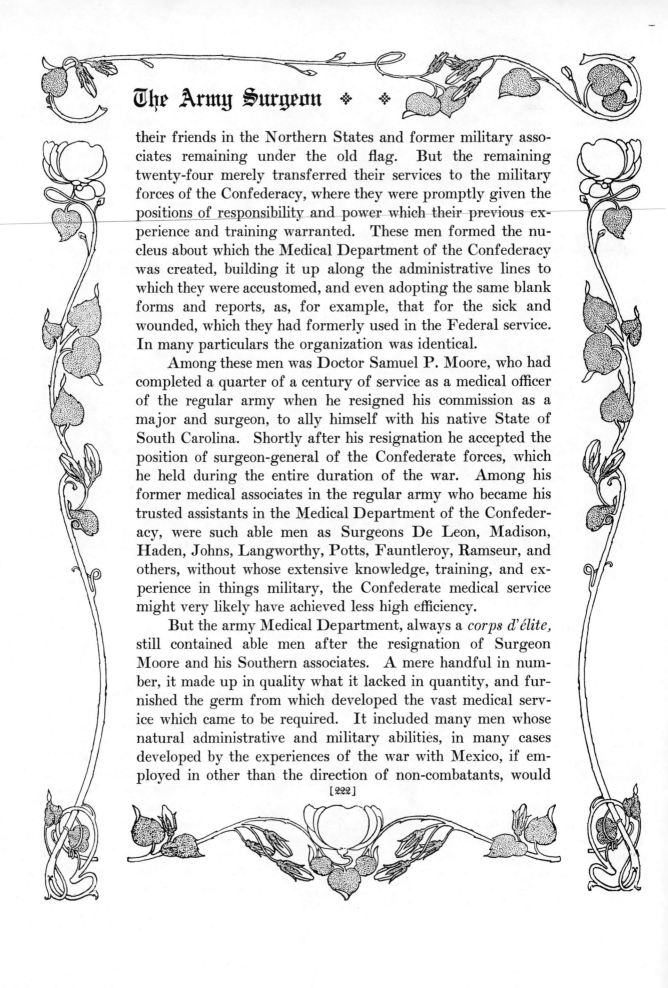

their friends in the Northern States and former military associates remaining under the old flag. But the remaining twenty-four merely transferred their services to the military forces of the Confederacy, where they were promptly given the positions of responsibility and power which their previous experience and training warranted. These men formed the nucleus about which the Medical Department of the Confederacy was created, building it up along the administrative lines to which they were accustomed, and even adopting the same blank forms and reports, as, for example, that for the sick and wounded, which they had formerly used in the Federal service. In many particulars the organization was identical.

Among these men was Doctor Samuel P. Moore, who had completed a quarter of a century of service as a medical officer of the regular army when he resigned his commission as a major and surgeon, to ally himself with his native State of South Carolina. Shortly after his resignation he accepted the position of surgeon-general of the Confederate forces, which he held during the entire duration of the war. Among his former medical associates in the regular army who became his trusted assistants in the Medical Department of the Confederacy, were such able men as Surgeons De Leon, Madison, Haden, Johns, Langworthy, Potts, Fauntleroy, Ramseur, and others, without whose extensive knowledge, training, and experience in things military, the Confederate medical service might very likely have achieved less high efficiency.

But the army Medical Department, always a *corps d'élite,* still contained able men after the resignation of Surgeon Moore and his Southern associates. A mere handful in number, it made up in quality what it lacked in quantity, and furnished the germ from which developed the vast medical service which came to be required. It included many men whose natural administrative and military abilities, in many cases developed by the experiences of the war with Mexico, if employed in other than the direction of non-combatants, would

BREVET LIEUTENANT-COLONEL A. A. WOODHULL

BREVET LIEUTENANT-COLONEL J. J. WOODWARD

ASSISTANT SURGEONS IN THE UNION ARMY WHO BECAME FAMOUS IN AFTER LIFE

A. A. Woodhull was advanced to the rank of brigadier-general April 23, 1904. He became a lecturer at Princeton University, and is the author of several medical works. J. J. Woodward took charge of the pension division of the surgeon-general's office and of the Army Medical Museum, and helped to collect material for the "Medical and Surgical History of the War of the Rebellion." He attended President Garfield after he was shot. Charles R. Greenleaf was chief surgeon with the army in the field during the Spanish-American War, medical inspector of the army, 1898–99, and chief surgeon, Division of the Philippines. John Shaw Billings was in charge of the Medical Museum and Library in Washington until his retirement from the service in October, 1895. The following year he was appointed director of the New York Public Library, comprising the Astor, Lenox, and Tilden Foundations, which were consolidated.

BREVET MAJOR CHARLES R. GREENLEAF

BREVET LIEUTENANT-COLONEL J. S. BILLINGS

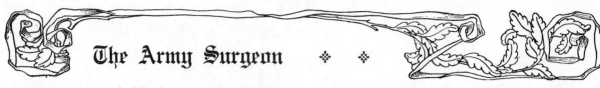

probably have made them national figures in the military history of the United States.

Some of the names on this medical roll of honor from the regular army are those of Finley, Hammond, Barnes, Crane, Murray, Moore, Sutherland, Baxter, Sternberg, and Forwood, all of them surgeons-general during or after the war. Others were Letterman, Smart, Woodward, Huntington, Otis, Woodhull, Smith, Greenleaf, and others whose great services might be mentioned. Many of these men became figures of national importance in a medical and surgical sense. Some in their time were recognized as the highest authorities the world over in respect to the professional subjects with which they had been particularly identified.

Contrary to the usual idea of the general public, army medical officers have many important duties outside the actual professional treatment of sick and wounded. Far-reaching health measures, under the direction of the commander, are in their hands. Vast hospitals must be organized, equipped, supplied, and administered, to which sick and wounded by the hundreds of thousands must be transported and distributed. This latter problem can advantageously be met only in the light of broad knowledge of military organization, methods, and purposes. There are subordinates to be enlisted, equipped, cared for, trained, and disciplined. An elaborate system of records, upon the accuracy of which the whole pension system of the Government rests, must be maintained. And upon the handful of trained regular medical officers the responsibility for efficient direction of the above-mentioned business management of the Medical Department had, at the outset of the Civil War, to devolve. From it, as a nucleus, there developed a scheme of organization of the medical service for war which remains the prototype upon which similar organization in all the armies of the world is now based, while administrative methods were worked out which still remain our standard for the management of similar conditions and emergencies.

SUPPLIES FOR THE MEDICAL DEPARTMENT IN WASHINGTON, 1865

"GLASS WITH CARE"

"Glass with care" is the label on the mound of boxes of medical supplies in the lower photograph. The elaborate organization of wagons, soldiers, clerks, buildings, and supplies shown in these two pictures was for the purpose not of making wounds but of healing them, not of destroying life but of preserving it. The place is Washington. In front of the supply depot guarded by three sentries and several officers is the rack used for tying horses. The street-car system in Washington had not yet de-

veloped. Because of the distances and mud no one walked who could avoid it. At the beginning of the war, each regimental surgeon was furnished with a suitable equipment for his regiment for field service in quantities regulated by the Supply Table. Later, when the regiments were brigaded and the regimental medical corps consolidated, the table was revised. The medical and surgical material available on the firing-line was practically that carried by the surgeon in his case, known as the "surgeon's field companion," and by his orderly in the "hospital knapsack."

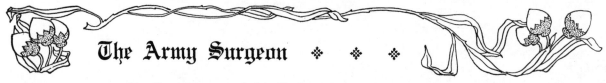

To the support of this little group, insignificant except in ability, the outbreak of the war promptly brought a vast number of the better type of medical men of the Northern States. Some of these physicians and surgeons had already achieved great fame and success in the practice of their profession, and their enrolment for the assistance of their country gave powerful incentive to similar action on the part of others of equal or less prominence. The younger medical men, lately graduated, flocked to the colors almost *en masse,* not only from motives of patriotism, but also because the practical training to be gained in the vast military hospitals was far more comprehensive and valuable than could be gained in any similar civil institution or walk of life. When, at the conclusion of the war, they undertook the practice of their profession in civil life, they found that their military experience placed them at once among the foremost of the local physicians and surgeons.

To give even brief mention of the self-sacrifice and achievements of the ten thousand medical men who, thus to aid their country, gave up the relative ease and the greater financial rewards of practice in civil life for the dangers and hardships of war, would require volumes. But it would be unfair not to recall the names of a few, whose services may have been of no whit greater value than those of others, who, for lack of space, must remain unmentioned, but whose professional standing during and after the war was such as to render them worthy of selection as representatives of the great volunteer medico-military class to which they belonged. Among such may be mentioned the names of Doctors Agnew, Ashhurst, Bacon, Bartholow, Bowditch, Bryant, Buck, Da Costa, Gouley, Gross, Hamilton, Hodgen, Pancoast, Shrady, Tyson, and Weir.

Under the agreement of the Geneva Convention, medical officers are now officially neutralized. This status cannot free them from the dangers of battle, in which they, of course, must share, but operates to exempt them from retention as prisoners

THE BOATS THAT BROUGHT MEDICAL SUPPLIES—APPOMATTOX RIVER, 1864

The upper photograph was taken about a mile above City Point. The supply-boat *Planter*, a familiar sight to soldiers, is lying at a little pier formed by a section of a pontoon-bridge. The lower left-hand photograph shows the *Planter* and more of the fleet in the service of the medical department. At the lower right-hand can be seen the steamer *Connecticut*, considered a "crack" boat in Long Island Sound navigation preceding the war. During part of the war she was used as an army transport on account of her speed. Immense quantities of supplies were shipped to the armies investing Petersburg, and the sight of these vessels gladdened the eyes of many a poor fellow in desperate need of what they brought, or waiting to be transported to the big hospitals or furloughed home.

THE BARGE AT THE MEDICAL LANDING

THE *CONNECTICUT*, FROM LONG ISLAND SOUND

[H—15]

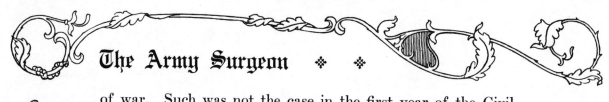

of war. Such was not the case in the first year of the Civil War, when surgeons were captured and immured in military prisons like combatant officers. Medical officers were thus often forced to make the hard choice of deserting the wounded under their care, often including patients from both sides who were urgently requiring attention, or of remaining and submitting to capture, with all the rigors and sufferings that this implied.

But General Jackson, after the battle of Winchester, in May, 1862, where he had captured the Federal division hospitals, took the ground that as the surgeons did not make war they should not suffer its penalties, and returned them unconditionally to their own forces. The neutral status of the surgeons, thus recognized for the first time, was subsequently formally agreed upon between Generals McClellan and Lee, though later the agreement was for a time interrupted. The idea that those engaged in mitigating the horrors of war should not be treated like those who create them, met with instant popular approval in both North and South, was subsequently advanced in Europe, and the humanitarian idea developed in this country was advocated until officially taken up by the great nations and agreed upon by them under the Geneva Convention.

In connection with the foregoing, the record of the casualties among the regular and volunteer Federal medical officers during the Civil War is of interest. Thirty-two were killed in battle or by guerillas; nine died by accident; eighty-three were wounded in action, of whom ten died; four died in Confederate prisons; seven died of yellow fever, three of cholera, and two hundred and seventy-one of other diseases, most of which were incidental to camp life or the result of exposure in the field.

The medical and surgical supplies for the Federal hospital establishments not accompanying troops were practically unlimited as to variety and amount. But with the material taken into the field with troops, considerations of transportation

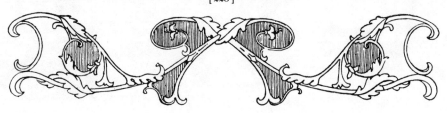

A HOSPITAL ON THE FIRING–LINE

CONFEDERATE CAMP IN FRONT OF PETERSBURG, CAPTURED JUNE 15, 1864

This abandoned Confederate camp fell into Federal hands June 15, 1864. It was used by the Union troops as a temporary hospital and camp. Three assaults had been made on Petersburg before this photograph was taken, June 24, 1864. The man with his arm in the sling is evidently one of the slightly wounded who was sent to this field hospital. It was not long before these rough shelters gave place to bomb-proofs and burrows. As the siege progressed the soldiers on both sides lived subterranean lives. Nothing was safe above ground within range of musketry fire. Even the resting-camps in which the relieving regiments took turns had to be heavily protected from dropping shells and long-range fire. It was in such exposed positions as this camp of abandoned winter-huts that some of the surgery had to be performed at the front.

were paramount. Generally speaking, ammunition was forwarded first, rations second, and medical supplies third. Owing to the tremendous number of men engaged, it was early demonstrated that road spaces occupied by marching troops had to be studied so that organizations could be moved and deployed as rapidly as possible. Nothing except the barest necessities could be brought to the front where large armies were contending. In spite of every effort, transportation always tended to increase. For example, when Grant entered upon his Wilderness campaign, it is said that his trains contained between five thousand and six thousand wagons, which, on a single road, would have made a column over fifty miles long. The first tendency of new troops is to overload, and to this neither the Civil War as a whole nor its medical service in particular proved exceptions. All finally came to realize that the nature and degree of sanitary relief which could be provided for troops at the front must partake of a compromise between what might be desirable and what was possible.

At the beginning of the war, each regimental surgeon was furnished with a suitable equipment for his regiment for field service, in quantities regulated by the supply table. This table, which was revised about a year later, seemed to contemplate the medical and surgical outfitting of regiments on the basis of independent service, and when they became brigaded much of the equipment so supplied was found to be not only unduly heavy and cumbrous but also unnecessary.

The medical and surgical material available on the firing-line was practically that carried by the surgeon in his case, known as the " surgeon's field companion," and by his orderly in the " hospital knapsack," a bulky, cumbersome affair weighing, when filled, about twenty pounds.

Wounds were expected—nay, encouraged—to suppurate, and that they could heal without inflammation was undreamed of by the keenest surgical imagination. Their repair was always expected to be a slow, painful, and exhausting process.

FEDERAL HOSPITALS IN THE CAROLINAS—"NO. 15" AT BEAUFORT, SOUTH CAROLINA, DECEMBER, 1864
CONVALESCENTS ON THE PORCH, STAFF AND FIRE DEPARTMENT IN FRONT

HOSPITAL OF THE NINTH VERMONT AT NEW BERNE, NORTH CAROLINA

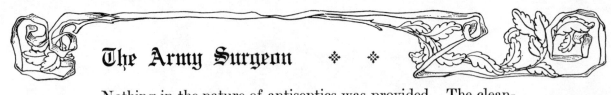

Nothing in the nature of antiseptics was provided. The cleanliness of wounds, except in respect to the gross forms of foreign matter, was regarded as of little or no importance. Even the dressings carried into action were few and scanty; where the soldier of the present carries on his person an admirable sterile dressing for wounds as part of his military equipment, in the Civil War the injured man covered his wounds as best he might with a dirty handkerchief or piece of cloth torn from a sweaty shirt. Elastic bandages for controlling hemorrhage were unknown, the surgeon relying, except in the case of larger vessels, on packing the wound with astringent, coagulant, and generally harmful chemicals. Medicines were carried in pill form, often largely insoluble and uncertain in result, or else in liquid form, difficult to carry and liable to loss. Soluble tablets were unknown. Crude drugs, like opium, were carried in lieu of their concentrated active principles, like morphine, now almost exclusively employed. Not a single heart stimulant of those regarded as most effective by modern medical science had place in the surgeon's armament carried in the field. A little chloroform was carried, but the production of surgical anesthesia was still a relatively new procedure, and several hundred major operations were reported during the war in which no anesthetic was employed.

In the first part of the war, each regiment had a hospital of its own, but the medicine-chest, mess-chest, and bulky hospital supplies were transported in wagons of the field-train, and hence were usually far in the rear and inaccessible.

Panniers containing the more necessary dressings, medicines, and appliances were devised to be carried along into action by pack-mules, but they were inconvenient and heavy, and were generally brought up in the ambulances after the fighting. Special wagons for medical supplies were then devised.

Surgical instruments were furnished by the Government to each medical officer, who receipted for and was responsible

CORONA COLLEGE, CORINTH, MISSISSIPPI

OFFICERS' HOSPITAL, NASHVILLE, TENNESSEE

McPHERSON HOSPITAL, VICKSBURG, MISSISSIPPI

CHESAPEAKE HOSPITAL, HAMPTON, VIRGINIA

MANSION HOUSE HOSPITAL, ALEXANDRIA, VIRGINIA

U. S. MARINE HOSPITAL, EVANSVILLE, INDIANA

HOSPITALS NEAR THE FIERCEST FIGHTING

Wherever great battles were fought, hospitals of more or less permanency, as well as temporary field-hospitals, were bound to spring up. At Corinth, which Rosecrans held stoutly against Van Dorn's impetuous attacks in October, 1862; at Nashville, where Hood was broken by Thomas in December, 1864; at Vicksburg, where Pemberton faced Grant until its fall, July 4, 1863; in Virginia, where the Army of the Potomac and the Army of Northern Virginia ranged over the ground again and again; even as far to the Union rear as Evansville, Indiana, hospitals were opened for the sick and wounded. Public buildings, schools, colleges, churches, hotels, and large mansions were all utilized for this purpose. Chesapeake Hospital in Hampton, Virginia, and Corona Hospital in Corinth, Mississippi, were female colleges before they were used as hospitals. At the Chesapeake about 700 wounded prisoners taken in the Seven Days' were treated.

FRIENDS' MEETING-HOUSE, CAPACITY 100

ST. PAUL'S CHURCH, CAPACITY 120

BAPTIST CHURCH, CAPACITY 150

GRACE CHURCH, CAPACITY 75

LYCEUM HALL, CAPACITY 80

CHRIST CHURCH, EPISCOPAL

CHURCHES USED AS HOSPITALS IN ALEXANDRIA

PRINCE STREET, WEST OF COLUMBUS, CAPACITY 95

CORNER OF KING AND WATER STREETS, CAPACITY 160

CLAREMONT GENERAL HOSPITAL, CAPACITY 174

WOLFE STREET GENERAL HOSPITAL, CAPACITY 100

NEW HALLOWELL GENERAL HOSPITAL, CAPACITY 50

GROSVENOR HOUSE HOSPITAL, CAPACITY 160

PRIVATE RESIDENCES USED AS HOSPITALS, ALEXANDRIA, VIRGINIA

for them. They were contained in four cases, one for major operations, one for minor operations, one a pocket-case, and one a field-case to be carried by the surgeon on his person into action. The instruments were well assorted, but they were used indiscriminately and without more than superficial cleansing upon both flesh and festering wounds, with the result that they habitually conveyed infection.

Under the surgical practice of the time, germs of blood poison, gangrene, and lockjaw were conveyed into the body. Moreover, it was the custom for the surgeons to undertake the most severe operations at the front, often under fire, under conditions in which even a pretense of surgical cleanliness could not have been maintained, even if the knowledge of the time had been sufficient to cause it to be attempted. What we would now term "meddlesome surgery" was not peculiar to the army but was characteristic of general surgical practice of the time. In fact, toward the end of the war the best surgeons in the country were probably those with the military forces, and the admirable results which they frequently achieved bear evidence, not only of their accurate anatomical knowledge and surgical dexterity but of the amount of injury and infection which the human organism can resist.

[For a further discussion of the personnel of the Federal Medical Department and the Surgeons-general and their work, see Appendices B and C.—THE EDITORS.]

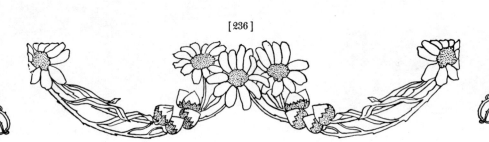

PART II
HOSPITALS

THE MEDICAL SERVICE
OF THE
CONFEDERACY

WHY THE AUTHOR OF THE FOLLOWING CHAPTER MUST RELY ON MEMORY AND PRIVATE SOURCES. —DESTRUCTION IN RICHMOND, APRIL, 1865 REACHING ALMOST TO THE CAPITOL ITSELF (IN THE REAR OF THE PICTURE), AND CONSUMING MEDICAL AND OTHER OFFICIAL RECORDS

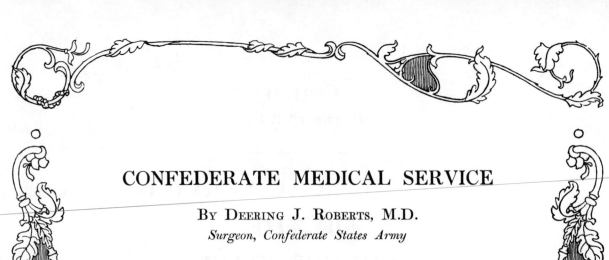

CONFEDERATE MEDICAL SERVICE

BY DEERING J. ROBERTS, M.D.
Surgeon, Confederate States Army

IN the conflagration in the city of Richmond, Virginia, on the night of April 2, 1865, on its occupation by the Federal army, two houses with their contents were completely destroyed; one occupied by Surgeon-General Samuel P. Moore as his office, and the one adjoining, in which were stored many papers, reports, and records pertaining to his office, and which had accumulated during the preceding four years.

While much has been placed on the printed page during the past forty years, including the numerous octavo volumes under the title of " The War of the Rebellion," and the larger but less numerous ones entitled " The Medical and Surgical History of the War of the Rebellion," in which other lines and departments of the Confederate States army, including their organization, acts and deeds, rank and file, field and staff, have place, giving records, reports, and facts, information relating to the Confederate Medical Department is scant and meager indeed. However, during the past few years, through the organization of the Association of Medical Officers of the Army and Navy of the Confederacy, a few material facts have been made accessible to the future historian, from which, with my own personal observations, limited though they were, was obtained the subject matter contained in the following pages.*

As the war dragged along, there was a greater want of medical, surgical, and hospital supplies among the citizens of the Confederate States in the territory not occupied by the

*See also Appendix D for information about the Organization and Personnel of the Confederate Medical Corps.

SAMUEL PRESTON MOORE
SURGEON–GENERAL OF THE CONFEDERACY

Dr. Samuel Preston Moore served as surgeon in the old army for many years. At the outbreak of hostilities he determined to follow his native State of South Carolina, where he had been born in 1812, and resigned from the army. He was almost immediately appointed surgeon-general of the Confederacy by President Davis, and served in that capacity until the end of the war. Dr. Moore did much with the scanty means to establish the Confederate medical service on a sure foundation. Though occasionally stern toward an offender, his words of encouragement were never lacking. Dr. Moore was a man of commanding presence. During the years after the war he became a noted and much beloved figure in the streets of Richmond, where he died in 1889.

Medical Supplies ❖ ❖

Federal lines than there was in the field and hospital service. The wholesale and retail dealers in drugs and medicines throughout the South usually kept large stocks on hand. The more prudent and far-seeing added to their usual stock in many of the larger cities and towns as the war-cloud darkened. These stocks were largely drawn upon by the medical purveyors, State and Confederate, and were supplemented by supplies from across the Atlantic, notwithstanding the rigid blockade of all Southern ports.

In connection with the ordnance bureau, an agency was established in London, with instructions to purchase and forward much-needed supplies for both Ordnance and Medical departments by every blockade runner, the vessels on their return trips carrying cotton to defray the expense. A separate agency for the Medical Department was established at Nassau. The cotton for the use of the Medical Department was purchased by special agents of the department, who were very active in the discharge of their duties, and supplies were shipped with commendable regularity.

From the time of the occupation of New Orleans by the Federals until the closing of the Mississippi River by the surrender of Vicksburg, considerable amounts of quinine and morphia were brought out of the Crescent City, at night, by fishermen in their small canoes or dugouts. The following incident is quoted from Dr. C. J. Edwards, of Abbeville, Louisiana:

Many and daring were the attempts of the distressed Confederates to obtain medicines during the war. In 1863, when Grant was besieging Vicksburg and his gunboats patrolling the Mississippi had cut the Confederacy in twain, my father was detailed from Wright's Arkansas cavalry, an independent command, to procure some quinine, calomel, and opium. He crossed the Mississippi River at Greenville, Mississippi, and proceeded with a buggy and horse to Canton, where he obtained the supplies. He made the return trip safely to the Mississippi River, only to find a gunboat in close proximity and no means of traversing the mighty stream, then bank-full. After considerable search he found an

THOMAS H. WILLIAMS
MEDICAL DIRECTOR OF THE FIRST
CONFEDERATE ARMY IN VIRGINIA

Dr. Williams was one of the regular army surgeons whose convictions led him to join the Southern cause. As medical director of the army in Utah under General Albert Sydney Johnston in 1859, he made an enviable record. In April, 1861, he resigned from the United States army, and on June 21st proceeded to Richmond. The following day he offered his services to President Davis, and was appointed surgeon in the Confederate States army. June 24th he was ordered to report to General Beauregard as medical director of the (Confederate) Army of the Potomac. He continued to hold this same position after General Joseph E. Johnston took command of the army. When General Johnston was wounded at the battle of Seven Pines, General Lee succeeded to the command. His medical director ranked Dr. Williams in the old army and therefore relieved him. Dr. Williams was afterward appointed medical director and inspector of hospitals in Virginia, and made his headquarters in Danville. He established nearly all the large hospitals in Virginia except at Richmond and Petersburg, and after a few months he was transferred to Richmond and put in charge of the "Medical Purveyors' Department," in which position he remained active till the end of the war.

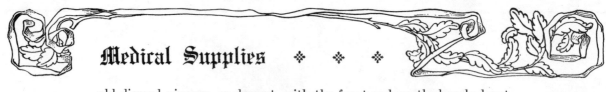

old disused pirogue, or dugout, with the front end partly knocked out. It was almost useless, but by loading only in the rear end he found the front would ride high enough to clear the water. He accordingly waited until night, when, under the convenient cover of darkness, he carefully loaded his frail craft with the precious burden, and stripping off, he swam the river in safety to the opposite side, pushing the dugout in front, keeping it properly trimmed.*

Supplies were brought into the Trans-Mississippi Department across the Rio Grande, from Mexico, close up to the time of General Richard Taylor's surrender to General Canby. Many petticoats were quilted in the shadow of the dome of the Capitol at Washington and in other Northern cities, worn through the lines by Southern ladies, and relieved of their valuable padding of quinine and morphia in Richmond. While "love laughs at locksmiths," love of country, inspiring brave hearts and stimulated by dire want, greatly aided in such important work.

In addition, on more than one occasion, valuable and greatly needed medical and surgical supplies were captured from the more bountifully supplied Northerners. Dr. J. B. Cowan, medical director of Forrest's cavalry, stated to the writer, that on one of Forrest's raids into western Tennessee, they captured and brought out a large wagon train, in which were three four-mule army wagons loaded with medical supplies, the remainder of which, after supplying his command very bountifully, were forwarded to Atlanta, Georgia. The value of that was estimated by Dr. George S. Blackie, medical purveyor there, to be fully equivalent to what would have cost the department at least one hundred and fifty thousand dollars in gold.

Finally, these means and measures were supplemented by a careful economy, and a resort to indigenous resources to be found in our hills and dales, fields and forests, mountains and

* *Southern Practitioner*, vol. xxx, page 535.

THE RICHMOND CITY HOSPITAL

Richmond, like Washington and Alexandria, became a collection of hospitals during the war. The accommodations of the City Hospital were soon exceeded, and the Chimborazo Hospital was one of those constructed to receive the overflow. The buildings composing it were beautifully located on a commanding eminence in the lower part of the city. The Confederate records of admissions to hospitals were destroyed in the burning of Richmond. Much of the nursing was done in private houses, and many of the soldiers wounded in the field were taken into adjoining houses, where they were concealed and guarded from capture. The total will never be known of the cases cared for by the women of the Confederacy, who fought for their side in combatting disease. When they were not nursing, their needles were busy in the cause. A soldier taken into a private house often went forth after his convalescence wearing a beautifully patched uniform and underwear made from the linen of the women, who sacrificed their own clothes and comfort for the benefit of the men at the front. Fighting on his own ground was a stimulus to defend the devoted and self-sacrificing women of the South.

THE CHIMBORAZO HOSPITAL, RICHMOND, VIRGINIA

valleys. There were probably at least three laboratories for the preparation of indigenous drugs established: one in Lincolnton, North Carolina; one at Macon, Georgia, and one west of the Mississippi, in which tinctures and extracts were manufactured to some extent.

One tincture in particular, well remembered and popularly known in field and hospital service as " old indig.," was used as a substitute for quinine in malarial fevers, a compound tincture of willow, dogwood, and yellow-poplar barks. Efforts were made to cultivate the poppy (*Papaver somniferum*) in Florida and North Carolina, and the unripe seed-capsules, when incised, yielded or exuded a dark gum, not unlike Turkish opium in its effects. Decoctions and tinctures of Jamestown or common jimson-weed, leaves and seeds (*Stramonium*), and maypop root (*Passiflora incarnata*) were employed for the relief of pain, both internally and as a local application. Boneset (*Eupatorium perfoliatum*) and yellow jasmin (*Gelsemium sempervirens*), the former used as an antipyretic and the latter to control nervous symptoms in fever; queen's-root (*Stillingia*), in all conditions of depraved blood; the inner bark and pith of the common alder for making salve for ulcers and chronic suppurating wounds; and fresh slippery-elm bark, the root and leaves of the mauva plant, and the leaves of the prickly pear, or cactus, when shorn of its spines, well pounded and macerated, as an emollient poultice, were among the most prominent of the indigenous remedies.

Many Confederate surgeons reported that at no time did they fail in having an ample supply of three most important drugs, quinine, morphia, and chloroform. Furthermore, in all the writer's service there was not a death from chloroform in field or hospital. Dr. Chaillé reported one case, immediately following an amputation just above the knee.

Other surgeons reported good success or " luck," among whom could be recalled Dr. J. B. Cowan, medical director, Forrest's cavalry; Dr. J. M. Keller, medical director, Trans-

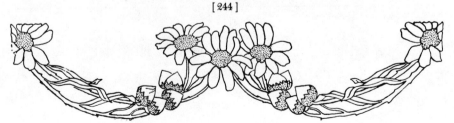

CONFEDERATE FIELD–HOSPITAL AT CEDAR MOUNTAIN, AUGUST, 1862

The Confederate loss at Cedar Mountain, known to the Confederacy as the battle of Cedar Run, was about thirteen hundred men. General Banks, who had the temerity to attack General Jackson with less than half that redoubtable Confederate general's force, suffered a loss of twenty-four hundred men. The medical corps of the Confederate army had not yet run short of medicines, books, surgical instruments, and supplies as it did later in the war. As the fighting dragged on, there was a greater want of medical, surgical, and hospital supplies among the citizens of the Confederate States in the territory not occupied by the Federal lines than there was in their field and hospital service. The Union had not yet developed an efficient cavalry corps, and among the supply wagons that fell prey to the swift-moving Confederate cavalry were some laden with medical supplies. The stocks accumulated by the wholesale and retail dealers in drugs and medicines throughout the South were largely supplemented from time to time by supplies from across the Atlantic.

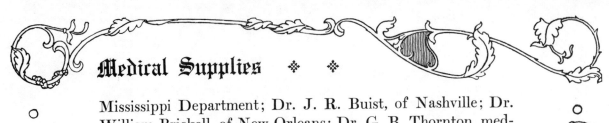

Mississippi Department; Dr. J. R. Buist, of Nashville; Dr. William Brickell, of New Orleans; Dr. G. B. Thornton, medical director of Stewart's corps, and others. Dr. Hunter McGuire, medical director of General T. J. Jackson's corps, collected fifteen thousand cases of chloroform anesthesia without a single death.

As for dressings, there were a few cotton manufactories in the South that made a fairly good quality of osnaburg from which bandages were made, in some instances rolled by the hands of fair women, or the medical officers and hospital attendants. Many households furnished old sheets and other worn cotton and linen garments, lint being made from the latter by scraping with a knife in some Southern woman's hands. Raw cotton, however, carded by hand, and in some instances separated from its seeds by the fingers of women and children, baked in an oven, in fact almost charred, was often substituted for lint, being rendered aseptic by this means, although we knew little of asepsis and antisepsis in that part of the "Sixties." When sponges became scarce, old but clean linen or cotton rags were used and then thrown away or burned, another aseptic procedure, although at the time that special designation had not been given it. Occasionally, silk for ligatures and sutures was limited, but it was as easily transmitted by blockade or the "underground" as were quinine and morphia; yet a few times I was forced to use cotton or flax thread of domestic make, and horse hair, boiled, to make it more pliant and soft—again accidental asepsis.

Water dressing for large wounds, amputations, resections, and extensive lacerations, was largely resorted to, by means of wet cloths applied from time to time, the nurse pouring small quantities on, or the automatic siphoning by means of a strip of cotton or linen, one end of which was immersed in a vessel of water suspended over the wound, the other hanging down a little lower than the bottom of the water. In that case a piece of oilcloth or part of an old piano cover was placed beneath the

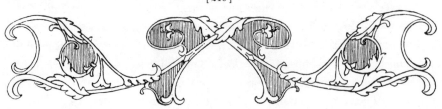

MRS. FELICIA GRUNDY PORTER
PRESIDENT OF THE WOMEN'S RELIEF SOCIETY
OF THE CONFEDERATE STATES

In the shadow of the Confederate Monument in the Mount Olivet Cemetery at Nashville, Tennessee, lie the remains of Mrs. Felicia Grundy Porter, who gave her time, devotion, and heart both during and after the war to the physical relief of the boys in gray. She was escorted to her last resting-place by Confederate soldiers riding on each side of the hearse, with many more following in its train. Mrs. Porter was born in Nashville, June 26, 1820. When the war broke out she set about establishing hospitals in Nashville for the wounded Confederate soldiers. She labored without stint as president of the Women's Relief Society, first of Tennessee, and then of the entire Confederate States. She collected a vast fund for this humanitarian purpose. As president of the Benevolent Society of Tennessee, she arranged for a series of concerts and tableaux in its towns and cities, the receipts from which were expended in buying artificial limbs for the disabled Confederate soldiers.

wound, so arranged as to drain the excess of water into another vessel on the floor at the bunk side. In some cases minor amputations, gunshot and incised wounds limited in degree of severity were hermetically sealed by adhesive plaster, or the starch bandage, securing " union by first intention." But suppuration was largely the rule, and in extensive wounds " laudable pus " was regarded as essential.

Instruments were procured by the medical bureau in the earlier part of the war from stock in the hands of dealers in the larger cities, later by blockade-runners, and by the handiwork of a few skilled workers in metals in the Southern States. Some were somewhat crude and clumsy, and lacked the beautiful polish and finish given by the experienced and well-equipped instrument maker. Occasionally a fortunate surgeon would acquire a good case of instruments by capture; but quite a number of our surgeons brought from their homes both amputating- and pocket-cases, their private property purchased before the coming on of hostilities.

Books were far more scarce than instruments. However, those who so desired could at times provide themselves in a meager way. Some surgeons made a point of calling on village and country practitioners in the vicinity of the army, and on more than one occasion, during such peregrinations, managed to make a purchase of medical works. The author has now in his library a copy of " Erichsen's Surgery," purchased from a Doctor Johnson in the vicinity of Clinton, Louisiana, just after the battle of Baton Rouge, August, 1862. The price paid was one ounce of " P. & W." sulphate of quinine, of which I had at the time an ample supply. I have also a copy of Wilson's " Dissector," 1857 edition, which I had carried with me from home, and managed to bring back with me, it being less cumbersome than the text-book of anatomy by the same author. Other books which I managed to secure from time to time by " barter and exchange," but was forced to abandon because of their size and weight, were

FOUR

DISTINGUISHED

CONFEDERATE

PHYSICIANS

CHRISTOPHER HAMILTON TEBAULT, M.D.

MEDICAL DIRECTOR A. J. FOARD

The Confederate medical service had to contend with lack of medicines, supplies, and ambulances, but the resourcefulness, energy, and tact of its members rose superior to all obstacles. Dr. Tebault served as a field surgeon with the 21st Louisiana and 10th South Carolina regiments, and afterwards as a hospital surgeon. Dr. Foard was medical director of the Army of Tennessee. Dr. Graham was surgeon of the Sixty-seventh North Carolina Infantry. Dr. Kellar was medical director of the Trans-Mississippi Department.

SURGEON JOSEPH GRAHAM

MEDICAL DIRECTOR J. M. KELLAR

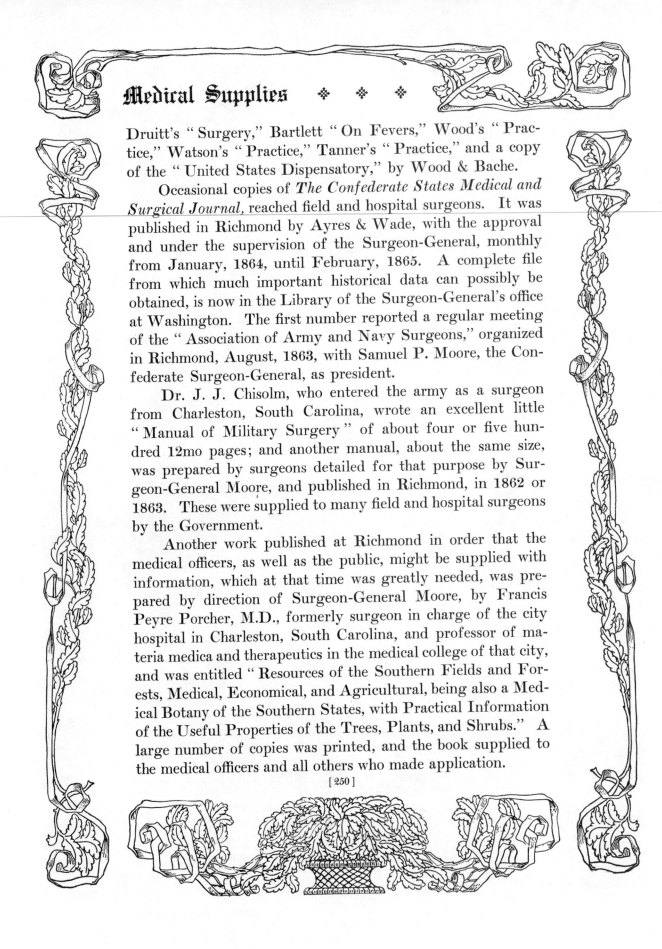

Druitt's " Surgery," Bartlett " On Fevers," Wood's " Practice," Watson's " Practice," Tanner's " Practice," and a copy of the " United States Dispensatory," by Wood & Bache.

Occasional copies of *The Confederate States Medical and Surgical Journal,* reached field and hospital surgeons. It was published in Richmond by Ayres & Wade, with the approval and under the supervision of the Surgeon-General, monthly from January, 1864, until February, 1865. A complete file from which much important historical data can possibly be obtained, is now in the Library of the Surgeon-General's office at Washington. The first number reported a regular meeting of the " Association of Army and Navy Surgeons," organized in Richmond, August, 1863, with Samuel P. Moore, the Confederate Surgeon-General, as president.

Dr. J. J. Chisolm, who entered the army as a surgeon from Charleston, South Carolina, wrote an excellent little " Manual of Military Surgery " of about four or five hundred 12mo pages; and another manual, about the same size, was prepared by surgeons detailed for that purpose by Surgeon-General Moore, and published in Richmond, in 1862 or 1863. These were supplied to many field and hospital surgeons by the Government.

Another work published at Richmond in order that the medical officers, as well as the public, might be supplied with information, which at that time was greatly needed, was prepared by direction of Surgeon-General Moore, by Francis Peyre Porcher, M.D., formerly surgeon in charge of the city hospital in Charleston, South Carolina, and professor of materia medica and therapeutics in the medical college of that city, and was entitled " Resources of the Southern Fields and Forests, Medical, Economical, and Agricultural, being also a Medical Botany of the Southern States, with Practical Information of the Useful Properties of the Trees, Plants, and Shrubs." A large number of copies was printed, and the book supplied to the medical officers and all others who made application.

PART II
HOSPITALS

———

THE SURGEON
IN
THE FIELD

———

PRAYER WITH THE WOUNDED AFTER SPOTSYLVANIA

THE PHOTOGRAPHER OF MAY, 1864, PRESERVED A MOMENT BREATH-
ING THE DEVOUT SPIRIT OF MILLET'S "ANGELUS." THE SURGEON'S
ASSISTANTS, HEADS BARED, AND THE NURSE STAND IN REVERENT
ATTITUDES; THE WOUNDED LIE LISTENING ON THE GROUND; WHILE
A CHAPLAIN POURS OUT A PRAYER TO THE ALMIGHTY THAT THE
LIVES OF THE STRICKEN SOLDIERS BEFORE HIM MAY BE SPARED.

ROUGH SURGERY IN THE FIELD

This is war. The man in the foreground will never use his right arm again. Never again will the man on the litter jump or run. It is sudden, the transition from marching bravely at morning on two sound legs, grasping your rifle in two sturdy arms, to lying at nightfall under a tree with a member forever gone. But it is war. The usual treatment of an ordinary wound during the Civil War consisted in shaving the part if necessary and washing it with warm water and a sponge. Asepsis was not yet understood. The sponge, used on any and all cases indiscriminately, soon became infected. Gross foreign bodies were removed and

FEDERAL WOUNDED ON MARYE'S HEIGHTS

the wound probed by instruments which were never sterilized and usually remained continuing sources of infection. The wound was usually protected by dressings of lint, the scrapings of which from cotton cloth by hand rendered its infection certain. Cloth or cotton compresses dipped in cold water were often used as dressings. Some surgeons used ointments spread on muslin. Flaxseed or bread poultices were often employed. In fact nearly every measure taken for the relief of the wounded was, through the irony of Fate and ignorance of infection, largely contributory in increasing the very suffering it was desired to prevent.

RED MEN WHO SUFFERED IN SILENCE

In modern warfare the American Indian seems somehow to be entirely out of place. We think of him with the tomahawk and scalping-knife and have difficulty in conceiving him in the ranks, drilling, doing police duty, and so on. Yet more than three thousand Indians were enlisted in the Federal army. The Confederates enlisted many more in Missouri, Arkansas, and Texas. In the Federal army the red men were used as advance sharpshooters and rendered meritorious service. This photograph shows some of the wounded Indian sharpshooters on Marye's Heights after the second battle of Fredericksburg. A hospital orderly is attending to the wants of the one on the left-hand page, and the wounds of the others have been dressed. In the entry of John L. Marye's handsome mansion close by lay a group of four Indian sharpshooters, each with the loss of a limb—of an arm at the shoulder, of a leg at the knee, or with an amputation at the thigh. They neither spoke nor moaned, but suffered and died, mute in their agony. During the campaign of 1864, from the Wilderness to Appomattox, Captain Ely S. Parker, a gigantic Indian, became one of Grant's favorite aids. Before the close of the war he had been promoted to the rank of colonel, and it was he who drafted in a beautiful handwriting the terms of Lee's surrender. He stood over six feet in height and was a conspicuous figure on Grant's staff. The Southwestern Indians engaged in some of the earliest battles under General Albert Pike, a Northerner by birth, but a Southern sympathizer.

HELPLESS WOUNDED DURING THE ACTION AT SPOTSYLVANIA

Written on the back of this print the editors of the PHOTOGRAPHIC HISTORY found the words: "On the battlefield of Spotsylvania, in the rear during the action." The place has been identified by comparison with many other photographs as Marye's Heights. Much of the battlefield surgery during the war was, in all probability, not only unnecessary but harmful. The rate of mortality after operation, 14.2 per cent., though shocking to the present generation, was inevitable, owing to the defective knowledge at the time as to surgical cleanliness. While the same number of operations could probably be performed by modern military surgeons with a small fraction of the Civil War death-rates, it is now recognized that most gunshot cases do better under surgical cleanliness, antiseptic and expectant treatment than by operation. The advantage of this conservative procedure was well illustrated by the war in Manchuria of 1903, where it is claimed that one-third of the Japanese wounded were able to return to the firing-line within thirty days.

FIELD AND TEMPORARY HOSPITALS

By DEERING J. ROBERTS, M.D.,

Surgeon, Confederate States Army

[The two articles which follow supply interesting personal reminiscences of hospital conditions within the Confederate lines. On the accompanying illustration pages will be found many examples of the hospitals and medical service in the Union armies, together with extensive description of Federal institutions and practice. The Appendices at the end of this volume supply some account of the system and organization, both Federal and Confederate, much of the latter appearing for the first time.—THE EDITORS.]

AS the records of the Confederate hospitals were burned in the surgeon-general's office at the fall of Richmond, it is difficult at this date to write of their work. But, from the writer's own experience and the accounts of others engaged in the work, it is possible to show something of what was attempted and accomplished in the face of difficulties which seemed insurmountable.

After some preliminary hospital experience at Hot Springs, and Bath Alum Springs, Virginia, I reported, in March, 1862, to Doctor S. H. Stout, who was just beginning his invaluable services as medical director of the hospitals of the Department and Army of Tennessee. Preferring active service, I was assigned to the Twentieth Regiment, Tennessee Infantry, with which I remained until paroled, after General J. E. Johnston's surrender.

On the morning of December 1, 1864, I received orders to go to Franklin, Tennessee, and make arrangements for the wounded of General Bate's division. I did so, taking with me my hospital steward, a detail of ten men, and two wagons.

MRS. SPINNER'S HOUSE IN 1862—USED AS A HOSPITAL IN 1861 DURING THE BULL RUN BATTLE

TWO OF THE FIRST FIELD–HOSPITALS

In such places as these the army surgeon worked, to the accompaniment of bursting shells which threatened to complete the havoc already begun, and destroy both the wounded soldiers and those who sought to relieve their agonies. The upper photograph shows Mrs. Spinner's house, between Centreville and the Stone Bridge, which was used as a hospital during the battle of Bull Run, July 21, 1861. Here the Honorable A.

THE STONE CHURCH AT CENTREVILLE—A HOSPITAL BEFORE BULL RUN

Ely, Member of Congress, and a large number of Federal troops were made prisoners by the Confederate cavalry. The Stone Church at Centreville, shown in the lower picture, had been used as a hospital only three days before, July 18, 1861, after the battle of Blackburn's Ford. The houses upon the field of battle, especially the first year, before the field-hospital system was perfected, were often utilized for army hospital purposes.

I found an old carriage- and wagon-shop about sixty by one hundred feet, two stories high. It had a good roof, plenty of windows above and below, an incline leading up to the upper floor on the outside, and a good well. This I immediately placarded as "Bate's Division Hospital," and put part of the detail to work cleaning out the work-benches, old lumber, and other débris.

Further up the same street, I found an unoccupied brick store, two stories high, eighty by twenty feet, and, on the corner of the square, the Chancery Court room, about forty feet square, both of which I took possession of, and put the remainder of the detail at work cleaning out the counters, shelving, empty boxes, and barrels from the one, and the desk, or rostrum, and benches from the other, sending the wagons into the country for clean straw.

Two assistant surgeons with additional detailed men reported to me and all worked diligently, so that, by the middle of the afternoon, the buildings were fairly well cleaned. The wagons did not have to go far afield, and each floor was soon covered with clean wheat-straw ten or twelve inches deep; and before midnight all the wounded were transferred from the field-hospital.

The provisional Army of Tennessee was at first, to some extent, supplied with spring vehicles as ambulances; but as the war progressed, hard usage and rough roads caused them to break down, and they were abandoned. Their places were supplied by ordinary wagons drawn by two mules and without springs. Staples on the sides of the body secured white-oak bows, covered with heavy cotton-duck cloth, with the name of the regiment, brigade, division, and corps painted on the sides of the white cover.

While such ambulances afforded somewhat rough riding for sick and wounded men, they were the best that could be supplied. Now and then, one or more well-built and equipped ambulances were captured; in which case it did not take long

INSTRUMENTS OF WAR AND MERCY—THE GUN AND THE CHURCH-HOSPITAL IN 1862

WHERE A WOMAN SERVED

In the foreground of the upper photograph appears a Confederate naval battery at Yorktown, Va., and in the background the Nelson Church Hospital. The photograph was taken July 1, 1862, after McClellan's army had swept past nearly to Richmond, leaving wounded and fever-stricken in its train. After the siege of Yorktown, the house which had been used as headquarters by General Cornwallis during the War of the Revolution was used as a hospital. It was placed in charge of Mrs.

CORNWALLIS' HEADQUARTERS A HOSPITAL IN 1862

John A. Dix, the wife of General Dix, then stationed at Fortress Monroe. Mrs. Dix was an enthusiastic Union woman who left her palatial home in New York to give her services to the suffering and wounded soldiers. The bricks of which this building was built were brought over from England. The hospital established here under the care of Mrs. Dix is said by old soldiers to have been one of the most convenient and pleasant of those established for the Union army in the early years of the war. Fortunately for the inmates it was never overcrowded.

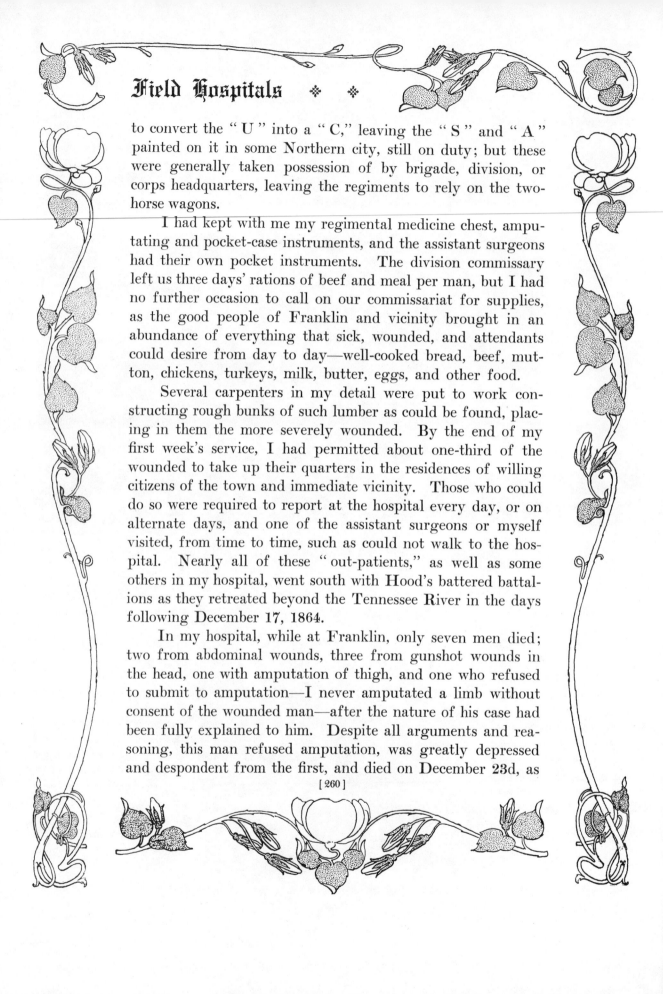

to convert the " U " into a " C," leaving the " S " and " A "
painted on it in some Northern city, still on duty; but these
were generally taken possession of by brigade, division, or
corps headquarters, leaving the regiments to rely on the two-
horse wagons.

I had kept with me my regimental medicine chest, amputating and pocket-case instruments, and the assistant surgeons
had their own pocket instruments. The division commissary
left us three days' rations of beef and meal per man, but I had
no further occasion to call on our commissariat for supplies,
as the good people of Franklin and vicinity brought in an
abundance of everything that sick, wounded, and attendants
could desire from day to day—well-cooked bread, beef, mut-
ton, chickens, turkeys, milk, butter, eggs, and other food.

Several carpenters in my detail were put to work constructing rough bunks of such lumber as could be found, placing in them the more severely wounded. By the end of my
first week's service, I had permitted about one-third of the
wounded to take up their quarters in the residences of willing
citizens of the town and immediate vicinity. Those who could
do so were required to report at the hospital every day, or on
alternate days, and one of the assistant surgeons or myself
visited, from time to time, such as could not walk to the hospital. Nearly all of these " out-patients," as well as some
others in my hospital, went south with Hood's battered battalions as they retreated beyond the Tennessee River in the days
following December 17, 1864.

In my hospital, while at Franklin, only seven men died;
two from abdominal wounds, three from gunshot wounds in
the head, one with amputation of thigh, and one who refused
to submit to amputation—I never amputated a limb without
consent of the wounded man—after the nature of his case had
been fully explained to him. Despite all arguments and reasoning, this man refused amputation, was greatly depressed
and despondent from the first, and died on December 23d, as

HOSPITAL WORK IN A FARM-HOUSE AFTER THE BATTLE OF FAIR OAKS—JUNE, 1862

The old farm-house in this photograph was serving as a hospital for the troops of Hooker's division after the battle of Fair Oaks, in the month of June, 1862, when McClellan had made his passage up the Peninsula in his celebrated campaign against Richmond. It lay to the right of the battlefield. To it the wounded were hurried in ambulances. The earliest arrivals were placed in the interior of the house and the slave-hut immediately adjacent. Those who were brought in later rested in the tents shown in the lower photograph.

Patients are visible in the windows of the building. Quite a number of the wounded soldiers who are able to walk have gathered in its shade and are giving earnest attention to the photographer. The medical department was charged with the transportation of the sick and wounded. This resulted not only in the organization of ambulance corps for duty on or near the battlefield, but in the organization and direction of wagon-trains, hospital railroad trains, and hospital ships plying from the field hospitals to those farther to the rear.

TENTS FOR THE OVERFLOW

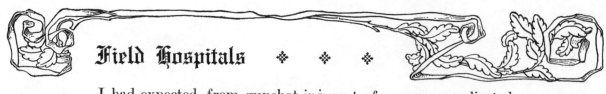

I had expected, from gunshot injury to forearm, complicated by nostalgia and despondency in an old man.

Largely predominating on both sides were the wounds inflicted by the rifled musket, carrying its conical ball of an ounce or more in weight. These wounds differed in some important and very material characteristics from all gunshot wounds in preceding wars, including that with Mexico; as well as those in our later experience with Spain, and those inflicted by the improved army-gun of the present day. The old round ball, of low velocity, caused many fractures in bones of the extremities. But it never produced such shattering, comminution, and amount of bone destruction and injury as did the heavy conical ball of increased velocity—both differing in character from the Mauser and Martini of the present day with their still greater increase of velocity—and its hardened or steel-jacketed projectile of smaller caliber, which often makes an almost clean-cut perforation, even through the shaft of a long bone.

The shattering, splintering, and splitting of a long bone by the impact of the minie or Enfield ball were, in many instances, both remarkable and frightful, and early experience taught surgeons that amputation was the only means of saving life. In the vicinity of a joint, the ends of the bone being more spongy, softer, and less brittle, the damage to the shaft of the bone was not so great, and the expedient of resection, largely resorted to and greatly developed by the surgeons, in many instances afforded a comparatively, if not perfectly, restored limb. Resections of the upper extremity afforded better results than those of the lower, although fairly good results were sometimes obtained in the case of the latter.

In some instances, I deemed it imperatively necessary to resort to a second, or even a third resection of the limb, even after the end of the bone had been sawn through, and while the patient was still under the influence of the anesthetic, the primary section furnishing the information that the bone had

CARING FOR THE WOUNDED FROM THE MISSISSIPPI TO THE POTOMAC

In the upper photograph are soldiers convalescing at Baton Rouge, Louisiana, from their wounds received on the Red River and Port Hudson expeditions, and below is Smith's farm near Keedysville, Maryland, close to where the battle of Antietam was fought in September, 1862. In the course of the day's fierce firing nearly twenty-five thousand men were killed and wounded. It covered a period of about twelve hours; few entrenchments or fortifications of any kind were used by either side. Dr. Bernard, surgeon of the One Hundred and Second New York, was made the chief of all the hospitals. One of the locations of his corps hospitals was on Smith's farm. In the background of the picture is a fine view of South Mountain. In the foreground the men are gathered about a fire.

AFTER ANTIETAM—ARMY SURGEONS, HUTS, AND TENTS FOR THE WOUNDED

been shattered, splintered, or split higher up than could be ascertained at first. Conservative surgery was, I might say, almost, if not entirely, a universal principle with the Confederate surgeon; conservatism, first, as to the life of the wounded soldier, secondly, as to his future comfort and usefulness.

Conical-ball wounds in the abdomen were nearly always fatal, far more so than those produced by the round ball with lower velocity. The intestines, in the former case, were generally perforated; in the latter, they often escaped this injury by being pushed aside by the slower moving round ball fired from the smooth-bore gun. The reverse of this was the case in wounds of the chest, since the round ball bruised and lacerated a large area of lung tissue, while the more swiftly moving conical ball often produced a clean-cut wound.

On December 25, 1864, my associates and myself, with the wounded of Bate's division, were all moved to Nashville, and placed in the large building on South College Street, built in the summer of 1861 for a gun-factory, where I, as the ranking surgeon, assumed charge of the twelve hundred wounded there assembled from the battlefields of Franklin and Nashville, assisted by nine other Confederate surgeons and assistant surgeons. On January 10, 1865, all the Confederate surgeons in Nashville were relieved by Federal surgeons, and we were sent by way of Louisville, Cincinnati, Pittsburg, Philadelphia, Baltimore, Fortress Monroe, and City Point to Richmond, reaching the capital, January 28th.

Remaining three days in Richmond, I visited every morning some part of Chimborazo Hospital, and other hospitals in the city. Leaving the capital, I went to Montgomery, Alabama, having thirty days' leave, and while waiting for the Army of Tennessee en route to the Carolinas, frequently visited a hospital there in charge of Doctor John Scott, an Englishman. He had been commissioned surgeon in 1861, assigned to duty at Pensacola until it was evacuated, and subsequently was stationed in Montgomery. The hospital was in a large

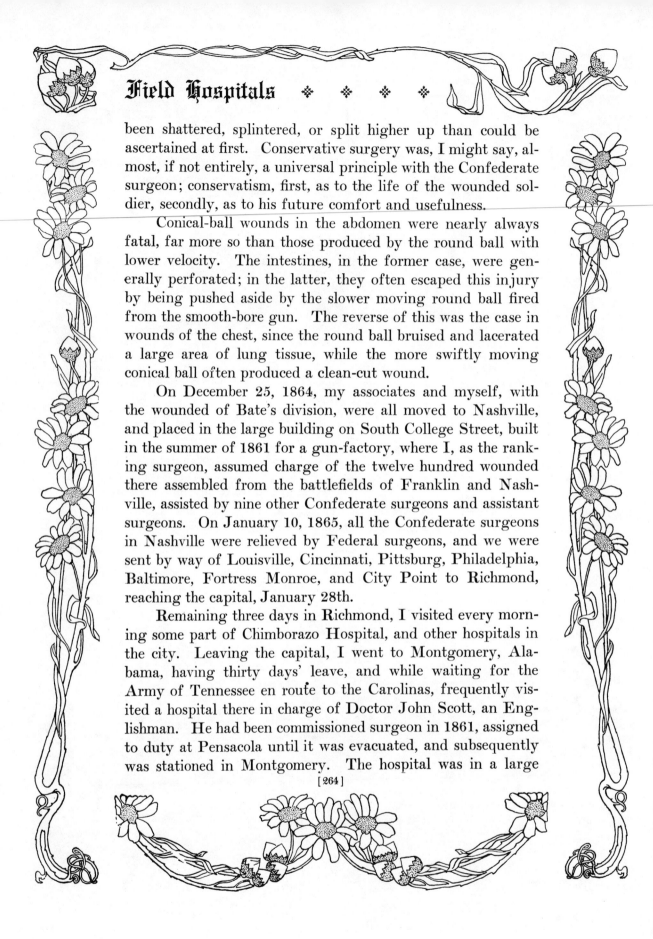

AN ARMY DOCTOR IN THE FIELD

C. K. IRWINE, SURGEON OF THE SEVENTY-SECOND NEW YORK INFANTRY

SEPTEMBER, 1863

Dr. Irwine is seen seated to the right of the tent pole, while the assistant surgeon faces him on the left. The quarters of a regimental surgeon were generally established on the line of the officers' tents, and he was usually open to calls at all hours. If he was a strict disciplinarian, he would only attend what was termed "the doctor's call" on the morning of each day. The words which the men humorously fitted to the notes of this call went: "Come and get your quinine, quinine, quinine; come and get your quinine—qui-i-ni-ine!" The Seventy-second New York took part in the battle of Gettysburg in July, 1863, and in the pursuit of Lee, and did duty along the line of the Rappahannock till October of that year. Its wounded were many, and the surgeons' duties were exacting during battle and for days thereafter.

SURGEON HAWKES, FIFTIETH NEW YORK ENGINEERS

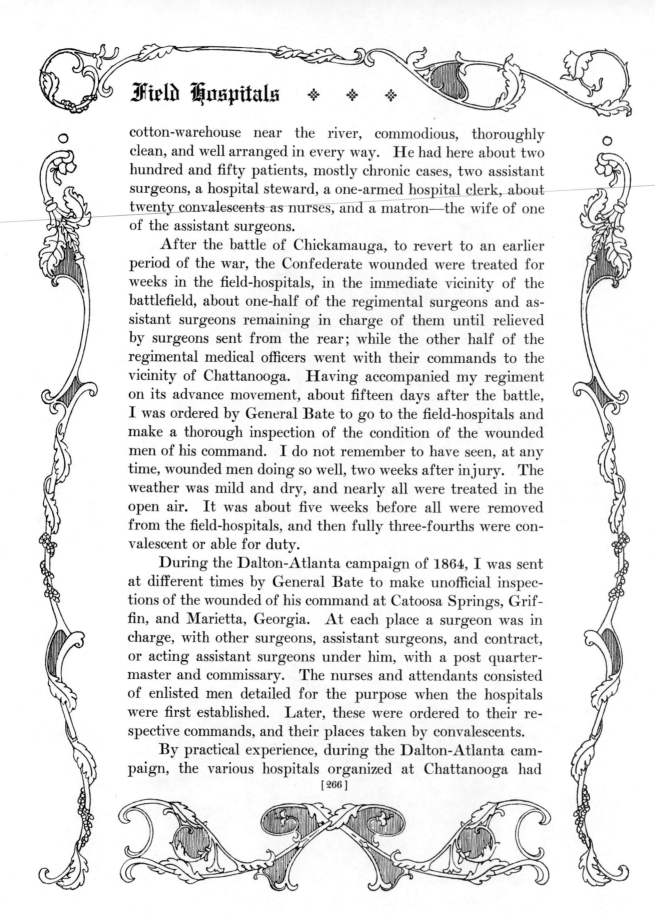

cotton-warehouse near the river, commodious, thoroughly clean, and well arranged in every way. He had here about two hundred and fifty patients, mostly chronic cases, two assistant surgeons, a hospital steward, a one-armed hospital clerk, about twenty convalescents as nurses, and a matron—the wife of one of the assistant surgeons.

After the battle of Chickamauga, to revert to an earlier period of the war, the Confederate wounded were treated for weeks in the field-hospitals, in the immediate vicinity of the battlefield, about one-half of the regimental surgeons and assistant surgeons remaining in charge of them until relieved by surgeons sent from the rear; while the other half of the regimental medical officers went with their commands to the vicinity of Chattanooga. Having accompanied my regiment on its advance movement, about fifteen days after the battle, I was ordered by General Bate to go to the field-hospitals and make a thorough inspection of the condition of the wounded men of his command. I do not remember to have seen, at any time, wounded men doing so well, two weeks after injury. The weather was mild and dry, and nearly all were treated in the open air. It was about five weeks before all were removed from the field-hospitals, and then fully three-fourths were convalescent or able for duty.

During the Dalton-Atlanta campaign of 1864, I was sent at different times by General Bate to make unofficial inspections of the wounded of his command at Catoosa Springs, Griffin, and Marietta, Georgia. At each place a surgeon was in charge, with other surgeons, assistant surgeons, and contract, or acting assistant surgeons under him, with a post quartermaster and commissary. The nurses and attendants consisted of enlisted men detailed for the purpose when the hospitals were first established. Later, these were ordered to their respective commands, and their places taken by convalescents.

By practical experience, during the Dalton-Atlanta campaign, the various hospitals organized at Chattanooga had

A WOMAN IN CAMP

"The touch of a woman's hands" came to have a meaning all its own during the war. The rough kindness of a comrade was as nothing compared to the gentle ministrations of a thrice-blessed damosel. This particular young lady seems remarkably bashful for one who has come to offer her services at Brandy Station, where a considerable portion of the army lay in camp in March, 1864. She can be seen again on the right of the photograph below, but her male escort has dwindled to only one or two, and she seems to have recovered her self-possession. In our admira-

tion of the ultimate efficiency of the medical department created in the Civil War, we must not overlook the fact that this was bought at the expense of such human agonies and sorrows as are, in the aggregate, beyond the estimate of the keenest imagination and sympathy. The Nation paid dearly, and in sackcloth and ashes, as it would pay in any future wars under similar conditions, for that policy of military unpreparedness, in which the medical service is necessarily made to share, which seems to form so fundamental and cherished a feature of our national policy of costly economy.

THE FEMININE TOUCH AT THE HOSPITAL

FIELD HOSPITAL OF THE SECOND DIVISION, SECOND ARMY CORPS, AT BRANDY STATION, VIRGINIA

A SANITARY–COMMISSION NURSE AND HER PATIENTS AT FREDERICKSBURG,
MAY, 1864

More of the awful toll of 36,000 taken from the Union army during the terrible Wilderness cam-
paign. The Sanitary Commission is visiting the field hospital established near the Rappahannock
River, a mile or so from the heights, where lay at the same time the wounded appearing on the opposite page.
Although the work of this Commission was only supplementary after 1862, they continued to supply many
delicacies, and luxuries such as crutches, which did not form part of the regular medical corps paraphernalia.
The effect of their work can be seen here, and also the appearance of men after the shock of gunshot wounds.
All injuries during the war practically fell under three headings: incised and punctured wounds, comprising
saber cuts, bayonet stabs, and sword thrusts; miscellaneous, from falls, blows from blunt weapons, and
various accidents; lastly, and chiefly, gunshot wounds. The war came prior to the demonstration of the fact
that the causes of disease and suppurative conditions are living organisms of microscopic size. Septicemia,
erysipelas, lockjaw, and gangrene were variously attributed to dampness and a multitude of other conditions.

WITH THE WOUNDED OF SPOTSYLVANIA COURT HOUSE, MAY, 1864

Examining the lawn closely, one perceives belts and bandages strewn everywhere. These recumbent figures tell more plainly than words what has been going on here. The stirring of the breeze in the leaves of the great oak which shades the wounded too often marks the sigh of a soul that is passing to its reward. The scene is Marye's Heights after the battle of Spotsylvania, May 11, 1864. The glory of the battle, the glitter of arms, the crash of artillery and musketry, and the pæans of victory echoing over the land after a great battle has been won are not all of war. The maimed and wounded soldiers who have fallen before the hail of shells and canister and grape realize at what price these pæans are bought. With limbs torn and bodies lacerated, they sometimes lay suffering excruciating torments for hours or even days after the battle had been fought. An insensible soldier passed over for dead by the ambulance corps, or lying unseen in a thicket, might recover consciousness to be tortured with thirst and driven frantic with the fear that he would be permanently forgotten and left there to die. Incongruous, but of interest to posterity, is the photographer's tripod on the right of the picture in front of the wounded lying in the shade of the house.

IN THE WAKE OF GRANT'S ADVANCE

This picture shows a warehouse on the banks of the Rappahannock to which wounded have been conveyed after the slaughter in the Wilderness. Grant had attempted to oust the Army of Northern Virginia from its position by a flank movement on Spotsylvania. Lee succeeded in anticipating the movement, and once again Grant hurled the long-suffering Army of the Potomac upon the unbroken gray lines of the Army of Northern Virginia. Two assaults were made on the evening of May 11th, but the position could not be carried even at a loss of five or six thousand men. The neighboring buildings were filled with the Federal and Confederate wounded. Around the factory above are the tents of a division hospital corps which have been found inadequate to care for so many wounded. They can be seen on every floor of the big structure. The hospital orderlies are hurrying about. At first tentage was not used by these field hospitals, but they were established in any existing buildings, such as churches, mills, and dwelling-houses. These, naturally,

[270]

A WAREHOUSE USED AS A HOSPITAL AFTER SPOTSYLVANIA, MAY, 1864

were not always convenient, but the first tent hospital was not used until the battle of Shiloh, April, 1862. The value of such shelter on this occasion was so manifest that hospital tents were soon after issued and ultimately used with troops almost exclusively in campaign as well as in periods of inactivity. These division or field hospitals, as finally developed in the war, proved to be thoroughly practicable and of the greatest value to the wounded in battle, while in camp they were set up and acted as temporary receiving hospitals to which sick were sent for more extended treatment or to determine the necessity for their removal to the fixed hospitals in the rear. Large in resources, they cared for wounded by the hundreds; always in hand and mobile, they could be sent forward without undue delay to where the needs of battle demanded and wheeled vehicles could penetrate. They embodied a new idea, developed by our surgeons, which was promptly adopted by all military nations with modifications to meet the demands of their respective services.

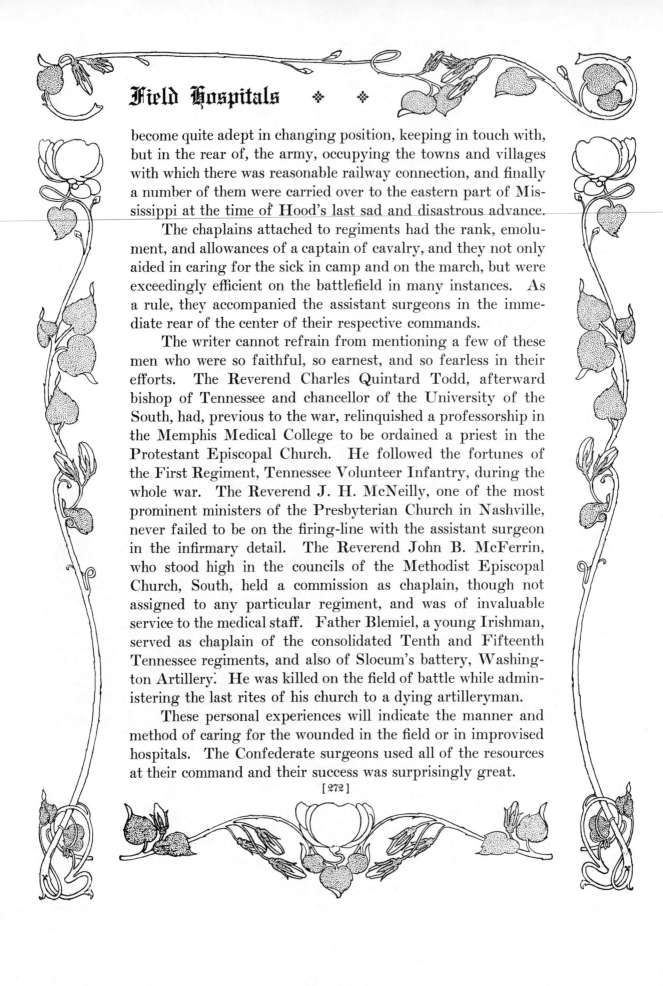

become quite adept in changing position, keeping in touch with, but in the rear of, the army, occupying the towns and villages with which there was reasonable railway connection, and finally a number of them were carried over to the eastern part of Mississippi at the time of Hood's last sad and disastrous advance.

The chaplains attached to regiments had the rank, emolument, and allowances of a captain of cavalry, and they not only aided in caring for the sick in camp and on the march, but were exceedingly efficient on the battlefield in many instances. As a rule, they accompanied the assistant surgeons in the immediate rear of the center of their respective commands.

The writer cannot refrain from mentioning a few of these men who were so faithful, so earnest, and so fearless in their efforts. The Reverend Charles Quintard Todd, afterward bishop of Tennessee and chancellor of the University of the South, had, previous to the war, relinquished a professorship in the Memphis Medical College to be ordained a priest in the Protestant Episcopal Church. He followed the fortunes of the First Regiment, Tennessee Volunteer Infantry, during the whole war. The Reverend J. H. McNeilly, one of the most prominent ministers of the Presbyterian Church in Nashville, never failed to be on the firing-line with the assistant surgeon in the infirmary detail. The Reverend John B. McFerrin, who stood high in the councils of the Methodist Episcopal Church, South, held a commission as chaplain, though not assigned to any particular regiment, and was of invaluable service to the medical staff. Father Blemiel, a young Irishman, served as chaplain of the consolidated Tenth and Fifteenth Tennessee regiments, and also of Slocum's battery, Washington Artillery. He was killed on the field of battle while administering the last rites of his church to a dying artilleryman.

These personal experiences will indicate the manner and method of caring for the wounded in the field or in improvised hospitals. The Confederate surgeons used all of the resources at their command and their success was surprisingly great.

PART II
HOSPITALS

———

GENERAL
HOSPITALS

———

1865—A PRESBYTERIAN CHURCH TURNED INTO A HOSPITAL WITH
41 BEDS, AT NASHVILLE

A PHOTOGRAPH WHICH HELPS TO EXPLAIN THE NATIONAL PENSION ROLL

The figure farthest to the right, with the white cross on his breast, was recognized as his own portrait, a generation after the war, by Henry W. Knight, of Company B, Seventh Maine Volunteers, one of the veterans associated with the preparation of this PHOTOGRAPHIC HISTORY. The cross is the corps badge of the Sixth Corps. The man on his right is Cephas McKelvey, of the Eleventh Pennsylvania Volunteers, who was wounded in the arm. Both men were convalescent. The personnel of these hospitals consisted of the surgeon in command, assisted by an executive and professional staff, and with the necessary number of stewards, clerks, attendants, cooks, laundry workers, guards, etc. Nursing and similar work was either done by details of soldiers from the line of the army or by civilians hired or volunteering for such duty. The guard, necessary for the maintenance of order, restraint of convalescent

CARVER HOSPITAL IN WASHINGTON, SEPTEMBER, 1864

patients and the protection of property, was usually composed of convalescent patients and members of the Veteran Reserve Corps. The surgeon in command of a general hospital had full military control over all persons and property connected with his institution, reported directly to the War Department and surgeon-general and received his orders therefrom. He usually had one or more assistants. The medical staff ordinarily numbered about one to each seventy-five patients. A medical officer of the day, detailed by roster, was always on duty, performing routine duties in relation to the proper management of the hospital and responding to any emergency in professional, administrative, or disciplinary matters. The ward surgeons had duties almost exclusively professional and similar to those performed by the resident physicians of civil hospitals. Two women are sitting by one of the cots.

The photographs on these two pages tell their own pathetic story—the story not of the wounded and suffering soldiers, but of their thrice-suffering womenkind. To this convalescent camp in Alexandria came the anxious wives and mothers, sweethearts and sisters to find their soldiers whom they had perhaps not seen for months or years. The mourning of the woman on the veranda tells the tale of a soldier-boy that is gone. Perhaps she has come to bring the aid and comfort to others which she was denied the privilege of lavishing on her brother or son. The quaint costumes of the time are very well illustrated in this photograph. Then a woman apparently put on a cap at forty, sometimes before. The little girls wear such

Gen. Heintzelman

voluminous draperies that one wonders how they could get about at all. These were the days of the hoop-skirt and the polonaise. In the photograph to the right they have removed their quaint small hats, and look less like premature little women. The little boys, in their " cunning " Kate Greenaway costumes on the left-hand page, have evidently just come up to get into the photograph. The officer lounging in the chair has turned his profile to the camera. A great change in the type of women's faces can be seen since that time. Women have changed more than men. The change is deeper than mere dress, and involves also her outlook upon the world. But she is as ready as ever to relieve distress and suffering in war.

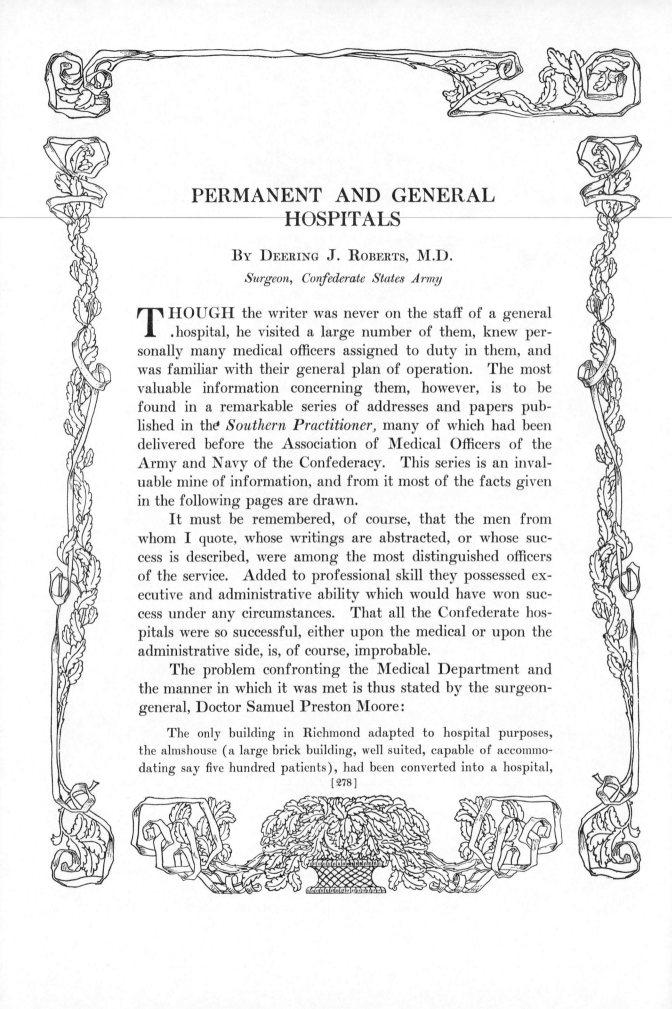

PERMANENT AND GENERAL HOSPITALS

By Deering J. Roberts, M.D.
Surgeon, Confederate States Army

THOUGH the writer was never on the staff of a general hospital, he visited a large number of them, knew personally many medical officers assigned to duty in them, and was familiar with their general plan of operation. The most valuable information concerning them, however, is to be found in a remarkable series of addresses and papers published in the *Southern Practitioner,* many of which had been delivered before the Association of Medical Officers of the Army and Navy of the Confederacy. This series is an invaluable mine of information, and from it most of the facts given in the following pages are drawn.

It must be remembered, of course, that the men from whom I quote, whose writings are abstracted, or whose success is described, were among the most distinguished officers of the service. Added to professional skill they possessed executive and administrative ability which would have won success under any circumstances. That all the Confederate hospitals were so successful, either upon the medical or upon the administrative side, is, of course, improbable.

The problem confronting the Medical Department and the manner in which it was met is thus stated by the surgeon-general, Doctor Samuel Preston Moore:

The only building in Richmond adapted to hospital purposes, the almshouse (a large brick building, well suited, capable of accommodating say five hundred patients), had been converted into a hospital,

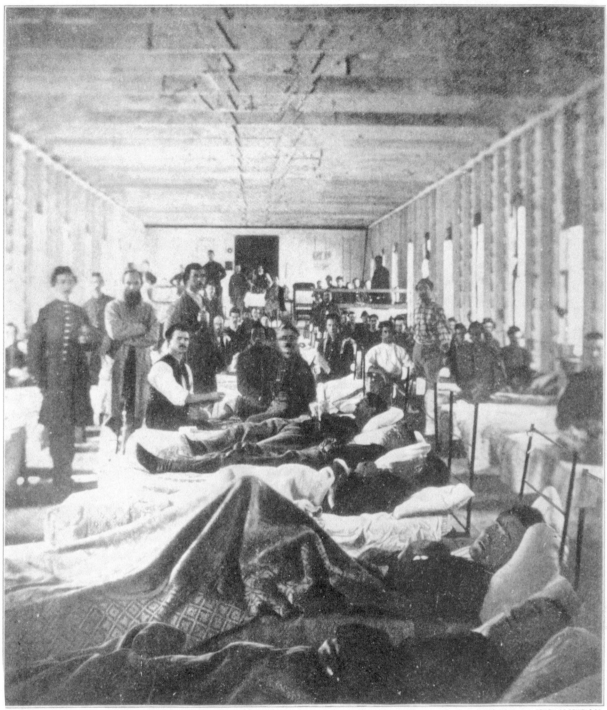

HOSPITAL WARD IN CONVALESCENT CAMP AT ALEXANDRIA

This is where thousands of fortunate soldiers got well from their wounds. When the regiments marched away to the front, their barracks and other available buildings were turned into improvised hospitals. Where the intended capacity was exceeded, tent wards were often pitched to supply the deficiency. Generally, however, other buildings were taken over to provide for the surplus wounded. These offshoots themselves were frequently forced to enlarge and, for facility of administration, were detached from the parent institution. For instance, in the middle of December, 1864, there were sixteen such institutions within the corporate limits of the city of Washington alone, and a total of twenty-five, with an aggregate bed capacity of 21,426, almost within cannon-shot of the Capitol. On this same date there were 187 general hospitals in operation, scattered all over the country from New England to New Orleans and from the Missouri to the Atlantic, and having the enormous total capacity of 118,057 beds, of which but 34,648 were then vacant.

and occupied by the wounded prisoners of the Northern army from the battle just mentioned [Manassas]. The Confederate wounded from the same battle were treated in private houses, in small, unoccupied wooden buildings, and small tobacco-factories improvised as hospitals. There were serious objections to this method of treatment of the sick and wounded, the principal being the liability of spreading contagious diseases among the inhabitants of the city; the aggregation of so many patients in the necessarily large wards of the factories, thereby contaminating the buildings, rendering them unfit for occupancy; and the impossibility of supplying by these means the further demands of the service.

To meet, as far as practicable, these requirements, the plan was adopted of erecting buildings, each one to be a ward and separate, of undressed planks set upright, calculated for thirty-two beds, with streets running each way, say thirty feet wide. From fifteen to twenty of such wards constituted a division, three or more divisions making a general hospital. Each division was separate and distinct, having all the appliances of a hospital, but under control and supervision of the surgeon in charge of the general hospital. There were five of these hospitals in the suburbs of Richmond, erected in 1861. At a rough estimate, twenty thousand patients were at one time treated at these general hospitals.

The plan proved to be excellent, and the temporary hospital buildings in the city were abandoned as soon as practicable, the larger factories only being retained and used. This segregation of the sick and wounded was highly beneficial. If the condition of a ward, from whatever cause, required its abandonment, it was done without trouble or much cost to the Government. It may be stated that cases of hospital gangrene were, as a rule, removed from wards and treated in tents, with decided benefit. General hospitals, on this plan, were established whenever and wherever deemed necessary. This was sometimes attended with delay; for the Medical Department, instead of being an independent bureau, building and furnishing hospitals, had to depend entirely upon the Quartermaster's and Commissary departments. Hence, much delay was experienced in obtaining proper hospital accommodations, and in such cases blame was attached to the medical bureau, which it never deserved.*

Southern Practitioner, vol. xxxi, pp. 492–493.

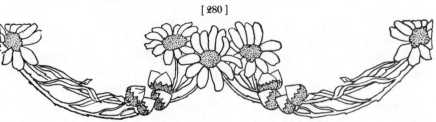

THE FIRST-HAND RECORDS OF THE PENSION SYSTEM
QUARTERS OF CHIEF OF AMBULANCE, FIRST DIVISION,
NINTH CORPS, IN FRONT OF PETERSBURG, 1864

The army surgeon in the field had clerical duties as well as medical.   An elaborate system of records, upon which the accuracy of the whole pension system of the Government rests, had to be maintained.   Here the mortality statistics of the first division, Ninth Corps, Army of the Potomac, were collected and preserved.   The field desks had handles on the end, as seen, and were easily portable.

PART OF THE GENERAL HOSPITAL AT CITY POINT—THE JAMES RIVER IN THE DISTANCE

General Hospitals ❖ ❖

Doctor John R. Gildersleeve, when president of the Association of Medical Officers of the Army and Navy of the Confederacy, in 1904, delivered an interesting address upon Chimborazo Hospital, Richmond. When the necessity for larger hospital accommodations became evident, Surgeon-General Moore, after consultation with Doctor James B. McCaw, of Richmond, chose Chimborazo Hill, on the outskirts of Richmond, as a site for the new hospital, and Doctor McCaw was placed in charge. Some of the buildings were opened early in 1862, and before the end of the war one hundred and fifty wards had been constructed. They were usually commodious buildings, one hundred feet long, thirty feet wide, and one story high, each ward having a capacity of from forty to sixty patients. The buildings were separated by alleys and streets, and the hospital presented the appearance of a town of considerable size. Five divisions were created, each in charge of a surgeon with the necessary assistants. These divisions were arranged, as far as possible, upon the basis of States. So far as possible troops from the same State were assigned to one division, and were attended by surgeons and attendants from that State.

The celebrated farm, "Tree Hill," was loaned to the hospital by Mr. Franklin Stearns, and afforded pasturage for a large number of cows and several hundred goats. The meat of young kids was found to be much relished by the soldiers. "The hospital trading canal-boat, *Chimborazo,* with Lawrence Lotier in command, plied between Richmond, Lynchburg, and Lexington, bartering cotton yarn and shoes for provisions. This was only one of the hospital's many resources." An additional fact is that the hospital never drew fifty dollars from the Confederate States Government but relied solely upon the money received from commutation of rations.

The total number of patients received and treated at Chimborazo Hospital amounted to seventy-six thousand (out of this number about

OFFICERS AND NURSES AT SEMINARY HOSPITAL, GEORGETOWN, APRIL 1, 1865

The two neat nurses in the window, with their old-fashioned black mittens, may be held responsible for the bird-cage hanging by the door. Neither they nor the chubby little boy sitting on the sidewalk in the foreground suggest war; yet this is a scene of April, 1865, before Lee's surrender. It is well-nigh impossible for a man surrounded by the sights and sounds and scents of every-day civilian life to realize what a touch of femininity meant to a sick soldier far from home after four years of rough campaigning. A chaplain was attached to most of these hospitals; his duties, besides those of a spiritual nature, having to do with correspondence with friends and relatives, supervision over the postal service, reading-room, library, amusements, etc. There was often much trouble in securing adequate nursing attendance, both in respect to the number and character of the personnel. There were female nurses at many hospitals; some were Sisters of Charity, and representatives of women's aid societies often took turns in nursing and assisting in the diet and linen-rooms. The sick were fed from the regular ration, or from articles purchased with the savings made on the unconsumed portions. The latter fund was in some cases scarcely sufficient.

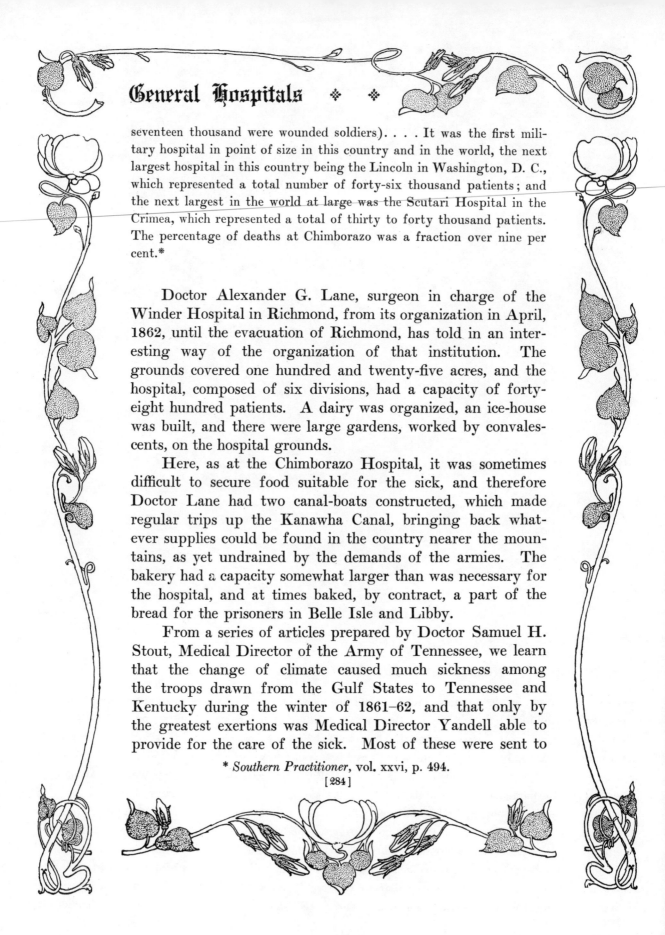

seventeen thousand were wounded soldiers). . . . It was the first military hospital in point of size in this country and in the world, the next largest hospital in this country being the Lincoln in Washington, D. C., which represented a total number of forty-six thousand patients; and the next largest in the world at large was the Scutari Hospital in the Crimea, which represented a total of thirty to forty thousand patients. The percentage of deaths at Chimborazo was a fraction over nine per cent.*

Doctor Alexander G. Lane, surgeon in charge of the Winder Hospital in Richmond, from its organization in April, 1862, until the evacuation of Richmond, has told in an interesting way of the organization of that institution. The grounds covered one hundred and twenty-five acres, and the hospital, composed of six divisions, had a capacity of forty-eight hundred patients. A dairy was organized, an ice-house was built, and there were large gardens, worked by convalescents, on the hospital grounds.

Here, as at the Chimborazo Hospital, it was sometimes difficult to secure food suitable for the sick, and therefore Doctor Lane had two canal-boats constructed, which made regular trips up the Kanawha Canal, bringing back whatever supplies could be found in the country nearer the mountains, as yet undrained by the demands of the armies. The bakery had a capacity somewhat larger than was necessary for the hospital, and at times baked, by contract, a part of the bread for the prisoners in Belle Isle and Libby.

From a series of articles prepared by Doctor Samuel H. Stout, Medical Director of the Army of Tennessee, we learn that the change of climate caused much sickness among the troops drawn from the Gulf States to Tennessee and Kentucky during the winter of 1861–62, and that only by the greatest exertions was Medical Director Yandell able to provide for the care of the sick. Most of these were sent to

* *Southern Practitioner*, vol. xxvi, p. 494.

AN AFTERNOON CONCERT AT THE OFFICERS' QUARTERS, HAREWOOD HOSPITAL, NEAR WASHINGTON

Hospital life for those well enough to enjoy it was far from dull. Witness the white-clad nurse with her prim apron and hoopskirt on the right of the photograph, and the band on the left. Most hospitals had excellent libraries and a full supply of current newspapers and periodicals, usually presented gratuitously. Many of the larger ones organized and maintained bands for the amusement of the patients; they also provided lectures, concerts, and theatrical and other entertainments. A hospital near the front receiving cases of the most severe character might have a death-rate as high as twelve per cent., while those farther in the rear might have a very much lower death-rate of but six, four, or even two

LOUISA M. ALCOTT,
THE AUTHOR OF "LITTLE WOMEN,"
AS A NURSE IN 1862

per cent. The portrait accompanying shows Louisa M. Alcott, the author of "Little Men," "Little Women," "An Old Fashioned Girl," and the other books that have endeared her to millions of readers. Her diary of 1862 contains this characteristic note: "November. Thirty years old. Decided to go to Washington as a nurse if I could find a place. Help needed, and I love nursing and must let out my pent-up energy in some new way." She had not yet attained fame as a writer, but it was during this time that she wrote for a newspaper the letters afterwards collected as "Hospital Sketches." It is due to the courtesy of Messrs. Little, Brown & Company of Boston that the wartime portrait is here reproduced.

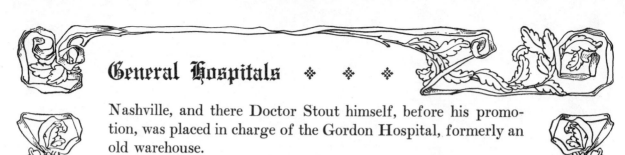

Nashville, and there Doctor Stout himself, before his promotion, was placed in charge of the Gordon Hospital, formerly an old warehouse.

This hospital had been in charge of a committee of ladies who had employed civilian physicians to attend the sick, and the hospital attendants were not under military discipline. Through the exercise of considerable tact, Doctor Stout reorganized the hospital and brought it under military rule without offending the sensibilities of the ladies. Doctor Stout was an excellent business man and required frequent statements from the commissary of the amount of money due the hospitals from commutation of rations, and the fund thus obtained was used liberally for the benefit of his patients, procuring for them articles of food to be had in the market. When chickens, butter, and eggs were not brought to the hospital in sufficient quantities, he sent out wagon-loads of cotton yarn purchased from the factories, and exchanged it for the much needed delicacies.

After his promotion to the office of medical director, Doctor Stout was particularly insistent that real coffee should be served the patients in the hospitals under his control, and sent subordinates to Wilmington and Charleston to purchase it from the blockade-runners. A bakery was established at every hospital, and the saving thus made inured to the benefit of the hospital fund.

He even went so far as to purchase at Chattanooga a printing outfit on which the numerous blanks needed for the use of the various hospitals were prepared. This was placed under the charge of privates detailed for the purpose and soon became a source of income.

Seeds were bought for gardens, and, when the number of convalescents was not sufficient to work them, labor was paid from the hospital fund. Cows, horses, and wagons were purchased whenever needed, without waiting for the formal approval of the surgeon-general. "I thought that economy of

EAST WARDS OF THE CONVALESCENT CAMP AT ALEXANDRIA—1864

A few of the convalescent soldiers in this photograph have been set to work, but the majority are idly recuperating. These east wards are much less attractive than those shown below, around headquarters. The buildings were poorly ventilated and poorly drained, and in wet weather stood in a sea of mud. The death-rate here was higher than at most hospitals or prisons. This was partly due to the fact that unoccupied soldiers are far more liable to disease than the soldier at work. These convalescent or parole camps made more trouble for the officers than did those of the active soldiers. "Camp Misery" was the title at first bestowed by the soldiers on this particular camp at Alexandria, Va. At first it consisted only of tents, and was badly managed; but later it was entirely reorganized, barracks were built, and Miss Amy Bradley of the Sanitary Commission did much to improve conditions. Two different types of ambulance stand before headquarters, as well as the old-fashioned family carriage.

CONVALESCENT CAMP AT ALEXANDRIA

General Hospitals ❖ ❖ ❖

expenditure was not to be considered urgent. The great undertaking was to find the materials needed."

At Chattanooga, Doctor Stout caused hospitals to be constructed upon an entirely new plan, which he maintained was far superior to that followed in the building of the Chimborazo Hospital, and which "was evidently an imitation of the models of such buildings long in use in the Federal service." His objections to the plan of Chimborazo were that its width afforded space for more than two rows of bunks and that, when windows and doors were necessarily closed on account of the weather, ventilation through the roof was not sufficient. He thus describes the new plan:

The pavilion wards erected under my direction, were of such width that only two rows of bunks could be arranged or accommodated in them. The bunks were placed crosswise of the room, the head of each being from one and a half to two feet from the side wall. Thus, an aisle or vacant space of from eight to ten feet in width was left in the middle of the ward throughout its entire length. Sometimes the wards were built one above another. Near the floor, and just under the ceiling overhead, were longitudinal openings with sliding shutters, one foot in width, that could be closed or opened at the will of the surgeon in charge. Overhead, in the ceiling, were also openings with sliding shutters, and latticed structures on the comb and in the gables, which were opened or closed as occasion required.*

Doctor Stout also provided a general register at his headquarters for all the hospitals under his direction. The surgeon in charge of every hospital was required to send daily any changes in his register. These were entered upon the general register, and it was therefore possible to find the whereabouts or the fate of any patient in a few seconds.

In addition to the general hospitals established for the treatment of patients until they were convalescent, "wayside" hospitals were established at every important junction-point.

Southern Practitioner, vol. xxiv, p. 213.

[288]

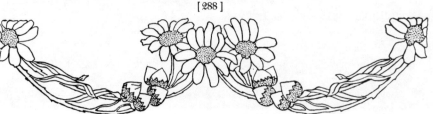

A FEDERAL OFFICER WOUNDED AT PINE MOUNTAIN, GEORGIA—AUGUST, 1864

This unusual photograph of an officer still on crutches, emaciated and suffering, was taken in August, 1864, near Pulpit Rock, Lookout Mountain, Tennessee. It is reproduced here through the courtesy of the officer himself—Major (later Colonel) L. R. Stegman, associated with the editors in the preparation of this work. In June, 1864, during Sherman's march to Atlanta, he was shot in the thigh, the shot fracturing the bone. Major Stegman was in command of the Hundred and Second New York, which was attached to the twentieth corps of the Army of the Cumberland. A wound of this character disabled the victim for many months. Colonel Stegman's companion in the photograph is Lieutenant Donner, of an Ohio regiment, also wounded in the thigh and using a cane for support.

General Hospitals ❖ ❖

In these were treated soldiers taken suddenly ill, convalescents who had overestimated their strength, and wounded whose condition forbade further travel.

Some of the general hospitals established received high praise from Federal sources. For example, the lamented Doctor Stanford E. Chaillé, of New Orleans, in a private letter written just before his death, tells of the capture of himself and his hospital at Macon, Georgia, by Wilson's cavalry, and goes on to say that he " was treated by General Wilson's medical director with marked consideration and to many favors, . . . and he urged me to continue in charge, on Federal pay, retaining my Confederate inmates, and admitting to separate wards Federal sick and wounded. My feelings were then too bitter to accept his generous offer."

At the beginning of the war, many private hospitals were established wherever troops were stationed for any length of time. These were generally under the control of a committee of women anxious to do something for the good of the cause, and under the charge of a citizen-surgeon of their own selection. The nursing was almost exclusively volunteer, but rations were furnished in some cases by the Confederate Government. Many of these were well conducted and did good service, particularly during that period before the general hospitals were built and the medical staff thoroughly organized.

When the Medical Department became able to take care of all the sick and wounded, it seemed best, for obvious reasons, that all sick and wounded should be brought under direct supervision of the Medical Department, and a majority of the private hospitals were discontinued. One of them, however, established in Richmond just after the first battle of Manassas (Bull Run) by Miss Sally L. Tompkins, deserves mention. Doctor William Berrien Burroughs says of this hospital:

Ten days after the battle, on July 30, 1861, entirely at her own expense she opened the Robertson Hospital (corner of Main and Third streets) which continued its mission of mercy to July 13, 1865. In

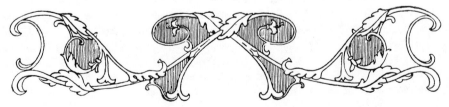

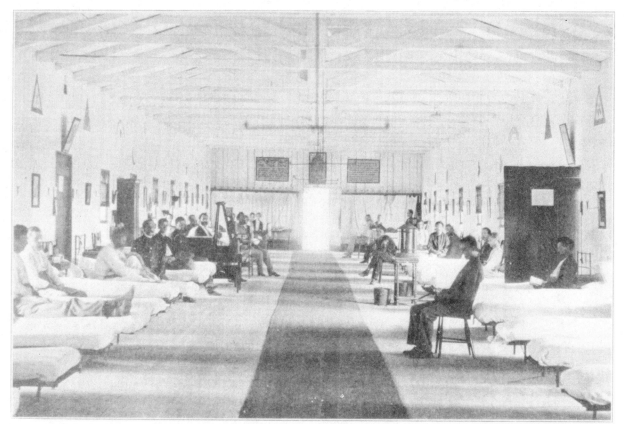

INSIDE A FEDERAL GENERAL HOSPITAL—THE ARMORY SQUARE, WASHINGTON

In the first part of the war, whenever the capacity of the regimental hospital canvas was exceeded, some neighboring dwelling-house would be taken over as a hospital annex. When it was fully recognized that the chief duty of the medical department at the front was the getting rid of the sick and wounded, after such preliminary assistance as put them in suitable condition to withstand the journey to the rear, the importance of the function which the general hospitals performed was better appreciated. At once the establishment of general hospitals, of suitable size and at convenient points, was pushed with great vigor. Shortly many such hospitals were in operation which, though perhaps in buildings of only temporary character, rivaled the best civil hospitals in completeness of equipment and professional service, and far surpassed the very largest of them in accommodations for patients. The best type of army hospital was constructed on the unit and pavilion system, which permitted prompt and almost indefinite enlargement at need.

ANOTHER VIEW OF WARD K AT THE ARMORY SQUARE

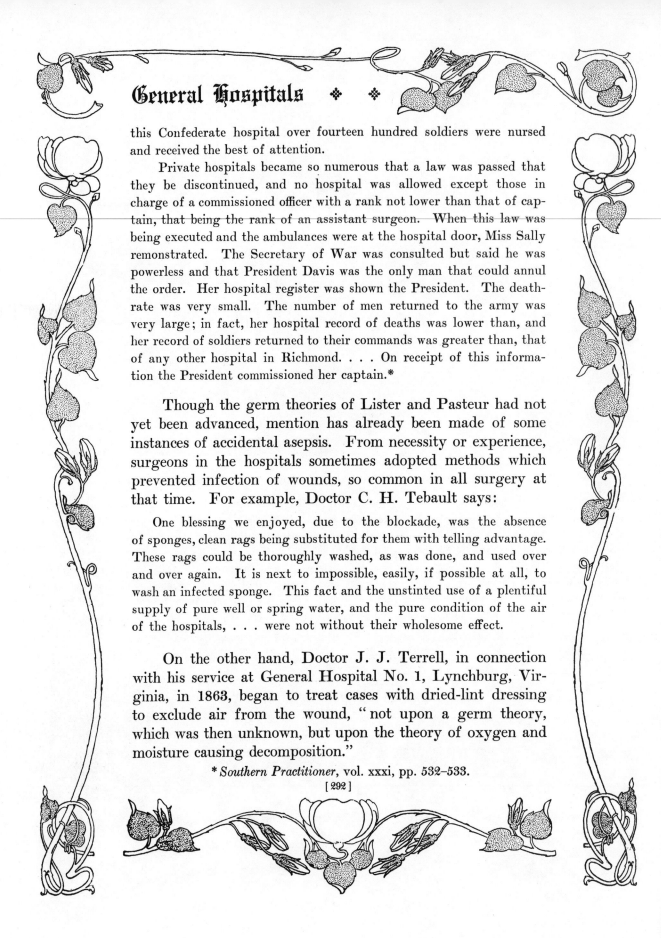

this Confederate hospital over fourteen hundred soldiers were nursed and received the best of attention.

Private hospitals became so numerous that a law was passed that they be discontinued, and no hospital was allowed except those in charge of a commissioned officer with a rank not lower than that of captain, that being the rank of an assistant surgeon. When this law was being executed and the ambulances were at the hospital door, Miss Sally remonstrated. The Secretary of War was consulted but said he was powerless and that President Davis was the only man that could annul the order. Her hospital register was shown the President. The death-rate was very small. The number of men returned to the army was very large; in fact, her hospital record of deaths was lower than, and her record of soldiers returned to their commands was greater than, that of any other hospital in Richmond. . . . On receipt of this information the President commissioned her captain.*

Though the germ theories of Lister and Pasteur had not yet been advanced, mention has already been made of some instances of accidental asepsis. From necessity or experience, surgeons in the hospitals sometimes adopted methods which prevented infection of wounds, so common in all surgery at that time. For example, Doctor C. H. Tebault says:

One blessing we enjoyed, due to the blockade, was the absence of sponges, clean rags being substituted for them with telling advantage. These rags could be thoroughly washed, as was done, and used over and over again. It is next to impossible, easily, if possible at all, to wash an infected sponge. This fact and the unstinted use of a plentiful supply of pure well or spring water, and the pure condition of the air of the hospitals, . . . were not without their wholesome effect.

On the other hand, Doctor J. J. Terrell, in connection with his service at General Hospital No. 1, Lynchburg, Virginia, in 1863, began to treat cases with dried-lint dressing to exclude air from the wound, "not upon a germ theory, which was then unknown, but upon the theory of oxygen and moisture causing decomposition."

*Southern Practitioner, vol. xxxi, pp. 532–533.

ARMORY SQUARE HOSPITAL—WHERE LINCOLN WALKED AMONG THE FLOWERS

Perhaps it was because of President Lincoln's habit of visiting the Armory Square Hospital in Washington that so much care has been bestowed upon the flowers. The walks are straight and even, and the scene, except for the ambulance standing near the curved walk, seems one of peace and not of war. The Capitol rises majestic in the background, and to the left is the little chapel attached to the hospital. Earnest people entered there to send up a prayer for the soldiers who were wounded in the cause of their country.

INTERESTED CONVALESCENTS

INTERIOR OF A WARD AT HAREWOOD GENERAL HOSPITAL, WASHINGTON, IN 1864

The mosquito-nettings which covered the couches of the sick and wounded have been draped above their heads to give them air and preparatory to the surgeon's visit. The time is evidently summer. In the vignette below, the white cloud has descended, and all is quiet save for the one patient seen crawling into his couch. Although the transmission of disease by mosquitoes had yet to be demonstrated, these soldiers were thoroughly insured. Against self-infection, however, they could not be protected. The number of surgical operations necessary on the quarter of a million men wounded on the Union side during the war does not appear, but as their wounds were practically all infected, with resulting pus-formation, secondary hemorrhage, necrosis of bone, and sloughing of tissue, it must be accepted as

very great. During the first eighteen months of the war, reports of surgical operations performed were not made by the surgeons, and no record exists of their nature and number. But such reports for the remainder of the war were very complete. They show, of ordinary accidents such as might occur in civil life, including burns and scalds, contusions, sprains, dislocations, fractures, incised and punctured wounds (not made by weapons of war), and poisoning, a total of 171,565 cases, with 3,025 deaths. Early in 1862, the aggressive movement of troops vacated a large number of rough barracks which they had previously occupied. Advantage was taken to fit them up hastily as hospitals to receive the sick removed from the troops thus taking the field. Generally speaking, none were wholly satisfactory for their new purpose, either from site, sanitary condition, arrangement, or construction. Nor were even water supply and sewage facilities always suitable. Toward the close of the first year of the war, the medical department, backed by the Sanitary Commission, urged the importance of building in advance well-planned hospitals, constructed on the pavilion principle, instead of waiting until emergency existed and then occupying hotels and other buildings poorly adapted for use as hospitals. The work of constructing such hospitals was shortly begun. As these were not intended to be permanent structures and were generally frame buildings of a simple character, the work of their construction could be rapidly accomplished. As an example of the rapidity of such work, the contractor for the Satterlee Hospital, in Philadelphia, agreed to construct it, with a capacity of twenty-five hundred beds, in forty days. Work was not entirely completed at the expiration of the contract period, but so much had been accomplished that its organization was begun by the surgeon in command on the very date specified. This hospital was subsequently expanded to a capacity of thirty-five hundred beds.

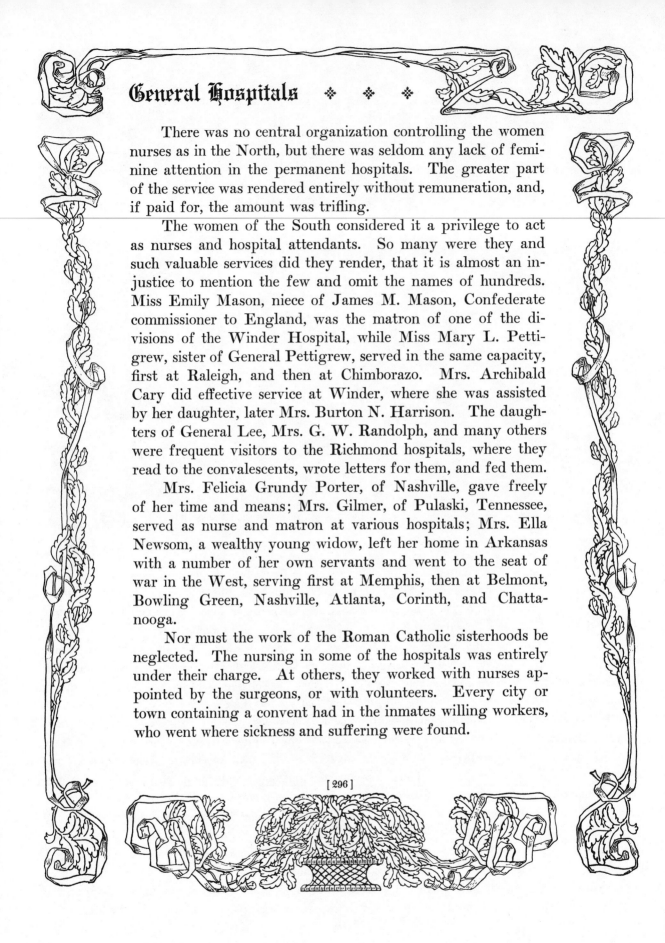

General Hospitals ❖ ❖ ❖

There was no central organization controlling the women nurses as in the North, but there was seldom any lack of feminine attention in the permanent hospitals. The greater part of the service was rendered entirely without remuneration, and, if paid for, the amount was trifling.

The women of the South considered it a privilege to act as nurses and hospital attendants. So many were they and such valuable services did they render, that it is almost an injustice to mention the few and omit the names of hundreds. Miss Emily Mason, niece of James M. Mason, Confederate commissioner to England, was the matron of one of the divisions of the Winder Hospital, while Miss Mary L. Pettigrew, sister of General Pettigrew, served in the same capacity, first at Raleigh, and then at Chimborazo. Mrs. Archibald Cary did effective service at Winder, where she was assisted by her daughter, later Mrs. Burton N. Harrison. The daughters of General Lee, Mrs. G. W. Randolph, and many others were frequent visitors to the Richmond hospitals, where they read to the convalescents, wrote letters for them, and fed them.

Mrs. Felicia Grundy Porter, of Nashville, gave freely of her time and means; Mrs. Gilmer, of Pulaski, Tennessee, served as nurse and matron at various hospitals; Mrs. Ella Newsom, a wealthy young widow, left her home in Arkansas with a number of her own servants and went to the seat of war in the West, serving first at Memphis, then at Belmont, Bowling Green, Nashville, Atlanta, Corinth, and Chattanooga.

Nor must the work of the Roman Catholic sisterhoods be neglected. The nursing in some of the hospitals was entirely under their charge. At others, they worked with nurses appointed by the surgeons, or with volunteers. Every city or town containing a convent had in the inmates willing workers, who went where sickness and suffering were found.

PART II
HOSPITALS

WITH THE
AMBULANCE
CORPS

WELL-EQUIPPED AMBULANCE BEARERS OF THE ARMY OF THE
POTOMAC, 1862—DRILL IN REMOVING WOUNDED

REMOVING THE WOUNDED FROM MARYE'S HEIGHTS, MAY 2, 1864

This spirited scene of mercy followed close on the assault and capture of the famous "Stone Wall" at Fredericksburg, May 2, 1863. The ambulances belong to the Fifty-seventh New York, which suffered a terrible loss when it helped, as a part of Sedgwick's Corps, to carry Marye's Heights. Out of one hundred and ninety-two men engaged, eight were killed, seventy-eight were wounded, and one was reported missing, a loss of forty-five per cent. Then the ambulance train was rushed to the front. Within half an hour all the wounded were in the field hospitals. The corps still had many of the short, sharply tilting, jolting two-wheeled ambulances whose

AMBULANCE CORPS OF THE FIFTY–SEVENTH NEW YORK INFANTRY

rocking motion proved a torment to sufferers.   Several four-wheeled ambulances appear, however, and later in the war the two-wheeled ambulances were entirely superseded.   The long lines of infantry drawn up in battle array in the background are ready to repel any further assaults while the wounded are being removed on the litters.   The one in the foreground (on the left) exhibits a device to elevate the patient's limbs.   The medical officer is gazing anxiously at the wounded soldier, and an orderly is hurrying over with some bandaging.   Directly behind the orderly, bearers are lifting another sufferer on a litter into the four-wheeled ambulance.

A FEW OF THE WOUNDED AT GETTYSBURG

To these rough tents, erected by the Second Federal Army Corps, the wounded have been rushed during the second and third days of the mightiest of all American battles, just decided at a cost of 6,664 dead and 27,206 wounded. Accommodations are simple. But cups hang at the front of the foremost tent wherewith to slake the sufferers' thirst, and at least one woman nurse is present to soothe their fevered brows with the touch of her cool hands. By this time the ambulance organization of the Union armies had been perfected. Such was the efficiency of its administration that on the early morning of the 4th of July, 1863, the day after the battle, not one wounded soldier of the thousands who had fallen was left on the field. The inspector-general of the army himself reported this

SECOND CORPS HOSPITAL, UNION CENTER, NEAR MEADE'S HEADQUARTERS

fact from personal investigation. During the Civil War, the number of battle casualties steadily increased, until in the year 1864 there were no less than 2,000 battles, actions, and skirmishes officially reported, and during the second quarter of that year more than 30,000 wounded were received in the Washington hospitals alone, while the total number of such admitted to all the hospitals during the same period exceeded 80,000. For the war period, May 1, 1861, to June 30, 1865, the cases admitted to hospitals for all surgical causes amounted to 408,072, with 37,531 deaths. Of this great number 235,585 were gunshot wounds, with 33,653 deaths. This gives a case-mortality among the wounded able to secure surgeon's care of 14.2 per cent., a terrible toll of the nation's young men.

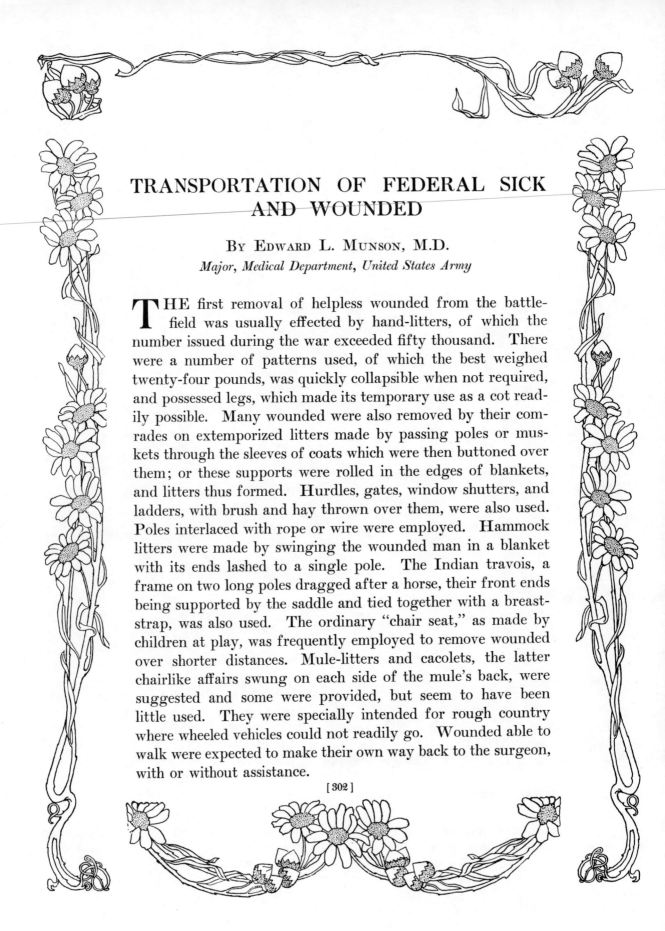

TRANSPORTATION OF FEDERAL SICK AND WOUNDED

By Edward L. Munson, M.D.
Major, Medical Department, United States Army

THE first removal of helpless wounded from the battle-field was usually effected by hand-litters, of which the number issued during the war exceeded fifty thousand. There were a number of patterns used, of which the best weighed twenty-four pounds, was quickly collapsible when not required, and possessed legs, which made its temporary use as a cot readily possible. Many wounded were also removed by their comrades on extemporized litters made by passing poles or muskets through the sleeves of coats which were then buttoned over them; or these supports were rolled in the edges of blankets, and litters thus formed. Hurdles, gates, window shutters, and ladders, with brush and hay thrown over them, were also used. Poles interlaced with rope or wire were employed. Hammock litters were made by swinging the wounded man in a blanket with its ends lashed to a single pole. The Indian travois, a frame on two long poles dragged after a horse, their front ends being supported by the saddle and tied together with a breast-strap, was also used. The ordinary "chair seat," as made by children at play, was frequently employed to remove wounded over shorter distances. Mule-litters and cacolets, the latter chairlike affairs swung on each side of the mule's back, were suggested and some were provided, but seem to have been little used. They were specially intended for rough country where wheeled vehicles could not readily go. Wounded able to walk were expected to make their own way back to the surgeon, with or without assistance.

[302]

UNION HAND–STRETCHERS AT WORK AT MARYE'S HEIGHTS IN MAY, 1864

Over fifty thousand hand-stretchers of various patterns were issued by the Union Government during the war. It was by means of them that the removal of the helpless wounded from the battlefield was effected. The best pattern of hand-stretcher weighed twenty-four pounds, was quickly collapsible when not required, and possessed legs which made its temporary use as a cot readily possible. This photograph shows the wounded on Marye's Heights after the battle at Spotsylvania, May 12, 1864. The wounded man on the stretcher is gazing rather grimly at the camera. His hand is bound up, and his foot showing at the end of the stretcher is bare. The poor fellow in the foreground seems pretty far gone. His face is as pale as the blanket which covers him. The whole group of strong men struck down typifies the awful effects of war.

Ambulance Service ❖ ❖

But the transportation results achieved in these ways were usually possible only over short distances. The organization of the medical service made no provision for removal of the wounded from the regimental collecting-points to hospital facilities further to the rear. There were no sanitary organizations in reserve, available to assist near the firing-line where their service might be needed, or to bridge with their succor, care, and transportation, the often tremendous gap between the relief stations of the regimental surgeons and the general hospitals, usually far in rear. Frequently surgeons with some regiments in action were overwhelmed by the number of casualties in their organizations, while others might be idly waiting with commands held in reserve. The need for organizations to play the part of intermediaries was obvious, but for some occult reason failed to appeal at first to those who had the direction of general military affairs in charge. The lack of such specially equipped and trained organizations resulted in a vast amount of suffering during the first eighteen months of the war, and gave rise to much criticism of the Medical Department which the latter in nowise deserved.

A carefully matured plan for the organization of a hospital corps, to belong to the Medical Department and take over work which was at that time being inefficiently done by some sixteen thousand enlisted men detailed from the line of the army, was submitted to the Secretary of War on August 21, 1862, but failed of adoption as a result of the opposition of General Halleck, general-in-chief. An appeal was then made as follows:

Surgeon-General's Office,
September 7, 1862.

Hon. Edwin M. Stanton,
    Secretary of War.

Sir: I have the honor to ask your attention to the frightful state of disorder existing in the arrangement for removing the wounded from the field of battle. The scarcity of ambulances, the want of organization, the drunkenness and incompetency of the drivers, the total absence of

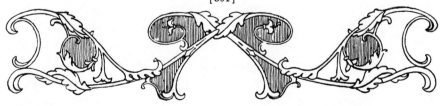

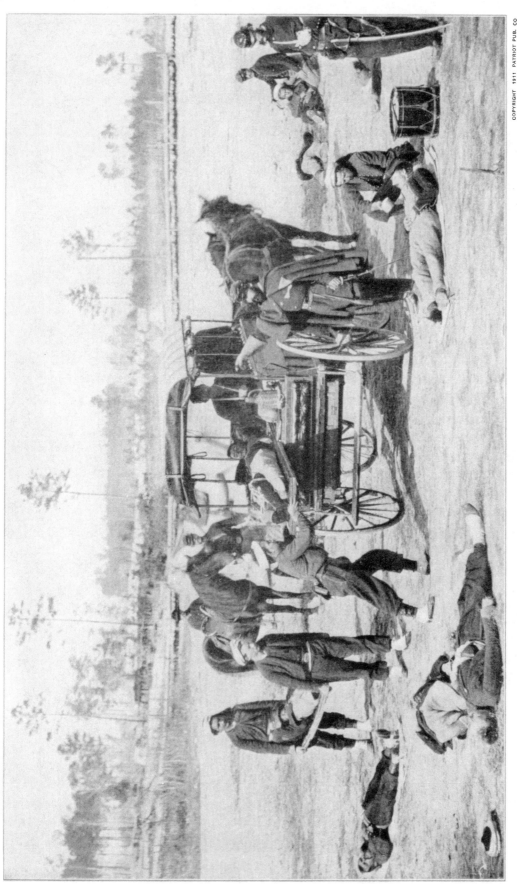

COPYRIGHT 1911 PATRIOT PUB. CO

AMBULANCE DRILL IN THE FIELD—THE NEWLY ORGANIZED CORPS SOON AFTER ANTIETAM

This busy scene of 1862 reveals an "ambulance drill" of the newly organized and well-equipped corps. On the left is a man on a litter with his arm thrown above his head. Another man on a litter with his leg encased in a sort of ready-made cast is just being loaded into the ambulance. On the right, near the drum, an orderly is presenting a cup of water to the "wounded" man comfortably reposing on a blanket. Beside him is a medical officer majestically directing affairs. Another orderly in the background on the right is kneeling by another "wounded" man, who is also gazing at the camera. The man in the foreground is playing his part well. He is lying on the bare ground, and his cap lies at a little distance from his head. This photograph would have comforted the anxious friends and relatives at home in '62, from its portrayal of the efficiency of the organization.

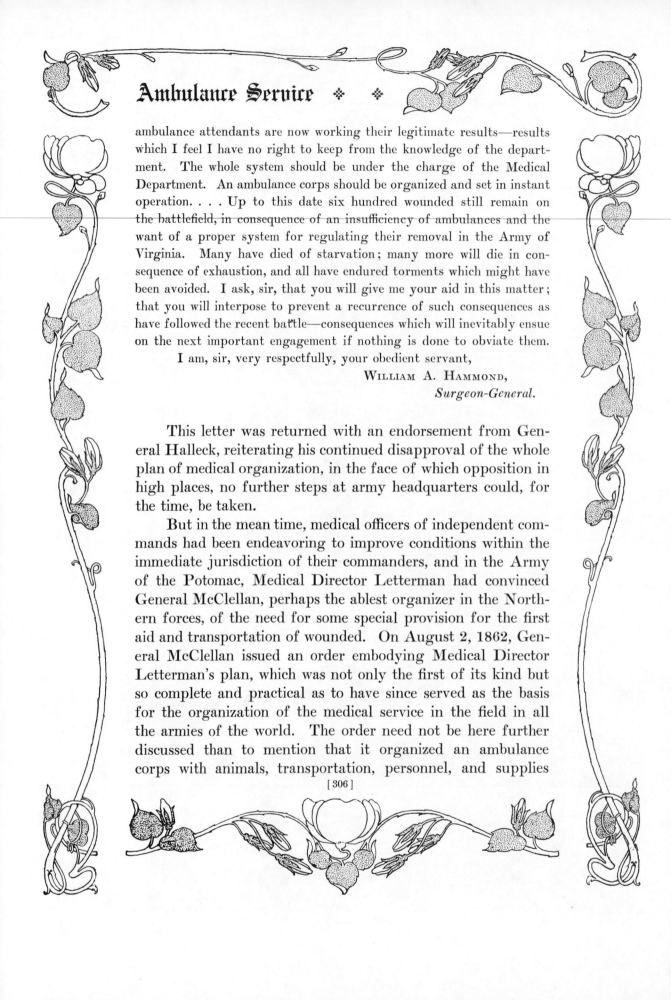

ambulance attendants are now working their legitimate results—results which I feel I have no right to keep from the knowledge of the department. The whole system should be under the charge of the Medical Department. An ambulance corps should be organized and set in instant operation. . . . Up to this date six hundred wounded still remain on the battlefield, in consequence of an insufficiency of ambulances and the want of a proper system for regulating their removal in the Army of Virginia. Many have died of starvation; many more will die in consequence of exhaustion, and all have endured torments which might have been avoided. I ask, sir, that you will give me your aid in this matter; that you will interpose to prevent a recurrence of such consequences as have followed the recent battle—consequences which will inevitably ensue on the next important engagement if nothing is done to obviate them.

I am, sir, very respectfully, your obedient servant,

WILLIAM A. HAMMOND,
Surgeon-General.

This letter was returned with an endorsement from General Halleck, reiterating his continued disapproval of the whole plan of medical organization, in the face of which opposition in high places, no further steps at army headquarters could, for the time, be taken.

But in the mean time, medical officers of independent commands had been endeavoring to improve conditions within the immediate jurisdiction of their commanders, and in the Army of the Potomac, Medical Director Letterman had convinced General McClellan, perhaps the ablest organizer in the Northern forces, of the need for some special provision for the first aid and transportation of wounded. On August 2, 1862, General McClellan issued an order embodying Medical Director Letterman's plan, which was not only the first of its kind but so complete and practical as to have since served as the basis for the organization of the medical service in the field in all the armies of the world. The order need not be here further discussed than to mention that it organized an ambulance corps with animals, transportation, personnel, and supplies

UNITED STATES HOSPITAL BOAT *RED ROVER* AT VICKSBURG

These two photographs show boats used for transporting the sick and wounded in the West and in the East. The hospital steamer *Red Rover*, shown in the upper picture, plied the Mississippi, while the steamer *Argo* and the schooner lying at her bow are two of the vessels that were used in bringing medical supplies to the Army of the Potomac in its operations near Petersburg. All transport boats were at first under control of the quartermaster's department, but later a number were placed under the exclusive control of the medical officers. These varied in type from the finest freight boats to the best types of speedy steamers.

HOSPITAL WHARF ON THE APPOMATTOX RIVER, NEAR CITY POINT

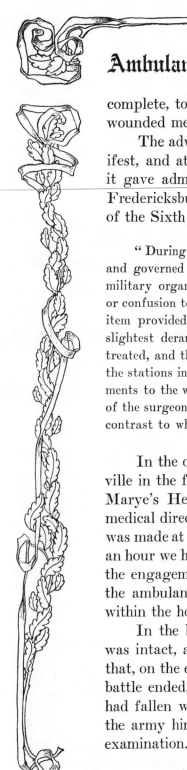

complete, to be used for succoring and transporting sick and wounded men, "and for nothing else."

The advantages of this organization became speedily manifest, and at the battle of Antietam, in the following month, it gave admirable service. Of its operation in the battle of Fredericksburg, Surgeon Charles O'Leary, medical director of the Sixth Corps, said in his official report:

"During the engagements of the 13th, the ambulances being guided and governed with perfect control and with a precision rare even in military organizations, the wounded were brought without any delay or confusion to the hospitals of their respective divisions. Not a single item provided for the organization of the field-hospitals suffered the slightest derangement, and the celerity with which the wounded were treated, and the system pervading the whole Medical Department, from the stations in the field selected by the assistant surgeons with the regiments to the wards where the wounded were transferred from the hands of the surgeons to be attended by the nurses, afforded the most pleasing contrast to what we had hitherto seen during the war. . . ."

In the operations at the time of the battle of Chancellorsville in the following May, the Sixth Corps charged and took Marye's Heights behind the town of Fredericksburg. The medical director of the corps, in his report, says: "The charge was made at 1 P.M.; the heights were taken, and in less than half an hour we had over eight hundred wounded. Two hours after the engagement, such was the celerity and system with which the ambulances worked, the whole number of wounded were within the hospitals under the care of nurses."

In the battle of Gettysburg the ambulance organization was intact, and such was the perfection of its administration, that, on the early morning of the 4th of July, the day after the battle ended, not one wounded man of the great number who had fallen was left on the ground. The inspector-general of the army himself reported this interesting fact from personal examination.

AMBULANCES GOING TO THE FRONT—BEFORE THE WILDERNESS CAMPAIGN

In the foreground of this photograph stand seven ambulances and two quartermasters' wagons, being prepared for active service in the field. The scene is the headquarters of Captain Bates, of the Third Army Corps, near Brandy Station. The following month (May, 1864) the Army of the Potomac moved to the front under General Grant in his decisive campaign from the Wilderness onward. A large quantity of stores lie upon the ground near the quartermasters' wagons ready for transportation to the front. As it became evident that any idea of providing each regiment with its individual hospital was impracticable in a large command, efforts were made to afford hospital facilities for each division at the front. As a result, the regimental medical supplies—the wagons containing which had usually been back with the field train when required during or after action—were largely called in and used to equip a single central hospital organization, which could be held intact and at once available to be brought forward in its wagons for use as needed. One of these hospitals was organized for each division, but sometimes the needs of the wounded in a given area would be such that several of these hospitals might be ordered to work near together.

The success of the plan under McClellan induced Grant to adopt it in the Army of the Tennessee, in an order dated March 30, 1863. Finally, Congress tardily passed an act, approved by the President on March 11, 1864, establishing a uniform system of ambulance service throughout the military forces. After it was once established, the value of this ambulance organization in the saving of life, suffering, and tears cannot be overestimated.

The ambulances were of a number of types, two- and four-wheeled. The former were soon found intolerable from their incessant rocking motion. The four-wheeled type was issued in various forms, successive models designed to avoid the demonstrated defects of their predecessors being issued. The Rucker ambulance was the final development toward the end of the war and gave much satisfaction. In a general way, it was the prototype of the improved ambulance now used in our army. One great fault of all these four-wheeled ambulances was their excessive weight in relation to their transportation capacity. After every great battle, any available supply wagons were used to supplement the ambulances. These were springless, but, with their floors well bedded with brush and hay, were made very comfortable for the wounded placed in them, while their canvas tilts served admirably to screen against rain and sun.

The medical-transport service in battle, as finally perfected, worked about as follows: The medical officers of regiments accompanied their organizations into action and established stations as near the firing-line as possible and usually at a sheltered point, with ready access from both front and rear. Hither the wounded resorted or were conveyed as the situation permitted, had their wounds dressed, and were set aside or started for the field hospital, if able to walk.

As soon as possible the ambulance corps came up and took over the helpless wounded, freeing the regimental surgeons and enabling them to accompany their organizations to

LESSONS
IN AMBULANCES

It was only after a great deal of experimenting with vehicles of various types, both two and four-wheeled, that the "Rucker" ambulance was accepted toward the end of the war as the final development. It gave complete satisfaction. In the accompanying photograph appear types of the two- and four-wheeled ambulances. The former were soon found intolerable; they transmitted every bump and depression in the road by a direct jolt to the suffering patient. One great fault of the four-wheeled

ambulances was their excessive weight in relation to their transportation capacity. The vehicle finally developed was the prototype of the improved ambulance now used in our army. The lower photograph shows a section of the vast system of repairs. The tremendous importance of general hospitals was recognized by Congress in February, 1865, in giving the rank of colonel to department surgeons having more than 4,000 hospital beds under their charge, and of lieutenant-colonel to those having less than that number.

THE MURDEROUS TWO–WHEELED AND MERCIFUL FOUR–WHEELED AMBULANCE

UNITED STATES AMBULANCE REPAIR SHOP AT WASHINGTON

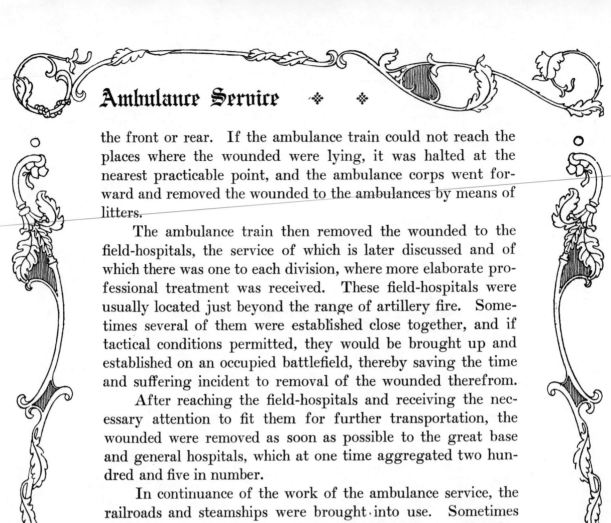

the front or rear. If the ambulance train could not reach the places where the wounded were lying, it was halted at the nearest practicable point, and the ambulance corps went forward and removed the wounded to the ambulances by means of litters.

The ambulance train then removed the wounded to the field-hospitals, the service of which is later discussed and of which there was one to each division, where more elaborate professional treatment was received. These field-hospitals were usually located just beyond the range of artillery fire. Sometimes several of them were established close together, and if tactical conditions permitted, they would be brought up and established on an occupied battlefield, thereby saving the time and suffering incident to removal of the wounded therefrom.

After reaching the field-hospitals and receiving the necessary attention to fit them for further transportation, the wounded were removed as soon as possible to the great base and general hospitals, which at one time aggregated two hundred and five in number.

In continuance of the work of the ambulance service, the railroads and steamships were brought into use. Sometimes conditions permitted trains to be run close to the scene of action and to receive wounded almost on the battlefield itself. This was the first war of great magnitude in which railroads were so employed.

The hospital trains were under the control of the Medical Department. The surgeon in charge was the sole head. Some were made up of passenger-cars which were regularly equipped or constructed by the railroad companies for the better care of wounded; some were hastily improvised at the front from ordinary freight-cars, merely emptied of the supplies which they had brought up and in which the wounded were merely laid on beds of boughs, hay, or straw. Between the two extremes there were all varieties of arrangements. Some cars were fitted with bunks; others with stanchions and supports,

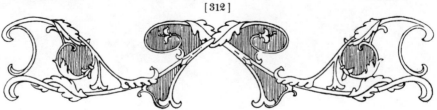

AN AMBULANCE TRAIN "PARKED" AT HAREWOOD HOSPITAL, THE MONTH GETTYSBURG WAS FOUGHT

AMBULANCES AND MEDICAL SUPPLY WAGONS "PARKED"—1864

A TRAIN OF AMBULANCES AT CITY POINT

AMBULANCE TRAIN
OF THE ENGINEER CORPS
AT FALMOUTH, VIRGINIA

1863

This photograph shows to what a state of perfection, in drill and equipment, the ambulance service of the Union armies had been brought by April, 1863. The castle on the ambulance curtains indicates the Engineer Corps. The little vignette below the larger photograph shows the train unharnessed and at rest. Starting with a medical department scarcely adequate for eleven thousand men in time of peace, the ambulance service was ultimately increased, developed, and organized into a vast administrative medico-military machine, working smoothly in all its ramifications and meeting efficiently the needs of a force aggregating, at one time, nearly a million men, exposed to the fire of an able opponent, and very often compelled to operate under unfavorable conditions and amid unhealthful surroundings. The department brought order out of chaos, health from disease, and surcease from suffering, in a manner and to a degree previously unparalleled. Its achievements must challenge the admiration of medical men for all time.

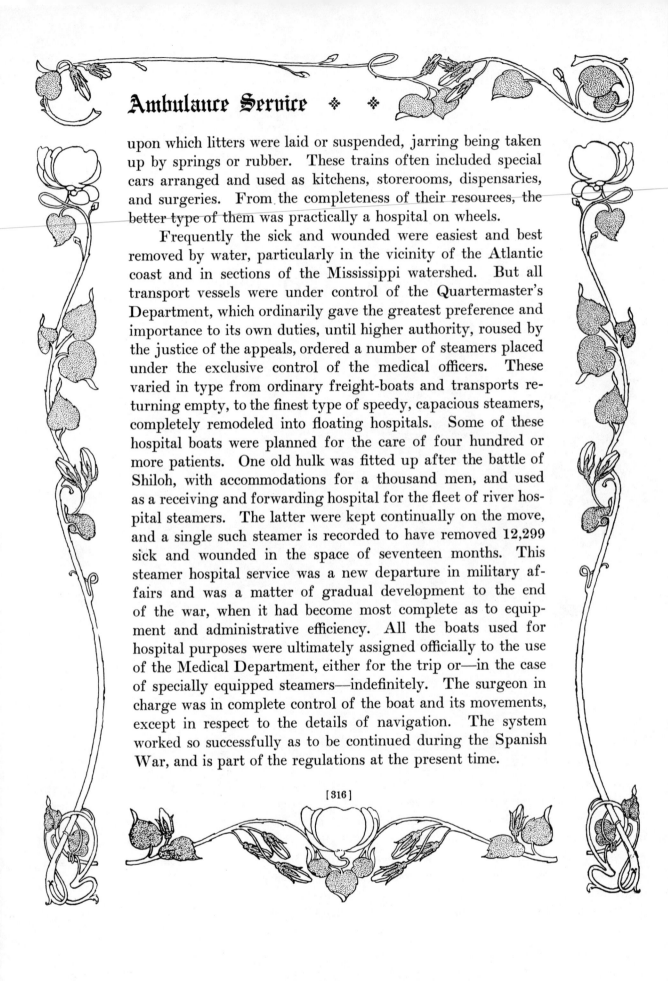

upon which litters were laid or suspended, jarring being taken up by springs or rubber. These trains often included special cars arranged and used as kitchens, storerooms, dispensaries, and surgeries. From the completeness of their resources, the better type of them was practically a hospital on wheels.

Frequently the sick and wounded were easiest and best removed by water, particularly in the vicinity of the Atlantic coast and in sections of the Mississippi watershed. But all transport vessels were under control of the Quartermaster's Department, which ordinarily gave the greatest preference and importance to its own duties, until higher authority, roused by the justice of the appeals, ordered a number of steamers placed under the exclusive control of the medical officers. These varied in type from ordinary freight-boats and transports returning empty, to the finest type of speedy, capacious steamers, completely remodeled into floating hospitals. Some of these hospital boats were planned for the care of four hundred or more patients. One old hulk was fitted up after the battle of Shiloh, with accommodations for a thousand men, and used as a receiving and forwarding hospital for the fleet of river hospital steamers. The latter were kept continually on the move, and a single such steamer is recorded to have removed 12,299 sick and wounded in the space of seventeen months. This steamer hospital service was a new departure in military affairs and was a matter of gradual development to the end of the war, when it had become most complete as to equipment and administrative efficiency. All the boats used for hospital purposes were ultimately assigned officially to the use of the Medical Department, either for the trip or—in the case of specially equipped steamers—indefinitely. The surgeon in charge was in complete control of the boat and its movements, except in respect to the details of navigation. The system worked so successfully as to be continued during the Spanish War, and is part of the regulations at the present time.

PART II
HOSPITALS

SURGEONS WITH THE NAVY

THE DOCTOR'S GIG ON THE MISSISSIPPI, 1864

DOUGLAS BANNON,
M.D.

SURGEONS
OF THE NAVY

No such losses in killed and wounded were experienced afloat as in the great battles ashore, yet the naval medical staff, especially on the Mississippi, the James, and the Potomac, were often called upon to coöperate with the army medical staff in caring for the wounded soldiers. There was a surgeon and sometimes an assistant surgeon on each ship. Hospital boats had medical staffs as large as the hospitals ashore. Beside the *Red Rover* there was the *City of Memphis*, which carried 11,024 sick and wounded in thirty-three trips up and down the Mississippi, and the *D. A. January*, in charge of Assistant Surgeon A. H. Hoff, which transported and cared for 23,738 patients during the last three years of the war. Other boats used as hospital transports were the *Empress* and the *Imperial*.

SURGEON BERTHOLET,
FLAGSHIP

MEDICAL STAFF OF THE RED ROVER

WILLIAM F. McNUTT, M.D.　　　GEORGE HOPKINS, M.D.　　　JOSEPH PARKER, M.D.

A "FLOATING PALACE"—UNITED STATES HOSPITAL STEAMER "RED ROVER" ON
THE MISSISSIPPI

This steamer was a veritable floating palace for the days of '61. It had bathrooms, a laundry, an elevator between decks, an amputating room, two kitchens, and the windows were covered with gauze to keep out flies and mosquitoes. When Island No. 10 was captured on April 7, 1862, several Confederate boats were taken. Among them was this *Red Rover*, an old side-wheel steamer which had been purchased in New Orleans for $30,000 the previous November. A shell had gone through her decks and bottom, but she was repaired at Cairo, Ill., and fitted up as a hospital boat by Quartermaster George M. Wise. The Western Sanitary Commission gave $3,500 for the purpose. Dr. George H. Bixby of Cairo was appointed assistant surgeon and placed in charge. Strange to say, the first serious cases placed on board were those of the commander and men of the gunboat *Mound City*, who had been severely scalded when the boiler was pierced by a shot in the attack on some Confederate batteries. This was the gunboat that had taken possession of the *Red Rover* when she was abandoned at Island No. 10, little more than two months previously. Before the *Red Rover* was placed in service, the army had chartered the *City of Memphis* as a hospital boat to take the wounded at Fort Henry to Paducah, St. Louis, and Mound City. There were several other hospital steamers, such as the *Louisiana*, the *D. A. January*, the *Empress*, and the *Imperial*, in service.

TIN CLAD 59, AND TUG OPPOSITE THE MOUND CITY HOSPITAL

A United States general hospital was constructed at Mound City, on the Ohio, a few miles above its junction with the Mississippi, early in the war. On September 29, 1862, Secretary Welles authorized the construction of a marine hospital also. The place was so named because of the existence of a slightly elevated bit of ground covered with trees, though at the beginning of the war only a few houses made up the "city."

A FULL LENGTH HOSPITAL SHIP "RED ROVER"

Smallpox epidemics caused 12,236 admissions to the Union hospitals, with 4,717 deaths. The patients were quarantined in separate hospitals or on boats and barges along the rivers, and the utmost care was taken to prevent the spread of the disease which was the cause of such a frightful mortality. The courage and devotion of the medical men and hospital orderlies who risked their lives to combat it cannot be praised too highly.

A SMALLPOX BARGE ON THE MISSISSIPPI

PART II
HOSPITALS

PRIVATE AGENCIES
OF
RELIEF

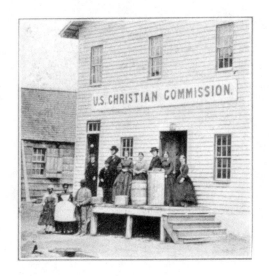

"BOXES FOR THE SOLDIERS" IN 1865

BOXES READY FOR THE BOYS AT THE FRONT

Though not so well known as the Sanitary Commission, the United States Christian Commission did an immense amount of valuable work during the Civil War, and appealed to those who preferred to make their contributions carry with them a positive expression of their faith. Though this organization did much relief work similar to that done by the Sanitary Commission, a large portion of its energies was directed toward improving the mental and moral welfare of the soldiers as well as their physical. Many thousand copies of Bibles and Testaments were distributed. Millions of tracts were sent out under its auspices. At every prominent camp reading-rooms were established, in which a point was made to secure papers published in all the States represented by the soldiers.

THE OFFICE OF THE UNITED STATES CHRISTIAN COMMISSION IN WASHINGTON

Writing materials were furnished free and stamps also; and every effort was made to induce the soldiers to remember the loved ones at home, since the officials believed that a keen remembrance of those left behind was one of the best safeguards against reckless living.   Its combinations extended through the Northern States.   Volunteers were solicited to contribute their services in the proper distribution of supplies, and a large number of men were regularly employed under salary.   Among the volunteers who went to the front were a large number of ministers who afforded great help to the wounded upon the field, and brought encouragement and sympathy to the hospitals where large numbers of ladies acted as nurses to the wounded soldiers.   The Government gladly availed itself of their aid.

TWENTY MILLIONS FOR RELIEF

THE CENTRAL OFFICE OF THE SANITARY COMMISSION IN WASHINGTON

From these general offices of the Sanitary Commission the various branches of the work were directed. The Commission was organized for the threefold purpose of inquiry, advice, and relief. During the first two years of the war, while the medical department was gradually increasing in efficiency, the Commission to a large extent cared for the wounded from many battlefields. In addition to the immense sum of money, nearly $5,000,000, expended by the Commission directly, several hundred thousand dollars raised under its auspices was spent directly by the different branches themselves. Supplies to the value of more than $15,000,000 were sent in addition to the money. The Commission also established rest-houses and accommodations for the sick, aided soldiers to correct any irregularities in their papers preventing them from receiving pay, bounties or pensions, and compiled a hospital directory.

[324]

THE SANITARY COMMISSION A SUCCESS—WOMEN IN THE FIELD, 1864

The creation of the Sanitary Commission was due to the desire of women to be of real, tangible help in the war. The plan at first met with little favor at Washington. The medical corps was indifferent, if not actually hostile, and the War Department was in opposition. But finally the acting surgeon-general was won over, and the plan took definite shape. The idea was to inquire into the recruiting service of the several States, to look into the subjects of diet, clothing, cooks, camping-grounds, in fact everything connected with the prevention of disease; and to discover methods by which private and unofficial interest and money might supplement the appropriations of the Government. During the first two years of the war, the camps of several hundred regiments were examined by inspectors appointed by the Commission, who advised the commanding officer as to proper location and sanitation.

COPYRIGHT, 1911, PATRIOT PUB. CO.

A LINK WITH THE FOLKS AT HOME

SANITARY COMMISSION OFFICERS AND NURSES AT FREDERICKSBURG, IN 1864

After the first enthusiasm of the different communities had passed, and "folks at home" realized that the boxes of edibles and wearing apparel they forwarded often reached, not their own dear ones but the Union soldier at large, speakers and organizers were sent out to stir the flagging interest in the work of the Sanitary Commission. Women who had been at the front, such as those shown sitting before the boxes and barrels in this photograph, told their experiences. Mrs. Mary A. Livermore began her career as public speaker by addressing such gatherings. The standard set was "a box a month for the soldiers." The presence of these nurses and supplies at the front after Spotsylvania was an incalculable blessing to the thousands of wounded soldiers and to the medical corps.

COPYRIGHT, 1911, PATRIOT PUB. CO.

SUPPLY WAGONS OF THE SANITARY COMMISSION AT BELLE PLAIN, 1864

After the Sanitary Commission proved its worth, it had no more ardent adherents than the medical corps. When a field-surgeon's requisitions were delayed, he would apply to the nearest Sanitary Commission official, who seldom failed to promptly forward the desired medicines. One of its activities was to publish pamphlets on sanitation, some of which were useful no doubt in theory but hardly practical for the soldier on the march. "When halting to rest," read one of them in substance, "never sit upon the ground. First unroll your rubber blanket, then spread on top of it your woolen blanket, and sit on that." Aside from the lack of such a plethora of blankets, the usual halt on the march was five minutes, exactly the length of time it took the soldier to roll up his blanket and strap it on his knapsack, ready for the march.

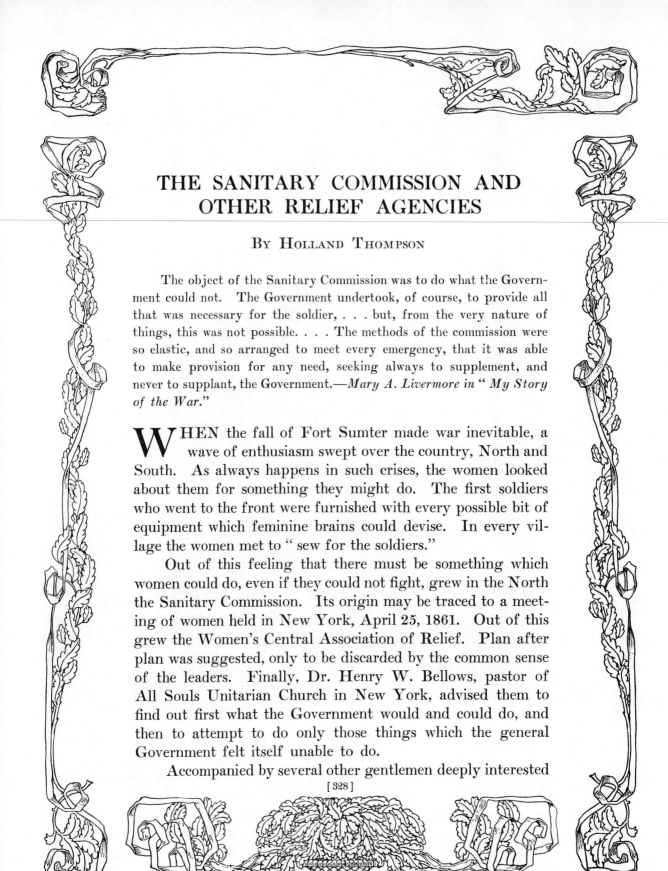

THE SANITARY COMMISSION AND OTHER RELIEF AGENCIES

By Holland Thompson

The object of the Sanitary Commission was to do what the Government could not. The Government undertook, of course, to provide all that was necessary for the soldier, . . . but, from the very nature of things, this was not possible. . . . The methods of the commission were so elastic, and so arranged to meet every emergency, that it was able to make provision for any need, seeking always to supplement, and never to supplant, the Government.—*Mary A. Livermore in " My Story of the War."*

WHEN the fall of Fort Sumter made war inevitable, a wave of enthusiasm swept over the country, North and South. As always happens in such crises, the women looked about them for something they might do. The first soldiers who went to the front were furnished with every possible bit of equipment which feminine brains could devise. In every village the women met to " sew for the soldiers."

Out of this feeling that there must be something which women could do, even if they could not fight, grew in the North the Sanitary Commission. Its origin may be traced to a meeting of women held in New York, April 25, 1861. Out of this grew the Women's Central Association of Relief. Plan after plan was suggested, only to be discarded by the common sense of the leaders. Finally, Dr. Henry W. Bellows, pastor of All Souls Unitarian Church in New York, advised them to find out first what the Government would and could do, and then to attempt to do only those things which the general Government felt itself unable to do.

Accompanied by several other gentlemen deeply interested

HOME WORKERS FOR THE SANITARY COMMISSION

These young women are hardly real nurses, but were thus photographed and the photographs offered for sale to secure money for the cause, in connection with a great fair held in New York. One of the most successful methods of raising money for the various activities of the Sanitary Commission was by means of such fairs in the great cities. Almost every conceivable variety of merchandise was sold. Often the offerings occupied half a dozen different buildings, one of which would perhaps be devoted to serving meals, another to the display of curiosities, another to art objects, another to fancy work, another to machinery, etc. Women gave their whole time for weeks to the preparation of the objects offered for sale, and then to the active work while the fair was open. Young girls acted as waitresses, sold flowers, served at the booths, and exerted all their charms to add to the fund "to help the soldiers." In New York and Philadelphia the great fairs realized more than a million dollars each, while that in Chicago was proportionately successful.

in the problem, he went to Washington to study the situation. The idea of the Sanitary Commission was a natural outgrowth of what they saw, but the plan at first met with little favor. The medical corps was indifferent if not actually hostile; the War Department was in opposition; President Lincoln feared that it would be a " fifth wheel to the coach." But finally the acting surgeon-general was won over and recommended the appointment of " a commission of inquiry and advice in respect to the sanitary interests of the United States forces," to act with the medical bureau. The committee was invited to put into a definite form the powers desired, and on May 23d suggested that an unpaid commission be appointed for the following purposes:

To inquire into the recruiting service in the various States and by advice to bring them to a common standard; second, to inquire into the subjects of diet, clothing, cooks, camping-grounds, in fact everything connected with the prevention of disease among volunteer soldiers not accustomed to the rigid regulations of the regular troops; and third, to discover methods by which private and unofficial interest and money might supplement the appropriations of the Government.

The plan was approved and, on the 9th of June, Henry W. Bellows, D.D.; Professor A. D. Bache, LL.D.; Professor Jeffries Wyman, M.D.; Professor Wolcott Gibbs, M.D.; W. H. Van Buren, M.D.; Samuel G. Howe, M.D.; R. C. Wood, surgeon of the United States Army; G. W. Cullum, United States Army, and Alexander E. Shiras, United States Army, were appointed by the Secretary of War, and his action was approved by the President on the 13th of the same month. The Government promised to provide a room in Washington for their use. The men at first appointed soon added others to their number, and as the movement spread over the country additional members were appointed until the commissioners numbered twenty-one. Frederick Law Olmsted, the distinguished landscape architect, was chosen general secretary

SHELTER FOR THE
WOUNDED ON
FURLOUGH

THE ONLY HOME
THAT MANY
SOLDIERS KNEW

The sick and wounded soldier with his strength and money spent found at all junction points where he had to transfer, when furloughed home, a lodge where he might find a welcome, a good meal, and, if necessary, spend the night. This

was partly to protect him from the hosts of sharpers and swindlers who met every train-load of furloughed soldiers and sought to prey upon them. The wives of the superintendents of these lodges were often an important factor in their success.

SOLDIERS' REST, ALEXANDRIA, VIRGINIA

WOUNDED SOLDIERS INSIDE THE "HOME"

THE "HOME" OF THE SANITARY COMMISSION—WASHINGTON

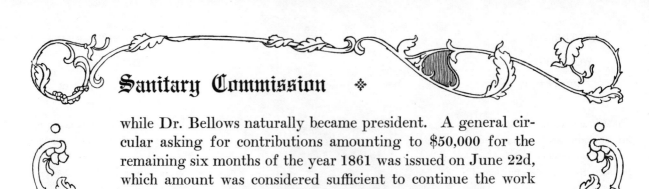

while Dr. Bellows naturally became president. A general circular asking for contributions amounting to $50,000 for the remaining six months of the year 1861 was issued on June 22d, which amount was considered sufficient to continue the work of inquiry and advice for that period.

Upon the authority thus given, an examination of the condition of the troops both in the East and in the West was undertaken by several members of the commission, with the result that unsanitary conditions were found almost everywhere. At once provision was made for the employment of expert physicians as inspectors of camps. Though the commission could pay only moderate salaries, it was found possible to secure inspectors of an unusually high type, many of whom resigned more remunerative positions to take up the work of the commission. Minute instructions were issued to them. They must not enter a camp without the approval of the superior officers, which was usually given as a matter of course. In their examination they were instructed to consider the location of the camp, its drainage, ventilation of tents or quarters, the quality of the rations, the methods of cooking, the general cleanliness of the camp and of the men. Wherever any of these fell short of a satisfactory standard, they were instructed to suggest tactfully to the commanding officers the points of deficiency and also to send their reports to the commission.

Their reports contained an immense number of physiological and hygienic facts, which were tabulated by the actuaries of the commission and digested by the physicians employed for the purpose. The effects of these inspections were almost invariably good. When a commanding officer once had his attention called to defects in the location of the camp or in drainage or in police, he was usually unlikely to make the same mistakes in the future, and every regiment in which sanitary and hygienic conditions were satisfactory was an example to the regiments with which it might be brigaded in the future.

Through the inspectors, eighteen short treatises prepared

A HOSPITAL AT NEW BERNE, N.C. LODGE No. 5 AT WASHINGTON, JULY, 1864

A LODGE FOR INVALID SOLDIERS TENTS AT BELLE PLAIN

Whether in permanent camp or on the field, the agents of the Sanitary Commission were always present with the armies, having ready some of the easily transported, yet invaluable hospital supplies of which the surgeons were so likely to run short. Many of the agents were accompanied by their wives, who often did good service in the hospitals. Nurses were also attached to the Commission officially or unofficially, and their service should be fully recognized. There were temporary shelters for invalid soldiers and members of the Sanitary Commission, their purpose being to furnish them with clean bedding and wholesome food and keep them out of the hands of sharpers or thugs who might otherwise prey upon them in their enfeebled condition. Here soldiers might await the coming of their relatives or the gaining of strength to enable them to travel to their homes. Aid was always given to secure pay, correcting papers which prevented them from receiving the same, and in a dozen other ways looking after their welfare. In all there were about forty of these lodges. The convalescent camp, at Alexandria, Virginia, intended for the care of those soldiers discharged from the hospitals but not yet able to resume their places in the ranks, was a special charge of the Commission, though not directly under its control. Other camps were established at Memphis, Cairo, and various other points in the West. Some of these rest-lodges are shown above.

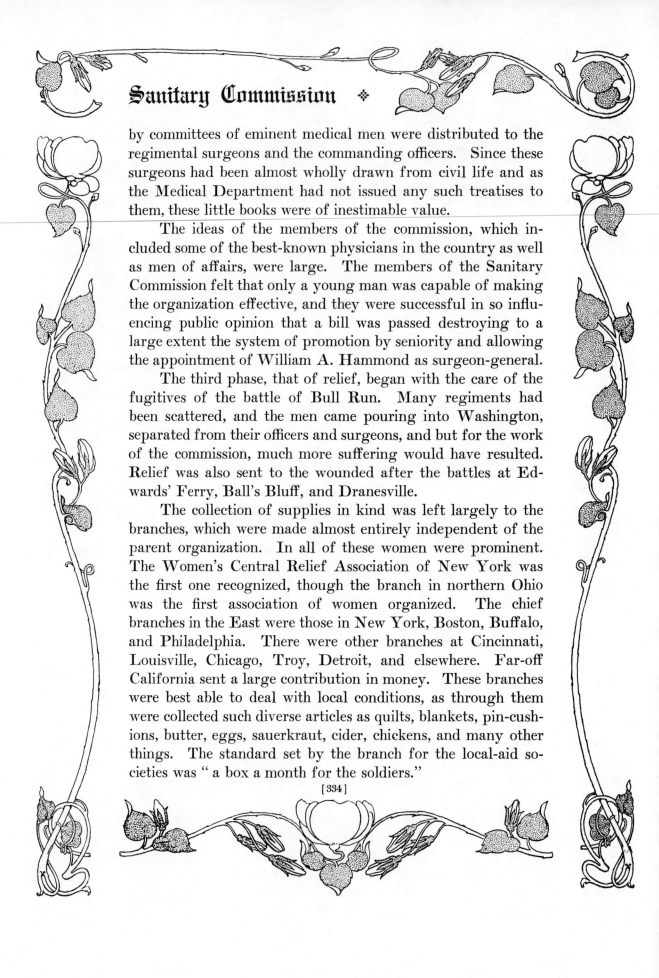

by committees of eminent medical men were distributed to the regimental surgeons and the commanding officers. Since these surgeons had been almost wholly drawn from civil life and as the Medical Department had not issued any such treatises to them, these little books were of inestimable value.

The ideas of the members of the commission, which included some of the best-known physicians in the country as well as men of affairs, were large. The members of the Sanitary Commission felt that only a young man was capable of making the organization effective, and they were successful in so influencing public opinion that a bill was passed destroying to a large extent the system of promotion by seniority and allowing the appointment of William A. Hammond as surgeon-general.

The third phase, that of relief, began with the care of the fugitives of the battle of Bull Run. Many regiments had been scattered, and the men came pouring into Washington, separated from their officers and surgeons, and but for the work of the commission, much more suffering would have resulted. Relief was also sent to the wounded after the battles at Edwards' Ferry, Ball's Bluff, and Dranesville.

The collection of supplies in kind was left largely to the branches, which were made almost entirely independent of the parent organization. In all of these women were prominent. The Women's Central Relief Association of New York was the first one recognized, though the branch in northern Ohio was the first association of women organized. The chief branches in the East were those in New York, Boston, Buffalo, and Philadelphia. There were other branches at Cincinnati, Louisville, Chicago, Troy, Detroit, and elsewhere. Far-off California sent a large contribution in money. These branches were best able to deal with local conditions, as through them were collected such diverse articles as quilts, blankets, pin-cushions, butter, eggs, sauerkraut, cider, chickens, and many other things. The standard set by the branch for the local-aid societies was " a box a month for the soldiers."

QUARTERS OF THE IMMENSE SANITARY COMMISSION ORGANIZATION
BRANDY STATION, VIRGINIA, IN 1863

Besides the active work at the front, departments or special bureaus were established at Washington, New York, Louisville, New Orleans, Baltimore, Philadelphia, Annapolis, and City Point, in addition to West Virginia, Texas, and the South. The report of the treasurer of the Sanitary Commission shows that from June 27, 1861, to July 1, 1865, the receipts from the Sanitary fairs in the principal cities were $4,813,750.64, and the disbursements $4,530,774.95, leaving a balance in the hands of the Commission of $282,975.69.

THESE QUARTERS AT BRANDY STATION WERE KNOWN AS THE "SHEBANG"

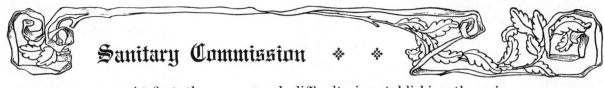

At first, there was much difficulty in establishing the principle of universality of relief. A community was willing to send a box to its own company or to its own regiment, but was less enthusiastic over the question of sending articles to men whom it had never seen. But after it had been shown that, on account of the frequent changes in the position of troops, thousands of such boxes lay in the express offices undelivered until their contents were often spoiled, the wisdom of the provision of a general-relief fund which should send aid wherever needed, came to be recognized.

One great difficulty to be overcome was the widespread belief in some sections that the soldiers did not get the contents of the boxes sent them. Rigid investigation disproved the existence of any considerable misapplication of stores, but the rumor was stubborn, and was believed by many whose zeal naturally was relaxed.

The commission proved its value during the Peninsula campaign of 1862. The transfer of troops to this new and somewhat malarious country soon brought on an amount of sickness with which the Governmental agencies were unable to deal. With the approval of the medical bureau, the commission applied for the use of a number of transports, then lying idle. The Secretary of War ordered boats with a capacity of one thousand persons to be detailed to the commission, which in turn agreed to take care of that number of sick and wounded. The *Daniel Webster,* assigned to the commission April 25, 1862, was refitted as a hospital and reached the York River on April 30th, with the general secretary, Mr. Olmsted, and a number of surgeons and nurses.

Other ships were detailed, though great inconvenience was suffered from the fact that several were recalled to the transport service, even when they had a load of sick and wounded, who, of course, had to be transferred at the cost, sometimes, of considerable suffering. At the same time, agents of the commission were near the front with the soldiers, offering such

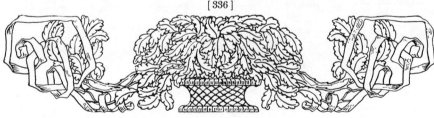

SANITARY–COMMISSION WAGONS LEAVING WASHINGTON FOR THE FRONT IN THE LAST DAYS OF THE WAR

This photograph shows how the Sanitary Commission worked. The four-horse team is harnessed to the covered wagon in which were carried those supplies which would be of most immediate use on the battlefield. It included stimulants of various sorts, chloroform, surgeon's silk, condensed milk, beef-stock, and dozens of other things. The mounted agent is ready to accompany the wagon, and the flag of the Commission is waving in the breeze. By this time the business of helping the soldiers was thoroughly systematized.

HEADQUARTERS OF THE CHRISTIAN COMMISSION IN THE FIELD, 1864

The following summary of the receipts of the Christian Commission up to January, 1865, will convey some idea of the magnitude of the work which it performed. In 1861 the receipts were $231,256.29; in 1863, $916,837.65; in 1864, $2,882,347.86, making a total of $4,030,441.80. During the year 1864, 47,103 boxes of hospital stores and publications were distributed, valued at $2,185,670.82.

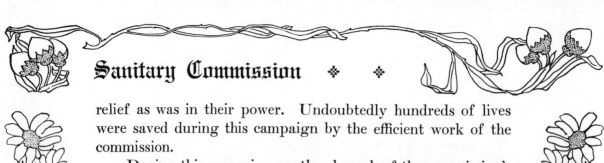

relief as was in their power. Undoubtedly hundreds of lives were saved during this campaign by the efficient work of the commission.

During this campaign another branch of the commission's activity developed. So many letters inquiring about sick, wounded, or dead soldiers were received that a hospital directory was begun, and before the 1st of April, 1863, this directory included the names of the sick and wounded soldiers in every general hospital. At the second battle of Bull Run the supplies sent forward by the surgeon-general were captured by the Confederates, and but for those furnished by the Sanitary Commission, the suffering would have been truly frightful. The work was continued at Antietam, where the supplies were brought to the field two days ahead of those of the Medical Department. The commission was also the main dependence after the battle of Fredericksburg, and not until the battle of Chancellorsville were the supplies of the Medical Department on the battlefield plentiful and accessible.

In the West, an organization in St. Louis, known as the Western Sanitary Commission, though having no connection with the larger body, was very efficient in the work of relief. It established and equipped hospitals, and was able to supply them. Many valuable contributions, however, were sent from the East. The Chicago, or Northwestern branch, also rendered valuable service. Scurvy was prevented by rushing carloads of fresh vegetables to Vicksburg and to the Army of the Cumberland.

After the reorganization of the medical bureau and the resulting increase in efficiency, the work of the commission became, as mentioned above, largely supplementary. And yet, to the end of the war, with every corps was a wagon carrying, among its supplies, chloroform, brandy, and other stimulants; condensed milk, beef-stock, bandages, surgeon's silk, and other articles of pressing need. A telegram from the inspector or relief agent on the spot to the nearest branch, demanding

CLARA BARTON—A WAR-TIME PHOTOGRAPH BY BRADY

Before the Civil War was over, Clara Barton's name had come to mean mercy and help for the wounded in war and peace alike. In the Civil War she took part in the relief work on the battlefields, described at length in the last chapter of this volume, and organized the search for missing men, for the carrying on of which Congress voted $15,000. She was active throughout the Franco-Prussian War, in the adoption of the Treaty of Geneva, in the founding of the National Red Cross in the United States, and in the Spanish-American War. Even later, in spite of advancing years, she appeared as a rescuing angel, bringing practical aid with sympathy to sufferers from the calamities of fire, flood, and famine.

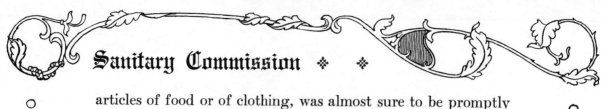

Sanitary Commission ❖ ❖

articles of food or of clothing, was almost sure to be promptly answered, while Government supplies were to be procured only on requisition, and necessarily passing through several hands, were sometimes much delayed. With the resulting lessening of the burden upon the energies of the commission, its activity was much broadened.

A "home" was established in Washington to give food and lodging and proper care to discharged soldiers. Those in charge were always ready to help soldiers to correct defective papers, to act as agents for those too feeble to present their claims at the pension office or to the paymaster, and to protect them from sharpers and the like. Lodges were established near the railway stations to give temporary shelter. Two nurses' homes were established, but these were largely used as temporary shelter for mothers or wives seeking their wounded sons or husbands.

In the West, a home was established by the Chicago branch at Cairo, Illinois, which was one of the main gateways through which soldiers passed, going toward or returning from the army. Rations were issued by the Government, and the building was furnished for the most part by the commission which assumed the management. It was, in effect, a free hotel for soldiers, and thousands were looked after and kept from harmful associations. Later it was much enlarged by order of General Grant, who instructed the officer commanding the post to construct suitable buildings. Much of the money raised by the Sanitary Commission was by means of fairs, some of which became national events, and lasted for weeks. During its existence the Sanitary Commission received $4,924,480.99 in money and the value of $15,000,000 in supplies.

No such well-organized instrumentality as the Sanitary Commission existed in the South. There were many women's-aid societies, and some of those in the seaport towns performed valuable services. The one in Charleston devoted its energies largely to procuring through the blockade the much needed

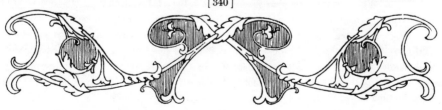

MICHIGAN STATE RELIEF ASSOCIATION MINISTERING TO WOUNDED AT WHITE HOUSE, VIRGINIA

There were various relief associations besides the Sanitary and Christian Commissions which did extremely efficient work. Here are some women from the West who are not only cooking on their stove in the open air, and broaching their boxes and baskets of delicacies, but seem to have cheered up the wounded soldier boys mightily. The soldier under the flag, with the girl in the white frock and little straw hat nestling close to him, appears far from discontented. The big sign "Michigan" over the entrance to the tent on which one can see the words "Michigan Headquarters," partially concealed, must have been a beacon of hope to many of the wounded soldiers from the far West of that day. The stoves and pans and kettles show that the inner man was cared for.

BUSY WITH GOOD WORKS FOR THE SOLDIERS

In this photograph one gets an actual glimpse of the manifold activities of the Christian Commission, especially as they appeared the first two years of the war. At the left a man with a hatchet is opening a box of such stores for the sick and wounded as the medical department did not supply—special medicines, jellies, chocolates, perfumes, and many others delicacies—which were greatly appreciated by the soldiers. In front of him stands a wounded soldier, his hand bound up and leaning upon a crutch, doubtless supplied by the Christian Commission, looking down gratefully at the woman in the poke-bonnet. Another woman is dipping into a tub, ap-

MEMBERS OF THE CHRISTIAN COMMISSION AT WHITE HOUSE ON THE PAMUNKEY

parently for something liquid, since the men behind her and the boy sitting on the grass in the foreground all have cups in their hands. In front of her is a man busy over a field stove. The men directly behind him seem to be constructing a temporary field oven, and in the background stands one of the Commission's supply wagons. The masts of the boat which has brought the delicacies for the soldiers to White House Landing are visible in the extreme background. This busy scene shows some of the practical good accomplished by the Christian Commission and how enthusiastically the women worked together with the men to alleviate the soldiers' woes.

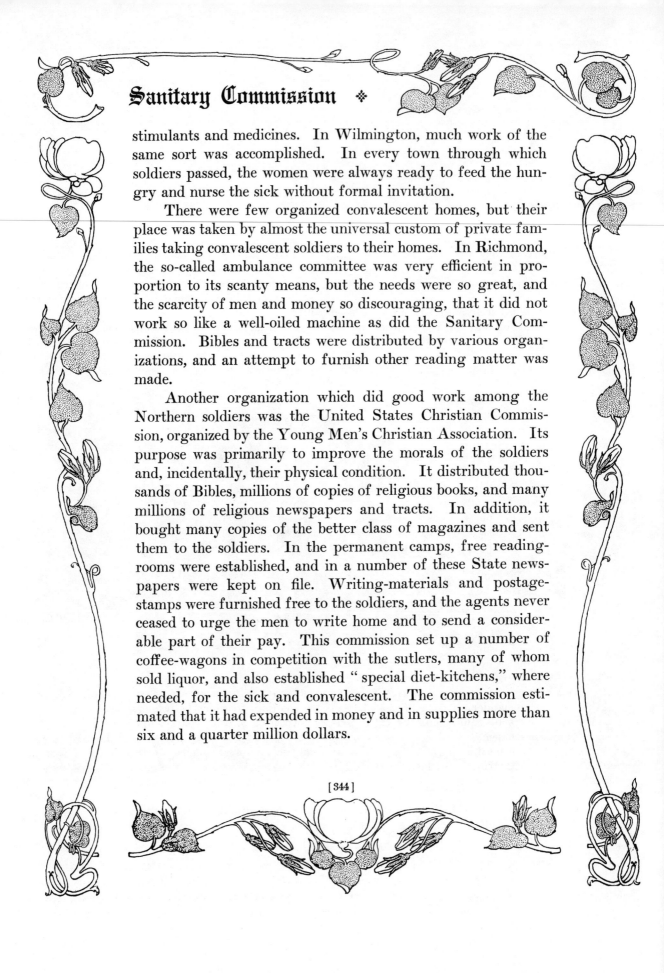

stimulants and medicines. In Wilmington, much work of the same sort was accomplished. In every town through which soldiers passed, the women were always ready to feed the hungry and nurse the sick without formal invitation.

There were few organized convalescent homes, but their place was taken by almost the universal custom of private families taking convalescent soldiers to their homes. In Richmond, the so-called ambulance committee was very efficient in proportion to its scanty means, but the needs were so great, and the scarcity of men and money so discouraging, that it did not work so like a well-oiled machine as did the Sanitary Commission. Bibles and tracts were distributed by various organizations, and an attempt to furnish other reading matter was made.

Another organization which did good work among the Northern soldiers was the United States Christian Commission, organized by the Young Men's Christian Association. Its purpose was primarily to improve the morals of the soldiers and, incidentally, their physical condition. It distributed thousands of Bibles, millions of copies of religious books, and many millions of religious newspapers and tracts. In addition, it bought many copies of the better class of magazines and sent them to the soldiers. In the permanent camps, free reading-rooms were established, and in a number of these State newspapers were kept on file. Writing-materials and postage-stamps were furnished free to the soldiers, and the agents never ceased to urge the men to write home and to send a considerable part of their pay. This commission set up a number of coffee-wagons in competition with the sutlers, many of whom sold liquor, and also established " special diet-kitchens," where needed, for the sick and convalescent. The commission estimated that it had expended in money and in supplies more than six and a quarter million dollars.

Appendix A

The Cartel of July 22, 1862

HAXALL'S LANDING, ON JAMES RIVER, VA.,
July 22, 1862.

THE undersigned, having been commissioned by the authorities they respectively represent to make arrangements for a general exchange of prisoners of war, have agreed to the following articles:

ARTICLE 1. It is hereby agreed and stipulated that all prisoners of war held by either party, including those taken on private armed vessels known as privateers, shall be discharged upon the conditions and terms following:

Prisoners to be exchanged man for man and officer for officer; privateers to be placed upon the footing of officers and men of the navy.

Men and officers of lower grades may be exchanged for officers of a higher grade, and men and officers of different services may be exchanged according to the following scale of equivalents:

A general commanding-in-chief or an admiral shall be exchanged for officers of equal rank, or for sixty privates or common seamen.

A flag-officer or major-general shall be exchanged for officers of equal rank, or for forty privates or common seamen.

A commodore carrying a broad pennant or a brigadier-general shall be exchanged for officers of equal rank, or twenty privates or common seamen.

A captain in the navy or a colonel shall be exchanged for officers of equal rank, or for fifteen privates or common seamen.

A lieutenant-colonel or a commander in the navy shall be exchanged for officers of equal rank, or for ten privates or common seamen.

A lieutenant-commander or a major shall be exchanged for officers of equal rank, or eight privates or common seamen.

A lieutenant or a master in the navy or a captain in the army or marines shall be exchanged for officers of equal rank, or six privates or common seamen.

Masters' mates in the navy or lieutenants and ensigns in the army shall be exchanged for officers of equal rank, or four privates or common seamen.

Midshipmen, warrant-officers in the navy, masters of merchant vessels, and commanders of privateers shall be exchanged for officers of equal rank, or three privates or common seamen.

Second captains, lieutenants, or mates of merchant vessels or privateers, and all petty officers in the navy, and all non-commissioned officers in the army or marines shall be severally exchanged for persons of equal rank, or for two privates or common seamen, and private soldiers or common seamen shall be exchanged for each other, man for man.

ARTICLE 2. Local, State, civil, and militia rank held by persons not in actual military service will not be recognized, the basis of exchange being the grade actually held in the naval and military service of the respective parties.

ARTICLE 3. If citizens held by either party on charges of disloyalty or any alleged civil offense are exchanged, it shall only be for citizens. Captured sutlers, teamsters, and all civilians in the actual service of either party to be exchanged for persons in similar position.

ARTICLE 4. All prisoners of war to be discharged on parole in ten days after their capture, and the prisoners now held and those hereafter taken to be transported to the points mutually agreed upon at the expense of the capturing party. The surplus prisoners not exchanged shall not be permitted to take up arms again, nor to serve as military police or constabulary force in any fort, garrison, or field-work held by either of the respective parties, nor as guards of prisons, depots, or stores, nor to discharge any duty usually performed by soldiers, until exchanged under the provisions of this cartel. The exchange is not to be considered complete until the officer or soldier exchanged for has been actually restored to the lines to which he belongs.

ARTICLE 5. Each party, upon the discharge of prisoners of the other party, is authorized to discharge an equal number of their own officers or men from parole, furnishing at the same time to the other party a list of their prisoners discharged and of their own officers and men relieved from parole, thus enabling each party to relieve from parole such of their own officers and men as the party may choose. The lists thus mutually furnished will keep both parties advised of the true condition of the exchange of prisoners.

ARTICLE 6. The stipulations and provisions above mentioned to be of binding obligation

Appendix A

during the continuance of the war, it matters not which party may have the surplus of prisoners, the great principles involved being, first, an equitable exchange of prisoners, man for man, officer for officer, or officers of higher grade exchanged for officers of lower grade or for privates, according to the scale of equivalents; second, that privateers and officers and men of different services may be exchanged according to the same scale of equivalents; third, that all prisoners, of whatever arm of service, are to be exchanged or paroled in ten days from the time of their capture, if it be practicable to transfer them to their own lines in that time; if not, as soon thereafter as practicable; fourth, that no officer, soldier, or employee, in the service of either party, is to be considered as exchanged and absolved from his parole until his equivalent has actually reached the lines of his friends; fifth, that the parole forbids the performance of field, garrison, police, or guard, cr constabulary duty.

JOHN A. DIX,
Major-General.

D. H. HILL,
Major-General, C. S. Army.

Appendix B

Personnel of the Medical Department of the Federal Army

BY MAJOR E. L. MUNSON, M.D., U.S.A.

THE surgeons from civil life entered the military service with varying status. At the outbreak of the war, the militia forces responding to the call of the President had one surgeon and one assistant surgeon with each regiment, in which they were commissioned as part of the regimental organization and from which they were seldom detached. They were commissioned by the governors of the several States, of whose military organizations they were a part. In the State troops later organized, professional assistance was similarly provided. But the need for additional medical men to help perform the tremendous administrative duties of the Medical Department was recognized, and volunteer medical officers were appointed medical directors of division, under the President's proclamation of May 3, 1861; while one surgeon was specified as part of the staff of each brigade of the force of five hundred thousand men authorized by the act of Congress of July 22, 1861. These staff-surgeons held the rank of major, commissioned by the President, and held equal rank and duties and possessed equal prerogatives with the members of the regular Medical Department, whether as medical directors of armies, corps, or departments, or in charge of hospitals. Besides the above, there was a class designated as acting assistant surgeons, who were civilian physicians, uncommissioned, serving under contract to do service in the field or in the hospitals.

Under the act of Congress of August 3, 1861, there was " added to the medical staff of the army a corps of medical cadets, whose duty it shall be to act as dressers in the general hospitals and as ambulance attendants in the field, under the direction and control of the medical officers alone. They shall have the same rank and pay as the military cadets at West Point." This same act also authorized the employment in general hospitals of such number of female nurses as might be indicated by the surgeon-general or the surgeons in charge.

During the years of the war the organization of the Medical Department of the regular army was increased so as to number one surgeon-general, one assistant surgeon-general, one medical inspector-general, sixteen medical inspectors, and one hundred and seventy surgeons and assistant surgeons. There were appointed 547 surgeons and assistant surgeons of volunteers. In addition, there were mustered into the service 2109 regimental surgeons and 3882 regimental assistant surgeons. During the same period there were employed under contract 85 acting staff-surgeons, and 5532 acting assistant surgeons. Even considering that some of these may have occupied several different positions, it is probable that, in round numbers, no less than ten thousand medical men gave direct assistance to the Northern forces during the war.

Appendix C

Union Surgeons-General and their Work

By Major E. L. Munson, M.D., U.S.A.

ON the death of Surgeon-General Lawson, of the United States regular army, which occurred shortly after the firing on Fort Sumter, Surgeon Clement A. Finley was, on May 1, 1861, appointed his successor. He was then the senior medical officer on the army list and sixty-four years of age, having had forty-three years of service in the Medical Department in all parts of the country and in various Indian wars. He was chief surgeon under General Scott in the Black Hawk War of 1832, receiving the official thanks of that officer for his efficiency; during the Mexican War he was at one time medical director of General Taylor's forces, and later was medical director of the army occupying Vera Cruz.

Surgeon-General Finley assumed the direction of affairs of his department at a most trying time. Congress had permitted no preparations for war to be made; supplies were neither on hand nor could they be obtained at short notice, and the number of trained medical officers was not sufficient to leaven promptly the mass of surgeons fresh from civil life, whose zeal, patriotism, and professional ability could not compensate for the profound ignorance of everything military which they necessarily entertained at the outset. In fact, conditions existed almost identical with those which again prevailed nearly four decades later at the outbreak of the Spanish-American War. Surgeon-General Finley did much to mold his excellent raw material into an administrative machine, but it took time to coordinate the resources now lavished without stint upon the Medical Department.

Politicians affected to be astounded that a thoroughly effective sanitary service could not be created out of raw material overnight. There was much suffering of the sick and wounded in the first part of the war for which the Medical Department was by no means wholly responsible, but political opponents of the administration endeavored to arouse feeling against its policy by working on the feelings of the mothers, wives, and sweethearts of the soldiers at the front. This had its effect on the War Department, culminating in abrupt rupture of the relations between the dogmatic Secretary of War Stanton and Surgeon-General Finley, and the sending of the latter away from Washington in the spring of 1862, without duty, to await retirement from the service.

After the relief from duty of Surgeon-General Finley, Surgeon Robert C. Wood served for several months as acting surgeon-general. It was evident that a man was needed as surgeon-general who should have large requirements and a broad mind—matured by years and experience, yet young enough to endure the labors, fatigues, trials, and disappointments that would confront the head of the Medical Department.

At this juncture, the Sanitary Commission, organized by civilians for the assistance of the army medical service, took a hand in affairs and, after careful consideration, recommended First Lieutenant William A. Hammond, who was appointed. Although low in rank, Doctor Hammond was far from being without military experience, having then had twelve years' service, of which eleven were under a previous commission as an assistant surgeon, which position he had resigned in 1860 to take a professorship in the University of Maryland, his native State. At the time of his appointment as surgeon-general he was approaching the age of thirty-five years, and had achieved a most enviable professional and scientific reputation in this country and abroad, especially in relation to physiology and physiological chemistry.

With the onset of the war, Doctor Hammond decided to reenter the army, though he would receive no credit for his previous eleven years of service. He was charged with the organization of the great general hospitals at Hagerstown, Frederick, and Baltimore, after which he was made medical inspector of camps and hospitals. So efficiently did he perform these tasks that a concerted movement was successfully started outside the army to make him General Finley's successor.

Of all the great medical figures of the Civil War, that of Hammond stands out in most heroic size. Of his work, no better picture can be given than in the glowing words of Stillé, in his "History of the United States Sanitary Commission":

"A new and vastly enlarged supply table, or

Appendix C

list of articles which the Government would undertake to provide for the inmates of the hospitals, was also issued by orders of the surgeon-general, embracing many things essential to their comfort, for the supply of which the hospital fund had been hitherto the only and most precarious source. Hospital clothing was also furnished to the patients under the new régime. As a means of securing the most competent men for the medical service of the army, he recognized the board of examination, and insisted upon a higher standard of attainment on the part of the candidate. He established also a new and complete system of hospital reports, which was designed to embody not merely a formal and barren statement of the number of patients in the hospitals and of those who were discharged or died, but also such facts concerning their condition as would constitute valuable material for a medical and surgical history of the war. . . . He instituted at Washington an army medical museum, in which was collected and arranged a vast number of specimens from the different hospitals, illustrating the nature of the particular diseases to which soldiers are liable, and the character of the wounds which are inflicted by the new missiles of war. . . .

"But the great central want of the system, which, if left unsupplied, all the other improvements suggested by the surgeon-general would have proved of little value, was the want of proper hospital buildings. Fortunately for the completion of the circle of his plans, the necessary cooperation of those officers of the Government outside of the Medical Department who were charged with the erection of hospitals, was at last obtained, and a large number were constructed on a vast scale in different parts of the country according to the pavilion system."

General Hammond was embarrassed by the fact that shortly after his appointment he, like his predecessor, incurred the displeasure of the Secretary of War. This culminated in the fall of 1863 in his removal from duty, after being found technically guilty of certain charges by a court martial. This led to dismissal from the service. In 1878, he had his case reopened and the evidence reexamined, and on this basis Congress reversed his sentence and placed him on the retired list of the army with the grade from which he had unjustly been deposed.

On the removal from office of Surgeon-General Hammond, on September 3, 1863, Colonel Joseph K. Barnes, medical inspector-general, was appointed acting surgeon-general, and this appointment was made permanent by his being commissioned surgeon-general on August 22, 1864. He was born in Philadelphia, in 1817, was educated at Harvard and the University of Pennsylvania, and at the time of his provisional selection had completed twenty-three years of service in the Medical Department of the army. He had served in various Indian wars, and actively participated in nearly all of the great battles in the War with Mexico. His experience stood him in good stead, and during the remainder of the Civil War the affairs of the surgeon-general's office were conducted with the highest efficiency, and the transition from war to peace was accomplished without a jar.

It is only fair to General Barnes' predecessors to say that they turned over to him a medical administrative machine which was working smoothly in all its parts, however loudly it had creaked under the stress of its emergency creation and development in the earlier years of the struggle. His efforts were greatly aided by the fact that he succeeded in retaining the friendship of Secretary Stanton, who thereafter omitted nothing that could conduce to the extension of the facilities and efficiency of the Medical Department. Surgeon-General Barnes continued in office for nineteen years, carrying out not only the well-devised plans of his predecessors, but others of his own conception. To him was due much of the development of the medical work of the army, the vesting of the control of general hospitals and hospital camps in the Medical Department, the inclusion of medical officers in the brevet commissions given at the end of the war, the development of the great Army Medical Museum and the superb library of the surgeon-general's office, the compilation of the medical and surgical records of the Civil War, and many other movements which redounded to the welfare of the sick, the efficiency of the troops, and the advantage of American military medicine. It fell to his lot to share in the care of two murdered Presidents, he being the first surgeon called to the bedside of Abraham Lincoln and, sixteen years later, summoned to assist in the treatment of James A. Garfield.

Appendix D

Organization and Personnel of the Medical Department of the Confederacy

By Deering J. Roberts, M.D., Surgeon, Confederate States Army

THE organization of the Confederate Medical Department was identical with that of the United States army at the breaking out of hostilities, and the army regulations under which rank and discipline were maintained were those of the United States, the only copies which came under the writer's observation being those printed prior to the war. The medical staff of the armies of the Confederacy embraced only three grades of rank, viz.: one surgeon-general with rank, emoluments, and allowances of a brigadier-general of cavalry; about one thousand surgeons with rank, allowances, and emoluments of a major of cavalry; and about two thousand assistant surgeons, with the rank of a captain of cavalry; among the latter, or possibly in addition thereto, were a number of contract surgeons or acting assistant surgeons, with the pay of a second lieutenant of infantry, who were temporarily employed; nearly all of these, however, at some period subsequent to their employment as contract surgeons were examined by an army board of medical examiners and were commissioned as surgeons or assistant surgeons, or dropped from the army rolls.

The following statement is quoted from an address by S. P. Moore, M.D., surgeon-general of the Confederate States army, delivered at Richmond, Virginia, October 19, 1875:

"*Congressional Legislation.*—To make the corps still more effective, to hold out rewards to distinguished medical officers, to offer incentives (if needed) to faithful and efficient performance of duties, and to confer additional and commensurate authority on those in most important positions, a bill was prepared creating the offices of two assistant surgeon-generals, one to exercise authority west of the Mississippi, the other to be on duty in the surgeon-general's office; medical directors, medical inspectors, medical purveyors, all with rank of colonel. This bill passed both Houses of Congress (they appearing willing always to aid the department in its effort toward a more perfect organization), but was vetoed by the President. It seemed useless to make further efforts in this direction." *

* *The Southern Practitioner*, vol. xxxi, 1909, p. 494.

To each regiment of infantry or cavalry was assigned a surgeon and an assistant surgeon; to a battalion of either, and sometimes to a company of artillery, an assistant surgeon. Whenever regiments and battalions were combined into brigades, the surgeon whose commission bore the oldest date became the senior surgeon of brigade, and although a member of the staff of the brigade commander, was not relieved of his regimental duties; sometimes, however, he was allowed an additional assistant surgeon, who was carried as a supernumerary on the brigade roster. To the senior surgeon of brigade, the regimental and battalion medical officers made their daily morning, weekly, monthly, and quarterly reports, and reports of killed and wounded after engagements, which by him were consolidated and forwarded to the chief surgeon of the division to which the brigade was attached; regiments and brigades acting in an independent capacity forwarded their reports to the medical director of the army or department, or to the surgeon-general direct. Requisitions for regimental and battalion medical, surgical, and hospital supplies, as well as applications for furlough or leave of absence, discharge, resignation, or assignment to post duty, on account of disability, were first approved by the regimental or battalion medical officer, after giving his reasons for approval and the nature of the disability in the latter instances, and forwarded by him to the senior surgeon of brigade, and by him to the chief surgeon of division and the other ranking officers in the corps and army for their approval. Independent commands reported to the medical director of the department or army, or the surgeon-general direct. Medical purveyors nearest to the army, as promptly as possible, forwarded all needed medical, surgical, and hospital supplies, on approved requisitions.

Assignments to the position of chief surgeon of division were sometimes made in accordance with seniority of rank of the senior surgeons of brigades, in other instances on application of the general commanding the division. His duties, in addition to approving reports coming from the senior surgeons of brigades, were to advise with the division commander in all matters pertaining to the medical care and hygiene of his command, and to have personal care of the attachés of the division staff and headquarters, and to advise and consult with his medical subordinates.

To each corps was assigned a medical director, a commissioned surgeon, his permanent assignment being made on personal application of the lieutenant-general commanding the corps; temporarily and when emergency demanded, his duties, which were similar to those of the chief surgeon of division as pertaining to the corps, devolved upon the chief surgeon of division whose commission bore priority of date; he, in turn, being succeeded by the ranking senior surgeon of brigade.

A medical director was assigned to the staff of each general commanding a department, or an army in a department, his selection usually being in deference to the general on whose staff he served and to whom was submitted for approval all reports and papers, from the various army corps, independent divisions, brigades, or smaller detachments. He also had charge of the staff and attachés of the department or army headquarters.

The non-commissioned medical staff consisted of a hospital steward for each regiment or battalion, with the rank and emoluments of an orderly sergeant, his selection as a rule being made by the ranking medical officer of the command, usually a graduate or undergraduate in medicine, or one having had previous experience in handling drugs; and his duties were to have charge of the medical, surgical, and hospital supplies under direction of the regimental or battalion medical officer, caring for and dispensing the same, seeing that the directions of his superior as to diet and medicines were carried out, or reporting their neglect or failure. The regimental band constituted the infirmary detail to aid in caring for the sick in camp and to carry the wounded from the field of battle, and when so occupied were under the surgeon or assistant surgeon. When necessary, additional detail was made from the enlisted men to serve temporarily or permanently on the infirmary corps. In some instances, an enlisted man was detailed as hospital clerk, and with the hospital steward was required to be present at sick-call each morning; these soldiers, with the infirmary detail, were relieved from all other regimental duty, such as guard duty and police detail.

The duties of the assistant surgeon were to assist or relieve the surgeon in caring for the sick and wounded in camp or on the march. On the field of battle he was expected to be close up in the immediate rear of the center of his regiment, accompanied by the infirmary detail, and to give primary attention, first aid to the wounded—this consisting in temporary control of hemorrhage by ligature, tourniquet, or bandage and compress, adjusting and temporarily fixing fractured limbs, administering water, anodynes, or stimulants, if needed, and seeing that the wounded were promptly carried to the field-hospital in the rear by the infirmary detail or ambulance.

The duties of the surgeons, in addition to caring for the sick in camp and on the march, were to establish a field-hospital, as soon as they could learn that the command to which they were attached was going under fire, at some convenient and, if possible, sheltered spot behind a hill or in a ravine, about one-half to one mile in rear of the line of battle, which was done under direction of a brigade or division surgeon. Here the combined medical staff of a brigade or division aided one another in the performance of such operations as were deemed necessary, as the wounded were brought from the front by the infirmary detail on stretchers or in the ambulance. Amputations, resections of bone, ligatures of arteries, removals of foreign bodies, adjusting and permanently fixing fractures, and all minor and major operations and dressings were made when deemed best for the comfort and welfare of the wounded men. As soon as possible after the permanent dressings were made at the field-hospital, and even in some instances while the troops were still engaged, the wounded were carried to the railroad and transported to the more permanent hospitals in the villages, towns, and cities, some miles distant.

The uniform worn by the medical corps was similar to that of the rank and file with only a slight difference. While the cloth and cut were the same, the facings of the coat collar and cuffs and the stripe down the sides of the trousers were black, while those of the infantry were light blue, the artillery, scarlet, and cavalry, buff; on the front of the cap or hat were the letters " M. S." embroidered in gold, embraced in two olive branches. On the coat sleeve of the assistant surgeon were two rows of gold braid, with three gold bars on the ends of the coat collar extending back about one and a half inches; while the surgeon had three rows of braid on the coat sleeves, and a single star on each side of the coat collar about an inch and a half from the end. The chevrons on the coat sleeves and the stripe down the trousers of the hospital steward were similar to those worn by an orderly or first sergeant, but were black in color.

The statement is sometimes made that many Confederate surgeons were inefficient, and in support of this contention a statement attributed to President Davis, in Surgeon Craven's "Prison Life of Jefferson Davis" is produced, in which he is reported to have said in conversation with the author, that "they had been obliged to accept as surgeons in the Southern army many lads who had only half finished their education in Northern colleges."

This statement would seem to indicate a scarcity of capable medical men who were willing to serve as such in the Confederate army, while the facts are that many of the infantry and cavalry battalions and regiments, as well as artillery companies, in addition to their usual complement of medical officers, bore on their rolls, either in field and staff, the commissioned officers of the line, or even in rank and file, capable and eminently well-qualified medical men, many of whom were subsequently transferred to the medical corps. The reports from Northern prisons where line officers or enlisted men often assisted the Federal surgeons in the care of the sick, confirm this statement.

It can be said, in all sincerity and confidence in the statement, that the students of the South who graduated from Northern and Southern medical colleges prior to the war between the States, were superior in scholastic attainments and mental qualifications to those of subsequent years. Not only is this the personal observation of the writer, but corroborative thereof are the following quotations from an address by Samuel H. Stout, M.D., late medical director of hospitals of the Department and Army of Tennessee.

"When I attended lectures in Philadelphia more than half a century ago, the number of students in the two schools there (the University, and the Jefferson) was a little more than one thousand, more than half of whom were from the Southern States. Of these latter, a majority were bachelors of arts, or had received a classical education. The Southern States in the slaveholding sections were, therefore, prior to the war well supplied with educated and chivalrously honorable surgeons and physicians. Such were the men who served at the bedside and in responsible positions in the medical corps of the armies and navy of the Confederacy." *

Finally, Samuel P. Moore, M.D., in an address delivered at Richmond, Virginia, October 19, 1865, published in the city papers of the following day, said, "The Confederate medical officers were inferior to none in any army"; and in another paragraph: "Although there were many capital

medical men in the medical corps, yet, from the easy manner by which commissions were obtained for medical officers appointed to regiments, many were supposed not to be properly qualified. It was therefore deemed advisable to establish army medical boards for the examination of medical officers already in service, as well as applicants for commission into the medical corps. These boards were to hold plain, practical examinations. The result was highly satisfactory."

In Tennessee, more than one instance can be mentioned where a good and well-qualified practitioner, on application to Governor Harris for a position in the medical corps, was by him urgently and earnestly advised and entreated to remain at home, as he would be needed there, because, as quite a number of his colleagues were to be found in the rank and file of the assembling soldiery, in addition to a full complement in the medical corps, the old men, the women and children, and the slaves at home must be cared for as well as the "boys" in the army. This measure prevailed in other States, and in only a few instances of rare emergency, that could not by any means have been avoided, and then only for a brief period, was there any dearth or scarcity of medical officers in the Confederate army, in the field or hospital.

Some States began organizing their troops before affiliating with the Confederacy, as in Tennessee. The medical officers received their commissions from the secretary of state, after examinations, both oral and written, by an army medical examining board appointed by the governor of the State. The medical examining board at Nashville was headed by Dr. Paul F. Eve, a teacher of surgery of wide experience, and a surgeon of both national and international reputation. His colleagues were Dr. Joseph Newman, who had served with the Tennessee troops in the war with Mexico, and enjoyed the confidence and esteem of a large clientele in Nashville during the intervening years, and Dr. J. D. Winston, also one of the leading practitioners of the capital city of the State. Boards of like character were serving the western division of the State at Memphis, and at Knoxville, in the eastern. When the State troops, then organized, were transferred to the Confederate States, they were recommissioned by the Secretary of War of the Confederacy, on recommendation of the surgeon-general, after examination and approval by the army medical examining boards of the Confederate army. As other troops were subsequently organized, they were supplied with medical officers who had passed a satisfactory examination before a Confederate army medical

* *The Southern Practitioner*, vol. xxiv, p. 437.

examining board and commissioned in like manner; the same measure was followed in the hospital service.

The examinations before State and Confederate army boards were thorough, complete, and eminently practical. Each applicant was required in a given number of hours to fill out the answers to a number of written questions, under supervision of the secretary of the board; and this being done, he was invited into an adjoining room and submitted to an oral examination to the satisfaction of the assembled board. The Confederate board of examiners serving with the Department and Army of Tennessee, as I remember, consisted of Dr. D. W. Yandell, of Louisville; Dr. J. F. Heustis, of Mobile, and Dr. Stanford E. Chaillé, of New Orleans, all being well-known teachers of medicine and surgery in their respective States, and at that time, or subsequently, of national reputation. Other medical examining boards were of like character.

The late Doctor Chaillé, the dean of the medical department of Tulane University, in a private letter, speaks of the work of the examining boards appointed in 1862 to report on the competency of the medical staff. The Confederate soldiers were almost exclusively volunteers who had elected their medical as well as other officers. Doctor Chaillé reported that his board caused the dismissal of a number of the surgeons and assistant surgeons, sometimes incurring the hostility of the officers and men in consequence, " because of the gross incompetence of laymen then *as well as now* to judge of the incompetence of medical men." He goes on to say that the incompetent were " exceptions to the superior merit of the vast majority of the members of the Confederate medical staff." This statement goes far to explain any apparent contradictions in the testimony regarding the competence of Confederate surgeons, and must be generally accepted.